Correctional Organization and Management

Correctional Organization and Management

Public Policy Challenges, Behavior, and Structure

ROBERT M. FREEMAN, Ph.D.

Shippensburg University

BUTTERWORTH
HEINEMANN

Boston   Oxford   Auckland   Johannesburg   Melbourne   New Delhi

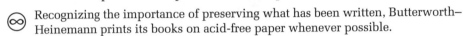
Library of Congress Cataloging-in-Publication Data
Freeman, Robert M., 1947–
    Correctional organization and management : public policy
  challenges, behavior, and structure / Robert M. Freeman.
      p. cm.
    Includes bibliographical references (p.) and index.
    ISBN 0-7506-9897-7 (pbk. : alk. paper)
    1. Prison administration—United States. 2. Correctional
institutions—United States—Administration. 3. Correctional
personnel—United States. 4. Prisons—Officials and employees—
United States. I. Title.
HV9469.F74 1999   98-47797
365'.068—dc21   CIP

British Library Cataloguing-in-Publication Data
A catalogue record for this book is available from the British Library.

The publisher offers special discounts on bulk orders of this book.
For information, please contact:

Manager of Special Sales
Butterworth–Heinemann
225 Wildwood Avenue
Woburn, MA 01801-2041
Tel: 781-904-2500
Fax: 781-904-2620

For information on all Butterworth–Heinemann publications available, contact our World Wide Web home page at: http://www.bh.com

10 9 8 7 6 5 4 3 2 1

Printed in the United States of America

To my wife, Diane, the nurse; my son, Eric, the engineer; and my son, Brian, the writer. Their support and patience made this book possible.

Contents

Preface

This is a book about the behavior of correctional organizations. The focus is the management and leadership practices that shape employee behavior through an ongoing process of environmental design. Having spent 21 years as a manager in both public and private corrections, I can confidently say that the effective management of a correctional organization is an exciting, demanding, complex responsibility that requires enormous dedication and commitment. The challenges are numerous and the work is rewarding.

My goal in writing this book is to provide an in-depth overview of the structure of correctional organizations and the environmental design process that defines organizational behavior. To accomplish this goal, I have drawn from personal experience, current information received from numerous correctional organizations, and the growing body of research examining management and leadership issues in organizations both inside and outside of corrections.

This book is written for students who are preparing to enter the world of corrections and practitioners who are meeting the challenge of managing complex organizations whose mission continues to evolve. There are three themes discussed in this book. The first theme is that there exists a complex relationship between public policy and the mission, behavior, and structure of correctional organizations. Public policy determines the mission of corrections. Once the mission has been specified, correctional managers use environmental design to shape the organizational behavior and structure necessary to accomplish that mission. Public policy is not static. It changes. Changes in public policy require changes in the organization's mission. Changes in mission require new organizational behavior and structure. The challenge for correctional managers is to define and implement those adaptive strategies that will reshape organizational behavior and structure to successfully accommodate the requirements of the new mission. The second theme is that the formulation of public policy is influenced by a complex ongoing interaction between elected officials, quasi-judicial government regulatory agencies, the judiciary, public-interest organizations such as the media, and single-interest groups such as unions. Thus, the external environment exerts an enormous influence over the mission, behavior, and structure of correctional organizations. The third theme is that the key to effective organizational behavior is a planned strategy of employee empowerment.

The exploration of these themes encompasses four areas: organizational theory, structure, and culture; the influence of external organizations on correctional management; fundamental management processes; and employee professionalization, social responsibility/ethical behavior, change management, and the future. To illustrate important concepts in these areas, I have made liberal use of material received from corrections professionals around the country. Much of this material is in the Boxes used to illustrate significant concepts and issues.

Chapter 1 brings the reader up-to-date on the evolution of correctional management theory. Chapters 2 and 3 define the internal environment of the correctional organization through a discussion of mission, values, goals, principles of organizational structure, and the organizational culture. Chapters 4 through 7 investigate the external political, fiscal, judicial, and special interest environment determinants of organizational behavior. Chapter 8 presents an in-depth overview of the distribution of power relationships in the structural subsystem of the correctional organization. Chapters 9 through 11 explain the roles of management and leadership, planning, decision making, communications, and motivation in environmental design. Chapters 12 through 14 emphasize the importance of employee professionalization, social responsibility and ethical behavior, and the management of change. Chapter 15 examines the challenges facing correctional managers and leaders as we enter the twenty-first century.

Each chapter is structured to provide an integration of management theory, research, and practice by illustrating theories and issues with examples of current correctional practices in both institutional and community corrections organizations. Every chapter begins with an introductory epigraph and Profile that introduces a concept important to the chapter topic. A list of learning objectives at the beginning of the chapter and discussion questions at the end provide a framework for discussing and understanding the flow of concepts in the chapter. The chapter summary provides a brief review of the chapter topic. Each chapter ends with a Critical Analysis Exercise (CAE) that presents a new concept or issue related to the chapter's primary subject. The CAE provides additional information and a set of critical analysis questions designed to stimulate integration of the CAE topic with the material in that chapter or, in some cases, with material introduced in earlier chapters.

Acknowledgments

A project this size depends on the support and encouragement of many people. In addition to my wife, Diane, and two sons, Eric and Brian, I am grateful for the active support and encouragement of Donna Hale and Tom Austin, two of my colleagues at Shippensburg University, who provided valuable insights and were available as a sounding board when I was having difficulty expressing a particularly difficult concept. Appreciation is also extended to Lori Konitski and Jennifer Britland, graduate students whose assistance was invaluable during the research phase of this book.

I am especially indebted to Reginald A. Wilkinson, Director of the Ohio Department of Rehabilitation and Correction and former President of the American Correctional Association. Director Wilkinson provided the Profile for Chapter 15 and some of the photographs used for illustration. I am also grateful to Dr. Ronald J. Waldron, Senior Deputy Assistant Director, Health Services Division, Federal Bureau of Prisons, and C. Allan Turner, Senior Fellow, Mount Vernon College, who provided the Telemedicine Box presented in Chapter 14.

A special thanks is extended to Anne Diestel, Archivist for the Federal Bureau of Prisons, and Kati Corsaut, Public Information Officer for the California Department of Corrections (DOC), who provided the majority of photographs used in this book. My appreciation for the DOC documentation from which many of the practical examples and illustrations were drawn is extended to Edward T. Brennan, Mike B. Evers, Dina Tyler, Bill Sprenkle, Russ Savage, Paul H. Korotkin, Susan J. Coley, James S. Wynn, Lynne Mosley, Roseanne Munafo, Chris Stunda, Tipton Kindel, and Vicky Myers.

I wish to thank Laurel DeWolf, Stephanie Gelman, and Rita Lombard, my editors at Butterworth–Heinemann, who provided invaluable assistance at every step of the process. Finally, my gratitude to the reviewers: Kevin E. Courtright, Ph.D., Lydia M. Long, Ph.D., M. L. Dantzker, Ph.D., James D. Stinchcomb, Ph.D., and Jeanne B. Stinchcomb, Ph.D. Their thorough review of my manuscript and valuable observations and insights provided guidance and direction. This book would not have achieved its present form without their help.

Writing *Correctional Organization and Management: Public Policy Challenges, Behavior and Structure* has been for me an educational and challenging experience. I hope this book will succeed in conveying a sense of the complexity associated with the management and leadership of correctional organizations as we enter the twenty-first century and will encourage its readers to take an active part in helping corrections meet the future.

One final note: I would like to invite readers to respond to this book by sending their comments or suggestions for improving the presentation of material directly to me. My address is: Department of Criminal Justice, Shippensburg University, Shippensburg, Pennsylvania 17257-2299.

1

The Evolution of Correctional Management

Learning Objectives

After completing this chapter, you should be able to:

- Define the fundamental concepts of organization, mission, environmental design, and organizational behavior.
- Compare and contrast Pre-DOC and DOC Corrections in terms of worker–task relationship; manager–worker relationship; and organizational structure.
- Identify and contrast six schools of management theory based on organizational behavior.
- Explain the influence of each management theory on the evolution from Pre-DOC Corrections to DOC Corrections.
- Summarize the contribution of Fayol's five management functions and 14 principles of management to defining the role of the DOC manager–worker relationship.
- Describe the organizational structure of a Department of Corrections using the principles formulated by Weber.

Key Terms and Concepts

Autocratic Warden
Bureaucracy
Bureaucratic Warden
Contingency Approach
Controlling
Coordinating
DOC Corrections
Directing
Employee Empowerment
Environmental Design
Fayol's Management Principles
Hawthorne Studies
Human Capital School
Human Relations School
Industrial Psychology
Line Staff (workers)
Managers
Method
Mission
The "New Agenda"
Organization
Organizational Behavior
Organizing
Planning
Policy
Pre-DOC Corrections
Procedure
Protestant Work Ethic
Scientific Management
Traditional Management
Wagner Act

[O]rganization . . . is a way of bringing order out of chaos, and thus it serves an important function. . . . [O]rganized human effort could not exist if human beings were not placed in certain relationships, told what to do, directed, and controlled. . . .

Douglas McGregor

Profile: From *The Waban* to the California Department of Corrections

The first California state prison, opened in 1852, was an old ship named *The Waban,* anchored in San Pablo Bay off Point Quentin. This ship was home to the 150 male and female inmates used to construct the California State Prison at San Quentin. After two years of backbreaking labor the inmates were moved into San Quentin, known at that time as the "Old Spanish Block." San Quentin was run by a private leasee until 1861, when the state of California assumed formal control of the institution and its inmates. In 1858, inmates began the construction of the California State Prison at Folsom, laboring for 22 years before Folsom opened its doors in 1880.

It was the practice in virtually every state prison in the 1800s that male and female inmates be housed in the same institution. In California, the female inmates were housed at San Quentin until 1933, when the first women's prison opened at Tehachapi. After an earthquake in July of 1952, the women were moved to the California Institution for Women at Frontera. Female inmates are now housed at Corona, Frontera, Stockton, Chowchilla (at 2,000 beds this is the largest U.S. women's prison), and Norco.

Each California prison was under the separate management of a warden until 1944, when the state legislature convened a special session to evaluate the state of California penology. The result was the creation of the California Department of Corrections (DOC), an organizational structure that brought all state prisons under the leadership of a Director of Corrections. Prison population increased from 1944 to the 1970s, when the number of inmates stabilized. Unfortunately, the politically motivated "get tough on crime" approach of the 1980s dramatically increased the inmate population from 24,500 to more than 114,000 between 1980 and 1993. The result was a series of authorizations between 1981 and 1990 for nearly $5 billion to construct 52,000 new prison beds. Between 1984 and 1993, the California DOC expanded three major institutions and either opened or began construction on 15 additional institutions (California Department of Corrections, 1996).

The California DOC now bills itself as the country's largest law enforcement agency. As of January 1, 1997, the DOC had 41,303 employees (Camp and Camp, 1997:116); 32 prisons, over 100 parole offices, and 12 Community Correctional Facilities (American Correctional Association, 1997:32–42); 148,072 inmates; 350,000 parolees and probationers (Camp and Camp, 1997: 2,140); and an annual budget of $3.9 billion (Camp and Camp, 1997:70).

Correctional organizations are complex arrangements of individuals and groups whose activities are managed within an organizational structure designed to achieve the formal mission that defines the purpose of the organization. Individual and group activities, given direction and structure by managers, create organizational behavior. Organizational behavior is the product of a continuous managerial process of environmental design that defines the worker–task relationship, the manager–worker relationship, and the organizational structure within which these relationships exist. Effective environmental design recognizes, and is influenced by, both the internal environment of the organization and the external environment. Environmental design has historically been influenced by management theories that constitute the field of investigation of a discipline known as Organizational Behavior (OB). OB postulates that organizational behavior is the result of three determinants of behavior: individuals, groups, and organizational structure.

The history of correctional organization and management is a history of the transformation of simple, stand-alone prisons ruled by autocratic wardens and "guards" into complex, bureaucratic systems managed by corrections professionals responsible for the activities of correctional officers and numerous categories of correctional personnel in both institutional and community environments. It is a history of moving from a managerial emphasis on the mechanics and structure of work to an emphasis on the human element in work, an evolutionary process that will be presented through a review of the influence of OB theorists on corrections during two periods of correctional management: Pre-DOC Corrections and DOC Corrections.

FUNDAMENTALS OF ORGANIZATIONAL BEHAVIOR

The Profile at the beginning of this chapter presents an example of organizational evolution: the growth of the California penal system from a boat anchored in a safe harbor to a massive bureaucratic system of interrelated correctional organizations scattered throughout a large state. To understand the nature of this evolution it is necessary to define four fundamental concepts: organization, organizational mission, environmental design, and organizational behavior.

Organization

An organization is a "consciously coordinated social unit, composed of two or more people, that functions on a relatively continuous basis to achieve a common goal or set of goals" (Robbins, 1993:3). Organizations achieve goals through the efforts of two groups of people—managers and workers (referred to as line staff, employees, or subordinates)—whose relationship to each other is defined in terms of expectations, skills, abilities, roles, and activities. Managers exercise control of the workers through decision making, planning, communication, allocation of resources, direction, and coordination processes designed to achieve a specific mission. Workers perform the specific tasks (work) defined by the managers. In the case of corrections, that work is the management of offenders.

Organizational Mission

The mission of any correctional organization is composed of a specific set of goals that has been determined by public policy makers and/or influenced by other external groups. The ability to achieve the mission requires correctional managers to have an in-depth knowledge of three elements: (1) the activities that correctional workers must perform to achieve the mission, (2) the nature of the internal and external correctional environment, and (3) the characteristics and activities of offenders. More specifically, the manager must ensure that specific worker activities are performed within a mission-congruent organizational structure. The complexity of the mission determines the complexity of the organizational structure. And mission complexity is influenced by the behavior of individuals, groups, and organizations in the external environment.

Environmental Design

The primary responsibility of managers is environmental design—"the design of an environment in which people working together in groups can accomplish objectives" (Koontz, O'Donnell, and Weihrich, 1986:13). Another term for environmental design is "job design," which is the "deliberate, purposeful planning of the job including all of its structural and social aspects and their effect on the employee" (Hellriegel and Slocum, 1979:413). In this book, we will use the term *environmental design* because "environmental" more accurately conveys the broad scope of management than does "job."

Environmental design provides three definitions. First, it defines the worker–task relationship by specifying the activities necessary to accomplish the tasks managers assign to workers. Second, it defines the manager–worker relationship (and, in the case of corrections, the manager–worker–offender relationship) by specifying the functions of the manager and the required methods of directing worker activities. Both sets of definitions are grounded in assumptions about the fundamental nature of both managers and workers. Third, environmental design defines the organizational structure within which the work will take place. The primary goal of any environmental design is effective individual and group behavior within an organization. "Effective behavior" is defined as behavior that achieves the mission.

Managers communicate the mission through the formulation and dissemination of policies, procedures, and methods. A policy is a general statement that reflects some aspect of the mission and serves as a guide for decision making. A procedure defines the specific sequence of steps to be taken to accomplish a task required by policy. A method specifies how a particular step in a procedure is to be performed, and it must therefore be more detailed than policy and procedure. For example, DOC policy requires that a priority of every prison manager is the maintenance of institutional security by limiting the ability of inmates to introduce contraband into the institution. Upon receiving this policy from the Commissioner, Superintendents issue a local policy statement requiring the routine search of all inmates on outside work details when they return to the prison. In response, Deputy Superintendents for Operations develop a procedure that requires all returning outside detail inmates to line up in front of the main gate, enter the receiving area one at a time to be greeted by at least two officers, remove their shoes for inspection, empty their pockets, and then be "patted down." The method to be followed for "patting down" is explained in detail: "Begin the search at the feet, checking all pants cuffs and pockets; run the hands up the outside and inside of the leg; check under the belt; run the hands up the shirt, under the arms; check under the collar; and inspect the hair for contraband." This sequence of policy–procedure–method defines the behavior of both inmates and officers when the goal is limiting the introduction of contraband into the facility.

Organizational Behavior

As noted above, the behavior of organizations is studied by a specific discipline, Organizational Behavior (OB). OB can be defined as "the field that seeks to comprehend and predict human behavior in organizational settings through the scientific study of individual processes, group processes, and organizational structure and function" (Baron, 1983:8). Thus, OB represents a distinct area of expertise built upon an evolving body of knowledge concerning the three determinants of behavior within an organization: individuals, groups, and organizational structure. OB theorists strive to improve organizational effectiveness by examining ten core processes (Robbins, 1993:7):

1. Motivation
2. Leader behavior and power
3. Interpersonal communication
4. Group structure and process
5. Learning
6. Attitude development and perception
7. Change processes
8. Conflict
9. Job design
10. Work stress

The result of the examination of these core processes is management theory.

OB theorists have traditionally focused attention on production industries and defined human behavior and organizational structure in terms of the requirements of machines and material product assembly. In human service work such as corrections, however, there is no material good that is the goal of production; rather, the product of corrections work is people. Nevertheless, basic OB principles can be applied to our discussion of correctional organization and management.

ORGANIZATIONAL BEHAVIOR AND CORRECTIONAL MANAGEMENT

Carrell, Jennings, and Heavrin (1997:5) divide OB into six schools of management theory: (1) Traditional Management (prior to

1880), (2) Scientific Management (1880 to 1920), (3) Human Relations (1920s to 1940s), (4) the Contingency Approach (1950s and 1960s), (5) Human Capital (1970s and 1980s), and (6) the "New Agenda" (1990s). Each of these schools defined a set of management beliefs, but each had implicit limitations that required the evolutionary development of the following school.

One of the areas of management belief that most sharply differentiates these schools involves the issue of employee empowerment. Employee empowerment is a conscious, organized process of managers involving employees in their work through a process of inclusion. That is, managers deliberately pursue a strategy of delegating authority; encouraging employees to participate in decision making; creating meaningful tasks that allow employees to feel that their efforts contribute to the well-being of the organization; educating and training employees to accomplish more difficult tasks than they were originally hired to perform; and allowing employees a high degree of flexibility in how they perform their jobs (Robbins, 1993:682–683). Employee empowerment represents a fundamental strategy of encouraging employees to view their jobs as meaningful and worthwhile. Traditional Management and Scientific Management did not recognize the concept of employee empowerment. However, beginning with the Human Relations movement, employee empowerment became a concern of management.

The history of correctional organization and management can be divided into two periods spanning approximately the same time period as OB. Pre-DOC Corrections, existing from 1812 to the early 1940s, had a remarkably simple mission: the punitive control of prisoners. This mission was to be accomplished in prisons dominated by an autocratic warden whose approach to management was independent of any centralized correctional authority (Bartollas and Conrad, 1992). Pre-DOC Corrections reflected the principles of Traditional Management and Scientific Management, emphasizing the mechanics and structure of work while largely ignoring the human element.

The rule of prisons by autocratic wardens was followed by DOC Corrections, extending from the early 1940s to the present, during which time the mission of corrections became considerably more complicated. In addition to providing custody and control, corrections was to foster offender rehabilitation through a variety of institutional and community-based treatment programs while providing humane living conditions in the prisons. To meet this increased mission complexity, the dominant role of the bureaucratic warden emerged as states created Departments of Corrections (DOCs) to provide centralized control of their state-operated prisons and community-based correctional organizations (Bartollas and Conrad, 1992). Relying extensively on Scientific Management principles for its structure, DOC Corrections has been strongly influenced by the schools of Human Relations, the Contingency Approach, Human Capital, and the emerging "New Agenda." We begin with Pre-DOC Corrections.

TRADITIONAL MANAGEMENT AND PRE-DOC CORRECTIONS

Traditional Management was guided by the principles of the Protestant Work Ethic:

1. Work is intrinsically rewarding.
2. Hard work will be recognized and rewarded by others and by God.
3. Owners have been chosen by God on the basis of their wisdom and ability and should be obeyed without question (Carrell, Jennings, and Heavrin, 1997:6).

The relationship between manager and worker embodied in the Protestant Work Ethic was unambiguous. Managers, superior in both ability and intelligence, performed all the managerial functions and provided total direction and control. Workers, considered to be generally equal to each other in ability, motivation, and productivity, were given the simple, routine jobs. Because workers were considered to be interchangeable units (cogs in the wheel) who could be easily replaced, their role was to obey orders without question. The belief that every employee has the potential to contribute to environmental design had not yet been articulated. Nor were Pre-DOC managers interested in developing a strategy of encouraging employees to assist them in environmental design. The concept of employee empowerment was unknown, and, if it had been verbalized by employees, this alien concept would have been quickly rejected by managers secure in their belief of God-given ability to direct and control every aspect of organizational life.

The Worker–Task Relationship In Pre-DOC Corrections

The Pre-DOC mission of the punitive control of prisoners provided managers with four primary goals: (1) prevent prisoners from escaping or engaging in violence, (2) make sure that prisoner labor is cost-effective, (3) maintain a minimum level of meeting prisoner basic needs, and (4) do nothing that would embarrass political leaders. To achieve these goals, managers assigned guards (the term *correctional officer* would not be introduced until the 1960s) specific tasks: maintaining close observation of prisoner behavior during every phase of activity; conducting periodic head counts; searching for contraband; guarding the prison perimeter; providing direct supervision during work and meals; maintaining basic control functions such as the lockstep formation and Silent System; and administering brutal physical punishment when rules were broken. It was simple, repetitive work organized around an emphasis on routine and characterized by a high level of boredom. The work was considered to be so unskilled that no hiring requirements other than physical size and strength were necessary. Nor was staff training deemed to be necessary. Lewis Lawes, a famous prison warden, noted that when he began his career in 1905 in New York his orientation on the first day

of duty consisted of being handed "a pair of sneakers and a club. The sneakers, to enable the guard to make his rounds noiselessly, so as not to disturb the sleeping forms within the dark cells, and the club to be used in emergencies should any of those forms become unduly active" (Lawes, 1932:12). The work of the guard was considered to be so simple that new employees were put to work the first day of employment.

The Manager–Worker Relationship in Pre-DOC Corrections

The most important manager in Pre-DOC Corrections was the autocratic warden. The relationship between warden and guard was strictly governed by the principles of the Protestant Work Ethic. Because the warden was considered to be a superior individual, he provided all direction and control. The untrained prison guards—expected to obey, not think—did as they were told and had little influence over the establishment of policy, procedures, and rules. Autocratic wardens required absolute loyalty. Guards who questioned the established policy could be immediately dismissed.

Typical of the autocratic wardens was Joseph Ragen, warden of Stateville and Joliet Penitentiaries in Illinois from 1936 to 1961. Ragen ruled his prisons with an iron fist and "required rigid adherence to formal rules and regulations covering virtually every aspect of prison life" (DiIulio, 1987:44). The source of those rules and regulations was Ragen, and Ragen alone. Although each warden had a complement of subordinate managers (captains, lieutenants, and sergeants), these individuals often had as little influence on policy development as the guards. In many cases, their function was simply to make sure that the orders of the warden were carried out exactly as given. They, too, were vulnerable to immediate dismissal unless they were fortunate enough to be in the good graces of the political leaders to whom their warden had to ultimately answer.

The quality of prison guards and the managerial attitude toward them can be clearly seen in this comment about Julian N. Frisbie, warden of the State Prison of Southern Michigan at Jackson, during the 1952 riot:

Warden Frisbie could not hire enough guards. The pay was lower than in near-by factories. He has said, "We would hire them if they were warm and alive." He got some bad ones. Nearly half the guards had jobs in town. Sometimes, exhausted by working two jobs, they were caught asleep on duty (Martin, 1954:35).

The challenge to the manager presented by this lack of work force quality was how to force the guards to accomplish the simple tasks involved in custody and control. Managers met this challenge by controlling guards in much the same way that the guards controlled prisoners. The concept that guards should be allowed to participate in environmental design was foreign and not supported by theory or the warden's personal experience. Because guards were considered to be interchangeable cogs there was no reason to attempt to develop their natural skills and abilities. They were not considered to be a resource.

The Organizational Structure of Pre-DOC Corrections

The mission of Pre-DOC Corrections required confinement of prisoners in the physical space enclosed by the prison walls. Any extension of corrections beyond the prison walls took the form of work gangs, agricultural work, and contracted labor to members of the community. There was no "community corrections" as we now understand the term nor centralized control by a headquarters staff. Reflecting this limited geography was an organizational structure that was primitive by today's standards. Each state prison was an independent unit

with an organizational structure embodying a rudimentary paramilitary prisoner control system that consisted of warden, guards, subordinate managers, and, in some cases, a physician or chaplain brought in on a part-time basis. Power and communication flowed from the warden, whose focus was almost exclusively on the internal environment. The external environment had limited influence on organizational behavior.

The Limitations of Traditional Management

Toward the end of the nineteenth century, three fundamental limitations of Traditional Management were readily apparent (Carrell, Jennings, and Heavrin, 1997:5). First, all employees do not adhere to the principles of the Protestant Work Ethic. Because employees are individuals with different value systems, not every individual embraced the Protestant Work Ethic with the fervor that managers would like. Traditional Management also ignored the profound influence of group values on employee behavior.

Second, employees possess the interest and initiative to perform some managerial duties (a fact readily incorporated in the Theory Y approach to employee motivation that is discussed in Chapter 11). Traditional Management provided the workers with no incentive to improve the way they accomplished their tasks or feel a sense of loyalty to the organization. Employees who lack a sense of participation frequently settle for doing the minimum amount of work possible and feel no loyalty to the organization or its principles. An unmotivated work force all too often results in a stagnant environment and failure to achieve the mission.

Third, all employees are not equal in skills and abilities. Assuming equality and assigning workers to tasks that they are unable to perform in an acceptable manner increases the potential for mission failure. In a factory, the consequences of mission failure may be a defective product and lowered revenues, but in corrections the consequences can be life-threatening. For example, assigning a corrections officer to work in a cellblock, a position that demands the ability to interact effectively with large numbers of inmates in confined quarters, can have serious negative consequences (such as increased violence) if that officer is more suited to working in a security tower. Assigning a probation officer who fears confrontation and interpersonal conflict to an Intensive Supervision Probation caseload can result in probationers successfully violating the rules and avoiding revocation because the P.O. is unable to effectively confront their inappropriate behavior.

Because the issue of unequal abilities was not recognized, Pre-DOC wardens were not interested in officer training or the use of corrective discipline. Workers who could not do the job were simply fired. The result was a high rate of worker turnover that left guards greatly outnumbered by growing numbers of angry prisoners who periodically expressed their dissatisfaction by rioting, which the guards were neither trained nor prepared to handle. Because of these limitations a new approach, Scientific Management, blossomed.

SCIENTIFIC MANAGEMENT (1880–1920)

Scientific Management began as a systematic effort to develop a "science of management" (Certo, 1985:27), the impetus for which in the noncorrections world came from public demands for elected and appointed officials to be held accountable for their performance in office (Denhardt, 1984:43) and the profit-driven need of business owners to increase worker efficiency.

In corrections, the need for accountability and a science of management was demonstrated far too often by graphic exposés of prison corruption and brutality. A typical example was the Elmira Reformatory in New York. Hailed as a model of the new penology of rehabilitation when it opened on July 24, 1876, the Elmira Reformatory was initially considered the very model of humane treatment of youthful offenders. Its warden, Zebulon Brockway, was considered to be the "Father of Rehabilitation." Yet, in 1894, the New York State Board of Charities, after five months of hearings, concluded that Elmira was "overcrowded, understaffed, and grossly mismanaged" (Pisciotta, 1994:33). Inmates were subjected to appalling levels of official brutality, homosexual rape orchestrated by inmate "Monitors," abuses of parole decision making, the absence of competent medical care, and an environment so dehumanizing that Brockway was forced to retire in 1900.

But Elmira was not atypical. Pre-DOC prisons were inhumane organizations in which each warden was permitted to determine the most appropriate means of achieving punitive inmate control.

Penitentiary prisoners often went hungry; firsthand accounts report prisoners begging for food from the prison kitchen and being punished for their temerity. Diseases ran rampant among poorly nourished prisoners. Even for the healthy and well-fed, life in the penitentiary was lonely and depressing and left no room whatsoever for adult autonomy (Johnson, 1997:33).

The demand for accountability required OB to move beyond the constraints of management by personal whim and philosophy. The physical sciences were achieving impressive gains through the use of scientific methodology. The newly emerging sciences of Psychology and Sociology were examining human behavior in terms of the scientific approach. It was time for managers to also adopt a more scientific approach.

The Managerial Component of Scientific Management

Frederick W. Taylor is generally acknowledged as the founder of the Scientific Management movement. In the early 1900s,

Taylor was a mechanical engineer at Pennsylvania's Middle and Bethlehem steel companies. Specialization and standardization were primitive, employees were unmotivated, and productivity was low.

Virtually no effective work standards existed. Workers purposely worked at a slow pace. Management decisions were of the "seat-of-the-pants" nature, based on hunch and intuition. Workers were placed on jobs with little or no concern for matching their abilities and aptitudes with the tasks they were required to do. Most important, management and workers considered themselves to be in a zero-sum game—any gain by one would be at the expense of the other (Robbins, 1993:701).

The preceding excerpt provides a perfect description of the lack of effective environmental design in Pre-DOC Corrections. There simply was no science involved in prison management. Taylor (1911) believed that the worker–task relationship was sufficiently complicated to deserve scientific study. Taylor also recognized that workers required motivation other than the intrinsic nature of the work itself. He proposed an economic man theory that management should focus on job design and employee motivation through a "scientific" approach to management that is based on four principles. First, the application of the methods of science to problems of management leads to increases in efficiency. Second, observation, measurement, and experimental comparison are among the principle methods of science that can be applied to problems of management. Third, the incentive of high wages and encouraging high productivity workers to stay on the job promotes worker–manager cooperation and promotes efficiency. Fourth, efficiency can be promoted through the standardization of working conditions and methods through motion and time study (Kazimer, 1974:4–7).

What Taylor was proposing was a dramatic change in the manager–worker relationship that required the managers to

1. Develop a scientific description for each element of a worker's job
2. Scientifically select each worker, then train, teach, and develop skill levels appropriate to the tasks to be assigned the worker
3. Cooperate with the workers to ensure that work is in accordance with the requirements determined by time and motion studies
4. Divide work and responsibility almost equally among managers and workers so managers are doing the work they are most qualified to perform

The end result of adherence to these principles? A more productive work force.

In 1913, in another important development in the science of management, Hugo Munsterberg made the argument that there should be a scientific study of human behavior that would identify general patterns as well as explain individual differences. Thus was born the field of Industrial Psychology, a discipline that would encourage the creation of DOC personnel management systems organized in terms of (1) the use of standardized psychological tests to improve employee selection, (2) an emphasis on the value of learning theory in developing and implementing training programs, and (3) the application of motivation theory as a management skill.

However, the wide application of these principles to correctional employees would not occur until the creation of the Federal Bureau of Prisons in 1930 and the emergence in the 1940s of state-level DOC Corrections.

What was missing from OB was a conceptualization of the manager–worker relationship that was more sophisticated than the Traditional Management assumption that managers simply were people who made sure workers did as they were told. The specific functions of the manager needed to be defined.

A Typology of Basic Management Functions

While Taylor was examining piecework for the Bethlehem Steel Company, the French industrialist Henri Fayol was examining the practices of top management in France. Based on his observations, Fayol proposed that management was something distinct from the typical business functions of finance, accounting, production, and distribution. He believed that management was an activity found in all organizations, regardless of their purpose, and that the activities of every manager could be defined in terms of five basic management functions: planning, organizing, directing, controlling, and coordinating (Fayol, 1916). Fayol declared that these functions were not independent of each other but, rather, were interrelated (Figure 1–1). The role of each of these functions in corrections will be briefly examined.

Planning

Planning involves a complex, ongoing process of "rational thinking, documentation, control, and monitoring" (Wright, 1994:158). Effective planning coordinates worker functions through an environmental design that begins with the development of a hierarchy of goals prioritized on the basis of criteria derived from the mission. Managers then develop and disseminate mission-congruent policies, procedures, and methods.

Planning encompasses every aspect of organizational behavior: the budget process, which determines the allocation of resources; the personnel selection processes of recruitment, evaluation, promotion, and dismissal of correctional employees; the classification of offenders and development of appropriate program designs; maintenance of the physical plant; provision of basic offender medical, food, housing, clothing, recreational, and religious activities; the relationship between treatment and security employees; the structure and programs of community corrections; relationships with other criminal justice agencies, the courts, legislatures, media, and special interest groups; and response to emergencies.

Organizing

Organizing consists of determining the activities to be performed within an organization, grouping those activities using a process

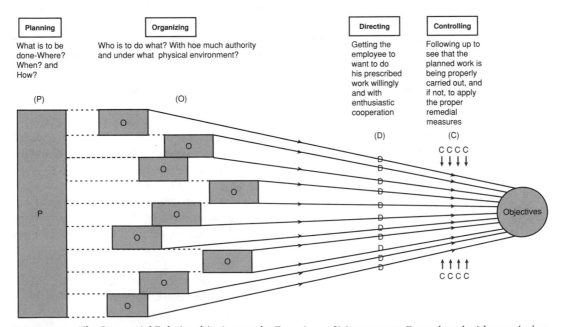

FIGURE 1–1   The Sequential Relationship Among the Functions of Management. Reproduced with permission.

called "departmentalization," and assigning managerial authority and responsibility in a manner that is clear to every employee. The resulting organizational structure is typically presented through the use of the organization chart, a written model that designates the formal organization of activities, authority relationships, and formal communications channels. As an organization expands, its growth may be represented on the chart in either a vertical or a horizontal direction. The addition of more levels of management is represented by vertical growth, while the addition of more functions (with the number of organizational levels remaining constant), is represented by horizontal growth.

The shape of the overall organizational structure is strongly influenced by the location of authority. Authority moves down the chain of command, with each position in the chain receiving the amount of authority necessary for its functions to be properly performed. The concentration of authority at the top managerial levels indicates managerial centralization and produces a multi-layered, vertical organization chart. The dissemination of authority throughout the organization represents a decentralization of managerial authority and produces a flattened organizational structure.

Some of these structural concepts are discussed further in Chapter 2. But with only our limited discussion of organizations thus far, we can nevertheless define the Pre-DOC Corrections organizational structure as one in which centralized authority created a narrow vertical structure in which all power and communication flowed from the warden to the guards through intervening layers of subordinate managers. (See chart below.) This simple structure stands in stark contrast to the complex DOC organization chart that is presented later in this chapter.

Directing

Directing focuses on providing appropriate levels of guidance and supervision to subordinates as they engage in the activities designed to achieve the mission. The directing function involves leadership, a complex process of motivating subordinates, directing their activities, maintaining an effective communication process, and resolving conflicts.

Controlling

Controlling involves a process of monitoring organizational behavior to ensure that employee activities and performance are in line with the requirements of the mission. A formal control process establishes

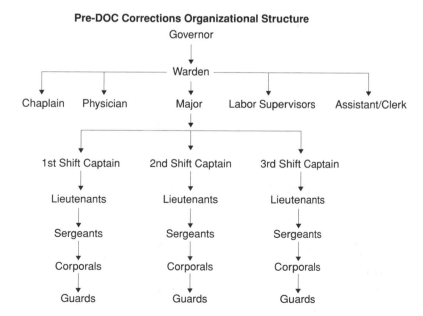

Pre-DOC Corrections Organizational Structure

standards, compares actual results with those standards, and takes corrective action when deviations from expected behavior are detected. The American Correctional Association (ACA) accreditation process, the budget process (both internal and external), written job descriptions and post orders, and formal annual employee evaluations are integral elements in a formal control process.

Coordinating

Today, coordinating is considered to be an objective of management, not a specific function (Kazimer, 1974:46). The successful coordination of activities occurs when the functions of planning, organizing, directing, and controlling have been effectively accomplished. Effective coordination provides a clarity of purpose, reduces the misuse and waste of resources, reduces employee and offender confusion, and increases the probability of mission success.

Fayol's Principles of Management

Henri Fayol emphasized that the importance of managerial ability increases as one moves up the chain of command. Thus, managerial skill is the most important component of job performance at the top level of management. Fayol noted that the failure to effectively perform each management function has serious consequences for any organization and he viewed mission failure as more than the result of poor workers. It was an outcome for which managers should be held accountable. Fayol proposed that job performance could be enhanced, and managerial failure minimized, by following 14 principles of management.

1. Division of Work: The specialization of employee activities increases productivity by making employees more efficient through the development of skills, confidence, and accuracy.

2. Authority: Managers have the right to give orders and the power to exact obedience. Along with authority goes managerial responsibility and accountability.

Authority and responsibility are two sides of the same coin. The manager is held responsible for the productivity of subordinates and any failure to achieve objectives.

3. Discipline: Employees must obey and respect the rules of the organization. Obedience and respect are created by effective leadership, common effort and agreement between manager and employee, and the judicious application of sanctions when rule violations occur.

4. Unity of Command: Orders received from two bosses will produce conflict and confusion. Therefore, an employee should be directly supervised by one person only.

5. Unity of Direction: A group of activities having the same objectives should be directed by one manager using one plan. To do otherwise creates confusion.

6. Subordination of Individual Interests to the General Interests: The interests of the organization as a whole take precedence over the interests of any individual employee or group of employees.

7. Remuneration: Employees must be paid a fair wage for their services, with fairness being determined by such factors as the cost of living, availability of employees, and general business conditions.

8. Centralization: This is an issue of proportion—the degree of employee involvement in decision making. Which degree of centralization or decentralization will lead to the greatest organizational efficiency?

9. Scalar Chain: The scalar chain is the line of supervision from top management to the lowest level of employee. Each level possesses more authority than the level below it. Communications and authority are organized in terms of this chain of command. Power and authority flow downward. The purpose of the chain of command is to promote organizational efficiency through the clear delineation of authority and communication channels.

10. Order: Employees and materials should be in the same place at the same time in accordance with an established social and material order.

11. Equity: Managers should treat their subordinates fairly and equally. Favoritism will create conflict and decrease organizational efficiency.

12. Stability of Tenure of Personnel: High levels of employee turnover create inefficiency. It costs money and time to train new employees. Employee retention should be a priority for managers. Managers should provide for orderly personnel planning and replacement of employees who have left the organization.

13. Initiative: Managers should provide employees the opportunity to initiate, propose, and execute ideas.

14. Esprit de Corps: Promoting team spirit through harmony and reduction of dissension between employees will build unity and create organizational efficiency.

Fayol's principles of management were logical and well articulated, and he believed that they should be taught in schools and universities. However, an essential question remained to be answered. In what type of organizational structure could his definition of the effective manager–worker relationship be most successfully achieved? That answer came from the German sociologist Max Weber.

The Structural Component of Scientific Management

While Henri Fayol was studying top management in France and Frederick Taylor was studying management at the shop level in the United States, Max Weber was developing a theory of authority structures and describing organizational activity in terms of authority relations (Weber, 1947). Weber was one of the first theorists to examine organizational behavior from a structural perspective. He believed that an effective organization consciously organized people and activities in order to achieve specific objectives. Weber described an ideal type of organization—the bureaucracy—that consisted of six elements:

1. Division of Labor: All jobs were broken down into simple, routine, well-defined tasks that would promote employee specialization.

2. Authority Hierarchy: Positions are organized in a hierarchy, each lower one being controlled and supervised by a higher one (Fayol's scalar chain).

3. Formal Selection: Every employee is to be selected on the basis of technical qualifications demonstrated by training, education, or formal examination, not on the basis of a personal relationship with the manager.

4. Formal Rules and Regulations: Managers must extensively rely on formal organizational rules if uniformity of activity and continuity of function are to be maintained during personnel changes.

5. Impersonality: Rules and controls must be applied uniformly to all employees, regardless of personalities, the manager's personal preferences, or personal involvement with an employee.

6. Career Orientation: Managers are professionals, not owners of the departments or organizations they manage. They work for a fixed salary and can pursue advancement (move up the "career ladder") within the organization.

The underlying theme of the bureaucracy was rationality. Weber believed that this rational, rules-oriented approach would be highly efficient because the "noise" generated by personal feelings, individual differences, and similar factors would be largely eliminated (Baron, 1983:510). Weber's theory became the prototype for the design of almost all of today's large organizations, including those in corrections. Weber was quick to recognize that the bureaucracy in its ideal form did not exist in the real world, but he believed that it could serve as the theoretical basis for discussing work and how it could be most effectively accomplished in large organizations.

The Limitations of Scientific Management

There are three fundamental limitations of Scientific Management (Carrell, Jennings, and Heavrin, 1997:5). First, employees are the heart of any organization. The success or failure of managers depends on the ability and dedication of the employees. However, the definition of workers as interchangeable factors of production with a limited ability to do more than routine work devalued the unique ability of each worker to effectively contribute to organizational effectiveness. For example, Taylor (1947:45–46) once declared: "One of the very first requirements for a man who is fit to handle pig iron as a regular occupation is that he shall be so stupid and so phlegmatic that he more nearly resembles in his mental makeup the ox."

Second, motivation is a complex phenomenon and economic gain is only one component of an individual's motivation, and not necessarily the most important component. The manager must be sensitive to a wide range of motivational factors, and understand a variety of motivational techniques, if employees are to be effectively motivated (as will be discussed in Chapter 11).

Third, highly specialized jobs are boring and this leads to low morale and employee problems such as dissatisfaction, alienation, absenteeism, and high rates of turnover. In their efforts to define the mechanics and

structure of the most effective worker–task and manager–worker relationship, Taylor, Fayol, and Weber overlooked two considerations: human beings form the core of every organization and human beings are social beings by nature. This lack of a "social" component in OB meant that the "people side" of organizational behavior was largely ignored. Consequently, OB theorists and managers alike remained ignorant of a valuable source of creativity and resourcefulness that could play an important role in their quest to make organizations more effective. This lack of a social dimension in management theory would be addressed by the Human Relations school, an approach that would be most clearly reflected in the 1960s rehabilitation model of inmate management and the growing recognition of a need for managers to encourage employee empowerment.

THE HUMAN RELATIONS MOVEMENT (1920s–1940s)

That the worker is a social being who deserves to be treated as more than a dumb beast of burden was articulated by two early OB theorists, Mary Parker Follett and Chester Barnard, whose ideas developed during the Scientific Management period but were not widely recognized until the 1930s (Wren, 1987). Both Follett and Barnard believed that workers were the organization's most valuable resources (Figure 1–2) and that the manager–worker relationship was more complex than previously realized.

Follett saw workers as unique individuals who had the potential to grow and develop. Thus, a poor worker should be encouraged to improve performance rather than be summarily dismissed. Individual potential, however, remained potential only until it was released through group association. In Follett's view, the job of the manager was to foster and promote a group ethic based on an understanding of manager and worker as partners in a common enterprise. Functioning in terms of this group ethic, the manager was to rely on personal expertise and knowledge as the means to motivate subordinates, rather than on the formal authority of the position. Group togetherness and team effort were to be the foundations of organizational efficiency.

Chester Barnard understood organizations as social systems that require human cooperation if they are to function effectively. He introduced the idea of communication as a means of acquiring this cooperation (Barnard, 1938). Barnard believed that the primary roles of the manager are to communicate and to motivate subordinates to attain higher levels of effort. He argued that organizational success depended on obtaining cooperation from employees and maintaining good relations with them. Barnard also broadened the scope of managerial attention. He proposed that organizational success also depended on maintaining good

relations with external organizations with whom there was regular interaction. Whether with employees or external organizations, the effective manager would maintain relationships through a process of examining interactions and making the organizational adjustments necessary to maintain an equilibrium. The need for DOC managers to be aware of the external environment, and respond appropriately to its influence, is examined in Chapters 4–7.

The Human Relations approach began to gain prominence in the 1930s through an emphasis on the social aspect of management theory. This emphasis was influenced by behavioral science research that began with a series of studies (1924–1932) at the Western Electric Company's Hawthorne Works in Cicero, Illinois. Numerous experiments in evaluating methods to increase employee productivity were carried out

FIGURE 1–2   The cardinal principle of the Human Relations movement is that people are an organization's most valuable resource. Every effort should be made to develop their potential. Source: Ohio Department of Rehabilitation and Correction.

during the eight-year period of the Haw-thorne Studies (Franke and Kaul, 1978). In one study, investigators determined that an increase in the light level of a room increased employee productivity. In another study, it was determined that an incentive plan had less impact on worker productivity than did group pressure and acceptance. The studies' conclusion that social norms or standards of the work group must be considered a key determinant of individual work was based on the finding that

---

behavior and sentiments were closely related, that group influences significantly affected individual behavior, that group standards established individual worker output, and that money was less a factor in determining output than were group standards, group sentiments, and security. These conclusions led to a new emphasis on the human factor in the functioning of organizations . . . (Robbins, 1993:707).

The Hawthorne Studies provided the impetus for OB theorists to officially recognize individuals as members of social groups and acknowledge that group values are a factor in organizational behavior that must be considered by managers. Consequently, the foundation for the role of organizational culture (the subject of Chapter 3) in organizational behavior was officially recognized in OB. These insights into human behavior produced by the Hawthorne Studies would eventually be supplemented by the work of a number of behavioral scientists. B.F. Skinner (1953), for example, raised awareness of the importance of employee motivation by demonstrating that behavior is a function of consequences: Desired behavior can be generated through the development of a reward system, and the most effective reward system is one in which a reward immediately follows the desired behavior while undesirable behavior is either punished or ignored. The increasing prominence of the behav-

ioral sciences in the 1960s encouraged correctional managers to explore issues of employee motivation and influenced the development of a variety of management styles (discussed in Chapter 9) based on the work of Abraham Maslow, David McClelland, Frederick Herzberg, and Douglas McGregor. In addition, the research of these theorists helped foster an awareness among correctional managers that there was a compelling need to develop strategies of employee empowerment. A discussion of the most prominent of these strategies will be presented in Chapter 11.

The Principles of the Human Relations Movement

The essential belief of Human Relations was that the key to higher productivity could be found in increasing employee satisfaction. The introduction of psychological and sociological factors into OB challenged previous principles governing the manager–worker relationship by emphasizing that managers should get to know their employees as individuals and consider their personal and emotional needs during the decision-making process, allow participation by employees in those decisions that affect their work, and strive to make their employees happy because the happy worker is a productive worker (Mayo and Roethlisberger, 1939). The primary difference between Human Relations and its predecessors was its belief that employees were more than factors of production. Recognition of their needs and feelings by managers would increase organizational effectiveness.

The Role of the Human Relations Movement in Creating DOC Corrections

The Human Relations recognition of the importance of the individual complemented the philosophy and activities of a group of social reformers known as the "Progressives," who were well-to-do individuals with an interest in improving social conditions for the disadvantaged. In the context of corrections, the Human Relations' emphasis on the worker as an individual meshed very nicely with the Progressives' belief that each offender was a unique individual whose needs and feelings should be recognized by corrections. The result of this meshing was a fundamental redefinition of the worker–task relationship; manager–worker relationship; and the organizational structure of corrections.

Redefining the Worker–Task Relationship

The Progressives argued that offenders were individuals who could benefit from treatment administered in accordance with their unique needs. Their focus on "moral regeneration" as a goal of corrections introduced a new concept of the offender as "a man who has suffered under a disease evinced by the perpetration of a crime" (quoted in Mitford, 1973:96). This new offender definition rejected the goal of punishment with its reliance on brutality, regimentation, and the lockstep and substituted the goal of treatment of the social and intellectual deficiencies that had produced an individual's criminal behavior. Achieving this goal required a new set of worker tasks: diagnostic interviews that relied on the ability to communicate and analyze; administration of formal testing instruments; report writing; development and implementation of educational and vocational training programs; classification of offenders in accordance with treatment needs; and the use of counseling skills and techniques.

As public policy makers accepted rehabilitation as a legitimate goal, it became increasingly obvious that uneducated guards were not capable of performing the complex tasks required by the new philosophical understanding of corrections:

Corrections is essentially a context in which mental health, resource management, and problem-solving skills merge into a dynamic continuum—one that requires the case manager to recognize and utilize interdisciplinary insights and strategies. The family, social institutions such as schools and churches, and community and institutional criminal justice environments all contribute to the context within which the correctional case manager works (Enos and Southern, 1966:v).

This shift in understanding made necessary the emergence of a new category of correctional employee: the treatment professional capable of performing the skilled diagnosis and treatment of offenders.

Redefining the Manager–Worker Relationship

The treatment professional was a new breed of employee. In marked contrast to the unskilled white male guard that was the hallmark of Pre-DOC Corrections, these new employees were highly educated. In addition, their ranks would increasingly be filled by women and minorities who would challenge the white male domination of corrections. Treatment staff were much more predisposed to challenge the autocratic warden's assumption of the right to be obeyed without question because they had specialized knowledge the warden lacked. They also had employment opportunities in the community (not available to guards who viewed corrections as their only possible livelihood) if corrections turned out to not be to their liking. "Treatment decisions" became the province of the treatment professionals who, because of the specialized nature of their functions, had to be under the supervision of managers who were equally, or better, educated. An increasingly significant element of organizational behavior slipped from the autocratic warden's control. More important, it became increasingly necessary that wardens be educated and possess a higher degree of flexibility and creativity than had previously been required.

Redefining the Organizational Structure

Because diagnosis and treatment by qualified treatment professionals was an integral part of the medical model, prisons began to develop classification systems; education and vocational education programs; and medical, psychological/psychiatric, and counseling services. The organization chart of the prison experienced both horizontal and vertical growth as treatment departments were added and new layers of management were created. But there was to be an even more profound effect on the organizational structure of corrections. By the 1920s the Progressives had succeeded in gaining wide acceptance of four reforms first proposed at the 1870 Cincinnati meeting of the National Prison Association: (1) probation, (2) indeterminate sentences, (3) parole, and (4) juvenile courts (Clear and Cole, 1994:62). By 1930 the federal government and 36 states had adult probation laws in effect. Probation and parole programs expanded the geography of corrections by permanently moving the correction mission into the community, an event that would play a role in creating the DOC organizational structure presented later in this chapter.

The Limitations of the Human Relations Movement

There were three fundamental limitations to the Human Relations approach (Carrell, Jennings, and Heavrin, 1997:5). First, the "happy worker is a productive worker" formula was a simplified concept of organizational behavior. The effectiveness of any employee is affected by a wide range of factors, many of which cannot be controlled by the organization. In corrections, prison overcrowding, the constant potential for violence, and the negative public perception of corrections adversely affect the lives of many correctional employees regardless of managerial efforts to improve the work environment. Second, workers are complex human beings with different needs and values. It is impossible for a manager to make everybody happy, regardless of the management style utilized. Third, the Human Relations approach failed to relate organizational objectives to employee objectives. A focus on meeting organizational needs as the main managerial priority diluted efforts to meet worker needs. Workers hearing that management was concerned about them, but seeing little concrete evidence of such concern, would eventually become so dissatisfied that they would demand the right to unionize.

THE EMERGENCE OF THE DEPARTMENT OF CORRECTIONS AND THE BUREAUCRATIC WARDEN

In the years immediately following World War II, governors and legislators demanded the creation of management systems that would ensure political control of governmental agencies, achieve greater efficiency, establish clear accountability for organizational behavior, promote higher standards of performance, and engage in a more efficient allocation of resources (Freeman, 1997b:286–292). In corrections, the need for creation of new management systems was announced by a devastating wave of riots. From 1951 to 1953, prison riots occurred in New Jersey, Michigan, Louisiana, North Carolina, Idaho, Georgia, Kentucky, California, Massachusetts, Ohio, Illinois, Pennsylvania, Utah, New Mexico, Arizona, Washington, Oregon, and Minnesota.

The investigations of these riots produced remarkably similar findings: Managers were unable to exercise effective control; guards were untrained; inmate classification procedures were almost nonexistent; prisons were run without formal rules; poor planning created a lack of direction; disciplinary practices were arbitrary and inconsistent; wardens were hired only because they could deliver political votes; employees were hired, promoted, and fired on the basis of managerial whim; operating procedures were unwritten and inconsistently applied;

there was a lack of inmate programs; and there existed throughout corrections an extraordinary lack of professional leadership. Interestingly, "[n]ot one of the official riot investigations challenged the basic assumptions of the prison system itself. All argued merely that its administration must be improved" (Martin, 1954:225). Heeding the call for change, correctional managers looked to Scientific Management principles for a new approach to management.

Applying Scientific Management to the Worker–Task Relationship

To effect meaningful change, correctional managers had to abandon the definition of the correctional worker as an interchangeable unit with limited potential and become more sophisticated in their structuring of the worker–task relationship. Managers turned to industrial psychology for help in structuring new processes of recruitment and selection, training, job assignment, and motivation.

Employee Recruitment and Selection

Recognizing that corrections increasingly required skilled workers, correctional managers created a new category of employee, the Personnel Officer. In the area of employee recruitment and selection, the responsibilities of the Personnel Officer would evolve to include responsibility for ensuring that potential employees were subjected to a battery of psychological tests, were interviewed with questions taken from standardized interview questionnaires organized in terms of the abilities and skills required for effective performance, and were refused employment if they did not meet standardized criteria related to job performance.

Training   The formal training of new recruits began to replace the traditional on-the-job training and would eventually lead to the creation of training academies staffed by yet another new category of employee—the professional trainer—who would be responsible for providing new employees with the knowledge and skills essential to effective job performance.

Job Assignments   DOC managers applied Taylor's principles to the creation of employee job descriptions that attempted to standardize job tasks in a way that maximized the ability to match worker and job assignment. Eventually, every category of employee would be defined in terms of the written criteria for the position and the description of the required duties. Every post assignment would have a set of written post orders. Heeding Munsterberg, managers began to identify individual abilities and, collective bargaining agreements permitting, make assignments based on the match between ability and task requirements. For example, a correctional officer lacking strong "people skills" would be assigned to a guard tower while the officer who had such skills would be assigned to a cell block. Probation and parole managers tried to match worker skills with offender types, realizing that a higher skill level is necessary to manage specialized caseloads, such as sex offenders.

Motivation   The need to motivate employees and offenders through the use of various types of communication (see Chapters 11–12) was reflected in employee training programs that began to incorporate teaching techniques designed to motivate both line staff and managers to higher levels of performance. Skinnerian principles began to be applied to employee training with trainers relying on the use of immediate feedback concerning trainee performance in test and hands-on exercises.

Applying Scientific Management to the Manager–Worker Relationship

The role of the manager had to change. Managers could no longer just hand a new officer a set of keys and give him a few simple instructions on guarding prisoners. To address the ills of corrections, managers had to make a commitment to the formal coordination of organizational behavior through an emphasis on planning, organizing, directing, and controlling the activities of their workers. This required the recruitment and training of a more educated, professional group of managers, a process that began slowly but rapidly accelerated in the 1970s.

The Conflict Between Mission and Employee Needs

Managers were also trying to heed the advice of Human Relations theorists to take employee needs into consideration in decision making, but the overriding managerial goal of achieving the mission often created employee resentment because of the level of personal sacrifice that goal routinely demanded. Working more hours than originally scheduled, with no ability to say no to the extra work, kept the employee from the family and increased exposure to the stressful correctional environment. Involuntary shift changes necessitated by high turnover disrupted personal lives and schedules and created resentment and hostility. As the rehabilitation model became prevalent, managers increasingly faced the challenge of frustrated correctional officers trying to balance the often conflicting demands of maintaining security and control while trying to assist the treatment professionals in effecting offender change. The lack of fit between correctional mission and employee needs created an employee perception that the manager–worker relationship had to be forced to change. The opportunity for this change was created by unionization.

The Wagner Act

In 1935, the U.S. Congress passed the Wagner Act. This piece of legislation recognized the right of private sector workers to join labor unions whose leadership had the power to collectively bargain with employers for improvement in working conditions, wages, and benefit packages. The Wagner Act legitimized the existence of trade unions and generated a rapid growth in private sector union membership.

The extension of the right to unionize to public sector employees gave birth to correctional employee unions in the 1970s. The power of these unions rapidly increased and correctional managers were forced to become more open to employee suggestions and demands concerning managerial policies. The powerful impact of these unions on the authority of correctional managers cannot be underestimated. DOCs now have large Personnel Departments whose responsibilities include salary/wage administration, grievance management, monitoring of health and working conditions, enforcement of collective bargaining agreements, training, recordkeeping, and a variety of other functions that Joseph Ragen and Zebulon Brockway could never have envisioned. Managerial discretion in virtually every aspect of the manager–worker relationship is now governed, and limited, by rules contained in collective bargaining agreements.

Scientific Management and the Structure of DOC Corrections

It was the prevailing political belief that an effective response to the thoroughly documented defects in corrections required the creation of an organizational structure based on the concept of Max Weber's bureaucracy. Thus, corrections began a process of centralization of organizational control by creating state departments of correction modeled on the Federal Bureau of Prisons created in 1930 by the U.S. Congress. The federal model impressed both politicians and inmates for three reasons. First, it had in place an effective inmate classification system: "Classification has been the federal system's great contribution to penology" (Martin, 1954:147). Second, inmate programs, which included factories, vocational and academic educational programs, religious programs, libraries, gyms, and a variety of recreational activities, were well organized and operated. Third, federal managers recognized the importance of the worker: "[T]he federal system chooses its guards with unusual care, gives them Civil Service status, trains them rigorously and well, pays them better than most states, and offers them a retirement plan (Martin, 1954:150).

Using the Federal Bureau of Prisons as a model, public policy makers in state after state voted to create a state DOC that would be headed by a Commissioner or Director responsible for coordinating all managerial functions in accordance with the principles expound by Fayol and Weber. The DOC, if it was to be effective, required a centralization of control and development of managers with the ability to view corrections in the context of an entire state, not a single prison. In California, for example, the current DOC Director is expected to manage the distribution of correctional organizations presented in Figures 1–3 and 1–4.

Bureaucratization required the replacement of the autocratic warden by the bureaucratic warden: An individual who could be effective in the new organizational structure and accept the definition of manager proposed by our next management theory.

THE CONTINGENCY APPROACH (1950s–1960s)

The Contingency approach developed in response to the growing complexity of organizations in general and was based on two broad principles. First, there is no one best way of managing all people in all situations. Second, when it comes to managing organizational behavior, there are no simple answers. Organizational behavior is a complex process of interacting factors that cannot be viewed in isolation (Baron, 1983:19). The manager does not have the luxury of the simple answer.

The Contingency approach defined the effective manager as the individual who could correctly analyze each individual situation, have knowledge of various managerial techniques, select the most appropriate alternative, and be capable of implementing that alternative as long as internal and external constraints permit one to do so. This definition of managerial effectiveness constituted the final nail in the coffin of the autocratic warden whose belief in total personal control made him unsuited for a job that required an acceptance that managers need the active support, commitment, and contributions of their staff to sustain organizational vitality.

Expanding the Scope of Environmental Design

The Contingency approach emphasized that there are no simple management answers because an organization's environment is constantly changing. This was certainly the case in corrections, where the influence of the rehabilitation model on organizational structure was increased when the 1967 President's Commission on Law Enforcement and Administration of Justice defined crime as a symptom of community failure and the task of corrections as including "building or rebuilding social ties, obtaining employment and education, securing in the larger sense a place for the offender in the routine functioning of society" (U.S. President's Commission, 1967:7).

Prison managers responded to the Commission's emphasis on rehabilitation by developing and expanding a network of work release, study release, furlough, and halfway house programs structured in accordance with the philosophy contained in the Federal Prisoner Rehabilitation Act of 1965 (McCarthy and McCarthy, 1991:177). Perhaps more important, the Commission provided the basis for public policy decisions that actively promoted community corrections as an alternative to prisons. Community corrections required a radical departure from the medical model's emphasis on treatment in prison to an emphasis on the use of probation with incarceration being reserved for a small number of violent offenders. Federal and state funds began to be diverted from other uses and applied to expanding the number of offenders in community corrections. Probation and

CORRECTIONAL FACILITIES:

INSTITUTIONS AND CONSERVATION CAMPS

. . . .

- ● City
- ★ Existing Prison
- ☆ Authorized New Prison
- ▲ Conservation Camp
- ▣ Female Camp

1. CSP, San Quentin
2. CSP, Folsom
3. California Correctional Institution, Tehachapi
4. California Institute for Men, Chino
5. Correctional Training Facility, Soledad
6. California Institute for Women, Frontera
7. Deuel Vocational Institution, Tracy
8. California Mens Colony, San Luis Obispo
9. California Medical Facility, Vacaville
10. California Rehabilitation Center, Norco
11. California Correctional Center, Susanville
12. Sierra Conservation Center, Jamestown
13. CSP, Solano County
14. CSP, Sacramento (New Folsom)
15. Avenal State Prison
16. Mule Creek State Prison, Ione
17. Richard J. Donovan Correctional Facility, San Diego
18. Northern California Womens Facility, Stockton
19. CSP, Corcoran
20. Chuckawalla Valley State Prison, Chuckawalla
21. Pelican Bay State Prison, Crescent City
22. Central California Womens Facility, Chowchilla

23. CSP, Wasco
24. CSP, Calipatria
25. CSP, LA County (Lancaster)
26. North Kern State Prison (Delano)
27. Centinela State Prison
28. Ironwood State Prison
29. CSP, Coalinga
30. CSP, Lassen County
31. CSP, Madera County II
32. CSP, Monterey County II

FIGURE 1–3   Correctional Facilities: Institutions and Conservation Camps. Source: California Department of Corrections. *Inside Corrections: Public Safety, Public Service* (1996a): 5.

FIGURE 1–4 Correctional Facilities: Parole Offices and Community Facilities. Source: California Department of Corrections. *Inside Corrections: Public Safety, Public Service* (1996a): 6.

parole departments increased in size and complexity of operation.

The Worker–Task Relationship in Community Corrections

As community corrections grew, so grew the need for correctional workers who had the specialized skills essential to the management and counseling of offenders outside of the traditional prison setting. An important component of this work was the ability to relate effectively to various members of the community, especially employers. The community corrections worker was assigned a set of tasks centering around postincarceration counseling of the offender and working with inmate families and employers to assist offender reintegration into society.

The Manager–Worker Relationship in Community Corrections

Managers had to adapt to the limited control structure of community corrections by emphasizing the development of communication and motivation skills. No longer was the threat of physical force an effective option in the management of offenders. Sharing a common educational background and community perspective, managers and employees often had a considerably more informal working relationship than that still prevalent in the prisons. Consensus decision making and a greater degree of flexibility and discretion became evident in many community correction organizations.

Expanding the Organizational Structure

The effect of community corrections on the vertical and horizontal complexity of the DOC is illustrated in the organization chart of the Ohio Department of Rehabilitation and Correction (ODRC) presented in Figure 1–5. The addition of community corrections as an ODRC function changed the ODRC organizational structure by necessitating the creation of a new department, Parole and Community Services. The addition of this department, and the creation of a new Deputy Director position, increased the vertical complexity of the ODRC. The creation of the offices of the Adult Parole Authority, Community Sanctions, Adult Detention, Victim Services, Parole Board, Parole Supervision, Probation Development, Interstate Compact, and the addition of Regional Parole Offices, significantly increased horizontal complexity.

Across the nation, similar changes in organizational structure were reflected in the distribution of correctional employees. As of January 1, 1997, the United States had 85.8 percent of correctional staff located in

prisons; 7.8 percent in community corrections; and 6.5 percent in central or regional offices (Camp and Camp, 1997:116).

Limitation of the Contingency Approach

Although the insights it provided were useful, the Contingency approach offered no new managerial techniques (Carrell, Jennings, and Heavrin, 1997:5). Attention shifted to the importance of the individual worker as a valued resource to be cultivated and nurtured.

THE HUMAN CAPITAL SCHOOL (1970s–1980s)

The Human Capital approach emphasized that employees are much more than just factors of production or individuals who only respond on the basis of feelings or needs. Employees are valuable investments that provide long-term returns to the organization if they are effectively developed and utilized. Employee knowledge, skills, and abilities were viewed as a valuable resource that should be appreciated and protected. It is the responsibility of management to engage in a process of environmental design calculated to meet both organizational and employee goals through effective behavioral programs based on Scientific Management and Human Relations principles.

Correctional managers heeded the call of the Human Capital approach and began to invest scarce correctional resources in the creation of training academies that utilized a variety of training strategies for all correctional employees, including managers (see Chapter 12). Various DOCs experimented with unit management, quality circles, management by objectives, and other forms of activity that allowed correctional employees a greater say in the daily operation of the prison. DOCs began to invest considerable amounts of money in recruiting, selecting, training, and attempting to keep employees.

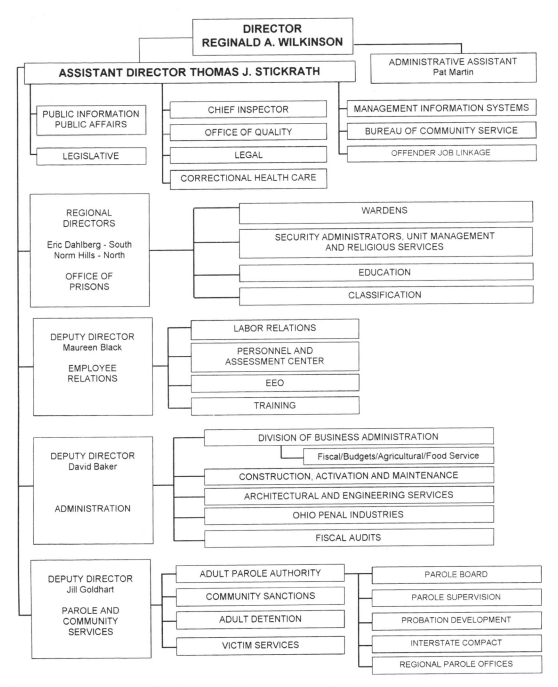

FIGURE 1–5 Organization of ODRC. Source: Ohio Department of Rehabilitation and Correction. *Annual Report: Fiscal Year 1994* (1996): 7.

Limitation of the Human Capital Approach

The primary limitation of the Human Capital approach was that it did not recognize the broad diversity of the work force and the impact of global issues (Carrell, Jennings, and Heavrin, 1997:5). This oversight would be addressed by the "New Agenda."

THE "NEW AGENDA" (1990s)

The "New Agenda" recognizes that diversification of the work force is changing OB practices because the dramatic increase in the number of women, minorities, and foreign nationals has altered the needs, desires, and motivations of the work force. In addition, technological advancement is occurring at a previously unimagined pace. For correctional managers, the 1990s have brought the challenge of meeting the needs of a diversified labor force and appropriately applying technology to an environment traditionally slow to change. These issues will be further explored in Chapters 14 and 15.

SUMMARY

Organizational Behavior is the study of how individuals, groups, and organizational structure affect the behavior of people in an organization. OB comprises a set of theories that have evolved from an emphasis on the mechanistic and structural aspects of the organization to an emphasis on understanding the value of people in organizations. These theories influenced the management of correctional organizations during Pre-DOC Corrections and continue to influence DOC Corrections. This chapter has examined managers and employees as individuals. In Chapter 2, we consider individuals as members of groups and the relationship between groups and organizational behavior.

Discussion Questions

1. What are the most significant differences between the six schools of management theory?
2. Which of Fayol's 14 principles of management were reflected in Weber's definition of bureaucracy?
3. How did the lives of managers, line staff, and offenders change as each school of management theory exerted its influence on corrections?
4. Which school of management theory had the greatest influence on organizational behavior in corrections? Why?
5. How did Pre-DOC and DOC Corrections differ on the issue of employee empowerment?

Critical Analysis Exercise: from Guard to Correctional Officer

The Pre-DOC guard role was defined solely in terms of being a keeper who engaged in custody, control, and surveillance:

The life of a guard is not an easy one. He is required to guard men to whom he is forbidden to speak except on business. He spends most of his waking hours behind bars. He is never more than a few feet from dangerous men who hate him. In a well-run prison, guards live under discipline almost as strict as convicts. No guard can get mixed up with the inmates . . . (Martin, 1954:171).

The relationship was one of high social distance between guard and inmate based on the constant use of force, physical coercion, and a rigid application of rules. The guard had only one priority—to maintain the order of the institution.

But DOC managers required guards to become correctional officers, human service workers who would

---

hunger for opportunities to improve the quality of life in the prison community and grasp them when they can. In the prison, the skills that matter are human relations and human services skills . . . that can be used to develop relationships and hence to reduce tension, defuse crisis, and conduct daily business in a civilized (and potentially civilizing) manner (Johnson, 1996:224).

The role of correctional officer as a human services worker requires closing the social gap between officer and inmate, and being flexible and willing to take risks in helping offenders change their behavior.

Critical Analysis Questions

1. How did Traditional Management and Scientific Management principles create the limited role definition of the guard?

2. What was the influence of the Human Relations movement on creation of the correctional officer?

3. What is the role of the manager in ensuring that new employees will be correctional officers, not guards?

2

Organizational Strategy, Structure, and Design

Learning Objectives

After completing this chapter, you should be able to:

- Define system, strategy, structure, and effectiveness.
- Explain the components of organizational structure in terms of seven fundamental principles.
- Describe the mechanistic and organic structures as defined by complexity, formalization, and centralization.
- Discuss organizational subsystems in terms of Mintzberg's five components of organizational design.
- Compare and contrast five Mintzberg design configurations.
- Relate three types of adaptive strategies and the role of learning and unlearning to environmental uncertainty.
- Describe the role of adaptive strategies in creating organizational effectiveness.

Key Terms and Concepts

System
Structural Subsystem
Technical Subsystem
Mission
Complexity
Vertical Differentiation
Formalization
Official Values and Goals
Managerial Subsystem
Strategy
Structure
Horizontal Differentiation
Spatial Differentiation
Centralization
Division of Labor
Authority and Responsibility
Functional Departmentalization
Geographic Departmentalization
Mutual Adjustment
Work Process Standardization
Skills Standardization
Lateral Coordination
Liaison Role
Project Teams
Mechanistic Structure
Design Configuration
Strategic Apex
Technostructure
Simple Structure
Divisional Structure
Professional Bureaucracy
Environmental Uncertainty
Innovation Strategies
Imitation Strategies
Innovative Learning
Unity of Command
Span of Control
Service Departmentalization
Unit Coordination
Direct Supervision
Output Standardization
Norms Standardization
Direct Contact
Task Force
Strategy-Structure Thesis
Organic Structure
Operating Core
Middle Line
Support Staff
Machine Bureaucracy
Adhocracy
Organizational Effectiveness
Adaptive Strategies
Cost-Minimization Strategies
Maintenance
Unlearning

Management is the dynamic force which converts human and non-human resources into organizations. It is a process which integrates unrelated resources into something that is greater than the mere sum of its parts. While the purpose of management is to coordinate the activities of people in organizations, its overall role is to facilitate the effective and efficient attainment of organizational goals and the personal needs of its members.

Anthony P. Raia

Profile: The Correctional Organization as a System

Every organization can be considered a system. All systems have seven fundamental characteristics (Holton and Jones, 1982). First, all systems have components (subsystems) that operate together toward the accomplishment of goals. Second, all systems operate as an identifiable whole and can be distinguished from one another by their boundaries. Third, the components of the system are interdependent: the activity of each component in the system affects the activities of the other components. Fourth, every system operates in an external environment that helps shape the output of the system. Fifth, every system has inputs (demands or supports) that shape organizational behavior. Demands are expressed as the expectations of society. Supports are the contributions from the external environment that support the system, such as tax dollars, legislation, and involvement by the private sector. The sixth characteristic is that every system produces identifiable outputs. The seventh is that all systems receive feedback from their environment, often in the form of challenges, that motivate the system to change.

Kast and Rosenzweig (1979:108–115) have proposed that organizations be understood as a set of five interacting subsystems: organizational goals and values, the psychological subsystem, the structural subsystem, the technical subsystem, and the managerial subsystem. Organizational goals and values reflect the conventional value system of the larger society within which the organization exists. The psychological subsystem consists of a psychological contract based on official, individual, and group values. The structural subsystem includes organizational procedures, the division of labor, policies, the formal chain of command, the informal power structure, channels of communication, and the built environment. The technical subsystem refers to the knowledge required to accomplish the mission of the organization. The managerial subsystem can be considered the glue that bonds the four subsystems of the organization together and provides continuity of policy, procedures, and behavior. All of the organization's activities occur within these subsystems.

A correctional organization can be defined as a system. It has distinct boundaries that distinguish it from other human service systems such as the educational system. Its subsystems are interrelated and work together to achieve the mission. The organization has an identifiable output: the offender who has completed the sentence of the court. Corrections exists in an external environment that, to a large extent, is a public policy environment. It is the recipient of demands, supports, and challenges from the external environment.

If an organization is to be effective, the relationships between individuals and groups of individuals within the organization must be controlled and regulated by managers whose guidance and direction is consistent with organizational values and goals. Employee activities are controlled and regulated through the processes of an organizational structure that is designed in accordance with the requirements of the organizational strategy. Fundamental principles of organizational structure must be considered during environmental design if the final product of that process is to be a structure and design that promotes organizational effectiveness. This chapter examines basic principles of organizational structure and design as they apply to correctional organizations and the effectiveness of those organizations. After briefly discussing official values, the structural, managerial, and technical subsystems of the correctional organization is considered (the psychological subsystem is discussed in Chapter 3).

Correctional organizations do not exist in a vacuum. They are influenced by an external environment that can introduce an element of environmental uncertainty when changes in that environment affect the organization. To remain effective in the face of environmental uncertainty, managers must aggressively pursue adaptive strategies that require employees to learn new behaviors and unlearn behaviors that are no longer effective.

ORGANIZATIONAL STRATEGY AND STRUCTURE

The Profile at the beginning of the chapter provides an overview of the correctional organization as a set of interacting subsystems whose activities are influenced by an external environment. If organizational behavior is to effectively meet the demands and expectations of the external environment, it must be guided by an organizational strategy that is responsive to those demands and expectations. We begin with a definition of organizational strategy.

Organizational Strategy

All organizations have a strategy. A strategy can be defined as "the pattern or plan that integrates an organization's major goals, policies, and action sequences into a cohesive whole" (Quinn, 1980:22). In its broadest sense,

[s]trategy may be viewed as a mediating force between the organization and its environment.

Strategy formulation therefore involves the interpretation of the environment and the development of consistent patterns in streams of organizational decisions ("strategies") to deal with it. . . . [M]anagers . . . develop an understanding of the environment; and in carrying out the duties of direct supervision, they seek to tailor strategy to its strengths and needs, trying to maintain a pace of change that is responsive to the environment without being disruptive to the organization (Mintzberg, 1983b:13–14).

Borrowing from the corporate literature, we can say that a well-defined strategy is one that addresses three areas of concern: (1) distinctive competence, (2) scope, and (3) resource deployment (Barnet and Griffin, 1992). A distinctive competence is something the organization does exceptionally well. The scope of a strategy specifies the range of markets in which an organization will compete. The resource deployment component of strategy involves the decision as to how an organization will distribute its resources across the areas in which it competes.

In the case of corrections, the distinctive competence is the management of offenders. The scope is both institutional and community corrections. The resource deployment component involves the distribution of resources across institutional and community corrections. Strategy, determined to a large degree by top management, outlines the organization's goals and the means of achieving those goals, influences the power of various work groups, and determines the resources top management is willing to allocate to those groups. Strategic decisions have consequences, especially when they involve a redistribution of resources. For example, in the 1960s, when Departments of Corrections (DOCs) throughout the nation embraced the concept of rehabilitation as a strategy, resources were channeled into treatment programs, the hiring of treatment staff, and correctional expansion into the community. One result of this shift in resources and priority was the perception by many correctional officers that their authority and ability to control inmates had been seriously diminished.

The Mission Statement

Strategy represents a blueprint of purpose for the organization that defines the organizational objectives. These objectives are formally expressed through the use of a mission statement. A well-developed mission statement also states the strategies, values, and commitments that provide guidance and direction to both managers and employees as they pursue accomplishment of the objectives. Citizens interested in a specific DOC can gain an overview of the purpose of that organization by reading its mission statement.

Each DOC has its own style of expressing its mission. For example, the mission statement of the Texas Department of Criminal Justice states that the purpose of the organization is to "provide public safety, promote positive change in behavior, and reintegrate offenders into society" (Texas Department of Criminal Justice, 1996:Foreword). The Illinois DOC mission statement states that their purpose is to "protect the public from criminal offenders through a system of incarceration and supervision which securely segregates offenders from society, assures offenders of their constitutional rights and maintains programs to enhance the success of the offender's reentry into society" (Illinois Department of Corrections, 1995:5).

The foundation of any mission statement is the official values of the organization. James Vander Zanden (1984:318) defines a value as an "ethical principle to which people feel a strong emotional commitment and which they employ in judging behavior." Values involve attitudes and feelings about different kinds of people, judgments concerning what constitutes "good" and "bad," what behaviors and conditions are acceptable and unacceptable, the criteria we find most useful for making decisions and choices, and a philosophy of what makes things work the way they should. Many DOC mission statements do not state the official values of the organization. An

exception is the Minnesota DOC, which has explicitly recognized the importance of organizational values in its mission statement. Minnesota's mission statement begins with the words "Our mission is to ensure that sanctions and services of the criminal justice system are designed and delivered to create a safer Minnesota" (Minnesota Department of Corrections, 1995:3). This overview is followed by a statement of core values and major goals. The value statement of the Minnesota DOC is as follows:

We value managing our services with openness, integrity, and accountability to the public. We value the dignity of individuals and their potential for growth and development. We value the rights of the victims. We value staff as our most valuable resource in accomplishing our mission, and we are committed to the personal welfare and professional development of each employee. We value leadership that encourages open communication and is responsive to innovation. We value the strength that comes from diversity. We value the safe, humane, and fair treatment of offenders (Minnesota Department of Corrections, 1995:3).

This value statement is followed by a statement of official organizational goals:

- To restore the victim, community and offender.
- To develop and support a range of correctional services and programs.
- To provide a safe, secure, humane environment for incarcerated offenders.
- To manage the organization effectively and efficiently.
- To educate and work cooperatively with other public and private organizations on common issues (Minnesota Department of Corrections, 1995:3).

An even more specific mission statement is that of the Arizona Department of Corrections. This statement (Box 2–1) clearly sets forth values, goals, and behavioral priorities.

BOX 2–1 MISSION STATEMENT
OF THE ARIZONA DEPARTMENT
OF CORRECTIONS

The mission of the Arizona Department of Corrections is to serve and protect the people of the State by imprisoning those offenders legally committed to the Department.

The Department will accomplish this by:

- Maintaining effective custody and control over offenders.
- Maintaining a healthy, safe, and secure environment for staff and offenders.
- Providing quality programs to offenders so they will have opportunities to learn more responsible behaviors and increase their chances of returning into society as law-abiding citizens.

To accomplish the above we recognize the need to:

- Develop and maintain a professional staff recognizing that each employee is an important contributor to the system.
- Assure that each employee has available the opportunities for personal and professional growth through training, education, and career development.

We believe the Department has the managerial and operational responsibility to be accountable to the public. This includes the Executive, Legislative, and Judicial branches of Government, the adult prisoners and, most importantly, the citizens of Arizona. In pursuit of this obligation the Department will maintain open lines of communication in a timely, professional, and efficient manner.

We further believe that by integrating priorities and expectations into unified operating plans which clearly state goals, objectives, professional standards, and direction, we will respond effectively to the changing demands placed upon the agency.

We value honesty and integrity in our relationships, and we place a high priority on quality of services and development of teamwork, trust, and open communication. We are committed to this goal internally and externally.

We will maintain an environment that is humane and fair to both employees and offenders, utilizing a grievance/discipline system that fosters due process and is consistently administered by the review and redress of wrongs. We will employee an objective classification system of offenders based upon behavior, criminal history, and performance.

We believe in encouraging, recognizing, and rewarding examples of professional leadership at all levels which contribute to the enhancement of our responsibility to serve and protect the people of the State of Arizona.

These beliefs are achievable to the extent that the resources necessary for their accomplishment are provided to the Department.

Source: Arizona Department of Corrections. *1995 Annual Report* (1996):4.

Organizational Structure

Regardless of how well expressed the mission is in writing, it cannot be achieved without structure. The structure of an organization can be defined as "the sum total of the ways in which its labor is divided into distinct tasks and then its coordination is achieved among these tasks" (Mintzberg, 1983b:2). Structure provides a means of organizing the activities of managers and workers in a way that will promote achievement of the mission. Structure establishes parameters, that is, it determines the tasks of employees and how and when they will perform them. More specifically, the parameters of structure provide answers to the following questions:

How many tasks should a given position in the organization contain, and how specialized should each task be?

To what extent should the work content of each position be standardized?

What skills and knowledge should be required for each position?

On what basis should positions be grouped into units and units into larger units?

How large should each unit be; how many people should report to a given manager?

To what extent should the output of each position be standardized?

How much decision-making power should be delegated to the managers of line units down the chain of authority?

How much decision-making power should pass from the line managers to the staff specialists and operators? (Mintzberg, 1983b:25)

The design of a correctional organization's structure must recognize (1) the nature of employee activities, (2) the characteristics of the organization's internal environment, (3) the activities of the offenders being supervised, and (4) the expectations and demands of the external environment.

THE COMPONENTS OF ORGANIZATIONAL STRUCTURE

The structural subsystem provides the structural framework for organizational behavior. Structure is made up of three components: complexity; formalization; and centralization. Complexity refers to the degree to which activities within the organization are broken up or differentiated. Formalization refers to the degree to which rules and procedures are used. Centralization refers to where the decision-making authority is found. Combined, these components create an organizational structure (Robbins, 1993:487–489).

Complexity

Complexity involves the degree to which activities within an organization are differentiated. Differentiation is the process of distributing those activities within an organizational structure. There are three types of differentiation: horizontal, vertical, and spatial.

Horizontal Differentiation

This type of differentiation establishes categories of employees that are distinguished from each other by the specialized knowledge and skills necessary to carry out their duties, as demonstrated in Figure 2–1. The required knowledge and skills of employees in the Florida DOC clearly differ as one moves across the organization chart from Health Services to Youthful Offender Program Services to Admission and Release to Security to Academic Programs.

Vertical Differentiation

This type of differentiation concerns the depth of the organizational structure. The more levels that exist, the more complex the organization. For example, the organization of the Ohio Department of Rehabilitation and Correction (ODRC) as presented in Figure 2–2 reveals a complex organizational structure headed by a Director who supervises central office and field activities with the assistance of an Assistant Director, two Regional Directors, and three Deputy Directors who work closely with wardens and subordinate central office managers.

Spatial Differentiation

Spatial differentiation refers to the degree to which the organization's physical facilities and personnel are geographically dispersed, as shown in Figure 2–3. As spatial differentiation increases, so increases complexity. A

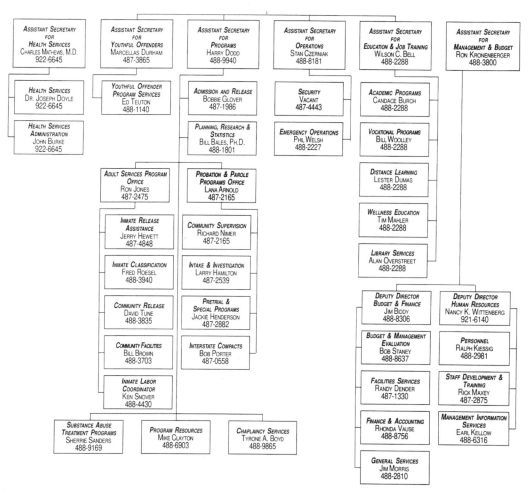

FIGURE 2–1 Organizational Chart: Florida Department of Corrections. Source: Florida Department of Corrections. *1994–1995 Annual Report: The Guidebook to Corrections in Florida* (1995): 7.

spatial differentiation as large as that of Florida's DOC results in an extremely complex organization because geographical diversity creates significant management and communication challenges. A commissioner located hundreds of miles from some of the system's facilities must be prepared to confront issues that would not arise if all the employees were concentrated in one physical location. A particularly significant aspect of this type of differentiation is that the challenges and issues faced by managers and employees in Region I might not be the same as those present in Region IV. These differences must be known and clearly understood if appropriate policy on a wide range of challenges is to be formulated by the central office. Otherwise, policy that is effective in Region I might actually damage organizational effectiveness in Region IV.

Formalization

Formalization refers to the degree to which functions within the organization are standardized—that is, the degree to which the use of individual discretion is limited by the expectation that all individuals performing a particular function will perform it in the same manner. Formalization is a process that increases the ability to predict and control behavior. The prediction and control of behavior are necessary if managers

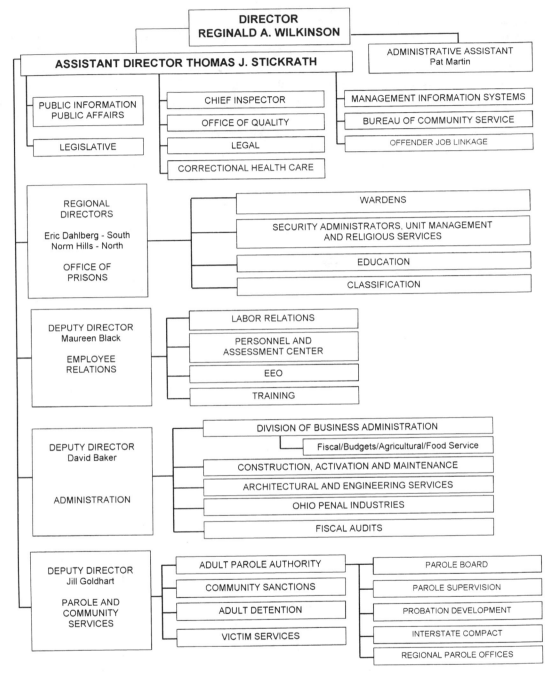

FIGURE 2–2 Ohio Department of Rehabilitation and Correction. Source: *Ohio Department of Rehabilitation and Correction Annual Report: Fiscal Year 1994* (1996): 7.

are to effectively (1) coordinate activities to prevent inefficiency, (2) ensure the consistency necessary for effective production or delivery of services, (3) ensure fairness to the recipients of services, and (4) create a sense of order (Mintzberg, 1983b:34–35).

Jobs in correctional organizations are highly formalized. Correctional workers

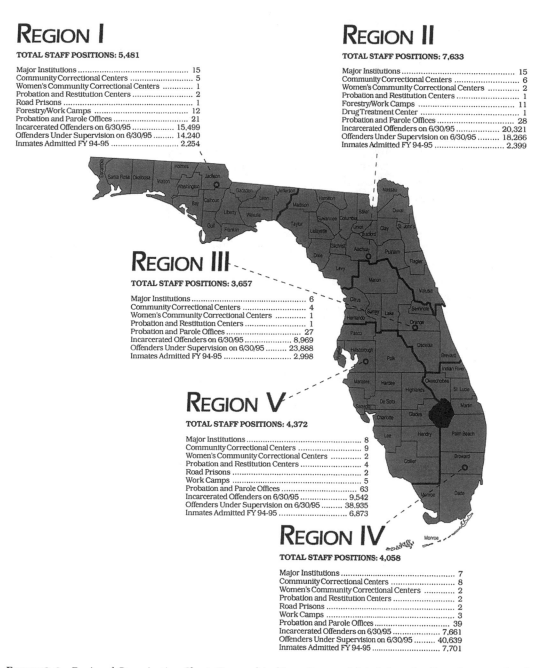

REGION I

TOTAL STAFF POSITIONS: 5,481

Major Institutions 15
Community Correctional Centers 5
Women's Community Correctional Centers 1
Probation and Restitution Centers 2
Road Prisons 1
Forestry/Work Camps 12
Probation and Parole Offices 21
Incarcerated Offenders on 6/30/95 15,499
Offenders Under Supervision on 6/30/95 14,240
Inmates Admitted FY 94-95 2,254

REGION II

TOTAL STAFF POSITIONS: 7,633

Major Institutions 15
Community Correctional Centers 6
Women's Community Correctional Centers 2
Probation and Restitution Centers 1
Forestry/Work Camps 11
Drug Treatment Center 1
Probation and Parole Offices 28
Incarcerated Offenders on 6/30/95 20,321
Offenders Under Supervision on 6/30/95 18,266
Inmates Admitted FY 94-95 2,399

REGION III

TOTAL STAFF POSITIONS: 3,657

Major Institutions 6
Community Correctional Centers 4
Women's Community Correctional Centers 1
Probation and Restitution Centers 1
Probation and Parole Offices 27
Incarcerated Offenders on 6/30/95 8,969
Offenders Under Supervision on 6/30/95 23,888
Inmates Admitted FY 94-95 2,998

REGION V

TOTAL STAFF POSITIONS: 4,372

Major Institutions 8
Community Correctional Centers 9
Women's Community Correctional Centers 2
Probation and Restitution Centers 4
Road Prisons 2
Work Camps 5
Probation and Parole Offices 63
Incarcerated Offenders on 6/30/95 9,542
Offenders Under Supervision on 6/30/95 38,935
Inmates Admitted FY 94-95 6,873

REGION IV

TOTAL STAFF POSITIONS: 4,058

Major Institutions 7
Community Correctional Centers 8
Women's Community Correctional Centers 2
Probation and Restitution Centers 2
Road Prisons 2
Work Camps 3
Probation and Parole Offices 39
Incarcerated Offenders on 6/30/95 7,661
Offenders Under Supervision on 6/30/95 40,639
Inmates Admitted FY 94-95 7,701

FIGURE 2–3 Regional Organization Chart: Geographical Locations and Administrative Data. Source: Florida Department of Corrections. *1994–1995 Annual Report: The Guidebook to Corrections in Florida* (1995): 9.

have a minimum amount of discretion in how and when specific activities will be performed. For example, a corrections officer working in a cellblock is expected to conduct inmate counts: physically count the number of inmates in their cells at des-

ignated times during the shift that officer is working. If the post orders for that block require a count at 8 A.M. and 1 P.M., then the officer is expected to conduct the count at those times. However, formalization is not limited to employees. The prison superintendent must develop budget proposals in accordance with detailed instructions from the central office that permit very little discretionary use of funds. The Food Services Manager must prepare and serve meals in accordance with a master menu that permits only minimal deviation.

This high degree of formalization means that correctional organizations are characterized by explicit job descriptions, a multitude of written rules, and clearly defined work procedures designed to limit the use of individual discretion at all levels of activity. The process of formalization requires managers to develop multiple volumes of policy and procedure manuals that, in most organizations, are reviewed and updated on an annual basis. This emphasis on formalization has led to a chronic staff complaint—that there is an excessive amount of paperwork. Virtually every required job task is described somewhere in the massive volumes of policy and procedure manuals that are the hallmark of the bureaucratic organization. And virtually every task must be documented in writing on one of the numerous report forms used to monitor employee activity.

Centralization

Centralization is the degree to which decision making is concentrated at one point within the organization. It has to do only with "formal" authority, that is, the rights inherent in the position. If top management makes the decisions with minimum input from employees, then the organization is centralized. If employees have the ability to make important decisions, then the organization is decentralized. Correctional organizations have always been centralized. They function in accordance with a command and control structure in which the authority flows downward through a strictly enforced chain of command. Managers do not easily tolerate violations of the chain of command, regardless of rationale or justification.

PRINCIPLES OF ORGANIZATIONAL STRUCTURE

The process of creating complexity, formalization, and centralization proceeds in accordance with seven fundamental principles: division of labor, unity of command, authority and responsibility, span of control, departmentalization, unit coordination, and lateral coordination.

Division of Labor

Division of labor means work specialization. Every job is broken down into a number of steps, with each step being completed by a separate individual, rather than each job being done by a single individual. The division of labor creates specialists. For example, the classification of an inmate to determine security and treatment needs is a job that consists of a number of separate activities. Counselors interview the new inmate and gather a variety of information about the inmate from external sources: law enforcement, family, schools, educators, the military. Psychologists administer psychological tests, interview the inmate, and create a psychological profile. Educators administer vocational and educational achievement tests and recommend remedial education programs. Medical department personnel conduct physical exams, compile medical histories, and prescribe medication or other courses of treatment. Block officers submit behavioral assessment reports based on their observations of the inmate during the classification period. Secretaries type and distribute the classification summary.

Unity of Command

This principle states that a subordinate should have one, and only one, superior to whom he or she is directly responsible. No individual should report to two or more superiors because of the inevitable confusion that will result. Therefore, correctional managers enforce a rigid chain of command based on the principle that every employee has only one immediate supervisor.

Authority and Responsibility

Authority is the inherent right of those in managerial positions to give orders and to expect the recipient of those orders to comply. Authority provides the foundation for the managerial subsystem that holds together the other subsystems. Each management position has specific inherent rights that are a characteristic of the position, not of the individual who occupies the position. To put it differently, authority stays with the position when the manager leaves. Thus, a superintendent can order any member of the correctional staff within the facility to perform professional functions while employed by the DOC, but as soon as retirement is taken all authority over the employees is lost. Authority, however, places demands on those who are given it. Once authority has been granted to an individual, that person is expected to accept a corresponding obligation to perform in an effective manner. This corresponding obligation is "managerial responsibility": the manager is expected to always act in the best interests of the organization, the employees, the offenders, and the public.

Authority Structures

Authority structures define who reports to whom, who makes decisions, and what decisions individuals or groups are empowered to make. The authority structure of corrections creates three levels of management: top managers; middle-level managers; and first-level managers.

Top managers, often referred to as the chief executive officer, include directors/commissioners of state DOCs, state prison superintendents, the Federal Bureau of Prisons director and that system's wardens, jail wardens, and directors of probation and parole departments. Deputy (assistant) directors, commissioners, superintendents and wardens are also included in this level

as part of an executive management team. These individuals establish "the big picture" policy, prioritize organizational goals, and allocate resources.

Middle-level managers are those managers, usually designated as department heads, who have lower-level managers reporting to them or are responsible for multiorganizational activities. The Chief of Medical Services in a state prison, for example, would be a middle-level manager, as would the Major of the Guard or a shift captain or lieutenant. Probation and parole supervisors are also middle-level managers.

The first-level manager (often referred to as a supervisor) directs the activities of the line staff who provide services directly to the offenders or to the organization. Sergeants supervise correctional officers; psychological service supervisors supervise psychologists; counselor supervisors supervise counselors; nurse supervisors supervise nurses; unit managers supervise a variety of line staff; and accounting supervisors supervise accountants and budget clerks.

It is tempting to attempt to create an artificial differentiation of these individuals by grouping them into four categories: administrators, managers, supervisors, and line staff. Such a typology would distinguish between these categories by referring to administrators as the individuals responsible for determining major policies and objectives; managers as the individuals responsible for managing a function but supervising no one; supervisors as the individuals responsible for supervising the staff assigned the responsibility of following policy and achieving objectives; and line staff as the workers. This approach, however, is too cumbersome and ignores the fact that administrators, managers, and supervisors share too many responsibilities and activities to justify an artificial differentiation. For example, in Figure 2–4, the Illinois DOC Table of Organization clearly establishes that the Director is responsible for the supervision of 11 individuals, and each Deputy Director is responsible for supervising various middle-level

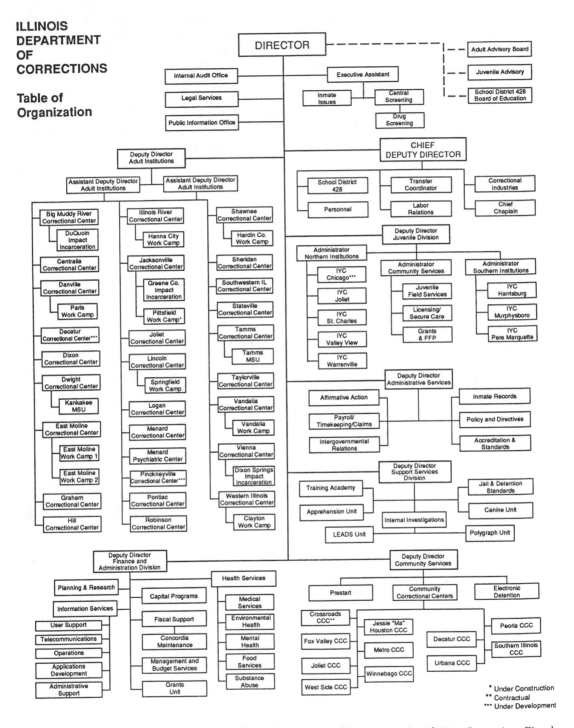

FIGURE 2–4 Table of organization. Source: Illinois Department of Corrections. *Insight into Corrections Fiscal Year 1995—Annual Report* (1995):4.

managers responsible for specific departments. The attempt to distinguish between directors, assistant directors, and department heads on the basis of some rigidly defining criteria such as supervision requirement versus no supervision requirement overlooks the reality that all managers are routinely involved in the simultaneous activities of managing and supervision of subordinates: "If someone supervises the work of other people . . . that person automatically manages because supervision of others requires specific planning and goal setting and the organizing, directing, and evaluating that is so essential to the management task (Rausch, 1978:14).

Line Staff as Managers

Before we leave our discussion of managerial authority and responsibility, it is valuable to look briefly at a situation unique to corrections. In corporate America, line staff are those individuals who do the work of production. Auto assemblers on an assembly line in Detroit are appropriately called workers, not managers. They do what they are told by managers. Their focus is the specific set of repetitive tasks they have been assigned. In prisons, line staff directly supervise, or provide services to, inmates and are given direction by managers. However, because of the unique nature of corrections, it would be inaccurate to place line staff such as correctional officers, laundry supervisors, food service supervisors, and maintenance supervisors in the same category as auto assemblers.

Prisons differ significantly, if not uniquely, from other organizations because their personnel hierarchies are organized down to the lowest level for the administration of the daily activities of men. The guard, who is the lowest-level worker in a prison is also a manager (Cressey, 1969:494).

The managerial aspect of correctional workers is probably most evident in the prison where all offender activities are regulated by line staff; indeed, all correctional staff in direct contact with offenders have significant responsibility for the management of their lives. This observation is true of all correctional organizations. Parole and probation officers and halfway house personnel are all managers of offenders. In its broadest sense, there are very few categories of correctional staff who do not manage someone.

Having said all of the above, in this book "managers" is meant to refer to those individuals who have the formal responsibility of planning, organizing, directing, and controlling the activities of subordinate employees providing direct services to either the organization or the offender population. The term is not to be applied to those individuals who only supervise offenders.

Span of Control

This term refers to the number of subordinates a manager can effectively direct. The designated span of control for an organization determines the number of vertical levels and managers that organization will need to accomplish its goals. For example, if a prison has 100 correctional officers working a shift, and the span of control is one lieutenant for every ten officers, then the number of lieutenants per shift will be ten. However, if the span of control is 20, then only five lieutenants will be necessary. Obviously, five lieutenants cost the organization less than ten lieutenants, but cost-effectiveness must be balanced against the need for safety. The number of lieutenants will subsequently determine the number of captains required to supervise the lieutenants.

Departmentalization

The specialists created by the division of labor need coordination if they are to effectively achieve organizational goals. This coordination is facilitated by grouping specialists together into departments under the direction of a manager, which is the process of departmentalization. There are three categories of departmentalization: functional, service, and geographic.

Functional Departmentalization A psychologist requires a different set of knowledge and skills than does a food service instructor. A correctional officer does not need the accounting and budget management skills so essential to a business manager but had better have a thorough knowledge of security procedures. In order to promote organizational efficiency, staff with similar specialized skills and orientations, who are expected to perform the same functions in the achievement of organizational goals, are grouped into departments. This type of departmentalization is functional departmentalization. Thus, a typical state prison places staff into different departments: security, counseling, psychology, specialized programs, education, vocational training, records, religious services, medical services, recreational activities, food services, budget, and physical plant maintenance (some of which are present in Figure 2–4).

Service Departmentalization This involves specialization within a department. For example, the Business Office in a prison will have staff who specialize in

budget preparation, the competitive bid process necessary for all purchases from community vendors, and management of inmate accounts and the inmate payroll. If the prison has a Corrections Industry division, there will be at least one Business Office employee expected to specialize in Correctional Industry recordkeeping. Personnel divisions require experts in a number of specialized areas, as can be seen in the organization chart of the Human Resources/Development Division of the Arizona DOC presented in Figure 2–5.

Geographic Departmentalization This is based on geography. Thus, the Florida Department of Corrections groups correctional institutions, community correctional centers, road prisons, forestry camps, drug treatment centers, work camps, and contract drug treatment centers by region, as shown in Figure 2–6.

Unit Coordination

It is not enough to have activities grouped together by departmentalization. The activities that occur within each department must be coordinated because unit members working together can achieve outcomes not

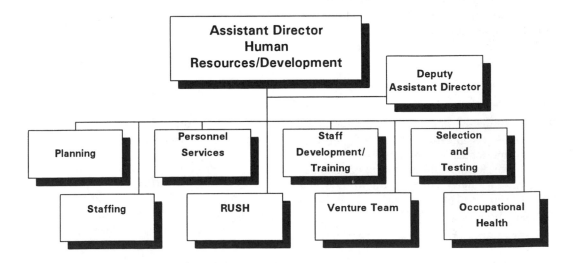

FIGURE 2–5 Human Resources/Development Division. Source: Arizona Department of Corrections. *1995 Annual Report* (1996):27.

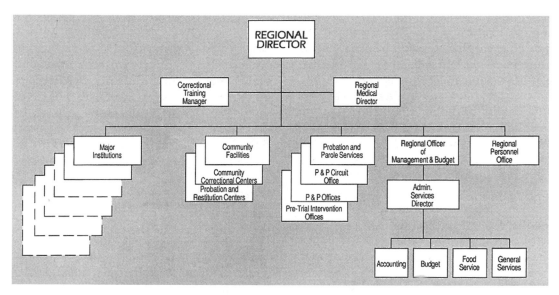

FIGURE 2–6   Florida Department of Corrections: Regional Organization and Function. Source: Florida Department of Corrections. *1994–1995 Annual Report: The Guidebook to Corrections in Florida* (1995):8.

possible for members working independently. There are three unit coordinating mechanisms: mutual adjustment, direct supervision, and standardization (Mintzberg, 1991:334). These mechanisms mesh activities together.

Mutual Adjustment   Coordination is achieved by a process of informal communication. Employees in a common work area who decide how to arrange the desks and subdivide the work space to meet individual needs and working styles are engaging in mutual adjustment.

Direct Supervision   This occurs when one person coordinates by giving orders to another person. A lieutenant is using direct supervision when telling the block officers to get the cellblocks ready for the major's weekly inspection. The commissioner is using direct supervision in announcing to the superintendents that they must each increase their prison's bed capacity by 10 percent.

Standardization   This is a process of coordination of work activities by providing unit employees with standards and proce-

dures to guide their performance of specific tasks. There are four types of standardization: standardization of work processes, output, skills, and norms (Mintzberg, 1991:334).

Work Process Standardization. This involves the development of procedures to be followed by workers who require minimal supervision and don't have to interact. Rules and regulations are used to standardize the work process. Returning to our example of the inmate classification process, the structure of every initial classification summary must be identical to every other classification summary. The exact sequence of contents (from Inmate Criminal History to Counselor Recommendations) is specified by policy and deviations are not permitted. The treatment staff contributing their specific sections require minimal supervision. Their training has prepared them to perform the functions necessary to generate the content required in the summary sections assigned to them. They do not have to interact during the preparation of the classification summary. In fact, typically, each individual independently gives their completed section to a secretary who types the information in the sequence required by policy.

Output Standardization. This involves the use of performance goals or output targets. The emphasis is on ensuring that the work meets certain standards. For example, a prison medical director is told that every new inmate must undergo a complete physical within 24 hours of reception so that health standards will be maintained. Food service managers are told that the evening meal must be finished by 6:00 P.M. so that there is no interference with inmate evening recreational activities.

Skill Standardization. This involves standardizing the worker instead of the work or the output. Each worker is taught the set of skills they will need for the job. Coordination occurs because the workers have learned what to expect from each other. The block officer knows what to expect from a nurse when it is necessary to call the infirmary to report an inmate complaining of chest pains. The counselor knows what to expect from the officers assigned to the classification unit. The food service supervisor knows what to expect from the maintenance supervisor called to fix a broken dishwasher.

Norm standardization. This occurs when workers share a common set of beliefs and can achieve coordination because of these beliefs. Norm standardization can benefit the organization when norms are consistent with official values and goals. But norms that are in conflict with official values and goals can create conflict and stress, as will be demonstrated in Chapter 3 when we discuss group values.

Differences in coordination occur from the way in which tasks are divided. Top management tends to use mutual adjustment while those areas with routine tasks (such as cellblocks, commissaries, kitchens, and laundries) rely on direct supervision, work process standardization, or output standardization. Work units staffed with educated professionals, such as medical, budget, and legal departments, rely on combinations of skill standardization and mutual adjustment (Hall, 1962).

Lateral Coordination

Departments also require coordination because they interact with each other and the frequency and volume of this interaction may vary. Lateral coordination involves the use of various mechanisms to improve information flow and horizontal cooperation: direct contact, liaison role, task force, and project teams (Jennings, 1993:68–74).

Direct Contact This is the simplest approach because it involves direct contact between managers who have a mutual problem. For example, the prison's Food Services Manager and the Laundry Manager prepare tentative, routine maintenance schedules for their equipment. The Maintenance Superintendent informs them that the schedules overlap and there aren't enough qualified maintenance personnel to service both sets of equipment simultaneously. The two managers get together and work out the problem by agreeing on schedule revisions. This process can also be viewed as a form of mutual adjustment.

Liaison Role When the volume of interdepartmental contact is large, an employee may be assigned to work with other departments as an intermediary. For example, every DOC has at least one Press Officer whose function it is to work with the media and provide information and assistance. DOCs also have legislative liaisons who work with elected officials interested in correctional issues. Accreditation coordinators at both the DOC and institutional level assist other departments in preparing for the American Correctional Association (ACA) accreditation process (discussed in Chapter 12). Commissioners, directors, superintendents, and wardens have administrative assistants who coordinate the interaction between the top manager and other members of the organization.

Task Force When several departments are involved in accomplishing a specific requirement or project, a task force of representatives selected from the involved departments will form a temporary committee assigned the responsibility of devising a mutually acceptable plan of action. For example, renovation of the prison dining room to bring it up to departmental standards will involve, at a minimum, representatives from Food Services, Maintenance, Purchasing, and Security. The task force disbands when the project has been completed.

Project Teams   Project teams provide the strongest horizontal linking mechanism and are used when organizations are involved in large-scale projects requiring extensive coordination among a number of different departments for several years. At the DOC level, virtually every department will have a representative on the project team assigned to new prison construction.

AN OVERVIEW OF ORGANIZATIONAL DESIGN

The previous section defined the structural components essential to the functioning of the organization. The next step in organizing employee activities to accomplish the mission is organizational design, which is the overall configuration of structural components into a single, unified organizational system. Structural components can be arranged in a number of ways to create a variety of organizational designs. The organizational design of the Pre-DOC prison was extremely primitive compared to the organizational design that has come to dominate DOC Corrections. How did this evolution in organizational design occur? Chandler's Strategy-Structure Thesis provides a framework to answer this question.

Chandler's Strategy-Structure Thesis

During the 1950s, a prominent organization theorist named Alfred Chandler studied approximately 100 large American corporations and concluded that organizations usually begin with a single product line (in the case of corrections, this single product line was incapacitation) that requires little organizational structure and can be administered by a single senior manager. As organizations grow, their strategies become more ambitious, product lines and their required activities increase, and a more elaborate organizational structure evolves. As growth continues, new strategies (such as rehabilitation in the case of corrections) are created that require new structures. Simply put, there is a direct relationship between organizational strategy and structure: changes in strategy precede and lead to changes in structure (Chandler, 1962). The organizational design subsequently changes in response to these structural changes. All organizations change through a process, planned or unplanned, of doing things in a different way. As organizations grow, their structural design becomes more elaborate.

The Influence of Size on Strategy and Structure   Chandler found that as an organization hires more employees, it will attempt to take advantage of the economic benefits of specialization by grouping employees together in a working arrangement that increases their effectiveness. The result is increased horizontal differentiation: the organization chart expands outward. As horizontal differentiation increases, the need for managerial control and coordination also occurs and vertical differentiation increases. The relationship here is straightforward: the greater the number of employees, the greater the reduction in the ability of existing managers to directly supervise each individual. Therefore, more layers of management are added and there develops an increased reliance on written policy, procedures, and rules. This increase in formalization generates more horizontal differentiation as departments are created to provide coordination and accountability. As the organization continues to grow, spatial differentiation is likely, as we have seen in the case of the California and Florida DOCs. Increased horizontal and vertical differentiation follow.

The relationship between size, complexity, formalization, and centralization is well established. The effect of size on complexity is an initial rapid increase in differentiation followed by a gradual decrease in the rate of differentiation (Blau, 1970:201–218). The greatest impact of size is on vertical differentiation as more levels of management are added to coordinate the growing number of employees and activities (Mileti, Gillespie, and Haas, 1977:208–217). As size increases, there is a corresponding increase in formalization. The need to control the behavior of employees forces managers to rely ever more extensively on formalized regulations (Rushing, 1980). The relationship between size and centralization is inverse. As size increases, top managers no longer have the time to make every decision, and decentralization of decision making must prevail (Child and Mansfield, 1972) if organizational effectiveness is to be maintained. In DOC Corrections, the top manager has the final approval on major decisions, but numerous daily decisions are the responsibility of lower-level managers.

Every organization creates a specific structure designed to facilitate the coordination of activities and control the behavior of employees. The two most common organizational designs are the mechanistic and the organic structure.

The Mechanistic Structure　　The mechanistic structure is machinelike and stresses efficiency through a reliance on written policies, procedures, and rules. Techniques for decision making are specified and well-documented control systems are emphasized. Managers emphasize routine as an essential tool of efficiency. A mechanistic structure closely fits the description of Weber's bureaucracy that was discussed in Chapter 1. It relies upon well-defined authority roles and a rigid chain of command and is characterized by high complexity, high formalization, downward communication, and low employee participation in policy formulation. The more mechanistic the structure, the less flexible it can be when it encounters challenges. The correctional organization is an example of the mechanistic structure.

The Organic Structure　　This structure is characterized by low complexity and formalization, a comprehensive information network, and high employee participation in decision making. Procedures are minimal and not formalized; work tasks are broadly defined and interdependent and subject to a continuous process of mutual adjustment. Flexibility and a willingness to adapt to changing conditions are considered critical. Organic designs are more like living organisms because they are innovative and can rapidly adapt to changing situations. Because of their flexibility, organic designs lack the stability to efficiently perform routine work. The more organic a structure, the more flexible, but less efficient it will be.

Every organizational structure has a specific design configuration. To understand the variety of possible design configurations, we turn to the work of Henry Mintzberg.

Mintzberg's Model of Design Configurations

Mintzberg (1983b) proposed that an organization is made up of five components, each of which designates a category of individuals responsible for a specific set of functions. These components are the operating core, the strategic apex, the middle line, the technostructure, and the support staff.

Operating Core

The operating core is the heart of the organization. Among its members are the employees who provide the direct services related to accomplishing the organizational mission: correctional officers, counselors, psychologists, probation and parole officers, nurses, teachers, food service and maintenance personnel, chaplains, and activity specialists. Operating core activities are closely monitored and regulated by managers striving to ensure standardization of employee performance.

Strategic Apex

The strategic apex contains the top-level managers charged with overall responsibility for ensuring that the organization "serve its mission in an effective way, and also that it serve the needs of those who control or otherwise have power over the organization (such as . . . government agencies, unions of the employees, pressure groups)" (Mintzberg, 1983b:13). As noted previously, management is the process of getting things done through employees by a process of ongoing engagement in planning, organizing, directing, and controlling employee activities. The strategic apex contains the members of the organization's executive management team.

Middle Line

The middle line consists of managers who have the formal authority to directly supervise members of the operating core, thus providing a linkage that connects the operating core to the strategic apex. Majors, captains, lieutenants, psychological services supervisors, directors of treatment, and probation and parole supervisors occupy the middle line.

The strategic apex and the middle line are the managerial subsystem of the organization. They work together to achieve the goals described in the epigraph at the beginning of this chapter. The managerial subsystem (Figure 2–7) represents the coordinating force in organizations.

Technostructure

The technostructure constitutes the organization's technical subsystem. Technostructure employees do not work directly with the offender population but serve the organization through activities that affect the work of all other employees. They design work, plan it, change it, or train the people who do it, but they do not do the work themselves. Rather, they use analytical skills to make the work of others more effective through standardization of policy and procedures and development of information management systems (work flow, research, data process-ing, strategic planning, financial control, and staff development) essential to the achievement of the mission. They also give technical advice to the strategic apex.

The technostructure secures and provides the technology needed to promote organizational efficiency. Technology is being used more extensively now than at any time in the history of corrections. Technostructure employees have the responsibility to acquire and introduce into the organization such technological advances as closed-circuit television, electronic perimeter surveillance and motion-detection systems, personal distress alarms, metal detectors, x-ray machines, computer-scanned identification bracelets for inmates, motion detectors, paging devices, pneumatic and electromagnetic locks, card-access buildings, video imaging, and computerized recordkeeping/ inventory/commissary/ and telemedicine systems.

Budget analysts, data processing analysts, computer programming specialists, accountants, personnel specialists, and fiscal control managers are examples of technostructure employees.

Support Staff

These are the people who provide indirect support services for the organization. They are not part of the operating core, but they provide support to the individuals in the other components of the organization. These individuals are different from those in the technostructure because they are not focused on standardization and are not primarily advice givers. Rather, they have their own specific functions to perform as they provide indirect services. Among the support staff are secretaries, payroll clerks, mailroom clerks, switchboard operators, attorneys, and public information officers.

Five Design Configurations

Any one of Mintzberg's five components can dominate an organization and produce one of five structural configurations: the simple structure, machine bureaucracy, divisional structure, adhocracy, or the professional bureaucracy.

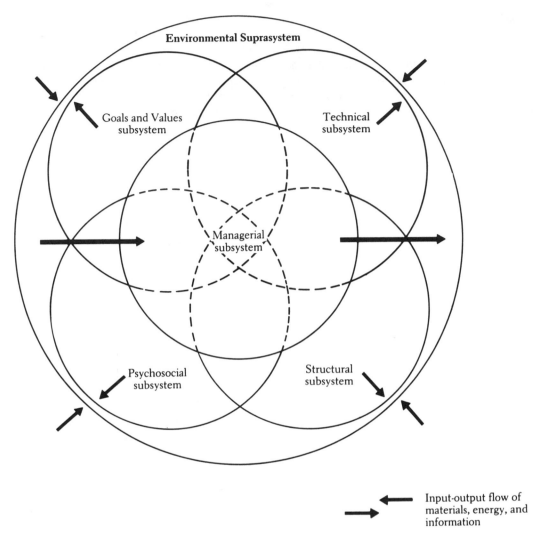

FIGURE 2–7   The Organization System. Source: Fremont Kast and James Rosenzweig. *Organization and Management: A System and Contingency Approach.* 3rd ed. New York: McGraw-Hill, 1979.

Simple Structure

An example of the simple structure is the prison commanded by the autocratic warden during Pre-DOC Corrections. In a simple structure, the strategic apex is dominant and control is highly centralized; structure is low in complexity, has little formalization, and has authority centralized in a single person (Mintzberg, 1983b:157). The simple structure was well-suited to wardens like Joseph Ragen who thrived on absolute control and centralized decision making, but it was unable to meet the increased effi-

ciency needs as DOC Corrections began to emerge.

Machine Bureaucracy

The configuration that could meet the efficiency needs of DOC Corrections was the machine bureaucracy. In this structure, the technostructure is dominant and control is exercised through standardization. Analysts and central office chiefs exercise enormous control by requiring adherence to standardized rules and procedures. Bureaucratization is used to create "an organization whose structure and operations are governed to a high degree by written rules" (Mann, 1984:28). A priority is placed on employees' carrying out strictly defined roles that "produce entirely determinable, impartial, and impersonal operation" (Mann, 1984:28). Standardization is the dominant theme of bureaucracy because standardized policies, procedures, and rules assist managers in coordinating and controlling the behavior of large numbers of employees. Routine and conformity in place of individual "shooting from the hip" are the organizational imperative.

The major strength of the machine bureaucracy is found in its ability to perform standardized activities in a highly efficient manner. The management of offenders, particularly in a prison, involves a high degree of structure in the form of a daily routine of activities. The reliance on written rules and regulations substitute for managerial discretion and reduces the confusion that would occur if employees and managers were free to exercise a high degree of autonomous decision making. In a machine bureaucracy, employees do well when confronting tasks for which they have been specifically trained, that have been previously encountered, and that are covered by the written rules. However, this strength also represents a primary weakness: the tendency for an obsessive emphasis on merely following the rules. This can promote inflexibility and difficulty in responding to new situations that require rapid change.

Divisional Structure

In a divisional structure, the power lies with middle management. A divisional structure is a set of autonomous units, each of which is a machine bureaucracy, coordinated by a central headquarters. Put another way, the divisional structure is a grouping of machine bureacracies whose activities are coordinated by a central headquarters. Because each unit is autonomous, the middle managers in charge of those units have considerably more control than the middle

managers in a machine bureaucracy. The divisional structure is typically a corporation with headquarters in one state and assembly and distribution plants in other states. Analogous to this corporate example is the DOC. In a DOC each prison and community corrections facility functions autonomously, yet in accordance with central office policy. Autonomy is exercised within central office-imposed constraints, a situation which creates frustration for prison and facility managers. Superintendents and facility directors are held fully responsible for the operation of their organizations at the same time they are required to make decisions in accordance with central office policy that may not take into consideration their unique needs and conditions.

Adhocracy

This configuration is an organic structure not found in corrections. In an adhocracy, the support staff is dominant and control is an exercise of mutual accommodation. Staff with highly specialized skills, such as doctors, attorneys, and computer specialists work together with very little control over each other. There are very few written rules and regulations and standardization and formalization are not conducive to the effectiveness of the members of the organization. Very little supervision of employees is needed because they are governed by an internalized set of professional rules. The adhocracy depends on decentralized teams of professionals making decisions and there is virtually no technostructure. There are no clear-cut distinctions between managers and employees and power is held by those individuals with a specific expertise, regardless of their position within the organization (Mintzberg, 1983b:261).

Professional Bureaucracy

In this configuration, the operating core controls and decision making is decentralized. A well-developed support staff may be present, but its purpose is to serve the operating core. Personnel work together in accordance with professional rules of behavior learned during programs of specialized study. These professionals function with a high degree of autonomy because the nature of their work requires autonomy. Doctors in a hospital, for example, function in accordance with a professional set of standards and perform their work with minimal supervision. Extensive employee empowerment is a feature of this design.

The history of correctional organization has been a history of evolution from the simple structure of Pre-DOC Corrections to the current complex structure of the machine bureaucracy and divisional structure. This evolution has seen the correctional organization transformed from the "patriarchal organization" based upon the traditional authority of the warden to a "rational-legal bureaucracy" in which a "professionally oriented central administration" formulates policy and comprehensive rules and regulations and unceasingly monitors the prison's day-to-day activities (Jacobs, 1977:73).

If structure and design are consistent with the mission, then organizational effectiveness, the subject of the next section, should result.

ORGANIZATIONAL EFFECTIVENESS

What is organizational effectiveness? It has been defined as the organization "doing the right thing" (Drucker, 1967:1–3). Mintzberg has suggested that organizational effectiveness will occur when the interplay of seven basic forces—direction, efficiency, proficiency, innovation, concentration, cooperation/culture, and competition/politics—is managed effectively (Mintzberg, 1991). Direction is the organization's sense of mission, the vision of what can be accomplished. Efficiency is the need to minimize costs, a growing concern of corrections in the 1990s. Proficiency is carrying out tasks with a high level of knowledge and skill. Innovation is the need to develop new services and approaches to chronic challenges.

Concentration is focusing organizational efforts on specific challenges. Cooperation/culture reflects the need for harmony and cooperation among diverse groups of people, a particularly powerful challenge in corrections because of the often conflict-ridden relationship between employees and offenders. Competition/politics involves the need for individual success and recognition, the lack of which can cause divisiveness within and between departments.

It is the responsibility of managers to consider each of these forces when they engage in environmental design. Ignoring a force can undermine effectiveness. For example, a lack of direction can result in a correctional organization whose employees lack the sense of purpose that leads to efficiency, concentration, and innovation.

But efficiency is not served if managers only focus on the internal environment of the organization. Reconsider the Profile at the beginning of this chapter and note that an important characteristic of a system is that its behavior is influenced by the external environment. Organizational effectiveness will be limited if managers do not consider the external environment in environmental design.

The External Environment and Organizational Effectiveness

Why should the external environment be of concern? It is of concern because events occurring outside of corrections can create environmental uncertainty for the organization. Generally, changes in the external environment can change the rules of the game for any organization. These changes can take the form of "emerging social and economic developments, legislative reform, drastic effects of war, new insights evolving from management experience, and research in the social and behavioral sciences" (Alexander, 1991:xi). (In Chapter 4 we begin our examination of the effects of these types of changes on the behavior of correctional organizations.)

Changing the rules of the game can create psychological uncertainty, a form of stress created by any situation or event to which an individual or organization must respond. Stress is the uncomfortable psychological state resulting from any encounter with the environment that is perceived as taxing resources or endangering well-being (Lazarus and Folkman, 1984). If an organization is to maintain its effectiveness, it must evolve over time. Correctional organizations are no exception. When events challenge existing strategy, correctional managers must change the existing structure through a process of adaptive strategy formulation.

Types of Adaptive Strategies

There are three basic types of adaptive strategies available to corrections organizations: innovation, cost-minimization, and imitation (Miles and Snow, 1978; Miller, 1987).

Innovation Strategy This form of adaptation involves changes made for the sake of meaningful innovation, not cosmetic change. The introduction of rehabilitation as an official goal required correctional managers to significantly change the organizational design. The result was prison treatment programs, the introduction of treatment staff into the work force, community corrections, and, more recently, creation of a variety of alternative to incarceration programs (such as house arrest) grafted onto the structure of traditional probation and parole departments. The modern commissioner of corrections facing severe overcrowding at every prison in the system can pursue an innovative strategy by requesting additional funding for prison construction, advocating the creation of new community-based correctional programs and facilities, and recommending that sentencing reform to eliminate mandatory sentencing and harsher penalties for nonviolent crimes become a political priority.

Cost-Minimization Strategy When the cost of operation exceeds the money allocated by government, managers must engage in a policy of strategic reduction of expenditures by either cutting costs or developing alternative revenue sources. As we will see in Chapter 5, correctional managers have devised a wide range of cost-cutting measures designed to benefit both corrections and the taxpayer. As for developing alternative sources of revenue, the inmate can be such a source. The most obvious examples of this strategy are the Pre-DOC Convict Lease System, the development of correctional industries, and the privatization movement and inmate-fee-for-services policies that are rapidly gaining popularity throughout the nation.

Imitation Strategy This is a strategy of watching what other organizations are doing, and then adopting those ideas and approaches that have been evaluated as most effective in achieving organizational goals. The use of various forms of alternatives to incarceration (such as house arrest and Intensive Supervision Probation) often began as an experiment in one DOC that attracted national attention and was closely watched by managers in other DOCs. Corrections may also adopt classification and counseling techniques used in other state agencies. Technological advances, such as computerized recordkeeping, are often developed in the private sector then duplicated in corrections after they have been proven to promote organizational efficiency.

Merely developing an adaptive strategy, however, is not enough to increase organizational effectiveness. The required employee behavioral changes must be incorporated into the daily routine of the employees that are the focus of the adaptive strategy. A process of learning must occur.

Adaptive Strategies and Learning

Adaptive strategies involve organizational learning, a process by which every level of an organization obtains new knowledge, tools, behaviors, and values, which are then "translated into new goals, procedures, expectations, role structures, and measures of success" (Bennis and Nanus, 1985:191).

There are two types of learning that occur within an organization: maintenance and innovative learning. Maintenance learning is defined as "the acquisition of fixed outlooks, methods, and rules for dealing with known and recurring situations" (Botkin, Mahdi, and Mircea, 1979:10). It is a type of learning that enhances problem-solving ability and is designed to maintain an established way of life. In correctional organizations, especially jails and prisons, maintenance learning has traditionally been well developed and institutionalized. The most effective method of organizing the inmate daily schedule of activities in a particular prison, for example, may consist of procedures and activities that have not changed significantly in years. In maintenance learning, current performance is compared only with past performance, not with what might have been done differently or the challenges of the future. Corrective action by managers addresses perceived weaknesses in the current way of doing things and learning tends to be restricted to those skills and techniques necessary to maintain the existing system.

For long-term effectiveness, particularly in times of turbulence, change, or discontinuity, innovative learning is required. Innovative learning encourages managers to look at problems in a different way, a way that is likely to bring about change, renewal, and restructuring. Innovative learning is much more difficult because it is focused on preparing employees for action in new situations. It is a process that requires the anticipation of future issues to be confronted without the luxury of a long period of trial and error. This type of learning relies on training, education, and unlearning.

Training and Education   Formal training processes are necessary to change the habits created by maintenance learning, to improve individual skills, and to encourage team building. Formal education is offered through the correctional training academy and in-service programs and is often supplemented or reinforced through formal communications channels such as newslet-

ters and bulletin boards (Bennis and Nanus, 1985:200) and the "read-at-roll-call" memo. Informal education takes place as a by-product of committee and task force participation and through briefings by vendors, consultants, and external auditors.

Unlearning   This involves the discarding of old knowledge that will interfere with the new behavior required by innovative learning. For example, addition of a community-based corrections component to a correctional system previously composed only of prisons will require a restructuring of the organizational hierarchy and a discarding of the philosophy that prisons are the only viable means of protecting the community from the convicted offender. New skills and thinking patterns suited to the less-structured reality of community-based corrections will have to replace behavior developed within a system based on the easy availability of physical instruments of control.

Adaptation must be an essential component of environmental design if organizational effectiveness is to be achieved.

SUMMARY

The correctional organization is a rational-legal machine bureaucracy; its employee activities are highly standardized, and conformity and "going by the book" are the fundamental operating philosophy. Because correctional organizations constantly interact with the external environment, processes of adaptation to the challenges and stress created by environmental uncertainty are necessary if organizational effectiveness is to be achieved. While structure and design are essential components in the creation of organizational effectiveness, the structural, managerial, and technical subsystems are not the only determinants of organizational behavior and effectiveness. A powerful set of determinants is located in the psychological subsystem. This subsystem is the focus of Chapter 3, where we examine the influence of employee and offender group values and behavioral norms on organizational effectiveness.

Discussion Questions

1. What is the relationship between strategy and structure? What is the effect of changes in strategy on structure?
2. How does bureaucracy promote organizational effectiveness?
3. What is the relationship between the structural components of an organization?
4. How do the structural, managerial, and technical subsystems contribute to organizational effectiveness?
5. Why are Mintzberg's five components of organizational design important to our understanding of correctional organizations?
6. What is environmental uncertainty and what is the role of adaptive strategy in the organization?
7. Which adaptive strategies would be most useful in corrections? Defend your answer.

Critical Thinking Exercise: The Feminine Model of Organization

Joyce Rothschild, an organizational sociologist, argues that gender-based value differences often lead women to prefer an organizational design that is significantly different from the bureaucratic structure proposed by Max Weber (1947). She calls this structure "the feminine model of organization" (Rothschild, 1991). The feminine model has six characteristics that distinguish

it from the Weber bureaucracy. First, people are treated as individuals with unique needs and values, not as the occupants of a particular office or organizational role. Second, relationships are seen as being intrinsically valuable, not just as the defined means of achieving organizational goals. Third, careers are defined in terms of individuals' being of service to others, not in terms of individual success, acquisition of power, and promotions. Fourth, feminine organizations provide personal growth opportunities for their members rather than an emphasis on job-required specialized skills and narrow ranges of expertise. Fifth, employees are considered to be members of a community based on trust and mutual care. Sixth, power and information are shared. Participatory decision making is encouraged.

Critical Analysis Questions

1. Are the feminine model and the traditional bureaucratic model mutually exclusive? Why or why not?
2. Are there any elements of the feminine model that would increase organizational effectiveness? If yes, what are they? How would they increase effectiveness?
3. Could the feminine model be adapted to community corrections? What issues would managers have to confront?
4. Are there any departments in the prison that could adapt to the feminine model? If yes, explain your choice.
5. What do you think the offender response would be to a correctional organization built on the feminine model?

3

The Organizational Culture of Corrections

Learning Objectives

After completing this chapter, you should be able to:

- Define organizational culture and explain the role of three systems of values and behavioral norms in that culture.
- Outline the process of employee socialization.
- Compare and contrast officer and inmate subcultural values.
- Summarize the managerial challenges presented by the presence of women and minority officers in prisons.
- Chronologically trace the evolution of the inmate subculture.
- Provide a description of a range of organizational responses to gang subculture and individual offender values.
- Establish the relationship between organizational culture and stress and identify managerial attempts to reduce stress.

Key Terms and Concepts

Organizational Culture
Official Values
Group Values
Psychological Contract
Socialization
Encounter Stage
C.O. Subculture
Custodians
   Lonely Braves
Female Correctional Officers
Institutional Role
Minority Correctional Officers
Inmate Code
Values Conflict
Wellness Programs

Values
Individual Values
Behavioral Norms
Subculture
Prearrival Stage
Metamorphosis Stage
Subculture
Supported Majority
Modified Role
Inventive Role
Inmate Subculture
Inmate Gangs
Stress
Mentoring Programs

[O]rganizational culture . . . is the culture that exists in an organization . . . similar to the culture in a society and consists of such things as shared values, beliefs, assumptions, perceptions, norms, artifacts, and patterns of behavior. It is the unseen and unobservable force that is always behind organizational activities that can be seen and observed

Stephen J. Ott

Profile: The Bureaucratization of a Probation Department

John Rosecrance's (1987) description of the bureaucratization of a California probation department provides an example of applying bureaucratic principles to improve the ability of managers and line staff to achieve the organizational mission. The probation department in which Rosecrance was employed was initially managed by a chief probation officer who had held the position for 20 years. An autocratic manager, the chief probation officer routinely engaged in "cronyism," that is, personnel decisions were made on the basis of personal relationships and perceived employee loyalty, not merit or professional qualifications. There was no formal written policy governing employee evaluation or promotion: "Chief _____ promoted only his buddies. He never paid attention to who was doing a good job; only to who was loyal to him" (Rosecrance, 1987:171). There was also a lack of standardized, written work rules. The chief probation officer "ran the place according to how he felt on that particular day" (Rosecrance, 1987:171). The lack of formal written policy created an organizational culture in which probation officers were permitted to develop an individual caseload management style based on the officer's personality. Discretionary decision making was unconstrained and a strong potential for the abuse of discretion existed. Because personal and professional independence were cherished, some probation officers made controversial court recommendations that created conflicts with district attorneys and judges. As one officer noted: "A few of the P.O.s [probation officers] had been getting out of hand. They were doing their own thing to such an extent that you hardly knew they worked for the probation department" (Rosecrance, 1987:173).

The new team of managers brought in to replace the chief probation officer slowly changed the rules of the game through bureaucratization. The use of individual discretion was sharply curtailed by the development of written policy, procedures, and rules designed to promote standardization of decision making and professionalism. The new managers emphasized that official regulations were to guide decision making and all recommendations to the court were to be departmental, not individual. New job specifications and duties were clearly spelled out so probation officers knew what was expected of them. Values organized around job performance, competence, group decision making, and ability to work with other agencies replaced the old values of autonomy and personal loyalty. Promotions, transfers, and dismissals were made on a merit, not a personal, basis. The standardization of employee behavior became the norm.

Fundamental to the ability of managers to effectively plan, organize, direct, and control is the understanding that every organization has an organizational culture that requires and prohibits certain beliefs, assumptions, and behaviors. The organizational culture exerts a powerful influence on the behavior of the people in the organization. In corrections, the organizational culture comprises three value systems: the organization's official values, the correctional officer subculture, and the inmate subculture. These values form the psychological subsystem of the organization. Values define standards of acceptable and unacceptable behavior, create behavioral norms, and form the basis for a psychological contract between individuals and groups of individuals. Subcultural values create unwritten, informal codes of conduct that may conflict with official values. Value conflicts can hinder achievement of the mission and create stress that requires managerial response.

DEFINING ORGANIZATIONAL CULTURE

The Profile at the beginning of the chapter provides an example of an organizational culture built around values of individual autonomy and discretion, loyalty to the manager, and the subordination of departmental mission and relationships with other agencies to individual employee styles. Bureaucratization modified this culture through the standardization of employee behavior. If bureaucratization and creation of a specific organizational structure were all that was involved in achieving the mission, the life of the manager would be easy. However, while bureaucratization and organizational structure provide the framework for employee behavior, they are not the organization's emotional center. Rather, the emotional center is the organizational culture, which can be defined as a set of key characteristics that describe the essence of an organization (Schein, 1985). The organizational culture defines the rules of the game:

[E]very organization develops a core set of assumptions, understandings, and implicit rules that govern day-to-day behavior in the workplace. . . . Until newcomers learn the rules, they are not accepted as full-fledged members of the organization. Transgressions of the rules . . . result in universal disapproval and powerful penalties. Conformity to the rules becomes the primary basis for forward and upward mobility (Deal and Kennedy, 1983:501).

Defining the rules creates the unique personality (climate) of the organization. This personality is based on values.

VALUES AND THE ORGANIZATIONAL CULTURE

As noted in Chapter 2, Vander Zanden (1984:318) defines a value as an "ethical principle to which people feel a strong emotional commitment and which they employ in judging behavior." Values involve attitudes and feelings about kinds of people; judgments concerning what constitutes "good" and "bad"; what behaviors and conditions are acceptable and unacceptable; the criteria we find most useful for making decisions and choices; and a philosophy of what makes things work the way they should. Chapter 2 also noted that every correctional organization contains a psychological subsystem. Values provide the content of the psychological subsystem. An organization's psychological subsystem is composed of three sets of values: official values; individual values; and group values. The relationship between different sets of values is referred to as a psychological contract. Therefore, the psychological subsystem can be conceptualized as an interlocking network of psychological contracts, some of which may be in conflict.

Official Values

Official values reflect the value system of the larger conventional society within which the organization exists, underlie the public philosophy of its managers, and guide employee behavior. The Florida Department of Corrections, for example, presents this statement of official values:

We, the members of the Florida Department of Corrections, believe:

- In the worth of the individual;
- Our word is our bond;
- In maintaining individual and collective integrity;
- That we recognize the right to be different and differ but shall not allow it to be divisive;
- Our most valuable asset is a well-trained, dedicated staff working as a team to meet any challenge;
- In an innovative approach to decision making based on sound correctional judgment;
- In treating all offenders firmly but fairly;
- That we have an obligation to be accountable and efficient in our use of resources (Florida Department of Corrections, 1995:4).

These values support a mission of public and staff protection and the maintenance of safe, secure, and humane environments.

Individual Values

Every individual is motivated by a set of personal values related to goals, job satisfaction, personal satisfaction, and the fit between their personal and organizational life. Values guide behavior; therefore, their influence on behavior can be either positive or negative. Positive personal values are expressed in beliefs such as respecting authority, standing up for your rights, respecting the rights of others, obeying the law, being tolerant of the beliefs of others, revering life, being honest, showing compassion, and helping people in need. Negative personal values are expressed in beliefs such as the white race is superior to other races, men are superior to women, the abuse of others is acceptable, compassion is weakness, only the strong survive, and the end justifies the means.

Individual values prescribe our behavior if we are acting as individuals. However, in a work environment, every individual is a member of a group whose shared values may be different from those of the individual.

Group Values

These are the values shared by the members of a particular group. Groups form subcultures. A subculture is a group of individuals "with a unique set of values, beliefs, and principles that operates within a larger environment" (Caudron, 1992:60–64). A subculture provides a powerful set of behavioral norms. The dominant subcultures in corrections are the correctional officer (C.O.) and the inmate subculture. Although correctional employees are organized into a variety of work groups based on similarities in function and each work group may have different behavioral norms, the lack of research concerning non-C.O. work groups norms, and the numerical dominance of C.O.s, limits our discussion to the correctional officer subculture.

The most important question that can be asked of any employee subculture is whether its values and norms are consistent with the organizational mission (Carrell, Jennings, and Heavrin, 1997:574). The importance of this question stems from the fact that employee subcultures provide an identity that new employees wanting to be accepted by the group usually learn and accept, even if the group values do not match individual values (Caudron, 1992:60–64) or the official values.

Psychological Contract

The psychological contract is an unwritten set of expectations that exist between managers and employees (Baker, 1985) that reflect their respective value systems. This contract defines the behavioral expectations that accompany every role. Managers expect line staff to be loyal, carry out their duties in accordance with their official job description and the organization's mission statement, and treat offenders in a professional manner. Line staff expect managers to be fair, be impartial in decision making, and do whatever is necessary to support the line staff. When these two sets of expectations mesh smoothly, a positive organizational climate is created.

There also exists a psychological contract between all correctional staff and the offenders under their supervision. Prison staff expect inmates to abide by the rules, go along with the program, and do whatever is necessary to achieve parole at the earliest time possible. Inmates expect to be treated fairly and provided the opportunity for programming and parole as quickly as possible. Probation and parole officers expect their clients to abide by the rules governing conduct within the community. Probationers and parolees expect to be treated like citizens, not inmates. If the expectations of the psychological contract are not met, staff may become repressive in their behavior, inmates may riot or engage in other forms of institutional disruption, and probationers and parolees may flee the jurisdiction or engage in new crimes.

New employees are not fully aware of the culture, or the psychological contract, of the organization into which they have been hired. Because new employees have their own views on how to do things, and these views may conflict with the organization's way of doing things, it is in the best interests of the organization to help new employees adapt to the work environment. This adaptation process is socialization, which we consider next.

SOCIALIZATION OF CORRECTIONAL EMPLOYEES

Socialization has three stages: prearrival, encounter, and metamorphosis (Maanen and Schein, 1977:58-62). In the *prearrival stage*, each employee joins the organization with a set of individual values, expectations, and attitudes that encompass both the work to be done and the nature of the organization. Employment is based on a selection process designed to ensure that only individuals who will "fit" are brought into the organization. An offer of employment means that managers have evaluated an applicant as being able to share and accept official values as the proper basis for organizational behavior. No offer of employment means that the applicant has been evaluated as having characteristics incompatible with official values.

During the *encounter stage* of socialization, the new correctional employee enters an environment where employee and offender behavior is structured by a rigid dependence on formal rules and procedures designed to ensure uniformity and regulate behavior. Upon entry into this bureaucracy the new employee confronts the possibility of conflict between personal expectations and organizational reality. If expectations are confirmed by actual experience, they will be reinforced during the encounter stage and official values and individual values will be compatible. However, if expectations are not confirmed, then the employee will be expected to undergo socialization because incompatible value systems and unmet expectations create dissatisfied employees, which happened to the case managers in the following description:

[T]he U.S. Bureau of Prisons has developed an outstanding ability to track the case management of inmates. The case manager's daily life is managed by SENTRY (an automated information system). The case management manual dictates the frequency of reviews and demands periodic updates in many categories of the system. The result is a manager's dream: quality control is excellent, the directors and regional directors are assured that functions are performed the same way on the West Coast as they are on the East Coast, and no inmate is forgotten. But what with high caseloads, slavish attention to paperwork, and auditors from the regional or central office who are insensitive to the demands of the job, the result is job dissatisfaction and burnout (Houston, 1995:73).

Employee incompatibility with, and failure to adjust to, the reality of the correctional environment has historically created high levels of employee turnover. During 1996, on average, 19.6 percent of correctional officers quit their jobs before completing the probationary period (Camp and Camp, 1997:126). Correctional managers asked to explain why employees resign have provided a range of reasons: low pay; the nature of the job (poor working conditions, long hours, stress from overcrowding or the threat of offender violence); and the nature of the employee—a poor fit between personal values and official values (McShane et al., 1991:220–225).

Finally, in the *metamorphosis stage* of socialization, the new employee must work out any conflicts discovered during the encounter stage. This resolution process may involve changes in personal behavior, and pressure to ensure conformity is exerted by managers through formal training programs designed to instill the new employee with the official values and job-specific information necessary to achieve the mission. Formal annual evaluations, informal mentoring, and the use of progressive discipline are also used to encourage compliance with official values. The metamorphosis is complete when the new employee is comfortable with the job.

However, managers spend relatively small amounts of time with new employees. A study of corporate managers revealed that they spend only 20 percent of their time in human resource management activities. The majority of their time is spent on formal management processes: decision making, planning, controlling, exchanging routine information and processing paperwork, and networking and interacting with outsiders (Luthans, 1988:127–132). There is little reason to believe that correctional managers, especially top managers, exhibit a different distribution of time and activities. Because new employees spend the greatest proportion of their time with their work group, that group's behavioral norms are a powerful influence on socialization. These norms can reinforce, or conflict with, official values.

CORRECTIONAL OFFICER SUBCULTURE

The origins of today's C.O. subculture are found in the white, uneducated, military-oriented, and male-dominated culture of Pre-DOC Corrections. The influence of the C.O. subculture on employee behavior cannot be overestimated:

The prison officer subculture may be as strong and significant as the inmate subculture. In fact, officers may become as "prisonized" as their inmate charges, the only difference being that officers are socialized into holding (or at least expressing) different values, observing a different—but probably no less stringent—"code," and following different behavior patterns. . . . Officers constitute a vastly outnumbered group, often scorned by their charges as well as the world outside, in need of each other to survive in a difficult and dangerous prison world (Kauffman, 1981:272).

The C.O. subculture immediately begins to teach new officers how to perceive inmates, anticipate trouble, and manage inmates (Crouch and Marquart, 1980) by instilling three fundamental custodial principles of prison work: security and control are paramount; maintain social distance from inmates; and be tough, be knowledgeable, and be able to handle inmates (Welch, 1996:143).

Subcultural Definition of Expected Correctional Officer Behavior

The C.O. subculture emphasizes the values of group solidarity and mutual support as a defense against being overwhelmed by a hostile inmate population capable of unpredictable violence. Kelsey Kauffman (1988:86–114) has identified a group of values that define the behavioral norms for three relationships: the officer–officer relationship, the officer–inmate relationship, and the officer–manager relationship.

Relationship Between Officers

Five values are important in defining this relationship. First, always go to the aid of an officer in distress. Prisons are dangerous environments. In 1996, 70 prison inmates died as the result of homicide (Camp and Camp, 1997:26); inmates committed 13,724 assaults against staff and 29,540 assaults against other inmates (Camp and Camp, 1997:36); and three members of staff were murdered (Camp and Camp, 1997:129). Officers only have each other to rely on if they experience a personal assault or must intervene to stop an inmate assault on another individual. This subcultural value is consistent with, and supports, the official value that officers will work together to meet the challenges of a dangerous environment.

Second, never make a fellow officer look bad in front of inmates. Because officers are concerned that any division in their solidarity will provide an opening for inmate manipulation, it is imperative that they show at least outward respect to their fellow officers and give no indication of personal disagreement or ill feelings. Third, always support an officer in a dispute with an inmate. Even if another officer is wrong, solidarity demands that all other officers provide support, even if there is disagreement with that officer's words or actions. To fail to provide support can invite inmate manipulation and create a rupture in group solidarity that can embolden inmates. Fourth, always support another officer's sanctions against an inmate. Officers do not always agree on the type of sanction that should be imposed when an inmate is caught in a rule violation. While two officers viewing the same violation may take different actions (one might file a formal misconduct report while the other might verbally counsel the inmate), they must set aside their personal feelings and support the sanctions imposed by other officers if group solidarity is to be maintained.

These first four values support the mission of promoting a safe and secure environment when the inmate being sanctioned is guilty of rule violations. Unfortunately, these officer–officer relationship values may undermine the mission of promoting a safe and secure environment if they result in officers keeping their silence when an officer allows personality conflicts, biases, or prejudices to guide his or her interaction with inmates. The C.O., for example, who witnesses another C.O. verbally or physically abusing an inmate and does not intervene or report the misconduct is allowing these loyalty values to create an unsafe environment. Abuse violates the official values of recognizing individual worth, fair treatment, and maintaining individual and collective integrity.

A fifth value for defining the relationship between officers is to show concern for fellow officers. A C.O. should be able to count on other officers to never leave a problem for them when their shift ends and to be available to help with personal problems. Kauffman (1988) contends that this particular norm is rarely upheld. If it is upheld, the official value of working together as a team to achieve the mission will be supported.

Relationship Between Officers and Inmates

First, don't "lug" drugs, that is, don't smuggle drugs for inmate use. Smuggling constitutes a violation of prison rules and the law. In addition, an inmate high on drugs can be very dangerous to both inmates and staff. This subcultural value supports the mission of providing a safe, secure, and humane environment and the official value of maintaining individual and collective integrity.

Second, don't be a white hat. An officer should never be sympathetic to inmates or identify with them or their needs. This value potentially may conflict with the official value of believing in the worth of the individual. However, according to Kauffman (1988), this norm is frequently violated. Officers in close proximity to inmates on a daily basis often try to help inmates by discussing their problems with them and giving advice, and an advisory relationship can gradually be transformed into a friendship.

Relationship Between Officers and Managers

First, maintain officer solidarity against all outside groups. C.O.s are generally quick to state that nobody, including their managers, understands the daily difficulties they encounter. They view officer solidarity as the only defense they have against an unappreciative environment that includes managers whose support of official goals often conflicts with subcultural values. Second, don't rat. Officers are not to "rat" on an officer to inmates or assist in the investigation of a fellow officer accused of the excessive use of force or otherwise breaking the rules. This is the same code of silence that prevails in policing and it is rooted in the same belief that the only person an officer can trust in an emergency is another officer. The staff member who reports corruption is "snitching" on a fellow officer and risks being left unprotected in a hostile environment by officers who no longer trust him. These subcultural values of the C.O. are the most troublesome because they violate the official values of maintaining individual and collective integrity, recognizing the worth of the individual, treating inmates fairly, and the officer's original commitment to "our word is our bond."

But a more subtle dimension to the code of silence is found in a pattern of complicity created by the reality that officers cannot follow every prison rule and still effectively manage inmates. The C.O., for example, who files a misconduct report for every instance of observed inmate rule violation will soon find that the entire shift has to be spent in front of the hearing examiner. The result will be resentment expressed by the officers who have to do that officer's work and overt, threatening inmate hostility. New officers quickly learn to ignore certain inmate behavior and overly restrictive prison rules in order to make their jobs manageable; but this behavior can justify a charge of employee rule violation and discipline if it is reported. Because other officers are aware of this rule breaking, an implicit conspiracy of silence develops. No one is turned in for anything because each of the others witnessing the rule violation are themselves guilty of rule violations that are witnessed by other officers (Lombardo, 1981:79).

Does the Officer Subculture Really Exist?

The officer subculture can be a source of conflict when its values conflict with the official values. But not everybody agrees that such a subculture exists. Although many in the field of corrections, such as Duffee (1975), testify to the existence of an officer subculture, there are those who disagree. Johnson (1987:122) has argued that "[t]here is no evidence that guards as a group are distinctly prejudiced or authoritarian, or indeed share any personality type at all." Klofas and Toch (1982:247) argue that the C.O. subculture, if it does exist, is not monolithic. Rather, there is a diversity in subcultural values and norms that supports three subcultural types: the "Subculture Custodians," the "Supported Majority," and the "Lonely Braves."

The Subculture Custodians, the smallest officer subgroup, are against inmates, possess antitreatment attitudes, and place a high value on security and control. The Supported Majority, the largest group, express attitudes that are supportive of inmates, the professionalization of C.O.s, and inmate treatment programs. The Lonely Braves believe they are being overwhelmed by the attitudes of the Subculture Custodians and are unable to express support for improving inmate conditions. In the sample of officers studied by Klofas and Toch, over 60 percent belonged to the Lonely Braves and Supported Majority.

If Klofas and Toch are correct, then correctional managers have a responsibility to learn as much about each subordinate as possible because this knowledge will assist in matching officers to the assignments for which they are most suited (collective bargaining agreements permitting). For example, a manager would not find it productive to assign a Subcultural Custodian to a thera-

peutic community where the officer is expected to participate in the treatment process. On the other hand, a Subcultural Custodian should be a very effective tower or perimeter patrol officer.

In the 1960s, the traditional white male domination of corrections generally, and the C.O. subculture specifically, was challenged by efforts to integrate the work force with women and minorities. That critical development is considered in the next sections.

FEMALE OFFICERS AND THE OFFICER SUBCULTURE

Women gained entrance into the working ranks of male prisons through a vigorous use of civil litigation against managers who refused to hire women as C.O.s. This litigation was based on the 1972 amendment to Title VII of the 1964 Civil Rights Act, which prohibited gender discrimination in employment decisions.

Pre-DOC managers refused to hire women to work in men's prisons because "[s]tereotypical feminine traits, such as seductiveness, fearfulness, and weakness create a perception that women would be a danger to themselves and their colleagues" (Pollock, 1995:102). These traits were associated with emotional softness while the subculture required emotional toughness. Male officers, and many managers, believed that women would be a liability because they would (1) lack the physical strength to provide effective back-up, (2) be vulnerable to assaults that would jeopardize officer safety and facility security, (3) be unable to enforce the rules because inmates would not follow their orders, and (4) violate inmate privacy and create inmate hostility (Hawkins and Alpert, 1989). Were male C.O.s and managers justified in their fears? We will briefly examine each concern.

Inability to Provide Back-Up Belknap (1991) found that female officers are less likely to use force to gain inmate compliance and are more likely to talk issues out

with inmates. This approach can be of benefit to correctional managers concerned
about the physical abuse of inmates,
although it may reinforce the perception
that women will not come to the aid of an
officer in distress. However, Belknap's finding has been challenged by another study.
Jenne and Kersting (1996) found few gender
differences in the use of aggression. Women
handled aggressive encounters with inmates
similarly to men and, where differences did
exist, the female officers tended to be more
aggressive, not less, than the men. The
authors concluded that this behavior may
be the result of women believing they have
to prove themselves. This finding suggests
that women are willing to provide back-up
when it is needed.

Vulnerability to Assault   Despite   the
widespread perception that women are
more vulnerable to assault, Shawver and
Dickover (1986) found little to confirm the
safety fears of male officers. In their study,
female officers were assaulted significantly
less often than male officers. There was no
relationship between percentage of female
officers and the number of assaults against
male staff.

Inability to Enforce the Rules   Many female
C.O.s believe they are more inclined than
men to treat inmates decently by listening
to their problems and being helpful, compassionate, and understanding (Pollock,
1986:89). It is this willingness to establish
an emotional tie with inmates that has led
many male officers to assume that female
officers will be unable to control male
inmates (Pollock, 1995:102). Such an inability to control would probably be most
apparent in the area of rule enforcement.

In a study of a medium-security state
prison in the Midwest, it was found that
female officers wrote approximately the
same number of misconduct reports for the
same types of violations as male officers,
and there was no difference in the likelihood of those reports being upheld by the
hearing officers or in the sanction that

would be imposed. The authors concluded
that the authority of female C.O.s is as legitimate as that of the male officers (Simon and
Simon, 1988). However, the perception of
female officers as unfit to manage male
inmates is still held by many male officers
(Progrebin and Poole, 1997).

**Female C.O.s as a Source of Inmate Hos-
tility**   Inmate reaction to the presence of
female C.O.s has, in fact, been mixed. Some
inmates are fearful that female officers cannot protect weaker inmates from the attacks
of predatory inmates. Other inmates share
the view of some male officers that a
woman's place is in the home, not in the
prison (Zimmer, 1986). However, in a survey of 120 male inmates in four Wisconsin
men's prisons, it was found that women
officers were liked by male inmates, first,
because they fulfilled a role as sex objects to
the inmates, and second, because they used
a more humane style of intervention than
the male officer (Petersen, 1982:452). The
feared uprising of male inmates in response
to the presence of female C.O.s has not yet
taken place.

Influence of Women on the Organizational Culture

The concern about female officers, however,
was about more than the physical safety
issue. There was also a fear that women
would bring into the prison environment a
new set of behavioral norms that would
undermine officer solidarity. Jurik and Halemba (1984:555–557), in a study of 40 female
and 139 male officers in a medium-mini-
mum security southwestern prison, found
that the female officers were more highly
educated, were more likely to come from a
professional and urban background, and
were more likely to be divorced, separated,
or single than were the male officers. The
women were also more likely to have an
interest in human service work and inmate
rehabilitation. Zimmer (1986:45) also found
that female officers in New York and New
Jersey were slightly more educated than

male officers and less likely to have a military background. A review of the literature by Zupan (1992) reported similar findings.

Studies indicate that female C.O.s favor a treatment approach and tend to use a more personal style of supervision than male officers (Jurik and Halemba, 1984; Crouch, 1985). The presence of female C.O.s in the men's prison has been promoted by many managers on the grounds that the personal style of supervision practiced by women can bring a "normalizing" influence into prison. The values underlying this "normalizing" influence contradict the "us versus them" mentality that can grow out of male subcultural values. Female officers will ask male inmates to do something, rather than order them; engage male inmates in conversations about children and families (Pollock, 1986); and more often explain an order than will male officers (Zimmer, 1986). The positive effect of female officers has been noted by Kissel and Seidel (1980), who report that 92 percent of male prison officers felt women made a special contribution to the facility, with 96 percent expressing the belief that female C.O.s increased the livability of the institution.

Zimmer (1986:150–151) believes that the presence of female C.O.s "constitutes a dramatic change for prisons and creates repercussions throughout the prison environment." One particularly powerful repercussion may involve the officer subculture. Arguing that worker homogeneity is a crucial element in subculture development and maintenance, Zimmer notes that female officers have been rejected from inclusion in the C.O. subculture, but increases in the number of female officers will present "a threat to the survival of the guard subculture as long as that subculture fails to assimilate women" (Zimmer, 1986:159).

Whether Zimmer is correct is not yet known. Because of a lack of empirical study (Pollock, 1995:107–108), the effect of female officers on organizational culture remains largely unanswered, as does the question of what effect a weakened officer subculture will have on prison organizational behavior.

Challenge of Female Officers to Managers

What has been clearly established, however, is that the introduction of the female officer into the all-male prison did introduce a powerful element of intraorganizational conflict to which managers had to respond. The days of prohibiting women from working in male prisons is long past and managers are expected to accept that reality. Thus, the male manager, who most likely has been, and may still be, immersed in the C.O. subculture (because of correction's tendency to promote from the ranks), is challenged by the professional obligation to identify and take action against male officer hostility toward female officers. The manager must develop, disseminate, and enforce policies prohibiting employees from making disparaging comments in the presence of both the female C.O.s and inmates, from spreading rumors of inappropriate sexual misconduct with inmates, or from engaging in any other behavior that would cause personal discomfort and/or have a direct impact on employment and career stability by causing women to resign. The enforcement of these policies can place the manager in the position of having to discipline officers with whom he has been friends for years.

Although progress continues to be made in recruiting and hiring women, they are still a numeric minority in most men's prisons. As of January 1997, women comprised only 19.7 percent of the DOC correctional officer staff (Camp and Camp, 1997:111). This lack of numbers makes the female C.O. highly visible. Zimmer (1986) argues that because of this visibility the appearance, demeanor, behavior, performance, and mistakes of female officers receive a disproportionate amount of attention; in particular, any mistakes, no matter the circumstances, are likely to quickly be communicated throughout the prison and repeatedly discussed. Zupan (1992) argues that the mistakes of one female officer are often generalized in such a way that the unsatisfactory performance by one female C.O. is assumed to be representative of all female officers.

How Different Are Female Officers?

Managers can point to a growing body of literature that refutes the basic proposition that because women are different they will have a different response to the job than male officers. Jurik and Halemba (1984) found only two differences between male and female officers in their respective perceptions of the job. The men wanted more discretion in carrying out their duties. The women wanted more structure and were more likely to express negative attitudes toward male co-workers, who they felt to be the cause of many of their problems at work. Both men and women officers tended to have negative attitudes toward their managers and to believe that the majority of their work-related problems were caused by those managers. In this respect, female officers are supporting the correctional officer subculture. There was little difference in levels of job satisfaction, which seemed to be little affected by the women's negative attitudes toward male co-workers.

Fry and Glaser (1987) found that the only difference between male and female officers was that the female officers were more negative in their evaluation of inmate services. Research has found no significant difference between male and female officers on the factors of punitive attitude or insensitivity to the identification of inmate needs (Jurik and Halemba, 1984; Zupan, 1986). It may be that the influence of the peer group outweighs any gender-based attitudes brought into corrections by women.

Management of the Female Officer

Male managers have traditionally assigned female C.O.s to low-risk assignments such as visiting rooms and control rooms where they have little direct inmate contact. This often paternalistic practice has the negative effect of limiting the officer's chance for promotion, denies her the opportunity to build confidence in her skills, and further antagonizes male officers who feel they are forced to work the more dangerous jobs while the women get the easy jobs (Zimmer, 1986; Jurik, 1985). Managers who practice differ-

ential treatment of female officers are violating a fundamental principle of management: Treat all employees equally unless their behavior signals the need for constructive differential treatment. The most effective managerial approach is to base the evaluation and job assignment of both male and female officers on individual job performance after they have undergone the identical formal training program.

In determining job assignments, managers must be aware that women may approach their work differently than men. Zimmer (1986) has suggested that women, experiencing the stress of the prison environment, may adopt one of three work styles: the "institutional role," the "modified role," and the "inventive role." In the institutional role, the female C.O. follows the rules and tries to maintain a highly professional stance. A preoccupation with obedience makes these women inflexible and rigid. In the modified role work style, the women believe they cannot perform the role as well as men and come to sympathize with the men who oppose women in corrections. These women fear inmates and avoid contact with them. They rely heavily on male workers for back-up. In the inventive role, women look to inmates for support, express little fear, and prefer work that involves direct inmate contact. It would be reasonable to expect women in the institutional and modified roles to be supportive of the officer subculture while women in the inventive role might challenge many of its values.

Managers who fail to recognize these role differences may create situations that have negative consequences. Placing a female C.O. who practices a modified role work style in a male inmate cellblock, for example, could create the chaos that many male officers have always predicted a woman on the block would cause. Having made this statement, it should be noted that Zupan (1992) argues that Zimmer has failed to make the case that these work styles are different from the styles adopted by male C.O.s, and Jacobs and Retsky (1975) have noted similar work styles among male officers. This area requires more research.

The female officer has not been the only threat to white male domination of the officer subculture. The minority officer has posed challenges to the corrections manager as well.

MINORITY OFFICERS AND THE OFFICER SUBCULTURE

The integration of the minority C.O. into the correctional work force in the late 1960s was the result of two powerful forces. First, because of an increased need for more employees, many prison managers found it necessary to look beyond the local white community from which C.O.s had traditionally been drawn. Second, inmates and community inmate advocacy groups demanded that C.O. diversity be implemented because it was necessary to have a sympathetic work force with which black inmates could identify (Jacobs and Kraft, 1978). Therefore, the first minority officers were African-Americans.

Challenge of Minority Officers to Management

This need for racial diversity was not readily accepted by veteran white officers, many of whom expressed fears that the "new breed" of nonwhite, urban guard was more pro-inmate and less trustworthy (Irwin, 1977) and would side with black inmates in officer–inmate disputes, a disruption of behavioral norms that would reduce C.O. solidarity. Managers had the difficult task of trying to integrate the two races and promote the concept of working together to achieve the mission. This task was made more difficult by the fact that many managers, particularly in the early days of DOC Corrections, were themselves influenced by racial fears.

The research on minority officer attitudes toward inmates has been mixed. Although

Jacobs and Kraft (1978) found that African-American C.O.s were more punitive than whites toward inmates, Jurik (1985) found that African-American officers had more favorable attitudes toward inmates than white officers. Klofas and Toch (1982) found that African-American officers also expressed a need for high social distance and concluded that they should be hired for reasons other than their assumed ability to relate better to minority inmates.

Racism on both a personal and institutional level has hindered the recruitment and promotion of minority officers. However, change has occurred and as of January 1997, 18.7 percent of adult system correctional officers were African-Americans and 9.1 percent belonged to other minority groups, with Hispanic officers (5.8 percent) being the second largest minority group (Camp and Camp, 1997:110). Unfortunately, racism in corrections still exists.

Cullen et al. (1985) found that African-American officers reported greater job dissatisfaction than white officers and speculated that minority officers receive less supervisory support than white officers. Philliber (1987) noted that studies have documented the tendency of African-American C.O.s to experience a level of stress that drives them to quit their jobs more often than whites. A primary explanation for leaving is conflicts with white managers. In a similar vein, Lasky, Gordon, and Strebalus (1986) observed that Hispanic C.O.s had significantly lower self-esteem than either white or African-American officers. Owen (1988:58) found that at San Quentin "racial conflicts and competition occur among the staff as they do among prisoners" with employment practices being a primary cause of animosity. White staff resented affirmative action programs that emphasized hiring and promoting minority officers. However, Wright and Saylor (1992) reported that African-American and Hispanic officers in the Federal Bureau of Prisons do not differ from white officers in their job satisfaction or opinions about management. Both African-American and Hispanic officers reported that they achieve satisfaction from working with inmates and African-American officers reported less stress than whites. The authors suggested that these findings may be the result of a managerial emphasis on professionalism and staff as "family."

The perception of racism has led many minority officers to create and join minority C.O. organizations that lobby for actions to reduce institutional racism. Some minority officers have gone to court for remedies for personnel hiring and promotion policies that were viewed as racially discriminatory. Zimmer (1986) argued that the failure to accept black officers will weaken the solidarity of the subculture in the same way as the failure to include female officers. As the number of black and other minority officers increases, a failure to accept them could seriously weaken the officer solidarity so cherished by the officer subculture. Because officer solidarity can support official values and promote the mission, the effective manager will seek to devise solutions that reduce conflict between white male officers and female and minority officers. The example of the Missouri DOC presented in Box 3–1 provides an overview of how DOC managers can meet the challenge of increasing both minority and female employment while reducing conflict.

BOX 3–1 THE MISSOURI DOC APPROACH TO EMPLOYEE DIVERSITY

Concerned about the low number of minority employees, DOC managers hired two additional human relations officers and placed them in charge of minority recruitment. These employees initiated a policy of establishing contact with churches and other religious groups, fraternities and sororities, chambers of commerce, and local chapters of the Urban League and National Association for the Advancement of Colored People and other ethnic and gender-based organizations. They also participated in Black Expos that enabled publicity and recruitment activities. In 1994, recruitment efforts were expanded to include volunteer and internship programs. To assist the largely white male staff in overcoming their resistance to diversity, the DOC implemented cultural diversity training sanctioned by the National Institute of Corrections. Each new employee receives a minimum of four hours of diversity training and an additional 16 hours is offered as part of the in-service training program. In addition, there are month-long observances of Black History Month, Women's History/Empowerment Month, Hispanic/Latino Heritage Month, and Asian/Pacific-American Month. Finally, the Human Relations Unit has become more active as an ombudsman to help employees resolve diversity-based conflicts (Braun, McKinney, and the Florida Team, 1995).

INMATE SUBCULTURE

The power of the correctional officer subculture in large part is a reaction to and is sustained by the values and behavioral norms of the inmate subculture. The inmate subculture is constantly evolving and can be divided into two periods: the 1800s to the 1950s and the 1950s to the present.

The Inmate Code and Pre-1950s Inmate Subculture

In every prison there exists "a complex, subtle, informal prisoner world with several subworlds . . . operating" (Irwin, 1980:11). The inmate world has a value system that generates a set of behavioral norms that become organized into the "inmate code." The inmate subculture is shaped by prisonization, and Sykes and Messinger (1960) have noted that the inmate code relies heavily on exaggerated images of masculinity that encourage "macho" behavior while condemning weakness, such as compassion, caring, sharing feelings and emotions, or expressing personal pain. The behavioral expectations of the inmate code emphasize loyalty to other inmates as expressed through noninterference with their activities, not "ratting" on them, avoiding the exploitation of other inmates, and minding one's own business. The inmate code also emphasizes that the "stand-up" inmate does not whine, cry, admit guilt, or try to curry favor with the staff by volunteering for work or accepting their view of the world. These behavioral norms conflict with official and employee subcultural values and norms. However, the inmate code is not always respected. Code violations can make the prison a very dangerous place because they often generate violence.

The inmate code is most frequently discussed in terms of prison inmates, but it can be argued that prisonization also influences the behavior of offenders in community corrections. The behavior of the parolee or probationer who has previously been incarcerated may still be governed to a large extent by the inmate code because its values and norms have become so deeply ingrained. Of particular concern to community corrections staff is the inmate code's fostering of distrust for criminal justice system employees and acceptance of violence. This distrust can lead to conflicts with probation and parole officers that limit their counseling effectiveness. The individual's acceptance of violence can jeopardize public safety as well as create a negative public perception of community corrections when a parolee commits a highly publicized crime such as rape or murder. Community corrections' staff concern about violence can be seen in the fact that as of January 1997, in 25 of 33 reporting state probation and parole agencies, officers carry weapons during at least some portion of their official duties (Camp and Camp, 1997:157).

The pre-1950s inmate code was based on three rules: "Do not inform, do not openly interact or cooperate with the guards or the administration, and do your own time" (Irwin, 1980:11–12). It reflected an inmate culture that was essentially an inmates-against-the-guards subculture that emphasized inmate group solidarity. However, the nature of subcultural values and behavioral norms changed as prisons entered the 1960s.

The Current Inmate Subculture

The inmate subculture began to experience rapid change during the 1960s and 1970s when some inmates, influenced by the social turbulence sweeping America, became politically aware and defined themselves as political prisoners (Fairchild, 1977). Envisioning themselves as heroes fighting a corrupt system, they began to challenge correctional managers by initiating litigation, some of which had a powerful effect on organizational behavior (see Chapter 7). This era of the political prisoner ended after the 1971 Attica riot for reasons still unclear (Pollock, 1997:247), but it left a legacy of black inmate militancy that challenged the power of white male C.O.s. Officers confronting a black inmate

FIGURE 3–1 Many of today's inmates are so dangerous that a simple trip to the law library requires shackling and officer escort. Courtesy of the California Department of Corrections.

would suddenly find themselves facing a hostile, black group (Carroll, 1976). Racial identity was becoming a powerful force in the inmate subculture (Jacobs, 1977) and "violence among inmates took on racial connotations, with formerly repressed black inmates rising to positions of dominance within the prison culture" (Johnson, 1996:144).

Carroll has argued that race now dominates every aspect of prison life with prisons "balkanized" and racial gangs holding territories such as portions of the yard, certain television rooms, and recreation room areas (Carroll, 1982). The result is that "[w]hat was once a repressive but comparatively safe 'Big House' is now often an unstable and violent social jungle" (Johnson, 1996:133). The growth in violence was also encouraged by the emergence of a prison drug culture in the early 1960s that increased the incidence of drug-related assaults, thefts, and inmate misbehavior (Figure 3–2). The increased incarceration of addicts in the 1970s also changed the nature of the inmate subculture because inmates "were generally younger than prisoners had been in the past and were characterized as having no loyalty to anyone or anything" (Bowker, 1977:110).

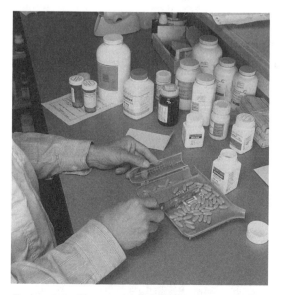

FIGURE 3–2 Drug use and trafficking is so prevalent in the current inmate subculture that tight control of all prescribed medication is a critical requirement.

To a large extent, the drug traffic in any prison is under the control of gangs. As early as 1970, gangs were exerting a powerful influence in Illinois and California prisons (Jacobs, 1977; Davidson, 1974). Racially based, maintaining strong ties to the community, and built around a structured power hierarchy, gangs came to dominate prison life. At least one author has argued that the inmate subculture is now the gang subculture (Pollock, 1997:251) because race-based gangs fulfill the same functions as the old subculture. They provide the inmate with a feeling of solidarity, provide services and protection, and help create and maintain a high level of self-esteem (Pollock, 1997:252).

The extent of gang influence was measured in a 1992 national survey that found 47,445 inmates throughout the country were members of 755 "security threat groups" operating in numerous prisons, especially in California, Illinois, New York, and Texas (American Correctional Association, 1993:4). Increased drug trafficking and gang domination of the inmate subculture has led to an increasingly high level of violence. The Texas Department of Criminal Justice, for example, in 1984 and 1985 witnessed 52 inmate homicides and more than 7,000 inmate and staff assaults, with 92 percent of the homicides and 80 percent of the assaults attributed to gang-related activities (Buentello, 1992:58). The Aryan Brotherhood gang was responsible for 18 percent of all homicides in the Federal Bureau of Prisons between 1982 and 1992 (Trout, 1992:62).

As new challenges to staff emerge, managers must modify employee behavior through a process of modification of the environmental design. Principles of organizational change are discussed in Chapter 14. For now we will concentrate on the need for environmental design modification directed at the inmate gang and the individual offender's value system.

Organizational Response to the Inmate Gang Subculture

The emergence of prison gangs and gang-related drug/violence has motivated managers to evaluate existing security, classification, and treatment approaches to determine more effective methods of reducing the threat posed by gangs. Many managers confronted with gangs have taken a two-pronged approach to changing the environmental design: creation of gang-specific inmate control policy and the use of treatment programs to change the individual value system so conducive to gang membership.

Creation of Gang-Specific Inmate Control Policy

A number of DOCs have created new policy, procedures, and rules in an effort to maintain institutional security and control in the face of the threat posed by gangs. For example, at the Washington State Penitentiary in Walla Walla, managers have allocated resources to train staff in gang member identification (Riley, 1992:68). The identification process begins during the initial classification of the inmate. Staff look for tattoos and scars indicative of gang affiliation; ask inmates if they are gang members; and, if the answer is yes, if separation from other gang members is necessary. Identified rival gang members are physically separated from each other through placement in one of three housing sections where movement and traffic is monitored and restricted. Special intelligence officers are used to prevent any gang from achieving a numerical superiority in any housing section.

The Texas Department of Criminal Justice has also diverted resources to pre-service and in-service staff training to focus attention on gangs and their activities. But Texas has gone even further in its attempts to control gangs. Managers have designated gang intelligence officers in each prison who gather gang-related information and identify gang members and leadership. Active cooperation in the sharing of information with other state and federal authorities has been initiated and identification of gang membership results in the inmate being placed in administrative segregation. This approach has apparently been effective in frustrating the ability of gang leaders to recruit new members and organize gang activities (Buentello, 1992:60).

Texas correctional managers have also reached out to the state legislature and lobbied for the enactment of legislation that (1) provides funding for a special prosecutor to focus on prison gang-related criminal activity, (2) makes it a felony for any inmate to possess a weapon, and (3) stipulates that any inmate convicted of a crime committed during incarceration will serve any sentence received consecutively. The result has been a breakdown in gang leadership and the ability of the gangs to be as effective as they were before these actions were taken (Buentello, 1992:60). The Federal Bureau of Prisons identified and separated gang members until the late 1980s when the changing nature of street gangs, and the threat presented by incarcerated members of drug cartels, created a shift to tracking "security threat groups." These are groups that do not meet the traditional definition of a gang but that appear to present a compelling potential threat: locksmiths, computer experts, electronic security experts, and explosives experts (Trout, 1992:66)

The Treatment Approach to Reducing Gang Membership

Programs that specifically target gang members for therapeutic intervention can be developed. For example, in 1993, when managers at the Hampden County Correctional Center in Massachusetts were confronted with inmate gang activity, they adopted an approach of physically segregating gang members after appropriate classification and providing a cognitive retraining program for them while they were in segregation status (Toller and Tsagaris, 1996). The program is offered by the counseling staff and involves group discussions and "homework." The goal of the program is reintegration into the Center's general population. A relapse component of monitoring and counseling is also included. One of the strong features of this program is that it recognizes that some inmates may have been coerced by peer group pressure into joining a gang and do not want to return to it. These inmates may be able to escape gang retribution for quitting gang activities by pointing out that they are being closely monitored by a staff willing to take action against them if they rejoin the gang.

Many inmates do not belong to gangs, yet their behavior is still directed by a set of individual values that promote violence, drug abuse, and gang membership. These values cannot go unchallenged if correctional organizations are to meet the mandate of staff/offender security and public protection.

Challenging Individual Offender Values

The effective challenge of inmate subcultural values requires a combination of education, skills training, and spiritual instruction (Figures 3–3 through 3–7). We will briefly review four examples illustrating this element of environmental design, beginning with the California DOC.

California   In 1990, the Richard J. Donovan Correctional Facility (RJD) adopted a drug treatment program pioneered at the Pima County Adult Detention Facility in Tucson, Arizona, in cooperation with the Amity Foundation of California, a private nonprofit organization specializing in drug offender

programs (Mullen et al., 1996). The program relies on a therapeutic community approach, a specific curriculum developed by Amity, and the rigorous cross-training of treatment staff and correctional officers. The centerpiece of the program is a spectrum of treatment approaches (see Box 3–2). The program has

FIGURE 3–4   Courtesy of the California Department of Corrections.

FIGURE 3–5   Courtesy of the Office of Archives, Federal Bureau of Prisons.

FIGURE 3–3   Courtesy of the California Department of Corrections.

FIGURE 3–6   Courtesy of the Office of Archives, Federal Bureau of Prisons.

reduced violence and drug use, and has proven to be cost-effective. A cost-benefit analysis reported that a 3,000 bed program would have an estimated seven-year cost savings of $29,705,000. The results have been so impressive that the DOC was able to persuade the California state legislature to commit $100 million to "build the largest dedicated prison drug treatment program in the world" (Mullen et al., 1996:123). It requires an enormous amount of planning, organizing, directing, and controlling to produce a viable treatment program. Box 3–3 provides an overview of the environmental design necessary to create this type of effective program.

BOX 3–2 CALIFORNIA INMATE DRUG TREATMENT PROGRAM

Two hundred men live in a housing unit on a yard with 800 other inmates. Amity participants share the yard with the rest of the inmates, but program space is isolated.

FIGURE 3–7   Courtesy of the Office of Archives, Federal Bureau of Prisons.

Twenty Amity staff, mostly ex-addicts and ex-offenders trained by Amity to work in prison participate in CDC security training for correctional officers to receive their security clearance.

All participate in a minimum of 40 hours per year of Amity immersion training to keep skills current.

Six "Lifers" (life with possibility of parole inmates) work with Amity staff as credible role models and help stabilize the program.

Forty program participants (inmates) work one week on, one week off, supporting staff in delivering the Amity program.

The Amity curriculum was developed more than 15 years ago by Naya Arbiter. A written and videotaped curriculum specifically designed to reach habitual offenders with chronic drug abuse histories, the curriculum involves encounter groups, seminars, video playback, psychodrama, and written and oral exercises. It addresses violence, family dynamics, gang involvement, and other issues relevant to this population.

A therapeutic community approach demands a very high degree of accountability from participants and staff.

A Correctional Counselor III and two Correctional Counselor staff members work with Amity staff and institutional staff to select inmates, conduct disciplinary proceedings, develop treatment plans, and develop discharge plans.

Reprinted with permission of the American Correctional Association, Lanham, MD.

BOX 3–3 ELEMENTS OF SUCCESS OF THE CALIFORNIA INMATE DRUG TREATMENT PROGRAM

The following are the elements of success for the Amity program that CDC administration, and institutional, treatment, and parole staff see as critical:

a director of corrections who saw the economic impact of drug abuse on the correctional budget (and public safety) and was willing to break new ground in addressing these issues;

central office staff who worked closely and effectively with the institution, parole, treatment staff in the prison, and the treatment program in the community;

a warden who was willing to take a risk and maintained a hands-on relationship with the program—insisting on fitting the program to the institution, but also treating the treatment staff with respect and giving them the independence needed to carry out their jobs;

the buy-in of the correctional staff in the institution to support the new program;

a correctional facility that was well managed and stable;

a treatment program that was experienced in working with offenders and committed to a joint-venture/collaborative approach to corrections;

a curriculum specifically designed for the inmate population served that was based on "emotional literacy" and issues particularly relevant to inmates in the program, including substance abuse, family dynamics, violence, racial prejudice, relapse prevention, moral development, building and maintaining positive relationships, and "how to get prison out of you";

a treatment program director who was willing and able to work cooperatively with the institution in implementing the program and maintaining it;

a treatment staff that was able to work side by side with the institution and maintain credibility to the inmates;

the incorporation of "Lifers" into the Amity in-prison program as credible role models and trainees;

regular cross-training of treatment, correctional and parole staff together to enhance understanding, cooperation, communication and a sense of joint ownership;

the assignment of a parole agent who worked in an integral fashion with corrections and treatment staff and was the catalyst for supporting parole program completers in the community; and

the development of a "linked" aftercare program for Amity prison parole completers that allowed a true continuance of treatment in the community.

Reprinted with permission of the American Correctional Association, Lanham, MD.

Massachusetts   In 1992, The Massachusetts DOC developed a system-wide skill-based program designed to target substance abuse, relapse prevention, anger management, and criminal thinking. The program can accommodate as many as 585 inmates at a time and involves both prisons and community corrections. The approach identifies criminal thinking patterns, teaches and rehearses prosocial skills, involves

out-of-class skill practice, and reinforces social skills through the use of maintenance groups and linkages to community services. Anecdotal evidence has been positive (Mitchell, Emodi, and Loehfelm, 1996).

Delaware   In June 1994, four DOC prisons began to offer inmates the opportunity to participate in a Life Skills Program designed to "reeducate clients socially, morally and behaviorally, while instilling appropriate values, goals and motivation" (Miller and Hobler, 1996:116). The goal of the program is to alter how offenders think and make judgments about what is right and wrong through the development of interpersonal relationship, communication skills, job and financial skills, and family values. A violence-reduction component includes anger control, stress management, and moral reeducation. Family involvement in the program is encouraged. The primary goal is reduced recidivism, and one-year follow-up results show a 8.1 percent recidivism rate for program participants compared to a control group rate of 34.9 percent. Although the target of this program is recidivism, it is reasonable to expect that a more prosocial value system can also reduce the attractiveness of gang membership.

Alabama   In recognition of the need to confront antisocial values in a cost-effective manner as early as possible, the Alabama Department of Youth Services has developed CITY—the Community Intensive Treatment for Youth Program (Earnest, 1996). This nonresidential treatment program provides needs assessment, an individualized treatment plan, GED training, family counseling services, individual and group counseling, the use of a behavior modification point system, and transitional follow-up services. Preliminary evaluations have been positive.

ORGANIZATIONAL CULTURE AND STRESS

Programming can change individual offender values, but treatment money is scarce, and many offenders never receive effective programming. The result is an intact inmate subculture that is a major source of employee stress. The vast majority of correctional stress research has focused on C.O.s, but the findings have not always been consistent.

The Extent of Correctional Stress   In a study of 147 federal C.O.s, Lasky, Gordon, and Strebalus (1986:324) observed "greater levels of psychological stress than expected from a nonpatient, normal male sample." Lindquist and Whitehead (1986:12), in a survey of 241 C.O.s, found that 38 percent viewed their jobs as very stressful, 29 percent reported moderate stress, and the remaining 32 percent "were in either the slightly or more than slightly stressful category." However, while Honnold and Stinchcomb (1985:48) noted frequent complaints of stress-related high blood pressure, migraine headaches, and ulcers, they noted that "the majority of correctional employees are apparently not plagued by debilitating levels of stress." It may be that the length of service of the employees being surveyed is an important factor. Brodsky (1982) found that a significant number of C.O.s experienced only minimal stress in their work after an initial period of adjustment during which they mastered the basic requirements of the job and adapted to the challenges of working in a prison environment. In this respect, stress may function as a screening mechanism that forces out employees not suited for corrections. However, Cheek and Miller (1983) make the argument that C.O.s are prone to deny their stress, a denial contradicted by objective data. Cheek (1984) reports that C.O.s have an average life span of 59 (compared to a national average of 75), twice the national divorce rate average, and experience high rates of suicide, alcoholism, heart attacks, ulcers, and high blood pressure.

Stress is not limited to prisons. Whitehead (1987), in a study of probation officers, found that 49 percent viewed their work as very or more than moderately stressful.

Sources of Stress for Line Staff   The stressors (sources of stress) for C.O.s are varied,

but Gerstein, Topp, and Correll (1987) concluded that it is the nature of the correctional environment that creates stress, not the personal characteristics of the employees. Stress is frequently linked to the characteristics of the work: danger; lack of predictability; feeling trapped in the job; low salaries; inadequate training; absence of standardized policies, procedures, and rules; lack of communication with managers; and little participation in decision making (Philliber, 1987). Cullen et al. (1985) and Lasky, Gordon, and Strebalus (1986) found that personal safety concerns increased as the security level of the prison increased. However, research has not found contact with inmates to be a primary source of officer stress (Adwell and Miller, 1985).

Rather, overriding the nature of the job as the primary stressor for the correctional officer is the structure of the correctional organization (Brodsky, 1982) and the activities of its managers (Whitehead and Lindquist, 1986). The failure of managers to support line staff has been emphasized by Lombardo (1981) and Brodsky (1982). This perceived failure to support constitutes a significant violation of the psychological contract between managers and officers. Lasky, Gordon, and Strebalus (1986) observed that role definition problems and role conflict from unclear expectations about the custodial/human service role play a significant role in officer stress. Zimmer (1986) and Jurik (1988) have found that female C.O.s report higher levels of stress than male C.O.s because of employee sexual harassment, limited supervisory support, and a lack of programs designed to integrate them into the male prison. However, Blau, Light, and Chamlin (1986), in a study of over 3,000 New York City correctional employees, did not find that line officers experience more stress than managers.

Sources of Stress for Managers   There is relatively little research available on managerial stress. Weinberg et al. (1985) found that manager–subordinate relations are a major source of stress for both managers and line staff; however, correctional managers only scored in the middle range of stress measures when compared to managers at state psychiatric hospitals, community mental health centers, and a general hospital. Most stressful to managers were subordinate decisions made without managerial consultation, poor subordinate productivity, and the need to discipline or terminate employees.

Effects of Stress on Organizational Effectiveness   The personal effects of stress on correctional employees have already been noted. On the organizational level, stress produces high employee turnover, reduced productivity on the job, high rates of absenteeism and use/abuse of sick leave, and inflated health care costs and disability payments. Researchers estimate that 40 percent of employee turnover is related to stress and that high rates of absenteeism and employee turnover are strong indicators of the amount of stress in a work environment (Slate, 1996). Organizations with high levels of employee stress are wasting money because every time an employee quits, the amount spent to recruit and train that employee is lost. And, as the ratio of new to seasoned staff decreases, the ability to maintain inmate control also decreases while the potential for disaster increases.

Methods for Reducing Stress   Cheek and Miller (1983) have suggested that managerial efforts to clarify job performance guidelines and practice more effective communication can reduce employee stress levels. Many managerial training programs now include skills training to move managers away from an emphasis on authoritarian styles of management. Rosefield (1981) has suggested training as a means of countering stress. Employees can be taught the recognition of stress-related symptoms and the use of stress management techniques during initial training and in-service programs. Managers can also reduce the level of stress through wellness programs and employee empowerment initiatives.

Wellness programs focus on increasing individual stress-coping ability by teaching the fundamentals of such activities as smoking cessation, health risk appraisals, back care, stress management, exercise/fitness, off-the-job accident prevention, nutrition education, blood pressure checks, and weight control. Although exercise programs typically offer high-exertion activities such as running or competitive sports, Arthur Hudson (1994), a New York City probation officer, suggested incorporating the slow movement, stretching, breathing, quiet sitting, and meditation elements provided by such disciplines as yoga and tai chi into exercise routines. Wellness programs are relatively easy to implement, although budgetary and physical space limitations may present initial obstacles.

Empowerment programs also offer the potential for stress reduction. In 1973, the National Advisory Commission on Criminal Justice Standards and Goals in Corrections recommended that managers adopt the concept of participatory management because giving employees more control over their work environment through active participation in the decision-making process can reduce stress. Participatory managers are associated with higher levels of employee morale and job satisfaction than are autocratic managers (Duffee, 1989) and engage in such employee empowerment initiatives as unit management programs and mentoring.

An excellent example of mentoring is the Federal Bureau of Prisons program, which pairs an experienced manager (mentor) with a less experienced employee (protégé) in every federal prison, regional office, and community corrections office. A mentor, after eight hours of training, may be paired with up to five protégés for a formal one-year relationship. This program has the potential to reduce employee stress because "enhanced communication, team work and staff perceptions of empowerment, productivity and job satisfaction are all objectives" (Edwards and Wrigley, 1995:102). The value of an empowerment program is that empowered employees identify problems and resolve them.

DEFINING THE ORGANIZATIONAL CULTURE OF CORRECTIONS

Based on the material presented in the first three chapters, we can describe the organizational culture of corrections as having the following characteristics. The organization is a unit of government charged with the responsibility of humanely managing offenders and protecting society. There are extensive rules and regulations that employees and offenders are expected to follow. Managers closely supervise the employees to ensure that there are no deviations from policy. Work activities are designed around individuals. There are distinct departments and lines of authority and communication organized in a formal chain of command. Conformity, loyalty, cooperation, and the avoidance of mistakes are highly valued and rewarded. The manager–worker relationship is regulated to a large extent by collective bargaining agreements. Management's exclusive concern with conformity and the mission can negatively affect employee morale and turnover. High levels of stress are produced by conflicting value systems.

SUMMARY

Organizational culture determines the personality of the organization. The organizational culture is the result of a dynamic interaction between three systems of values and behavioral norms. Conflict between these systems create managerial challenges, such as the integration of women and minorities into the work force and the reduction of employee stress. The effective manager must understand the subcultures operating within the correctional environment and their effect on the ability of the organization to achieve the mission. Those values and norms that conflict with the mission must be identified and addressed by managers through modification of the environmental design. Clearly, the internal environment of the organization influences organizational behavior. However, there is another powerful determinant of organizational behavior: the external environment. In the next chapter, we highlight the influence of the external environment on organizational behavior.

Discussion Questions

1. What values do the C.O. subculture and the inmate subculture have in common? How do they differ?
2. What challenges does the C.O. subculture present to managers?
3. How can new employee socialization efforts be improved?
4. What effect have female and minority correctional officers had on the prison organizational culture?
5. What challenges are presented by the inmate subculture?
6. What actions can correctional managers take to change gang and individual offender values and norms?
7. What are the sources of employee and manager stress?
8. How can employee stress be effectively reduced?

Critical Analysis Exercise: Reducing the Use of Physical Violence

In Pre-DOC Corrections, physical violence was an ingrained element of the "guard" subculture and it was not uncommon for "goon squads" to violently assault and brutalize inmates. Such behavior is no longer condoned. Professional managers now enforce a policy that all correctional employees (prison as well as community corrections) are to use physical force as a defensive tactic only. Training academy staff emphasize the prohibition of the excessive use of force and the use of verbal and defensive control ("come-along" holds) techniques. Managers sometimes encourage employees to engage in martial arts training as long as the skills learned are for defensive purposes only. The prevailing DOC policy addressing the use of force is as follows: (1) only the amount of force needed to control an assailant and/or eliminate or minimize the danger of serious bodily harm or death to self or others will be used; (2) the use of force stops as soon as the threat of physical harm is over; and (3) force is never to be used as a form of punishment (Paul Brown, 1996:78). Official values promoting a willingness to physically "mess up" an inmate have been replaced by official values promoting the control of violent inmate behavior through nonlethal techniques.

Critical Analysis Questions

1. Which elements of the Pre-DOC correctional officer subculture were supportive of the use of excessive officer force?
2. Do you think the introduction of female correctional officers has weakened the value placed on physical force? If so, how?
3. What actions can managers take to ensure employee compliance with limited-use-of-force policies?
4. How can mastering self-defense techniques reduce stress?

4

The Political Environment of Corrections

Learning Objectives

After completing this chapter, you should be able to:

- Define the relationship between the conservative revolution and prison overcrowding.
- Contrast the political and correctional manager perspectives on increasing incarceration rates as a crime control policy.
- Outline the organizational, human, and economic consequences of prison overcrowding.
- Establish the limitations of building out as a primary adaptive strategy for overcrowding.
- Explain the effect of adaptive strategies on organizational structure and design.
- Develop a plan of action for management of prison overcrowding that would not emphasize the use of incarceration.
- Identify the changes in the correctional technostructure produced by the actuarial model and adaptive strategies.
- Discuss the issues involved in advising elected officials.

Key Terms and Concepts

Public Policy	Official Goals
Operative Goals	Political Ideology
Liberal Realism	Conservative
Politicization	Ideology
of Crime	Conservative
Sentencing Reform	Revolution
Prison	Parole Reform
Overcrowding	Overcrowding
Building Out	Challenges
Front-end	Leasing Out
Strategies	Back-end
Increasing	Strategies
Complexity	Decreasing
Increasing	Centralization
Formalization	Actuarial Model
Technostructure	Technology
Changes	Legislative
Advising	Liaison Office
Extending	
Confinement	

Prison management will become a tougher job now that more and more inmates will be serving longer and longer minimum terms. There is little incentive for good behavior from an offender who is 32 years old and looking at 40 hard years and knowing he would be 72 years old if and when he finally gets out. This . . . hardening of the system . . . presents special challenges to prison management. . . . It is both challenge and opportunity on a grand scale.

Texas Department of Criminal Justice, 1995.

The formulation of America's current crack cocaine control policy began with an effort in 1986 to provide law enforcement agencies with the tool of tougher sentences for crack cocaine traffickers. By 1988, the U.S. Congress had enacted legislation that required federal judges to impose a mandatory five-year prison sentence for possessing crack cocaine in an amount that was only one-hundredth of the amount of powder cocaine necessary to trigger mandatory sentencing. The process by which this 100:1 differential was created was strongly influenced by public fear of drug crime, media sensationalization of the death of basketball player Len Bias in 1986 from a drug overdose, the political need to be tough on crime for reelection purposes, and a widely held perception that crack cocaine was more dangerous than powder cocaine. The results of the legislation were massive overcrowding in the federal prison system and perceptions, both offender and public, that the crack cocaine laws were racially biased—88.3 percent of the crack cocaine convictions involved black defendants (Gest, 1995). Repeated efforts in 1996 and 1997 to reduce the 100:1 ratio in response to the perception of racial bias in sentencing were repelled by legislators fearful of being publicly labeled "soft" on drug crime.

Because correctional organizations are open systems, their managers must be responsive to the demands and expectations of four types of external environment, each of which presents a unique set of correctional challenges. This chapter examines the political environment within which corrections exists. Chapter 5 discusses the fiscal environment. Chapter 6 examines the special interests environment. And Chapter 7 considers the legal environment. We begin with the political environment because it is the legislation formulated by public policy makers that creates the mission of the correctional organization and gives overall direction to employee behavior. Every mission can be defined in terms of sets of official and operative goals that combine to form a body of organizational goals that direct organizational behavior. As the mission changes, implementation of adaptive strategies change employee functions, organizational structure, and design. This chapter examines the relationship between public policy making, correctional mission, and prison overcrowding; the changes in organizational structure and design resulting from prison overcrowding-related adaptive responses; and the role of managers in public policy formulation.

PUBLIC POLICY, MISSION, AND GOALS

The Profile at the beginning of the chapter provided an example of the type of public policy formulation that can significantly influence the organizational behavior of corrections. How do we define public policy? "A policy is a plan of action. Public policy regarding crime is really no more than a plan of action targeting the various crime phenomena of a society" (Hancock and Sharp, 1997:1). More simply, Thomas Dye (1981:1) has defined public policy as "whatever the government chooses to do or not to do." This last point needs to be emphasized. Correctional managers have historically had little direct influence over the public policy shaping their organization's behavior. Their role has been one of creating a mission-appropriate environmental design derived from public policy created by bodies of elected officials who may or may not have sought the advice of correctional managers.

Official and Operative Goals

To fulfill the requirements of public policy, correctional managers must formalize two types of goals: official goals and operative goals (Perrow, 1961). Official goals provide the public with the rationale for the organization's existence by expressing public policy and the formal mission. Operative goals specify the mechanics of achieving the official goals. Official goals can be met only through the achievement of operative goals. Consider, for example, the official goals of the Florida Department of Corrections (DOC):

[T]o protect the public, provide a safe and humane environment for staff and offenders, to work in partnership with the community to provide programs and services to offenders, and to supervise offenders at a level of security commensurate with the danger they present (Florida Department of Corrections, 1995:4).

How are these official goals to be achieved? The operative goals of the Florida DOC are outlined in Box 4–1. They provide a blueprint for organizational behavior by specifying the activities to be undertaken and the methods to be used for measuring the success or failure to achieve individual goals. The source of organizational goals is located in the political process that creates the mission.

BOX 4–1 FLORIDA DOC RECOMMENDATIONS FOR IMPROVEMENT

As required by F.S. 20.315(16), the Department of Corrections has developed recommendations for improving correctional services in the state. Based on accomplishments during the last fiscal year and objectives defined in the Department's Strategic Plan, it is recommended that action be taken and/or resources provided to accomplish the following departmental objectives:

Reduce the escape rate from major institutions and the rate of felony crimes committed by offenders while in prison.

Increase the percentage of single cell housing units commensurate with the increase in violent and disruptive inmates.

Conduct formal risk and needs assessments for 97 percent of offenders sentenced to prison.

Conduct formal risk and needs assessments for all offenders placed on Community Control, probation, or other community supervision programs.

Reduce the number of probationers and community controlees revoked and committed to prison for technical violations.

Reduce the commitment rate for drug offenders who have received treatment.

Establish security components in all facilities commensurate with accepted professional standards and mission requirements.

Link the data received from sentencing guidelines with the department's other automated databases.

Increase development of partnerships with private and public agencies.

Expand the Community Work Squad Program to 75 percent of department facilities.

Reduce by 10 percent the proportion of lesser offenders sentenced to state prison.

Substantially reduce the commitment rate of released inmates.

Implement programs and services which will result in a 10 percent reduction in the rate of supervised revocations.

Meet at least 85 percent of identified needs associated with department programs and services based on results of needs assessments.

Increase employee awareness of agency issues, policy, and practices.

Increase awareness of media, educators, students, business/civic leaders, and the general public on the role and scope of the Department.

Achieve the level of funding required for new beds and for all strategic plan strategies.

Compensate correctional officers and other career service employees equitably when compared to state law enforcement officers and staff of other state agencies.

Maintain correctional officer turnover and correctional probation officer turnover at a rate not exceeding 10 percent annually.

Employ a work force which reflects the community in terms of all races, genders, and cultures in the available labor market.

Implement a work force plan based on emerging needs of a majority of department employees.

Train 500 staff in Corrections Quality Managerial Leadership (CQML) principles.

Establish a Quality Assurance Program to include all major department components.

Adopt the Sterling Award criteria to validate departmental productivity increases.

Establish new sites for correctional officer basic training programs.

Standardize training curricula.

Reduce Employees' travel time away from work for training purposes.

Replace overloaded distributed processes with client/server LAN-based technology.

Acquire capacity upgrade for the mainframe computer.

Increase technical support staff to adequate levels.

Implement according to their projected schedules the innovative technology projects identified in the Information Resources Management Plan.

Equip central office, regional offices, and 50 percent of major institutions to receive satellite broadcast programs.

Source: Florida Department of Corrections. *1994–1995 Annual Report: The Guidebook to Corrections in Florida* (1995): 5.

Legislative Creation of the Mission

The prevailing definition of the mission of corrections depends on which political party is controlling the legislative process. The mission of corrections is only one element in an overall criminal justice system crime control strategy.

The Role of Political Parties in Public Policy Formulation

Political parties are based on a political ideology: a system of beliefs and assumptions about human behavior that influence crime control strategy. The definition of correctional mission at any given time reflects the ideology of the political party in power. There are two primary political ideologies in America: the conservative and the liberal (Walker, 1989). The conservative ideology assumes that criminals are individuals who have failed to assume responsibility for their behavior by not exerting sufficient self-control. Therefore, deterrence, retribution, and incapacitation are the appropriate crime control goals. The liberal ideology views criminals as the victims of negative social forces such as poverty, discrimination, and lack of equal opportunity. Rehabilitation of the offender by providing programs to correct societally induced individual deficits is the goal and the key to crime control—a goal that is based on the assumption that people can change their behavior if they receive the assistance of trained professionals.

As noted above, the mission and organizational goals of corrections will depend to a large extent on which political ideology is dominant. The emphasis on rehabilitation by the liberal ideology creates a set of organizational goals significantly different than those created by the conservative ideology.

Political Ideology and the Evolution of Mission

Public policy is not static. It changes in response to changes in the external environment. When changes in public policy occur, the mission and organizational behavior of corrections also changes. The most dynamic changes occur when a shift in public policy produces a mission that requires the creation of new organizational goals and/or a new organizational structure.

SHIFT FROM LIBERAL REALISM TO THE CONSERVATIVE REVOLUTION

Public policy is influenced by events in the external environment. The Progressive Era of the early 1900s emphasized the role of society in creating social harm, which in turn provided the foundation for shifting the mission of corrections from retribution to rehabilitation. The euphoria that gripped America after World War II provided energy for the liberal perspective that created the rehabilitation model.

The Liberal Perspective on Crime During the 1950s and 1960s, thinking about crime was dominated by "liberal realism" (Currie, 1997:52). Crime was conceptualized as a social problem—a symptom of basic inequalities often rooted in racism—that had festered to the point of threatening American society. The offender was viewed as a victim of a society flawed by social inequality in income distribution, educational opportunity, and the availability of employment. On July 23, 1965, President Lyndon Johnson established the President's Commission on Law Enforcement and Administration of Justice for the purposes of investigating the causes and nature of crime, collecting criminal justice system

information, and providing recommendations about how the criminal justice system might better meet "the challenge of crime." The 1967 final report of the Commission reflected the liberal perspective that crime could be prevented if social inequalities were corrected and cited the failure of prisons to prepare inmates for life in the community after release. The Commission recommended a "substantial upgrading" of corrections and a reorientation "toward integration of offenders into community life" (President's Commission, 1967:183). Thus, rehabilitation became an official goal.

The Conservative Revolution But the liberal influence was short-lived, rendered unacceptable by a "conservative revolution" born of an increase in the crime rate that saw the total number of reported Index crimes grow from 4,710,000 in 1965 to 14,872,883 in 1991 (Uniform Crime Report, 1986:41; 1991:5). The conservative revolution redefined crime as a criminal justice problem and rejected social explanations of, and social solutions to, crime.

A significant aspect of the process of public policy formulation since the 1970s has been the "politicization" of crime. This phenomena can be traced to the 1964 presidential election when Barry Goldwater promoted a "law and order" theme and challenged Lyndon Johnson's "war on poverty" as a soft-headed response to crime (Cronin, Cronin, and Milakovich, 1981). The Goldwater campaign signaled the beginnings of the conservative revolution in political thinking about crime and the role of the criminal justice system that became a centerpiece of future political campaigning, as both liberal and conservative candidates emphasized the need for strong measures to combat drug trafficking and violent street crime.

The public's fear of crime that accompanied, and was fostered by, this process of politicization led to acceptance of a conservative ideology that "was only one facet of a much broader transformation in American social thought and policy on domestic issues" (Currie, 1997:51). The criminal justice element of this transformation focused on the nature and origins of criminal behavior. Prominent scholars such as Harvard's James Q. Wilson (1975) proposed that some individuals are inherently evil or "wicked." Conservatives argued that the social permissiveness of the 1960s and early 1970s had undermined the effectiveness of the criminal justice system by weakening the concept of personal responsibility to such an extent that many people saw nothing wrong with engaging in criminal behavior. This perspective was given credence by the statistical evidence that crime rates were rising at a time when incomes were rising, national unemployment was falling, and more money than ever before was going into programs for the socially disadvantaged. The result for liberals was an "etiological crisis," (Young, 1988): if the liberal cures for crime are in place, but there is an increase in crime, then this increase logically must be the result of the leniency of a "soft" criminal justice system whose liberal philosophy has actually bred crime (Currie, 1997:53).

What has been the effect of the conservative revolution on corrections? The most significant effect has been prison overcrowding, a formidable challenge that has produced changes in organizational philosophy, structure, and design. We consider this critical issue facing corrections in the next section.

THE CONSERVATIVE REVOLUTION AND PRISON OVERCROWDING

A major aspect of the conservative revolution has been state and federal "get tough on crime" sentencing reforms that replace judicial discretion in the sentencing of offenders with mandatory minimum sentences. The result is longer periods of incarceration than would otherwise occur if judicial discretion were allowed to operate; this is the "hardening of the system" referred to in the epigraph at the beginning of this chapter.

Mandatory Drug Use Sentencing Laws and Prison Overcrowding

Laws requiring mandatory sentences for specific offenses (particularly violent and drug crimes) have been passed in 49 states (Adler, Mueller, and Laufer, 1994:357). The effect of drug crime sentencing reform has been prison overcrowding. A 1994 National Institute of Justice survey found that 88 percent of the correctional managers surveyed cited the increased number of sentenced drug offenders as the primary cause of overcrowding. One warden commented that drug offenders serving long sentences filled about 75 percent of the available cells (National Institute of Justice Update, 1995b:1). Almost 80 percent of new admissions to the Federal Bureau of Prisons between fall 1986 and fall 1988 were for drug offenses. The number of inmates incarcerated for nondrug crimes increased only 5 percent during this period as compared to a 31 percent increase in drug offenders (U.S. General Accounting Office, 1989a). Much of this increase is the result of the 1988 Anti-Drug Abuse Act (U.S. General Accounting Office, 1989b:15) described in the Profile at the beginning of this chapter.

Largely because of mandatory drug sentencing laws, the percentage of inmates in state prison for a drug crime rose from 6 percent in 1979 to 21 percent in 1991. Over eight times as many inmates were serving a state prison sentence for a drug law violation in 1991 (150,300) than in 1979 (17,600). Inmates sentenced for a drug offense accounted for 30 percent of the increase in prison population from 1979 to 1991 (Beck and Brien, 1995:51). A Texas study reported that the crime that most frequently resulting in a prison sentence was drug possession (22 percent) and 53 percent of all drug offenders (possession and trafficking) sentenced to prison were convicted for possession of one gram or less of the illegal substance (Fabello, 1993). Irwin and Austin (1997:27–28) noted that nearly 30 percent of all prison sentences in 1992 were for drug crimes (with one third being for simple possession) compared to 1981 when the figure was 9 percent and to 1960 when only 5 percent of all new prison admissions were for drug crimes. In 1994, drug offenses constituted 31 percent of state court felony convictions and 41 percent of federal court convictions. Drug crimes comprised 30 percent of state prison sentences and 55 percent of federal prison sentences (Bureau of Justice Statistics Bulletin, 1997a:3).

Parole Reform as a Cause of Prison Overcrowding

The impact of sentencing reform has been compounded by probation and parole reform. Many legislatures have identified parole as a system conducive to abuse of the individual while failing to protect society. As a result, between 1976 and 1984, California, Colorado, Illinois, Indiana, Maine, New Mexico, Florida, Minnesota, North Carolina, and Washington either eliminated or severely limited the use of parole (Rhine, 1996:347). Parole is no longer a part of the federal system. The Comprehensive Crime Control Act of 1984 created the U.S. Sentencing Commission and scheduled the U.S. Parole Commission for phasing out in 1997 (Rhine, 1996:347). The conservative rationale for rejecting parole can be clearly seen in the explanation in Box 4–2 by Virginia's governor of that state's decision to abolish parole.

BOX 4–2 ABOLISHING PAROLE SAVES LIVES AND PROPERTY

On Father's Day 1986, Richmond Police Detective George Taylor stopped Wayne DeLong for a routine traffic violation. DeLong, recently released from prison after serving time for murder, shot and killed Taylor.

On another occasion, Leo Webb, a divinity student at Richmond's Virginia Union University, was shot to death at the bakery where he worked. His killer, James Steele, was on parole for a malicious wounding.

What makes these incidents so disheartening is that they could easily have been prevented. Both killers, incarcerated earlier for violent crimes, spent only a fraction of their sentences in prison.

When I took office in 1994, Virginians were suffering the consequences of a lenient criminal justice system that refused to take punishment seriously. From 1988 to 1993, Virginia witnessed a 28 percent increase in violent crime. Three out of every four violent crimes were committed by repeat offenders.

The people of Virginia were tired of seeing criminals walk free after serving a fraction of their sentences. Public safety is a top responsibility of state government. Education, economic development, and health care all suffer when people feel threatened.

As one of my first acts as governor, I created the Commission on Parole Abolition and Sentencing Reform, a bipartisan commission of prosecutors, judges, crime victims, law enforcement officers, business leaders, and legal scholars. I called for a special session of the General Assembly in September 1994 to focus the public's and the legislature's attention on this issue.

A complete overhaul was necessary. Convicted felons were serving about one third of their sentences, and many were serving only one sixth. Violent criminals were no exception. First-degree murderers were given average sentences of 35 years, but spent an average of only 10 years behind bars. Rapists were being sentenced to nine years and serving four. Armed robbers were receiving sentences averaging 14 years and serving only about four. Even those who had already served time for similar offenses were receiving the same sentences and serving the same amount of time as first-time offenders.

On Oct. 13, 1994, I signed into law legislation that prevents thousands of crimes, saves lives and money, and restores trust in the criminal justice system. Under the new law, we have eliminated discretionary parole, which allows a parole board to release an offender after he has served only part of his sentence, and established truth in sentencing.

Under Virginia's system, inmates convicted of a violent crime serve a minimum of 85 percent of their sentences. Data shows that more than 4,300 felony crimes would have been prevented between 1986 and 1993 if the current system had been in place. This is based on actual convictions and real cases, not projections.

We eliminated "good time." However, in order to encourage good behavior among inmates and allow correctional officers to maintain order, the commission proposed a system of earned-sentence credits, which allows inmates to earn a maximum of 54 days per year, a dramatic reduction from the average 300 days they had been given before.

To determine appropriate sentencing increases, the commission evaluated the relationship of recidivism to time served and age of release. Data showed that the longer an offender remained behind bars, the less likely he or she would be to commit another crime after finishing his or her sentence. Although preventing offenders from committing further acts of violence was the primary goal, sentencing increases needed to reflect the notion of retribution as well. Virginia now sends the message to violent criminals: "We will not tolerate violence, and if you commit a violent crime, you will stay in prison until you're too old to commit another one."

Since we enacted these landmark sentencing reforms, the commonwealth has witnessed an overall 12 percent reduction in violent crime. Violent offenders are spending more time in prison. Under our plan, we have built two low-cost work centers which each house 150 first-time and nonviolent offenders. These work centers operate at about half the cost per inmate as a standard prison, and they ensure that inmates work while incarcerated.

The principle that has guided our efforts, and should guide policy makers in all issues, is honesty. Easy-release rules prevented judges and juries from preempting the community's judgment about the proper punishment for illegal conduct. Under the new law, judges do not have to play guessing games when imposing sentences. Police officers do not have to see the same criminals out on the streets only a year after their last arrest. Criminals know that they cannot beat the system. Crime victims and their families finally are seeing justice done. Virginia's citizens can trust that their government is working to make this Commonwealth a safe place to live, work, and raise a family.

Source: *Corrections Today* 59(4) (1997): 22–23. Reprinted with permission of the American Correctional Association, Lanham, MD.

Where parole has not been eliminated outright, there has nevertheless been a tightening up of probation and parole criteria that has affected prison overcrowding. Taxman (1995:46) noted that in 1986, 74 percent of probationers successfully completed their terms. By 1990, that figure had dropped to

60 percent. Austin (1995:2) has also noted the impact of probation and parole violators returning to prison: in 1993, approximately two thirds of all Texas prison admissions were probation or parole violators.

Extent and Impact of Prison Overcrowding

The conservative revolution has created an "unparalleled explosion of the prison population" (Irwin and Austin, 1997:xvii). Getting tough on crime through increasing the rate of incarceration has created a condition of almost overwhelming prison overcrowding throughout the United States: "In the 1990s the most pressing political crisis in the prison system is crowding" (Crouch et al., 1995:65). Between 1985 and June 30, 1996, the state and federal prison population rose from 487,593 to 1,112,448; county jail populations increased from 256,615 to 518,492; and the total incarcerated population rose from 744,208 to 1,630,940 (Bureau of Justice Statistics, 1997b:1). As of January 1, 1997, only eight DOCs were operating at 95 percent or less of capacity; 15 DOCs were operating at between 95 percent and 105 percent of capacity; and 27 DOCs and the District of Columbia were operating at greater than 105 percent of capacity. The Federal Bureau of Prisons was at 124.4 percent of capacity (Camp and Camp, 1997:63).

Statistics tell only a small part of the story. To understand the full impact of prison overcrowding, it is necessary to look at its consequences.

Organizational Consequences
The national warehousing of inmates creates a significant level of organizational strain that is unavoidable because managers lack the authority to refuse to accept new commitments from the courts. In an interview of 90 prison managers (Camp and Camp, 1989), four types of organizational strain were emphasized.

Decreased Physical Plant Longevity
Overcrowding places strain on the prison infrastructure through the overuse of plumbing, electrical, heating, air conditioning, and sewage systems, as well as equipment used for food and laundry services. Equipment and systems designed to work under normal conditions are often operated at an intensity and frequency that far exceeds design specifications. This overuse causes expensive breakdowns and a constant need for repairs that increase tension, divert money from treatment budgets, and wear out overextended maintenance staff. The operational life of a prison infrastructure can be significantly shortened by this type of abuse.

Impaired Levels of Staff Functioning
Although the managers in the Camp and Camp (1989) study reported that recruitment and training efforts were not adversely affected by overcrowding, they did cite staff turnover and excessive overtime as significant problems. The need to maintain adequate levels of staffing as the inmate population steadily increased in each prison required many correctional officers to work an excessive number of hours. Overtime work leads to fatigue, which leads to mistakes as well as increased use of sick leave. The increased use of sick leave, in turn, increases the amount of overtime managers must order. A vicious cycle is created. The inability to adequately supervise the large numbers of inmates led staff to believe that inmates were able to violate prison rules with little risk of detection. Overcrowding results in employees experiencing high levels of stress, a problem frequently cited when they terminate employment.

Inadequate Opportunities for Constructive Inmate Activities
Inmate population increases are rarely matched by corresponding increases in programming and employment opportunities. The Camps (1989) found that approximately 20 percent of the inmates in their study had no jobs and many of those with assigned jobs had little to do. In many prisons, inmates are assigned to be "tier workers," a job that usually requires sweeping the block for several

minutes each hour of the work shift. Inmate idleness is critical because the old adage "Idle hands do the Devil's work" is particularly meaningful in a prison setting. Inmate idleness is often implicated as a precipitating factor in prison riots and other forms of violence and rule violation. In addition, the lack of work and programming opportunities increase the probability that inmates will not be rehabilitated.

Inadequate Levels of Inmate Control

Camp and Camp (1989) found that a reduced ability to supervise inmates led to an increase in thefts in living areas and increased the difficulty of controlling the introduction of contraband, especially in the visiting rooms. Clayton and Carr (1984) found a strong relationship between crowding and inmate rule violations. It is difficult to maintain a close watch on "problem" inmates when overcrowding exists. This problem is especially acute when those problem inmates are prone to violence. Logically, overcrowding should increase the vulnerability of inmates to violence. Gaes (1985:95), for example, found that "prisons housing significantly more inmates than a design capacity of sixty square feet per inmate are likely to have high assault rates." The Camps (1989) found that in overcrowded prisons the fear of weaker inmates that predatory inmates will have a greater opportunity to victimize them results in an increased demand for protective custody placement. They also reported that during the early 1980s there was an increase in the inmate suicide rate in crowded prisons.

However, not all of the literature correlates prison overcrowding with increased levels of violence. Lillis (1994), in a survey of 41 states, the District of Columbia, and the Federal Bureau of Prisons, found that between 1983 and 1993 the annual number of prison suicides actually dropped from 131 to 100 and the overall number of homicides dropped from 135 in 1983 to 50 in 1993; inmate assaults on correctional staff decreased from 6,047 to an estimated 5,840; and inmate-on-inmate assaults decreased

from about 14,000 to approximately 10,000. Thus, there was actually a significant reduction in reported inmate violence during a ten-year period that saw the inmate prison population more than double. And both Camp and Camp (1989) and Lillis (1994) reported a significant decline in escapes in the early 1990s. Clearly, additional research concerning the relationship between prison overcrowding and violence is needed.

Psychological and Medical Concerns

The reduction of living and programming space reduces inmate privacy, creates a higher overall level of tension, and limits access to programming (Camp and Camp, 1989). Greater population density increases the psychological strain already existing in prisons (Cox, Paulus, and McCain, 1984) and generally reduces the quality of prison life. It reduces employee effectiveness in the primary functions of classification, housing assignments, food and medical services, security, and providing specialized treatment programs. It disrupts the daily routine of the facility and increases the cost of operation.

The psychological effects of overcrowding include stress-related anger, hostility, anxiety, and depression. Inmates living in open areas, like dormitories, tend to use medical services more and have higher blood pressure (Crouch et al., 1995:66), and there is increasing concern about the potential for spread of communicable diseases like tuberculosis in densely populated prisons (Durham, 1994:54). This concern is well-founded. A 1996 study by the New York DOC found that in 1992 inmates with active tuberculosis were present in 43 of its 69 prisons and 466 employees had tuberculosis. One third of the prison employee infections were the result of occupational exposure (New York Department of Corrections, 1996:2). Improved surveillance in the form of more rapid diagnosis and physical isolation of inmates with active tuberculosis has since been undertaken to decrease the risk of employee infection.

In an attempt to reduce the negative consequences of prison overcrowding, correctional managers have adopted a variety of innovative and imitation strategies to decrease prison population densities. These strategies, which run the gamut from building out to emergency population release mechanisms, are examined in the next section.

ADAPTIVE STRATEGIES TO MANAGE PRISON OVERCROWDING

Once the design capacity of a prison has been reached, managers must resort to the use of adaptive strategies. One of the most destructive strategies, but generally the first to be enacted because it can be done rapidly and at minimal cost, is the "cannibalization" of prison space through the use of such not-so-temporary measures as crowding bunk beds into makeshift dormitories installed in basements or program areas such as gymnasiums, weight rooms, class rooms, and hallways. For example, in 1995, the Pennsylvania DOC had to locate 7,000 prison-based emergency beds. The solution: cots set up in gymnasiums, day rooms (inmate leisure activity areas), and storage areas (Mahan, 1996:B8). This is a haphazard approach that employees and inmates alike resent because it disrupts the delivery of services and places inmates in living areas where supervision is difficult and less secure.

Building Out

Cannibalization, at best, provides short-term population relief. As makeshift prison beds fill up, longer-term strategies must be implemented. In his survey of state correctional managers, Vaughn (1993:16) found that the most common long-term innovative response has been new prison construction (47 out of 50 states) followed by double- and triple-bunking of inmates (42 states). In a number of states where the rate of population increase has been so dramatic that DOCs have been unable to build prisons quickly enough, managers have "leased out" inmates to other states fortunate enough to have a surplus of beds. Figure 4–1 identifies the DOCs that had adopted leasing out by 1996.

In addition, the Federal Bureau of Prisons contracts for 2,800 beds in Texas (Stanley Brown, 1996:44). Leasing out can be both temporary and expensive. A state with vacant jail or prison beds this year may not have them next year. And, as of December 1995, the per diem rates for medium custody inmates ranged from $35 to $75 per day, depending on the services provided (Stanley Brown, 1996:46). Therefore, a state with 100 inmates leased out will at minimum spend $1,277,500 a year and, at maximum, $2,737,500 a year. In return for this expense, leasing out permits only a minimal amount of overcrowding relief (Stanley Brown, 1996:47).

State	Private Beds/ Facility In State	Bed Contract Out of State
Alabama	●	
Alaska	●	
Arizona	●	
California	●	
Colorado	●	●
Florida	●	
Indiana	●	
Iowa	●	
Kansas	●	
Kentucky	●	
Louisiana	●	
Minnesota	●	●
Mississippi	●	
Missouri		●
New Mexico	●	
New York	●	●
North Carolina		●
Oklahoma	●	●
Oregon		●
Rhode Island	●	
Tennessee	●	
Texas	●	
Utah		●
Virginia		●

FIGURE 4–1 States Contracting for Beds or Facilities. Source: *Corrections Today* 58(1) (1996): 46. Reprinted with permission of the American Correctional Association, Lanham, MD.

While leasing out is certainly costly, building out is enormously expensive. From 1972 to 1992, the number of correctional employees in the United States increased 108 percent. Annual spending for corrections rose from $9.1 billion to nearly $32 billion, almost one third of the annual U.S. expenditures for the entire criminal justice system. Spending on corrections is the fastest-growing item in state budgets (Irwin and Austin, 1997:13–14). "Building out" of overcrowding by constructing wave after wave of new prisons accounts for the largest proportion of the increase in state and federal budgets for corrections. In fiscal year 1995 alone, for example, state and federal governments allocated $5.1 billion for construction of new prison space (Edna McConnell Clark Foundation, 1995). Box 4–3 provides an overview of prison overcrowding and the building-out response by one DOC.

BOX 4–3 THE CONSERVATIVE REVOLUTION AND THE ARIZONA DOC

During the period of 1980 to 1994, the annual inmate population of the Arizona DOC grew by 185 percent: from 370 new inmates received in 1980 to 1,898 new inmates received in 1994. This increase was the result of the convergence of six events. First, Arizona experienced an increase in the state population of 46.7 percent. An increase in the number of state residents logically translates into additional criminal activity and higher prison populations. Second, the number of active law enforcement officers increased with a resulting increase in arrest activity. Third, while the overall crime rate in Arizona decreased, the violent crime rate increased 41.5 percent between 1983 and 1993. The result was a disproportionate increase in the number of violent offenders incarcerated. These new receptions also tended to have longer sentences than nonviolent offenders. The increase in gang activity

in Arizona contributed to this trend. Fourth, Arizona experienced an increased emphasis on drug enforcement that dramatically increased the number of drug offense commitments. Statewide adult arrests for drug trafficking increased by 66.4 percent between 1988 and 1993, resulting in a 109 percent increase in imprisoned drug offenders between 1989 and 1994: from 2,038 inmates to 4,257. Fifth, the most dramatic increase in prison population came from an increased revocation rate for inmates placed on probation and parole. The number of revoked probationers sent to prison increased from 2,343 in 1992 to 3,362 in 1994, a 43.5 percent increase. The number of parole revocations increased 52.1 percent between 1993 and 1994 as Arizona implemented "get tough on crime" strategies. Finally, various categories of release from prison decreased as release policies were readjusted to make release criteria more stringent. As a result, on June 30, 1995, the Arizona Department of Corrections had 2,647 more inmates than beds. In response, the department set up Quonset huts, assigned 484 inmates to tents, and placed temporary beds in areas not designed for housing. Between 1996 and 2001, the DOC is scheduled to build 11,625 additional beds at an estimated cost of $322,650,000. Arizona will be building three types of prisons: minimum security ($28,000 per bed); medium security ($30,000 per bed); and maximum security ($35,000 per bed). In addition, Maximum Special Management Unit beds will be placed where needed at a cost of $55,000 per bed. By June 30, 2001, the projected bed deficit will still be 2,095.

Source: Arizona Department of Corrections. *1995 Annual Report* (1996).

Building out does not solve the problem of overcrowding. It only distributes the problem throughout a wider geographical area. Typifying the failure of building out is the projection that the state of Florida will have to add 58,000 prison beds in a ten-year period just to keep up with the projected rise in convictions. Projected cost: $1 billion in construction and $2 billion a year in operational expenditures (Furniss, 1996:40). Because of the increasingly prohibitive cost of building out and leasing out, DOCs are turning to the private sector for assistance. The issue of the privatization of correctional services is considered in Chapter 5.

There is also a legal dimension to building out. On January 1, 1997, 22 DOCs had 198 prisons under court-mandated population limits (Camp and Camp, 1997:55). However, there has been some recent improvement. On January 1, 1995, there were 36 DOCs with 227 prisons under a population limit (Camp and Camp, 1996a:6).

A more effective response to prison overcrowding requires the use of adaptive strategies that will reduce the number of prison inmates instead of simply trying to find beds for them.

Front-End and Back-End Strategies

The public policy makers who have created sentencing reform and prison overcrowding are increasingly forced by economic reality to legislatively approve front-end and back-end prison population control strategies. Front-end strategies involve the use of alternatives to incarceration programs such as traditional probation and intermediate sanctions including intensive probation, house arrest, electronic monitoring, and shock probation or split sentences (Clark, 1994:105). Back-end strategies generally involve the acceleration of early release, either through good time credits or parole (Clark, 1994:105). A number of states also use emergency release mechanisms (such as adding on good time credits) when the institution is under a court decree not to exceed a certain population limit (Durham, 1994). Box 4–4 provides a description of both front-end and back-end strategies as they are used by the Florida DOC. Although these strategies permit discretionary decision making, the use of discretion is severely restricted by criteria set forth by the Florida legislature. And much of this restriction is time specific, a characteristic that reflects the evolution of public policy on crime control issues.

BOX 4–4 TYPES OF COMMUNITY SUPERVISION IN THE FLORIDA DEPARTMENT OF CORRECTIONS

I. Court Originated Sanctions

Probation
A court-ordered term of community supervision under specified conditions for a set period of time not to exceed the maximum sentence for the offense of conviction, which may be either a felony or a felony reduced to a misdemeanor.

Community Control
Intensive court-ordered supervision in lieu of prison involving quasi-confinement of convicted felons to their homes with numerous monthly contacts by officers having restricted caseloads. At the direction of the court or election by the department, Community Control may involve electronic monitoring of offenders.

Pretrial Intervention
A supervision program intended to divert persons charged with any nonviolent felony of the third degree from further prosecution and possible adjudication of guilt. Approval of the program administrator, the state attorney, the judge, and the victim allow the charged person to enter Pretrial supervision, the successful completion of which results in a dismissal of charges.

Drug Offender Probation
An intensive, treatment-oriented form of supervision administered by officers with restricted caseloads for offenders with chronic substance abuse problems and convictions on drug offenses.

Administrative Probation
A noncontact supervision program for low-risk offenders requiring only compliance with all laws.

II. Supervision as a Condition for Early Prison Release

Parole
At the discretion of the Florida Parole Commission, a conditional extension to the community of the limits of confinement for inmates whose prison terms resulted from convictions occurring prior to the advent of Florida's Sentencing Guidelines in October 1983.

Conditional Release
For certain violent and chronic offenders perpetuating their crimes on or after October 1, 1988, a prison release supervision program whose terms and conditions are set by the Florida Parole Commission. The maximum term of supervision cannot exceed the inmate's prison sentence.

Control Release
Created to maintain the state's prison population within the mandated capacity, Control Release is managed by the Control Release Authority (CRA), made up of the members of the Parole Commission. The CRA uses a system of uniform criteria to determine the number and types of inmates released to supervision prior to the expiration of their sentences. Inmates convicted of crimes occurring on or after October 1, 1983, are eligible, with the exception of habitual

offenders, sex offenders, offenders committing crimes against a law enforcement officer, and offenders serving minimum mandatory sentences. Supervision time cannot exceed the inmate's prison sentence.

Administrative Control Release
As an option effective May 25, 1992, the Control Release Authority may, at its discretion, waive supervision contacts and require only that inmates placed on Control Release live within the law.

Supervised Community Release
A release program, at the discretion of the department, for selected inmates who are within 90 days of release from a prison term for an offense occurring before July 1, 1988, or later than that date if no Provisional Credits have been earned.

Conditional Medical Release
Upon recommendation by the department, the Florida Parole Commission may release under conditions at its discretion any inmate judged to be physically incapacitated or terminally ill.

III. Other Supervision

Upon request, the department may supervise offenders subject to parole or work release from a county jail. In addition to supervising offenders, Probation and Parole Services performs a number of related duties, which include collecting court-ordered payments from offenders, conducting drug tests, and preparing offender investigations. In FY 1994–1995, probation and parole officers collected $52,405,030 in court-ordered payments from offenders.

Source: Florida Department of Corrections. *1994–1995 Annual Report: The Guidebook to Corrections in Florida* (1995): 92–93.

In the long-term these strategies, if their use is expanded, may maintain prison population stability, but real reductions in prison populations are unlikely if the current sentencing reforms remain in place. The key to a significant reduction in the incarceration rate is new sentencing reform legislation.

Recall that Chandler's Strategy-Structure Thesis states that a change in strategy produces specific changes in organizational structure. Prison overcrowding has done more than fill up the prisons and make the creation of new bed space a critical managerial priority. The adaptive strategies used to address prison overcrowding have brought about changes in organizational structure and design.

Effect of Adaptive Strategies on Organizational Structure

Adaptive responses to prison overcrowding are driving a variety of changes in organizational complexity, centralization, formalization, and the technostructure.

Increasing Complexity

Management strategies to reduce prison overcrowding have increased the degree of spatial, horizontal, and vertical differentiation in virtually every DOC.

Increasing Spatial Differentiation   The Texas Department of Criminal Justice expanded from 40 prisons to 114 during the period of 1990 to 1995 (Texas Department of Criminal Justice, 1996:7). As the total number of prisons in a DOC increases, new employees must be hired for the existing Central Office departments responsible for technostructure and support functions for the prisons. Expansion of community corrections programs increases spatial differentiation as the need for new work sites is identified and new offices are created. Leasing out of beds and the use of private corrections further expands spatial differentiation, frequently into other states.

Overcrowding may also change the spatial distribution of specific functions. For example, one of the biggest challenges overcrowd-

ing creates is the need to maintain an effective inmate classification system as bed space becomes increasingly limited. In some DOCs (Pennsylvania, South Carolina, and New Mexico, for example), the need to improve efficiency in the classification process has led to a modification in organizational structure. Specifically, the practice of having each prison receive and classify new inmates, or having several regional classification centers, is being discarded in favor of creating a centralized diagnostic center where every male inmate is initially sent (female offenders are generally still classified at female prisons).

Increasing Horizontal Differentiation

As Central Office workload increases, and the department experiences "growing pains," horizontal differentiation occurs. The Commissioner, for example, may decide that living within the departmental budget during a period of expansion requires the creation of a new function: coordination of the simultaneous construction of new prisons across the state so that the operative goals of cost-effective construction and the avoidance of an unnecessary duplication of services can be achieved. Because functional changes require structural changes, the degree of horizontal differentiation increases when Central Office creates the new Engineering Services Unit responsible for coordination of all new prison construction. The use of front-end and back-end strategies also increases horizontal differentiation because new departments dedicated to specific community-based functions that had previously not existed must be established.

A change in the spatial distribution of functions may also change horizontal differentiation, especially at the prison level. For example, diagnostic centralization may well result in a change in the horizontal differentiation structure of the prisons involved. The prison that is now the centralized diagnostic facility increases horizontal differentiation if this is a new function. The prisons no longer involved in classification may lose certain departments, or at a minimum see them downsized.

Increasing Vertical Differentiation Vertical differentiation increases as the Commissioner's span of control begins to stretch too thin. A Commissioner who could effectively supervise six superintendents is going to find that effective supervision of the nine additional superintendents made necessary by the building of nine new prisons is simply not possible. A Deputy Commissioner position, or layer of Deputy Commissioner positions, must be inserted between Commissioner and superintendents. Changes in the strategic apex and the departmental chain of command will occur as new managerial positions are created in an effort to improve the ability of the Commissioner to govern.

As the use of state-operated community corrections grows in response to the increase in numbers of offenders being diverted or released from prison, vertical differentiation also increases as new layers of managers are added to maintain standardization and efficiency. An example of the effect of the implementation of overcrowding reduction strategies on organizational structure can be seen in Figure 4–2, which shows the organization chart for the Ohio Department of Rehabilitation and Correction. In the early days of DOC Corrections in Ohio, the organization chart would have been dominated by prisons. Today, a significant element of the chart consists of Parole and Community Services.

Merger of Independent Agencies In the case of Texas, an even more dramatic change in organizational structure occurred when three independent adult criminal justice agencies—the Department of Corrections, Board of Pardons and Paroles, and adult Probation Commission—were merged into one

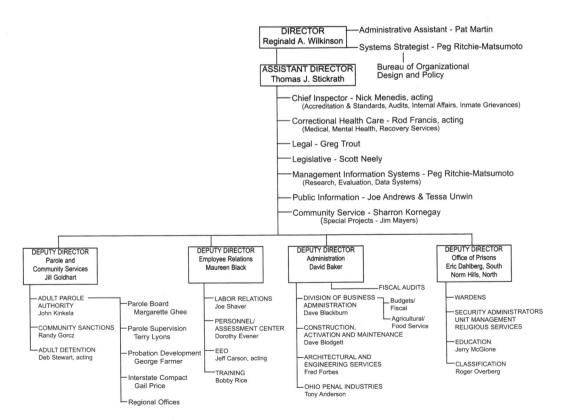

FIGURE 4–2 Organization of Ohio Corrections. Source: Ohio Department of Rehabilitation and Correction. *Annual Report: Fiscal Year 1995* (1996):2.

"seamless" agency, the Texas Department of Criminal Justice. When agencies merge, a new organization chart is created as departments are modified, or eliminated, in a systematic attempt to eliminate redundancy and duplication of services. Horizontal and vertical differentiation may be significantly modified. It can take years to effect the changes required by agency merger, and managers must show sensitivity to the fears and concerns of the employees affected by merger by maximizing the flow of communication and working to allay fears of termination.

Decreasing Centralization

As new managers are added, the system of decision making grows more and more decentralized. Decisions that were once the exclusive domain of top managers are pushed lower and lower in the hierarchy because of workload volume and time constraints limiting the ability of top management to handle every decision. It is clear from the Ohio DOC organization chart as depicted in Figure 4–2 that the director is separated from the prison and community facilities staff by multiple layers of Central Office managers, technocrats, and support staff. The managers in each department must assume an increasingly large portion of the decision making in their area of jurisdiction because the director simply does not have the time to micromanage each department. In fact, as DOC directors become increasingly involved in working with political leaders, more and more decision making falls on their assistants and those managers subordinate to that position. The result can be a director who is increasingly isolated from the rest of the system. To maintain control, directors must develop communication systems designed to provide them with information concerning critical problem areas and potential solutions.

Increasing Formalization

As more new employee functions are created, additional Central Office departments such as Planning, Security Audit, Classifica-tion and Population Management, Privatization Services, and Community Services come into existence to provide the structural framework and support for those functions. Formalization increases as new department managers actively promulgate policy statements governing the activities of the employees under their jurisdiction. These new departments must standardize employee behavior, often in areas with which existing employees have no experience, and the result is the creation of new policy manuals and a vast array of documentation-of-service-provided forms. New Central Office functions and structures are often duplicated in the prisons. As functions evolve, the modified organizational structure may bear little resemblance to the earlier structure.

Adaptive responses to prison overcrowding went beyond changing organizational structure, however. They came to include changing the philosophy of offender management. As a result, the policies of the rehabilitation model are being gradually displaced by the policies of the actuarial model.

PRISON OVERCROWDING AND THE ACTUARIAL MODEL

Correctional managers frantically attempting to meet the challenges posed by prison overcrowding in the 1980s began to believe that the safety and security concerns created by the massive increase in inmates (and the negative changes in inmate subculture) required a change in the philosophy of offender management. The result was policy changes that defined an offender management approach known as the "actuarial model."

A New Penology

Cohen (1985) and Reichman (1986) have noted an increasing tendency of correctional policy to view inmates as members of specific offender categories and subpopulations rather than as individuals. Feeley and Simon (1992:449–474) argued that a new penology is emerging that is shifting the focus of correctional employees from the missions of individual rehabilitation and promotion of equity in offender management (the justice model, which is discussed in Chapter 7) to a mission of management of "aggregates of dangerous groups." This emerging philosophy of corrections does not emphasize punishment, rehabilitation, or achieving equity. Instead, the emphasis is on coordinating managerial processes dedicated to classifying offenders into risk groups and "managing a permanently dangerous population while maintaining the system at a minimum cost" (Feeley and Simon, 1992:463). This new penology (Feeley and Simon do not use the term *actuarial model*) uses a language of probability of risk that is replacing the language of rehabilitation.

Shifting the Emphasis of the Inmate Classification Process Security has always been king in the prison, but a major focus of the rehabilitation model was the identification of individual inmate programming needs. The official philosophy was that every offender was a unique individual. Under the actuarial model, however, the individual offender is viewed as a member of a specific risk group. This philosophical change has shifted the focus of inmate classification processes from the rehabilitation model's emphasis on clinical diagnosis and individual programming requirements to an emphasis on determining individual security levels.

The language of classification no longer emphasizes clinical diagnosis, needs, and programming capabilities. It is now a language that increasingly emphasizes the determination of individual offender security risk in accordance with a prison classification system divided into five security levels. Level V prisons are maximum security prisons (sometimes referred to as end-of-the-line prisons) that provide secure housing and a secure perimeter. Programming is limited and all out-of-cell activities

are closely monitored and supervised. The ultimate Level V prison is the super-max prison. Level IV prisons allow inmates daylight movement within sight of a correctional officer and eligibility for all programs and activities within the main perimeter, which is secure. Level III prisons have external perimeter security similar to level IV and V prisons but allow a wider variety of programs and greater freedom of movement. Level II prisons have a perimeter consisting of a single fence or intermittent external patrols. Housing is open (dormitory, single, and multiple occupancy rooms) and there is an emphasis on programs and activities. Level I facilities are nonsecure community-based facilities that include prerelease centers and halfway houses.

Although the identification of treatment needs is not totally ignored, these needs are considered secondary to the identification of security and control needs.

Increasing the Ability to Control Offenders The actuarial model emphasizes the efficient control of specific risk groups through the development of inmate management approaches that favor the increased utilization of technology and techniques that treat offenders as members of risk groups rather than as unique individuals. In prisons, correctional officers work in steel and glass "bubbles" from which they monitor inmate activity by the use of closed circuit cameras and microphones instead of moving about freely and interacting with the inmates. In community corrections, probation and parole officers increasingly are involved in monitoring functions that rely on drug testing and surveillance technology while their active involvement in the offender behavioral change process is decreasing. Counseling of the probationer/parolee is being replaced by a strategy of rapid incarceration for rule violations.

The Growth of Community Corrections from the Actuarial Model Perspective
The 1980s witnessed an increased use of house arrest (with or without electronic

monitoring), shock probation, boot camps, day fine centers, and Intensive Probation Supervision programs. Although these initiatives are frequently viewed as innovations in rehabilitation, an understanding of the actuarial model suggests that these programs may actually be mechanisms for controlling the behavior of low-risk offenders in a cost-effective manner (this issue is considered more fully in Chapter 5). That is, these innovations may actually represent "control processes for managing and recycling selected risk populations" (Feeley and Simon, 1992:465). Even the concept of recidivism changes when viewed from the perspective of the new penology. A high recidivism rate is viewed by the rehabilitation model as an indicator of failure to reintegrate the offender into the community. Under the actuarial model, recidivism is viewed as "evidence of efficiency and effectiveness of parole as a control apparatus" (Feeley and Simon, 1992:455).

The inmate control characteristics of the actuarial model of inmate management are nicely illustrated in the description of the Georgia DOC's "get tough" approach in Box 4–5. Note that virtually every aspect of inmate life has been modified and even the official name of the DOC has been changed to reflect the change in organizational mission.

BOX 4–5 BACK TO BASICS IN GEORGIA'S PRISONS

Georgia was one of the most responsive states to enact "tough on crime" legislation with its 1994 "Two Strikes and You're Out" law. Now, Georgia is getting tough in the prisons.

In October 1995, Governor Miller ordered the Department of Corrections to get tougher on criminals— keep them working while they are incarcerated and make prisons a place for punishment for one's crime. Agencywide, Corrections has undergone many changes.

More Work

All able-bodied inmates are required to do unpaid work to help repay their debt to society, including working in inmate construction, food and farm services, and in the communities. Educational or substance abuse classes are arranged around an inmate's full-day work schedule.

Reduce Privileges

In FY96, all weight equipment and nonathletic recreational equipment were removed by the inmates and donated to local schools across the state. In order to reduce any idle time and to promote good health, all inmates are required to walk 4.5 miles per day.

Inmates are only allowed to watch television after work hours, and then only as a tool for educational purposes or behavior management, not simply for entertainment. Basic cable television connection is limited only to those prisons where normal TV reception is poor.

All inmate and probation detainee uniforms are labeled with "State Prisoner" or "State Probationer" on the back of their shirt for easy identification in the community.

No Furloughs

Eliminated in January 1996, the furlough program had allowed some prisoners to go home for a few days during a holiday or the summer. No longer can any inmate leave prison for Christmas or for any other holiday.

Name Change

In May 1996, the State Board of Corrections passed a resolution to immediately change the names of the state institutions. All facilities formerly known as correctional institutions are now known as state prisons.

Prison Sweeps

Immediately upon Wayne Garner's appointment to the Georgia Department of Corrections, the Commissioner instituted a plan to have prison tactical squads perform surprise prison sweeps, eliminating contraband to keep prisons safe for the inmates and staff. Because of these sweeps and that prisons are now performing in-house sweeps, Georgia's prisons are cleaner, safer, and more secure for staff and prisoners alike.

Systemwide Changes

Remove weights and nonathletic recreation equipment from prisons. Weights were donated to local schools.

Cease all special leave programs. No holiday furloughs.

Require all inmates to walk 4.5 miles per day.

Mark uniforms "state prisoner" or "state probationer."

Toughen boot camp programs; cease graduation ceremonies.

Substitute a cold sandwich for lunch—no hot lunch.

Change name of facilities from Correctional Institution to Prison.

Source: Georgia Department of Corrections. *Annual Report: Fiscal Year 1996. Tough Issues, Hard Facts* (1997): 13.

Fortunately, research is beginning to demonstrate that an emphasis on control and monitoring does not necessarily eliminate rehabilitation efforts. Fulton et al. (1997:308) have found that probation and parole officers involved in Intensive Supervision Programs (ISPs), which are a centerpiece of the actuarial model, actually have "a much stronger focus on the rehabilitative function of probation and parole and on strategies for promoting behavioral change than regular supervision officers." One possible explanation for this finding may be ISP training programs that emphasize principles of effective behavioral intervention. Or it may just be that rehabilitation is a difficult concept to eradicate. This type of finding is always open to debate.

What is not open to debate, however, is the fact that a current correctional priority is the management and control of offender risk groups. Nor can it be denied that the use of adaptive strategies and the emergence of the actuarial model have modified organizational design.

MODIFYING THE ORGANIZATIONAL DESIGN

As organizational structure and philosophy change, the organizational design also changes. The number of individuals in the strategic apex, operating core, and middle line rises and the structures of functional departments increase in complexity. For example, a Central Office personnel department that started with a Chief, one middle-level manager, and 12 employees may now have a Chief, three middle-level supervisors, and 38 employees.

However, the most dramatic change occurs in the technostructure, as the strategic apex need to improve the flow of information necessary for effective decision making rapidly increases. This increased need for information stems from two sources: (1) the new knowledge required by the need to implement adaptive strategies, and (2) the actuarial model's emphasis on offender management and control that demands that new solutions be found to old problems of maintaining prison security and protecting the safety of employees and the public. As a result of this convergence of adaptive strategies and the actuarial model, the last decade has witnessed technological innovation becoming an increasingly important element in environmental design, with the technostructure assuming a greater importance than ever before. The most important technological changes are occurring in prison security, information management systems, and community corrections offender management.

Prison Security   Corrections has greatly benefited from the downsizing of the military because defense firms have now turned to corrections as a source of revenue for new technology. The corrections-specific technology currently in use or under development for prisons reads like science fiction: pulsed radar technology such as the Ground Penetrating Radar system used at the Lompoc Federal Correctional Institution in 1993 to locate an escape tunnel; lethal electric fences around every California DOC prisons; a heartbeat monitoring system that can detect inmates attempting to hide in containers in vehicles exiting the prison through the sally port; satellite monitoring to detect the location of offenders placed on house arrest programs; the use of inmate smart cards—a plastic card embedded with a computer chip that contains every available piece of information known about the offender carrying or wearing it; "officer-down" bracelets that report an officer in distress as well as identify the inmates in the immediate vicinity; devices for narcotic and explosives detection; x-ray body scanners that test for contraband concealed in body cavities; noninvasive drug testing using eye scans and skin patches; a smart gun that is computer coded so it cannot be fired by anyone other than the registered owner; a language translator to be used for communication with non-English-speaking offenders; and walk-through metal detectors that can pinpoint the exact location of the metal (deGroot, 1997a).

In the future, correctional managers should have the capability to create a computer-generated map of each prison that will plot each critical incident involving an inmate and provide guidance for staffing reallocations, placement of security devices, and overall improvement of inmate management (Wilkinson and Ritchie-Matsumoto, 1997:66).

Information Management Systems   In addition to computerizing virtually every database imaginable, DOCs are beginning to explore the use of Internet technology systems to coordinate the sharing of information with not only other prisons but the rest of the criminal justice system (Wilkinson and Ritchie-Matsumoto, 1997). The use of Internet technology will make it possible for database information developed in each prison to be rapidly shared with police departments and other government agencies for use in police investigations, adult and juvenile classification processes, and to prevent abuses of social security, workers' agencies, and compensation boards. Medical information can be shared with hospitals and private physicians through the use of telemedicine, now in service in 18 DOCs (Gailiun, 1997:69).

Correctional organizations now have the technology available to create Internet home pages that will educate the public about corrections and provide information to potential job applicants (Figure 4–3). The ability to communicate within the organization can be enhanced by the use of electronic mail, electronic bulletin boards, and the use of electronic forms.

Community Corrections Offender Management   The Washington Division of Community Corrections recently installed the Graphically Enhanced Network Information Enterprise (GENIE) in four of their field offices (Geiger and Shea, 1997). GENIE is an automated reporting center into which minimum-risk offenders key in their answers to a series of questions. This replaces the need for face-to-face meetings with low-risk offenders and allows the parole officer more time to supervise high-risk offenders. GENIE also has a built-in system for tracking offenders who don't report on schedule. Failure to report results in GENIE automatically alerting the officer and sending a letter to the offender notifying them of their delinquency and ordering immediate compliance with the reporting schedule.

Future uses of technology could include the use of global positioning systems, using

State of New Mexico

Corrections Department

Welcome to the Corrections Department Home Page!

The Corrections Department provides public safety
through a continuum of custody, control, supervision,
programs and services for offenders,
with professionalism, progressive management
and fiscal responsibility.

For detailed information on the Corrections Department,
choose from the following.

Office of the Secretary

Annual Report

Corrections Quarterly

The Guardian

Directory of Facilities

Frequently Asked Questions

Education Bureau

Statistics

Correctional Industries
Products and Services

FLASH

Press Releases

Contact us at:
Corrections Department
Post Office Box 27116
Santa Fe, New Mexico 87502-0116
phone: (505) 827-8710
fax: (505) 827-8220

For Employment Information call: 1-800-260-6399
NM Corrections Department is an Equal Opportunity Employer
EEO Officer: Virgil Garcia (505) 827-8619

OR via e-mail

FIGURE 4–3   State of New Mexico Department of Corrections home page.

satellites to automatically determine the location of every sex offender and any other offender deemed to be a significant risk to the community and transmit that location to a probation or parole officer (Dalton, 1997).

Training Staff to Use the New Technology   Once managers understand the value of technology, and how it can be used in their particular facility, it is not enough for them to bring new technology into the system. They must also demonstrate to employees that the technology will make their jobs easier, not unnecessarily complicate it. This can be accomplished through the development of training programs that effectively demonstrate the benefits of the technology as well as how to operate and care for it. Failure to provide appropriate levels of training will create staff frustration, resistance to change, and stress that otherwise could have been avoided.

While the changes in function, structure, and design created by the development and implementation of adaptive strategies have been impressive, they have also greatly increased the complexity of the managerial role in corrections. What is the correctional managers perception of the conservative revolution?

THE MANAGER'S PERSPECTIVE OF THE CONSERVATIVE REVOLUTION

A 1994 survey of 157 superintendents and 925 state prison inmates in California, Delaware, Florida, Illinois, Michigan, Ohio, Texas, and Pennsylvania (Simon, 1994a) revealed a marked lack of support for the crime control policies of the conservative revolution. Rather, the superintendents favored (1) an increase in the number of community prevention programs, (2) the smarter use of prison resources, (3) the repeal of mandatory minimum sentences, and (4) the expanded use of alternatives to incarceration.

The superintendents were in favor of community crime prevention and treatment in the form of improving the educational quality of schools and education programs that would teach young parents to be better parents. They rejected the "one size fits all" approach to the sentencing of drug offenders and expressed the belief that many of the individuals currently incarcerated for drug offenses do not represent a threat to society. Ninety-two percent of the managers believed that greater use should be made of alternatives to incarceration, such as home detention, halfway houses, boot camps, and residential drug programs.

Managers overwhelmingly supported the use of recidivism-focused prison programs: drug treatment; vocational training; psychological counseling; and educational programs. These responses appear to be in tune with the results of inmate surveys regarding the causes of crime: drugs and alcohol, no employment, a bad family life, and limited education.

In marked contrast, the Republican "Contract with America" advocated a public policy agenda of: (1) $10 billion for law enforcement grants, (2) $10.5 billion for prison construction, partly conditioned on a showing that "the state has increased the average prison time actually served in prison" and, (3) federalizing of a vast number of local gun crimes by creating new mandatory sentences for any state or federal drug or violent crime that involves possession of a firearm (Simon, 1994b:23).

This difference in perspective may reflect the different realities facing politicians and correctional managers. Public policy makers view crime control as only one of a number of pressing challenges. They can pass crime control legislation, then move on to the next problem area. Correctional managers, on the other hand, must live daily with the consequences of crime control policy. Having to struggle constantly with the challenges created by prison overcrowding, they are more likely to see the need for alternatives. This leads us to the question: What is the role of the correctional manager in public policy formulation? Some answers are given in the next section.

ROLE OF THE STRATEGIC APEX IN PUBLIC POLICY FORMULATION

We have noted the apparent gap in perception between many correctional managers and the politicians responsible for crime control legislation. This suggests that these managers may privately be at odds with the prevailing political sentiment. How freely can the manager dissent from official policy?

Organizational Relationship Between Director and Public Policy Makers

The answer to the question just posed is that while top correctional managers may privately dissent, their public behavior must always be guided by public policy. No matter what the private opinion, a manager's first responsibility is to carry out the legislated mission through an ongoing process of effective environmental design. The ability to freely speak out against a specific public policy is constrained by the organizational relationship between director and governor: "[T]he correctional administrator remains caught between the pragmatic knowledge that many persons in our prisons can safely be dealt with elsewhere, and the requirement to remain politically consistent and loyal to an administration's desires" (Riveland, 1991:11).

Top managers in corrections are at-will employees, that is, they can be summarily dismissed by the executive branch without cause or explanation. Historically, political preferences have played a significant role in the length of tenure of top correctional managers. State prison superintendents and wardens reportedly have the highest attrition rate of all categories of prison employee (Benton, Rosen, and Peters, 1982:18). As of July 1997, the average length of service for the directors of adult correctional agencies was 3.6 years (Camp and Camp, 1997:106). Lunden (1957) examined 612 wardens who had held office in 43 states over a 50-year period: 37 percent of the wardens served two years or less; 24 percent served three to four years; and 26 percent served between five and nine years. Sixty-one percent of the wardens were in office for less than five years. In Missouri, no warden served over four years in the period from 1880 to 1920; the warden changed whenever the governor changed (Schroeger, 1984). Recently, superintendents with the longest tenure have served for an average of 14.1 years (Camp and Camp, 1997:107).

The manager accepts the appointment with the explicit understanding that the politicians legislate public policy and the manager implements that policy. However, this does not mean that the manager cannot attempt to influence public policy.

Influencing Public Policy Makers

Correctional managers are not robots who mindlessly perform in accordance with political commands. They can influence public policy by proposing and implementing innovative strategies. When these strategies are successful, public policy makers may pay attention and be persuaded to reallocate financial resources. For example, public policy makers concerned about maintaining prison security while reducing recidivism may be impressed by treatment initiatives even in these days of the conservative revolution. An example of this was pointed out in Chapter 3 when we discussed the success of the California DOC in persuading their legislature to approve $100 million for drug treatment programs. Managers can also formally advise on pending corrections-related legislation. The managers who would appear to have the most to offer in this area are the director and the superintendent.

The Director as Advisor

The role of advisor requires a director to be "a harbinger projecting the resources that will be required and, preferably, as one who can shape a course of sound public policy through the political process" (Riveland, 1991:10). This shaping can be achieved in two ways: first, by direct contact between director and public policy makers; and second, by modifying the organizational structure to create a new function and category of employee: the legislative liaison officer.

Direct Contact   DOC directors are usually members of the governor's cabinet and, as such, have access to a wide range of policy makers. As cabinet members they have a responsibility to meet personally with key political leaders and attempt to influence their decision making on policy critical to corrections by presenting as much relevant information as possible. There are undoubtedly many candid opinions expressed by managers in private meetings with elected officials. However, directors don't have enough time to personally intervene on every corrections-related legislative issue because the amount of such legislation during any given year can be quite large, even for a small department. For example, the Arkansas DOC in 1995 saw the 80th Arkansas General Assembly pass legislation that established mandatory minimum sentences for certain crimes and parole eligibility for habitual offenders, amended the statute on capital punishment to include inmates who commit premeditated murder, extended the definition of sexual abuse to include sexual contact by DOC employees with individuals under DOC jurisdiction, prohibited state licensing agencies from disciplining medical staff involved in legal executions, made possession or use of weapons by inmates a criminal offense, allowed the DOC to contract with private businesses to use inmate labor, and repealed prohibitions on publishing details of executions (Arkansas Department of Corrections, 1996:5).

The depth and breadth of corrections-related legislation clearly requires modification of the organizational structure.

Legislative Liaison Officer   Organizational structure can be modified to create a substitute for the top manager—the Legislative Liaison Officer (LLO). The office is often named the Office of Intergovernmental Relations. The LLO generally reports directly to the Commissioner and functions as the link between the DOC, the legislature, and the governor's office. The LLO job description is to oversee all corrections-related legislation, alert top managers to newly introduced bills, arrange sponsorship of DOC proposed legislation, and attempt to stop or amend legislation harmful to the DOC. These functions require working with House and Sen-

ate staff, legislators, and special interest groups and organizations during the process of drafting and/or amending legislation. The LLO also arranges for the DOC to provide testimony on legislation and assists legislators on corrections-related constituent problems and questions (Illinois Department of Corrections, 1997:9).

LLOs must possess the necessary communications skills to work with legislators who have different political beliefs on a variety of issues and they must have a thorough knowledge of corrections. One of the communication tools frequently used is the Annual Report. The majority of DOCs and the Federal Bureau of Prisons issue an annual report. While the size, contents, and use of sophisticated graphics may vary, Annual Reports provide a general summary of the current status of the department and are frequently used to call attention to organizational efforts to effectively address critical problem areas, such as overcrowding. Annual Reports often have a wide distribution and are sent automatically to elected state and/or federal officials.

The Superintendent as Advisor

Directors spend a considerable amount of time involved in the political process because that is the nature of their role in a political system that demands agency accountability. But what about superintendents? They are on the front lines of managing the consequences of the conservative revolution. How active can they be in public policy advising? Superintendents appear to play a relatively small role in political advising for several reasons. First, directors often have a policy that the DOC should only speak with one voice. That is, the director speaks for the agency at the Capitol and superintendents are not encouraged to become politically involved at that level. Second, many superintendents are located in rural areas and political contact is limited to those politicians representing the jurisdiction in which the prison is located. Third, the operational priorities of their job do not allow time for extensive political advising.

Operational Priorities of the Superintendent In a survey of 487 correctional superintendents, McShane and Williams III (1993) found that these managers had an internal environmental focus, that is, their priorities were on achieving operative goals, not public policy formulation. Typically, superintendents spend the most time on internal personnel issues, resource management, inmate management, meetings with security staff, and planning/programming activities. Considerably less time is spent on meetings with state officials, community relations/media activities, or contacts with community agencies or individuals. When custody levels were examined, there were no significant differences in activity (McShane and Williams III, 1993:39).

The superintendents expressed grave concern about the external constraints directly affecting the day-to-day management of their prisons: tight budgets, low-quality staff and staff shortages (often created by low legislatively determined salary structures), overcrowding, and negative court and legislative decisions. These factors are, to a large extent, the result of public policy formulation. Yet, while they acknowledged the importance of external influences, most of the managers still focused most of their energy on the daily prison routine.

A major reason for this focus on operative goals may be found in the superintendent's professional commitment to achieving the mission. This is a commitment that leaves little time for external activities. There is also the possibility that inmate disturbances or other situations can lead to negative media coverage and political scapegoating that can ruin an otherwise promising career. Thus, the focus is on monitoring the internal environment as closely as possible.

SUMMARY

The political environment confronting today's correctional managers is formidable. The conservative revolution has created three major challenges for managers. The first challenge is the official goal of maintaining safe, orderly, and humane prisons by developing a broad range of effective adaptive strategies to manage overcrowded prisons. The second challenge is developing an effective advisory strategy to use during the formulation of corrections-related public policy. The third challenge, briefly touched upon in this chapter, is that managers must manage in accordance with a politically mandated requirement of fiscal conservatism that requires an emphasis on cost-minimization strategies. We examine this challenge more fully in the next chapter.

Discussion Questions

1. What is the relationship between the conservative revolution and prison overcrowding?
2. What are the challenges created by prison overcrowding?
3. What adaptive strategies have managers developed to manage prison overcrowding?
4. How have these adaptive responses changed organizational structure and design?
5. How would you explain the unexpected relationship between inmate violence levels and overcrowding?
6. What can a director do to educate elected officials about the consequences of the conservative revolution?

Critical Analysis Exercise: Extending the Confinement Of Sexual Predators

On June 23, 1997, the U.S. Supreme Court, in a 5-4 decision, ruled that states can lock up sex offenders in mental institutions even though they have already served their full prison sentence. The ruling involved a Kansas sexual predator law designed to ensure that authorities have a mechanism for indefinitely keeping child molesters confined. Under the Kansas law, an inmate can be kept in a mental institution if he has been convicted of a sexually violent crime, had a mental abnormality or personality disorder, and was judged likely to engage in future predatory acts of sexual violence. Thirty-eight states and the District of Columbia had urged the Supreme Court to uphold the law. In doing so, the Court ruled that mental hospital confinement does not constitute a double punishment and that the use of a civil hearing to determine dangerousness as a justification for continued confinement is constitutional. The decision, viewed as a dramatic public policy shift in criminal justice strategy (Biskupic, 1997), adds involuntary hospital confinement to the existing arsenal of harsher sentences and community sex offender notification laws. It is anticipated that many states will now pass similar sexual predator legislation.

Critical Analysis Questions

1. Is it fair to confine an individual because the authorities believe he may commit a crime in the future? Defend your answer.
2. What should be the role of correctional staff in determining the future dangerousness of an incarcerated sex offender?
3. What challenges could this type of legislation create for correctional employees and managers?
4. What actions can be taken to manage these challenges?
5. Will this law protect the public? Defend your answer.

5

The Fiscal Environment of Corrections

Learning Objectives

After completing this chapter, you should be able to:

- Define fiscal conservatism as a goal and the roles of the budget process and the Request For Proposal in achieving this goal.
- Contrast the three categories of cost-minimization strategy.
- Summarize the methods each category of strategy employs.
- Define privatization as a cost-containment and a revenue-enhancement strategy.
- Outline the issues in the privatization controversy.
- Describe the role of the manager in effective privatization.

Key Terms and Concepts

Fiscal Conservatism
Request For Proposal
Cutback Budgeting
Cost-Containment Strategies
Front-end Strategies
Administrative Good Time
Meritorious Good Time
Cost-Reduction Technology
Controlling Construction Costs
Prefabrication
Revenue Enhancement
Offender Service Fees
Inmate Labor
Service Brokerage
Alternative Financing
Governmental Use Model
Corporate Model
Good Time
Earned Good Time
Emergency Good Time
Cost-Reduction Policy Changes
Prototypes
Design/Build
Inmate Reimbursements
Technology Surcharging
Privatization
Partial Services Privatization
Total Services Privatization
Joint-Venture Model
Free Enterprise Model

We must turn away from the excessive use of prisons. The current incarceration binge will eventually consume large amounts of tax money, which will be diverted from essential public services such as education, child care, mental health, and medical services . . . that will have a far greater impact on reducing crime than building more prisons.

John Irwin and James Austin

Profile: Fiscal Conservatism in the Michigan Department of Corrections

Between 1985 and 1995, the share of the state budget allotted to the Michigan Department of Corrections (DOC) increased from 6 percent to 15 percent. The rate of budget growth between 1984 and 1990 was 26 percent per year. One in four state government employees was working in state corrections by 1995. However, fiscal conservatism mandated that corrections "do more with less." In response, the DOC reduced the rate of budget growth to 9 percent per year from 1991 through 1996 by implementing a process of cutback budgeting that included the following measures:

1. Double bunking of inmates to create 7,000 new beds (estimated savings: $750 million—$285 million in operating costs and $462 million by avoiding new prison construction).

2. Remodeling the Huron Valley Women's Facility instead of building a new 400-bed psychiatric inpatient facility (estimated savings: $65 million) and converting the former Newberry State Hospital into an 800-inmate medium security prison instead of building a new prison (estimated savings: $10 million).

3. Increasing the number of parole agents from 612 in 1991 to 867 in 1995 to produce a reduction in caseload size from 90 in 1991 to 69 in 1995. The result of increased supervision was a 50 percent reduction in the number of parolees returned to prison with a new felony conviction. This helped decrease the rate of increase of overcrowding between 1991 and 1995.

4. Increasing the number of offenders under community supervision by 8 percent, from 56,300 in 1991 to 61,000 in 1995, while prison intake dropped by 50 percent for low-risk offenders who were previously sent to prison with minimum sentences of 12 months or less and 17 percent for those with minimum sentences of 13 to 24 months.

5. Creating Technical Rule Violations Centers (TRV Centers) to correct the behavior of rule-breaking parolees or inmates on community status. This eliminated the return to prison of 1,400 low-risk offenders in 1995.

6. Expanding the boot camp option and establishing a residential aftercare program for boot camp graduates in an effort to reduce recidivism. In addition, DOC-operated detention centers were opened to provide judges an intermediate sanction for technical rule violators as an option to incarceration.

7. Encouraging county jails to incarcerate low-risk felony offenders rather than sending them to prison in return for state reimbursements that increased from $4.4 million in 1991 to $12.7 million in 1995, the equivalent of 969 prison beds.

8. Implementing a health care policy (the "Work Fit Injury Care Program") that developed an off-site employee injury care facility designed to reduce the number of employee worker compensation claims (estimated savings: $1.5 million).

9. Increasing revenue for state government, and reducing the DOC's need for general fund appropriations, by a system of inmate telephone surcharges (estimated revenue: $8 million).

10. Reorganizing the use of the DOC training academy to reduce employee travel expenses (estimated savings: $1.5 million in four years) (Michigan Department of Corrections, 1996b:8–20).

The massive prison overcrowding created by the conservative revolution's sentencing and parole reform initiatives has created an economic crisis for government at all levels. Tax revenues are not unlimited and, as correctional budgets have grown at the expense of other state agencies, elected officials have increasingly demanded that corrections assume a proactive role in reducing the burden on the taxpayer. Fiscal conservatism is an official correctional goal to be achieved through the development and implementation of cost-minimization strategies. There are three categories of cost-minimization strategy (cost containment, controlling construction costs, and revenue enhancement) designed to reduce the public tax burden. An increasingly important component of fiscal conservatism is the privatization of correctional services traditionally provided by government.

FISCAL CONSERVATISM AS AN OFFICIAL GOAL

In its simplest form, fiscal conservatism as a public policy can be translated as: "Do more with less." There are two reasons why fiscal conservatism is today a critical goal. First, there is the issue of the growth in correctional spending. State general fund appropriations for corrections totaled $8 billion in 1987 (Hunzeker, 1992). Eleven years later, in 1998, the estimated state spending on corrections was approximately $23 billion and estimated federal spending was $3.2 billion (Camp and Camp, 1997:72). Although most of this increase was the result of building out, the increased service demands from a growing number of special-need inmates (the elderly, female, addicted, gang members, mentally ill/retarded, and HIV-positive) who require a disproportionate share of resources has also increased spending.

Second, this growth in correctional budgets is incompatible with the philosophy of the conservative revolution that America needs less government and reduced public sector spending. It also conflicts with the reality that the taxpayer is not an unlimited source of revenue. Politicians fear the political consequences of raising taxes, but must answer the question: "Where are we going to find the additional money needed for corrections?" One strategy has been to take from higher education budgets. In California, for example, state spending for corrections increased 25 percent (to $3.3 billion) from Fiscal Year 1990–1991 through 1993–1994 while funds for higher education declined by 25 percent (to $4.4 billion). In many states, cutting higher education programs in order to fund new prison construction (Salahi, 1994; Gottfredson, 1995) has become policy. Money from other social service programs is also being diverted into corrections, the concern about which is expressed in the epigraph at the beginning of the chapter. In reviewing the growing diversion of public funds into corrections,

Dwyer and McNally (1994:277) state: "In essence, social and economic costs associated with incarceration are holding businesses, taxpayers, and other necessary publicly funded programs hostage in the 1990s."

As a result of these developments, correctional managers are increasingly under the gun to reduce the cost of corrections to the taxpayer. The pressing question for correctional managers is: "How are we to achieve fiscal conservatism?" The answer to this question is found in the development and implementation of cost-minimization strategies. These strategies require the use of two management tools: the budget process and the Request For Proposal (RFP).

Budget Process

A budget is a planning and control document created by accountants, financial advisers, and managers; "a plan or schedule adjusting expenses during a certain period to the estimated income for that period" (Bittel, 1989:187); a financial standard for a particular agency or program or activity that is derived from planning goals and the requirements of the mission. Budgeting can be defined as "[t]he process of planning and controlling the future operations of a business by developing a set of financial goals and evaluating performance in terms of those goals" (Brock, Palmer, and Price, 1990:g-1). Note the use of the word *business* in this definition. Correctional managers are expected to approach the task of budgeting in the same way as managers in the private sector.

The budget is a tool for achieving maximum efficiency in the use of financial resources. As such, a budget can be viewed as a set of targets that will guide organizational behavior; it is a working document to be used and modified as conditions change. To effectively engage in budgeting, correctional managers must be aware of seven fundamental principles that apply to every budgeting process (Brock, Palmer, and Price, 1990). First, the budget must reflect reasonably attainable goals. Second, the budget should be prepared from basic data that reflects both past results and future expectations. Third, the budget period should be of reasonable length (most correctional organizations are on a one-year budget cycle). Fourth, the individuals responsible for achieving the results should have a part in developing the budget. In corrections, input is primarily the function of middle-level and top managers. Fifth, there should be a thorough review of every budget proposal designed to detect and eliminate needless duplication of services and ineffective use of resources. Sixth, after the budget has been approved by the pertinent governmental authority, each departmental manager should be provided a written copy of their department's budget to use as a planning guide. Finally, frequent comparisons of actual results with the budget should be made. This helps ensure individual accountability and operational efficiency.

Request For Proposal

The Request For Proposal (RFP) is a planning document given to private sector service providers bidding on a contract. It defines the expectations the correctional managers have for the service provider and provides a foundation for the legal contract that will govern the relationship between corrections and the contractor.

In Chapter 10, different types of budgeting systems will be explored. For now our discussion is limited to a budget process referred to as "cutback budgeting": the process of reducing costs through the use of cost-minimization strategies.

DEVELOPMENT OF COST-MINIMIZATION STRATEGIES

Cost-minimization strategies can be divided into three categories: cost containment, controlling the cost of new prison construction, and revenue enhancement. An effective cost-containment strategy requires achievement of two operative

goals: (1) reducing the number of inmates and (2) reducing the daily cost of incarceration. Controlling the cost of new prison construction involves the operative goal of replacing traditional construction methods with technologically improved, cost-effective construction. Revenue enhancement attempts to develop nontaxpayer revenue sources through the implementation of three strategies: (1) inmate reimbursement, (2) surcharging the inmate use of technology, and (3) the construction of beds for leasing out. All three strategies can involve the use of inmate labor and varying amounts of interaction with the private sector. We begin with cost containment.

STRATEGIES OF COST CONTAINMENT

As noted in Chapter 4, efforts to increase available bed capacity through "cannibalizing," building out, and leasing out are often prohibitively expensive. Because the most critical issue for cost containment is the number of inmates, inmate population reduction is potentially the most effective cost-containment strategy.

Reducing the Inmate Population

The fiscal logic for reducing the number of offenders incarcerated at any given point in time is compellingly simple. For example, the Georgia DOC reports a daily cost of incarceration that ranges from $33.71 to $62.23 (the $124.39 per-day cost of the Augusta State Medical Prison is excluded from this calculation), depending on the security level of the prison. The daily cost of community supervision is, on average, $1.36 (Georgia Department of Corrections, 1997:18, 30). It is obvious, therefore, that the greater the number of offenders who are not incarcerated, the greater the reduction in prison-related expenditures. Inmate population reduction can be achieved through the use of community-based alternatives to incarceration and/or the use of a good time system. In many states, public policy makers have assisted corrections by approving both.

Community-Based
Alternatives to Incarceration

Convicted offenders can be diverted from incarceration through the use of a variety of front-end strategies. The diversion strategies that have been the most politically popular have been boot camp, house arrest (with or without electronic monitoring), and Intensive Supervision Probation (ISP). Achievement of cost-effectiveness through the use of these front-end diversion strategies is predicated on three assumptions. The first assumption is that these programs will reduce recidivism. Therefore, over the long term, fewer inmates will return to corrections as parole violators or repeat offenders. This reduction in new commitments to the DOC will translate into a reduced inmate population and a reduction in the amount of money which must be budgeted for corrections.

The second assumption is that front-end diversion programs are inherently less expensive because they do not require the massive physical plant and large staff required by prisons and jails. Therefore, the inmate per-day cost of front-end diversion alternatives will be lower than the inmate per-day cost of incarceration.

The third assumption is that the use of front-end diversion programs will reduce prison overcrowding. Fewer inmates packed into a prison lowers the number of inmates who have to be maintained and reduces the expensive wear and tear on the prison infrastructure (especially kitchen and laundry equipment). Fewer inmates and longer life spans for the infrastructure translate into a lower overall cost of incarceration. More important, front-end diversions such as boot camps should allow correctional managers to avoid the expense of new prison construction (Clark, Aziz, and MacKenzie, 1994:8).

The theory is common sense and appealing, but the question is: Are these assumptions met when front-end diversion programs are used? The research is mixed and not particularly encouraging.

Boot Camps   Does a day in a boot camp cost less than a day in prison? Logically, this should be the case. After all, the amount of time an offender spends in a boot camp is usually less than the amount of time spent in prison. However, research suggests that not all boot camps have equal potential for achieving cost reduction. In fact, a review of current data suggests that only one type of boot camp (the state probation boot camp) has a lower cost than incarceration. What is the basis for this conclusion? As of January 1, 1997, the average daily cost of imprisonment was $54.25. During this time period, 35 DOCs and the Federal Bureau of Prisons operated boot camps housing a total of 7,250 inmates at an average cost per inmate per day of $56.77 (Camp and Camp, 1997:75, 97–99). State probation boot camps held another 2,005 offenders and state parole boot camps held 1,237 offenders. The average daily cost was $49.26 and $61.00 respectively (Camp and Camp, 1997:171).

To put this in a more easily visualized form (using $54.25 as a baseline figure):

Prison	Boot Camps	Probation	Parole
$54.25	$56.77	$49.26	$61.00
	+$2.52	−$4.99	+$6.75

Thus, it appears that the use of probation camps have the potential to reduce the cost of offender management by, on average, $4.99 per offender per day. The question of why there is such a difference between the cost of state probation camps and state parole camps requires further study.

What about the ability of boot camps to achieve cost-effectiveness through the reduction of prison overcrowding and recidivism? MacKenzie and Souryal (1997) examined boot camps in Florida, Georgia, Illinois, Louisiana, New York, Oklahoma, South Carolina, and Texas and found evidence that boot camps can reduce prison overcrowding. However, this reduction occurs only if boot camps house those offenders who were otherwise prison-bound. If the camps house inmates that were not prison-bound, then a net widening effect can occur that will increase prison overcrowding (MacKenzie and Souryal, 1997:398) and the long-term cost of corrections.

MacKenzie and Souryal (1997) concluded that there is little evidence that boot camps reduce recidivism. A 1994 National Institute of Justice study also concluded that boot camps in Louisiana and New York have not been successful in reducing recidivism.

House Arrest Nearly every state uses house arrest to increase the supervision of low-risk parolees or probationers. The estimated cost of house arrest per offender is about $1,500 to $7,000 a year, while electronic monitoring increases the cost about $1,000 a year (Petersilia, 1988). As of January 1, 1996, only 9,346 offenders were being electronically monitored (Camp and Camp, 1996b:160).

Intensive Supervision Programs Deschenes, Turner, and Petersilia (1997), in evaluating Minnesota's ISP, determined that the program reduced the cost of corrections by $5,000 per offender per year while presenting no increase in risk to public safety. However, during the period of evaluation, prison admissions were reduced by less than 5 percent. The overall research findings on the effectiveness of ISPs as an alternative to incarceration in reducing costs are mixed. Petersilia and Turner (1993) offer a generally pessimistic view while Baird and Wagner (1990) and Pearson and Harper (1990) are more optimistic.

Advocates of front-end strategies suggest that these programs have already saved millions of taxpayer dollars. However, comparing the cost of incarceration versus the cost of front-end strategies is a complicated process and "glib claims about cost savings associated with intermediate punishment often do not stand up to careful scrutiny" (Morris and Tonry, 1990:234). Becker (1997:398), for example, is concerned that most intermediate sanctions may simply widen the correctional net because offenders who would ordinarily receive a prison

sentence still receive a prison sentence. Thus, cost savings may only be temporary.

Good Time Strategies

Even if front-end strategies are able to achieve a degree of cost-effectiveness, the high rate of incarceration frequently requires correctional managers to lobby elected officials to provide additional relief in the form of giving legislative approval to the back-end strategy of awarding good time credits that permit early parole. The back-end strategy of early parole based on the accumulation of good time credits will reduce the actual amount of prison time served for selected inmates and thus reduce the total cost of their incarceration.

There are four types of good time system: administrative, earned, meritorious, and emergency (Weisburd and Chayet, 1996:220–223). The *administrative good time system* permits the automatic award of good time credits to inmates upon commitment to custody. The actual time served will depend on whether credits are revoked in response to rule violations. Administrative good time is used to punish misbehavior, not as a reward for good behavior, and may be considered a disincentive, or punishment, system (Ross and Barker, 1986). Lost credits are frequently restored to inmates approaching their parole date as managers exercise discretion in response to the level of overcrowding (Jacobs, 1982). In an *earned credit system,* good time functions as a reward for positive behavior. The time served is reduced by involvement in prison treatment programs and, sometimes, employment in correctional industries. The *meritorious good time system* is often used to complement the earned credit system. Good time credits are awarded to inmates who perform exceptional acts: participation in charity runathons, community service projects, donating blood, or assisting staff in emergency situations. *Emergency good time credits* are used in overcrowded prisons and jails, often operating under a court-ordered population cap, that need a method of quickly releasing inmates during periods of extreme overcrowding. An emergency release program allows correctional managers to grant groups of inmates a block of credits if they meet criteria such as nonviolent commitment offense and close proximity to release (Austin, 1986), that permit early release.

Are Good Time Systems Fair? As of January 1, 1997, ten DOCs and the District of Columbia were authorized to use an emergency release program. In 1996, a total of 2,517 inmates were released, with the largest number (954) being released by the District of Columbia (Camp and Camp, 1997:53). Good time systems are not without controversy. Good time credits can be considered a hidden system of discretionary decision making (Clear, Hewitt, and Regoli, 1978) that results in fundamental inequality of treatment, especially when eligibility is based on participation in programs not equally available to all inmates. Due process rights may be abused when good time revocation decisions are based on race, age, and place of incarceration (Flanagan, 1982). Correctional managers must make every effort to ensure that their good time system is an equitable one. Otherwise, inmate resentment may increase already high employee and inmate stress levels.

Does the Use of Good Time Threaten Public Safety? Critics of good time legislation often oppose this back-end strategy on the grounds that it may endanger the public. How safe is good time? Between 1980 and 1993, the Illinois DOC released more than 21,000 inmates an average of 90 days early because of severe overcrowding with little impact on the state's crime rate and an estimated savings of $50 million. Based on these findings, the state expanded its use of good time by an additional 90 days and is now saving more than $90 million per year (Austin and Bolyard, 1993). A recent study of an Oklahoma preparole program found that inmates could be released three to six months early without influencing the state's crime rate, at a cost savings of $9,000 per inmate (Austin and Hardyman, 1992).

This level of savings is impressive. For the Illinois DOC, a projected savings of $90 million dollars a year helps reduce the annual budget request, which for Fiscal Year 1998 was $1,073,825,300 (Camp and Camp, 1997:72). However, too great a reliance on good time systems can create a public perception that criminals are evading punishment. It also increases the probability of a sensational crime by an early release offender, which can damage the DOC's reputation and may even scuttle the good time program. Correctional managers must develop and implement written policy that provides specific release criteria and procedures, establishes employee accountability, and limits the use of discretion.

Reducing the Daily Cost of Operations

The unfortunate reality is that even effective front-end and back-end strategies are frequently not enough to return inmate population levels to the design capacity of the prison. These strategies must be supplemented by the development of strategies to reduce the daily cost of operating the prison. Managers have developed a number of such strategies.

Eliminating Staff Positions Through Technology
Because nearly half the total annual cost of operation of a jail or prison involves correctional officer (C.O.) salaries and benefit packages (Beilen and Krasnow, 1996:131) many managers are recognizing the cost-containment value of replacing C.O.s with technology. In November 1993, the California DOC began a program of replacing continuously staffed guard towers at some of its prisons with lethal electrified perimeter fences. The operative goal: elimination of as many as ten towers requiring 48.3 staff positions for an annual savings of $1.5 million, with the cost of each fence being paid back within the first or second year of operation. A reduction of 750 positions because of guard tower elimination could translate into yearly savings of $40 million (Hoffmann et al., 1996:66–68).

The construction costs of a new facility represent only about 10 percent of the total cost of operation over a typical 30-year life cycle (Beilen and Krasnow, 1996:131). Therefore, designing new facilities with the goal of reducing the number of fixed correctional officer posts to save money over the long run is a priority in new prison construction. For example, expansion of the Niagara County Jail (New York) in 1995 incorporated an efficient unit design that allowed 224 inmates to be supervised by only five officers and promised annual cost savings of $164,000 (Beilen and Krasnow, 1996:131).

Changing or Eliminating Employee Functions

Changes in monitoring procedures in 1995 allowed the Connecticut DOC to reduce C.O. overtime by 300,000 hours, saving an estimated $7 million (Connecticut Department of Corrections, 1996:5). In 1995, the Commissioner of the Pennsylvania DOC touched off a storm of protest from C.O.s when he announced a plan to reduce officer overtime costs by $5 to $6 million a year by eliminating guard tower positions at five prisons (*Evening News,* 1996:B1, B4).

Correctional officers are not the only employees targeted by budget reductions. In 1996, Maryland's governor tried to balance the budget by eliminating all academic and vocational education programs, except special education. In Rhode Island, academic and vocational educators were laid off (Vogel, 1996:120). And, in 1997, the District of Columbia DOC closed two of its three halfway houses in order to transfer 37 community corrections staff to the understaffed Lorton Correctional Complex, an action that eliminates the need to hire an additional 37 prison employees (Thompson, 1997:D03).

Although a strategy of reducing the personnel complement can effect both short-term and long-term cost savings, there is a price to be paid. Any managerial action which eliminates jobs will meet with bitter resistance from employees and their unions. Unions will engage in information pickets, talk to the media, and aggressively pursue a strategy of warning the public that management's actions will decrease employee safety and increase public risk. Downsizing the work force, even if this involves only a few positions, can be interpreted by employees to mean that management's talk about encouraging employee empowerment is just that— talk. Correctional managers considering an employee reduction strategy must carefully look at the negative psychological impact of those lost jobs on the remaining employees.

The trust between employees and managers is often fragile. The belief that management is more interested in saving money than helping employees can be a powerful threat to that trust. Therefore, an employee reduction strategy should not be implemented without prior discussion with employees and their unions. In many states, the CBAs require such discussion, but even if the employees are not unionized, this traumatic issue should be publicly discussed before any employee reduction policy is implemented. At a minimum, employees should be informed of the need for the policy; the basis for determining that employee reduction is the best course of action; the savings to be derived; and the manner in which the policy will be implemented. If an employee reduction strategy requires the elimination of positions currently filled, the dismissal of those employees is the course of action most likely to arouse employee anger. If the reductions can be achieved through attrition (not filling positions as they become vacant through retirement or transfer), the likelihood of a negative employee reaction can be significantly diminished.

Reducing Inmate Activities and Services

An increasingly utilized approach to reducing the daily cost of operations has been to selectively target inmate activities and services by declaring them to be nonessential and, therefore, eligible for elimination. The most frequent targets are inmate recreational activities, especially weight lifting, which is often viewed as a security threat. That is, inmates bulking up can be more powerful than correctional employees and, thus, represent a physical threat to them. In addition, weight-lifting can be the cause of expensive inmate injuries. In 1995, the Arizona DOC identified inmate weight-lifting injuries as a source of excessive medical expenditures. Removal of weight-lifting equipment resulted in an estimated savings of $101,900 through a reduction in orthopedic costs (Arizona Department of Corrections, 1996:26). The leader in the aggressive pursuit of fiscal conservatism in the 1990s has been Sheriff Joseph Arpaio in Maricopa County, Arizona, who achieved a national reputation by housing inmates in tents and reportedly saving $100,000 a year by banning coffee. The sheriff also replaced hot lunches with cold sandwiches, thereby reducing the cost of jail meals to as low as 30 cents compared to the $2 a meal in other jails (Banisky, 1996:A1, A8). These types of actions can create inmate anger and resentment which, combined with idleness, can create the potential for violent disturbances.

On November 17, 1996, an inmate riot in Arpaio's Tent City Jail caused an estimated $130,000 in damages and injured eight sheriff's employees. The inmates were in control of Tent City for five hours. Critics of Sheriff Arpaio were quick to see a link between the riot and the harsh conditions of Tent City. However, a 2,100 page internal report blamed the riot on the inappropriate actions of a Detention Officer who used pepper spray on an inmate instead of considering other alternatives. It should be noted that "Sheriff Arpaio refused to provide records from a separate probe of the riot conducted by internal affairs investigators" (*Dallas Morning News,* 1998:21A).

Unfortunately, conservative politicians have increasingly targeted inmate educational programs as nonessential. In 1994, Congress eliminated inmate Pell grants and inmate "college programs that had developed gradually over a 20-year period collapsed seemingly overnight" (Linton, 1998:18). This action was taken despite the body of literature demonstrating a relationship between college education and lowered recidivism. In addition, governors in a number of states have eliminated funding for prison libraries, high school courses, and vocational training programs.

The negative impact of program elimination on inmate morale is substantial. Fortunately, some elected officials understand the value of educational programs and have approved funding for "no-read, no-release" educational programs which feature basic skill instruction. Congress has also recently funded a provision in the Higher Education Act which finances postsecondary education for some inmates (Linton, 1998).

Modernizing Basic Service Delivery Systems

One area of potential savings in any prison is the kitchen. The introduction of food service technologies such as advanced meal preparation systems with reheating facilities, the use of a blast-chilling component that reduces labor and allows the cooks to use products with a limited shelf life, and the introduction of meal assembly and delivery systems that decrease assembly and distribution time can save millions of dollars over the life of the equipment (Gatland and Bowers, 1997:78–81).

Using Inmate Labor for Public Sector Projects

This strategy reduces the cost of corrections by housing inmates in less expensive work camps. It has the added public relations value of allowing corrections to claim credit for reducing, to some small degree, the overall cost of state government by substituting cheap inmate labor for expensive civilian labor. In 1996, 4,000 California inmates in 33 camps reportedly spent an estimated 2 million hours on firefighting (Figure 5–1) and fire prevention and 6 million hours on conservation projects and community service activities. This use of inmate labor saved an estimated $70 million (California Department of Corrections, 1996b:1–3). The Arizona DOC also has inmate firefighters and estimates that in 1995 Arizona saved $150,000 by using inmates to fight fires (Arizona Department of Corrections, 1996b:18–19).

FIGURE 5–2   Inmates can help managers achieve the goal of fiscal conservatism by performing basic institutional services and making craft products for sale to the public. Courtesy of the Ohio Department of Rehabilitation and Correction.

FIGURE 5–1   The California DOC makes extensive use of inmate firefighters, an approach that saves tax payer money. Courtesy of the California Department of Corrections.

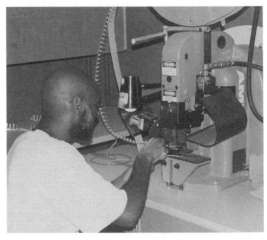

FIGURE 5–3   Courtesy of the Ohio Department of Rehabilitation and Correction.

Using Inmate Labor for In-House Projects

Inmates have a variety of skills that can be used to reduce costs (Figures 5–2 through 5–4). In Kentucky, an estimated $100,000 was saved by using inmates to complete the multipurpose addition to the chapel at Blackburn Correctional Complex and relocate and expand the Medical Building, and an estimated $200,000 was saved by using inmate labor in the restoration of the Central Kentucky Treatment Center located in Louisville (Kentucky Department of Corrections, 1996:34–35). Inmate-managed orchards and gardens saved Arizona an estimated $91,705 in 1995 (Arizona Department of Corrections, 1996b:19).

How Effective Are Daily Cost-Reduction Strategies?

How do the above cost-reduction savings noted compare to the total cost of the DOC? Consider the data from four states (from Annual Reports and Camp and Camp, 1996b:64, including new construction costs):

FIGURE 5–4   Courtesy of the Ohio Department of Rehabilitation and Correction.

STATE	SAVINGS (Proposed or Actual)	FISCAL YEAR 1996 BUDGET
Arizona	$251,900	$414,105,900
California	$110,000,000	$3,725,516,000
Connecticut	$7,000,000	$414,587,134
Michigan	$3,000,000	$1,268,796,000

These savings, when viewed within the context of the total budget, have limited effectiveness in achieving fiscal conservatism and can be easily outweighed by the cost of building new prisons. Therefore, correctional managers must control the cost of new prison construction.

CONTROLLING THE COST OF NEW PRISON CONSTRUCTION

Before the era of DOC Corrections, the expense of building new prisons was met in part by using the labor of the inmates themselves (Figures 5–5 and 5–6), as we discussed in the Profile at the beginning of Chapter 1. More recently, some DOCs have tried to avoid the construction of new prisons by acquiring unoccupied state hospitals or military bases and converting them into prisons, a process that involves less money and time than new prison construction. But there are not enough state hospitals and abandoned military bases to support the level of inmate increase most DOCs have witnessed and it is frequently necessary to build new prisons despite the best efforts of correctional managers to secure suitable conversion sites. Therefore, managers have been under pressure to develop effective construction cost-containment strategies.

Prototype Prison Construction

A widely used innovative construction strategy is the prototype prison. The prototype approach involves using a design that has already been used at another site. It is possible to save time using a prototype because the project team can work from a set of design plans that have been tested

FIGURE 5–5 During Pre-DOC Corrections, the cost of new prison construction was controlled by the use of inmate labor. Courtesy of the Office of Archives, Federal Bureau of Prisons.

FIGURE 5–6   Courtesy of the Office of Archives, Federal Bureau of Prisons.

through the actual construction of another prison where potential construction problems have already been encountered and resolved (Figure 5–7). The larger the DOC, the greater the savings that can be realized by prototype prison construction. Pioneering efforts in California are being imitated all across the country, even in small facilities. For example, the Niagara County Jail project previously mentioned involved a prototype process that reduced average construction time from 30–36 months to 24–27 months (Beilen and Krasnow, 1996:131).

Prefabricated Prison Construction

Prototype construction often involves the use of prefabricated building components. Prefabricated components are elements of a building that are assembled off-site, trucked to the building site, and put together in much the same way that a giant puzzle would be assembled: numbered components are connected at predetermined connection joints. The Delaware DOC, for example, in adding 600 beds to the Delaware Correction Center and 300 beds to the

Sussex Correction Center, used prefabricated (precast) ceilings, wall panels with security windows cast into the panel, and precast concrete guard towers. The result was a reduction in construction costs and time. The DOC also saved money by using inmate labor to assemble the tower components (Donohue and Greloch, 1997:90–92).

Design/Build

This approach is a project delivery system in which one firm assumes total responsibility for the design and construction of a project. This approach is becoming popular with correctional managers because it enables them "to meet very tight construction schedules, guarantee budgets in the early phases of construction and simplify construction administration" (Reilly and Grothoff, 1997:75). Eliminated is the time-consuming process of awarding separate parts of a project to different firms that must then establish effective communication channels and coordinate a variety of activities over a period of years.

FIGURE 5–7 This line-of-sight supervision unit at Ohio's Allen Correctional Institution is an example of prototype construction. Courtesy of the Office of Archives, Federal Bureau of Prisons.

Multiple communication channels frequently create miscommunication and coordination of activity problems between contractors which can increase the length (and therefore, the cost) of any project. The unintended results of such problems can also be embarassing. This author once toured a DOC's new training academy. The tour was led by the Commissioner of Corrections who proudly pointed out the various features of the academy. Pride turned into embarrassment, however, when the Commissioner realized that the men's rooms lacked urinals and the beautifully carpeted hallways could not be vacuumed because there were no electrical outlets in the hallways. The problem? The electrical contractor, the plumbing contractor, and the general contractor had not communicated effectively with each other or with the project architects. The build/design approach eliminates this type of miscommunication and coordination problem.

An example of this approach is found in Missouri where the DOC needed to construct a 1,200-bed facility. Based on past experience, correctional managers anticipated that it would take three years to build the prison. The design phase alone would require 15 to 18 months. Because of inmate population pressure, DOC managers decided to try the design/build process, which would permit construction to begin before the architectural drawings were complete. Build/design increases efficiency by having a design/build team working to complete the plans for the prison while the design/build contractor is negotiating with subcontractors and beginning work on such tasks as site preparation and utility line installation. In Missouri, design/build compressed construction time to such an extent that it was only 24 months from the awarding of the contract to turning the prison over to the DOC (Reilly and Grothoff, 1997:75).

Developing the Construction Request For Proposal

Project needs are communicated to prospective project bidders through the use of the RFP. In the case of the Missouri DOC, their RFP provided (1) two bound sets of performance specifications indicating the items to be supplied and minimum levels for quality and performance, (2) a bound set of equipment cut-sheets defining requirements for specific medical, dental, laundry, and food service equipment, (3) a site plan showing the location of the proposed entrance, perimeter security road, and security fencing, and (4) a preliminary soils report with limited drilling information. An RFP organized in this manner will prevent a multitude of time-consuming problems.

Federal Project Financing

The U.S. Department of Justice's (DOJ) Violent Offender Incarceration/Truth-in-Sentencing Incentive Grant Program gives grants to states interested in building or expanding correctional facilities if they can guarantee they will implement truth-in-sentencing laws requiring violent offenders to serve a substantial portion of their sentences. Approximately $10 billion has been authorized by this program through Fiscal Year 2000 (Dallao, 1997:70).

STRATEGIES OF REVENUE ENHANCEMENT

A major drawback of every successful strategy for increasing bed capacity is that the manager is also increasing the cost of the daily operation of corrections by increasing the total number of inmates. This requires that correctional managers develop cost-minimization strategies to reduce the economic burden on the taxpayer through revenue enhancement. The operative goal here is to increase nontaxpayer sources of revenue. If successful, the taxpayer burden of supporting corrections will be held to a lower rate of increase than would occur if nontaxpayer sources were not developed. The most politically popular strategies have been those that require the inmate to pay for some portion of the cost of incarceration.

Inmate Reimbursement Strategies

There are three major areas targeted for inmate reimbursement of services traditionally received free of charge.

Legal/Administrative Costs   In 1996, the Georgia legislature approved a policy of placing the costs of paying court costs and fees on inmates who file malicious or frivolous actions and requiring that the DOC deduct funds from the inmate's account until all costs are paid. The DOC was also authorized to make deductions from inmate accounts to pay for damage to state property, medical injuries to themselves or others, and for costs to quell a disturbance (Georgia Department of Corrections, 1997:7). The Minnesota DOC, during Fiscal Year 1994–1995, collected $518,000 from employed inmates to fund services for crime victims. State law requires all inmates making more than $50 in Correctional Industries to have between 5 and 10 percent of their pay deducted for funding victim services (Minnesota Department of Corrections, 1995). This approach has been taken a step further by a national citizens group—VOCAL (Victims of Crime and Leniency)—which in 1997 began lobbying the U.S. Congress for a constitutional amendment that would require convicted offenders to fund victim's rights programs (Sommers, 1997).

Health Care Services   Charging inmates for visits to the infirmary to see a physician or nurse is a particulary controversial practice. Inmates are entitled to receive appropriate medical treatment when they are ill. Given their lifestyles, offenders often come into the prison with a mulitude of physical problems, some of which (HIV-related infections, for example) are extremely expensive to treat. It is unconstitutional to deny necessary medical care on the grounds that it is expensive. However, some inmates abuse the prison health care system by going to the infirmary when they are not ill. Rather, they want to visit with the nurses or see a friend who is ill, or be treated for a routine cold for which the only treatment is bed rest and plenty of fluids, or just to break the monotony of the daily routine by going to a different part of the prison. This type of inmate activity diverts the attention of physicians and nurses from those inmates who genuinely need medical treatement. Therefore, an increasing number of correctional managers believe that a small fee-for-service is justified for three reasons. First, a fee-for-service requires inmates to pay a small portion of the cost of their medical care and this is an act in service of the goal of fiscal conservatism. Second, it reduces inmate abuse of the health care system. Third, it allows physicians and nurses to pay more attention to inmates who are genuinely in distress. As of January 1, 1997, 23 DOCs charged inmates for routine health services and three DOCs were in the process of implementing a pay-for-medical-services program. Charges per visit ranged from $2 to $4 (Camp and Camp, 1997:74–75).

Monthly Supervision Fees Twenty-three states now allow both probation and parole departments to charge supervisory fees. The average monthly fee is $22.62, with a range of $10.00 in Kentucky and Montana to $40.00 in New Hampshire and Oklahoma (Camp and Camp, 1997:165). In 1990, Texas collected more than $57 million in fees—a nice offset of the $106 million spent on supervision (Finn and Parent, 1992:2,12). The cost of drug detection tests is often included as a cost of supervision. Box 5–1 provides a description of the system of offender fees used by the Kansas DOC.

from an average of 15,172 contacts per month in 1994 to 7,364 per month in 1995. DOC representatives are quick to note that no inmates are denied medical care because of an inability to pay and fees are not charged for follow-up visits for the same condition or complaint. Inmates are charged $5.35 for the actual cost of drug tests with positive results. During the first year of the program, $2,017 was collected. Fees are used to offset the costs of drug test administration. Offenders on parole and postrelease supervision are charged a supervision fee of either $15 or $25 a month. During the first year of the program, $187,628 was collected; $46,906 of this amount was transferred to the Crime Victim's Compensation Fund. In addition, offenders on parole are charged a fee of $10 for a positive drug test and $30 for a confirmation test with a positive result. If the initial test is positive, but the confirmation test is not, the $10 fee for the initial test is waived (Kansas Department of Corrections, 1996:3.10).

BOX 5–1 THE OFFENDER FEE APPROACH

Beginning in 1995, the Kansas DOC initiated a system of offender fees that requires inmates to pay a fee of $1 per month for administration of their inmate trust accounts. A total of $464,847 was collected during the first year and transferred to the Crime Victim's Compensation Fund. Inmates are also charged a fee of $2 for each inmate-initiated primary visit to a prison sick call. During the first year of the program $26,257 was collected and medical contacts were reduced

Service fees are resented by inmates, but to date there is no empirical evidence that this resentment has risen to the level of individual or collective action. Inmate bank accounts are not the only source of revenue enhancement. The inmate use of technology services can also provide revenue.

Technology Surcharges

A common feature in prisons and jails is a telephone system that allows inmates to make collect phone calls. In 1995, the Arizona Department of Corrections modified the inmate telephone system contract to allow a technology surcharge that reportedly generated $1.5 million for the inmate Activity and Recreation Fund (Arizona

Department of Corrections, 1996:23). The experience of Michigan with this strategy was noted in the Profile at the beginning of this chapter. In virtually every DOC today, technology surcharging is an increasingly popular method of raising revenue.

This practice is arousing a considerable amount of interest because DOCs can make a substantial amount of money, and this is in the service of fiscal conservatism. However, controversy is created by the fact that the source of that money is the inmate family, the vast majority of whom have very limited financial resources. Critics of phone surcharges believe it is unfair to use financially stressed inmate families as a source of both private sector profit and DOC revenue enhancement. Advocates of the practice point out that inmates voluntarily make the phone calls, should be aware of their families' financial status, and have the power to make the phone call as short as those finances require. Thus, inmates are expected to exercise financial responsibility. Advocates also point out that a requirement that the calls be collect is necessary to prevent inmates from using the cellblock telephones to perpetuate phone scams on unsuspecting members of the community. This debate will undoubtedly continue; however, more and more correctional managers, driven by the political and public demand for fiscal conservatism, are studying the possibility of the technology surcharge as a primary source of revenue enhancement.

Construction of Beds for Leasing Out

Electing to build more cells in new construction (or renovation) projects than will be needed for the projected inmate population in order to have excess cells to lease out is another revenue enhancement approach that can be profitable. Revenue derived from leasing out can be used to offset the operational costs for the entire prison. For example, in 1995, the Arizona DOC received $991,900 for the incarceration of illegal aliens (Arizona Department of Corrections, 1996:18).

So far, we have considered cost containment and revenue enhancement strategies that primarily involve the internal environment of corrections. But the external environment as a source of assistance cannot be ignored. We turn now to the critical issue of privatization.

PRIVATIZATION

In its broadest sense, privatization involves "turning to the private sector for new ideas and possibly untapped expertise" (Travis, Latessa, and Vito, 1985:11). The need for correctional managers to practice fiscal conservatism has created an eagerly seized opportunity for the private sector to enter corrections: "Where demand for a service outstrips supply and where prices seem unreasonably high, conditions are ripe for competition and for the emergence of new sources of supply" (Logan and Rausch, 1985:303). However, corrections cannot enter into privatization unless the state legislature has passed an enabling statute that gives correctional managers the authority to contract out correctional services to the private sector.

Privatization as a Cost-Containment Strategy

Walker (1994:572) discusses privatization in terms of "service brokerage." That is, the private sector is in possession of a variety of basic services needed by corrections and can provide these services in a more cost-effective manner than the public sector. Service brokerage can be analyzed on three levels of service delivery: community field service, community residential service, and institutional service (Walker, 1994:572).

Community Field Services
This type of brokerage involves services provided totally within the community by already existing private agencies. To receive these services, correctional manag-

ers will enter into a contract with a private company able to provide mental health and substance abuse counseling, educational services, and job training/placement services. Clients using these types of services are primarily adult and juvenile parole and probation departments. This is the type of privatization that is the least controversial. Advocates view it as a cost-effective method of ensuring the availability of specialized services provided by qualified community professionals. For example, in 1995, the Health Services Division of the Arizona DOC negotiated five-year discount contracts with community health care providers using a system of capped rates to prevent inflation. Estimated savings: $2,059,600 (Arizona Department of Corrections, 1996:26).

Community Residential Services

Mullen, Chabotar, and Cartow (1985) view community residential services as a form of management contracting, that is, the management of inmates on a per diem basis by private contractors. This type of brokerage involves contracting with a private company for the total operation of halfway houses, group homes, prerelease centers, or jails. Correctional managers using this strategy generally report cost savings (Camp and Camp, 1984).

Contracting for Institutional Services

This type of brokerage can take three forms: partial services (reduction of the cost of daily operation), alternative financing (reducing the cost of construction), or total services (reducing the number of inmates in public prisons).

Partial Services Brokerage   A private contractor provides direct food, medical, laundry, counseling, or educational and vocational training services to inmates. As of January 1, 1997, 70,216 inmates were receiving contracted food services and 418,211 inmates were receiving contracted medical services (Camp and Camp, 1997:77). This

type of privatization is cost-effective because union employees (with generous salary and benefit packages) are replaced by nonunionized employees who lack state salary and benefits.

Alternative Financing   This strategy involves the use of private funds to quickly finance the construction of publicly operated jails and prisons. After construction, the new facility is turned over to the public sector. Advocates citing the cost-effective benefits of alternative financing point to such examples as the Corrections Corporation of America (CCA), which in 1984 built a 68,000-square-foot detention center in Houston designed to hold undocumented aliens in six months for $14,000 per bed. Typically, the Immigration and Naturalization Service would need 2.5 years to complete this type of project and the average cost would be $26,000 per bed (Seligman, 1992:111).

Total Services Brokerage   This is alternative financing followed by complete operation of the facility by a private corporation (Mullen, Chabotar, and Cartow, 1985). This is the most controversial form of privatization because a private for-profit corporation assumes total control of an inmate population. This form of total services brokerage is also known as the "prison management" component of privatization. Private companies such as CCA contract to build prisons and then manage the inmates incarcerated within those prisons. As of January 1, 1997, 14 states had contracts with 47 privately operated prisons housing a total of 20,987 offenders. Seventeen of the prisons were minimum security and 16 were medium security (Camp and Camp, 1997:79). The number of inmates housed in private prisons is increasing at the rate of about 25 percent each year (Thomas, 1994:5–6).

However, privatization can go far beyond cost containment. Increasingly, it is a source of revenue enhancement.

Privatization as a Revenue Enhancement Strategy

Inmate labor can be used for more than saving money on in-house or community projects. It can be used to produce goods and services that can generate a profit within the framework of the "prison-industrial complex" (Donziger, 1997:325) (Figure 5–8). Today, there are four organizational models of inmate labor in use: the governmental use model, the joint venture model, the corporate model, and the free enterprise model (Dwyer and McNally, 1994:285).

Governmental Use Model

The governmental use model is followed by the traditional Correctional Industries operation that produces, for example, license plates. Prison inmates produce products whose sales are restricted to state and local government agencies—a limited, but secure, market. Private sector involvement is minimal and usually in the form of an advisory role on issues of management advice or technical assistance. Inmates are typically paid a small stipend, although some industries may provide production bonuses.

The advantage of this model is that correctional managers maintain control of the industry and can maximize inmate employment as a means of reducing inmate idleness. A disadvantage is that these industries generally produce products and teach skills that have no equivalent or widespread private sector counterpart. The work does not prepare inmates to reenter the community work force. Nevertheless, the governmental use model is the most prevalent of the Correctional Industries (Grieser, 1987:1).

Joint Venture Model

In this model, correctional managers contract with a private sector business to produce private-firm products or purchase a product name and design for sales within the governmental use model. Managerial control is shared between the public and private sector. Private sector involvement in the areas of design, production, marketing, and distribution is greater than in the governmental use model. An example of the joint venture model

FIGURE 5–8 Correctional industries have become a major source of revenue enhancement. These inmates are going to their correctional industry jobs in the U.S. Penitentiary at Leavenworth. Courtesy of the Office of Archives, Federal Bureau of Prisons.

is Corcraft, which is the New York State Correctional Services Prison Industry. Some correctional manager control is lost using this model, but inmates can benefit from learning skills that have a community equivalent.

Corporate Model

The prison industry that assumes a corporate model is a semi-independent organization that emulates private sector businesses. Correctional managers are primarily concerned with issues of security and maximizing inmate involvement in the industry. Control and profitability are heavily influenced by private sector managers. Profit is a primary motivation and inmates can learn valuable work skills because their work environment closely approximates that of the outside community, at least where productivity expectations and adherence to the work ethic are concerned. An example of the corporate model is PRIDE— Prison Rehabilitative Industries and Diversified Enterprises, Inc.—which is a component of the Florida DOC. PRIDE is an example of the marriage of the goals of fiscal conservatism and rehabilitation. As the material in Box 5–2 illustrates, PRIDE is economically profitable and these profits are used to expand inmate work opportunities during incarceration as well as underwrite a variety of noncorrectional taxpayer-supported programs such as victim restitution and compensation. At the same time, inmates can learn marketable skills and gain legitimate employment in the community, two activities that appear to significantly reduce recidivism. PRIDE is also an excellent example of correctional managers making effective use of a variety of resources available in the external environment.

BOX 5–2 PRIDE INDUSTRIES, FISCAL YEAR 1994–1995

Areas of Responsibility

Prison Rehabilitative Industries and Diversified Enterprises (PRIDE), Inc., was authorized by the Florida legislature in 1981 to operate the state prison industries. A nonprofit corporation, PRIDE has contributed over $73 million to the state of Florida over the years, including inmate compensation, victim restitution, and investment in state assets.

Inmate On-the-Job Training

In the 1994–1995 fiscal year, 4,648 inmates trained and worked 4,611,255 hours in PRIDE's multi-businesses. The corporation offers over 400 different skill paths required by 2,838 inmate positions within 40 industries and 12 operations located in 21 prisons. PRIDE inmate workers were paid $1,771,469 in 1995 and $265,720 was paid to victim restitution.

Opportunities for Inmates

PRIDE's variety of businesses provide job training experiences consistent with the private sector companies in Florida. PRIDE integrates market-based customer-driven goals, objectives, and measurements with industrial job training and employability education. Within this private enterprise mode, inmate workers assigned to PRIDE by the Department of Corrections learn marketable job skills demanded by today's business world.

Accredited Training

Seventy-six percent of the PRIDE industries have been certified or recognized by national business/trade associations and accredited institutions such as the Department of Education, Clemson University School of Textiles, Clemson Apparel Research, the University of Florida (Institute of Food and Agricultural Sciences), Florida A&M University/ Florida State University, the

National Institute of Automotive Service Excellence (ASE), the American Welding Society as well as Pittsburgh Paint and Glass Co. (PPG).

Postrelease Support

Prior to release, inmate workers receive job readiness training and are advised to contact the PRIDE job developers, using a toll-free number provided. Upon release, referrals and job interviews are scheduled for the ex-offenders, with an emphasis on matching the job with job training received at PRIDE. Critical transitional support such as housing, transportation, clothing, and tools (if needed) are provided to the ex-offenders.

PRIDE Prison Industry Consistently Wins International Awards

For the past four years PRIDE's Cross City Screen Printing Industry has competed with over 200 companies from 32 countries in an international screen printing contest. To date, the inmate workers' award-winning samples have garnered seven top awards: three First Place (Golden Squeegee Awards), two Second Place (Silver Squeegee Awards), and two Third Place (Bronze Squeegee Awards). PRIDE has been the only prison-based industry to enter this competition.

Economic Impact

PRIDE has averaged $36 to $40 million in economic impact each year through PRIDE staff payroll and purchases of goods and services from over 3,500 Florida-based companies. This impact on the state is valued annually between $60 to $80 million, based on the 1.2 to 2 multiplier effect.

Recommittment Study

A four-year tracking study shows that of the 4,710 PRIDE inmate workers released into the community, 719 or 15.2 percent have returned to prison. Of the 4,710 inmates released, 2,068 inmates worked for PRIDE for six months or more. Only 230, or 11.1 percent of those were recommitted.

Source: Florida Department of Corrections. *1994–1995 Annual Report: The Guidebook to Corrections in Florida* (1995): 27.

Free Enterprise Model

Of the four organizational models, this model offers the most private sector autonomy. Business and employment decisions are made by the private sector employer and minimum or market wages are paid to the inmates who are typically charged for room and board (and restitution, in most cases). By the end of 1995, the Kansas DOC had nine free enterprise industries using 147 maximum-, medium-, and minimum-security inmates in four prisons (Figure 5–9). These industries are totally freestanding, profit-making organizations that can provide inmates with competitive labor market skills while providing the prison an independent source of revenue.

The Extent of Inmate Labor Privatization

In Fiscal Year 1996, 48 DOCs reported total DOC-operated industry sales of $1.4 billion. Privately operated prison industry sales were $6.3 million in four DOCs. Thirty-two DOC-operated programs reported an average profit of $1,509,547. Seven DOCs lost $2.9 million. Profits and losses ranged from a high of $12.1 million profit at the Federal Bureau of Prisons to a loss of $894,782 in Illinois (Camp and Camp, 1997:85).

The fact that Correctional Industries can be a losing proposition should sound a cau-

COMPANY NAME	TYPE BUSINESS	NO. INMATE EMPLOYEES	LOCATION
Zephyr Products, Inc.	Metal Fabrication	25	Leavenworth
Heatron Inc.	Industrial Heating Elements	43	Leavenworth
Henke Inc.	Manufacture Snow Plows	12	Leavenworth
Jensen Engineering Inc.	Computer Assisted Drafting	5	Lansing
Hearts Designs Inc.	Childrens Clothing	15	Lansing
United Rotary Brush Inc.	Street Sweeper Brushes	4	Lansing
Impact Design Inc.	Embroider Sports Wear	13	Lansing
Michaud Cosmetics Inc.	Hotel Amenities	7	Topeka
Century Manufacturing Inc.	Lucite Products	23	Ellsworth
TOTAL		147	

FIGURE 5–9   Private Industries Employment. Source: Kansas Department of Corrections. *Corrections Briefing Report* (1996): 9.4.

tionary note. For the advocates of the privatization of inmate labor, however, there are four selling points. First, correctional managers gain access to private-sector enterprise and the presence of private-sector personnel helps to "normalize" prison life. Second, inmates can provide financial support to their families while learning skills to increase future employability. Third, taxpayers benefit from inmate payment of room and board and of state and federal income taxes, which contribute to general revenues and fund special programs such as victim restitution. Fourth, private-sector businesses facing overseas competition gain a valuable labor resource (Auerbach et al., 1988:2).

However, there are constraints on the privatization of inmate labor that are imposed by public policy concerns and the prison's internal environment.

Public Policy Constraints on the Privatization of Inmate Labor

Public policy makers have not always encouraged the privatization of inmate labor. Since 1870 there have been periods of strenuous public and organized labor opposition to the use of inmate labor because of fears that it would render free world workers unable to compete in a free market. Between 1801 and World War II, there was a steady increase in the passage of legislation

restricting prison industry markets (Auerbach et al., 1988:71) such as the 1929 Hawes-Cooper Act, which effectively prohibited the sale of inmate made goods because of fears that free world labor could not compete with inmate labor.

However, because of the lobbying of correctional managers and the private sector, the U.S. Congress relaxed prohibitions against the use of inmate labor in the 1960s through passage of the Department of Labor's Manpower Development Training Act (MDTA), which allowed inmates the opportunity for education, training, and meaningful work. In 1979, President Carter signed the Prison Industries Enhancement Act, which was amended in 1984 as the Justice Assistance Act. This legislation continued to exempt prison industries from federal restraints and encouraged private sector involvement. As a result, by 1992 there were 23 states involved in pilot projects linking corrections and the private sector, collectively known as the Prison Industry Enhancement (PIE) project (Dwyer and McNally, 1994:283–284).

Such pilot projects, however, fail to approximate the real labor world in one very important respect. Economic rewards are the most common incentive to productive labor in the community. Gordon Hawkins (1983) has observed that the public is strongly opposed to paying inmates minimum or market wages and he considers this "principle of least eligibility" to be the most significant obstacle to the development of productive prison labor programs. Today, very few inmates receive even the minimum wage for their labor. The average daily wage ranges from $1.86 to $7.26 in the DOC-operated industry, $28.34 to $37.86 in the privately operated industry, and $0.85 to $4.03 in the DOC-operated nonindustry (Camp and Camp, 1997:89). Clearly, inmates are not paid a free market wage. To do so would significantly increase the cost of corrections and reduce profits.

Internal Prison Constraints on the Privatization of Inmate Labor

Even when public policy makers endorse the concept of using inmate labor for revenue enhancement, there are further constraints imposed by the internal environment of the prison. The first such constraint is that older prisons lack the physical space in which to locate and operate a profitable correctional industry; the costs of modifying the physical plant would far outweigh the economic benefits to be derived from an industry. In addition, rural prisons may experience significant problems in the transportation of raw materials and finished products that make it difficult to keep manufacturing costs at a reasonable level. However, even in newer prisons designed with inmate labor in mind, there are other significant internal constraints.

Private employers require a work force that can spend eight hours a day on the job. In prisons, the work day can be interrupted by regular counts, unannounced contraband searches of the work site, escapes and the subsequent lockdown of the entire prison, and callouts for visits and medical, education, religious, or counseling sessions. Inmates can be transferred to another prison, placed in a disciplinary unit because of rule infractions, or simply quit work. Inmate turnover rates far exceed those of private industry and it is difficult to

attract and keep competent civilian supervisors in a prison work environment (U.S. General Accounting Office, 1982).

Further, there can also exist managerial resistance, especially if the managers have no prior experience with industry. The goals of operating a prison and the goals of a for-profit company are not complementary. Correctional managers are not accustomed to being judged by profit and loss statements. In addition, security must always be a priority. Increased inmate activity within the prison, access to tools and raw materials that can easily be converted into weapons, presence of large groups of inmates in industrial shops where flammable materials are readily available, and the constant entrance and exit of vehicles carrying the raw materials and finished products necessary for a business raise a variety of security concerns for even the most progressive manager.

Kinkade and Leone (1992:58–65), in a study of 699 correctional managers, found that the managers with the greatest number of years of correctional experience were least likely to favor the use of inmate labor for profit. The managers who accepted this approach preferred the governmental use model. Correctional managers were also generally opposed to the private management of general inmate populations but did support private management of such special-need offenders as drunk drivers and illegal aliens.

Taken together, privatization-related cost reduction and revenue-enhancement strategies can help achieve fiscal conservatism. But privatization is not without controversy.

THE PRIVATIZATION CONTROVERSY

Privatization, especially total services privatization, constitutes a major shift in correctional behavior. It permits the external environment to become involved in the daily operation of a critical public sector function. Before correctional managers embrace privatization there are serious issues that they must explore. Durham (1994) identifies eight major issues: the right to punish, the profit motive, legal liability, actuality of cost savings, quality of services, governmental dependency, encouragement of excessive use of incarceration, and abuse of inmates. These issues are best understood as questions:

1. Is the right and power to punish offenders exclusively reserved to the government or can it be delegated to private individuals?
2. Is government legally liable for the mistakes of private correctional managers who are guilty of mismanagement?
3. Are correctional services a legitimate source of profit?
4. Is privatization truly cost-effective?
5. Will the quality of services be diminished by cost cutting in the name of profits?
6. What happens if government becomes dependent on a private company that later goes bankrupt?
7. Will profitability encourage the excessive use of incarceration because it is good for business?
8. Will the abuse of inmates occur more frequently in private prisons?

These questions can be consolidated into one major concern: Does privatization serve the public good? The expansion of total services privatization has been limited because many elected officials and correctional managers are not yet confident of the answer to this question. Durham's questions can be grouped into constitutional issues, safety issues, and fiscal issues.

Is Privatization Constitutional?

Durham's first two questions raise constitutional issues: Is it constitutional to delegate correctional functions to private corporations? The U.S. Supreme Court has not established a clear answer to the question of whether correctional functions can be transferred to the private sector (Robbins, 1995:592–594). Absent a specific legislative or legal prohibition against such delegation, many states have proceeded with privatization initiatives. This may not be as risky as it sounds because the U.S. Supreme Court has not invalidated any governmental delegation of authority to the private sector in more than 50 years (Robbins, 1995:593).

Another constitutional question asks whether private corrections employees are operating "under the color of state law." Put another way, can private corporations be sued because of their policies or the actions of their employees? Citing a series of U.S. Supreme Court decisions, Robbins (1995:589–592) has concluded that from a constitutional perspective a private corrections corporation is considered to be the equivalent of a governmental agency for the purposes of legal liability and action. The reasoning of the Court has consistently been that to say otherwise would allow government to avoid its constitutional obligations to offenders simply by delegating governmental functions to the private sector.

Durham's third question concerning the right of private corporations to make a profit off of offenders has received no constitutional objection. There is no legal objection to earning a profit as long as private sector behavior is legal.

Is Private Corrections Safe?

This issue encompasses Durham's questions 5 and 8. To date, the answer to these questions has been mixed. There have been incidents that have raised concern. For example, a 1995 riot at an Immigration and Naturalization Service (INS) detention center for illegal immigrants in Elizabeth, New Jersey, injured 20 detainees and produced $100,000 in property damages. The riot's causes included a corporate policy of using untrained, poorly paid staff, serving substandard meals to inmates, and shackling detainees in leg irons when they met with their attorneys (Donziger, 1997:329–330).

Offering more encouragement is a study that compared a private women's prison in

New Mexico to a state and federal women's prison on the basis of eight dimensions of confinement: security, safety, order, care, activity, justice, conditions, and management. "The private prison out-performed the state and federal prisons, often by quite substantial margins, across nearly all dimensions" (Logan, 1992:601). Suggested explanations for the superior performance of the private prison included (1) a well-designed facility, (2) greater operational and managerial flexibility, (3) decentralized authority, (4) higher morale, enthusiasm, and sense of ownership among line staff, (5) greater managerial experience and leadership, and (6) strict "by the book" control of inmates (Logan, 1992:602).

In his review of private corrections, Donziger (1997:330) concludes that "it appears that some private corrections companies manage inmates better than some state-run facilities." But are they more cost-effective?

Is Private Corrections More Cost-Effective?

This issue involves Durham's fourth question. Private correctional facilities claim to operate with a cost savings of 10 percent to 20 percent over state-operated facilities (Donziger, 1997:328). Is this statement supported by experience and research? The Louisiana DOC claims to be saving $1 million a year through contracts with Wackenhut Corporation and CCA. Wackenhut reportedly spends $24.52 per day while CCA spends $25.41 and the state spends $25.92 (Fields, 1996:3A). In 1986, Kentucky saved $400,000 a year by hiring CCA to manage the Marion Adjustment Center (Bryce, 1993). In a survey of correctional experience with privatization, state DOCs reported that contracted services were cost-effective, that the agencies could not provide them at a similar cost, and that expansion plans were being developed (Camp and Camp, 1985). Logically, the ability of private contractors to use nonunion labor and to bypass the time-consuming, cumbersome bid processes that public correctional organizations are bound by should effectively reduce

costs. And, as one private contractor has noted: "[T]he contractor has an investment in providing services in the most cost-effective, program-efficient manner possible because its business future depends on successful and credible service delivery" (Cotton, 1995:80).

This logic is not accepted by everybody. For example, in 1991, the American Jail Association went on record as being opposed to the privatization of jails. Among the concerns cited was the belief that private jails are actually more expensive than public jails (American Jail Association, 1991).

Durham's questions 6 and 7—concerning the possibility of governmental dependency on private corporations and the profitability of those corporations encouraging the excessive use of incarceration—remain to be addressed as private corrections continues to expand. However, these questions deserve serious study. If private corrections firms lobby for legislation that has the practical effect of increasing the number of offenders under correctional supervision, or go bankrupt and leave correctional managers with limited ability to immediately restore services, the future problems of correctional managers will be immeasurably increased.

THE CORRECTIONAL MANAGER'S ROLE IN EFFECTIVE PRIVATIZATION

Because of the increasing use of privatization, many DOCs have increased their technostructure by adding a Privatization Office. Top managers have a responsibility to ensure that the allocation of financial and technological resources is sufficient for support staff and technostructure employees to gather the information, and conduct the detailed analysis, necessary for managers to decide if specific correctional services should be privatized. The budget process can provide a realistic assessment of the cost savings a private contractor can provide.

Once a service has been targeted for privatization, the manager must make available an RFP to every potential bidder. An example of an effective RFP is found in the Alabama DOC's 1991 RFP for comprehensive inmate health care services. This RFP reported the number of inmates to be serviced in each year of a four-year contract, requested the bidder's projected annual cost per inmate, monthly cost per inmate, total estimated cost of the contract by year, and the total estimated cost of the contract over its life. The RFP contained 12 pages of DOC requirements and 59 pages of federal and state law and court rulings governing the provision of Alabama inmate health care services. Each bidder was required to post a $250,000 Guarantee of Good Faith as a show of financial stability. The time and date for a Bidder's Conference was provided (Alabama Department of Corrections, 1991).

Each submitted bid must be thoroughly reviewed by Central Office and field staff to determine if it meets the requirements of the RFP. Although the lowest bid is the one that is most preferred, the selected contractor must have a proven track record. Many managers ask for a list of current and previous contracts so they can verify previous contractor performance. After contractor selection, the RFP becomes the foundation for the legal contract between corrections and contractor.

After the contract has been signed by both parties, there must be a series of start-up meetings in which Central Office and field staff work with the contractor to define and resolve as many potential problems as possible. Once the actual work is under way, quarterly reports of performance submitted by the contractor must be carefully reviewed by Central Office and field staff responsible for contract monitoring. In addition, frequent unannounced on-site inspections should be conducted to ensure that what is on the quarterly reports truly reflects performance. Any deviation from the contract must be immediately addressed. Every contract must provide that the DOC can terminate services if contractor performance is unacceptable.

Privatization is likely to be the wave of the future in corrections. The forces of fiscal conservatism are powerful because the ability of the community to continue to fund the ever-growing correctional budget is limited. The correctional manager philosophically opposed to privatization will not be able to avoid it. Therefore, correctional managers have the responsibility to ensure that the privatization of correctional services is properly implemented and the activities of private corrections' employees are carefully monitored.

SUMMARY

The requirements of fiscal conservatism confronting today's correctional managers are formidable. Unable to control the rate of commitment of new inmates to prison, correctional managers are still expected to live within the boundaries of budgets that, despite a phenomenal rate of growth, never seem to be quite large enough. Cost-minimization strategies located in the internal and external environment of corrections are helping corrections meet the challenges of fiscal conservatism. The use of these strategies is sometimes influenced by a variety of special interests groups that will be discussed in the next chapter. Of particular importance are public employee unions and the media.

Discussion Questions

1. What do the three cost-minimization strategies have in common? How do they differ?
2. How effective will cost-minimization strategies be if sentencing reforms are not modified?
3. What is the role of technology in fiscal conservatism?
4. What are the opportunities and the risks associated with the privatization of correctional services?
5. What is the role of the correctional manager in achieving effective privatization?

Critical Analysis Exercise: Inmate Labor Versus Free World Labor

The December 9, 1996, issue of *U.S. News and World Report* presented an article with the provocative title of "Are Prisoners Stealing Your Job?" This article reported on the use of inmate labor by private manufacturers who have located their factories behind prison walls. Examples cited included inmates wrapping software for Microsoft in Washington, making lingerie for Victoria's Secret and graduation gowns for Jostens in South Carolina, making IBM electronic circuit boards in Texas, taking TWA airline phone reservations in California, and marketing a line of blue jeans in Oregon with the slogan: "Made on the inside to be worn on the Outside." The article ended with the statement:

As prison labor becomes more widespread, the bigger concern is that inmates will begin to steal—jobs, that is. Reports that companies are leaving the outside world to set up prison factories could leave American workers wondering if they have to go to prison to find work. After all, 20 years with hard labor—and pay—might not sound so bad to some jobless souls on the outside (Cohen, 1996:67).

Critical Analysis Questions

1. What official and operative goals are served by private-sector employment of inmates?
2. Are there public benefits from the employment of inmates? If your answer is yes, what are these benefits?
3. Can public harm result from private companies employing inmates in jobs like reservation clerks? If so, what type of harm? How can managers minimize the possibility of such harm?
4. What would be the consequences of not allowing correctional industries to expand into the private-sector market?
5. What would be the most likely consequences of abolishing privatization programs?
6. Should inmates employed by correctional industries be paid the same wage as employees in the private sector? What are the pro and con arguments?
7. Is there a moral argument for the privatization of inmate labor? If so, what is it?

6

The Special Interests Environment of Corrections

Learning Objectives

After completing this chapter, you should be able to:

- Summarize the influence of quasi-judicial, public interest, and single-interest organizations on correctional behavior.
- Define the major components of the Americans with Disabilities Act and establish its influence on organizational behavior.
- Describe the relationship between the media and corrections.
- Outline the most effective managerial strategies for developing a positive relationship with the media.
- Define the role of public employee unions in correctional policy formulation.
- Explain the evolution of Victim Services and its impact on the organizational structure.
- Describe the role of private corrections corporations in the formulation of corrections-related public policy.
- Contrast Pre-DOC managerial goals with DOC managerial goals.

Key Terms and Concepts

Quasi-Judicial Regulatory Agencies
OSHA
Civil Rights Act of 1964
Americans with Disabilities Act Access to Public Services
Pre-employment Offer
Gratuitous Vilification
News Media Communication Strategies
Public Employee Unions
Collective Bargaining Agreement
Privatization
Managerial Goals
EPA
Civil Service System
Equal Employment Opportunity
ADA Compliance
Reasonable Accommodation
Entertainment Media
Public Information Officer
Single-Interest Organizations
Collective Bargaining
Victim Services Unit
Iron Triangle

Given that the United States is a pluralistic and geographically diverse country, the public policy process is designed to discourage any group or small number of groups from dominating the process while encouraging a high level of interaction among different individuals, groups, and organizations.

Barry Hancock and Paul Sharp

Profile: The Evolution of Correctional Health Care Standards

In 1870, the Congress on Penitentiary and Reformatory Discipline promulgated the first set of corrections standards: the Declaration of Principles. Principle 33 specified that adequate medical services should be provided to inmates, but Pre-DOC correctional managers generally failed to comply with this standard. DOC Corrections brought about a renewed interest in correctional health care:

1966—The American Correctional Association (ACA) published an update of the 1870 Declaration of Principles, entitled Standards for Correctional Institutions.

1968—Correctional managers, motivated by a growing internal movement to professionalize corrections, created the Project on Self-Evaluation and Accreditation to develop standards, including medical, for correctional organizations.

1972—The American Medical Association (AMA) conducted a major study of jail health care delivery systems.

1974—The Commission of Accreditation for Corrections was established by the ACA.

1975—The Law Enforcement Assistance Administration (LEAA) published a manual, *Prescriptive Package, Health Care in Correctional Institutions,* the most comprehensive description of an adequate correctional health care program.

1975—The American Correctional Health Services Association (ACHSA) was organized.

1976—The AMA published *Standards for the Accreditation of Medical Care and Health Services in Jails.* These standards also applied to prisons and were used in accreditation.

1976—The American Public Health Association published *Standards for Correctional Health Care.*

1976—The AMA granted accreditation to 16 jails in six states.

1977—The Commission of Accreditation published a comprehensive set of standards for jail and prison operations. Included in those standards were health care standards.

1977—The American Bar Association (ABA) published a set of standards for correctional health care.

1978—The LEAA awarded the Michigan DOC a $1 million grant to develop a prison health care program. The program produced 19 resource manuals for use by correctional organizations throughout the United States.

1978—The U.S. General Accounting Office (GAO) published a report that recommended the need to coordinate federal efforts to improve medical and dental care in jails and prisons.

1979—The GAO report was endorsed by the American Public Health Association.

1982—The AMA accredited the Georgia State Prison in Reidsville.

1982—The National Commission on Correctional Health Care (NCCHC) was established as a separate organization from the AMA.

1995—The NCCHC had accredited health care systems in over 350 facilities, including jails and prisons (Hemmons, 1997:1–2).

The existence and activities of special interest organizations in the external environment cannot be ignored by correctional managers. As the chapter epigraph suggests, corrections-related public policy formulation is a process that can have many participants. It is not just the province of politicians being advised by correctional managers. Special interest organizations help shape organizational behavior by making their views known during the debates that are part of the process of public policy formulation. The above Profile presents an example of how correctional behavior can be shaped by governmental and special interest organizations concerned about a specific correctional function, such as the delivery of inmate health care services. However, special interest views incorporated into public policy not directed exclusively at corrections can also impact on correctional behavior, as we will see in our discussion of the Americans with Disabilities Act. Special interest perspectives are important because their incorporation into public policy frequently limits the use of correctional managers' discretion, especially in the critical areas of personnel practices and offender management, and can promote changes in organizational structure. Of greatest relevance to corrections are the quasi-judicial government regulatory agencies that ensure compliance with legislation, public interest organizations such as the media, single-interest organizations such as public employee unions and victim's rights groups, and private corrections corporations. Correctional managers must be sensitive to the agendas of all of these organizations when engaging in environmental design.

QUASI-JUDICIAL GOVERNMENT REGULATORY AGENCIES

In Chapter 5, the impact of legislative sentencing and parole reform on corrections was discussed. Legislative bodies also pass legislation designed to assist selected categories of citizens (such as those with disabilities) and the interaction between the legislative and executive branches of government have produced a complex system of quasi-judicial regulatory agencies that have the responsibility of ensuring that government agencies are in full compliance with applicable legislation. These agencies are empowered to regulate the behavior of government agencies by monitoring that behavior, investigating complaints, and ordering that inappropriate policies be changed. During Pre-DOC Corrections, the autocratic wardens were exempt from legislation governing other types of organizations, such as schools and hospitals. That exemption no longer exists.

Two important quasi-judicial regulatory agencies are the Environmental Protection Agency (EPA) and the Occupational Safety and Health Administration (OSHA). The EPA monitors and enforces compliance with environmental laws and has the authority to issue corrective orders and impose penalties if environmental laws are being violated. OSHA requires employers to maintain a workplace free of recognized hazards that are likely to cause serious injury or death to workers (Hood and Hardy,

1983:155). Federal and state OSHA inspectors have the power to enter and inspect the workplace and issue citations, corrective orders, and establish penalties.

Both EPA and OSHA can influence the creation of correctional operative goals. For example, corrections' official goal of providing a safe and humane environment in a prison will be declared unmet if an OSHA inspector discovers asbestos in a prison's cellblocks. The resulting corrective order will mandate that the asbestos be removed because it constitutes a health threat. This corrective order requires the superintendent to create the operative goal of removing asbestos from all cellblocks, a process that is time-consuming, expensive, and often involves the entrance of outside contractors into the prison. Such a process is generally disruptive to the orderly operation of the prison, but by order must be undertaken. EPA representatives will be concerned about the possibility of asbestos getting in the air and acting as a form of air pollution during the removal process. Thus, the correctional managers charged with renovating the old cellblocks will find their procedures being monitored by both OSHA and EPA inspectors. This does not have to be an adversarial relationship. Agencies such as EPA and OSHA are a valuable resource for correctional managers.

Quasi-judicial regulatory agencies also ensure compliance with legislation governing the managerial functions of hiring, promoting, and dismissing employees. Of greatest importance in this area are federal and state Civil Service systems.

Civil Service System

When Pre-DOC Corrections was the corrections model, the hiring and promotion of correctional employees was more often a function of political patronage—party loyalty, personal friendship, or family loyalty—than it was merit. But patronage systems are disruptive because staff can change as often as the political power, or the warden, changes. Recognizing the need for employee stability as a foundation for encouraging accountability and professionalism in corrections, post–World War II government emphasized the replacement of patronage systems with Civil Service divisions designed to severely limit the ability of the autocratic wardens to arbitrarily hire, promote, and fire. Civil Service Commissions have the responsibility of ensuring that government employment decision are based on considerations of merit and fitness for the job. For bureaucratic managers, hiring is a complex process of adhering to written, standardized procedures set by Civil Service divisions that have the legal authority to determine objective, standardized minimum education and experience qualifications for positions, advertise vacancies, administer objective pre-employment and promotion examinations, develop applicant interview standards and rules, enforce legal requirements for hiring based on examination performance, and establish rules for employee promotion and dismissal. Personnel management practices must be in compliance with established policy, regulations, and rules that , if violated, can subject the manager to investigation and administrative discipline.

The Civil Service systems do more than standardize hiring, promotion, and dismissal policies for all applicants. They specifically safeguard the rights of groups of individuals that Pre-DOC managers had systemically excluded from employment, as discussed in the next section.

CIVIL RIGHTS ACT OF 1964

While it is not a corrections-specific piece of legislation (like parole reform), corrections is still covered by the provisions of the Civil Rights Act of 1964, which makes Civil Service divisions responsible for ensuring that correctional managers do not discriminate against specific groups of individuals. The Act makes it illegal to deny employment on the basis of race, color, religion, age, national origin, and gender, and resulted in the creation of Affirmative Action programs monitored by Civil Service. All DOCs now issue Equal Employment Opportunity (EEO) policy statements that forbid employment discrimination. A typical EEO policy statement is that of the Arkansas DOC:

The ADC is an equal opportunity employer providing equal employment opportunities without regard to race, color, sex, religion, national origin, age, disability, or veteran status. This policy and practice relates to all phases of employment including, but not limited to: recruiting, hiring, placement, promotion, transfer, lay-off, recall, termination, rates of pay or other forms of compensation, training, use of all facilities, and participation in all Department sponsored employee activities and programs. All members of ADC management staff are familiar with this statement of policy, the philosophy behind it, and their responsibility to apply these principles in good faith for meaningful progress in the utilization of minorities and women (Arkansas Department of Corrections, 1996:39).

Implementation of EEO policy is the responsibility of field and Central Office personnel officers. Allegations of EEO violation will be investigated by internal affairs units and, if found to be true, the responsible managers and/or employees can be subjected to disciplinary action, including suspension and dismissal.

But minorities were not the only groups excluded from corrections in the Pre-DOC era. Individuals with disabilities were also excluded. This practice was ended by a second important piece of legislation, which we consider next.

AMERICANS WITH DISABILITIES ACT OF 1990

The Americans with Disabilities Act (ADA), which aims to protect the approximately 43 million Americans who have some form of disability, has been labeled the first major civil rights legislation in 30 years (Morton and

Anderson, 1996:86). The ADA defines disability as a physical or mental impairment that substantially limits one or more major life activities: caring for oneself, walking, seeing, hearing, performing manual tasks, speaking, learning, working, and breathing (Appel, 1995:85). ADA requirements are applicable to corrections because correctional employees and offenders are not exempt from having a disability. For corrections, ADA covers physical plant structure and design, personnel practices, and inmate access to programs.

Physical Access to Public-Sector Services

The first ADA requirement is that individuals with disabilities must have physical access to public-sector services. The Architectural and Transportation Barriers Compliance Board has issued guidelines, which took effect on June 20, 1994, to the Department of Justice and the Department of Transportation establishing standards for state and local government buildings subject to the ADA. Section 12 of these standards covers specific prison issues such as special inmate entrances, door hardware, glazing, escorted exit routes, cell design and hardware, and the number of cells that must be disability accessible.

Title I of the ADA presents staff accessibilty requirements. Title II presents standards for inmate and public accessibility to governmental services. These standards are quite specific. For example, doors to program areas and employee officces "must have a clear travel space of at least 32 inches wide and open at least 90 degrees, with a threshold no higher than a half inch" (Appel, 1995:85). The precise nature of the accessibility standards for which correctional managers are responsible is illustrated in Box 6–1.

both inmates and visitors. If the visiting area serves only nonaccessible inmate cells or rooms, only the visitor's side needs to be accessible. To be accessible, the cubicles must have 27 to 29 inches of clearance for knee space, be at least 36 inches wide and have at least 8 inches of counter space extending from the partition between inmate and visitor. In cubicles where there is a solid partition or security glazing separating the inmate from the visitor, there must be a method to facilitate voice communications. These methods may include grills, talk-through baffles, intercoms, or telephone handset devices and must be at a height accessible to both those in wheelchairs and those who have difficulty bending or stooping. If telephone devices are used, at least one must be equipped with volume controls. For contact visiting areas, fixed seating should be designed for ease of wheelchair transfer and must be 17 to 19 inches off the floor. If moveable seating is provided, wheelchairs can be substituted and any tables must have 27 to 29 inches of clear knee space. All visiting areas must be located on an accessible route from the entrance of the facility. If that route contains a fixed metal detector, it must be at least 32 inches wide. Better yet, hand-held devices should be used because metal wheelchairs (and other types of metal appliances that may be used) will set off metal detectors. If the accessible route to the visiting area includes log-in counters, locker rooms, vending machine areas, or waiting areas, they must also meet ADA standards for such areas.

Alan Appel. "Requirements and Rewards of the Americans with Disabilities Act." *Corrections Today* 57(2) (1995): 85–86. Reprinted with permission of the American Correctional Association, Lanham, MD.

BOX 6–1 ADA DESIGN OF THE INMATE VISITING ROOM

For noncontact visiting, at least 5 percent, but no fewer than one, of the cubicles must be accessible for

Cost of ADA Compliance For correctional managers, specific requirements like those presented in Box 6.1 have affected staff training (Figures 6–1 through 6–3) and have raised two concerns. First, what will be the financial cost of complying with ADA requirements? A partial answer comes from the Philadelphia County Prison system. For a 192-bed dormitory-style facility, the estimated cost of ADA compliance is 3.6 percent of the total construction costs. For a 2,000-bed intake and close-custody facility, the estimated cost of ADA compliance is 0.83 percent of the total construction costs (Appel, 1995:85).

FIGURE 6–1   Given the complexity of ADA rules and regulations, extensive training of managers and line staff is critical. Courtesy of Ohio Department of Rehabilitation and Correction.

FIGURE 6–2   Courtesy of Ohio Department of Rehabilitation and Correction.

FIGURE 6–3   Courtesy of Ohio Department of Rehabilitation and Correction.

Cost is such a particularly perplexing problem for small-jail managers. Fearful that their limited budgets will not cover the cost of ADA modifications, that some of them are pursuing a strategy of putting off ADA activities until they can build a new jail (Thompson and Ridlon, 1995). Correctional managers must remember that for facilities constructed or renovated before January 26, 1992, structural changes are required only when there is no other way to make programs accessible. Historic facilities may be exempt from the requirement to make changes (Sickle, 1995:106). The second question involves safety and security concerns. Can ADA-required modifications be accomplished without creating an undue administrative burden or security risk? This raises the issue of reasonable accommodation.

Reasonable Accommodation

According to the ADA, a reasonable accommodation

means making already existing facilities readily accessible to and usable by individuals with disabilities; job restructuring, part-time or mod-

ified work schedules, reassignment to a vacant position, acquiring or modifying equipment or devices; appropriately adjusting or modifying examinations, training materials, or policies; and providing qualified readers or interpreters; as well as other similar accommodations for individuals (Coleman and Furr, 1992:8).

A reasonable accommodation does not include modifications that would directly threaten the safety of the employee or others, or cause an undue or administrative hardship. Correctional managers frequently envision that efforts to achieve a reasonable accommodation will require massive changes that will create a nightmare of paperwork and physical plant changes. These fears are often groundless. For example, a wheelchair-bound employee assigned to work in a prison control room cannot enter the control room if it is three steps above the floor. The simple, and relatively inexpensive, solution is to install a ramp or lift to allow the employee access to the control room (Collins, 1996:303).

Bernsen and Gauger (1995) note that some ADA requirements have the potential to create a security risk. For example, lever-type door handles can be broken off and used as weapons; grab bars can be used for assault or suicide. To reduce the possibility of such an event, levers and bars must be fastened to a solid structure as securely as possible. In addition, cells set aside for inmates with disabilities must be on an accessible path of travel so effective fire evacuation is possible.

So far, we have discussed the impact of the ADA on the physical environment of corrections. However, the ADA has an even greater impact on management personnel policies and practices.

Employee Hiring Practices

The ADA specifically states that when engaging in personnel functions, employers are prohibited from refusing to hire, or promote, an individual with a disability when that individual is otherwise qualified for the job. Interviewers are permitted to ask an applicant about their ability to perform a job "but cannot ask about disabilities or conduct tests that tend to screen out individuals with disabilities" (Coleman and Furr, 1992:6–7). The development of acceptable interview questions can be a very complicated process and this personnel function is a potential source of litigation. The content of interview questions is constantly being redefined as case law concerning the ADA evolves. The following guidelines should be followed by Personnel Directors as they standardize interview questions:

1. The employer may ask the individual whether he or she can perform the essential functions of the job.

2. The employer cannot ask questions about disability on application forms or at interviews, and an identified disability can be discussed only after a formal job offer (usually referred to as a conditional offer of employment, pre-offer, or pre-employment offer) has been made to the individual, and even then only in reference to the individual's ability to perform the job.

3. The employer cannot engage in any pre-offer activities that are designed to detect hidden disabilities, such as hearing impairment, epilepsy, or mental illness.

4. If there is a disability known to the employers, they may ask specifically how the individual can perform the functions of the job and whether an accommodation will be needed. The nature of the required accommodation can be discussed; however, the focus of the interview must be on the individual's ability to perform the essential functions of the job, not on the disability.

But why must an individual with a disability be hired? The goal of the ADA is to bring into the work force those citizens who have historically been discriminated against by traditional employment practices that automatically assumed that the disabled cannot be productive employees. The ADA provides an access to those individuals who can be productive and this access should benefit both employee and employer. Put more simply, it is now wrong to discriminate against individuals who are different from the majority. This leads to the issue of how to structure the hiring process so that it is not discriminatory. We begin with the issue of employee medical tests as an element in the determination of applicant ability to perform the job.

Definition of Medical Test
The ADA states that a job offer may be conditioned on the results of a job performance-related medical examination only if it is required of every new employee in the job category. The test should be related to the essential functions of the job and have a clear organizational necessity. The applicant cannot be questioned about prior or current legal drug use if doing so would lead the applicant to reveal the existence, nature, or severity of a disability. The issue of pre-employment drug and alcohol testing is particularly complex and is considered more fully below.

Psychological exams that could provide evidence of a psychological disorder are not permitted at the pre-employment offer stage, but tests that measure the ability to perform the job are permitted. Polygraph exams are not addressed by the ADA, but questions that would elicit the existence or nature of a disability, such as "Do you have any mental disorders?" would not be permissible unless a conditional offer of employment had been made. Background checks that involve disability-related injuries are prohibited, but checks of high school and college transcripts, credit checks, and state police and FBI checks are allowed. Job-related vision tests are permitted as long as they are not used to establish evidence of a medical disability.

Alcohol and Illegal Drugs

There is a great deal of confusion about the application of the ADA to individuals using illegal drugs and individuals who are alcoholics. The ADA carefully defines controlled substances and the illegal use of drugs by references to the Controlled Substances Act and other provisions of federal law, but it does not define "alcoholic, alcoholism, or alcohol addiction" (Shaw, MacGillis, and Dvorchik, 1994). The ADA exempts current illegal drug users from protection of the law. Those individuals who are currently using illegal drugs can be refused employment or fired. The ADA does not prevent employers from testing applicants or employees for current illegal drug use or from making employment decisions based on verifiable results. A test for the illegal use of drugs is not considered a medical examination under ADA rules; therefore, it is not a prohibited medical examination. However, if the illegal drug user is no longer engaging in the illegal drug use and has successfully completed or is currently participating in a supervised rehabilitation program, or has been certified as rehabilitated, that individual is considered an individual with a disability (Shaw, MacGillis, and Dvorchik, 1994).

Testing for alcohol is not mentioned in the ADA (Bulmer, 1992); however, alcoholics are not excluded from ADA protection (Shaw, MacGillis, and Dvorchik, 1994). Individuals who are alcoholic are defined as suffering from an ADA-covered disability. They cannot be denied employment because of their alcoholism. But employers can hold the alcoholic to the same high performance standards as any other employee as long as they make a reasonable accommodation, such as providing Employee Assistance Programs (EAPs) that engage in "constructive confrontation." Such EAP strategies involve confronting employees who demonstrate unsatisfactory job performance and who are suspected of having problems with alcohol, spelling out the consequences of continued poor performance, and offering assistance in obtaining treatment for alcohol abuse (Sonnenstuhl, 1988).

Alcoholics can be subjected to discipline, including dismissal, if they violate organizational policies that forbid using alcohol on the job or being under the influence of alcohol at work, as long as these policies are applicable to every employee, not just the alcoholic (Shaw, MacGillis, and Dvorchik, 1994). The ADA also permits employers to consider their obligation to ensure workplace safety in determining if an alcoholic is qualified for a position. That is, the employer may consider whether the alcoholic poses a "direct threat to the health or safety of themselves or others" (Federal Register, 1991). The determination of "direct threat" involves a process of (1) identification of significant risk of substantial harm; (2) identification of the specific risk factor, which must be a current risk, not one that is speculative or remote; (3) assessment of risk that is based upon objective medical or other factual evidence regarding a particular individual; and (d) even if genuine significant risk of substantial harm exists, consideration of how the risk can be eliminated or reduced below the level of a "direct threat" by reasonable accommodation (quoted in Shaw, MacGillis, and Dvorchik, 1994:113).

Conducting the Pre-offer Interview

Disability-related inquiries during the pre-employment offer interview are prohibited.

This can be a very complicated area and Personnel Department employees often require legal assistance in developing a standardized set of legal interview questions. For example, questions about why an applicant had an attendance problem with a former employer cannot be asked because it could elicit information about a disability. There can be no questions about an applicant's work compensation history or job-related injuries. Questions about why an applicant does not have a job-related license or certificate are permitted, however, and interviewers can ask about lifestyle, with some exceptions. For example, applicants can be asked if they eat three meals a day, but they cannot be asked if they eat small snacks at regular intervals because this can lead them to reveal a disability, such as diabetes. An applicant can be asked if they drink, but not how much because alcohol addiction is a disability (Rubin, 1995a:118–119). A basic rule of thumb is that if a pre-employment offer question could lead an applicant to reveal the existence or extent of a disability, the question should not be asked. For this reason, correctional managers must establish a policy of using standardized, pre-approved questions from which deviation is not permitted.

Inmate Access to Programming

Inmates with disabilities are not to be physically excluded from treatment programs because of their disability. If physical access to the program is the problem, then the ADA requires that the program site be moved to a more accessible location unless that would constitute an undue burden on the organization. If the disability affects the offender's ability to learn, then accommodations to enhance their ability to learn must be made as long as those accommodations do not significantly alter the program. Acceptable accommodations include the use of computers, sign language interpreters, Braille books, and programs designed to permit early parole (Rubin, 1995a:120).

MANAGERIAL RESPONSE TO THE AMERICANS WITH DISABILITIES ACT

Managers may believe that compliance with specific ADA standards will create an administrative burden that they cannot manage. When this occurs, correctional managers can legally challenge specific ADA standards and, by so doing, request the courts to determine issues of appropriate cost and impact on organizational effectiveness of the standard being contested. The effectiveness of ADA has been limited because the definition of disability is open-ended and terms such as "reasonable accommodation" are vague (Mishra, 1995).

It is up to the courts to settle many ADA-related issues. For example, in 1998, lawyers for the state of Pennsylvania took the issue of ADA applicability to state prisons to the U.S. Supreme Court in a case involving an inmate named Yeskey, who sued the Pennsylvania DOC on the grounds that denial of entrance into a boot camp because of his hypertension constitutes a violation of the ADA. Pennsylvania argued that the ADA was never intended to apply to prisons because it limits the powers of the state in the core function of running its prisons (Corrections Alert, 1998).

An area of particular concern for correctional managers has been the issue of the ADA and the mentally ill applicant or employee (see Box 6–2). And there are other situations where the ADA modifications may be felt to create too great a burden. However, Appel (1995:86) has argued that correctional managers have a professional responsibility to embrace ADA standards and plan to implement them as effectively as possible because the ADA is the law. The failure of correctional managers to abide by the law sends the wrong message to offenders, employees, and the community.

The U.S. Supreme Court agrees with Appel's position concerning ADA applicability to corrections. In response to *Pennsylvania Department of Corrections v. Yeskey,* the high court ruled that the ADA covers prisons:

In an unanimous opinion authored by Justice Antonin Scalia, the justices held first that the "public entity" term in the ADA clearly includes state prisons and prisoners within its coverage.

Then they flatly rejected the argument posed by Pennsylvania's attorneys that prison boot camps do not provide inmates with "benefits" to "programs, services] or activities" as further defined in the statute. "Modern prisons provide inmates with many recreational 'activities,' medical 'services,' and educational and vocational 'programs,' all of which 'benefit' the prisoners," Justice Scalia wrote. (*Corrections Professional* [1998]. "ADA Clearly Applies to Prisons, Supreme Court Rules: Physical and Program Accomodations Are Necessary." 3 [20]:1,8).

The impact of the high court's ruling on corrections has yet to be determined and many correctional managers are taking a wait-and-see approach. Reflective of this approach is the statement by Matt Davis, a spokesman for the Michigan DOC: "We're going to assess to see what's going on [before making any policy changes]. What we're trying to avoid is exorbitant costs" (quoted in *Corrections Professional* [1998]:8). The court did not address the question of whether the U.S. Congress exceeded its authority by stipulating that states cannot be immune from ADA lawsuits.

BOX 6–2 THE ADA AND MENTAL DISABILITY CLAIMS

Some disabilities are physical and obvious: a missing limb or blindness, for example. But other disabilities, such as a learning disability or mental illness, are not readily obvious. Many correctional managers have been concerned that the ADA will be used by unruly, disruptive, even violent employees and offenders as a mechanism for avoiding appropriate disciplinary action. For example, an otherwise acceptable employee diagnosed as suffering from depression or delusional paranoid disorder becomes angry, disruptive, even verbally and/or physically threatening to other employees, managers, and offenders. Can this type of employee be effectively disciplined, including termination, or will management's actions constitute a violation of the ADA because no reasonable accommodation was made for the mental illness? After all, the ADA is designed to protect the rights of individuals with psychiatric illnesses. This issue is made increasingly complicated by the fact that the handbook of mental disorders, the *Diagnostic and Statistical Manual,* now identifies more than 300 disorders, up from 106 just 18 years ago (Herbert, 1998:63).

Employer concerns about employee misuse of the ADA may be unfounded. In a brief review of relevant cases, Herbert (1998) noted that the courts appear to be moving in the direction of increasing employee accountability for their behavior rather than creating a new class of victims entitled to legal protection. Current legal interpretation appears to be saying that a psychiatric disability that interferes with the ability to function on the job, but does not persistently interfere with other major life activities, is validation that the individual is not "otherwise qualified for the job." As Herbert (1998:64) noted: "When it comes to dysfunction, judges are saying, 'Deal with it.'" Indeed, such behaviors as insubordination and the ability to get to work on time have been ruled to be employer-actionable offenses regardless of the cause of the behavior and, therefore, not eligible for ADA protection.

The issue of ADA protection for offenders with psychiatric illnesses may be more challenging. In 1997, a federal court ruled that the Pennsylvania DOC had violated an inmate's rights when they did not make reasonable accommodations for his Tourette's syndrome, a neurological disorder characterized by uncontrollable motor and verbal tics that occur at unpredictable times and may be misunderstood by other inmates. Nor did the prison accommodate the inmate's joint disease that prevented him from standing for long periods of time. The specific violations of the DOC were to deny the inmate a chair for his nonhandicapped cell after removing him from a previously assigned handicapped cell and to make him stand for counts. Furthermore, the inmate was disciplined for returning to the privacy of his cell when he was experiencing an episode of tics even though he had previously been authorized to do so by a physician (*Corrections Professional*, 1998:12). The courts may be more receptive to allegations of ADA violations from inmates because of their incarceration status.

The ADA can assist managers in helping inmates change their behavior by increasing inmate access to meaningful programs. Correctional managers can also use the ADA as a budget lever. That is, when submitting the annual budget proposal, they can emphasize that certain requests are based on an ADA requirement. This can help persuade the budget-approving authority to increase the budget.

Cost of Noncompliance

Noncompliance with the ADA can have adverse consequences. Applicants or employees who believe they have been discriminated against because of a disability may file a complaint with the Equal Employment Opportunities Commission (EEOC), which may investigate the complaint and try to resolve it through negotiation. If this fails, EEOC may file suit against the agency or issue a "right to sue" letter to the complainant. A court, if it decides in favor of the plaintiff, may award injunctive relief (reinstatement and back pay) and damages up to $300,000 for organizations with 500 or more employees (Collins, 1996:303). Offenders may also file litigation alleging disability-related discrimination. Whether the plaintiff is an inmate, employee, or applicant, if the court finds in favor of the plaintiff it may issue an injunction prohibiting the organization from continuing with a discriminatory practice, order reasonable accommodations (such as providing an interpreter for hearing-impaired inmates at disciplinary hearings), and order payment of the legal costs and compensatory damages for unlawful and intentional discrimination (Sickle, 1995:108).

Compliance and the Organizational Structure

The placement of individuals and departments in an organization chart reflect the importance of their functions to that organization. Note that in the Florida DOC (Figure 6–4) the Inspector General's Office and Legal Services, two departments that will play an important role in the investigation and review of AA and ADA violation allegations, are under the direct supervision of the Secretary. Thus, these departments, the functions they perform, and the legislative mandates they are empowered to enforce, are designated as important enough to receive the direct attention of the DOC Secretary.

PUBLIC INTEREST ORGANIZATIONS AND CORRECTIONS

Quasi-judicial regulatory agencies are not the only organizations that influence public

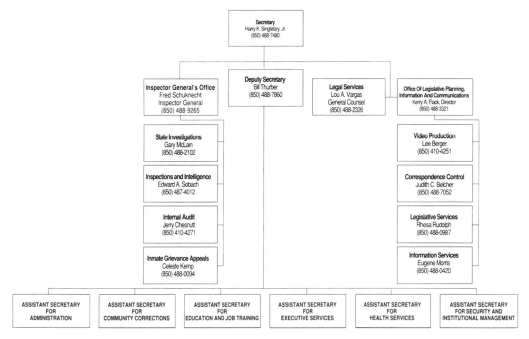

FIGURE 6–4 Department of Correction Organization Chart. Source: Florida Department of Corrections 1996–97 Annual Report: The Guidebook to Corrections in Florida. 1997

policy and correctional behavior. Public interest groups do so as well. A public interest organization is an organization that is concerned with the general public interest rather than with only the interests of a specific, well-defined group within the community. Common Cause, for example, monitors the activities of government in general in an effort to safeguard citizens from government abuse. One of the most powerful public interest groups is the media.

The Media, Public Perception, and Public Policy

Prior to 1970, correctional managers had little concern about the media (newspapers, radio, television, and magazines) because both organizations had little interest in each other. This lack of interest ended in the 1970s as a growing community social and judicial activism focused on prison conditions and was empowered by the Freedom of Information Act of 1966, which gave the news media

access to previously inaccessible government documents (Marsh, 1996:332).

Corrections–Media Relationship

There is a powerful belief, held by both correctional managers and employees, that the media has shaped a negative public perception of corrections by presenting stories that are almost universally biased and negative:

Many corrections workers believe the public image of the corrections field is quite bad. Actually, it is nowhere that good. . . . The public view of corrections in this country is, frankly, terrible. The major stories that reach the public about corrections are almost universally negative (Schwartz, 1989:38).

M. Wayne Huggins, Director of the National Institute of Corrections in 1989, has stated: "I believe no profession has been more unfairly, inaccurately or intentionally distorted than ours" (Huggins, 1992:58). In a recent article on correctional officer (C.O.) suicide, the author reports that one source of C.O. stress is the fact that "the work of correctional officers is neither understood nor appreciated by the public at large (Kamerman, 1996:23).

Is there empirical support for this belief that the public has a negative perception of corrections? A 1979 survey of a random sample of registered voters in Illinois, Indiana, and New Hampshire asked citizens to rate the performance of the police, courts, and corrections on a scale of good, fair, and poor. The rating for police performance was 57 percent good, 43 percent fair. The courts had a rating of 11 percent good, 47 percent fair, and 42 percent poor. The rating for corrections was 15 percent good, 20 percent fair; and 65 percent poor (Graber, 1979).

In a more recent study conducted for the Florida DOC by the University of Florida's Bureau of Economic and Business Research (*Corrections Journal,* 1997), Floridians rated DOC effectiveness in three areas: inmate rehabilitation, escape prevention, and providing drug and alcohol treatment. The ratings are depicted in Table 6–1. These findings can be interpreted as a public perception that the Florida DOC is generally effective in protecting the public by preventing escapes, but less effective in protecting the public by rehabilitating offenders. The survey also found that both the public and the media have severely limited knowledge about corrections, its purposes, and activities. Basic information about length of time served by Florida inmates was missing and there were misperceptions about such issues as C.O. entry-level salaries and the basic routine of prison life (*Corrections Journal,* 1997:6). For example, survey respondents assumed that all inmates have air conditioning when only 7 of the 55 DOC prisons have it. They also believed that prison overcrowding was a major problem when, in fact, Florida now has a bed surplus because of massive building out.

Ken Kerle, Managing Editor, in 1996, of *American Jails,* published by the American

TABLE 6–1   Public's rating of DOC effectiveness in Florida

	Inmate Rehabilitation	Escape Prevention	Inmate Programs
Excellent Job	1%	13%	3%
Good Job	13%	51%	24%
Fair Job	43%	31%	40%
Poor Job	42%	5%	34%

Jail Association, believes that the emphasis of media coverage on the negative events in corrections has created an unfortunate stereotyping ("gratuitous vilification") that presents correctional staff as "a bunch of noncaring, selfish, greedy, corrupt individuals" (Kerle, 1996:5). How has this "gratuitous vilification" been created? The influence of the entertainment and news media are most frequently cited as sources of negative public perception.

Entertainment Media and the Public Perception of Corrections

Most Americans have no personal knowledge of corrections or its employees. Their perception of the profession is heavily influenced by the entertainment media and too often "the perpetuation of the stereotype that correctional officers and administrators are disgruntled alienated hacks prone to violence under pressure misleads the public, giving it an unrealistic view of the corrections profession" (Zaner, 1989:65).

A review of 60 years of prison movies establishes strong evidence of negative stereotyping, especially of correctional officers (Zaner, 1989). Movies such as *The Big House* (1930), *Caged* (1950), *I Want To Live* (1958), *Birdman of Alcatraz* (1962), *Cool Hand Luke* (1967), *The Longest Yard* (1974), and *The Shawshank Redemption* (1994) consistently portray C.O.s as either indifferent, helpless pawns of a brutal system or sadistic hacks who are the source of the system's brutality. Inmates are presented in equally stereotyped roles: the lovable hero, Cool Hand Luke, or the vicious prison wolf who rapes young inmates. Even when there is a sympathetic warden, such as portrayed by Robert Redford in *Brubaker* (1980), audience identification with the warden is attained through contrasting his nobility with the brutality and corruption of sadistic prison staff abusing pathetic, helpless inmates. This imagery can be taken to ridiculous extremes. For example, in an October 1995 episode of the popular television series *The X-Files,* a warden in a maximum-security prison beats to death two Death Row inmates in a shower room while a C.O. indifferently stands guard.

Entertainment media images of correctional brutality and corruption can be riveting. But entertainment imagery is not reality. Reality is competent, caring, dedicated, hard-working corrections professionals who are "living rebuttals to the popular stereotypes of prison workers" (DiIulio, 1991:51). Why haven't the news media presented this reality to the public?

News Media Coverage of Corrections

The news media are frequently criticized for focusing on correctional "failures" that present corrections in the worse light, sensationalizing corrections' problems, and failing to provide a balanced view of correctional issues. In order to further explore this issue, consider the following two case studies.

Case Study One: A Parole "Failure"　Parole boards are a particularly good target for media criticism. As John Curran Jr., Chairman of the Massachusetts Parole Board in 1989, has noted:

Police are in the business of catching criminals. Prosecutors can boast of being tough crime fighters, and judges have the lofty role of punishing the guilty and letting the innocent go free. But parole boards let admittedly guilty felons out from behind the bars every day (Curran, 1989:30).

Thus, when a mistake is made, the media coverage can be intense and highly critical. For example, in February 1995, a 43-year-

old convicted murderer named Robert "Mudman" Simon was paroled from the State Correctional Institution at Graterford, a huge maximum-security prison located north of Philadelphia. A member of the Warlocks motorcycle gang, Simon murdered a New Jersey police officer in May 1995, an event that generated a high level of media coverage and scathing editorial calls to reform the Pennsylvania parole system.

The intense public and media criticism of the release of Simon led to a reorganization of the Pennsylvania Board of Probation and Parole and significantly reduced the use of parole. The result was a 60 percent reduction in parole releases and a 1,000 inmate increase in the DOC inmate population between May and July of 1995 (*Evening News* 1995:B1, B10).

The media emphasis on the tragic murder committed by one parolee was distinctly one-sided. Rarely if ever mentioned were the thousands of parolees who never committed a new crime or the difficulties inherent in trying to predict human behavior, especially criminal behavior. The political response to the media coverage was to toughen up the system, a response that increased prison overcrowding and raised the stress levels of everyone who worked there. Because of one parolee, thousands of inmates and correctional employees were negatively affected. The media had played a significant role in shaping public policy.

Case Study Two: A Prison "Failure"　On January 8, 1997, six inmates successfully escaped from the maximum-security State Correctional Institution at Pittsburgh (SCIP) after spending months digging a 70-foot tunnel under the prison's massive stone walls. The result was an onslaught of media coverage, criticism, and demands for changes, often cast in the form of editorial cartoons. Typical of these cartoons are the ones presented in Figure 6–5.

Once again, media coverage had created a specific public perception of corrections and its employees. This type of criticism stings and fails to provide a balanced look at

FIGURE 6–5 Editorial Cartoons Commenting on the SCIP Escape. Source: Randy Blish. Editorial cartoons, *Tribune Review* (February 1997), Greensburg, Pa. Courtesy of Randy Blish.

Pennsylvania state law allows prison inmates to wear civilian clothing.

Pennsylvania state prisons have allowed them to wear them on their way to Mexico.

FIGURE 6–5 *(Continued)*

corrections. An internal investigation of the SCIP escape concluded that a communication failure had played a key role in the escape: a Regional Deputy Secretary had failed to require corrective action by the SCIP staff after being notified through an audit report that SCIP lacked an adequate tool control system. It was this lack of tool control that permitted the inmates to tunnel under the wall. Prior to the escape, prison audit reports were sent to the Regional Deputies with no requirement that they forward the reports to the Secretary or provide evidence of follow-up.

Having determined that there had been a breakdown in communication between Central Office and the field, the Secretary formalized the relationship between the Secretary, three Regional Deputy Secretaries, and 23 superintendents by increasing formalization. As of April 1997, each superintendent is required to file weekly status reports with the Secretary that will establish managerial accountability and allow the Secretary to detect and respond to any problems before they can develop. The Regional Deputy Secretaries are required to visit each facility in their jurisdiction eight times a year and submit quarterly inspection reports to the Secretary.

The Language of Gratuitous Vilification

Correctional staff also argue that it is not just the emphasis on negative events that reinforces gratuitous vilification. It is the language news media professionals often use when the subject being covered has only a peripheral involvement with corrections. For example, a *Time* magazine article on comedian Tim Allen's incarceration for cocaine possession stated:

Allen found humor useful in prison. He made the *meanest* (italics mine) guard laugh by putting pictures of Richard Nixon in the peephole of his cell when they made their rounds. . . . Once, while riding a bus to another prison, he managed to slip out of his hand-cuffs. The only thing he could think to do was to bum a cigarette off the old bank robber sitting in front of him (Zoglin, 1994:80).

The term *guard* is resented by corrections professionals because it so clearly conveys the image of the Pre-DOC employee whose sole interest was punitive control. And the Tim Allen story suggests that not only are C.O.s mean, they are also so incompetent that they cannot even properly handcuff an inmate. Stereotyping also applies to correctional managers. In an April 29, 1996, *Time* article on Timothy Leary, the reporter states: "So here we were for one more try, in the visitor's tank at the federal pen in San Diego, waiting for the *stone-faced* (italics mine) warden to decide whether or not to allow our visit (Ressner, 1996:73)." The language in both of these examples reinforces the negative stereotyping created by the entertainment media.

MANAGERIAL RESPONSE TO THE MEDIA

How does the DOC reassure the community that a problem has been corrected or that it has accomplishments it rightfully can be proud of? Managers must engage in a strategy of modifying organizational structure and developing communication strategies (Figure 6–6).

Modifying the Organizational Structure

Correctional managers are faced with two fundamental truths. First, crime and corrections are news and the news media will either report the official view of corrections or they will provide news from other sources that may, or may not, accurately present the issue at hand. To "circle the wagons" and avoid all contact with the media is counterproductive and "No comment" responses to media questions are likely to

FIGURE 6–6 One method of influencing public opinion is the use of inmates in community projects. The inmates in these pictures are helping to rehabilitate low income housing. Courtesy of the Office of Archives, Federal Bureau of Prisons.

fuel speculation that correctional managers have something to hide. The media will report corrections' news with or without the cooperation of correctional managers. Second, the news media is, in fact, a powerful shaper of public opinion and public policy. Therefore, it is in the best interests of corrections for its managers to proactively establish a formal working relationship with the media that encourages open communication. This can be accomplished through the process of horizontal differentiation by the creation of a new unit, the Public Information Office, and of a new category of employee, the Public Information Officer.

The Public Information Officer (PIO) is responsible for maintaining a high level of contact with the news media by efficiently responding to media inquiries about specific or general correctional issues, arranging tours of facilities and interviews with staff, issuing press releases on correctional activities that might be of interest to the general public, and advising correctional managers on media-related issues. A particularly thorny issue between corrections and the media concerns the issue of interviews with inmates. Most correctional managers have a policy of not allowing this type of media access because it takes up staff time and may give the selected inmates too much status with the inmate population. This policy, like every other policy, can be subject to change, however. In 1997, the Virginia DOC, after a high-profile debate in the state legislature about media access to inmates (a debate that was decided in the DOC's favor) decided to permit media–inmate interviews and 42 of its 52 facilities were designated as locations for reporter interviews. This decision not only improved the corrections–media relationship, it put to rest an issue that the legislature was tired of hearing about (*Corrections Journal*, 1997:1–2).

PIO Qualifications The effective PIO will have a communications or media background that provides a thorough understanding of how the various components of the media work. The PIO will understand media needs (such as the pressure to meet daily deadlines and have effective sound bites) and will have mastered the art of packaging information so the organization can be presented in the best light possible. The PIO should be a "people person" who recognizes the value of networking and establishing positive, informal relationships with media managers and reporters that will encourage the media to get both sides of a story before publication. The PIO must have the integrity to acknowledge "mistakes" but also be skilled at presenting an informative rationale that emphasizes the complexity of the issue under scrutiny. Thus, a PIO commenting on the "Mudman" Simon incident would stress that while such tragedies can occur, they are infrequent and there is an elaborate screening process in place to min-imize the risk to the public. A PIO com-menting on the SCIP escape would stress the overall positive record of the DOC in preventing escapes and keep the media informed of the progress of the internal investigation and subsequent policy changes and personnel actions (demotions, dismissals, and suspensions resulting from internal administrative actions).

Marsh (1996:333) has established six rules for an effective PIO. First, always tell the truth. A single instance of lying or creat-ing the perception that ill-advised action is being hidden will be quickly spotted by the media and can poison the corrections–media relationship for years. Second, develop a personal relationship with pub-lishers, editors, and reporters, which can prevent hasty judgments on the part of the media, save embarrassment for both sides, and provide the public with comprehensive information. Third, do not play favorites. Treat every news representative equally and ensure that all news outlets receive the same information at the same time. Playing favorites only sets the organization up for unfavorable reporting by media representa-tives "out of the information loop." Fourth, establish a clearly stated public relations policy in writing and stick to that policy. All employees should receive training in the policy and adhere to it. Correctional managers must enforce the policy. Fifth, educate the public by providing informa-tion about specific programs and policies. As the 1997 Florida study demonstrates, the public often has misconceptions about the most fundamental correctional issues. Sixth, the PIO should maintain contact with the media when there are no problems so editors and reporters have positive, current background information.

Communication Strategies

The PIO cannot create a positive relation-ship without the help of correctional manag-ers. Richard J. Koehler, the Commissioner of the New York City Department of Correc-

tions in 1989, advocated an aggressive, open approach of correctional managers meeting with the media on a regular basis in order to provide a perspective that balances correc-tional problems with successes (Koehler, 1989:16–17). In addition, managers must be open to permitting media tours of their facil-ities, meeting with local editorial boards to discuss corrections in general, inviting responsible journalists to spend a day with staff and see firsthand how business is con-ducted, and appearing on talk shows and other forums when the operation is running smoothly. The production of brochures and short videos for public information dissemi-nation can effectively educate both the media and the public (Curran, 1989:32).

One avenue of communication open to correctional managers that is frequently overlooked is serving as a guest columnist for a local newspaper. This activity provides an excellent opportunity for educating the public on a variety of corrections-related topics. Box 6–3 provides an example of a state prison superintendent educating the public about a recent walkaway from his institution. Notice how this superintendent seeks to reassure and educate the public about inmate walkaways and the organiza-tional response to those events by thor-oughly explaining the response activities designed to protect the community and voicing sensitivity to their concerns. The promise to provide further information in the future signals his interest in maintaining an ongoing process of communication and response to community concerns.

BOX 6–3 "ON THE INSIDE LOOKING OUT"

I had a meeting with the Pennsylvania state police and local police, as well as 911 representatives on January 27 on preparations in the event of an escape. As luck would have it, that afternoon SCI-Albion had its first "walkaway" from the institution as reported in the *Albion News*.

Fortunately, our correctional officers apprehended the fugitive within an hour of his untimely departure. Consequently, some neighbors in the immediate area were not notified because the search was called off as soon as the prisoner was located.

The institution's escape plan appeared to work very well. As I have told many groups upon my arrival over four years ago, someday we would experience an emergency via an outside work crew, and it has finally happened.

One always wonders why inmates do such things, especially when this particular inmate had recently received a release date for a Community Corrections Center in Erie. Impulsive acts can be expected from time to time and they never cease to amaze me.

However, back to our emergency plans for such an event. We have had numerous unannounced drills and training on escapes and that has paid off in quick response from our corrections staff, as well as the state and local police. During our meeting on January 27, we discussed a warning system for the community and we plan on installing a steam whistle to alert the local community of any such emergencies at the institution.

We will also develop a code system to indicate when the situation is resolved, as well as routine tests of the whistle. Additionally, we have updated our plan to include sending out a special patrol to cover both the elementary, middle school, and the high school should any future walkaways occur.

During last week's "walkaway" we sent staff house-to-house to alert residents of the event. We apologize if any residence was missed, but the plan for doing so was not com-pletely developed from our morning meeting.

We heard that the color tan of our Correctional Industries and maintenance staff was confused with the inmate "browns," and some residents were concerned. Should this occur again, the staff will present their official Department of Corrections' identification cards with their picture, job title, and the Superintendent's signature.

It should also be noted that the inmate "browns" are closer to maroon than brown. Outside inmate workers are dressed in the inmate browns (maroon) and gray uniforms. The brown or maroon denotes direct supervision by staff and the gray denotes intermediate supervision, meaning they will be placed on a job on the institutional grounds and receive periodic checks from the institution's patrol, as well as their job area supervisor (tan uniforms).

In any event, I will be sending out more information on our new steam whistle and more information on our emergency procedures. I assure you we take every precaution to avoid such problems and treat these incidents extremely seriously; however, they may happen from time to time, and we all need to be alerted when they do. You should also know that the inmate has been charged with a new offense and now faces an additional seven years in prison, and I assure you, not at SCI-Albion.

Thanks again for your continued support and, as always, I promise you I will keep you advised of any developments.

Source: Edward T. Brennan. "On the Inside Looking Out." *Albion (Pa.) News*, Wednesday, 12 February 1977, p. 19. Reprinted by permission.

Promoting a Positive Image

Schwartz (1989) and Freeman (1996a) have suggested that correctional managers need to become more aggressive in promoting a positive image of corrections. This involves more than establishing a positive media relationship. Creating a positive public image involves making corrections, especially prisons, visible to the public in a favorable way. Suggested approaches include (1) annual facility open houses and staff participation in college job fairs, (2) the sponsorship of community youth activities, (3) participation in reputable radio, television, and college discussion groups or programs, (4) the use of organized letter writing campaigns to protest negative stereotyping in the entertainment and news media, (5) official opposition to the use of prisons for movies presenting only negative staff stereotypes, (6) the use of community volunteers, (7) immediate professional letter to the editor responses to negative media coverage, (8) creation of Speaker's Bureaus in which staff as well as inmates speak to the public, (9) encouragement of staff to participate in community events, and (10) work with academia to ensure that research reflects the reality of modern corrections (Freeman, 1996a).

The media is powerful, but it is not the only external organization that can influence corrections. Single-interest groups focused on the needs of a well-defined subgroup of society can also influence correctional behavior.

SINGLE-INTEREST ORGANIZATIONS AND CORRECTIONS: EMPLOYEE UNIONS AND VICTIMS' RIGHTS

The Profile at the beginning of the chapter referred to the AMA, ABA, ACA, and the ACHSA. These organizations represent a specific constituency (physicians, attorneys, correctional employees, and correctional health care administrators, respectively) and expect that professional principles will govern the behavior of their members when they are involved in the delivery of services. Thus, the AMA and the ACHSA will be concerned about the delivery of health care services to inmates. The ABA will be concerned with the ability of offenders to have access to the courts and receive justice. Correctional employees will be concerned about professionalism. All such professional organizations may try to influence public policy concerning corrections.

In addition, there are external organizations that provide advocacy for correctional employees and victims.

Public Employee Unions

A labor union is an organization made up of employees that has been legally created for the express purpose of acting collectively to protect and promote employee interests. The fundamental purpose of unions is to improve employment conditions for its membership through collective bargaining. Collective bargaining "is the process whereby representatives of the employees meet with representatives of management to establish a written contract setting forth working conditions for a specific time" (Bennett and Hess, 1992:231). The first prison employee unions with collective bargaining rights were established in 1956 in Washington, D.C., and New York City. In the 1970s, numerous states authorized correctional employees, especially C.O.s, to unionize and engage in collective bargaining. Correctional employee unions usually affiliate with a larger union, such as the American Federation of State, County, and Municipal Employees (AFSCME).

Union–Management Relationship
Jacobs (1978:44) argues that unionization "has redefined the prison organization in adversary terms so that wardens are bosses and complaints are grievances." The result has been a clear separation between managers and employees. Many correctional managers believe that unions deny managers the

ability to make the most effective use of employees, efficiently allocate resources, or develop and maintain a professional work force. A frequent complaint of management is that public employee unions function in accordance with a "union model" that has the philosophy: "We protect our own no matter what happens. If we have to pick between the young, educated professional and the old, established worker, we go with the old one every time" (Bennett and Hess, 1992:235). The "union model" can create a high level of managerial frustration because its successful challenge of managerial authority and use of discretion has changed the manager–employee power differential.

Challenging Managerial Authority and Discretion

Because unions represent employees, not managers, the needs of the two groups can easily conflict. In order to satisfy the employees whose dues support the union and its leadership, union leaders have traditionally challenged the authority of correctional managers to dictate conditions of employment and have successfully weakened that authority. Union strategies aim to influence managerial authority and discretion in decisions concerning fundamental management functions: determining staffing levels; setting work schedules and job assignments; controlling correctional operations and budgets; setting standards of employee conduct on and off duty; establishing hiring, promotion, transfer, termination, and disciplinary procedures; setting work performance standards; creating organizational goals, policies, procedures, and rules; establishing training programs and training requirements; and formulating and enforcing the organization's Code of Ethics.

Today, correctional managers cannot unilaterally determine pay and benefit packages, promotional standards, disciplinary procedures, policy, and working conditions. Union victories in achieving higher salary and benefits packages have also confronted managers with a loss of control over the budgetary process with funding increases often going to current staff instead of being used to hire new staff or modify the prison environment.

Decreasing the Manager–Employee Power Differential

Unions have successfully decreased the manager–employee power differential. In a manager–employee dispute, managers no longer face an individual employee. Instead, they face an employee who is a member of a powerful external organization. Because of the potential for conflict and misunderstanding that is present in any relationship where there is a power differential, especially one that is changing, the union–management relationship (and, by extension, the manager–employee relationship) is governed by a written document: the collective bargaining agreement.

Collective Bargaining Agreement

The primary mechanism for incorporating labor union influence into the correctional policy structure is the collective bargaining agreement (CBA)—a document negotiated by management and the union that defines the professional conduct expected of both employee and manager. The CBA limits the use of managerial discretion in employee-related decision making by specifying rules and procedures that cannot be violated without penalty. The CBA defines every aspect of the manager–employee relationship.

Typically CBAs are carefully crafted to strike a balance between union and management power, and the language striking that balance is carefully chosen for maximum specificity. For example, the Ohio CBA Overtime articles strike a balance between the union's emphasis on seniority and management's need to have adequate staffing levels:

Insofar as practicable, overtime shall be equitably distributed on a rotating basis by seniority among those who normally perform the work. Specific arrangements for implementation of these overtime provisions shall be worked out at the Agency level. Absent mutual agreement to the contrary, overtime rosters shall be purged at least every twelve (12) months . . . [I]f a sufficient number of employees is not secured through the above provisions, the Employer shall have the right to require the least senior employee(s) who normally perform the work to perform said overtime (Ohio Contract, 1994:33).

The Challenge of Multiple CBAs   One of the challenges correctional managers face is that there frequently are multiple unions, and CBAs, governing the manager–employee relationship. Take for example, the issue of rate of accrual for vacation. A correctional manager may be responsible for employees who are represented by different unions. The first union (A) may have negotiated the following rate of accrual:

Length of State Service	Accrual Rate
1 year or more	80 hours
5 years or more	80 hours
10 years or more	120 hours
15 years or more	180 hours
20 years or more	200 hours
25 years or more	240 hours

Thus, a 25-year veteran can take six weeks of vacation per year. But the second union (B) may have negotiated a different rate of accrual. As follows:

Length of State Service	Accrual Rate
1 year or more	40 hours
5 years or more	60 hours
10 years or more	120 hours
15 years or more	160 hours
20 years or more	180 hours
25 years or more	200 hours

In this case, a 25-year veteran is only entitled to five weeks of vacation a year. The correctional manager who forgets about this difference in contract language can create chaos when employees represented by union A apply for vacation time and the manager denies requests on the basis of "insufficient time accrued" because he or she is thinking in terms of union B's CBA language.

Multiple CBAs frequently provide different language governing specific management functions. And there is just enough difference in this language to cause conflict and misunderstandings if employees and managers do not thoroughly understand that there are language differences in the CBAs applicable to different employee groups. Because of the complexity of CBAs and the potential for conflict created by contract language differences, DOCs have created the Central Office position of Labor Relations Coordinator in the Personnel Services division. This individual provides guidance to managers confronting contract issues. The position is frequently duplicated at the field level.

Unfortunately, no matter how precise the language, there will inevitably be conflicts in interpretation. The most feared result of such conflict is the organized employee strike, although most states now prohibit C.O.s from striking.

Union–Management Conflicts

Any conflict between corrections management and union in Ohio is governed by Article 25 ("Grievance Procedure") of the Ohio AFSCME contract, which in 11 pages describes the grievance and arbitration processes designed to formally handle issues of conflict. If a conflict cannot be resolved at the local level, the union always has the right to take the issue to outside arbitration. Because an arbitrator's ruling is often binding, both union and management are motivated to strive to informally resolve CBA disputes rather than be bound by a ruling that may limit their ability to resolve future issues.

Working with the Union Leadership

The days of the autocratic warden are gone. Managers now have a professional obligation to work with labor unions to achieve organizational goals through the development of policy that recognizes such issues as seniority, employee safety, overall working conditions, staff–inmate relationships, and the staff right to due process protections in disciplinary procedures. When union and management interests overlap (such as the need for more C.O.s and security equipment), unions can be a powerful ally for managers making their case for more money and legislative support. When interests diverge, there will be fundamental differences of opinion. For example, a majority of correctional Personnel Directors favor making some degree of college education a hiring requirement for C.O.s (Sechrest and Josi, 1992), yet C.O. unions have always vigorously opposed any change from the entry-level requirement of a high school diploma or GED.

The Role of the Manager in Conflict Resolution   Effective top managers work to avoid management–employee disagreements from ballooning into conflict by encouraging the resolution of disagreements at the lowest level possible. This means encouraging supervisors to carefully listen to employee concerns, apply their knowledge of the governing CBA to the situation, and attempt to resolve the conflict through persuasion and discussion.

The effective manager takes every available opportunity to develop negotiation and conflict resolution skills and will use those skills in official Meet and Discuss meetings as well as in informal meetings. The key to a successful management–union relationship is the refusal to personalize issues. As long as the relationship is professional, most issues can be resolved without resorting to arbitrators.

The Employee Union and Public Policy Formulation

It is in the best interests of the union to influence public policy that will increase the number of correctional employees. C.O. unions have a vested economic interest in expanding the number of prisons. In Illinois, the C.O. union is credited with pushing through legislation that banned the privatization of prisons and increased sanctions against inmates in possession of weapons. The Michigan union has opposed proposals to lower the rate of incarceration by making inmates eligible for boot camps (Donziger, 1997:334). In California, the California Correctional Peace Officers Association has claimed that 38 of 44 bills it pushed in the state legislature have become law and that in a decade the union's membership has increased from 4,000 to 23,000; the average salary has increased to $55,000, more than a public school teacher or tenured associate professor with a Ph.D. in the California state university system (Foote, 1993:12). The California union is the second-largest campaign donor in the state and spends about $1 million per election cycle to gubernatorial and legislative candidates who promote prison expansion (Alexander, 1993). C.O. unions can be a powerful force in maintaining the domination of the conservative ideology, and consequently contributing to prison overcrowding, that poses such critical challenges to corrections.

However, unions are not the only external organizations that influence corrections. There are also external organizations that represent the interests of victims of crime.

Advocating the Rights of Victims

Beginning in the early 1980s, both the community and correctional managers began to pay attention to the issue of victims and the services they need. A 1991 nationwide study by the National Victim Center found that 31 DOCs and 29 juvenile correctional agencies notify victims of changes in inmates' status. In addition, 26 DOCs, 15 state juvenile correctional systems, and 22 state parole agencies have representatives active in local, state, and regional coalitions of crime victim and crime service providers. Nineteen DOCs, 12 state juvenile correctional agencies, and 20 state parole agencies provide information, training, and technical assistance by agency professional staff to crime victims and service providers within their states (National Victim Center, 1991). This process of providing victim services began with parole departments.

Parole Departments and Victim Services

In 1982, the Final Report of the President's Task Force on Victims of Crime included four recommendations to improve parole department delivery of victim services. First, parole boards should notify crime victims and their families in advance of parole hearings, if they have provided the parole department with their names and addresses. Second, parole boards should allow victims, their families, or their representatives to attend parole hearings and deliver a victim impact statement. Third, parole boards should implement policy that ensures that parolees who violate the rules will be immediately returned to custody until their case can be adjudicated. Fourth, parole boards should not apply the exclusionary rule to parole revocation hearings (President's Task Force on Victims of Crime, 1982).

The task force did not address the issue of victim services in probation or institutional corrections. However, in 1992, the American Probation and Parole Association (APPA) started a Victim Issues Committee and, in 1994, adopted a policy statement on victims that requires probation, parole, and other community-based corrections professionals to be sensitive to the needs of victims while engaged in their daily duties (American Probation and Parole Association, 1994). In response, many states have initiated programs designed to demonstrate this sensitivity. For example, the Ohio Parole Board has a Victims Section whose employees have constant contact with victims' families; answer calls about victims' issues; correspond with judges, prosecutors, legislators, and criminal justice agencies; and operate a victim notification program. Each Ohio state prison now has a Victim Coordinator on staff (Clayton, 1997:71).

Institutional Corrections and Victim Services

In 1986, the ACA developed a broad policy on victim services and formed the Task Force on Victims of Crime. In 1988, the Task Force published 15 recommendations that became the foundation for four training and technical assistance projects funded by the U.S. Department of Justice Office for Victims of Crime. The ACA Task Force recommended that institutional corrections should (1) establish communication channels with victims to provide notification of offender status whenever that status changes (transfer or release); (2) develop offender-directed educational and offender supervision programs (restitution, community service and fines, and "no contact with victim" orders); (3) develop programs to respond to employees who have become victims, or witnessed victimization of other employees or inmates, by inmates engaged in violence, riots, or hostage situations; and (4) become involved with community victim service providers by joining their coalitions, sponsoring joint training, supporting the development of advisory boards for correctional Victim Services units, and improving public awareness of correctional victim services.

A model for this interaction of corrections and community victim services is found in the Minnesota DOC. The DOC helps fund the Minnesota Coalition Against Sexual Assault, a statewide coalition for sexual assault services that provides outreach to member programs, service-related technical assistance, and statewide efforts to increase awareness of sexual violence issues. The DOC Victim Services Unit Battered Women Program provided over $12 million in grants to 66 battered women programs serving 20,000 women and children throughout the state during 1994–1995. In addition, the DOC Victim Services Unit awarded state and federal funds to 48 community-based sexual assault centers that provide direct services to victims, training for professionals who work with victims of sexual assault, and community awareness education programs that educated 294,000 citizens during 1994–1995 and provided funding and technical assistance to programs for general crime victims. Its Department for Abused Children administered state and federal funds for 32 child abuse programs (Minnesota Department of Corrections, 1995:18).

In addition, the Minnesota DOC has developed a Critical Incident Stress Debriefing (CISD) program conducted by peer members and mental health professionals trained to help employees who have experienced or witnessed violence. CISD staff engaged in 19 debriefings of 125 staff during 1994–1995. The debriefings "manage stress responses, mitigate the impact of incidents, and accelerate a return to normal job activity" (Minnesota Department of Corrections, 1995:17).

So far, we have focused on groups in the special interest environment of corrections that have a people-oriented focus. But there is one last influence on correctional behavior that is somewhat different: the private corrections corporation.

PRIVATE CORRECTIONS CORPORATIONS

The privatization of correctional services is an integral element of any effective strategy of fiscal conservatism. Correctional managers have frequently benefited from privatization and there is no doubt that privatization has been a profitable enterprise for many private corrections corporations. Corrections Corporation of America (CCA) had a 57 percent increase in profits between 1992 and 1993 (Ramirez, 1994:1) and has been listed as a "theme stock" for the 1990s because of an expected "dramatic increase in the number of prisoners being served by private companies" (Goins, 1994). CCA has engaged in an extensive marketing campaign to increase the size of the private corrections market, and to strengthen its position within that market, by retaining lobbyists to push for legislation favorable to

correctional privatization (Securities and Exchange Commission, 1994:11). Partial service providers are also doing well and have an incentive to lobby for privatization legislation. For example, in 1994, Correctional Medical Services (CMS) of St. Louis was providing medical care for 150,000 inmates, three times its service level in 1987 (Meddis and Sharp, 1994:10A). But profitability becomes a negative for corrections if it encourages private companies to support legislation that is not in the best interests of corrections.

Supporting Legislation Unfavorable to Corrections Nils Christie has suggested that "companies that service the criminal justice system need sufficient quantities of raw materials to guarantee long-term growth. . . . [T]he raw material is prisoners" (Donziger, 1997:326). This statement suggests that private corrections has a vested interest in the judiciary providing a steady stream of convicted offenders. Paulette (1994:A1) has suggested that the private corrections industry uses the "war against crime" rhetoric as a lucrative marketing strategy in much the same way that defense contractors used Cold War rhetoric to persuade Congress to finance big-ticket armament contracts. Thus, there exists an "iron triangle" of government bureaucracy, private industry, and politicians with a shared interest in expanding the criminal justice system.

This "prison-industrial complex" involves some of the largest investment houses on Wall Street competing to underwrite jail and prison construction with tax-exempt bonds that do not require voter approval (Donziger, 1997:327). Industrial giants like Westinghouse have created divisions to retool from defense products to criminal justice products. And CCA and Wackenhut are listed on the New York Stock Exchange: "Private companies are growing rapidly as the correctional population expands, and they are aggressively 'exporting' their formulas for private jails and prisons to other countries" (Donziger, 1997:327). As a result, the rate of growth of private facilities is four times the rate of growth for public facilities (Thomas, 1995:vii). To stay in business and grow, these private facilities need offenders.

Thus, public correctional managers may be at risk of seeing prison populations grow if private corrections is successful in lobbying for increased sentencing. The result will be increased complexity, problems, and challenges for correctional managers that would have been avoided if prison populations had decreased. Therefore, correctional managers must be sensitive to the activities of private corrections companies and be willing to challenge those activities whenever they believe they are not in the best interest of corrections.

SPECIAL INTEREST INFLUENCES, GOALS, AND ORGANIZATIONAL STRUCTURE

The combined effect of the special interest influences we have discussed in this chapter have rendered obsolete the Pre-DOC autocratic warden's goals of maintaining punitive control and not embarrassing the governor. The bureaucratic manager must function in accordance with a much more complicated set of goals: (1) the maintenance of a safe, secure, and humane offender environment in accordance with legislative and fiscal conservatism mandates; (2) maintenance of two-way communication with employees, inmates, elected officials, union leadership, community leaders, private corrections executives, government regulators, and special interest groups; (3) sponsorship of an environment that fosters racial, gender, cultural, and personal diversity; (4) humane but cost-effective management of offender risk groups; (5) encouragement of ongoing education and training of staff; (6) development of employee professionalism; (7) effective rehabilitation planning; and (8) future-oriented planning.

It is not only the goals that have changed. The organizational structure of corrections has also changed.

Special Interest Influences and Organizational Structure

The influence of special interest organization activities on correctional structure is considerable.

Increasing Horizontal Differentiation

Using the Minnesota DOC as an example (Figure 6–7), we can see that the activities of quasi-judicial regulatory agencies, employee unions, victim rights groups, and private corrections corporations have significantly increased horizontal differentiation. In response to the influence of external organizations, the Minnesota DOC over a period of time added the Office of Diversity to the Commissioner's span of control and expanded the Management Services division by adding the Hearings and Victim Services units. The functions of the Facilities Inspection and Enforcement unit and the Investigations unit have been expanded through EEO and ADA legislation and made more complex by the new standards to be considered in facility inspections and investigations of policy violation allegations.

Every public policy requirement for corrections that is influenced by a special interests organization can increase, or change to some extent, employee functions in any of the units noted on the organization chart. For example, the use of a Victim Services unit as a channel for state and federal grants increases the number of functions in the Financial Services division. Correctional managers at every level must acquire a working knowledge of applicable legislation in order to effectively plan employee activities. The Executive Budget Officer, in particular, will need to be aware of the financial implications of ADA, Victim Services, CBA changes, and privatization.

Formalization and Centralization   For-malization will increase as new policies, procedures, and rules are promulgated to inform employees and inmates of relevant changes. As these policies are incorporated into the daily routine, centralization will

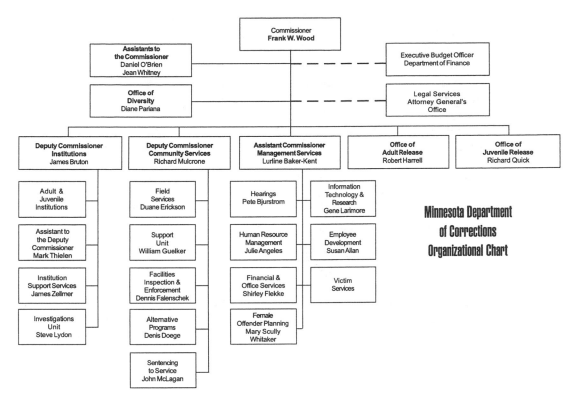

FIGURE 6–7 Minnesota DOC Organization Chart. Source: Minnesota Department of Corrections (1995).

decrease because new responsibilities and increased functions always decrease the ability of managers to monitor every employee decision. The Human Resource Management division will see an increase in CBA-related issues and questions as policy changes create new areas of disagreement between union and management. The Legal Services department will see an increase in workload as questions about, and litigation concerning, special interests legislation come in from the field. The Employee Development training curriculum will need to be revised.

SUMMARY

Quasi-judicial regulatory agencies and special interest organizations exert a powerful influence on correctional behavior through a process of public policy formulation that

imposes standards that constrain managerial discretion and require modifications of the organizational structure. The result has been an increasingly complex role for correctional managers as well as a professionalization of corrections. However, legislative bodies and special interest groups do not have the final say on correctional behavior. When disputes between corrections and other organizations and groups arise, correctional managers enter the legal environment of corrections. There they encounter the judiciary. In the next chapter, we examine the legal environment of corrections.

Discussion Questions

1. What has been the impact of EEO and ADA on correctional personnel practices?
2. How has the organizational structure changed in response to the actions of

quasi-judicial regulatory agencies and special interest groups?

3. How has the media shaped the public perception of corrections and influenced corrections-related public policy formulation?

4. What has been the impact of public employee unions on the use of managerial discretion?

5. How can Victim Services units help shape a positive public perception of corrections?

6. How do DOC correctional managers goals differ from Pre-DOC manager goals?

Critical Analysis Exercise: Improving Community Relations

Marilyn Ford (1996:105) has suggested that correctional managers can strengthen the corrections–community relationship and counter the negative portrayal of corrections in the media through a process of opening the prison to the community by developing policy to encourage and support inmates and correctional employees becoming active in the community. She suggests that inmates can provide low-cost labor for government, nonprofit agencies, and charitable events. Correctional employees can speak to neighborhood watch and civic groups about their facility and corrections in general. They can participate in child safety programs by fingerprinting children, informing the public about crime techniques, and helping in community charity events. Some prisons currently permit citizens to attend educational and vocational programs behind the walls. In addition, correctional managers can welcome community volunteers into the prison to assist in religious, educational, and treatment programs. The use of volunteers brings community churches, universities, and self-help groups into the prison. These volunteers can provide assistance to inmates and help educate citizens to increase their understanding of a demanding profession.

Critical Analysis Questions

1. What are the potential benefits of involving inmates and correctional employees as participants in the community?

2. What are the potential risks?

3. What activities other than the ones mentioned could involve inmates and staff?

4. What could be the role of community corrections offenders and staff in strengthening the corrections–community relationship?

5. In what type of community activities should correctional managers become involved?

6. What will be the role of written policy, procedures, and rules in offender and employee involvement in the community?

7. What role can the PIO play in strengthening the corrections–community relationship?

8. What role can Victim Services' employees play in strengthening the corrections–community relationship?

7

The Legal Environment of Corrections

Learning Objectives

After completing this chapter, the reader should be able to:

- Differentiate between the hands-off doctrine, judicial activism, and judicial retrenchment.
- Outline the process of institutional reform litigation.
- Identify the constitutional standards judicial review has established for institutional and community corrections.
- Explain the psychological effects of judicial activism on inmates, elected officials, and staff.
- Summarize the approaches used in formalizing the correctional litigation process.
- List and explain the legal rights of employees.
- Relate judicial activism to organizational structure.

Key Terms and Concepts

Building Tenders System
Slave of the State
Judicial Review
Hands-off Doctrine
Jailhouse Lawyer
Judicial Activism
American Civil Liberties Union
American Bar Association
Judicial Function of Management
Cruel and Unusual Punishment
Deliberate Indifference
Due Process
Consent Decree
Managerial Resistance
Strategic Planning
Inmate Legal Assistance Programs
PELR Model
Event Reconstruction
Inmate Grievance System
Vicarious Liability
Judicial Retrenchment
Alabama Federal Intervention Syndrome
Totality of Conditions
Liberty Interests
Reform Litigation
Habeas Corpus
Managerial Acceptance
Ombudsman
Routine Legal Response Model
Legal Response Coordinator
Alternatives to Litigation
Complaint Officer
Section 1983 of the Civil Rights Act of 1871
Civil Rights of Institutionalized Persons Act of 1980

By focusing attention on the severe deficiencies of the correctional system, the litigation created pressure for management reforms. Contemporaneously with the litigation, or soon thereafter, a broad range of important changes occurred. Those changes assumed different forms—new organizational structure, increased funding, new administrators, changes in personnel policies, new facilities, additional personnel, improved management procedures, etc. These changes were generally considered beneficial.

M. K. Harris and D. P. Spiller

Profile: Judicial Activism and Organizational Behavior in Texas

In 1980, Judge William W. Justice presided over *Ruiz v. Estelle,* a class action lawsuit that alleged that Texas Department of Corrections (TDC) policies in the areas of health care, access to courts, fire and safety, sanitation, and inmate discipline were unconstitutional and, in many cases, represented a threat to inmate safety. TDC attorneys argued that a TDC record of low levels of violence (only 16 inmates murdered between 1970 and 1978), as well as low assault and disturbance rates established that there was no unconstitutional threat to inmate safety. An area of especially sharp disagreement was TDC's "Building Tenders" (BT) system that used tough inmates to control the inmate population through psychological intimidation and physical violence.

On December 12, 1980, Judge Justice issued a 248-page memorandum opinion that ordered a wide range of specific changes in TDC organizational behavior. The most important changes were (1) dismantling the BT system, (2) doubling the number of correctional officers (C.O.s) and retraining veteran officers, (3) liberalizing good time policies, (4) revising the handling of inmate grievances and establishing a more elaborate hearing process, (5) revising the classification system designed to reduce the number of inmates placed in maximum security status, (6) requiring a single cell per inmate, (7) closing or upgrading the prison hospital at the Walls unit, (8) dividing prisons into management units of no more than 500 inmates, (9) requiring that the court approve all TDC construction plans, and (10) stipulating that the findings of the court-appointed monitor of prison conditions be treated as findings of fact. In 1982, a three-judge appeals panel overturned Judge Justice on orders six through ten (*Ruiz v. Estelle,* 1982). Despite some initial problems in implementing the court's orders, not the least of which was managerial resistance, *Ruiz v. Estelle* had a positive impact. The replacement of the BT system with 1,000 new C.O.s, reinvention of the classification system, and development of administrative segregation units effectively addressed the unconstitutionality of the TDC.

Correctional managers must consider the legal ramifications of policy, procedures, and rules before they are disseminated to employees and offenders. The days when correctional managers managed their organizations in accordance with personal experience and philosophy (often expressed with the phrase "gut-level feeling") instead of in accordance with the U.S. Constitution are long gone. The relationship between the courts and corrections can be divided into three distinct periods. During Pre-DOC Corrections, the courts favored a hands-off doctrine of judicial deference to the expertise of the autocratic wardens. In the 1960s, bureaucratic wardens implementing the rehabilitation model were confronted with an era of judicial activism that brought corrections under the umbrella of the Constitution and significantly changed organizational behavior. As the actuarial model began to emerge in the 1980s, the courts shifted to judicial retrenchment, a middle-of-the-road position characterized by a less aggressive approach to offender rights. The cumulative effect of judicial activism has been the reduced use of managerial discretion in the management of both offenders and employees. This chapter examines the continually evolving relationship between corrections and the courts.

COURTS AND PRE-DOC CORRECTIONS

In 1787, the U.S. Constitution set forth the fundamental right of habeas corpus (the right to challenge the legality of one's confinement) but did not specifically refer to inmates. In 1789, the Bill of Rights provided constitutional safeguards for individuals accused of crimes, but it was not until 1966 that the federal courts (*Coleman v. Peyton,* 1966:907) recognized that the right of access to the courts is one of the constitutional rights a convicted offender clearly retains.

The Hands-Off Doctrine

From 1787 until the 1960s, the federal courts followed a hands-off doctrine of declining jurisdiction in nearly all inmate litigation. There appear to be two schools of thought about why the hands-off doctrine prevailed. The argument most commonly given is that the federal courts did not recognize inmates as individuals guaranteed constitutional protection. Often cited as the basis for this view is *Ruffin v. Commonwealth* (1871), which defined the legal status of the inmate as "a slave of the state" with no rights other than those that his keepers were inclined to give him. Consequently, a prison manager's exercise of discretion and authority was not to be scrutinized by the courts.

However, Donald Wallace (1997) argues that the "slave of the state" language of *Ruffin* is contradicted by a number of state court decisions contrary to *Ruffin,* including *Westbrook v. State* (1909), in which the Georgia Supreme Court noted that inmates have all the rights of an ordinary citizen except those rights that the law has specifically removed. It is Wallace's contention that the federal courts did recognize that inmates have constitutional rights but did not accept inmate litigation because they felt constrained by five public policy concerns: (1) the separation of powers doctrine, (2) their lack of judicial expertise in corrections, (3) a fear that judicial intervention would undermine prison discipline, (4) a fear that accepting inmate litigation would result in a flood of litigation, and (5) the view that the principles of federalism precluded consideration of state inmate claims by the federal courts (Haas, 1977).

Regardless of the source of the hands-off doctrine, its practical effect was to allow the autocratic wardens to manage prisons in accordance with their personal philosophy. The U.S. Constitution did not exist inside prison walls. The result was the brutal system that has provided a basis for the gratuitous vilification of correctional employees discussed in Chapter 6.

COURTS AND DOC CORRECTIONS

In the post–World War II era, American courts began to express a concern for the rights of minorities in reaction to the horrors resulting from the extreme violation of human rights in Germany and the Soviet Union (Smith and Pollack, 1996:168). The beginning of judicial activism in corrections occurred when the U.S. Supreme Court, in *Brown v. Board of Education* (1954), extended constitutional rights and protections to disadvantaged groups (Marquart and Sorensen, 1997:229). By the late 1950s, blacks were a majority of the inmate population in many state prisons. As the Civil Rights movement grew, Black Muslim inmates, often assisted by lawyers with civil rights experience, began to successfully challenge correctional policies and procedures. Between 1961 and 1978, there were 61 reported federal court decisions pertaining to Muslims (Jacobs, 1997:233). Many of these decisions involved the right of Muslims to practice their religion. A landmark case was *Cooper v. Pate* (1964), which permitted Muslim inmates to challenge religious discrimination (the refusal of prison officials to allow Muslims to possess the Koran and hold worship services) under Section 1983 of the resurrected Civil Rights Act of 1871: "The success of the Muslims on the constitutional issue of free exercise of religious rights brought the federal courts into the prisons" (Jacobs, 1997:233).

Encouraged by the Muslims' successes, other inmates became active in litigation. Since 1964, federal judges in virtually all states have ordered state governments to dramatically change the way they operate their prisons and jails (Chilton, 1991). The foundation for successful inmate litigation was, and continues to be, Section 1983 of the Civil Rights Act of 1871, which we examine next.

Section 1983 of the Civil Rights Act of 1871

Originally passed in an effort to fight the Ku Klux Klan in the aftermath of the Civil War, Section 1983 provides that any person acting under color of state or local law who violates the constitutional or statutory rights of another individual can have their actions challenged through civil litigation. Under Section 1983, inmates may challenge violations of their First Amendment freedoms of speech, religion, and association and any prison policies that restrict their access to the courts.

Section 1983 has been the most effective device for redressing the grievances of state prisoners (Turner, 1979) because the U.S. Supreme Court in *Monroe v. Pape* (1961) interpreted it to give the federal courts original jurisdiction over any claims alleging violations of federal constitutional rights by local or state officials. The practical effect of this ruling was to allow individuals suing local or state officials under Section 1983 to bypass state courts (thus avoiding a time-consuming and financially costly process)

and go directly to federal court. In *Cooper v. Pate* (1964) the U.S. Supreme Court made it clear that state inmates could use Section 1983 to register allegations of unconstitutional treatment by local and state officials.

Need for External Legal Assistance

Although judicial activism recognized offender rights, offenders often were poorly equipped to prepare written documents and make effective legal arguments. Because of the high level of functional illiteracy among the general inmate population, "jailhouse lawyers" became an unofficial, and controversial, source of legal expertise. In a 1969 case, *Johnson v. Avery,* the U.S. Supreme Court provided official recognition to jailhouse lawyers by ruling that when prison officials fail to provide inmates with adequate legal services, inmates cannot be punished for providing legal assistance to each other. In 1974, *Wolff v. McDonnell* extended the jailhouse lawyer's authority of representation to civil rights suits attacking prison policies and conditions.

Because jailhouse lawyers were most often self-educated in the law, however, they frequently were unable to successfully argue their cases in court owing to the legal complexity of the issues involved. What the inmates needed was the assistance of professional attorneys. This need was recognized by the social activists of the 1960s and 1970s and met by the involvement of the American Bar Association (ABA) and the American Civil Liberties Union (ACLU) in the arena of correctional litigation.

THE AMERICAN BAR ASSOCIATION, THE AMERICAN CIVIL LIBERTIES UNION, AND THE PRISONERS' RIGHTS MOVEMENT

In 1970, the ABA "gave the prisoners' movement the imprimatur of the established legal community" (Jacobs, 1997:235) by creating the Commission on Correctional Facilities and Services for the purpose of advocating correctional reform. The Commission's Resource Center for Correctional Law and Legal Services provided a central clearinghouse for information and resources coordination for prisoners' rights groups and inmates filing litigation. Numerous state bar associations followed the lead of the ABA, as many established special committees dedicated to prison reform. Funding was secured from a variety of sources and by the mid-1970s inmates had a powerful community ally in their demands for constitutional conditions of confinement. Inmates were further assisted by the ruling in *Bounds v. Smith* (1977) that the Constitution imposed upon the states the obligation to provide inmates with either law libraries or adequate assistance from individuals trained in the law.

The ABA commitment to inmate rights was welcome, but many of the critics of corrections believed that a more aggressive approach was needed. This approach was provided by the ACLU.

The American Civil Liberties Union

The ACLU is a nonprofit group of attorneys that actively pressures federal, state, and local governments to avoid public policy that will infringe on the individual's constitutional rights. A division of the ACLU is the National Prison Project (NPP): eight full-time attorneys who handle a regular caseload of 20 to 25 active cases involving correctional issues. The NPP originated in 1972 in the aftermath of the 1971 Attica prison riot (Hickey, 1996:329). The purpose of the NPP is to safeguard adult and juvenile offenders' Eighth Amendment rights to be free from cruel and unusual punishment. It also serves as a resource center for the law governing the policies of corrections.

The NPP influences correctional behavior in three ways. First, it is extensively involved in prison reform litigation. NPP attorneys have effectively used class action lawsuits to attain extensive organizational reforms in Alabama, Colorado, New Mexico, Oklahoma, Rhode Island, South Carolina,

and Tennessee. They have successfully challenged behavior modification programs in Connecticut, Georgia, Kentucky, Hawaii, Virginia, Arizona, and the federal prison in Marion, Illinois. They have pioneered the use of court-appointed "Special Masters" to oversee correctional reforms (Hickey, 1996:329).

Second, the NPP is active in taking a public position on correctional issues in order to influence public policy making. NPP attorneys frequently draft model legislation reaffirming offenders' rights and advise state legislatures about alternatives to incarceration. They lobby legislatures and oppose legislative initiatives or correctional projects believed to be contrary to the best interests of offenders. For example, in Chapter 5 we noted the opposition of the American Jail Association (AJA) to the privatization of public jails. The AJA, an organization often at odds with the ACLU, was actually preceded in their opposition on this issue by the NPP, which in September 1986 passed a resolution opposing the development of private prisons. The rationale for this opposition was the belief that private prison inmates would be likely to suffer deprivations beyond those suffered in public prisons, have lessened substantive and procedural legal rights, be exposed to ineffective enforcement of health and safety standards, and be exploited under poor working conditions without pay; the NPP also felt that private prisons would encourage the overuse of incarceration (Ryan and Ward, 1989:35). These concerns have been echoed by the ABA (Gentry, 1986).

Third, the NPP is adept at forming alliances with community groups and exerting group pressure to prevent controversial correctional projects. For example, in Tennessee in the late 1980s, the state's ACLU chapter joined with the American Federation of State, County, and Municipal Employees (AFSCME) and local prison reform activists in a successful effort to stop an attempt by Correctional Corporation of America (CCA) to privatize the entire state correctional system (Immarigeon, 1987). In Pennsylvania, the local ACLU chapter joined with the state

AFL-CIO, the Pennsylvania Council of Churches, the Urban Coalition, the Guardian Civic League, a black police officers' organization, and AFSCME to oppose Buckingham Security's proposal to build a private prison for protective custody inmates. The proposal was defeated and the coalition was also able to persuade the legislature to approve a measure prohibiting any further attempts at prison privatization until more research had been undertaken (Hornblum, 1985).

Effect of the NPP on Managerial Discretion NPP reform litigation and political lobbying can significantly limit the use of discretion of correctional managers. As a result, correctional policy must always be formulated with the possibility of a legal challenge in mind. For this reason, top managers have their Legal Services Division routinely review organizational policy to determine if it is open to constitutional challenge.

The relationship between the NPP and correctional management is basically adversarial, but this is not necessarily negative. The NPP serves the valuable function of ensuring that correctional managers keep the Constitution in mind when engaged in environmental design. This awareness assists in the professionalization of corrections. But how does the NPP translate its concerns into correctional reform? The NPP lacks the authority to directly initiate correctional change. NPP attorneys cannot tell correctional managers how to do their jobs. But they can persuade the judiciary to tell correctional managers what they can, and cannot, do in the area of offender management. The NPP can, through the filing of 1983 litigation, set in motion a powerful process known as judicial review.

JUDICIAL REVIEW AS A CONSTITUTIONAL CONTROL MECHANISM

Judicial review is the "power of a court to declare acts of governmental bodies contrary to the Constitution null and void."

(Neubauer, 1996:411). This power is derived from the Constitution and is the mechanism used by the courts to ensure that each state failing to meet constitutionally mandated requirements is brought into compliance with the Constitution (Johnson, 1995:218–219). A primary focus of judicial review is the correctional manager's exercise of judicial authority.

Managerial Exercise of Judicial Authority

It is the correctional manager's responsibility to create an environmental design that will effectively and constitutionally implement applicable legislation. Inherent in this process is the exercise of a judicial function created by a rule-making power that has been legislatively delegated to managers (Duffee, 1980b:329). Managers exercise judicial authority in the sense that they must make rules for situations that are not specifically addressed by statute. It is the manner in which this judicial function has been exercised that the courts examine during the process of judicial review. Judicial review was rarely exercised during the era of the hands-off doctrine, but it is the cornerstone of judicial activism. We begin with the judicial review of organizational policy.

Review of Organizational Policy
Courts may examine the organizational policy that defines the totality of prison conditions or it may engage in selective intervention by examining only the policy in one specific area.

Examining the Totality of Conditions *Ruiz v. Estelle* (1980) involved more than the BT system. It involved a full range of major issues that, taken together, established a totality of conditions that Judge Justice declared cruel and unusual for TDC inmates. Allegations of the unconstitutionality of a totality of conditions are presented in a "conditions of confinement" lawsuit. As of January 1, 1997, 333 prisons in 30 DOCs were involved in conditions of confinement suits (Camp and Camp, 1997:54). These are the lawsuits with the greatest potential for dramatically changing systemwide behavior.

Use of Selective Intervention   Selective intervention generally targets a specific area such as medical/mental health services, food services, religious services, access to law libraries, or inmate discipline. Many inmate lawsuits alleging deficiencies in a specific area are class action lawsuits filed in the name of all DOC, or specific prison, inmates. As of January 1, 1997, there were 135 class action lawsuits filed against 46 DOCS (Camp and Camp, 1997:54). Class action suits are time-consuming, involve a high level of legal preparation, and are financially and emotionally draining. But they do serve to test the constitutionality of specific correctional practices.

For example, in *Holt v. Sarver* (1970), a federal judge ruled that the Arkansas DOC could no longer use the "Tucker Telephone" as a method of inmate discipline. Because prison lawsuits routinely invoke the Eighth Amendment prohibition against cruel and unusual punishment, *Holt* is important because it defined "cruel and unusual punishment" as any condition that "amounts to torture, or that is grossly excessive in proportion to the offense for which it is imposed, or that is inherently unfair, or that is unnecessarily degrading, or that is shocking or disgusting to people of reasonable sensitivity" (cited in Bartollas and Conrad, 1992:453).

Review of Individual Employee Use of Discretion
The power of judicial review can also be invoked to examine an individual's exercise of discretion. Individual employees can be named as defendants in inmate litigation if their behavior is part of unconstitutional organizational policy (such as use of the Tucker Telephone); but they can also be named because it is alleged that their individual use of discretion has produced unconstitutional behavior. For example, in

Smith v. Wade (1983), the U.S. Supreme Court found against a C.O. who had placed a young inmate in a cell with two inmates known to be violent. The result was a night of rape and torture. *Smith* affirmed that a prison employee, not just the organization, may be held liable for punitive damages in litigation alleging cruel and unusual punishment. When employees act with reckless or callous disregard for health or safety, the inmate is entitled to punitive damages.

It is possible to get an understanding of the process by which judicial review changes organizational behavior by examining the following specific model of institutional reform litigation.

A Model of Institutional Reform Litigation

Phillip J. Cooper (1988) has postulated a four-stage model of institutional reform litigation: the trigger phase, the liability phase, the remedy phase, and the post-decree phase.

Trigger Phase
Long-standing policies and practices create high levels of inmate frustration until some critical event in the internal or external environment convinces inmates that they have no choice except to enter the legal arena by filing a lawsuit. For example, the litigation that led to the total redesign of DOC inmate disciplinary systems was triggered by correctional officers abusing coercive power, i.e., inmates were being placed in disciplinary segregation solely on the whim of officers who simply did not like them. Much of the litigation filed by Black Muslim inmates was triggered by the nation's Civil Rights movement, which sensitized inmates to the unconstitutionality of such historical correctional practices as segregated cellblocks and routine denial of religious freedom. The history of landmark correctional litigation is one of correctional managers implementing and enforcing policies that cannot stand the scrutiny of judicial review.

Liability Phase

This phase is largely controlled by the attorneys. Its purpose is to determine if there is a violation that justifies a remedy and, if so, the extent of any injury suffered by the plaintiffs. This phase can last for years. *Ruiz v. Estelle* (1980) was filed as a class action suit in April 1974 but did not go to trial until October 1978. The trial lasted 161 days; 349 witnesses testified and 1,530 exhibits were entered into evidence (Martin and Ekland-Olson, 1987:xxvi).

To Settle or to Fight?   This is the basic legal dilemma every correctional manager faces. Taking a lawsuit all the way to a verdict can involve an enormous financial and emotional expense. Box 7–1 provides an excellent example of the complexity involved in inmate-filed class action litigation during the liability phase especially if inmates are demanding that the legal issues be formally resolved through the judicial process instead of through a less costly and time-consuming process, such as agreeing on a consent decree. The material in the Box also illustrates the intense frustration corrections managers can experience when confronted with such litigation and a judge perceived to be more sympathetic to the inmates than to the DOC. Finally, the actions of the Michigan DOC in publishing the newsletter presented in Box 7–1 represent an interesting, and rare, attempt to educate the public about a legal situation that is being funded entirely by taxpayer money. Losing a court case can also be very expensive. In addition to the cost of implementing court-ordered changes, there is the possibility of the inmates' being awarded nominal damages, compensatory damages, and punitive damages (Collins, 1993).

BOX 7–1 ONE-YEAR BIRTHDAY FOR LEGAL MONSTER: TAXPAYERS CONTINUE TO GET SOAKED FOR JUDGE'S PRIVATE PARTY

Tulips will bloom in Holland, Michigan, this year; Castro will continue to rule over Cuba—and there will be a prisoner-sponsored lawsuit against the state, kept alive by an Ingham County circuit judge bent on imposing his view of the Constitution on Michigan's citizens. April 11, Friday, marks the one-year anniversary of the trial in which Michigan prisoners are suing the state, alleging their rights would be violated if corrections officials are able to regulate the type and amount of property offenders can have while locked up. The prisoners also want to set the rules on their access to courts and to reconfigure the state's system for placement in various levels of security. The suit was filed ten years ago, and the trial finally started nine years later. The issues in the case are not easily understood by most outside the field of corrections, nor do most common folk even care. To those who work in the department, though, and especially for those who work in prisons, the outcome of those issues could be the difference between life and death. For example, Ingham County Circuit Judge James Giddings once signed an order prohibiting the Michigan Department of Corrections from taking seam rippers from inmates. A seam ripper has a small, very sharp blade and can easily be used to cut the seams from a garment—or the throat of a corrections officer. The judge has also, in the nine years after the suit was filed and before the trial started, allowed prisoners to keep other dangerous items or those that could easily be crafted into what prisoners commonly call a "shank," or homemade weapon. The decisions made—or, more accurately, the decisions he refuses to make—are also a continued burden to taxpayers. The first year of the trial has cost more than $1 million, when the costs for transportation of prisoners. housing, security, and supplies are tallied. That does not include the thousands of legal hours that assistant attorneys general have spent on the case. Nor does it include the added cost of transporting more than 100 dangerous offenders to and from court in the 140 days the court has been in session. The result? The current operations of the department are not very different than on the first day of the trial, after one year of hearings and thousands of hours of work by lawyers, clerks, and corrections staff. The judge has been active, handing down more than 75 orders. He has decided that the department can serve freeze-dried chili instead of frozen chili in the prisoner store; he decided that Prison Legal Services, which represents the prisoners in the case and is housed at taxpayer expense in a correctional facility, may install a microwave oven in its office; he has decided that the department cannot put a prisoner into administrative segregation for substance abuse; he has decided that lawyers for the prisoners can have conference calls with prisoners, forcing staff to accommodate that order; he has decided that lawyers for the prisoners deserve as much as $200 per hour (yes, that's taxpayer money) for their work on the case; he has decided that all attorneys, including prosecutors and, should it occur, other judges, must be searched before entering a prison. Judge Giddings has also decided, perforce, that the trial will last for many more years if it continues at its current pace. More than 700 potential witnesses are listed for the plaintiffs and plaintiff-intervenors (female prisoners). So far, only 155 witnesses have appeared.

Quoted from *The Insider*, A Public Information Service of the Michigan Department of Corrections. April 9, 1998:1–2.

Nominal damages (usually in the amount of $1) are awarded when inmates have sustained no actual harm but there is sufficient evidence to establish that their rights have been violated. Compensatory damages refer to actual loss and can include inmate out-of-pocket expenses or compensation for pain and suffering and mental anguish. In *Sostre v. McGinnis* (1971), a federal appeals court sustained an award of $9,300 imposed on a warden and Commissioner of Corrections as compensation ($25 per day) for the 372 days inmates spent in a solitary confinement judged to constitute cruel and unusual punishment. Punitive damages are awarded when the wrongful act was done intentionally and maliciously or with reckless disregard for inmate rights. In *Smith v. Wade* (1983), the inmate that was raped and tortured by two other inmates received $25,000 in compensatory damages and $5,000 in punitive damages because the court ruled that the C.O. should have known that an assault was likely. In some cases, the court may award attorney's fees to the plaintiff, although jailhouse lawyers are not entitled to such an award (Mushlin, 1993).

Consent Decree Because of the enormous expense of a protracted trial, litigation is frequently settled by both parties agreeing to enter into a consent decree, which is a negotiated change in practices and conditions that does not require the defendants to admit guilt. The court must approve all the terms of any settlement. Although a settlement may be viewed by some people as an admission of guilt, a consent decree spares both parties the expense and uncertainty of a protracted trial and minimizes the risk of ongoing negative publicity.

Remedy Phase

Two processes are involved in this phase. The first is the development of a plan of action designed to correct constitutional deficiencies. Second, when there has been a finding of liability (i.e., no consent decree is in effect), there may be an appeal that, when completed, may alter the original plan of action. The role of the court in developing a remedy can be either deferential or directive. In the deferential role, the judge will mandate that correctional staff correct a deficiency but provide little or no specific guidance. In *Holt v. Sarver* (1970), for example, the federal judge finding major violations in Arkansas's largest prisons ordered general improvements in prison conditions but did not become involved in the development of a formal plan of action (compliance monitoring). In the directive role, the court plays an active role in both development of a remedy and the enforcement of compliance, as was the case in *Ruiz v. Estelle* (1980).

Post-Decree Phase

During this phase the remedies are implemented, evaluated, and correctional compliance is monitored. An irony of this phase is that the managers who may have fought tooth and nail in court defending the constitutionality of their actions are now legally responsible for changing organizational behavior. This issue becomes especially critical in conditions of confinement cases where the changes tend to be dramatic.

Court-Appointed Monitor The court-appointed monitor (or Special Master) is an individual the judge believes to be capable of monitoring correctional compliance with all provisions of the court order, conducting effective negotiations with correctional managers to resolve problems, and providing recommendations to the judge for coercive compliance actions if negotiation fails. As of January 1, 1997, 157 prisons in 15 DOCs had a court-appointed monitor (Camp and Camp, 1997:54).

Judicial Compliance Mechanisms Judges have a variety of compliance mechanisms available if correctional response is too slow. Judges can (1) levy fines after issuance of a contempt citation, (2) strip the current managers of authority and appoint a receiver, and (3) order a facility closed. For example, the Rhode Island DOC was fined $189,000 by Judge Raymond Pettine after

failing to comply with the orders in *Palmigiano v. Garrahy* (1977). Judge Wayne Justice threatened the Texas DOC with $24 million in fines if compliance was not forthcoming (Martin and Ekland-Olson, 1987). In Alabama, Judge Johnson relieved the Board of Corrections of its authority and transferred it to a newly elected governor who had promised prison reform (Yackle, 1989).

In the original decree in *Palmigiano*, Judge Pettine had ordered Rhode Island's 100-year-old maximum security prison closed, but over a period of time allowed the state to make physical changes until the state won the right to keep the prison open indefinitely (Carroll, 1996:273).

However, corrections does not always lose the case, as Box 7–2 illustrates. In reading the material contained in this Box, notice, again, the frustration of corrections managers. Also note the attention being given to communication with staff, inmates, and the community concerning the new property policy.

BOX 7–2 THE PROPRIETY OF PROPERTY: TEN-YEAR LEGAL AND LEGISLATIVE ISSUE FINALLY NEARS COMPLETION

Personal property, like life and liberty, is a pillar of the American political and legal landscape. So it came as no surprise that prisoners (who already have a propensity to sue for the most picayune excuses) sought through legal action to determine the type and amount of property they could have. What is surprising—shocking, even, to those who have not followed the history of *Cain v. MDOC,* which was filed in 1988—is that the MDOC had to wait until September, 1998, before it could finally begin to confiscate property from prisoners. Finally, after ten years of ad nauseum legal activity, the MDOC was able to implement a property policy that, like those of most other states and the Federal Bureau of Prisons, was aimed at protecting the security of institutions and the safety of those within. For the department, it meant putting certain prisoners in uniforms; it meant eliminating excess property that is used to hide contraband, such as drugs and weapons, and delay shakedowns. And it meant that a new property policy was established and will be the basis for all others in the future. The concerns of the department, though, did not hold sway with Ingham County Circuit Judge James Giddings until late last year. In December, after several months of trial in the ten-year-old, infamous *Cain* case, the judge issued an opinion that supported the right of the MDOC to control property in its prisons.

Giddings wrote:

"It is further ordered that [the MDOC] may properly declare what items of property prisoners will be allowed to possess or acquire in a correctional facility."

Even that statement, though, was not enough to keep additional hurdles from being thrown in the MDOC's path. Nonetheless, despite the delays, the week of Oct. 26 is the planned completion date of the policy, when all restricted inmate gear is to be packed away and sent home or donated to charity. The entire property policy—including details about shipping and clothing exchange for some inmates—was communicated to staff and prisoners at least two days in advance of the pickups. Wardens also were encouraged to bring the topic up at their community forums and address any questions or concerns prison neighbors would have. A notice was also posted in the living areas of affected prisoners. Certain types of clothing are now pro-

hibited, such as: clothing that looks like uniforms worn by corrections staff; clothing worn traditionally by various professionals; hooded clothing or ski masks; and ponchos. Before the new policy began, prisoners were allowed to send restricted personal belongings out of the facility at their expense or with a visitor. It is likely that no one will be able to fully appreciate the enormity of the undertaking until the final tally has been made of all the truck-loads, boxes, and personal items confiscated from prisoners. Given the new property policy and a stock population of 43,000 prisoners, the final numbers will be...(To be continued next issue).

Quoted from *The Insider,* A Public Information service of the Michigan Department of Corrections. October 27, 1988:1–2.

PSYCHOLOGICAL IMPACT OF JUDICIAL ACTIVISM

The discussion has thus far centered on the legal process. But what is the psychological impact of judicial activism? Because criminals are a minority population, the 1960s and 1970s saw "a generous interpretation of the Bill of Rights in their favor" (Smith and Pollack, 1996:168). This "generous interpretation" had a powerful psychological effect on inmates, line staff, elected officials, and correctional managers.

Inmate Empowerment

For inmates, the courts' willingness to hear their allegations of constitutional violations and order correctional reforms produced a sense of having gained some control and "there can be no doubt that their self-image [was] dramatically altered" (Cohen, 1972:864). As a result, the number of federal petitions filed by local and state inmates increased from 218 in 1966 to 2,030 in 1970, 12,397 in 1980, and 16,741 in 1981 (Howard, 1982:379; Advisory Commission of Intergovernmental Relations, 1984:149). In 1981, 20 percent of federal court cases involved inmates (Moore, 1981:1). From 1989 to 1995, the number of lawsuits increased from 18,389 to 36,672 (Camp and Camp, 1996b:51).

Line Staff Powerlessness

Line staff, particularly correctional officers, perceive the ability to maintain strict control of inmate behavior as essential to their personal survival. They resent inmate access to the courts and complain that judges too frequently order changes that work against the rights and safety of C.O.s. Court decisions favorable to inmates introduce an element of uncertainty about the legal validity of all staff behavior and encourage additional inmate challenges to staff control. The result is a deterioration in working conditions for correctional employees who, in their frustration, begin to view the courts as always siding with the inmates. They feel betrayed and "sold out" by agencies that should support their authority (Carroll, 1974:54). The result can be excessive personal stress, union-involved conflict, high levels of personnel turnover, low morale, and, sometimes, retaliation against inmates.

Challenging the Authority of Elected Officials

Frequently, federal judges will order sweeping reforms that require large financial expenditures: "There is little doubt that correctional systems have been forced to increase their expenditures as a result of court orders" (Welsh, 1996:208). Elected officials are the only individuals with the power to increase the correctional budget to the level necessary to implement reform. If they do so, then correctional managers can more easily implement court-ordered

reforms. If elected officials refuse to make the necessary budgetary changes, however, then organizational behavior will generally continue as before.

Court intervention is generally resented by elected officials because they view the operation of their prisons as their responsibility. In addition, funds required to make the changes must come from the budgets of other state agencies and may not be forthcoming when elected officials have given prison reform a low priority. The advocates of the conservative revolution fervently resist spending large amounts of money to make inmate life more pleasant and legislatively initiated reform is often very slow in coming. This resistance has been termed the "Alabama Federal Intervention Syndrome," which is defined as the tendency of state officials to duck responsibility for changing prison conditions until being forced to do so by federal judges, who can then become the buffer between the elected officials and a public angry about "coddling criminals" and the increased level of correctional expenditures (McCormack, 1975:523, 536).

The resistance of elected officials places correctional managers in a difficult position. Even if they are in agreement with the court-ordered changes, they are dependent on the state legislature to provide the necessary funding. For example, in *Pugh v. Locke* (1976), a federal judge ruled that the Alabama DOC had not achieved minimum standards of incarceration because of a failure to alleviate prison overcrowding and establish a meaningful classification system. Governor George C. Wallace openly refused to initiate court-ordered reforms and delayed badly needed prison reform for nearly a decade (Yackle, 1989).

Correctional Manager Role Reversal

Correctional managers tend to view themselves as professionals whose personal experience makes them the most qualified architects of organizational behavior. Inmate litigation dramatically challenges this basic assumption by redefining managers as defendants who must explain their policies in a public forum: the courtroom. Involvement in litigation as a defendant is more than the filing of motions, elicitation of testimony, and legal interpretation of law and policy. It is an emotional experience for many managers because the litigation, and the entire court process, is viewed as a formal questioning of personal and professional honesty, integrity, and worldview. Managers may experience the psychological pain that comes from a "failure to persuade the courts of the wisdom and 'rightness' of correctional methodology. Thus, frustration, bitterness, confusion, and demoralization inevitably result" (Bershad, 1977:61). This frustration is often compounded by the fact that their defeat is publicly imposed (Harris and Spiller, 1977:213–214). This public humiliation can lead to resistance to court-ordered reforms.

Managerial Resistance to Court-Ordered Reforms

The attitude of correctional managers concerning court-ordered changes is important because it influences the reactions of subordinates. The managers who personalize litigation may come to perceive themselves as embattled protectors of the right way of doing things. They resent what they take to be a personal attack on their competence and integrity by judges who have never had to cope with the harsh reality of managing inmates and don't understand the daily challenges faced by correctional managers (Harris and Spiller, 1977:213–214). Managers who personalize the results of litigation in this way may take actions that are contrary to both the court decision and principles of effective management, delay necessary adaptation, and precipitate further judicial intervention.

Delaying the Inevitable Managers who have personalized the outcome of litigation often do everything in their power to delay implementation of court-ordered changes.

In the case of *Ruiz v. Estelle* (1980), after Judge Justice had rendered his ruling the litigation dragged on for three more years with bitter charges and countercharges coming from both sides and "anti-TDC" corrections professionals cheering at the idea that Judge Justice was "dragging those good old boy wardens kicking and screaming into the twentieth century" (DiIulio, 1987:215–216).

Retaliation Against Jailhouse Lawyers

Korn (1995) has noted that Soviet psychiatrists recognized a delusion referred to as "litigation mania"—a condition in which "a patient continually claims that his confinement is a violation of his civil rights" (Korn, 1995:335). Although rejected by American psychiatrists, a frustrated correctional manager may frequently be tempted to use this approach in managing chronic inmate litigators. For example, in 1974 a chronic writ writer in the Georgia DOC named Bobby Hardwick was transferred from Reidsville prison to a solitary confinement unit for "incorrigibles and security risks" located in H-House of the Georgia Diagnostic and Classification Center (GDCC). The reason given for the transfer by Reidsville Warden Joseph Hopper was the numerous writs Hardwick had filed, a behavior that the warden viewed as "antisocial" and justified the transfer that would hopefully "change his devious trend" (Korn, 1995:336). Instead, Hardwick's legal challenge to being placed in solitary confinement for four years was ruled successful in 1978 when a judge found that conditions in H-House were in violation of the Eighth and Fourteenth Amendments.

Managerial Acceptance of Court-Ordered Reforms

While managerial resistance may be a tempting response to judicial activism, the effective manager understands that there is a professional responsibility to accept the court's decision. The most productive managerial response to court-ordered changes is to incorporate those changes into strategic planning.

Strategic Planning and Implementing the Court Order   Although planning will be discussed extensively in Chapter 10, it is appropriate at this point to briefly mention the concept of strategic planning. This long-term planning approach involves anticipating the organizational activities and changes that must be implemented over a specific time period and incorporating the requirements of those changes into the budgeting process. For example, the court-ordered development of an inmate mental health services system would require creation of a task force to (1) study the mental health service models used in other DOCs, (2) anticipate as many implementation problems as possible for each model, (3) determine the benefits of each model, (4) select the most appropriate model (the traditional imitation adaptive strategy), (5) establish the degree of formalization (type of services-provided documentation) the model will require, (6) develop a time frame for implementation of the model, (7) forecast the budgetary impact of the program, (8) develop a training program for managers and employees, (9) educate current and new inmates to the model by including it in the inmate handbook, and (10) monitor the use of the model after it has been implemented, making course corrections as necessary. Frequently, a court order requiring change can give managers the leverage necessary to fund this type of strategic planning.

Although the psychological impact of judicial activism has been impressive, an even more profound consequence of judicial activism has been its effect on environmental design. Judicial activism brought the justice model into corrections. The justice model is a model that emphasizes legal principles and provides and enforces the requirement that environmental design must be constitutional: principles of legal fairness must be incorporated into policies, procedures, and methods. Correctional managers failing to recognize the requirements of the justice model can be taken to court and forced to comply with the Constitution.

JUDICIAL ACTIVISM AND THE JUSTICE MODEL

Institutional Corrections

One of the critical consequences of judicial activism was that it helped legislatures usher in the justice model. With regard to institutional corrections, the justice model required correctional managers to modify environmental design to achieve the goals of retribution, deterrence, and incapacitation within a framework of legal fairness. A critical area of employee–inmate interaction affected by the justice model is the administration of inmate discipline. Prior to 1974, the typical inmate disciplinary policy was a "Captain's Court" system where inmates had no right to due process and the unsupported word of a C.O. to a superior officer was sufficient to justify severe sanctions. In 1974, the U.S. Supreme Court ruled in *Wolff v. McDonnell* that inmates facing serious disciplinary action have the right to basic due process procedures that include (1) written notification of the charges at least 24 hours prior to appearance before an impartial prison hearing board where charges could be rebutted, (2) the right to present documentary evidence and call defense witnesses unless this would jeopardize prison safety and security, (3) the right to assistance of a "counsel substitute" (another inmate or a staff member) if illiterate or if the issues are unusually complex, (4) the right to a written statement of the evidence supporting the decision and the rationale for any actions taken from the hearing board, and (5) an acknowledgment (not a right) that the board could permit the accused to cross-examine witnesses (*Wolff v. McDonnell*, 1974). A model of effective compliance with *Wolff* is the inmate disciplinary system developed by the Oregon DOC.

Oregon DOC Inmate Disciplinary Policy

The Oregon DOC inmate disciplinary policy consists of 28 pages of rules, eight of which define inmate rule violations and violation reporting procedures. The stated goal of the policy is to (1) provide for a safe, secure, and orderly operation, (2) establish norms of acceptable inmate conduct and consistent and fair procedures for the processing of inmate Misconduct Reports, (3) establish a comprehensive range of appropriate disciplinary sanctions for rule violations, and (4) provide a consistent departmental response to "like types of misconducts committed by inmates with similar misconduct histories" (Oregon Department of Corrections, 1996:1–2).

Rule Violation Categories　　Inmate rule violations are grouped into four categories: Property Violations; Violations Against Persons; Violations Involving Fraud or Deception; and Violations Against the Orderly Operation of the Department/Facility, Including Weapons and Escape Devices (Figure 7–1).

Discretionary Decision Making　　The Oregon DOC specifically recognizes and defines the use of employee discretion in reporting inmate rule violations:

Corrective Action: Employees shall be expected to use less than formalized procedures if the act(s) of misconduct do not constitute a threat to life, health, facility security or good order, employee authority or property. Corrective action may include: reprimand, warning and counseling, and as authorized by the functional unit manager, loss of leisure activities for no more than eight hours. The officer-in-charge shall review and approve or disapprove all employee recommendations for loss of leisure time activities (Oregon Department of Corrections, 1996:10).

Filing the Misconduct Report　　If a rule violation justifies the filing of a misconduct report, the officer must file that report within 24 hours of the rule violation; the reviewing supervisor must certify report accuracy and ensure that the inmate has received a Notice of Hearing and Inmate Rights (Figure 7–2) within 24 hours of the filing; and a formal hearing, unless waived by the inmate, will be held no later than five working days after the inmate has received a copy of the report.

Types of Hearing　　If the rule violation is a major misconduct, the hearing will be formal, unless waived by the inmate. The formal hearing is the responsibility of a hearing officer, who is an employee of the Inspections Division assigned to review and dispose of major, and certain minor, misconduct reports through formal hearing. If the rule violation is minor, the hearing will be informal, unless a formal hearing is requested by the inmate. Informal hearings are the responsibility of an adjudicator.

The Role of the Hearing Officer/Adjudicator　　The hearing officer and adjudicator are finders of fact and any finding of guilt is to be based on the legal standard of proof of a preponderance of the evidence, defined as "the greater weight of evidence (e.g., 51 percent vs. 49 percent). It is such evidence that, when weighed with that opposed to it, has more convincing force and is more probably true and accurate" (Oregon Department of Corrections, 1996:13).

Imposition of Sanctions　　Sanctions are imposed in accordance with the Oregon DOC Major Violation Grid (Table 7–1) or the Minor Violation Grid (Table 7–2). If the sanctions include a loss of privileges, the inmate must be given a Loss of Privileges Sanction Order (Figure 7–3).

Limiting Disciplinary Segregation　　The most punitive form of sanction is disciplinary segregation because it involves physical removal from the general population. Disciplinary segregation is a form of sanction that is easy to abuse. Therefore, the Oregon DOC provides that no inmate shall serve more than 180 days in disciplinary segregation at any one time.

The Oregon DOC model effectively defines inmate rule violations, misconduct

OREGON DEPARTMENT OF CORRECTIONS
<u>NOTICE OF HEARING</u>
NOTICE OF INMATE RIGHTS

TO:_____
    LAST NAME   FIRST   INITIAL   SID#   CELL/BUNK #

A Hearing concerning the attached Misconduct Report will be scheduled within five (5) working days. The Adjudicator will classify this Misconduct Report as <u>Major</u> or <u>Minor</u>. Major Reports are scheduled for Formal Hearings and Minor Reports are scheduled for Informal Hearings. You will be mailed a Hearings Schedule Card informing you of the time and date of your hearing. The Rule(s) of Prohibited Conduct you are alleged to have violated is/are reflected on your copy of the Misconduct Report.

Notice of Hearing and Notice of Rights Served: Time_____(am/pm) Date:_____

                  By:_____
                        Printed Name/Signature   Title

1. PROPERTY VIOLATIONS

__ **a.** **ARSON:** An inmate commits arson if he/she starts an unauthorized fire or causes an explosion.

__ **b. DESTRUCTION, ALTERATION OR FAILURE TO PROTECT OR PRODUCE PROPERTY:** An inmate commits Destruction, Alteration or Failure to Protect or Produce Property I when he/she, except as authorized by an employee, destroys, abuses, alters, damages, defaces, misuses, tampers with, or wastes materials or property, or fails to properly protect or produce property issued to him/her in a timely manner. Destruction, Alteration or Failure to Protect or Produce Property I can be committed in the following ways:

(A) The property involved exceeds $75 in value; or

(B) The misconduct involves the functioning of a security device (e.g., locks and cell doors, or fire alarm systems); or

(C) The misconduct involves a threat to the safety, security or orderly operation of the facility.

__ **c. DESTRUCTION, ALTERATION OR FAILURE TO PROPERLY PROTECT OR PRODUCE PROPERTY (minor violation):** An inmate commits Destruction, Alteration or Failure to Properly Protect or Produce Property II when he/she, except as authorized by staff, destroys, alters, abuses, damages, defaces, misuses, tampers with or wastes materials or property or fails to properly protect or produce property issued to him/her in a timely manner.

__ **d. CONTRABAND I:** An inmate commits Contraband I if:

(A) He/she possesses any controlled substance; or

(B) He/she possesses or distributes intoxicants; or

(C) He/she possesses any drug paraphernalia; or

(D) He/she has any controlled substance in his/her urine or blood; or

(E) He/she fails to provide or refuses to submit a urine sample for the testing of the presence of controlled substances; or

(F) He/she alters, taints or contaminates a urine sample; or

(G) He/she possesses money in excess of $1.

__ **e. CONTRABAND II:** An inmate commits Contraband II if he/she possesses contraband other than that listed in Contraband I (OAR 291-105-0015(d)(A-G)) and Contraband III (OAR 291-105-0015(f)):

Contraband II may be committed in the following ways:

(A) An inmate possesses contraband which creates a threat to the safety, security or orderly operation of the facility (e.g., razor blades, checks, tobacco or smoking paraphernalia, tattoo equipment or paraphernalia, unauthorized medication (except self-medication which has expired) and items of barter, such as jewelry or canteen items not purchased by him or her); or

(B) An inmate possesses contraband which was obtained by threats of or actual violence or obtained by theft (including services), forgery, or coercion.

__ **f. CONTRABAND III (minor violation:)** An inmate commits Contraband III if he/she possesses contraband other than that listed on Contraband I (OAR 291-105-0015(d)(A-G)) and Contraband II (OAR 291-105-0015(e)(A-B), including money in an amount of $1 or less, uncancelled stamps, self-medication which has expired, legal material belonging to another inmate or property in excess of that authorized by staff members.

__ **g. UNAUTHORIZED USE OF A COMPUTER:** An inmate commits Unauthorized Use of a Computer if he/she, except as authorized by the Director or attendant to participation in an educational/vocational program, operates or uses any Department of Corrections computer equipment including, but not limited to terminals, personal computers, minicomputers, work stations, controllers, printers and communication devices; or exceeds the conditions of use or access granted by the Director.

2. VIOLATIONS AGAINST PERSONS:

__ **a. ASSAULT I:** An inmate commits Assault I if:

(A) He/she causes physical injury to an employee, visitor or volunteer; or

(B) He/she throws bodily fluids on an employee, visitor or volunteer, including feces, urine, spit, semen and blood; or

(C) He/she causes serious physical injury to another person other than an employee, visitor or volunteer; or

(D) He/she causes physical injury to another person and uses a dangerous/ deadly weapon; or

(E) He/she commits a unilateral attack in a location or under circumstances which creates a threat to the safety, security, or orderly operation of the facility, such as the dining hall or the recreation area; or

(F) He/she commits a sexual assault upon another; or

(G) He/she has knowledge that he/she is HIV positive and engages in non-assaultive sexual intercourse with another, either oral, vaginal, or rectal; or

(H) He/she refuses to stop his/her assaultive behavior after being ordered to do so and which necessitates a staff member(s) becoming physically involved to stop the assaultive behavior.

__ **b. ASSAULT II:** An inmate commits Assault II if:

(A) He/she throws bodily fluids on another inmate, including feces, urine, spit, semen and blood; or

(B) He/she commits a unilateral attack and causes physical injury to another person; or

(C) He/she is involved in a mutual fight in a location or under circumstances which creates a threat to the safety, security, or orderly operation of the facility, such as a dining hall or recreation area.

__ **c. ASSAULT III:** An inmate commits Assault III if:

(A) He/she commits a unilateral attack; or

(B) He/she is involved in a mutual fight and causes physical injury to another person.

__ **d. ASSAULT IV:** An inmate commits Assault IV if he/she is involved in a mutual fight.

__ **e. DISRESPECT I:** An inmate commits Disrespect I if he/she directs hostile, sexual, abusive or threatening language or gestures, verbal or written, towards or about another person involving a physical threat to the other person.

__ **f. DISRESPECT II:** An inmate commits Disrespect II if he/she directs hostile, sexual, abusive or threatening language or gestures, verbal or written, towards or about another person the expression of which or under circumstances which create a threat to the safety, security or orderly operation of the facility (including, but not limited to, when one or more persons are present, or in a location such as a dining hall or recreation yard.

__ **g. DISRESPECT III (minor violation):** An inmate commits Disrespect III when he/she directs hostile, sexual, abusive or threatening language or gestures, verbal or written, towards or about another person.

CD 146D p2 (6/96)

FIGURE 7–1 Oregon DOC Notice of Inmate Rights: Notice of Hearing. Source: Oregon Department of Corrections. *Prohibited Inmate Conduct and Processing Disciplinary Actions* (1996).

__ **h. EXTORTION I:** An inmate commits Extortion I if he/she compels or induces an employee or any other person who is not an inmate to act or refrain from acting by threats, force or intimidation. (Extortion includes the use of threats, force or intimidation to collect gambling and other types of debt).

__ **i. EXTORTION II:** An inmate commits Extortion II if he/she compels or induces an inmate to act or refrain from acting by threats, force or intimidation. (Extortion includes the use of threat, force or intimidation to collect gambling and other types of debt).

__ **j. HARASSMENT - RACIAL/RELIGIOUS/SEXUAL:** An inmate commits Racial/Religious/Sexual Harassment if he/she directs offensive language or gestures towards another person or group, or about another person or group, or subjects another to physical contact because of the other person's or group's race, sex, color, religion, national origin, age, marital status, or disability.

__ **k. HOSTAGE TAKING:** An inmate commits Hostage Taking if he/she interferes with another person's personal liberty by taking him/her hostage. CD 146D (4/93)

__ **l. NON-ASSAULTIVE SEXUAL ACTIVITY:** An inmate commits Non-assaultive Sexual Activity if he/she engages in sexual activity which produces or is intended to produce sexual stimulation or gratification in the present of another person and the sexual activity is conducted without violence, threat of violence, coercion, or use of a weapon.

__ **m. TATTOOING:** An inmate commits Tattooing if he/she marks or allows to be marked his/her skin, or the skin of another, with a pattern by puncturing it and inserting a dye or other material to make a pattern.

3. VIOLATIONS INVOLVING FRAUD OR DECEPTION

__ **a. BRIBERY:** An inmate commits bribery if he/she confers, or offers or agrees to confer any benefit upon another person, which may influence an employee's judgment, action or decision, or an employee's exercise of discretion in an official capacity, or during the course of an employee's employment.

__ **b. FALSE INFORMATION TO EMPLOYEES I:** An inmate commits False Information to Employees I if he/she presents or causes the presentation of false or misleading information to an employee which creates a threat to the safety, security or orderly operation of the facility. False or misleading information shall include gestures, and auditory and/or written communication.

__ **c. FALSE INFORMATION TO EMPLOYEES II (minor violation):** An inmate commits False Information to Employees II when he/she presents or causes the presentation of false and misleading information to employees. False or misleading information includes gestures, and auditory and/or written communication.

__ **d. FORGERY:** An inmate commits Forgery if he/her falsely makes, completes, alters or presents a written instrument.

__ **e. GAMBLING (minor violation):** An inmate commits Gambling when he/she wagers anything of value in games of chance, or an inmate possesses paraphernalia associated with gambling or possesses the proceeds of gambling activity, money or otherwise.

__ **f. MAIL FRAUD:** An inmate commits mail fraud if he/she uses the mail (U.S. Postal Service or inter-departmental) to deceive another person or business in order to obtain money, property or something of monetary value.

4. VIOLATIONS AGAINST THE ORDERLY OPERATION OF THE DEPARTMENT/FACILITY, INCLUDING WEAPONS AND ESCAPE DEVICES

__ **a. DISOBEDIENCE OF AN ORDER I:** An inmate commits Disobedience of an Order I when he/she overtly refuses to promptly or in a timely manner, comply with valid orders which create a threat to the safety, security, or orderly operations of the facility (such as when one or more other persons are present).

__ **b. DISOBEDIENCE OF AN ORDER II:** An inmate commits Disobedience of an Order II if:

(A) He/she overtly refuses to follow a valid order; or

(B) He/she fails to comply with a valid order which creates a threat to the safety, security or orderly operation of the facility (such as when one or more other persons are present).

__ **c. DISOBEDIENCE OF AN ORDER III (minor violation):** An inmate commits Disobedience of an Order III when he/she fails to comply with a valid order.

__ **d. DISTURBANCE:** An inmate commits a Disturbance if he/she advocates, creates, engages in, maintains or promotes an unreasonably annoying condition or disorder, characterized by unruly, noisy, or violent conduct or unauthorized group activity, which disrupts the orderly administration of or poses a direct threat to the security of a facility, facility programs or the safety of employees or other persons.

__ **e. DRUG SMUGGLING:** An inmate commits Drug Smuggling if he/she distributes, has distributed to him/her or manufactures any controlled substance.

__ **f. CONTRABAND SMUGGLING:** An inmate commits Contraband Smuggling if he/she distributes contraband or has contraband distributed to him or her which creates a threat to the safety, security and orderly operation of the facility.

__ **g. EMPLOYEE/INMATE - RELATIONSHIPS:** An inmate commits a prohibited Employee/Inmate Relationship when he/she knowingly engages in any personal or business transactions, either directly or through his/her family or friends, with an employee or volunteer of the Department of Corrections, except as authorized in advance by the employee's job description or functional unit manager.

__ **h. ESCAPE:** An inmate commits Escape if he/she departs without authorization from:

(A) Within the security perimeter of a facility;

(B) The immediate control of Department of Corrections staff while outside the facility security perimeter;

(C) The grounds of a minimum security facility without a security perimeter; or

(D) The direct supervision of non-Departmental personnel authorized to supervise inmates while outside the facility security perimeter.

__ **I. UNAUTHORIZED DEPARTURE:** An inmate commits Unauthorized Departure if he/she departs without authorization while on temporary release or transitional leave from a facility and not under direct supervision.

__ **j. POSSESSION OF A DANGEROUS/DEADLY WEAPON OR AN ESCAPE DEVICE:** An inmate commits Possession of a Dangerous/Deadly Weapon or an Escape Device when he/she possesses such a weapon or escape device as defined in this rule (OAR 291-105-0010(8) and (15)).

__ **k. UNAUTHORIZED AREA I:** An inmate commits Unauthorized Area I if he/she is in any location not designated by assignment, programmed activity, call-out of staff directive:

(A) He/she is present in an area which can result in harm to another; or

(B) He/she is present in any location which is not authorized by staff or programmed activity and which creates a threat to the safety, security or orderly operation of the facility; or

(C) He/she fails to be in any location in which inmate has been ordered to be which creates a threat to the safety, security or orderly operation of the facility. (For instance, failure to be present for a count).

__ **l. UNAUTHORIZED AREA II (minor violation):** An inmate commits Unauthorized Area II when he/she is in any location not designated by assignment, programmed activity, call-out or staff directive.

__ **m. UNAUTHORIZED ORGANIZATION I:** An inmate commits Unauthorized Organization I if, except as specified by Department of Corrections Rule on Group Activities (Inmate) (OAR 291-145) or by the functional unit gang information manager, the inmate creates or actively promotes, recruits, or participates in any club, association or organization which is a gang.

__ **n. UNAUTHORIZED ORGANIZATION II:** An inmate commits Unauthorized Organization II if, except as specified by Department of Corrections Rule on Group Activities (Inmate) (OAR 291-145) or by the functional unit gang information manager, the inmate supports, displays, or endorses through verbal, visual or written communication, any club, association or organization which is a gang or engages in a petition drive without specific authorization from the functional unit manager.

__ **o. UNAUTHORIZED ORGANIZATION III (minor violation):** An inmate commits Unauthorized Organization III if, except as specified by Department of Corrections Rule on Group Activities (Inmate) (OAR 291-145) or by the functional unit manager, the inmate creates, promotes, or participates in any club, association or organization.

(5) An inmate who attempts or conspires to commit conduct in violation of a rule(s) of misconduct shall be found in violation of the rule(s), and shall be subject to appropriate sanction(s) on the same basis as if the inmate had committed a completed violation(s). (See definitions for attempt and conspiracy).

CD 146D p3 (6/96)

FIGURE 7–1 *(Continued)*

NOTICE OF INMATE RIGHTS
<u>RIGHTS IN FORMAL AND INFORMAL HEARINGS</u>

(1) HEARING: You are entitled to a hearing whenever a Misconduct Report is filed against you. Prior to your hearing, you will be provided a copy of the Misconduct Report, a Notice of Hearing and a statement of your rights in a disciplinary hearing. You will be scheduled for a hearing within five days (excluding Saturday, Sunday and holidays) after you receive your Misconduct Report. Your hearing will be conducted in accordance with the provisions contained within the Department of Corrections rule governing Prohibited Inmate Conduct and Processing Disciplinary Actions (OAR 291-105-0005 through OAR 291-105-0080).

If you are charged with one or more major rule violations, you will have a formal disciplinary hearing before a hearings officer. If you are charged with only minor rule violations, you will have an informal disciplinary hearing before a disciplinary adjudicator; unless you specifically request that the minor charges be heard at a formal hearing. Formal hearing proceedings will be tape recorded, however informal hearings will not.

You may be allowed to receive assistance from another person during the hearing, in those instances where there may be a language barrier or where a question of your competence or capacity to understand the charges or surrounding facts may arise.

You may decline to attend your hearing, however, the hearings officer/adjudicator may make a determination in the case at issue, regardless of whether you appear or not. Additionally, you may not be allowed to attend your hearing if your inappropriate behavior warrants your exclusion from it.

(2) EVIDENCE: You have a right to speak on your own behalf and to present evidence at the hearing. However, the hearings officer/adjudicator may exclude evidence that is determined to create a threat to the safety or security of the facility or that would not assist with the resolution of the disciplinary action. The hearings officer/adjudicator may consider evidence which is considered confidential and you will not be provided the names of individuals providing the information or any specific statements they may have given.

(3) INVESTIGATION/WITNESSES: You may *request* that an investigation be conducted related to the charges against you. In a *formal hearing* you may also *request* that witnesses be called to testify on your behalf. However, you will need to submit your request for witnesses to the hearings officer, in writing, prior to your hearing. In either situation, you must provide the hearings officer/adjudicator with sufficient evidence to conclude that the results of the investigation and/or the testimony provided by witnesses, will either constitute a defense to the charge(s) or substantially lessen the severity of the violation(s). Otherwise, the hearings officer/adjudicator may deny your request.

(4) POSTPONEMENT: Your hearing may be postponed for good cause and reasonable periods of time; including preparation of a defense; gathering of additional evidence; avoiding interference with an ongoing police investigation; etc.

(5) SANCTIONS: If you are found in violation of a rule of prohibited conduct, the hearings officer/adjudicator may impose sanctions. These sanctions may include, but are not limited to: disciplinary segregation, loss of privileges and monetary fines.

(6) REVIEW: Within fifteen (15) working days (excluding Saturday, Sunday and holidays) of the conclusion of your formal hearing, the hearings officer will prepare and submit to the functional unit manager, a written Finding of Fact, Conclusion and preliminary Order. You should direct concerns or issues regarding your hearing, to the functional unit manager, as soon as possible after the conclusion of your hearing. The functional unit manager will review the preliminary Order and; sign the Order, making it the final Order; amend the Order and sign it, making it the final Order; or order the hearings officer to reopen the hearing to consider additional evidence not considered at the original hearing. If the functional unit manager fails to act on the preliminary Order within five (5) days (excluding Saturday, Sunday and holidays) it will become the final Order, unless there has been a deviation ordered by either the hearings officer or the functional unit manager.

If you are found in violation of a major infraction which is located on Level I or Level II of the Major Violation Grid, you may request an Administrative Review of your case by the Inspector General for the Department of Corrections. You must file such a request with the Inspector General, within 30 calendar days after the Final Order has been signed. Your request must minimally contain; a copy of the Misconduct Report and a copy of the hearings officer's written Finding of Fact, Conclusions and Order. The Inspector General will only review your case based upon the following criteria: was there substantial compliance with the rule; was the finding based upon a preponderance of the evidence; and was the sanction imposed in accordance with the provisions of the rule (OAR 291-105). *The Inspector General <u>will</u> <u>not</u> review your request in terms of the severity of the sanction imposed.*

There is no review procedure related to informal hearings.

For more specific, detailed information regarding your rights in a disciplinary hearing, you may review the Department of Corrections rule mentioned above (OAR 291-105-0005 through OAR 291-105-0080.)

(See reverse side for further instructions regarding informal hearings)

CD 295p.1 (6/96)

FIGURE 7–2 Oregon DOC Notice of Inmate Rights: Rights in Formal and Informal Hearings. Source: Oregon Department of Corrections. *Prohibited Inmate Conduct and Processing Disciplinary Actions* (1996).

* ATTENTION *

If you are charged only with a minor rule violation(s) and are scheduled for an informal hearing, you should bring this form with you to the hearing.

I understand my rights in formal and informal disciplinary hearings as stated in this Notice of Inmate Rights form.

_____ _____
Inmate's Signature   Date

_____ _____
Adjudicator   Date

          _____
          Case Number

I, _____ request a formal hearing

in the case of a Misconduct Report I received on _____

___ for alleged violation of rule(s) _____.

CD 295 p.2 (6/96)

FIGURE 7–2 *(Continued)*

reporting procedures, conduct of impartial hearing procedures, and the sanctions that can be imposed. Although the need for employee discretion is recognized, it is defined and limited by written policy. Thus, a finding of guilty in an Oregon DOC disciplinary hearing will have been reached within an organizational framework far more legalistic than the unlimited discretion framework of the Captain's Court.

Community Corrections

The above discussion of the justice model focused on the legal rights of prison inmates. But the justice model also applies to offenders under community corrections supervision. In prisons, the courts have emphasized the prohibition of cruel and unusual punishment. In community corrections, the courts have been most concerned

OREGON DEPARTMENT OF CORRECTIONS
LOSS OF PRIVILEGES SANCTION ORDER

Name _____ Case # _____ Date _____

SID # _____ Housing _____ Hour _____

RULE(S) VIOLATED: _____

_____ *Days loss of all designated leisure time activities as follows:*

_____ *ALL · LISTED ACTIVITIES*

_____ Hobby Shop   _____ Dayroom (movies / television)

_____ Canteen   _____ Recreation Yard / outside activities

_____ Cardroom   _____ Multipurpose Building / inside activities

_____ Picture-taking program   _____ Library - recreation reading program (except Legal Library)

_____ Telephone   _____ All inmate organization meetings (except AA / NA)

_____ Other _____

*Effective from:*_____*Through 2400 hours (midnight):*_____

_____Hours extra duty to be completed by 2400 hours (midnight) on:

COMMENTS: _____
_____
_____
_____

If an inmate is on loss of all privileges, unless otherwise exempted by the terms of this Sanction Order, she/he must remain in her/his assigned cell/bunk area except for: meals, call-outs, work assignments, assigned educational, professional and/or technical training classes, and visits. If Canteen privileges are restricted, an inmate may purchase seven (7) envelopes each week during the period that she/he is on loss of Canteen privileges. Inmates on loss of all privileges may attend one denominational worship service of her/his choice each week that she/he is on loss of all privileges.

Emergency and legal phone calls may be made in accordance with the Department of Corrections rule on "Telephones (Inmate)" and the established procedures of the facility of confinement. An inmate must make arrangements for emergency/legal phone calls with the appropriate designated staff member. Failure to do so constitutes a violation of the written Sanction Order.

If an inmate under sanction is transferred from one Oregon Department of Corrections facility to another during the effective period of this Order, the inmate remains subject to the terms of the Order unless otherwise exempted by administrative action.

A "Sanction Order" is a valid written order. Inmates violating the terms of a Sanction Order may receive an additional Misconduct Report, and if the violation is established, additional disciplinary sanctions.

The Department of Corrections rule of "Prohibited Inmate Conduct and Processing Disciplinary Actions" does not provide for the appeal of disciplinary hearing decisions to the Functional Unit Manager. Within 15 working days following the conclusion of the hearing, the Hearings Officer shall prepare and issue a Preliminary Order containing the Hearings Officer's Findings of Fact and Conclusions of law. Once issued, the Preliminary Order shall be delivered to the Functional Unit Manager or designee for her/his processing in accordance with the terms and limitation of OAR 291.105-031.

_____
Signature of Hearings Officer

COPIES: WHITE (Hearings), YELLOW (Staff), PINK (Inmate)   CD 103D (6/96)

FIGURE 7–3   Oregon DOC Loss of Privileges Sanction Order. Source: Oregon Department of Corrections. *Prohibited Inmate Conduct and Processing Disciplinary Actions* (1996).

TABLE 7–1 Major violation grid: Inmates misconduct history scale. Source: Oregon Department of Corrections.

# Rule	A 6 or More Prior Major Violations Within Last 4 Yrs.	B 4–5 Prior Major Violations Within Last 4 Years	C 2–3 Prior Major Violations Within Last 4 Years	D 0–1 Prior Major Violations Within Last 4 Years
I (1) (a) Arson (2) (a) Assault I (4) (d) Disturbance (4) (e) Drug Smuggling (4) (h) Escape (2) (h) Extortion I (2) (k) Hostage Taking (4) (j) Poss Dang/Dead Wpn/Escape Dev (4) (m) Unauthor Org I	Fine: $200 max Seg: 120 days LOP: 28 days max	Fine: $200 max Seg: 120 days LOP: 28 days max	Fine: $200 max Seg: 120 days LOP: 28 days max	Fine: $200 max Seg: 120 days LOP: 28 days max
II (2) (b) Assault II (3) (a) Bribery (1) (d) Contraband I (4) (g) Employee/ Inmate Relationship (2) (i) Extortion II (1) (g) Unauthor Use of Computer (4) (f) Contraband Smug (4) (l) Unauthor Depart	Fine: $100 max Seg: 42–84 days LOP: 28 days max	Fine: $100 max Seg: 35–49 days LOP: 28 days max	Fine: $100 max Seg: 28–42 days LOP: 28 days max	Fine: $100 max Seg: 28–35 days LOP: 28 days max
III (2) (c) Assault III (1) (b) Destruct/Alter of Property I (4) (a) Disobedience I (2) (e) Disrespect I (3) (d) Forgery (3) (f) Mail Fraud (2) (l) Non-Assault Sexual Act (2) (j) Racial/Rel/Sex Harassment (4) (k) Unauthor Area I (4) (n) Unauthor Org II	Fine: $75 max Seg: 14–28 days LOP: 14–28 days	Fine: $75 max Seg: 14–21 days LOP: 14–28 days	Fine: $75 max Seg: 7–21 days LOP: 14–21 days	Fine: $75 max Seg: 7–14 days LOP: 14–21 days
IV (2) (d) Assault IV (1) (e) Contraband II (2) (f) Disrespect II (2) (m) Tattooing	Fine: $50 max Seg: 7–21 days LOP: 14–28 days	Fine: $50 max Seg: 7–14 days LOP: 7–21 days	Fine: $50 max Seg: 0–14 days LOP: 7–14 days	Fine: $50 max Seg: 0–7 days LOP: 7–14 days
V (4) (b) Disobedience II (3) (b) False Infor I	Fine: $25 max Seg: 0–14 days LOP: 7–21 days	Fine: $25 max Seg: 0–14 days LOP: 7–14 days	Fine: $25 max Seg: 0–14 days LOP: 7–14 days	Fine: $25 max Seg: 0–14 days LOP: 7–14 days

TABLE 7-2 Minor violation grid: Inmates misconduct history scale. Source: Oregon Department of Corrections.

# Rule		
VI	(4) (c) Disobed III (2) (g) Disrespect III (4) (o) Unauth Org III	Fine: $25 max Seg: 0–7 days LOP: 7–14 days
VII	(1) (c) Destruct/Alter of Property (3) (c) False Info II (3) (e) Gambling	Fine: $15 max Seg: 0–5 days LOP: 7–10 days
VIII	(1) (f) Contraband III (4) (1) Unauth Area II	Fine: $10 max Seg: 0–3 days LOP: 0–7 days

about the protection of liberty interests and have placed constitutional restrictions on the conditions of supervision of offenders who have received community corrections sentences. The most significant restrictions apply to the legal requirements of contract conditions, probation revocation, and parole revocation.

Legal Requirements of Probation/Parole Conditions

Although parole officers (P.O.s) have wide latitude in the behavioral contracts they develop with their clients, case law has established that contract conditions must (1) serve either the purpose of protecting society or promoting rehabilitation, (2) be clear and explicit in outlining what the client can and cannot do, (3) be reasonable, that is, not excessive in expectations or impose an unreasonable burden, and (4) be constitutional (Del Carmen, 1985).

If these conditions are met, P.O.s have two constitutional methods they can use to enforce the contract. First, random drug testing is constitutional. In fact, probationers may be subjected to random drug testing even if their crimes were not drug-related (*State v. Morris,* 1991). Second, in many states, P.O.s can search a client's home without a warrant and use illegally seized evidence in a revocation hearing. In general,

P.O.s may enter a client's home without a search warrant as long as they have reasonable grounds to believe that contraband is inside and they have their supervisor's permission (*Griffin v. Wisconsin,* 1987).

Probation Revocation

In 1973, *Gagnon v. Scarpelli* established that due process is required in probation revocation hearings: (1) written notification of the charges, (2) advance written notice of the revocation hearing to allow time to prepare a defense, (3) client attendance at the hearing is permitted as is the presentation of evidence, (4) the right to confront and cross-examine accusers must be upheld, and (5) a probationer may have legal counsel if the case is so complex that they are beyond the understanding of an ordinary person. Probation can be revoked if the client has been convicted of a new crime or violated the conditions of probation. The decision to revoke can be appealed to a court, but the courts are generally reluctant to become involved in this area of organizational behavior.

Parole Revocation

In 1972, *Morrissey v. Brewer* established that parole revocation hearings must also be governed by due process procedures, as listed above. The procedures are remarkably similar to those for probation clients, but the right to an impartial hearing board is specifically granted. Regardless of placement, offenders cannot be denied their fundamental constitutional rights, especially the right to due process. But does the justice model apply to correctional employees? Yes, it does.

The Justice Model and Employee Rights

The principles of fairness, legal rights, the obligation of correctional managers to set policy that is constitutional, and the right of individuals to sue correctional managers if policy is unconstitutional is not reserved exclusively to offenders. Correctional employees also benefited from the introduction of the justice model into corrections. Correctional employees have the right to seek, and secure, a legal remedy against a manager who has implemented employee policies which are violative of individual rights.

Laws Governing Personnel Management Procedures

Managers can be held legally accountable if their personnel practices violate the following laws: the Civil Rights Acts of 1964 and 1970, which prohibit race discrimination in employment practices; the Equal Pay Act of 1963, which prohibits discrimination in wages on the basis of gender; the Age Discrimination in Employment Act of 1967, amended in 1978, which prohibits discrimination based on age for people between the ages of 40 and 70; the Rehabilitation Act of 1973, amended in 1980, which prohibits discrimination against handicapped individuals by federal contractors and the federal government; the Pregnancy Discrimination Act of 1978, an amendment to Title VII, which prohibits employment discrimination based on pregnancy, childbirth, and related conditions; the Civil Service Reform Act of 1978, which requires a federal workforce "reflective of the nation's diversity"; the Immigration Reform and Control Act of 1986, which prohibits discrimination against qualified aliens on the basis of national origin; and the Americans with Disabilities Act of 1990. Correctional Managers can be held legally liable for three types of violations of employment legislation.

Negligence in Employment Practices

All of these laws are enforced by the Equal Employment Opportunity Commission (EEOC) and can provide the foundation for employee litigation. A correctional manager can be sued if deemed to have been "negligent" in the hiring, assignment, retention, direction, supervision, or training of subordinate personnel. Litigation is permitted if the manager is deemed to have violated an employee's rights when failing to promote, in disciplinary action, and in the dismissal process. Section 1983 can even be used in an action for unfair failure to hire a person (Barrineau, 1994:71–72).

Failing to Warn of Hazardous Working Conditions

Correctional managers can be sued under Section 1983 for failure to warn of hazardous working conditions; however, the courts are generally not sympathetic to these types of claims. In Oklahoma, for example, a female librarian raped by an inmate sued facility managers for negligence for providing lax security. She lost in court because she had been told at the time of hiring that she would be in contact with inmates who had a history of violence (*Corrections Professional*, 1997d:14). In *Walker v. Rowe*, (1986:511), an appeals court overruling a lower court judgment in favor of C.O.s killed or injured in a riot noted: "The state must protect those it throws into snake pits, but the state need not guarantee that volunteer snake charmers will not be bitten."

Failure to Permit Appeal

Correctional managers can also be held liable for not granting an employee a proper hearing to appeal hiring, promotion, discipline, and termination of employment decisions. In order to legally fire an individual, a correctional manager must, at a minimum, show that (1) there are substantive reasons for the dismissal, (2) the organization has established a proper procedure to be followed in every case of dismissal, (3) the established procedure was followed in the case under discussion, and (4) the behavior cited as the rationale for the dismissal had an adverse impact on the organization or the public (Barrineau, 1994:76). However, the employee does not have to complete the organization's appeal process prior to filing an employment discrimination civil suit under Section 1983.

JUDICIAL ACTIVISM AND ORGANIZATIONAL STRUCTURE

The impact of judicial activism on corrections can be summarized as follows:

1. The tradition of management as "art" has been replaced by bureaucracy.
2. A new generation of managers has been created.

3. Procedural protections for inmates have been expanded.
4. Public awareness of prisons has been increased.
5. Inmates have been politicized and their expectations heightened.
6. Prison staff have been demoralized.
7. It is now more difficult to maintain control over inmates.
8. A professional movement within corrections to establish national professional standards has been created (Jacobs, 1997: 241–244).

In addition, the organizational structure of corrections has changed as new functions have been created.

Increasing Horizontal Differentiation

Horizontal differentiation has increased through a process of functional departmentalization as correctional organizations adapted to the need for new categories of employees, functions, and departments. One of the most important adaptations was the creation of the Legal Affairs Division. For example, the California DOC has a Legal Affairs Division composed of three separate units. The Correctional Law Unit acts as house counsel; it offers legal opinions and advice and coordination of litigation support is provided by the Attorney General's office and other trial counsel. The Employment Law Unit provides and coordinates representation in court litigation and administrative hearings on such employment issues as adverse actions, employment discrimination, affirmative action, selection and standards, and health and safety. The Arbitration Defense Unit handles the DOC's legal defense in the arbitration of prison claims not resolved by the Planning and Construction Division. The California DOC has also created an Office of Health and Safety that administers the workers' compensation and disability benefit programs, manages the return-to-work programs that

aid the return of employees after illness or injury, administers the Hazardous, Toxic, and Volatile Substances program to ensure safety in the handling, storage, use, and disposal of hazardous substances, and coordinates the Employee Assistance Program (California Department of Corrections, 1996a:25, 28).

In Missouri, the DOC has created an Office of Constituent Services that has the responsibility of responding to citizens' questions about conditions of confinement in DOC prisons. Every question and concern about DOC policy is either answered directly by Constituent Services employees or referred to managers who can respond. This process alerts correctional managers to developing problems and provides information that they can use to evaluate and, if necessary, modify policy. As a consequence, since January 1994, the number of lawsuits pending against the department has fallen from 1,825 to 462, while the inmate population has increased by 47 percent (deGroot, 1997b:77).

Increasing Formalization

In adapting to an environment of judicial activism, correctional managers have done more than create new departments. They have increased the degree of formalization. For example, the once underground process by which inmates research and prepare their litigation has now been formalized.

Formalizing the Pretrial Litigation Process

The constitutional right of inmates to sue correctional organizations has resulted in the creation of formal inmate legal assistance programs governed by organizational policy and funded through the organization's annual budgetary process. Currently, there are two types of inmate legal assistance programs: (1) prison-supported networks of jailhouse lawyers and (2) resident counsel programs staffed by attorneys.

Prison-Supported Networks of Jailhouse Lawyers In Nebraska, jailhouse lawyers receive good time credits if they assist other inmates in filing litigation. In Pennsylvania, jailhouse lawyers in each prison offer free legal services to other inmates with work credit, supplies, office space, and a law library provided by the prison (Rudovsky, Bronstein, and Koren, 1983). The supervision of these jailhouse lawyers is most frequently the responsibility of the prison librarian, who also has the responsibility of annually updating the inmate law library.

Resident Counsel Programs Staffed by Attorneys The resident counsel program involves jailhouse lawyers and law students or paralegals under the supervision of lawyers (Alpert and Huff, 1991:339). Resident counsel programs are probably more effective than prison-supported networks because of the involvement of attorneys; however, they are more expensive.

The practice of correctional managers providing inmates with a mechanism for initiating effective litigation against the organization and its employees can be a source of resentment for employees and managers alike. However, effective correctional managers have learned that both programs can serve the valuable function of reducing prison tension. Cardarelli and Finkelstein (1974) reported that over 80 percent of a large sample of state Commissioners, superintendents, and treatment directors agreed that legal services provide a safety valve for inmate grievances, reduce inmate power structures and tensions from unresolved legal problems, and contribute to rehabilitation. A second nationwide survey of prison managers (Haas and Champagne, 1976) found that resident counsel attorneys helped reduce problems with jailhouse lawyers and friction between staff and inmates.

In addition to formalizing the inmate pretrial litigation process, correctional managers have also formalized the process by which the organization responds to inmate litigation.

Formalizing the Organizations' Litigation Response

The volume of inmate litigation produced by judicial activism required managers to develop an efficient model of litigation processing that would be the responsibility of a new category of employee: the Litigation Response Coordinator (LRC). Litigation response coordination can also be a new function assigned to an already existing employee category, most frequently the superintendent's administrative assistant. The most commonly used model of litigation response is the reactive Routine Legal Response (RLR) model. It functions as follows: (1) a lawsuit is received, either by the top manager or an individual employee; (2) allegations are investigated by the LRC; (3) an institutional response is submitted to the court; (4) plaintiff interrogatories are responded to through the preparation of defendant declarations after additional discussion and investigation; (5) the judge conducts a pretrial conference; (6) employees scheduled to provide testimony review the facts of the case with counsel; and (7) staff testify in court and undergo cross-examination (Freeman, 1996b:100). Each step in the process is governed by written policy and requires documentation. Each lawsuit is treated as a unique event and is individually processed.

The RLR model works well under normal conditions when a variety of lawsuits are received on an as-filed basis; but Freeman (1996b) has suggested that the efficiency of the RLR model breaks down when managers are confronted with the large volumes of inmate litigation that typically follow a correctional emergency, such as a riot, especially if there has been widespread physical plant damage and injury. He suggested that correctional organizations can more efficiently process large volumes of post-emergency litigation by preplanning for such an event through development of a proactive Post-Emergency Litigation Response (PELR) model based on three assumptions: (1) the major theme of each post-emergency lawsuit will be very similar, if not identical, (2) the majority of litigation themes can be anticipated simply by the staff's talking to inmates after the emergency, and (3) event reconstruction (determining what was done, who did it, and who authorized it) of critical decisions and staff actions can be under way well before the first lawsuit is received.

The PELR model provides a system for employee legal training, documenting decisions during the emergency, creating a multi-agency Litigation Response Team consisting of DOC and Attorney General staff who begin work as soon as the emergency is over, counseling support for staff called to testify and mandatory posttrial debriefing to better prepare staff called to testify in subsequent post-emergency litigation (Freeman, 1996b:103). The PELR is designed to decrease staff anxiety and reduce the financial and time costs involved in the hundreds of inmate lawsuits filed in the years after an emergency by providing a rapid, coordinated anticipation of litigation by the individuals who will have to defend each case in court. Instead of each lawsuit being treated as unique, and preparation beginning after it is received, each lawsuit is treated as a member of a category of lawsuits, the response to which has already been developed and, in many cases, tested in court.

Inmate litigation is an unpleasant fact of life for correctional managers. They can, however, act to reduce the amount of litigation through a process of communication formalization designed to create alternatives to litigation, as we consider in the next section.

Formalizing Alternatives to Litigation

Litigation is extremely time-consuming, labor-intensive, financially expensive, and an exceedingly slow method of conflict resolution. Managers wanting to reduce the potential for inmate litigation can institute one of two types of conflict resolution system: the ombudsman or the inmate grievance system. The services of jailhouse lawyers may prove useful in both systems.

Ombudsman   An ombudsman is an outside public official who has the qualifications to investigate an inmate allegation and render a recommendation. An ombudsman may also mediate negotiations between inmates and managers. Their decisions may be binding or advisory, depending on legislative intent.

Inmate Grievance Systems   In 1967, the President's Commission on Law Enforcement and the Administration of Justice recommended the establishment of prison inmate grievance procedures. The Commission argued that inmates should always have an administrative recourse for grievances against officials that is subject to review by some outside authority (Cory, 1982:23). Concerned about the rising number of Section 1983 lawsuits, the U.S. Congress in 1980 passed the Civil Rights of Institutionalized Persons Act, which required inmates to "exhaust the internal prison grievance" process before a Section 1983 suit would be heard by a federal court. This requirement provided 90 days for the prison to resolve the matter informally. If there is no grievance system, the suit can go directly to federal court. A 1980 study conducted for the National Institute of Corrections showed that approximately 75 percent of the state DOCs surveyed, and many of the largest jails, had initiated such a system after the 1971 Attica riot (Cory, 1982:24). The Federal Bureau of Prisons initiated its grievance system in 1974 (Cory, 1982:22).

An inmate grievance system is established by policy and provides a formal communication channel through which inmates can submit complaints to managers with the authority to change organizational behavior. The most effective systems have five components: (1) a requirement that managers attempt to informally resolve the complaint, (2) the formal investigation of unresolved complaints by a complaint officer (who may also be the LRC), (3) a process of attempting an informal resolution by the complaint officer, (4) a written superintendent's response that explains either the resolution of the complaint or why it cannot be resolved at the institutional level, and (5) a procedure for inmate appeal to the Commissioner for further review and resolution attempt.

A consequence of the grievance system's emphasis of informal resolution is that centralization of decision making is reduced.

Reducing Centralization

A policy of informal resolution of inmate concerns and problems at the lowest level possible means that top managers frequently have no involvement in legal issues until they are notified of a pending lawsuit. The prison librarian, complaint officer, legal assistance attorneys, first- and middle-level managers, and concerned employees are constantly making decisions that will either reduce or increase the probability of litigation on a specific issue. For example, in Missouri, employees in the Office of Constituent Services recognized that the friends and families of inmates frequently had questions about DOC visiting procedures, mail, and telephone privileges. To formally address these questions, the employees authored a handbook entitled *For Friends and Family* that is now automatically sent to the families of newly incarcerated inmates (deGroot, 1997b:77). This has undoubtedly played a role in the reduction of lawsuits cited earlier. Individuals who have a ready source of reliable information and correctional employees to whom they can present concerns are less likely to encourage inmate, or external, litigation. Individuals who feel that nobody in the department cares about them or their loved ones often view litigation as the only option open to them.

The legal environment is complex and very few correctional managers have formal legal training. If they are to steer the organization through the legal maze confronting it, they must receive enough in-house training to allow them to identify potential legal issues when they engage in environmental design.

LEGAL TRAINING FOR MANAGERS

Although managers are not personally liable in most lawsuits because they are consid-

ered to assume the identity of the government that employs them, they can be held personally liable for their subordinates' unconstitutional actions if they knew, or should have known, of the existence of a pattern of gross abuse and did nothing about it after gaining such knowledge. This is known as vicarious liability (Bennett and Hess, 1992:211).

There are two exceptions to the "pattern" requirement. A manager may also be liable, first, if there is a clear disregard of clearly established law involved in the actions, and second, if the failure to supervise or the lack of proper training programs is so severe as to constitute "gross negligence" or deliberate indifference to the plaintiff's constitutional rights (Barrineau, 1994:67). Under these conditions, the manager can be held liable not only for damages but, if found liable in a Section 1983 civil action, for opposing counsel's attorney's fees as well.

Defense and Lawsuit Prevention Strategies   Correctional managers enjoy a qualified or good faith immunity if they can persuade a jury that their actions were in good faith and the disputed conduct was reasonable. This is an affirmative defense based on their assurance that their conduct did not violate clearly established statutory or constitutional rights that a reasonable person would have known. A correctional manager can also acknowledge that a deprivation of rights occurred, but an "acceptable beginning" has been undertaken to correct the problem that led to the deprivation of rights. This defense works if the actions were taken prior to the litigation, not as a consequence of the litigation. Invalid defenses are those that involve clearly unreasonable or outrageous conduct, even if unintentional (Barrineau, 1994:79–82).

The most effective means of preventing both offender and employee litigation is to have an organizational strategy that (1) emphasizes the rule of law, (2) provides constitutionally based written policies, procedures, and rules, (3) sponsors effective training that goes beyond meeting minimum standards, (4) provides close supervision of employees, (5) establishes formal grievance and informal conflict resolution mechanisms (for employees, the Collective Bargaining Agreement [CBA] will structure conflict resolution approaches to a high degree), and (6) requires complete documentation of all training and disciplinary actions (offender and employee). Although many managers have an aversion to documentation-related paperwork, a thorough record of management functions can make the difference between a legal victory and a legal defeat.

JUDICIAL RETRENCHMENT

We have seen in this chapter thus far how judicial activism has significantly increased the complexity of correctional management; but the tide is beginning to turn. By the mid-1970s, the U.S. Supreme Court had become reluctant to further expand the rights of inmates and, in some cases, began to restrict them. There were three reasons for this retrenchment: (1) prison populations had more than doubled between 1972 and 1982 and most jurisdictions had fewer financial resources to implement court-ordered reforms, (2) public attitude had hardened in favor of more punitive treatment of offenders, and (3) the character of the U.S. Supreme Court had changed as several liberal Justices appointed during the 1950s and 1960s retired to be replaced by conservatives (Silverman and Vega, 1996:319).

This movement toward a more restrictive interpretation of inmate rights is seen in *Bell v. Wolfish* (1979) and *Rhodes v. Chapman* (1981). In *Bell*, detainees in the Metropolitan Correctional Center (MCC) in New York City challenged double-celling and strip searches. The Court upheld MCC and noted that correctional managers "should be accorded wide-ranging deference in the adoption and executing of policies."

In *Rhodes*, the U.S. Supreme Court examined allegations by inmates at the Southern Ohio Correctional Facility at Lucasville, a prison holding 2,300 inmates although design capacity was 1,600. The Court ruled that over-crowding in and of itself could not be the measure of the constitutionality of a prison because crowding does not necessarily indicate how prison conditions affect inmates. The Court ruled that unless conditions were "deplorable" or "sordid" (the "totality of conditions" approach), the courts should defer to prison officials. The new focal point of the courts became "how bad conditions and their effects had to be before they violated the Eighth Amendment, what conditions were relevant, and how various conditions should be weighed in relation to one another. The state of mind of defendants was irrelevant in answering these questions" (Collins, 1995:274).

Daniels v. Williams (1986) established that inmates can sue for damages in federal court only if officials had intentionally or deliberately inflicted damage. *Wilson v. Seiter* (1991) established that the standard for the review of official conduct is whether state policies or staff actions constitute "deliberate indifference" to constitutional rights. While it is unlikely that the federal courts will return to the hands-off doctrine, they do appear to be giving correctional managers wider latitude in their use of discretion. However, this does not absolve managers from ensuring that their environmental design is constitutional.

SUMMARY

The legal environment of corrections is a complex maze of court decisions creating legions of rules and regulations that constrain the exercise of managerial discretion and affect every aspect of organizational behavior. Although the judicial activism of the 1960s and 1970s has apparently been replaced by judicial retrenchment, correctional managers must always be aware of the power of the courts to intervene and force organizational changes if judicial review establishes that the responsibility to provide a constitutional environment for offenders and employees alike has not been met.

Having explored the evolution, structure, design, and environments of correctional organizations in the first seven chapters, it is time to turn our attention to the processes that shape organizational behavior. In the next chapter we examine the power relationships in a correctional organization.

Discussion Questions

1. Has judicial activism been a positive force or a negative force? Explain your answer.
2. Was judicial activism really necessary or would correctional managers have begun to make changes on their own in the 1960s?
3. Do court-ordered changes weaken the ability of staff to control inmate behavior? If so, how?
4. What specific due process rights are incorporated into the Oregon DOC inmate disciplinary policy? Do these rights weaken or strengthen officer authority? Defend your answer.
5. What can managers do to help line staff accept unpopular court-ordered changes?
6. What constitutional protections apply to inmates, community correction offenders, and employees?
7. What mechanisms can be developed to encourage informal resolution of offender and employee grievances?
8. Will judicial retrenchment result in a return to the abuses of the hands-off era? Why or why not?

Critical Analysis Exercise: Limiting Inmate Access to the Courts

The Prison Litigation Reform Act (PLRA) signed into law by President Bill Clinton on April 26, 1996, states "that before an inmate can file a civil rights action in Federal court the inmate must

- exhaust all available administrative remedies before filing the case, whether or not the facility's grievance

procedures were certified by the Department of Justice or the Federal Court, and
- show physical injury to receive damages for mental or emotional injury suffered while in custody.

Additionally, the Act generally prohibits an inmate from filing a petition in forma pauperis (as an indigent without liability for court fees and costs) if the inmate has filed three or more actions in Federal Court that were dismissed as frivolous or malicious or for failing to state a claim on which relief can be granted. Further, inmates filing petitions in forma pauperis are required to pay the appropriate filing fees (and costs, where applicable) from their existing funds or any funds available to them through their trust fund accounts within the correctional system.

This act also provides for sanctions to be imposed on Federal inmates who abuse the court system. The act authorizes the Federal courts to order the revocation of any unvested good time of Federal inmates whose petition was dismissed because it was filed for malicious purposes, solely to harass the other party, or because the inmate presented false testimony or evidence" (Quoted in *Bureau of Justice Statistics* [1997]. "Prisoner Petitions in the Federal Courts, 1980–96." Washington, DC: U.S. Department of Justice, Office of Justice Programs:16) Proponents justify the PLRA legislation by citing the following cases of frivolous lawsuits:

An Ohio car thief who claimed his constitutional rights were violated because he could not wear sunglasses. A Texas inmate who sued because he received chunky, not smooth, peanut butter. A California serial killer who had kidnapped, raped, and tortured five girls sued because his sandwich was soggy and his cookie broken. A Florida murderer who filed a lawsuit on the basis that the piece of cake he received at dinner was too small. A Florida inmate who killed two adults and burned three children alive who has filed 63 lawsuits: his cell is too hot; his food too cold; and his

TV programs contain violence. A Michigan inmate who sued because he did not receive what he claimed to be the winning sweepstakes mailing that would have made him a multimillionaire (*Philadelphia Inquirer*, 1996:A30).

Critical Analysis Questions

1. What are the arguments for and against the PLRA?

2. How do you think inmates will respond to the PLRA? Should this even be a consideration? Why or why not?

3. Would an inmate grievance system be as effective as the proposed legislation in reducing frivolous lawsuits? Why or why not?

4. How should the terms "frivolous" and "malicious" be defined? Who should have the responsibility for defining these terms? On what do you base your answer?

8

Power Relationships in a Correctional Organization

Learning Objectives

After completing this chapter, you should be able to:

- Define power and identify the bases and sources of power.
- Provide a description of the formal power relationships within a Department of Corrections (DOC).
- Trace the evolutionary shift of organizational power from the managerial subsystem to the technical subsystem.
- Define political behavior and summarize its effects on organizational effectiveness.
- Develop a managerial strategy of response to political behavior.
- Explain the shift from the individual exercise of power to the collective exercise of power by inmates.
- Outline and summarize the effective managerial uses of power.

Key Terms and Concepts

Texas Control Model
California Consensual Model
Dependency
Power Relationships
Power Recipient
Bases of Power
Coercive Power
Reward Power
Sources of Power
Authority
Traditional Authority
Control of Resources
Employee Empowerment
Resistance
Organizational Politics
Illegitimate Political Behavior
Role Ambiguity
Michigan Responsibility Model
Power
Managerial Dependency
Power Holder
Compliance
Legitimate Power
Referent Power
Expert Power
Formal Position
Position Power
Personal Attributes
Control of Information Flow
Learned Helplessness
Control Analysts
Legitimate Political Behavior
High Self-monitor
Defensive Behaviors
Inmate Power
Power Tactics

Webster's Dictionary defines power as the possession of control, authority, or influence over others, and the ability to act or produce an effect. In the workplace, power is seen as the ability to get things done by exerting influence over others. And while titles and authorities may differ, people within an organization can almost always identify those with the power.

Micheal Carrell, Daniel Jennings, and Christina Heavrien

Profile: Three Models of Correctional Management

The Texas control model of management operated in the Texas DOC prior to the 1980 decision in *Ruiz v. Estelle*. This model was based on a correctional philosophy that emphasized inmate obedience, work, and education. Every DOC prison was designated as maximum security and run accordingly. Correctional officers (C.O.s) were organized in accordance with a rigid paramilitary chain of command. Official rules and regulations, even the most minor ones, were vigorously enforced, violations were swiftly punished, and power was firmly located in the hands of the correctional employees. Correctional managers allowed a portion of this power to be given to Building Tenders who were allowed to dominate other inmates through force and intimidation. The primary organizational goal was the firm control of inmate behavior through a well-defined system of rewards and punishments. Inmates were not allowed to form organizations or engage in collective behavior.

In contrast, the Michigan responsibility model placed a premium on measures that maximized developing inmate responsibility for their behavior. An elaborate classification system attempted to fit every inmate into the most appropriate but least restrictive prison setting. The paramilitary features of institutional life were minimized and inmates were encouraged to express their feelings and perceptions. Tight security was considered undesirable because it reduced the opportunities for inmates to engage in normal behavior. The prevailing philosophy was that inmates were to be given the greatest amount of freedom consistent with their security status, then held accountable for their actions. C.O.s were encouraged to informally handle inmate rule violations through counseling and informal conflict resolution techniques. The formation of inmate organizations in the name of normalizing the prison environment was encouraged. An elaborate inmate grievance system was a hallmark of this model.

The California consensual model developed a strong classification and inmate grievance system. Inmates were encouraged to organize and were offered a variety of treatment programs. The paramilitary control structure was modeled along the lines of the Texas control model, although rule enforcement was largely discretionary. California managers and employees were very sensitive to the ability of the inmates to take over prisons and a management by consent policy was a hallmark of the consensual model, that is, management is accomplished by brokering compromises among the system's most powerful inmate gangs. California has attempted to steer a middle course between the tight paramilitary control of the Texas model and the inmate-oriented approach of the Michigan model (DiIulio, 1987:104–137).

The Profile presents three models of correctional management. These models rely on the use of power, but each model emphasizes a different base of power and achieves a different balance of organizational versus inmate power. All organizational behavior is determined by a complex interplay of power relationships based on different bases and sources of power. Both the organizational and offender exercise of power has undergone an evolutionary process. Bureaucratization has produced a shift in organizational power from the managerial subsystem to the technical subsystem. The advent of inmate gangs has shifted the exercise of power from an individual basis to a collective basis. The use of power directs individuals toward the achievement of individual and organizational goals and can have both negative and positive consequences. Power used in the service of organizational goals has positive consequences. Power used in the service of political behavior that places personal goals above organizational goals may have negative consequences. It is the responsibility of the correctional manager to effectively use power to achieve the mission.

THE EXERCISE OF POWER

Power can be defined, in its simplest terms, as the extent to which one individual can get another individual to do something that individual would otherwise not do (Dahl, 1957). The chapter epigraph provides a working definition of power, but it does not answer a fundamental question: Why do individuals engage in behavior that they otherwise would not choose when another individual tells them to do so? The answer to this question is found in the notion of dependency.

Dependency and the Exercise of Power

Robbins (1993:407) noted that "probably the most important aspect of power is that it is a function of dependency." On the simplest level, dependency is a condition in which one individual (A) has something that another individual (B) needs or wants. In order to obtain this something, B will act in a manner desired by A. Therefore, power can be defined as the capacity for one individual to influence the behavior of another individual to do something they would otherwise not do because compliance will provide the individual with something they need or want. This definition implies both a dependency relationship and the assumption that both individuals have some discretion over their behavior (Robbins, 1993:407).

Creation of Dependency

A person, group, or organization can have power only when they have control over a resource—something that someone else wants or needs. Dependency is created when an individual controls resources that are important, scarce, and cannot be substituted for (Mintzberg, 1983a:24). To create dependency, the resources the individual controls must be important to the organization. Specialized knowledge such as computer skills, legal expertise, and knowledge of information management technology are important because they provide the information correctional managers need for effective strategic planning in increasingly volatile internal and external environments. The individuals in possession of special-

ized information can persuade decision makers to take a course of action they might otherwise ignore. When this occurs, power has been exercised.

A resource needs to be perceived as scarce in order for it to create dependency. Money is a scarce resource in any correctional organization. The ability of managers to control the distribution of discretionary funds provides them with a source of power. Subordinates desiring funding for a new program, creation of a secretarial position to assist them, enlargement of office space, or promotion with a salary increase will be inclined to obey the orders of the manager who can influence the distribution of funds and promotional opportunities. That a resource cannot be substituted for has to do with the elasticity of power. That is, the more a specific resource has no readily available substitute, the more power the control of that resource provides. For example, attorneys, doctors, technology specialists, and fast-track construction experts have a great deal of power because there is no substitute for their skills.

Relationships between individuals, groups, and organizations, and any combination of relationships among all three entities, can be defined in terms of power based on a dependency relationship. More specifically, a dependency relationship can be defined as constituting a power relationship.

POWER RELATIONSHIPS AND ORGANIZATIONAL BEHAVIOR

A power relationship is an exchange relationship that involves two categories of individual: the power holder and the power recipient. Power relationships can be either formal or informal. The formal power relationship is based on the official, chain-of-command power differential that exists in relationships among individuals, groups, or organizations. It provides the foundation for the formal managerial regulation of group and organizational behavior through the control of individual behavior. The prison superintendent who issues a policy requiring inmates to adhere to a new grooming standard is regulating a specific aspect of inmate behavior. The Medical Director who requires nursing staff to adhere to a specific protocol in treating tuberculosis is regulating employee behavior. In both cases, the power differential between the power holder and the power recipients provides the managers with the authority to impose disciplinary actions on any individuals who violate policy. Thus, the superintendent and the Medical Director are the power holders and the inmates and the nursing staff are the power recipients, respectively.

The informal power relationship frequently involves peers. For example, Officer Smith, a seasoned veteran, working a cellblock with newly hired Officer Jones observes that Officer Jones is allowing inmates to spend more than the allotted time in the shower room. Officer Smith talks to Officer Jones and persuades him to adhere to the shower schedule no matter how much the inmates argue that they need more shower time. This is an example of an informal use of power. Officer Jones does not have to do as Officer Smith says because both C.O.s have equal rank, but he chooses to do so because he respects Officer Smith and understands the value of accepting the advice of a more experienced officer. Officer Smith is the power holder and Officer Jones is the power recipient. The resource possessed by Officer Smith is his ability to give respect and acceptance to Officer Jones.

The greater the power recipient's dependency on the power holder, the greater the power exercised by the power holder. Thus, a probationary employee may be quicker to obey a manager than would a seasoned employee with full union protection. However, power does not have to be used to be effective in influencing behavior. The fact that the potential exists to use power is often all that is necessary. The chain of command that is the structural backbone of the correctional organization consists of a series of well-defined power relationships in which the subordinate is dependent upon

the manager for positive reports and support and is always aware of the ability of the manager to make unfavorable reports, take disciplinary action, or withhold support. The manager does not have to exercise this power to gain compliance. It is enough that both individuals recognize the potential for that exercise of power.

Evolution of the Manager–Employee Power Relationship

In Pre-DOC Corrections, the power relationship between managers and employees was one-sided because there were so few constraints on the exercise of managerial power. Employees were completely dependent upon the good will of the manager. The bureaucratization of corrections has modified the manager–employee power relationships. Although power continues to reside primarily in the manager, employee dependency has been reduced by the ready availability of active challenges to managerial power: the union, the courts, Civil Service, pro-employee legislation, and the drive of managers toward employee empowerment and professionalism. The power relationship between managers and employees is no longer one-sided.

Managerial Dependency on Subordinates Dependency is in fact not a one-way street in the manager–employee relationship. Managers also experience dependency in their relationship with employees. The organizational mission can only be achieved through the concerted efforts of employees. If subordinate staff do not do their jobs, the manager will soon be in great difficulty because he or she is ultimately responsible for achieving the mission.

Managerial Dependency on Central Office Managers are not immune to being power recipients. For example, a superintendent receives a memo from the Central Office Chief of Correctional Industries. The memo mandates a change in the wage structure for inmates in the prison's mattress fabrication plant. The previous formula of calculating inmate daily pay on the basis of the number of mattresses produced per day has created quality control problems because inmates are rushing the work to increase their pay. In addition, fiscal conservatism demands that Correctional Industries (C.I.) costs be reduced. The new policy is to pay a flat hourly rate unrelated to the number of mattresses produced. In effect, a bonus system has been eliminated. The superintendent knows that the C.I. inmates will object to this change, but the new policy has already been approved by the Commissioner. The Chief of Correctional Industries is the power holder and the superintendent, like the C.I. inmates and their supervisors, is the power recipient.

The relationship between power holder and power recipient constitutes a compliance relationship. Amitai Etzioni, a theorist of administration, defined compliance as a person's behavior being in accordance with orders or directives given by another person. For a compliance relationship to exist, the order giver must have the ability to induce or influence the order recipient to carry out the order or directive (Etzioni, 1961:3). This ability to induce or influence is created through the power holder's ability to manipulate specific bases (types) of power.

BASES OF POWER

The term *base of power* refers to possession of a specific type of resource that gives the power holder his or her power. French and Raven (1968) expanded Etzioni's work by postulating the existence of five bases of power that can be manipulated in order to gain the compliance of subordinates: reward power, coercive power, expert power, referent power, and legitimate power (Kanter, 1977). Reward power is based on the perception of the power recipient that the power holder can, and will, reward compliance to orders and directives. Coercive power is based on the belief of the

power recipient that failure to follow directives or obey the rules will result in punishment. Expert power is based on the power recipient's belief that the power holder has a high level of specific expertise. Referent power is based on the positive identification of the power recipient with the power holder. Legitimate power is most closely aligned to Weber's (1947) concept of authority: power recipients follow orders because of a belief that those above them in the chain of command have the legal right to impose rules and regulations.

A base of power provides the means to induce or influence the behavior of other individuals, but what is the source of these bases of power?

SOURCES OF POWER

The source of power can be located in a formal position of authority, personal attributes conducive to the influence of others, the control of organizational resources, especially information, and employee empowerment.

Formal Position of Authority

Authority can be understood as power legitimized over time (Pfeffer, 1981). Formal authority is authority vested in the formal position the individual holds within the organization—a position recognized as having power, of being a "boss." This is known as position power (or traditional authority). In an organization, positions based on traditional authority often have been in existence for decades or longer. Obedience to the individuals in these positions is expected to be automatic because their authority is legal: it is based on legislative statute and the rules, regulations, and hierarchy of an organization expressed through a formal chain of command.

The easiest element of position power to understand is the official control over rewards and punishments. This power is fundamental to the exercise of traditional authority. Correctional managers reward individuals by promoting them or working to advance their potential for promotion by giving them highly prized assignments. For example, a respected Deputy Superintendent for Operations may find his or her advancement potential enhanced by being assigned to the Central Office investigation of a sensational prison escape or riot. A valued probation or parole officer will be given the assignment of drafting the policy, procedures, and rules for a new Intensive Supervision Probation Program (ISP) for managerial review. Acceptable performance in these types of tasks will then be used as justification for promotion. However, deputies and parole officers who are not respected will find no such assignments forthcoming.

The use of traditional authority is dependent upon subordinates accepting the position and being willing to follow the directives of the individual holding the position. The chain of command in a correctional organization represents the official hierarchy of positions possessing traditional authority. Subordinates who adhere to the chain of command do so for three reasons: (1) organizational behavior is interdependent—it is usual for one individual to lead another if success is to occur, (2) most people believe that the person in charge has the expertise to get the job done and, therefore, should be obeyed, and (3) deferring to authority becomes automatic and institutionalized in a bureaucracy—employee reactions tend to be consistent with the organizational culture organized around the chain of command (Carrell, Jennings, and Heavrin, 1997:318).

Merely being in a position that carries formal authority is not enough, however; the individual occupying that position must be willing to acquire power and exercise it in an effective manner.

Ability to Effectively Use Power   Managers who will effectively use power have been described as possessing the following characteristics: (1) the energy, endurance, and physical stamina that permits the long hours in the office necessary to outperform other individuals and provide a positive role model; (2) a focus not only on the mission but on the details that must be taken into consideration for successful mission achievement; (3) flexibility as expressed in the ability to listen to the opinions of others and modify a position in response to those opinions; (4) a high tolerance for conflict and the ability to manage conflict situations; and (5) the ability to share the limelight with others who have worked on a project or made a contribution (Carrell, Jennings, and Heavrin, 1997:327).

Personal Characteristics

Personal characteristics can be so powerful that an individual can exercise power even if position power is lacking. This is known as charismatic authority and lies in the personal attributes that allow an individual to influence others without granting or withholding organizational rewards and punishments. Charismatic authority is often based on the ability to persuade, lead by example, or attract others to try and emulate the charismatic individual. The individuals who possess position power may or may not also possess charismatic authority. An example of a top manager who possessed both position power and charismatic authority was Dr. George Beto, the director of the Texas DOC from 1962 to 1972, whose reputation was summarized by an inmate's testimony: "Old Beto couldn't be beat, the preacher man with a baseball bat in one hand, a Bible in the other" (cited in DiIulio, 1987:197). Individuals with charismatic authority are respected regardless of their formal position and are often informal leaders.

Control of Organizational Resources

The amount of power an individual has through control of a resource depends on the value of that resource to others in the organization. Managers exercise power through the use of their authority to distribute organizational resources (especially funds, employee positions, and equipment) through the annual budget process. Providing an adequate level of funding to a specific program or project will allow it to expand and achieve its potential. Restricting the flow of funding will limit potential and may even result in the termination of the program. Salavik and Pfeffer (1977) have suggested that certain departments in an organization may become powerful because of their ability to acquire and control critical resources. One of the most critical resources in corrections is information.

Control of Information Flow Bacharach and Lawler (1980) identify the control of the information flow in the organization as a type of power. This ability requires a physical position within a communications network that permits access to valuable information. For example, a physical proximity to power allows the superintendent's secretary and administrative assistant to have immediate access to an enormous amount of confidential information about personnel, budgets, pending policy, and Central Office initiatives and concerns. Being close to a person in power has traditionally been a source of power, especially when the individual can control the information reaching the boss. Both secretaries and administrative assistants are in a position to facilitate, delay, or prevent the flow of information others want communicated to the superintendent or Commissioner.

In a very real sense, secretaries and administrative assistants are the gatekeepers to the top manager. The intelligent subordinate manager will quickly learn the practical value that can be realized from developing a cordial relationship with the top manager's personal secretary or administrative assistant. A cordial relationship can increase access to the top manager, provide information (gleaned from casual conversations) that would otherwise remain unknown, and even influence promotion

decisions. For example, top managers frequently discuss the performance of subordinate managers with their administrative assistant and, sometimes, with their secretaries. The opinion of these individuals about the person under discussion can carry weight. Therefore, it is best for the subordinate manager if that opinion is positive. This author once witnessed the superintendency of a new prison decided at lunch where the author and the Commissioner were joined by the Commissioner's secretary and administrative assistant. The comments by both convinced the Commissioner to promote an individual not generally considered to be in the running for the promotion. It is always wise to be on friendly terms with gatekeepers.

Individuals can also become power holders because their position in the organization chart provides access to specialized information that is vital to achievement of the mission but is often unknown to managers, including superintendents and Commissioners. Technostructure department heads in the Division of Business Administration, Management Information Systems, and Employee Relations (see Box 8–1 on page 199) can become extremely powerful because of the control they exercise over the information deemed critical in top managerial decision making and strategic planning. These individuals have no direct authority over security or treatment departments, but they frequently influence policy development in these areas through their specialized knowledge of the availability of discretionary funds, grants, external sources of revenue, consultants, and a wide variety of external sources of highly technical information and expertise.

Finally, power can be derived from the withholding of information. Many managers are adept at retaining information about specific policy and budget decisions within the strategic apex until it is time "to go public" and inform the rest of the organization. Information can also be withheld through the use of technical jargon, a common complaint lodged against psychologists and computer experts. As we will shortly see, the ability to control the flow of information has dramatically shifted the balance of power within the correctional organization.

Employee Empowerment

As noted in Chapter 1, empowerment is a process of allowing employees who previously had little or no ability for independent action to act with more autonomy. Employees who are empowered are able to exert influence on organizational policy development. Many correctional managers have embraced the concept of work teams and total quality management (TQM) as a method of empowering employees. These approaches are discussed in Chapter 11. Empowered employees provide an additional base of power because the manager delegates certain responsibilities to them (as in unit management) and this delegation allows managers more time and energy to focus on strategic planning activities. Employees able to assume a higher level of responsibility than previously permitted are able to achieve results otherwise not possible.

Process of Employee Empowerment   Tracey (1990:163) has suggested that the process of employee empowerment requires managers to (1) tell employees their specific responsibilities, (2) assign authority equal to the responsibilities, (3) set standards of excellence, (4) provide the training necessary to achieve the standards, (5) provide knowledge and information relevant to achieving the responsibilities, (6) provide performance feedback, (7) recognize achievements, (8) trust employees to have the ability to do the job, (9) give employees permission to fail, and (10) treat employees with dignity and respect. Achieving standards, acquiring information and skills, and being recognized for outstanding performance empowers employees and benefits the organization by creating employee loyalty and a desire to achieve organizational goals.

To summarize, sources are where the power holder gets the power. Bases are what the power holder manipulates to induce or influence power recipients to behave in a desired manner. Having defined the bases and sources of power, we can turn in the next section to defining the structure of the correctional organization in terms of the formal power relationships as these are usually diagrammed on an organization chart.

FORMAL ORGANIZATIONAL POWER RELATIONSHIPS

Power relationships in a correctional organization can be analyzed using elements of two models introduced in Chapter 2. From the Kast and Rosenzweig (1979) model, we will take the concept of managerial and technical subsystems. From the second model, Mintzberg's (1983b) model of organizational design, we will take the five groupings of function: the operating core, strategic apex, middle line, technostructure, and support staff. Using the perspective provided by these elements, our analysis of DOC organizational structure is based on three propositions:

1. The strategic apex and the middle line constitute the managerial subsystem.
2. The technostructure and support staff constitute the technical subsystem.
3. Both subsystems work to control operating core behavior.

In examining the power relationships in a correctional organization, we will periodically refer to the organization chart of the Ohio DORC shown in Box 8–1, which presents the structure of power relationships in that DOC. Because the focus of the managerial and technical subsystems is the behavior of the operating core, we begin our analysis of organizational power at that level.

Power and the Operating Core

Employees in the operating core "perform the basic work related directly to the production of products and services" (Mintzberg,

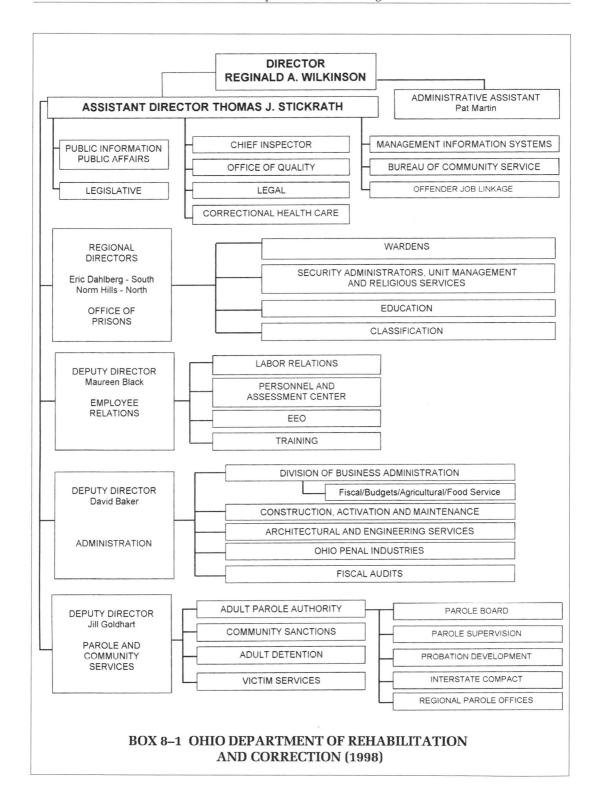

**BOX 8–1 OHIO DEPARTMENT OF REHABILITATION
AND CORRECTION (1998)**

1983b:12). In the case of the DOC, the product is the offender and the services are all those activities involved in managing the offender population. Although there are Central Office staff who play a role in the providing of services to offenders, they do not work directly with offenders. Therefore, for our purposes, the operating core will be defined as those field employees who work directly with the offender population in either an institutional or a community corrections setting. The prison operating core consists of three groups of staff: the correctional officers, the treatment staff, and ancillary staff (food services, trades and maintenance, groundskeeping, and correctional industries). The community corrections operating core consists of probation/parole officers, residential facility staff, and private corrections and public agency employees. The correctional employee–offender power relationship involves the skillful use of the five bases of power, defined by French and Raven (1968).

Correctional Officers

The C.O. is a social control agent responsible for the enforcement of prison rules and maintenance of institutional control and security. In order to effectively enforce the rules, the C.O. must have the power to control the behavior of a hostile inmate population.

Legitimate Power and Rule Enforcement   The legal authority of the C.O. to be a social control agent rests on the legitimate power inherent in the structural relationship between officer and inmate. The position of the officer in this relationship confers the right to have orders obeyed and authority respected. The position of the inmate in the relationship conveys the duty to obey all orders. Legitimate power provides the basis for the C.O.'s control of inmate behavior through the giving of orders, informal resolution of conflict situations, overall direction of activities, and use of formal disciplinary procedures in response to inmate rule violations. All C.O.s possess legitimate power. It comes with the position.

Expert Power   Not all C.O.s have expert power. Those officers who do possess expert power are perceived by inmates to have some special skill, ability, talent, or expertise that can be of benefit to the inmate if the officer so chooses. Cressey (1965) has suggested that the organizational goals of a prison make a difference in whether inmates perceive an officer to possess expert power. Power based on technical competence, academic knowledge, and judgment is more likely in a setting where the officer is expected to participate in the treatment decision making process. That is, if the goal of a prison is strictly custody, as is the case with a super-max prison, officers may be viewed as having legitimate power but not expert power because their sole focus is custody and control. However, an officer in a treatment-oriented prison offering a broad variety of in-house programming and prerelease programs might be expected to play a formal role in program decision making. This officer is more likely to be viewed as possessing expert power than the super-max officer.

Referent Power   Referent power is a type of personal authority not shared by all officers. The officers who do have this power are able to earn the respect of inmates by respecting the human dignity of all persons and not acting out of personal malice. C.O.s who are impartial and fair in their management of inmates, keep their promises, and treat inmates with dignity and respect possess referent power (Hepburn, 1985:149) because inmates who respect an officer are more likely to willingly comply with that officer's orders. Inmates who do not view an officer as having referent power may be more motivated to violate the rules and even become aggressive when they believe they are being unfairly treated.

Reward Power   Stojkovic (1987) found a strong reliance on reward power among the C.O.s he studied. Reward power is part of an official system of rewards based on the awarding of privileges. Positive officer reports often play a role in decisions concerning job and housing assignments, in-house employment, and eligibility for outside work details, community corrections, furloughs, and parole. Officers may also informally reward inmates by ignoring minor rule violations.

The degree of reward power available to C.O.s depends on inmate perception. Reward power exists only if inmates believe officers have that power. To varying degrees, the traditional strength of officer reward power has been undermined by the primary role of treatment staff in the formal classification process that determines custody and programming levels.

Coercive Power Coercive power is based on the inmate perception that officers have the ability to formally punish prison rule violations through the writing of a formal misconduct report that can lead to loss of good time credits and parole denial, or to informally punish violations through physical beatings or psychological abuse. DOC policies that have formalized due process rights in inmate disciplinary procedures, implemented inmate grievance systems, legitimized the use of jailhouse lawyers, and promoted access to the courts have significantly undermined the ability of C.O.s to use coercive power and have, in fact, provided inmates with a countervailing power (Poole and Regoli, 1981). For inmates, the coercive power wielded by C.O.s now exists in a far more symbolic form than the brutality that existed during Pre-DOC Corrections. In DOC Corrections, the message of coercive power is most frequently conveyed to inmates through the presence of armed tower and perimeter officers; random strip searches; officer access to handcuffs, mace, batons, and firearms; cell searches; and C.O. and inmate uniforms. One of the most powerful examples of the exercise of coercive power is found in the recent movement toward the routine creation of state DOC super-max prisons. Other states, like California (Figure 8–1), have also created super-max institutions.

Treatment Staff

Legitimate, reward, expert, and coercive power are possessed by all treatment staff. Legitimate power is by virtue of their positions, which are officially defined. Reward power is based in the decisive role of the treatment staff in the formal, ongoing classification process that determines job and housing assignments, transfers to a more desirable prison, specialized program involvement, furlough and work release participation, and recommendations for transfer to preparole community corrections facilities. Expert power has its source in the inmates' perception of counselors, psychologists, teachers, and vocational instructors as individuals possessing specialized academic skills that both inmates and C.O.s lack. Treatment staff control over the parole recommendation process can be considered a formidable form of coercive power: given the typical inmate's desire for parole, treatment staff have a powerful "club" over the head of any inmate who does not "go along with the program." Referent power is not necessarily accorded treatment staff but must be earned. If treatment staff are perceived as unfair, biased, and insensitive, they are not going to be respected.

Ancillary Staff

All ancillary staff possess legitimate power because their positions are officially defined and legal. They often have expert power because of their specialized job skills. The reward power of the ancillary staff lies in their ability to recommend pay raises and influence decision making by the treatment staff. Extremely skilled ancillary staff may also have referent power in the eyes of inmates who would like to master a skill possessed by the employee. A skilled auto mechanic, for example, may enjoy a high degree of status in the eyes of the inmates working in the prison garage. A skilled baker may be held in respect by inmates who enjoy the rolls, biscuits, and pies the baker creates. Coercive power is found in the ability of ancillary staff to file misconduct reports based on inmate rule violation, to dismiss

FIGURE 8–1   California's most secure prison facility, the high-tech Security Housing Unit (SHU), is located within the maximum custody Pelican Bay State Prison. Its purpose is to protect staff and inmates from the few most violent, predatory offenders in the California DOC. Courtesy of the California Department of Corrections.

inmates from valued work details, or assign inmates to the least desirable tasks of a job. A lawn detail inmate assigned to use a weed whacker on a steep hill, for example, will have a less pleasant day than the inmate assigned to drive the riding mower.

Community-Based Corrections Staff

Probation/parole officers and community corrections facility staff have basically the same power relationship with their clients as do the prison-based treatment staff. They all possess legitimate power because their positions are officially defined. Expert power is based in the qualifications for entry into the position and the specialized people skills treatment staff use. Coercive power is based in the power to return the offender to the harsher prison environment. Reward power is based in the ability to award privileges, such as extended home furloughs, and place offenders in desirable community treatment programs and employment. Referent power may, or may not, be granted.

The overall exercise of power by the operating core is controlled by the managerial subsystem, which we examine next.

Power and the Managerial Subsystem

The correctional organization has two levels of managers: the strategic apex managers who engage in policy formulation and set the overall direction of organizational behavior, and the middle-line managers who provide direct supervision to the employees in the operating core.

Strategic Apex

The strategic apex exists at both the Central Office and the field level. It contains the policy formulation element of the managerial subsystem. Strategic apex behavior, at both the Central Office and field level, is guided by four operative goals: (1) developing organizational strategy, (2) monitoring the organization's performance, (3) ensuring that organizational behavior is in accordance with the organizational goals and values contained in the mission statement, and (4) correcting any significant deviations in required organizational behavior. The managers in the strategic apex "allocate resources, issue work orders, authorize major work decisions, resolve conflicts, design and staff the organization, monitor employee performance, and motivate and reward employees" (Mintzberg, 1983b:13). The strategic apex also manages the organization's relationship with the external environment.

Central Office Strategic Apex In the Central Office strategic apex, the policies defining appropriate organizational behavior for the entire DOC are approved by the Director through a complicated process of formulation and consultation with the Assistant Director and the various Regional Directors, Deputy Directors, and department heads distributed throughout the Central Office chain of command (see Box 8–1).

Managers below the rank of Director are responsible for monitoring field compliance with policy, (2) providing advice and appropriate resources to field managers experiencing serious conflicts or problems, (3) reviewing and recommending changes in current policy in their area, (4) drafting new policy for director approval, (5) overseeing the implementation of new policy at the field level, and (6) coordinating preparation for external auditing processes such as American Correctional Association (ACA) accreditation. The Assistant Director, for example, is extensively involved in the formulation and monitoring of policy governing the quality of health care services provided to every offender within the Ohio Department of Rehabilitation and Correction.

Field Strategic Apex Smaller strategic apexes are also located in the field. Superin-

tendents, deputy superintendents, and residential directors are responsible for (1) transforming Central Office policy into the local policy, rules, and procedures that will direct staff and inmate behavior, (2) responding to questions concerning those policies, (3) monitoring staff and inmate compliance with local policy and correcting deviations, and (4) advising Central Office of unique local problems creating a need for new policy or modification of existing policy.

Sources of Strategic Apex Power The legitimate power underlying organizational policy, procedures, and rules has its source in the legislative statutes governing the correctional organization and in any judicial decisions in favor of those policies. The policy generated by Central Office also provides legitimacy for field policy, procedures, and rules. Reward power is located in the ability to provide desirable assignments, approve promotions, publicly recognize outstanding performance, and use the budgetary process in a manner favorable to specific individuals or work units. Coercive power is located in the ability to control and discipline employee behavior in accordance with legislative statutes and collective bargaining agreements (CBAs). Expert power is located in the specialized skills necessary to manage a correctional organization. A sampling of these skills includes a knowledge of prison security and control devices; the ability to effectively manage both employees and offenders; a working knowledge of every department under a manager's jurisdiction; effective public relations and communications skills; the ability to oversee the budget process and effectively allocate organizational resources; an understanding of principles and techniques of education; the ability to speak intelligently with employees in a wide range of occupations and professions; an understanding of the legislative requirements of the Occupational Health and Safety Administration (OSHA) and the Environmental Protection Agency (EPA); familiarity with basic legal principles; an overall understanding of personnel policy; and the ability to effectively plan (Wright, 1994:177).

Referent power is located in the ability of the correctional manager to present a vision of the future to employees and persuade them to share that vision.

The Middle Line

The middle line connects the operating core to the field strategic apex. The middle line is the direct supervision element of the managerial subsystem. It is the responsibility of the commissioned officers, casework managers, infirmary supervisors, shop foremen, and parole supervisors to ensure that their subordinates are doing their jobs in accordance with policy. The middle line oversees the transformation of written policy into behavior through the direct supervision of subordinates. For example, if policy requires block officers to conduct three inmate counts per shift, the area lieutenant checks to ensure that those counts are actually being performed.

During Pre-DOC Corrections the power relationship between the strategic apex and the middle line was simple. The warden told the middle line when, how, and what to do and was obeyed without question. This is no longer the case. Some DOCs now have a unionized middle line; and commissioned officers, through their union, can influence the use of power by both levels of the strategic apex. Even if there is no union representation, the opposition of commissioned officers to a specific policy is not something to be taken lightly by either superintendents or the Commissioner. After all, it is the middle line that is responsible for enforcing policy in the prisons when the superintendent and Commissioner are not available. The top manager who alienates the commissioned officers does so at great risk.

Limitations of the Strategic Apex

There is an old saying that knowledge is power. The strategic apex is required to provide overall policy direction, but it lacks the vast array of specialized skills and knowledge necessary to accomplish the task of formalization in a large bureaucracy. Cor-

rections is too complex an enterprise for the strategic apex to "know it all." The bureaucratization that brought an end to the power of the autocratic warden also changed the distribution of power within the correctional organization. The expert, reward, and coercive power concentrated in the autocratic warden gradually shifted from the managerial subsystem to the technical subsystem.

Power and the Technical Subsystem

It is the analysts in the technostructure and the experts in the support staff who make up the technical subsystem of the DOC. These individuals shape organizational behavior by providing the specialized knowledge that informs policy decisions, constrains the arbitrary use of discretion, and resolves policy disputes. Every level of the correctional organization is now dependent on the specialized knowledge located within the technostructure and support staff. For example, while it is the Director of the Ohio Department of Rehabilitation and Correction who formally requests funding for construction of a new prison, it is the analysts in the Architectural and Engineering Services and Division of Business Administration who possess the expertise to develop a specific funding proposal. Resolution of a management–union conflict concerning a complex CBA paragraph defining the use of personal leave will come from a Central Office Labor Relations Coordinator. Concerns expressed about the effectiveness of clean-up procedures for HIV-infected blood spills will be responded to by Correctional Health Care. Whether a magazine received by inmates is pornographic will be resolved by the Legal Personnel.

Technostructure

Control of the operating core is exercised through the technostructure's standardization of employee behavior through creation and enforcement of an elaborate regulatory structure composed of thousands of rules and regulations. It is the technostructure that provides the strategic apex with the capability of developing strategy, monitoring organizational behavior, and correcting deviations in that behavior.

Technostructure Exercise of Expert Power

The technostructure consists of the analysts who serve the DOC by making the work of the operating core more effective. Of particular importance are the control analysts, defined as those individuals who are responsible for standardizing the work of the operating core. There are three types of control analysts: (1) work-study analysts who standardize work processes, such as the analysts who develop standard reception procedures for the processing of all new inmates received by a prison; (2) planning and control analysts who standardize outputs, such as the correctional industry analysts who develop quality control procedures for each product line and the parole analysts who standardize criteria for parole; and (3) personnel analysts who standardize skills, such as the training specialists who develop the training academy curriculum and the personnel analysts who standardize recruitment, interview, hiring, and promotion procedures.

In the Ohio Department of Rehabilitation and Correction, Central Office analysts are located in Correctional Health Care, Management Information Systems, Labor Relations, EEO, Training, Division of Business Administration, Construction, Activation and Maintenance, Architectural and Engineering Services, Ohio Penal Industries, Fiscal Audits, as well as the Adult Parole Authority. To varying degrees, elements (such as Employee Relations) of the Central Office technostructure will have their counterparts in the field. Every prison, for example, has a personnel department whose activities are carefully reviewed by Central Office's Employee Relations. The activities of the prison budget director will be monitored by the Division of Business Administration.

Technostructure Constraint of Reward Power

In corrections, the most obvious rewards include opportunities for promotion, job security, preferred shift/duty assignments, and salary/benefit increases. But the exercise of reward power is no longer the prerogative of strategic apex discretion that it was in Pre-DOC Corrections. Commissioners and superintendents cannot arbitrarily grant favored employees pay raises, benefit changes, or promotions. The exercise of reward power by the strategic apex has been sharply constrained by the CBAs and Civil Service rules that the technostructure must enforce if the organization is to avoid successful legal challenges from the unionized operating core. Today, reward power is standardized through bureaucracy: defined and regulated by Civil Service commission rules and CBAs policed by elements of the Central Office technostructure such as Employee Relations. No matter how much a superintendent wants to give a productive employee a pay raise, that reward may be constrained by a personnel officer saying: "His next merit increase isn't due for six months. He'll just have to wait his turn."

Technostructure Constraint of Coercive Power

Civil Service rules and CBAs have greatly diminished the ability of the strategic apex to use coercive power. Superintendents frequently complain that disciplinary procedures are so complicated, and employee-oriented, that it may take years of concerted action before an obviously poor employee can be dismissed. Only in the most flagrant cases of criminal conduct is immediate dismissal of an employee possible.

Support Staff

Creation of the support staff also shifted expert and coercive power away from the managerial subsystem. The support staff provides indirect support to both the strategic apex and the middle line. These individuals are not preoccupied with standardization and are not primarily advice givers (although that may be one of their duties, especially when the strategic apex is involved in policy development that has legal ramifications). Rather, they have distinct functions to perform. The attorneys in Legal, for example, represent the employees of the DOC in court when they have been named as defendants in inmate litigation. The Bureau of Community Service oversees the operation of the DOC's community corrections programs while Legislative personnel work with elected officials on corrections-related legislation. The Division of Business Administration prepares the annual budget request, engages in contract preparation, and audits the books. It is this last office that is duplicated at the field level. In general, the support staff are confined to Central Office. (Note: *Support staff* is a term that can also be used to identify the secretaries, clerks, and mailroom staff who regulate the vast amounts of bureaucratic paperwork and the switchboard operators who channel phone communications. These individuals are located throughout the DOC on an as-needed basis.)

The organizational structure with its rigid chain of command and myriad administrative and operations manuals dictates the organization's formal power relationships. But formal structure is not the only channel for the exercise of power. The use of power can also be on an informal basis, in the form of employee political behavior.

THE INFORMAL EXERCISE OF POWER: ORGANIZATIONAL POLITICS

Every organization is political in the sense that individuals and groups within the formal organizational structure will attempt to exert influence, earn rewards, and advance their careers. Political power involves the use of some base of power to affect organizational decision making or engage in behaviors that are self-serving and nonsanctioned by the organization (Vredenburgh and Maurer, 1984). Political behavior can be defined

as "those activities that are not required as part of one's formal role in the organization, but that influence, or attempt to influence, the distribution of advantages and disadvantages within the organization" (Farrell and Petersen, 1982:405).

Political behavior is located outside of the formal duties and responsibilities specified by the chain of command and requires some attempt to use an individual's power bases for personal gain. A political behavior can be either legitimate or illegitimate (Drory, 1988). Legitimate political behaviors are "normal" behaviors that include complaining to your immediate supervisor, bypassing the chain of command, forming coalitions to influence a specific policy, developing contacts outside the organization through professional development activities, obstructing organizational policies or decisions through inaction or excessive adherence to the rules, exchanging favors with other employees for mutual benefit, and lobbying for or against some organizational policy or program. Illegitimate political behaviors include sabotage of the decision-making process by withholding critical information from decision makers, whistle-blowing, spreading rumors about other employees or important events, leaking confidential information to the media or public policy makers, groups of employees calling off sick the same day or shift in protest of an organizational policy or decision, and wearing clothing or symbols that will be offensive to other employees and offenders. The use of illegitimate political behavior is risky because it can result in dismissal; severe sanctions, such as suspension or demotion, which limit the ability to exercise legitimate power; or loss of reputation.

Factors Contributing to Political Behavior

Political behavior is encouraged by individual employee characteristics or organizational factors that provide favorable outcomes to those individuals pursuing a political agenda.

Employee Characteristics

Personality Type   The type of individual most likely to engage in political behavior is the "high self-monitor" (Ferris, Russ, and Fandt, 1989). These individuals are more sensitive to social cues, exhibit higher levels of social conformity, and are more highly skilled in political behavior than are "low self-monitors." They believe they can control their environment, are more likely to take an active stance in conflicts, and will attempt to manipulate situations in an effort to further personal self-interest. High self-monitors are adept at reading situations and can mold their appearance and behavior to make a good impression in different situations. They are skilled in the use of flattery, excuses, providing favors, name-dropping, minimizing the severity of personal mistakes, and agreeing with the boss (Cialdini, 1989). High self-monitors are frequently found on the fast track to promotion. Low self-monitors are more likely to "go along with the program," abide by the chain of command, and display the same appearance and behavior regardless of the situation. These are often the workhorses of the organization, the ones to whom high self-monitors delegate the routine, boring tasks that must be completed if the mission is to be achieved.

Investment in the Organization   Employees who have made an emotional investment in the organization expect to be rewarded for that investment and have a great deal to lose if forced out; they are less likely to exercise illegitimate political power (Farrell and Petersen, 1982:408). Employees who feel a sense of personal security because they have alternative job opportunities, and therefore little to lose, are much more likely to exercise illegitimate political agendas. In a prison, treatment staff may be more likely to pursue an illegitimate political agenda because they are better equipped to leave corrections and enter a lucrative civilian job market than are most C.O.s.

Expectation of Success   An employee with a low expectation of success is less likely to exercise illegitimate political power because the risks associated with managerial discovery of that exercise are too high. High expectations of success are usually associated with powerful employees with polished political skills or inexperienced and naive employees who misjudge their changes of success (Robbins, 1993:425).

Organizational Factors

Certain situations and organizational cultures promote high levels of political behavior. For example, when organizational resources are declining, or changing, political behavior is more likely to occur (Hardy, 1987). Organizational cultures characterized by low trust, role ambiguity, unclear performance evaluation systems, low rewards, democratic decision making, high pressures for performance, and self-serving senior managers will create political behavior (Fandt and Ferris, 1990). In corrections, all of these factors became applicable to C.O.s when rehabilitation became a formal goal of the mission.

Rehabilitation and C.O. Political Behavior   The introduction of the correctional rehabilitation model in the early 1960s attempted to modify the C.O.'s traditional custodial role of strict supervision and control by adding the role of human service worker. Suddenly, in addition to providing custody, the officer was expected to be a provider of mental health services "who resonates to adjustment prob' ''s of humans-in-crisis, and seeks to /   to inmate suffering. Such activity   human services realm and   on-custodial" (Toch, 1

Officers train'
control were expe
maintain order, a.
operation of the pr
inmates and expressing
problems. They were ex
the rules yet use discretion
ment when "bending the ru

inmates adjust to the harshness of prison life. They were expected to maintain enough social distance to avoid manipulation and corruption yet allow sufficient contact to encourage inmates to "open up" about their problems. Decision making was to be "democratic" in the sense that inmate needs were to be taken into consideration and flexibility used. Such conflicting custodial and treatment goals created role conflict: "If they enforce the rules, they risk being diagnosed as 'rigid'; if their failure to enforce rules creates a threat to institutional security, orderliness, or maintenance, they are not 'doing their job'" (Cressey, 1965:1025). C.O.s were no longer certain how their performance was to be evaluated, but they quickly learned that they could be severely punished for mistakes made during their attempts to manage the conflicting requirements of custody and rehabilitation. Role conflict created an officer belief that the strategic apex no longer supported them and, as a result, they (1) were being treated more unfairly, and had less influence over policy decisions, than inmates, (2) lacked real power, (3) were being abused by inmates, (4) were unappreciated by their superiors and the public, (5) were fighting a lost cause, and (6) had no incentive to care about the organization (Poole and Regoli, 1981). The result was low trust, a perception that rewards would be few and far between, and a sense that managers were self-serving.

The alienation from their job felt by many officers was expressed through intense feelings of anxiety, frustration, and anger. The perceived failure of the strategic apex to support C.O.s was viewed by those officers as a failure of legitimate authority. And the failure of legitimate authority has consequences: "When legitimate authority fails, political behavior arises" (Tosi, Rizzo, and Carroll, 1986:527). One of the most pro-

nd consequences of the resulting legiti-

itical behavior by C.O.s was the

ization as the only salvation

ent filled with conflict and

THE CORRECTIONAL MANAGER AND ORGANIZATIONAL POLITICS

Gandy and Murray (1980:244) found that nearly 75 percent of business employees surveyed thought that political behavior had a negative effect on their organization. Political behavior will be harmful to the organization if it monopolizes the energy of employees and managers; results in rewards not based on merit; relies on hasty decision making; and encourages such defensive employee behaviors as rigidly adhering to rules and regulations instead of looking at the nuances of a particular situation, passing the buck, avoiding unpleasant tasks by falsely pleading ignorance or inability to do the work, treating other people as objects instead of individuals, stalling so it looks like work is being accomplished when it actually is not, scapegoating (blaming others for your mistakes), lying, and resisting positive changes (Ashforth and Lee, 1990). Defensive behaviors delay decisions, increase interpersonal and intergroup tensions, restrict change efforts, and can lead to a highly politicized environment characterized by low employee morale and rigidity that makes the organization unresponsive to the need to change organizational behavior in response to external changes.

How is a manager to reduce the negative potential contained in political behavior? Carrell, Jennings, and Heavrin (1997:334) suggest that the effective manager will (1) recognize the importance of each interest group to the organization and ensure an even distribution of organizational resources, (2) understand the perspective of organizational units and groups, (3) accept the need to exercise power in order to get things done, (4) understand power strategies, dynamics, and motivations in order to use appropriate tactics in specific situations and understand how others use power, and (5) recognize how power is lost— especially understand the consequences of lack of patience, pride, or lack of control over resource management in undermining the willingness of employees to cooperate.

The effective exercise of power by managers and employees is a function of both the organizational structure and culture. But there is one final group of interest in any discussion of the exercise of power in corrections: the offenders.

THE INMATE AS HOLDER OF POWER

There are five types of power that can be discerned as part of inmate culture: coercive, referent, legitimate, provision of resources, and expert (Stojkovich, 1984).

Coercive Power   The willingness to exercise coercive power has always been the primary basis for respect in the inmate culture. The ability to use physical violence, to effectively initiate or defend against a physical assault, is highly prized in the supermacho prison environment. The respected inmate is the one who "stands ready to kill to protect himself, maintains strong loyalties to some small group of other convicts (invariably of his own race), and will rob and attack or at least tolerate his friends' robbing and attacking other weak independents or their foes" (Irwin, 1980:192–195).

The rise in the 1960s of inmate gangs, racial polarization, and fragmentation of the white-based inmate social structure shifted the ability to exercise coercive power from individuals to groups, particularly the gangs. This shift also decreased the power differential between employees and inmates. Today, an organizational or individual employee overreliance on physical coercion as a routine compliance measure can produce an equally powerful coercive power response from inmates in the form of organized assaults on staff or riots.

Referent Power   Referent power is a mechanism of compliance traditionally used by various inmate religious groups. The Black Muslims have been successful in controlling inmate behavior through the use of religious ceremony and readings. Increasingly, however, referent power is being exercised by gang leaders.

Legitimate Power   Legitimate power has traditionally rested with those inmates who are older and have been confined for long periods of time because they are often given special privileges by employees because of their perceived ability to keep other inmates under control (Korn and McCorkle, 1954:191). In the 1960s, legitimate power began to shift to inmate gang leaders because their official position in the gang hierarchy provided them with the position power to control the behavior of large numbers of inmates and sources of contraband. This ability to control can seriously disrupt organizational behavior and the ability of gang leaders to cause correctional managers sleepless nights is an indication of just how powerful many gangs have become.

Provision of Resources Power   Provision of resources power can be observed in the ability of some inmates, particularly Lifers, to work their way into jobs that allow them the means to make the lives of other inmates more comfortable (or uncomfortable) through the arrangement of cell and job transfers or allow them access to information not readily available to others. For example, two officers talking about an impending shakedown of a cellblock may forget that the inmate assigned to clerical duties in their area is listening to every word and will be able to trade that information for a personal reward upon returning to the cellblock.

The domination of inmate gangs in many prisons has removed control of prized resources (such as drugs) from the hands of individuals and placed it in the hands of the gangs. In some prisons, virtually every type of contraband is controlled by gangs. The result is an enormous amount of collective power.

Expert Power   Expert power has traditionally been held by the jailhouse lawyers whose successes in achieving court-ordered increases in inmate power have reinforced the widespread officer perception that inmates actually possess more power than staff (Fox, 1982; Hepburn, 1989). However, expert power can express itself in other forms of behavior. Inmates known to be escape artists, or who have mastered a variety of methods to introduce contraband into the facility, or have some technical knowledge such as a legitimate skill can also exercise expert power. Inmate gang members known for their skill in physical combat or psychological intimidation are also regarded as having expert power.

The Organization–Inmate Power Relationship   In the Profile at the beginning of the chapter, we saw how the organization–inmate power relationship can vary depending on the managerial perception of mission and circumstances. In the Texas control model, the power relationship was definitely one-sided and in favor of the C.O.s because of their reliance on coercive power. In the Michigan responsibility model, every effort was made to grant inmates power and, in effect, to equalize the power relationship through an emphasis on inmate accountability for their personal behavior. Expert and reward power as an organizational strategy was emphasized. In the California consensual model, it can be argued that the organization–inmate power relationship was one of unofficially shared power. California has also emphasized reward and expert power.

MANAGERIAL STRATEGIES OF EFFECTIVE POWER USE

The effective manager is the individual who quickly learns to use power to effectively motivate staff to work together in achieving the organizational mission. If the manager has achieved a position of formal power, but has not learned how to effectively use that power, the results can be a badly demoralized work force.

Two particularly negative features of a demoralized work force are learned helplessness and resistance (Tosi, Rizzo, and Carroll, 1986). Learned helplessness is a condition characterized by psychological dependency and withdrawal: employees passively await orders from superiors because of a fear of taking the initiative in difficult situations. Typical symptoms include a lack of loyalty and a just-put-in-my-time-and-go-home ("Nothing I do or say matters anyway") attitude. The result will be a lackluster performance that is not responsive to the need of the organization for proactive employees.

Resistance is a condition that can manifest itself in more aggressive ways: not following through on requests for a specific action, attempts to gain power to offset the manager's, and even retaliation (Kotter, 1979:44). The resistant individual may try to modify power relationships through the use of passive-aggressive behavior such as the "misunderstanding" of orders or overtly aggressive attempts to sabotage the organization through abuse of inmates, undermining of policy, and destruction of property.

In the long term, the manager who is unable to effectively use power may find career advancement stifled. Employee performance is seen to be affected to such an extent that the manager is no longer perceived as an asset to the organization. To avoid being an ineffective manager requires an understanding that employees (and offenders) will respond differently to the use of the bases of power. The key to successful management is learning how to read a situation and choose the most effective base of power when developing a strategy to manage the situation.

In general, expert power is most strongly related to effective performance (Rahim, 1989). Employees respond in a very positive manner to competence, which can produce high levels of employee performance. Position power does not appear to be related to effective performance (Ivancevich, 1970). The use of reward and coercive power is not particularly effective either. Employees tend to hold a negative view of the use of both rewards and punishments as reasons for complying with managerial requests and these bases are associated with low employee performance; coercive power is also negatively related to group effectiveness and creates resistance (Bachman, Bowers, and Marcus, 1968). Thus, the bottom line seems to be that effective managers will lead by competent example and rely as little as possible on the use of reward and coercive power.

Strategies of Influence

Kipnis et al. (1984) have described how managers influence other managers and employees through the use of a variety of power tactics (strategies) that include the following:

1. Reason—the use of facts and data to make a logical presentation of ideas
2. Friendliness—the use of flattery, creation of goodwill, assumption of a humble attitude, or use of friendliness prior to making a request
3. Coalition—getting the support of other individuals to support your request or program
4. Bargaining—the use of negotiation through the exchange of benefits or favors
5. Assertiveness—the use of a direct and forceful approach such as demanding compliance or giving orders or pointing out that rules are made to be obeyed
6. Higher authority—gaining the support of organizational superiors
7. Sanctions—using organizationally derived rewards and punishments such as promising or withholding a salary increase, threatening to give an unsatisfactory performance evaluation, or approving or withholding a promotion

Obviously, the ability to use sanctions as a strategy in corrections is severely limited by legislation, Civil Service procedures, CBAs, and the organization's own technical subsystem. However, this can be an effective approach to use with at-will employees who have no Civil Service or legal protections.

The use of a specific strategy depends on the manager's relative power, objectives, expectations of the recipient's willingness to comply, and the organizational culture.

Relative Power Managers who control resources valued by others, or who are perceived to be in positions of dominance, use a greater variety of tactics than do those with less power. The superintendent who wants to institute a new policy that will change the daily routine of correctional officers can select from the entire menu of power tactics described by Kipnis et al. (1984). For example, a superintendent who wants to implement a Unit Management system has the ability to use every power tactic from reason to sanctions. However, the correctional officers who do not accept Unit Management can only use the tactics of reason, friendliness, coalition, and bargaining in expressing their disapproval of the new policy. They lack the power to use the tactics of assertiveness or sanctions, and going to a higher authority carries a substantial risk of retaliation, although unions can exercise this tactic.

The power relationship is critical to the choice of strategy. Managers attempting to influence superiors choose to use (in descending order) the strategies of reason, coalition, friendliness, bargaining, assertiveness, and higher authority (Kipnis et al., 1984:62). Given the rigidity of the chain of command in corrections, resorting to higher authority can be a very dangerous choice if the manager's superior views the activities as "going over my head to get your own way."

Managers attempting to influence subordinates choose to use (again, in descending order) the strategies of reason, assertiveness, friendliness, coalition, bargaining, higher authority, and sanctions (Kipnis et al., 1984:62).

Managerial Objectives Managers seeking benefits from superiors tend to use friendliness, but they use reason when pushing a desired project or program. They use reason to sell ideas to subordinates and friendliness to obtain favors.

Expectations of Success   When past experience indicates a high probability of success, simple requests are used to gain compliance. When success is less predictable, there is a temptation to use assertiveness and sanctions.

Organizational Culture   The organizational culture in which a manager works will influence the choice of strategies. The organizational culture of corrections tends to encourage the use of assertiveness and sanctions, although managers in small organizations such as halfway houses are likely to rely on reason, friendliness, and bargaining.

The effective manager knows how to match strategy to situation for maximum results. The above discussion has focused on the manager–employee relationship, but what about the manager's relationship with individuals and organizations in the external environment? In dealing with the media, unions, quasi-judicial regulatory agencies, special interest groups, citizens, and other Criminal Justice System (CJS) agencies, correctional managers must rely almost exclusively on reason, friendliness, bargaining, and coalition. The ability to use assertiveness, sanctions, and appeal to a higher authority are severely diminished by the lack of the formal power relationship found in the internal environment. The need for correctional managers who have mastered the skills of reason, friendliness, and bargaining is especially acute in community corrections because this level of organization cannot set itself apart from the community in the way that prisons can.

SUMMARY

Power is distributed throughout the correctional organization in accordance with bases and sources of power that are influenced by individual and organizational characteristics. The formal distribution of power is governed by the official relationship between the strategic apex, middle line, technostructure, support staff, operating core, and offender population. Bureaucratization has significantly shifted the control of coercive, reward, and expert power from the strategic apex to the technostructure and support staff. The rise of prison gangs has shifted inmate power from individuals to groups. The ineffective use of managerial power can encourage the development of informal political behavior that may have negative consequences for the organization if correctional managers do not recognize and respond to that behavior. In the next chapter, we examine the exercise of power through leadership.

Discussion Questions

1. Why is a power relationship an exchange relationship?
2. Would the current DOC distribution of power relationships exist if correctional bureaucratization had not occurred?
3. What can managers do to ensure their effective use of power?
4. What individual and organizational characteristics contribute to organizational politics?
5. What actions can correctional managers take to minimize the negative effects of employee political behavior?
6. What are the bases of inmate power? How does their use of power differ from the organizational use of power?
7. Is unionization a form of staff resistance? Why or why not?

Critical Analysis Exercise: The Super-Max Prison

The Illinois DOC Closed Maximum Security Correctional center in Tamms, Illinois, is designed to provide the highest level of security and the most restrictive movement of 520 of the DOC's most violent and difficult inmates. The basic organizational element is the inmate housing pod—ten cells in each of six cellblocks arranged around a control station strategically placed to permit visual access to both tiers of each cellblock. Each pod has special-purpose areas: a medical assessment room; two library cells; multipurpose space for use by clergy, psychologists, and others; and outdoor exercise enclosures. Inmate access to these areas is on a one-at-a-time basis and all services are delivered to the inmate in the cell whenever possible. Cell furniture is a concrete sleeping platform with a pad, a wall-mounted writing surface and shelf, a stainless-steel "combi unit"—water closet, lavatory, and drinking fountain—and a small stainless-steel mirror. Because of the security risk these inmates present, they are confined to their cells as long as 23 hours a day with an hour allowed for personal hygiene and exercise. Three showers a week are offered. Food, library, and even minor medical services are delivered to inmates in their cells. All routine inmate activities are conducted in solitude. Inmates are transported out of cell only for visitation, court proceedings, and major medical procedures. They are always handcuffed, restrained, and escorted by C.O.s during any transport. Continuous inmate surveillance is provided by 103 cameras. Recognizing the potentially negative consequences of sensory deprivation, DOC psychologists and sociologists complete a baseline assessment of each inmate during initial processing and reevaluate inmate psychological status at specified times during incarceration. The facility also houses the Illinois DOC execution chamber, which is designed for multiple executions (Shepperd, Geiger, and Welborn, 1996).

Critical Analysis Questions

1. Does the super-max prison represent an abuse of organizational power? Defend your answer.
2. Do you think the courts will find the super-max prison to be a form of cruel and unusual punishment? Why or why not?
3. What types of inmate behavior justify this confinement?
4. The super-max prison represents a use of coercive power. Is there another type of power that might be more effective in controlling inmate behavior? If so, which one?
5. How effective do you think a super-max prison is in changing inmate behavior? Will these changes be positive or negative?
6. What adverse psychological effects should psychologists be concerned about?
7. What do you think the public response will be to the expanded use of super-max prisons?

9
Correctional Management and Leadership

Learning Objectives

After completing this chapter, you should be able to:

- Define the effective manager and the effective leader.
- Present a typology of management functions, skills, and roles.
- Develop the argument that management and leadership are not synonymous terms.
- Define the trait approach, contingency, and path-goal theories of leadership.
- Compare and contrast the theories of leadership.
- Develop a typology of leadership skills and styles.
- Outline and summarize the elements of an effective leadership practices model.

Key Terms and Concepts

Manager
Management Functions
Management Roles
Leadership
Contingency Theories
Situational Leadership Theory
Path-Goal Theory
Authoritarian
Transactional Leadership
Manager-Leader Model of Leadership Practices
Environmental Design
Management Skills
National Institute of Corrections
Trait Approach
Fiedler's Contingency Approach
Leader–Member Exchange Theory
Leadership Styles
Participative
Transforming Leadership

Effective correctional leaders go beyond managerial tasks to adapt to a new paradigm that embraces risk-taking, provides a vision of the future, and fosters cooperation both internal and external to their organizations. Leaders know how to manage change. One of the key contributions to a leader's success is the ability to deal with those in the external environment whose cooperation and support are important and sometimes critical.

Marie Mactavish

Profile: James V. Bennett, Former Director of the Federal Bureau of Prisons

James Van Benschoten Bennett (Figure 9–1) was director of the Federal Bureau of Prisons (FBOP) from 1937 to 1964. Prior to his appointment, the U.S. federal prison system consisted of three penitentiaries and two reformatories, each operating almost independently of each other because there was little central direction from Washington. The prisons were woefully underfunded and overcrowded, and the wardens were political appointees. Staff were poorly trained, most inmates were idle because of a lack of work and programming, living conditions were unhealthy, food and medical services were primitive, and there was a systemic reliance on brutality as a control measure.

In 1928, Bennett proposed a centralized system of federal correctional institutions that would have a greater access to resources, be empowered to construct more humane prisons, and have a mandate to develop and implement innovative programs that would promote rehabilitation. He also urged the establishment of specialized facilities to treat narcotics offenders. Bennett helped draft the legislation, enacted in 1930, that created the FBOP. Bennett then served as assistant director from 1930 to 1937. In 1934, he created the Federal Prison Industries, Inc., and significantly reduced inmate idleness. In addition, he helped abolish the corporal punishment of inmates, rooted out political corruption and patronage, developed inmate classification programs, built a series of new prisons to reduce overcrowding, developed inmate grievance procedures, and entered into a partnership with the U.S. Public Health Service to establish a prison hospital and two narcotics treatment facilities. When he became director in 1937, Bennett pushed for better educational and vocational training programs, work and study release, increased community involvement in rehabilitation programs, and liberalized mail and visiting procedures. In the late 1930s and 1940s, Bennett opened special prisons for juvenile delinquents. He also codified a uniform policy structure for all federal prisons, imposed a systemic audit process that allowed headquarters staff to oversee field operations, converted FBOP employees to Civil Service status, enhanced staff development through a system of awards, training programs, and merit promotions, and improved communications throughout the system. In 1961, the FBOP opened three halfway houses, among the first in the nation. As a last official act, Bennett championed the 1965 Federal Prisoner Rehabilitation Act (Roberts, 1996).

FIGURE 9–1 James V. Bennett (1894–1978) was director of the Federal Bureau of Prisons for almost three decades. Courtesy of the Office of Archives, Federal Bureau of Prisons.

The Profile's review of the career of James V. Bennett provides an example of an individual who can be described as both an effective manager and a successful leader. As a manager, he engaged in the basic management functions of planning, organizing, leading, and controlling employee behavior. As a leader he provided a vision of the direction he thought the Federal Bureau of Prisons should be heading and the inspiration to motivate employees to act in accordance with that vision. "Manager" is a formal role and title defined by position power and hierarchical placement in the organization chart. Therefore, every correctional organization has managers. Leadership is another matter, however. The formal designation of manager does not necessarily mean that the individual is also a leader. Management and leadership are not synonymous. The skill requirements and philosophies of these roles are different. Corrections has historically had both managers and leaders. However, the complexity of corrections is currently increasing so rapidly that a fundamental organizational challenge is the need to transform managers into leaders. The effective correctional organization of the future will be the organization in which managers have made the transition from manager to leader. In this chapter, we define and contrast management and leadership.

DEFINING MANAGEMENT

We begin this chapter with a basic question: What is a manager? The simple answer is that a manager is an individual whose position power confers the responsibility of creating "the design of an environment in which people working together in groups can accomplish objectives" (Koontz, O'Donnell, and Weihrich, 1986:13). Effective employee activity is made possible by managers who understand that the difference between an organization in a state of chaos and an organization efficiently accomplishing the mission is an ongoing environmental design process built on a foundation of the basic management functions of planning, directing, organizing, and controlling.

Management Functions and Environmental Design

The four fundamental management functions share the goal of creating and coordinating an effective environmental design.

The process of management is a continuum made up of many overlapping and interwoven activities. To summarize, planning defines organizational goals, develops organizational strategy, and determines the priority of operative goals. It can be a short-term process, such as determining the day's activities, or it can be a long-term process of strategic planning that projects goals and activities five years into the future. Organizing formalizes the activities of groups of employees through departmentalization and creates the chain of command that holds together the organizational structure. Organizing basically involves making decisions about the division of labor. Leading (leadership) applies the specialized processes of motivation, direction, communication, and conflict resolution to employee behavior. Controlling is an evaluative process that matches progress against goals, monitors employee performance, and makes adjustments or new decisions to correct any deviations from required behavior.

Distribution of Management Functions

The priority placed on each function is largely dependent upon the manager's formal position in the organization. Top managers may spend 70 percent to 80 percent of their time engaged in broad-based, long-term planning and organizing. First-level managers may spend 80 percent to 90 percent of their time in directing and controlling daily activities (Phillips and McConnell, 1996:47), while middle managers may divide their time equally between the four management functions. The higher in the hierarchy a manager rises, the greater the necessity to take the "big picture" view of the organization and not get bogged down in daily operational issues.

Top managers must avoid micromanaging: they must reject the often powerful temptation to review every subordinate decision and manage every detail of the jobs being performed. Micromanagement can create an atmosphere of distrust and low morale and can stifle creativity. The micromanager frequently becomes a bottleneck in the flow of communication and decision making, and the organization may in fact be better off without the micromanager (Geary, 1990:16). The effective manager will empower employees by delegating to each individual as much responsibility and authority as their experience, intelligence, training, and job requirements allow.

This overview provides us with an initial definition of a manager as the individual responsible for developing an effective environmental design. But our definition is incomplete. A manager is more than a collection of functions. A manager must also possess a specific set of skills.

Management Skills

How well does a manager perform the various functions required throughout the course of a career? That answer depends on the degree of proficiency the manager has developed in the technical, human, and conceptual skills (or competencies) so essential to effective management (Katz, 1974:90–102).

Technical Skills   Technical skills involve the ability to apply specialized knowledge or expertise. For managers, the technical expertise should be in decision making (Chapter 10), communication, and motivation (Chapter 11). A manager lacking any one of these skills will most likely exhibit poor performance when attempting to perform management functions.

Human Skills   These involve the ability to understand, work with, and motivate people, individually and in groups. They are essential if the manager is to achieve organizational goals through the efforts of subordinates. Many managers have a high level of technical proficiency. They understand the mission and can develop plans of action for implementing policy designed to support the mission, conceptualize new programs, prioritize goals, and develop realistic budget proposals. But they cannot

effectively manage interpersonal conflicts, listen to subordinates or inmates, or motivate in a positive manner.

For example, a cardinal principle of good management is that employee discipline is always done in private. A technically proficient manager with poor "people" skills can quickly destroy group morale by publicly reprimanding subordinates in front of other employees or offenders. The principle that an effective manager educates staff can be violated by interpreting sincere questions about policy and procedure as a defiance of authority and responding "If you don't like the way I do it, don't let the door hit you on the way out." The principle that people should be commended for positive performance can be violated by a manager who ignores employee performance except when there is a mistake.

Conceptual Skills   A multitude of complex problems can get in the way of successfully accomplishing the mission. Conceptual skills constitute the ability to intellectually analyze and diagnose complex problems through a logical, sequential process of (1) definition of the problem, (2) definition of objectives, (3) development of alternative solutions, (4) development of plans of action, (5) troubleshooting to determine what might go wrong, (6) communication of the selected plan of action to staff, and (7) implementation of the plan of action (Lyles, 1982:10).

The effective manager is able to apply conceptual skills to a wide range of problems. The value of this manager to the organization is even greater if there is a personal commitment to teaching those skills to subordinates, especially those individuals being groomed for promotion. Our definition of manager is now enlarged: A manager is an individual who understands management functions and also possesses the technical, human, and conceptual skills necessary for effective environmental design. The process of defining the manager is not yet complete, however. Functions and skills must be expressed through a set of activities known as management roles.

MANAGEMENT ROLES

In 1973, Henry Mintzberg proposed that the behavior of managers can be defined in terms of managerial roles grouped into three categories of activity: interpersonal, informational, and decisional. A manager can be compared to a single actor performing in a multirole play, required by the demands of the play to shift from role to role as circumstances dictate but never permanently staying in one role.

Interpersonal Role

Managers have an official people function that requires three types of interpersonal role: the figurehead, the leader, and the liaison.

Figurehead The figurehead is a ceremonial role that has both social and symbolic value for the organization. For example, the Commissioner who presides over the annual Employee of the Year Award Ceremony, presents the official plaque, shakes the award recipient's hand, and poses with the recipient for the public relations photo is representing the Department of Corrections (DOC) in a social event that expresses the organization's gratitude for a job well done.

Leader The leadership role involves responsibility for the personnel process: employee hiring, training, motivating, promotion, and discipline. The leader rarely has a hands-on involvement in these processes but does have the overall responsibility for ensuring that they are functioning properly.

Liaison The liaison role involves developing and maintaining a network of contacts with individuals and groups inside and outside the organization who can provide information and assistance. These networks can be both formal and informal. Interaction with the legislature is formalized through the Legislative Liaison Office and contacts with the media are formalized

through the Public Information Officer, but managers may also have informal contacts with community leaders and media representatives as well as judges, attorneys, law enforcement personnel, inmate advocacy groups, and other managers.

Informational Role

Managers also collect and disseminate information that is relevant to organizational behavior. There are three types of informational role: monitor, disseminator, and spokesperson.

Monitor The manager continually receives information from Central Office, professional journals, letters from the public, inmate complaints, inquiries from judges and legislators, and through discussions with counterparts, both locally and nationally. This information is sifted and evaluated for relevance in achieving the mission.

Disseminator Relevant information is transmitted to appropriate staff throughout the organization. For example, updated information about HIV-infected inmates from the Center for Disease Control in Atlanta will be sent to the Medical Director. A study of the effectiveness of mace and stun guns in controlling a disruptive inmate during a cell extraction would be sent to the Deputy Superintendent for Operations and Training Lieutenant. The effectiveness of electronic monitoring will be distributed to probation and parole officers. Managers, especially top managers, are bombarded with a steady flow of information that they must read, evaluate, understand, and introduce into the chain of command.

Spokesperson This role involves representing the organization to outsiders, frequently in an attempt to educate them about corrections. The Commissioner who participates in a college panel discussing the effects of prison overcrowding, for example, is officially representing the DOC. Similarly, the parole officer who speaks to a business group about the potential for offenders to be good employees is functioning as a spokesperson.

Decisional Role

The manager must constantly make choices. This involves four roles: the entrepreneur, the disturbance handler, the resource allocator, and the negotiator.

Entrepreneur This role involves initiating and overseeing new projects that will improve the quality of organizational behavior. For example, a superintendent might direct treatment staff to develop a proposal for implementation of a sex offender treatment unit or direct the in-service training coordinator to develop an ethics curriculum.

Disturbance Handler Managers are responsible for taking corrective actions when disturbances develop. But a disturbance is not necessarily a dramatic event, such as a riot. In fact, a better term for this role is *change manager*. Managers must manage the response to any event that changes the traditional way of doing things. Judicial decisions, legislative mandates, union initiatives—all challenge the way things are done in corrections and it is the responsibility of correctional managers to integrate these changes into the existing environmental design. A prime example of this challenge was considered in an earlier chapter: the Americans with Disabilities Act (ADA) of 1990, which has radically changed the managerial approach to correctional architecture by requiring correctional managers to incorporate accessibility design standards into all phases of facility renovation and construction, including communications systems.

Resource Allocator This role involves the allocation of human, physical, and financial resources. The superintendent's development and submission of the annual budget request to Central Office is an essential element of this role.

Negotiator Managers must represent the organization in situations where the focus of discussion is the allocation of resources or conflict resolution. For example, in most DOCs each superintendent has the opportunity to meet with the Commissioner to discuss the superintendent's budget request after it has been evaluated by Central Office. During this meeting, it is the responsibility of the superintendent to persuasively argue the justification for approval of the requested budget priorities. The superintendent's conflict resolution role may come into play during discussions with outside agencies, such as the Environmental Protection Agency (EPA), that have expressed concern about specific correctional practices.

Once again we must revise our definition of a manager: A manager is an individual who understands the four basic management functions necessary for effective environmental design, possesses technical, human, and conceptual skills, and is capable of demonstrating that knowledge and those skills in a variety of roles. This naturally leads to another question: Who are the current correctional managers and how do they prepare for their jobs?

CORRECTIONAL MANAGER PROFILE AND PREPARATION FOR THE JOB

A 1989 survey of 512 wardens and superintendents in state and federal prisons determined that correctional managers, as a group, have a relatively homogeneous demographic makeup. They are predominately white, college-educated males in their mid-forties who have worked in corrections for nearly two decades. Two thirds of these managers have a military background and, prior to becoming correctional managers, one third were correctional officers (C.O.s) and a majority had come from the treatment ranks (Cullen et al., 1993:76). Each correctional manager is influenced by a personal philosophy of what his or her organizational mission should be. The primary goal of the 512 survey respondents was incapacitation, but there was also support for rehabilitation as a secondary, but fundamental, goal of corrections. The researchers concluded that rehabilitation is a "core element of the orientation of America's correctional elite" (Cullen et al., 1993:85).

But there is more to being a correctional manager than possessing a personal philosophy and having the title of manager. There is the issue of preparation to manage. Are these 512 wardens and superintendents adequately prepared to effectively manage their correctional organizations? This question has been the focus of an ongoing debate. Because management involves a continued response to complex and demanding challenges, it stands to reason that correctional managers should be trained in the art of management. The requirement of achieving the mission creates a powerful need for managerial competency. After all, a prison superintendent is responsible for managing a multimillion dollar budget, an expensive physical plant, possibly thousands of inmates, and hundreds of employees within an internal environment of different subcultures and an external environment that is increasingly intrusive. Community corrections can be just as challenging with the added dimension of the offender being free in the community. Do correctional managers possess this level of competency?

The Debate About Competency

Duffee (1980a:8) has reported that most correctional managers have been promoted from within and have no formal training in management. Shannon (1990) found that while many managers did have an "on-the-job" background in management, their formal education was in the social sciences, and few had corrections-related college training. Their organizational skills had to be adapted to corrections.

The debate about competency concerns the impact of this lack of formal management training on professional competence.

One of the standard arguments in favor of the privatization of corrections is that private sector managers can be more effective because they are trained to think in terms of bottom-line accountability whereas correctional managers think in terms of managing inmates. Cohn (1991) argued that the effectiveness of correctional managers is questionable because they merely apply techniques learned as they rose through the ranks and, therefore, have difficulty planning and anticipating future challenges. However, Silverman and Vega (1996:278–280) countered that the college and in-service training most prison managers receive adequately prepare them for their professional responsibilities.

Many corrections professionals will argue that corrections is such a unique environment that the most effective manager will be the individual who has come up through the ranks. The perception, and fear, is that managers coming into correctional management from other fields will make too many mistakes as they try to adjust to the challenges of offender management.

In considering this debate, it is important to recognize that the criteria for the selection of managers has changed since the 1960s. For example, in 1978, Bartollas and Miller reported that every warden in the Illinois DOC in the mid-1960s had risen through the ranks from a C.O. position. Less than ten years later, no warden had started as a C.O. This decreased emphasis on the value of line experience may reflect a political acknowledgment that correctional management is far more complicated than simply knowing how to handle inmates on a direct contact level.

Preparing for a Career in Corrections

An increasing number of correctional managers enter the field as an early career choice. They have not entered corrections after years in a totally unrelated occupation. Rather, they have prepared for the field by majoring in criminal justice. College programs in criminal justice often have a corrections track that provides an academic exposure to correctional management issues and processes. These tracks frequently provide students the opportunity to have an internship in a correctional organization that provides a firsthand view of correctional managers on the job. This initial exposure provides the foundation on which the correctional organization can build.

However, the issue of where correctional managers come from may not be as relevant as it used to be. Because of the rate of change confronting managers in every type of organization, it has been noted that "[t]here is an axiom that by the time a person reaches his or her mid-career plateau, those who have learned the lessons of management and leadership through experience have honed and shaped their skills for a world that no longer exists" (Ault and Brown, 1997:136). There is no reason to believe that this axiom does not apply to corrections. As a result, every three to five years, current and future correctional managers need a minimum of two weeks of formal, intensive training provided by skilled training professionals in a setting outside of the work site (Ault and Brown, 1997:136).

Formal Training of Correctional Managers

Regardless of where managers come from, they must be trained, and periodically updated, in the art of correctional management. Top managers are increasingly emphasizing the need for current and future managers to receive more than on-the-job training; correctional organizations at every level routinely provide at least a minimum amount of formal management training. External training resources are also available.

The National Institute of Corrections Contribution to Managerial Training
The National Institute of Corrections (NIC) Academy is an excellent source of training for both entry-level managers who must learn the basic principles of management and senior managers who want a refresher course in specific areas of interest. In 1998, the NIC offered the following courses:

Management Development for the Future
Management Development for Women and Minorities
Strategies for Building Effective Work Teams
Public and Media Relations
Public and Media Relations for CEOs and PIOs
Orientation for Parole Board Members
Operational Framework and Goals for Community Corrections
Restorative Justice: Principles, Practices, and Implementations
Evaluation and Accountability Strategies for Correctional Programs
Women Offenders: Developing an Agency Plan (with Technical Assistance)
Training for Offender Employment Specialists

In addition, the NIC offered six jail management workshops covering services, planning, design review, and audit procedures and six prison management seminars covering emergency planning and a variety of strategies for prison management (National Institute of Corrections, 1997:23–35). Figure 9–2 provides an overview of the NIC technical and training services. Box 9–1 describes the NIC's service delivery strategies.

BOX 9–1 NIC'S SERVICE DELIVERY STRATEGIES

Two strategies are used to carry out NIC's programs and services:

A proactive and leadership approach to influence national policies, practices, and operations by identifying and developing programs that address areas of emerging interest and concern to correctional executives and practitioners as well as public policy makers,

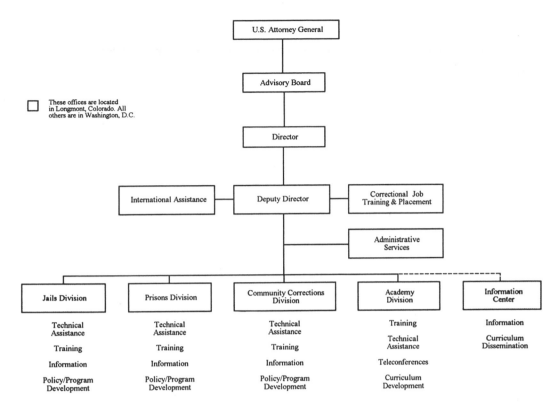

FIGURE 9–2 National Institute of Corrections Organization and Services. Source: National Institute of Corrections. *NIC Service Plan for Fiscal Year 1998: Training Technical Assistance.* Washington, DC: U.S. Department of Justice, 1997.

Responsive assistance and services to client agencies and staff to improve their correctional systems.

Programs and services are delivered through the following mechanisms:

Direct technical assistance to provide expertise to the requesting agency. There is no award of funds to the agency, and the technical assistance is usually accomplished through on-site assistance. Technical assistance is generally provided for a period of three to five days for a maximum cost of $10,000. Individuals retained by NIC or NIC staff provide the assistance.

Special emphasis programs are available in specific areas in which NIC has completed developmental work and has established a coordi-nated, multifaceted approach to assisting agencies in successful program implementation. Activities can include technical assistance, training, peer consultation, and information dissemination. NIC staff facilitate or participate in these activities.

Training services are provided through seminars conducted at the NIC Academy, at state and local sites, and regionally; videoconferences; and workshops provided as technical assistance and at conferences. These services are supported by ongoing curriculum development and refinement, a network of regional trainers, and a clearinghouse for correctional staff training materials. Technical assistance providers and NIC staff provide training services.

Information services are closely related to the technical assistance and training services, but also support all other NIC programs. Corrections-related materials and NIC publications are disseminated to corrections practitioners by the NIC Information Center, which is operated by a private contractor. Information is also disseminated through the NIC divisions.

Networking activities are sponsored by each of the NIC divisions to provide the opportunity for correctional executives and administrators to interact with their peers from other jurisdictions. These activities provide a forum for the exchange of information and experiences on current issues. NIC staff facilitate these meetings.

Source: National Institute of Corrections. *NIC Service Plan for Fiscal Year 1998: Training Technical Assistance.* Washington, DC: U.S. Department of Justice, 1997.

Clearly, the NIC offers a broad range of formal training and technical assistance programs to virtually every type of correctional organization. Formal training is designed with the specific goal of producing a manager who has all the competencies necessary for effective correctional management. But, does the training we have described produce a leader? After all, one of the management functions listed by Fayol (1916) was leading and one of Mintzberg's interpersonal roles was that of leader. Can we assume the effective manager is also a leader?

The answer is no. Far too often, managers able to effectively plan, organize, direct, and control are not leaders. Management and leadership are not the same thing: not all leaders are managers and not all managers are leaders. To understand why this is so, we begin by defining leadership.

DEFINING LEADERSHIP

The chapter epigraph provides a useful working definition of leadership. Leaders establish the direction of the organization and inspire their employees to want to achieve the goals set by the leader. Vance Packard (quoted in Kouzes and Posner, 1987:1) has defined leadership as "the art of getting others to want to do something that you are convinced should be done." Leaders are able to communicate their vision of the organization's future, articulate the strategies for achieving that vision, and execute those strategies by inspiring employees to overcome technical, personal, and bureaucratic challenges (Kotter, 1990).

Kouzes and Posner (1986), in a survey of 10,000 public and private organization managers, found that leaders are people who are (1) honest, (2) competent, (3) able to communicate their vision for the future, (4) able to provide inspiration, (5) have credibility, (6) display a willingness to challenge the status quo, (7) foster mutual trust and team building, (8) provide a positive role model for subordinates, and (9) able to recognize and celebrate subordinate successes.

While it is true that managers may be also be honest, competent, have credibility, provide a positive role model for subordinates, and recognize and celebrate subordinate success, there are substantial differences between managers and leaders.

Comparing Managers and Leaders

A fundamental difference between managers and leaders is that management is a function of location within the organizational structure. The specific tasks required of a manager depend on one's location within the organization and the position power assigned to that location. Leadership is not dependent upon organizational location. It is more a quality of the individual: "Leaders differ from managers in that they emphasize intangibles such as vision, values, and motivation" (Legnini, 1994:1570).

It is only the leader who can develop and communicate a vision of the future that challenges the status quo while inspiring "a sense of excitement about the significance of the organization's contribution to society" (Bennis and Nanus, 1985:226).

Procedures versus Change   Ultimately, management is about developing and implementing the practices and procedures the organization needs to cope with complexity. It is about routine planning, directing, organizing, and controlling. Leadership is about coping with change. The leader must have the ability to identify those changes in the environment that will affect the organization, develop appropriate change strategies, effectively communicate those strategies, and inspire employees to welcome and participate in the process of change (Kotter, 1990:7).

Summarizing the Differences Between Management and Leadership   There are nine fundamental differences between managers and leaders:

1. The manager administers, the leader innovates.
2. The manager focuses on systems and structure, the leader focuses on people.
3. The manager relies on control, the leader inspires trust.
4. The manager has a short-term view, the leader has a long-term view.
5. The manager asks how and when, the leader asks what and why.
6. The manager has his concentration on the bottom line, the leader is focused on the horizon.
7. The manager accepts the status quo, the leader actively challenges the traditional way of looking at issues.
8. The manager is the classic good soldier, the leader is his own person.
9. The manager does things right, the leader does the right thing (Bennis, 1989).

One final note needs to be made about leaders. Leadership is not necessarily a characteristic possessed solely by individuals in formal management positions in the organizational structure.

Formal Versus Informal Leadership

Every organization has two types of leaders: formal and informal. The formal leaders are those managers defined by their position in the organizational structure. They may or may not possess the characteristics identified by Kouzes and Posner, but their official duty is to lead as well as manage. The informal leaders are the individuals who do not have position power but do have the respect of their peer group because they possess a set of psychological characteristics (such as honesty, competence, toughness, and the ability to persuade) that influence their peer group to look to them for advice and guidance. Frequently, in corrections, the peer group trusts informal leaders more than they trust the formal leaders. Employees concerned about the effects of a new policy presented by management will be influenced in their response to that policy by the support, or lack of support, it receives from the organization's informal leaders.

What makes an individual an effective leader? Many answers have been offered to this fundamental question, but there are three explanations (models) that have received the most attention.

Trait Model of Leadership

The earliest model of leadership proposed that leaders are those rare individuals who are born to lead. They are born to lead because they naturally possess the characteristics necessary for effective leadership.

Trait Approach

Trait theory (sometimes referred to as the "great man theory") assumes that leaders are individuals who are born to lead. That is, a leader is an individual who has the good fortune to be born possessing highly desirable personal characteristics: (1) intelligence, analytical judgment, and verbal ability, (2) the ability to consistently achieve in scholarship and athletics, (3) emotional maturity and stability, (4) persistence, dependability, and a drive for achievement, (5) social skills and adaptability to different groups, and (6) a desire for social and socioeconomic status (Stogdill, 1948:35–64). The apparent validity of this argument can be seen in a literature review by Kouzes and Posner (1990). When 7,500 employees were asked "What values (personal traits or characteristics) do you look for and admire in your supervisors?" 87 percent cited honesty, 74 percent cited competence, 67 percent were impressed by a vision of the future, and 61 percent valued the ability to inspire others. Honest, ethical personal behavior was rated as the most important overall characteristic.

There is a certain intuitive attractiveness to this approach and it is not unusual to hear people refer to other individuals as being born to lead. But even a brief review of history suggests that too many world leaders have been lacking in one or more of Stogdill's defining criteria for this approach to be valid. This overly simplistic approach has largely been discarded because of a recognition that leadership is more than a function of personal characteristics. Leadership occurs in an environment that influences decision making and the exercise of authority.

Contingency Model of Leadership

Tannenbaum and Schmidt (1958:95) noted that the study of leadership by organizational theorists now emphasizes group dynamics "with its focus on members of the group rather than solely on the leader." Contingency theories broaden the focus of discussion to include the situation that requires the exercise of leadership and the followers who are to be the object of that leadership. This interaction can be expressed as

$$SL = f(L,F,S)$$

where SL = successful leadership, f = function of, L = leader, F = follower, and S = situation (Certo, 1985:319). This equation suggests

that successful leadership depends on a manager's ability to "read" a situation and adjust personal behavior accordingly. The superintendent eager to have the prison pass an American Corrections Association (ACA) accreditation audit will function as a coach and a salesperson and motivate staff through a bureaucratic process that involves committee meetings and other forms of democratic group discussion. The superintendent faced with an inmate riot will adopt the authoritarian approach of the autocratic warden.

Fiedler's Contingency Theory

According to Fiedler (1967), whether leadership is effective is a function of three critical situational factors: (1) the leader–follower relationship, (2) a task structure, and (3) position power. Leader–follower relationships are either good or poor. A good relationship exists when there is a condition of follower trust and affection for the leader. A poor relationship exists when followers distrust and dislike the leader. The degree of trust and confidence employees have in a leader depends, to a large extent, on that leader's expert and referent power. Task structure is either high or low. A high task structure consists of a well-defined mission statement supported by written policies, rules, and procedures that spell out goals, individual responsibilities, and organizational expectations. A low task structure has a minimal amount of policy, rules, and procedures and permits the excessive use of individual discretion in decision making. Finally, position power is either strong or weak. Strong position power exists when the leader can hire, promote, and fire. Weak position power exists when the leader lacks this level of authority. In other words, position power depends on the extent of the leader's legitimate, reward, and coercive powers.

According to Fiedler, therefore, a leader's effectiveness is determined by the leader's personal traits and by various structural elements of the situation. Thus, in any discussion of leadership, both the leader and the nature of the situation must be considered.

Defining the Leader   Fiedler studied the psychology of leaders and defined a "leader" in terms of a specific psychological measurement: the attitude toward the least-preferred co-worker (LPC). As used by Fiedler, LPC refers to the way the leader tends to evaluate the individual with whom she or he has found it most difficult to work. Leaders who perceive this individual in negative terms tend to be primarily concerned with attaining successful task performance. Fiedler referred to these leaders as "low LPC leaders." Another term for this type of leader is "task-orientated leader" or "directive leader." These individuals are most concerned with getting the job done, meeting deadlines, and not exceeding the budget. They tend to prefer highly structured situations where the focus is the bottom line.

Those leaders who perceive the least-preferred co-worker in positive terms are mainly concerned with having good relations with employees. These are "high LPC leaders," also known as "human relations-oriented leaders" or "supportive leaders." They tend to be permissive, more people-oriented, and supportive in their relationships with subordinates. They also prefer unstructured situations that require creativity.

Defining the Situation   Situations can be defined in terms of leader–follower relationship, task structure, and position power. Fiedler suggests that the effectiveness of low LPC leaders and high LPC leaders is a function of how much control a leader has over subordinates in any given situation. The term Fiedler used to describe this element of leadership is situational control, a variable which can be located on a continuum of low to moderate to high:

Low_____Moderate_____High

Leader–follower relationship, task structure, and position power are the elements that define situational control. Fiedler states that the more positive the leader–follower relationship, the more highly structured the job, and the stronger the position power, the more control or influence a leader has, i.e., the higher the level of situational control. The more negative the leader–follower relation-

ship, the less structure present in the job, and the weaker the position power, the lower the level of situational control. To illustrate this concept, we will examine two individuals: a county jail warden and a prison superintendent. Both these individuals are defined as top managers and, therefore, should be leaders but, as we will see, their situational control is markedly different.

The DOC superintendent is well respected (good leader–follower relationship); directs activities—such as budget preparation, policy development, and oversight of subordinate performance—that are clear and specific (high task structure); and has a high degree of freedom to reward and punish subordinates (strong position power). The Commissioner of Corrections allows the superintendent a large amount of discretion as long as DOC policy is followed. The DOC superintendent is highly effective because her situational control is high. However, the county jail warden is in a less favorable leadership position. Although his direction of activities is highly structured in much the same way as the DOC superintendent's is structured, the county jail warden lacks position power. He has no authority to hire, promote, or fire any employee. Instead, the County Board of Commissioners has retained that authority. All the county jail warden can do is make personnel recommendations to the board. Because these recommendations are frequently ignored, the warden's employees have learned the fine art of playing county politics with the result that individuals not recommended by the warden have been hired, promoted, or dismissed. The result is a lack of employee respect for the warden that borders on contempt. Thus, it is safe to say that there exists a very poor leader–follower relationship. Because of this low situational control, the county jail warden is highly ineffective and, in fact, recently resigned in frustration.

Matching the Leader to the Situation
Effective group performance depends upon the proper match between leadership style and the degree to which the situation gives

control and influence to the leader. Different situations require different leadership approaches. Fiedler, Chemers, and Mahar (1977) concluded that task-oriented leaders tend to perform better in situations in which they have either a great deal of influence or very little influence.

Fiedler suggests that the effectiveness of low LPC leaders will be superior to that of high LPC leaders when situational control is either very low or very high. However, the effectiveness of high LPC leaders will be superior when situational control falls in a middle range between these two extremes. What is the basis for these statements?

According to Fiedler, in situations of low situational control (i.e., negative relations, unstructured tasks, and low position power), employees require a considerable amount of guidance and direction if the mission is to be accomplished. Because low LPC leaders are task-oriented they are more likely to provide a higher degree of structure than are high LPC leaders. On the other hand when there is high situational control (i.e., positive relations, highly structured tasks, and high position power), conditions are already very favorable to accomplishment of the mission. The leader has to do very little in the way of structuring the task; therefore, there is time and energy to dedicate to improving relations with subordinates and the result is a tendency to adopt a relaxed, "hands-off" style that employees appreciate. The employee reponse is increased performance.

However, in the same situation, the high LPC leader, confident in the relationship with employees, may shift attention to task performance, an unnecessary behavior which employees may interpret as micromanaging. The result can be impaired employee performance. As to the issue of moderate situational control, conditions are mixed, and the promotion of good manager–employee relations is often a priority. High LPC leaders have an advantage in this type of situation because they already have an interest in people and being supportive. The low LPC's focus on task is likely to be perceived as an expression of autocratic leadership and the result can be reduced employee morale and effectiveness.

Criticisms of Fiedler's Approach　　Fiedler implies that leaders can be either task-oriented or human relations-oriented, but not both. The theory does not provide for a leader being high on both dimensions. If this assumption is correct, leaders possess an inflexibility that will harm the organization as it experiences changes to which the leader cannot readily adapt. Thus, there are only two ways to increase leader effectiveness. First, you can change the leader to fit the situation. That is, replace a task-oriented leader with a human relations-oriented leader. Second, you can change the situation to fit the leader by restructuring tasks or increasing the leader's position power. Klofas, Stojkovic, and Kalinich (1990:134) note two important problems with this position. First, field observation of correctional managers will readily suggest that many managers exhibit both styles of leadership, depending on the situation. Second, the traditional rigidity of correctional organizations makes both of Fiedler's solutions difficult to implement.

There is clearly more to leadership effectiveness than the factors defined by Fiedler. Leaders and situations are only part of the contingency equation. A more thorough understanding of leadership requires the further consideration of the nature of the followers.

Hershey-Blanchard Situational Leadership Theory

Paul Hershey and Ken Blanchard (1974; 1982) have developed a contingency theory that discusses leadership effectiveness as a function of the maturity level of a leader's followers.

Defining the Leader　　Leader effectiveness depends on the activities of followers. Followers either accept or reject the leader. Hershey and Blanchard have developed four leadership styles based on a low–high ordering of the Fiedler's task and relationship dimensions. These styles are telling, selling, participating, and delegating.

The telling leader (high task–low relationship) emphasizes directive behavior by defining roles and explicitly telling subordinates what, how, when, and where to perform various tasks. The selling leader (high task–high relationship) takes a balanced approach of providing both directive behavior and supportive behavior. The participating leader (low task–high relationship) allows subordinates to share in decision making, with the main role of the leader being to facilitate and communicate. The delegating leader (low task–low relationship) provides little direction or support because subordinates are motivated to perform at high levels. Which leadership style is most effective? The answer depends on the maturity level of the followers.

Maturity Maturity of the followers, as defined by Hershey and Blanchard, is the ability and willingness of people to take responsibility for directing their own behavior. Maturity has two components: job maturity and psychological maturity. Job maturity is defined in terms of job-related knowledge and skills. Psychological maturity is defined in terms of the willingness or motivation to do something. Individuals high in job and psychological maturity need little external control. They are able to function quite capably on their own. There are four stages of maturity:

M1—low job maturity and low psychological maturity: People are both unable and unwilling to take responsibility. They are neither competent nor confident. Their most frequently used phrase would probably be: "I don't know how to do that job. Give it to somebody else." These subordinates need clear and specific policy and procedures. The most effective leadership style is telling.

M2—low job maturity and high psychological maturity: People are unable but willing to do the necessary job tasks. They are motivated but lack appropriate job skills. Their most frequently used phrase would probably be: "I'd like to help you out, but you'll have to tell me what to do." The most effective leadership style is selling.

M3—high job maturity and low psychological maturity: People are able but unwilling to do what the leader wants. Their most frequently used phrase would probably be: "I can do that, but I don't think it's in my job description." These individuals can also be described as burned out. They know how to do the job, but no longer have any interest in doing so. The most effective leadership style is participating.

M4—high job maturity and high psychological maturity: People are both willing and able to do what the leader asks. Their most frequently used phrase would probably be: "No problem. Just let me at it." This is the easiest situation for a leader because subordinates are both willing and capable of assuming responsibility for their tasks. The more mature the work force, the less direction the leader must provide. The most effective leadership style is delegating.

Clearly an important characteristic of a correctional manager is the ability to accurately assess both the job maturity and psychological maturity of individual employees. But it is not just the maturity of the followers that is important. The manager must also consider the maturity of the organization as a whole.

An organization (such as a recently opened prison or parole office) with a majority of employees new to corrections requires leaders to provide a high level of structure and support. This organization should be at the M2 level. If it is at the M1 level, the correctional managers face a severe challenge that will be extremely difficult to meet. However, as the maturity of the followers increases, effective leadership requires less structure and support. The organization that achieves an M4 level of maturity will require the least structure and support. Ten years after the new prison or parole office has opened, employees should have attained a level of competence that requires minimal structure and support. Thus, organizational effectiveness and leadership style are both highly dependent upon the maturity of the followers (Hershey and Blanchard, 1974). An essential management skill, then, is the ability to accurately assess the maturity level of the manager's staff. This is particularly important for the top manager taking over a new DOC, prison, jail, or community corrections department. An initial faulty assessment can waste resources and eventually create manager–staff conflict.

In applying this theory, correctional managers must always keep in mind the fact that an organization, especially one as large as a DOC, is highly unlikely to have only one maturity level. The maturity levels of different prisons, units within individual prisons, and Central Office departments are likely to vary. Top managers, therefore, must possess the ability to develop specific strategies for specific prisons, units, and departments.

Leader–Member Exchange Theory

Graen, Novak, and Sommerkamp (1982:109–131) have elaborated on situational leadership theory by suggesting that leaders do not treat all followers in the same manner. Leader–member exchange (LMX) theory suggests that followers belong to one of two categories: the in-group and the out-group. The in-group are trusted, receive a disproportionate amount of the leader's time, and are more likely to receive special privileges. The out-group members receive less of the leader's time, fewer rewards, and have leader–follower relations based on formal authority interactions. Research has not clearly established the basis of in-group membership selection, but there is evidence that leaders favor those followers who are similar to them in gender, racial, age, and personality characteristics (Duchon, Green, and Taber, 1986:55–60).

LMX theory is important because of the negative consequences that can result from a staff perception, correct or not, that a leader or manager is "playing favorites." Staff morale can be seriously damaged. Managers should never underestimate the negative reaction a perception of favoritism can create. In a worst-case scenario, unhappy staff will "keep book" on the manager. That is, they will document every instance of managerial wrongdoing they can uncover and at some point send the "book" to the offending manager's superior, who may be prompted to initiate an internal affairs investigation.

Although follower maturity is important, our discussion of the role of the follower in defining leadership effectiveness has not been completed. Follower perceptions of what the leader has to offer them must also be accounted for if we are to advance our understanding of leadership.

Path-Goal Model of Leadership

According to path-goal theory, a leader's behavior is acceptable to subordinates to the degree that it is viewed by them as an immediate source of satisfaction or a source of future satisfaction. Path-goal theory asserts that the primary function of the leader is to (1) clarify and establish goals with subordinates, (2) help subordinates determine the best paths for achieving goals, and (3) remove obstacles to goal achievement.

Types of Leaders   According to path-goal theory, effective leadership is related to making subordinate need satisfaction contingent on effective performance and the degree of coaching, guidance, support, and rewards that a leader is able to provide to followers. Using this approach, House (1971) identified four types of leaders: the directive leader, the supportive leader, the participative leader, and the achievement-oriented leader.

The directive leader emphasizes the expectations of the leader, the tasks to be performed, and the policy and procedures to be followed in attaining organizational goals. The supportive leader emphasizes a managerial concern for the well-being of subordinates that conveys to staff the message that meeting the needs of employees is as important as meeting the needs of the organization. The participative leader rejects the autocratic role and emphasizes collaboration and consultation between leader and subordinates in decision making. The achievement-oriented leader focuses on setting challenging goals and expects that subordinates will achieve organizational goals. By all accounts, James V. Bennett, profiled at the beginning of the chapter, was an achievement-oriented leader.

Effective Leadership   Path-goal theory, in direct contrast to Fiedler's approach, suggests that leaders are flexible and there is no one style of leadership to fit every situation confronted by correctional managers. The effective leader is the individual who is able to tailor the leadership style to the specific situation at hand. If a manager's assessment of a situation is incorrect, then the application of an inappropriate leadership approach can have negative consequences.

The Influence of Organizational Reality
There are two aspects of organizational reality that must be taken into consideration in any discussion of path-goal theory. First, managers must be careful to design paths and goals that are reasonable and attainable. The superintendent who decides that the goal of increasing the inmate population to 190 percent above design capacity is reasonable and attainable is likely to find that both staff and inmates sustain a level of stress that will create difficulties for all concerned.

Second, inherent in the path-goal model is the suggestion that subordinates who are instrumental in helping the leader achieve organizational goals will be rewarded with positive performance evaluations and promotion. Yet, correctional leaders typically have little control over reward distribution. While they can readily provide a positive evaluation of employee performance, the ability to promote is dependent upon a vacancy occurring in the desired position. Even if such a vacancy occurs, the ability to promote will undoubtedly be limited by

Civil Service rules and promotion criteria and procedures spelled out in collective bargaining agreements. Promotion may also be limited by court decisions concerning the percentage of women and minorities who should be moved into the supervisory ranks.

Having examined a variety of leadership theories, it is now time to explore in greater detail the nature of the leader–employee relationship. We turn to the issue of leadership styles.

LEADERSHIP STYLES

Leadership styles can be defined in terms of the amount of input employees have in the decision-making process. When it comes to decision making, leaders can be classified as either authoritarian or participative (democratic). The authoritarian leader, such as Joseph Ragen, makes decisions based on personal experience, training, and intuition, without input from others. The authoritarian leadership style is reactive. Because of the rigidity of their chain of command, a problem often becomes serious before leaders are aware of it. This hinders the ability of the organization to limit the damage that problems can create. This limitation has been addressed by participative leadership.

Participative Model

The participative model requires leaders to share their leadership authority with subordinates rather than unilaterally making all the decisions. This leadership approach is based on three principles: (1) the worker knows his or her job better than anyone else, (2) employees can and will accept the responsibility for managing their work, and (3) intelligence and creativity exist among all employees at all levels of the organization (Weisz, 1985).

A prominent example of correctional participative leadership is the unit management concept. This form of inmate supervision places each inmate housing unit under the management of a team of staff (C.O.s, case managers, mental health service providers, counselors, and clerical support staff) to whom management has delegated a great deal of decision-making responsibility regarding individual inmates and the operation of their particular housing unit. Unit management is extensively used by the Federal Bureau of Prisons and has been adopted by a number of state DOCs. Wright (1991) has emphasized that encouraging staff participation increases employee trust and organizational effectiveness, helps to train future leaders, and reduces staff turnover. However, correctional leaders who are fearful that sharing decision-making authority will diminish their importance will resist the unit management concept.

Advantages of Participative Leadership

The participative leadership style, with its emphasis on employee involvement and communication, encourages a proactive employee approach. Staff feel free to communicate problems they see developing without fear of criticism, offer solutions, and work with leaders to keep a small problem from becoming a large problem. For example, under the authoritarian model, C.O.s hearing inmate complaints about the quality of the meals may be slow to forward those complaints up the chain of command. As a result, leaders may be caught off guard when the inmates launch a sitdown strike in the dining hall. However, under the participative model, C.O.s are likely to immediately advise leaders of an impending problem and actively suggest solutions.

When leaders respect their employees and allow them to participate in decision making, the organization is more likely to benefit from innovative ideas and methods (Rotemberg and Salener, 1993). Employees involved in the decision-making process experience an empowerment that gives meaning to their work and increases their sense of personal accomplishment. They are also more likely to readily accept a course of action that has been developed with their input, and professional development will be enhanced to a greater degree than merely following orders permits. The focus of leadership is on what the employee can become, not what they currently are.

There is, however, a broader, more encompassing way to define leadership styles, which is to identify them as either transactional or transformative. We consider these next.

Transactional Versus Transformational Leadership

James Burns (1978) identifies two types of leadership: the transactional and the transforming. Transactional leadership is bureaucratic in nature and involves the exchange of one thing for another: exemplary performance in return for a promotion, for example. The vast majority of correctional managers practice transactional leadership. They enforce policy, procedures, and rules, and guide and motivate employees in the direction of organizational goals by clarifying task and role requirements; but their relationship with subordinates is essentially pragmatic: "We've done a good job today because we kept the lid on."

Transforming leadership is much more complex. It attempts to actualize the potential of both follower and leader by creating an organizational climate that recognizes and develops the unique qualities of the employee, a process that may ultimately convert followers into leaders. These leaders provide individualized consideration, intellectual stimulation, and often possess charisma. They change employee awareness of old problems by encouraging them to look at old problems in new ways. It is the quality of transformation that most distinguishes leaders like James Bennett from managers.

Both transactional and transformational leadership are necessary elements of an effective organization (Seltzer and Bass, 1990). Transactional leadership provides the foundation for both organizational behavior and transformational leadership.

Transformational leadership produces levels of employee performance that go beyond what would occur with a transactional approach alone: it is associated with lower turnover rates, higher productivity, and higher levels of employee satisfaction (Bass and Avolio, 1990). Transformational leadership functions in the service of employee empowerment.

Having defined the various leadership styles, there is one more point of interest in any discussion of leadership. What are the strategies of leadership?

STRATEGIES OF LEADERSHIP

After interviewing 161 individuals in top leadership positions in six continents, Charles Farkas and Philippe DeBacker (1996) concluded that there are five distinct leadership strategies:

1. Strategic Approach: The leader is the organization's top strategist, systematically envisioning the future and providing the direction to get the organization there. This approach was successfully employed by James Bennett.

2. Human Assets Approach: The leader manages for success through people policies, programs, and principles. This leader will emphasize strategies designed to increase employee empowerment.

3. Expertise Approach: The leader possesses a particular expertise that can be used to focus the organization. A Commissioner who is an attorney may, for example, use legal knowledge as a means of directing organizational behavior.

4. Box Approach. The leader builds a set of rules, systems, procedures, and values that essentially control behavior and outcomes within well-defined boundaries. This is the approach favored by the transactional leader.

5. Change Approach: The leader acts as an agent of radical change, trans-

forming bureaucracies into organizations that embrace the new and different. James Bennett, as a transformational leader, successfully used this approach in creating the Federal Bureau of Prisons.

The most popular leadership style in private industry is the human assets approach, with 30 percent of corporate leaders "emphasizing teamwork, building leaders, and true empowerment" (Farkas and DeBacker, 1996:109). In corrections, however, the box approach is the preferred style of leadership.

Not all managers are leaders and not all leaders are managers. A technically competent manager may be a disastrous leader, unable to motivate staff to achieve more than the minimum necessary for continued employment. A revered leader may be so unskilled in basic management principles that a successful organization falls apart after the leader dies or retires. Both of these realities can be avoided by training managers to be leaders.

MAKING THE TRANSITION FROM CORRECTIONAL MANAGER TO LEADER

John DiIulio (1987; 1991) has noted that while leadership styles may differ, managers who are also effective leaders can be identified by six behavioral patterns. First, successful manager-leaders focus on outcomes by establishing the mission statement and allocating the resources necessary to achieve the mission. Essential to this focus on outcomes is the ability to engage in strategic planning. Second, prison security and custody are defined as the top priority for every employee: all employees are trained to think of themselves as C.O.s first. This is the "correctional worker" concept, and both Hambrick (1992) and DiIulio argue that this sharing of priorities will strengthen morale and focus attention on the mission. Third, there is the "management by walking around (MBWA)" principle: effective manager-leaders spend as much time in the prison as possible, engaging inmates and staff in conversation and personally observing organizational behavior. Community corrections managers make a point of visiting their field staff, observing their performance, and discussing issues of concern. Managers who fail to engage in MBWA, regardless of how busy they are, will be perceived by both employees and offenders as disinterested in what is happening in their lives. The manager viewed as nothing more than a figurehead will not be a leader. Fourth, they enter into strong relationships with powerful community individuals and groups. Effective manager-leaders understand the value, especially in a small community, of such activities as joining the Kiwanis, Lions, and Rotary; faithfully attending meetings; and volunteering for community service projects. Coaching in youth sports leagues can also provide a opportunity for positive community visibility. Fifth, successful manager-leaders do not often innovate, but when they do, the changes are far-reaching and made slowly so that staff and offenders can adjust to the new way of doing things. The rule that rapid change can invite disaster is religiously adhered to during the planning phase of any change. The final factor is longevity. Successful manager-leaders have a tenure of at least six years, enough time to really learn the dynamics of their organization and to make effective changes in organizational behavior.

These behavioral patterns are important for understanding the traits of the successful manager-leader, but they do not completely define the individual we are seeking.

Developing a Personal Philosophy of Leadership

The manager who wants to become a leader must adopt a personal philosophy that requires a policy of (1) coaching and developing employees' potential, not simply giving orders, (2) providing sufficient employee autonomy so they become self-managed to as great a degree as the organizational structure permits, (3) participating in and encouraging teamwork as much as possible, (4) encouraging decision making by those employees closest to a situation, (5) encouraging innovation and risk taking to meet the constant challenges facing the organization, (6) and treating employees as assets, not expenses, by investing organizational resources in their training and development (Robinson, 1989).

But there is more to making this transition from manager to leader than developing a personal philosophy. Klofas, Stojkovic, and Kalinich (1990:124–126) have defined leadership as an operational process that (1) effectively accomplishes organizational goals, (2) can be learned by managers who then apply specific concepts of leadership to real world situations, (3) employs groups that are influenced to accomplish the tasks essential to goal achievement, and (4) is political, that is, the external environment cannot be ignored. This definition suggests that a manager who wants to be a leader can be taught leadership skills.

Teaching Leadership Skills

Corrections is too complex a field for leadership to be a trial-and-error process. The fortunate leader-to-be will have a senior manager who takes the time to engage in mentoring. This process of guiding professional development and self-development can be intrinsically rewarding to both parties as well as pay dividends to the organization. However, while mentoring can be of great benefit, it must be complemented by formal training. Recognizing the differences between management and leadership, the NIC in 1998 offered correctional managers a variety of training programs: the NIC Executive Excellence Program; Correctional Leadership Development; Executive Leadership Training for Women; Executive Training for Deputy Directors; Executive Training for New Wardens; and Executive Orientation for New Probation CEOs (National Institute of Corrections, 1997:19–22). Clearly, the entire spectrum of correctional organizations is represented in NIC efforts to foster the development of leadership.

The depth of training provided can be gauged by a brief review of one of these programs: the NIC Executive Excellence Program. This program involves two weeks of intensive assessment and training that culminates in the development of a personal Executive Leadership Development Plan (ELDP). Essential to development of the ELDP is the identification of deficiencies during a pretraining individual assessment process that uses a variety of self-assessment inventories designed to measure competence in six core areas of ability needed by correctional leaders: interpersonal, leadership, decision making, communication, personal development, and professional knowledge. The program ends with a personal growth assessment that measures progress.

Training covers such topics as leading correctional change and innovation; strategic management; building organizational vision and conveying values; ethics of decision making; creating the correctional agenda for the future; executive communication skills; group dynamic and facilitation skills; organizational transformation; executive fitness; politics and policy development; conflict management; power and influence; managing diversity; public and media relations; effective correctional policy strategies; continuous quality improvement; budgeting, economics, and fiscal management; and the information age in corrections (National Institute of Corrections, 1997:19).

Each manager also develops a field assignment project based on their individual ELDP that is carried out after the two-week training program has been completed. This assignment often involves assisting the individual's organization in implementing a major change or program. Mentoring and technical assistance may be provided by the NIC while the field assignment is under way. In addition, participants become part of an alumni network and may be asked to serve as mentors and faculty for future lead-ership programs (National Institute of Corrections, 1997:19). This provides an opportunity for ongoing personal growth and contribution to the field.

The end result of periodic formal leadership training is the ability to provide the sort of leadership every correctional organization needs—a leader who will function in accordance with the following model of leadership.

AN EFFECTIVE CORRECTIONAL LEADERSHIP MODEL

Effective correctional leadership involves a set of practices that acknowledges both the internal and the external environment of corrections. Marie Mactavish (1997) has devised a Correctional Leadership Practices Model based on practices drawn from Kouzes and Posner's (1987) Leadership Practices Inventory. Mactavish's model provides a framework for defining positive leadership practices that encompass the internal environment, the internal–external environment, and the external environment. The discussion that follows is organized around these dimensions.

Leadership Practices Within the Internal Environment

In developing a team approach to accomplishing the organizational mission, the effective leader will model the way, encourage the heart, enable others to act, and resolve problems.

Modeling the Way   The leader will set high standards, clearly articulate personal values and beliefs, and have a strong commitment to hiring employees who will contribute to accomplishing the mission. Personal and professional behavior will be consistent with these values and beliefs and the leader will be visible to the employees. Leading by example is a powerful form of motivation because employees are sensitive to the behavior of their leaders. They carefully observe that behavior and leader behavior that is out of line with the vision being shared can hinder the process of achieving the mission.

Encouraging the Heart   A leader lets people know that they are appreciated and publicly and privately emphasizes that achieving the vision relies on a team approach. Employees must be recognized and it is the smart leader who stays in the background when the organization is being praised and officially recognized. When a correctional organization receives ACA accreditation, for example, the individuals who are publicly acknowledged and cited should be the employees, not the managers. In addition, when employees have reached a specific individual or department goal, or accomplished a challenging task, they should be publicly recognized for their efforts. A personal letter from the top manager, copied to the personnel file, and/or a public recognition ceremony can help keep employees involved in organizational life.

Enabling Others to Act   This refers to building trust; engaging subordinates in planning, problemsolving, and conflict resolution; and creating a strong team spirit that emphasizes the ability of individuals to make meaningful contributions. The successful leader will not micromanage. Qualified, trained employees do not need and will resent the manager who is constantly looking over their shoulder to make sure they know what they're doing. As previously noted, micromanagement will deflate employee morale and negatively affect performance.

Resolving Problems   The resolution of problems, especially employee conflicts, is often unpleasant, but the successful leader will not ignore problems. When a problem arises, it should be investigated, alternatives should be examined, and a solution implemented and evaluated. The most successful problem resolution is that which involves employee input and consensus building. This encourages employees to refine their own conflict resolution skills.

Leadership Practices That Span Internal and External Environments

Because the external environment has such a powerful impact on corrections, correctional leaders must acknowledge that impact through five practices: inspiring a shared vision, challenging the process, changing, influencing, and collaborating.

Inspiring a Shared Vision   The leader will create a vision of the "big picture" and nurture an environment in which employees share, and want to achieve, this vision. The creation of a safe, humane, and secure correctional environment is made possible by a leader who can articulate the processes that will shape that environment. In creating and sharing the vision, the leader will be enthusiastic and engender a sense of excitement that will increase the motivation of employees. MBWA provides an excellent opportunity to demonstrate this enthusiasm.

Challenging the Process   A rapidly changing external environment requires new methods and approaches and the ability to try the new when the old is no longer working. Leaders will encourage employees to experiment and make changes in resolving problems. This is one of the advantages of the unit management system. It allows a group of employees to make their own decisions and, by doing so, to learn what works and what doesn't.

Successful leaders will challenge the status quo. Those correctional leaders who introduced rehabilitation as an official goal of corrections were going against a long history of punitive control and disregard for inmate rights and needs. The early pioneers in community corrections were going against both an organizational and a societal status quo that viewed the use of incarceration as the best crime control policy. Such policy initiatives require personal courage and an understanding of the difficulty of introducing and managing change. Innovation is a hallmark of the successful leader.

Changing   This refers to the leader's ability to adapt—to provide a sense of purpose and direction to employees who are experiencing confusion and disorientation as change is introduced into the organization. Effective leaders are constantly challenging where their organization is going and how and when it is going to get there. And the effective leader is not afraid of receiving bad news. There is a tendency for employees to want to protect the leader from unpleasant news. This tendency may be rooted in a desire to not upset the boss, or it may be the result of a fear of a "kill the messenger" response when they deliver the bad news. Regardless of the reason, it is counterproductive to deprive leaders of information that may affect decisions currently being formulated. Leaders will surround themselves with people they can trust to give them bad news and return that trust by not responding negatively to the messenger (Bennis, 1990).

Influencing   This refers to the ability to persuade others to follow a course of action without relying on position power. It is the ability to influence employee behavior through effective communication and the use of reason.

Collaborating   This involves shared responsibility and consensus building in the effort to achieve common goals that cannot be achieved by the individual. Collaboration can be both informal and formal. Informal collaboration involves employees and leaders informally discussing a specific situation and possible courses of action. Formal collaboration frequently takes the form of an official mentoring process or creation and support of a unit management system.

Leadership Practices in the External Environment

As has been noted in previous chapters, corrections does not exist in a vacuum. Powerful organizations in the external environment have their own interests, goals, and agendas. Correctional leaders cannot control these organizations, but they should try to influence their behavior toward corrections.

The challenges the conservative revolution has presented to correctional organizations were presented in Chapters 4 and 5. The political perspective that Commissioners and directors can easily translate political rhetoric into correctional reality, and the danger of the Commissioner becoming a political liability, and thus politically expendable, if problems do occur in translating rhetoric into reality (Chase and Reveal, 1983), create a tendency for correctional leaders to be cautious rather than innovative. The willingness of the correctional leader to present the correctional view of issues and to effectively use the Legislative Liaison Office, as presented in Chapter 4, represents the best antidote to caution based on fear of political reprisal.

Interacting with the Media   Mactavish (1997:70) noted that "[t]he media's public reach is awesome. . . . Astute correctional leaders know that the media can make or break them." The effective correctional leader will follow the strategies for media interaction presented in Chapter 6.

SUMMARY

Management and leadership are critical elements in any discussion of organizational behavior. Management is the ability to accomplish the mission through the efforts of others while leadership is the ability to create a vision of the future and communicate it so effectively to subordinates that they willingly work to achieve that vision. The study of organizational behavior provides a working definition of management, and our understanding of leadership has progressed from the relatively simple trait approach through a variety of contingency theories that emphasize the importance of the interaction between leaders, followers, and situational factors to path-goal theory, which has sharpened our view of the responsibilities of a leader. An essential element of both effective management and leadership is the ability to effectively engage in two processes: decision making and planning. These organizational processes will be discussed in the next chapter.

Discussion Questions

1. Why was James V. Bennett an effective leader?
2. When is a manager also a leader?
3. Which situational factors would be most important in an evaluation of prison leadership? Or community corrections leadership? Or would there be any difference?
4. Which theory, or combination of theories, provides the most comprehensive view of leadership? Defend your answer.
5. Which style of leadership will be most effective in prison? In community corrections? Why?
6. What is the process by which a leader is created?

Critical Analysis Exercise: The Perception of Gender-Based Leadership Differences

Historically, research has overwhelmingly associated masculine characteristics with the ability to provide organizational leadership, but recent studies have found that both masculine and feminine characteristics are commonly possessed by organizational leaders (Kent and Moss, 1994). In fact, male and female managers, when surveyed, generally select the same set of skills needed to be successful. However, there still exists gender-based stereotyping by employees. The first stereotype is that female managers cannot control their emotions, tend to fall apart under pressure, respond impulsively, lack commitment to the organization, and do not understand the concept of being a team player. The second stereotype is that women have stronger communication and empathy skills: they show concern for others, listen more carefully, are responsive to meeting the needs of others, and are more likely to provide emotional support. In general, males express more stereotypes about women managers than women do about male managers (Baack, Carr-Ruffino, and Pelletier, 1993).

Critical Analysis Questions

1. Where is gender stereotyping more likely to occur—in institutional corrections or community corrections?
2. How great an obstacle is gender stereotyping to women who want to advance into top leadership positions in corrections?
3. What is the effect of gender stereotyping on organizational behavior and effectiveness?
4. What can female managers do to reduce gender stereotyping?
5. What can male managers do to reduce gender stereotyping?

10
Decision Making and Planning

Learning Objectives

After completing this chapter, you should be able to:

- Define the three elements of a decision.
- Contrast individual and group decision making.
- Summarize the advantages and disadvantages of individual and collective decision making.
- Define five approaches to overcoming groupthink.
- Contrast three models of decision making.
- Demonstrate the relationship between prediction models, base rates, and prediction errors.
- Explain the relationship between decision making and planning.
- Differentiate between short-term and strategic planning.
- Outline a strategy of planning for correctional emergencies.
- Summarize the planning and cost-containment functions of the budgeting process.
- Develop a budget for a correctional organization.

Key Terms and Concepts

Decision
Programmed Decision Making
Nonprogrammed Decision Making
Decisive Decision Makers
Hierarchical Decision Makers
Collective Decision Making
Groupshift
Brainstorming
Nominal Group Technique
Delphi Technique
Electronic Meetings
Stepladder Technique
Optimizing Model
Satisficing Model
Prediction
Statistical Methods
False Negatives
Predictive Validity
Short-term Planning
Budget Process
Emergency Planning
Mitigation
Individual Decision Making
Flexible Decision Makers
Integrative Decision Makers
Groupthink
Information Management
Bounded Rationality
Intuitive Model
Clinical Methods
Base Rates
False Positives
Planning
Strategic Planning
System Review
Emergency Life Cycle
Preparedness
Recovery
"All Levels" Approach
Capital Budget
Variance Report
Budgeting
Operating Budget
Revenue Budget
Audit
Response

At its best, strategic planning requires broad-scale information gathering, an exploration of alternatives, and an emphasis on the future implications of present decisions. It can facilitate communication and participation, accommodate divergent interests and values, and foster orderly decision making and successful implementation.

John M. Bryson

Profile: Strategic Planning in the Louisiana Department of Public Safety and Corrections

As of July 21, 1995, all Louisiana state prisons were under federal court supervision. Attorneys for the inmate plaintiffs had successfully argued that the Department of Public Safety and Corrections (DPSC) was unconstitutional in its management of four critical areas: prison overcrowding, violence, inmate programming, and medical services. In an effort to regain state control of its prisons, DPSC managers engaged in a process of strategic planning that produced a Master Plan designed to correct the specific deficiencies cited by the court.

Prison Overcrowding: An additional 3,007 state beds were to be created through new construction by the end of Fiscal Year 1997–1998. In addition, the DPSC would execute Cooperative Endeavor Agreements with local jails to obtain access to 800 beds, initiate a study of the feasibility of diverting juvenile status offenders to traditional community social service agencies, and expand the community corrections concept through the increased use of DOC and private contractor community facilities and evaluation of electronic monitoring program expansion potential.

Violence Management: The DPSC modified its classification process to assign violent, special needs, and high-risk offenders to state facilities and low-risk inmates to parish facilities. It also required all new juvenile facility correctional officers to receive 120 hours of intensive training prior to assignment.

Treatment Programming: The DPSC planned to implement a U.S. Army computer-based literacy program (Job Skills Education Program (JSEP)) in all juvenile institutions and five adult prisons. It collaborated with the LaSalle Parish Hospital District to construct and operate a 276-bed facility to provide substance abuse counseling, vocational training, and continuing education. DPSC managers also proposed development of a substance abuse treatment program for incarcerated juveniles.

Medical Services: The DPSC proposed construction of a geriatric and chronic convalescent facility in Caddo Parish designed to provide a centralized nursing facility for the chronically ill and the centralization of medical and psychiatric services at Elayn Hunt Correctional Center through construction of a $33 million Skilled Nursing/Mental Health/AIDS-HIV Unit housing 594 chronically ill offenders. In addition, medical staff developed a protocol for the annual testing of all staff and inmates for Multiple Drug-Resistant Tuberculosis (TB), a highly contagious disease not controlled by medication. The construction of negative air pressure rooms used to isolate and treat TB inmates at three adult institutions was undertaken (Source: Louisiana Department of Public Safety and Corrections, 1995).

The Profile provides an example of two critical management processes: decision making and planning. The ability of managers to make correct decisions is essential to the effective direction of every type of organizational behavior. Decision making is a fundamental process by which individuals or groups choose one alternative over all other recognized alternatives. If decision making is to be effective, the decision makers must have access to accurate information and possess the ability to effectively apply that information to the situation or event under examination. Relevant information is received from both internal and external sources. Planning is a process of coordinating decision making in service of the goal of improving decision making at every level of the organization. Planning can take two forms: short-term and strategic. The Profile provides an example of strategic planning generated by an unfavorable court decision. Each step in the development of a Master Plan involved a decision-making process in which multiple alternatives had to be evaluated and numerous decisions made. However, strategic planning concepts also apply to routine correctional operations. Planning, whether short-term or strategic, is a process of coordinating ongoing decision making to ensure that employee behavior is structured to achieve organizational goals and that appropriate resources are provided to support organizational activities.

DEFINING THE DECISION-MAKING PROCESS

Decisions are organizational responses to problems or opportunities that provide the means to achieve organizational goals. A decision can be defined in terms of three components: "a goal, the existence of alternatives, and information upon which the decision may be based" (Gottfredson and Gottfredson, 1986:213).

Goals in Decision Making

Any situation defined as a problem can also be defined as an opportunity. The effective manager is one who can view any given problem as a situation that provides an opportunity to correct deficiencies and improve organizational behavior. This positive perspective on decision making structures thinking so that a decision will represent both a response to a problem and a response to an opportunity. A problem exists when there is a difference between an organizational goal and organizational performance. Inherent in that difference is the opportunity to improve organizational performance. For example, the Louisiana DPSC in the Profile had a problem because prison overcrowding, high levels of inmate violence, and a lack of inmate programming and medical services conflicted with the goal to provide a safe, secure, and humane environment for offenders and employees. Judicial confirmation of these problems provided

DPSC managers with the opportunity to improve overall organizational performance.

The Decision as Goal-Oriented Behavior

All decisions are goal-oriented; that is to say, every decision represents the intent to achieve a certain goal. In addition, any given decision can have multiple goals. For example, in Louisiana, the challenge was to regain state control of the prisons and end judicial intervention. The mechanism by which state control was to be regained was the American Correctional Association (ACA) accreditation process. DPSC managers had three accreditation goals: (1) achieving a credential that identified the DPSC as stable, safe, and constitutional; (2) creating a better-trained, cohesive, and consistent workforce; and (3) encouraging employee pride and achievement (Louisiana Department of Public Safety and Corrections, 1995:9). These goals not only represented a response to a problem (judicial control), they acknowledged the opportunity to create a better organization.

Existence of Alternatives

Was ACA accreditation the only possible response? No, it was not. It is difficult to imagine any issue so narrowly defined that only one decision is possible. The effective decision maker realizes that there are always alternative courses of action, each of which has specific strengths and weaknesses. DPSC managers could have chosen alternatives other than ACA accreditation, such as passive resistance through implementing court-ordered changes as slowly as possible or filing a series of legal appeals. There are always multiple alternatives for decision makers to consider.

Information and Decision Making

An effective decision maker does not pull answers out of the air when confronted with a problem and opportunity. Rather, the decision maker attempts to gather relevant information on which to base a decision. The possession of comprehensive, accurate, current information in decision making is critical. How is the decision maker to obtain adequate amounts of relevant information? Some information may already be known because of the manager's previous personal experience with similar situations. But decision makers increasingly must rely upon information provided by information specialists in the technostructure and support units of the organization. The complexity of correctional decision making has generated the need to modify organizational structures through the creation of Management Information Service Bureaus (MISBs), which are data collection and research units charged with providing accurate information to decision makers: "Knowledge is power, and information provides that knowledge, yet the real skill in information management is to package information so that the client can make informed decisions" (Labecki, 1996:1). A considerable amount of MISB activity is directed toward providing and updating baseline statistical data such as inmate demographic information. A typical example of this type of data is seen in Table 10–1, which provides a detailed description of the adult inmate population in the Minnesota Department of Corrections (DOC).

TABLE 10–1   Minnesota DOC adult inmate profile.* Source: Minnesota Department of Corrections. *1994–1995 Biennial Report* (1995): 24.

Population:

Total	4644	
Males	4424	95.3%
Females	220	4.7%

Return Rate: (1992 supervised releases, intensive community supervision, paroles, discharges) N=1894

Follow-up Period	W/New Sent	W/O New Sent	Total
12 months	11.7%	15.6%	27.3%
24 months	18.5%	17.3%	35.9%

Commitments:	*1994*	*1995*	*Change*
January–June	1256	1246	–.8%
July–December	1098		
Total	2354		

Releases–Fiscal Year 1995:

Supervised Release/Parole	2156	82.2%
Intensive Community Supervision	180	6.9%
Discharge	286	10.9%
Total	2622	

Admissions–Fiscal Year 1995:

New Commitments	2217	75.8%
Release Return W/O New Sent	579	19.8%
Release Return W/New Sent	127	4.3%
Total	2923	

Average Sentence Length (sentenced in FY95, includes jail credit, excludes Lifers): 46.7 months. For comparison purposes, the average sentence length in FY85 was 38 months.

Offenses (top six): N=4615

Sex Offenses	1007	21.8%
Homicide	776	16.8%
Assault	614	13.3%
Burglary	522	11.3%
Drugs	513	11.1%
Robbery	466	10.1%

TABLE 10–1   *(Continued)*

Types of Offenses: N=4615

Person	2933	63.6%
Property	998	21.6%
Drug Offense	513	11.1%
Other/Not Reported	171	3.7%

Current Inmates Age 50 or Older: 254

Number of Lifers: 215 (258 including non-Minnesota)

Race:

White	2381	51.3%
Black	1609	34.6%
Indian	317	6.8%
Hispanic	250	5.4%
Other	87	1.9%

Educational Level:

Grades 0–8	272	5.9%
Grades 9–11	1513	32.6%
High school graduate	1210	26.1%
GED	783	16.9%
College and up	638	13.7%
Other/Unknown	228	4.9%

Average Age: 32.3

Marital Status:

Single	3026	65.2%
Married	790	17.0%
Divorced/Separated	648	14.0%
Other/Unknown	180	3.9%

Religion:

Catholic	717	15.4%
Lutheran	475	10.2%
Baptist	470	10.1%
Muslim	125	2.7%
American Indian religions	95	2.0%
Other Christian	609	13.1%
(Note: 43.5% unknown or no preference)		

Population by Institution:

Stillwater	1364	29.4%
St. Cloud	813	17.5%
Faribault	759	16.3%
Lino Lakes	724	15.6%
Oak Park Heights	401	8.6%
Willow River/Moose Lake	302	6.5%
Shakopee	216	4.7%
Red Wing	65	1.4%

Industry:

Inmates Employed	1067

Average Population–Fiscal Year 1995: 4492

Certified Juveniles:

Certified at Commitment	131
Current Inmates Under Age 18	22

*Data as of 7/1/95 (unless noted)

Baseline data plays a critical role in decision making. Managers who do not have a numbers base from which to operate are going to have difficulty making accurate decisions. Making a decision without baseline data is akin to trying to pick the jack of diamonds out of the deck when blindfolded. A lack of reliable baseline data can lead to erroneous conclusions, unresolved disputes, and the directing of staff activity to areas that do not require it. As we will see in Chapter 14, the management of change is heavily dependent upon an information processing system that can provide managers with the specific data they need when developing, implementing, and evaluating adaptive strategies.

The MISB is an essential management tool, regardless of the type of decision that has to be made. And there is more than one type of decision to be made.

Types of Decisions

Decisions can be classified as either case management or organizational. Both of these categories of decision making can be further classified as programmed or nonprogrammed.

Case-Management and Organizational Decisions

Case management decision making has a narrow scope—generally the individual offender—and focuses on such issues as security classification status, in-house and community programming needs, potential for program success, eligibility for prerelease programs, and parole eligibility. The prison classification unit staff, probation and parole officers, and community correction center employees are the ones primarily engaged in case-management decision making.

Organizational decision making involves correctional managers and has a much broader scope. It focuses on the development of the massive amount of policy, procedures, and rules necessary to formalize employee and offender behavior.

Programmed and Nonprogrammed Decisions

A programmed decision is more or less routine because it involves a well-structured situation in which decisions are frequently made, standard decision-making procedures have been established, and there is a minimum of uncertainty involved. A programmed decision rests on a foundation of written policies, procedures, rules, and past practices that function to standardize the final decision.

For example, a programmed case-management decision-making process exists in inmate classification systems. Classification Center managers typically develop written procedures that make it possible to process large volumes of people in a relatively short period of time. Examples of programmed organizational decisions are found in the functions of payroll processing, vendor payment, and the reordering of standard inventories of food, supplies, and equipment. Programmed decision making is ensured by the formalization process through which managers develop standard operating procedures in every type of organizational activity to achieve the goal of having every employee "on the same page."

Nonprogrammed decisions involve unstructured situations of a novel, nonrecurring nature in which information is often incomplete and there is a lack of accepted methods of resolution. A high level of subjective judgment and even intuition may be involved in this level of decision making. Over time, the process of formalization can convert nonprogrammed decision situations into programmed decision situations. For example, when correctional managers were first confronted in the 1970s with the need to build out of prison overcrowding, there was confusion and uncertainty about how to design and construct new prisons. In the 1990s, the construction of new prisons in many DOCs has become routine because managers have adopted the principles and practices of prototype prison construction.

In the 1980s, correctional managers were confronted with a new medical scourge:

AIDS. Initially, every decision that had to be made about an HIV-positive offender was nonprogrammed. Today, every correctional medical department has written protocols for the management of HIV-positive inmates from initial diagnosis to death, if that occurs while under correctional jurisdiction.

Although decision making can become routine, not every individual viewing a specific issue will make the same decision. Just as there are different types of decisions to be made, the process by which decisions are made can also differ.

Individual and Collective Decision Making

The decision-making process in a correctional organization can involve either an individual or a collection of individuals.

Individual Decision Making

Individual decision makers can be classified in terms of four basic styles: decisive, flexible, hierarchial, and integrative (Junsaker and Junsaker, 1981).

Decisive Decision Maker This type of decision maker will process a minimum amount of information to arrive at one firm conclusion. The emphasis is on speed, efficiency, and results. Long, detailed reports full of complicated analysis, graphs, and charts will be skimmed, ignored, or turned over to a subordinate for review and creation of an executive summary. The decisive decision maker likes to reduce complex problems to their simplest form. A typical response to the presentation of a complicated situation is "What's the bottom line?" Decisive decision makers are reluctant to take the time necessary for in-depth evaluations of complicated issues. A Commissioner facing a class action lawsuit regarding the conditions of confinement may greet the attorney's request for an in-depth discussion of the issues with the question: "What will a settlement cost us?"

The decisive decision maker frequently uses personal experience to rank the impor-

tance of individual bits of information as they are received instead of waiting for all the information to be collected. When what is assumed to be the most important information is received, a decision may be made before the less important information is even reviewed. This type of decision maker may jump the gun on a decision only to find that postdecision problems could have been avoided if additional information had been considered.

Flexible Decision Makers These decision makers prefer concise reports containing a wide variety of briefly stated alternatives to be considered through a process of consensus building that often requires extensive discussions with other individuals. The process of gaining acceptance of an evolving solution is fundamental to the actions of the flexible decision maker. The method of analysis is sequential: one alternative is offered, considered, then accepted or rejected before a second alternative is considered.

Hierarchial Decision Maker This decision maker will carefully analyze large amounts of material in a methodical search for the one best possible solution. Perfection, precision, and thoroughness are prized. The brief report favored by the decisive decision maker will be rejected as woefully inadequate. This is the type of manager who will rely extensively on the creation of a committee, or committees, to study every relevant issue prior to any formulation of a solution.

Integrative Decision Maker The integrative decision maker will use masses of information to generate a variety of alternatives that are considered simultaneously. This type of decision maker prefers to have each alternative subjected to a process of complex analysis; the final solution will be one which has undergone multiple reviews and modifications prior to formal approval. The integrative decision maker is extremely dependent on technostructure and support employees to provide the majority of the information necessary for an informed decision.

These categories represent decision making approaches that are determined by individual preference, but it is important to note that the effective decision maker is the manager who is inconsistent in approaching both problems and opportunities. By "inconsistent" we mean that there is a recognition that different situations require different approaches. Ineffective decision makers will always use the same approach, regardless of the situation. An adaptable style is more conducive to effective decision making than a single, permanent approach (Skinner and Sasser, 1981).

Collective Decision Making

Collective decision making involves a group of individuals whose attention is focused on the same situation. This category of decision making offers both advantages and disadvantages when compared to individual decision making (Maier, 1967; Hill, 1982; Schwartz and Levin, 1990).

Advantages of Collective Decision Making   The advantages of this type of decision making include (1) a more complete set of information and knowledge is available because a group of individuals are pooling their experience and training, (2) an increased diversity of views is represented and this increases the probability of more alternatives being considered, (3) the process creates ownership of the decision by the people who have participated in the decision making process, and (4) increased legitimacy is bestowed upon the final decision.

The primary strength of a collective decision-making process is found in the diversity of viewpoints and information that can be represented: the more diversity, the less the likelihood of overlooking a critical alternative or piece of information. In addition, employees often resent decisions made by one individual because they view this type of decision making as undemocratic, arbitrary, and capricious. Many employees believe that collective decision making confers legitimacy on the decision, with the greatest legitimacy belonging to those processes that include employee representatives. This legitimacy encourages employees to be more willing to accept and behave in accordance with the decision. Collective decision making encourages employee empowerment because it allows employees to feel that they are an important part of the organization.

Disadvantages of Collective Decision Making   There are several disadvantages associated with collective decision making: (1) it is a time-consuming process that may create inefficiency and limit management's ability to respond quickly to a situation, (2) social pressures to conform can squash disagreement and promote conformity, (3) domination of the group by one person or a few individuals may decrease effectiveness, and (4) responsibility is ambiguous. The first of these disadvantages is obvious. A discussion of the other three is included below in the discussion of groupthink and groupshift.

Measuring Decision-Making Effectiveness

Which is more effective: individual or collective decision making? Research indicates that, in general, decisions reached through the collective decision-making process are more effective (Michaelsen, Watson, and Black, 1989) than decisions reached by the average individual in the group but are seldom better than the performance of the best individual in the group (Miner, 1984). What does this mean? It means that decision-making effectiveness can be defined in terms of speed, creativity, acceptance of the final decision, and efficiency.

In terms of speed, individual decision making is superior, but groups tend to be more creative and the final decision more acceptable. Groups, however, are generally less efficient than individuals. Managers having to choose between an individual and a collective decision-making process must keep these factors in mind. In addition, the manager must consider two other characteristics of groups that can create an obstacle to effective decision making: groupthink and groupshift.

Groupthink

Groupthink is related to group norms. A group is a social situation and, therefore, exerts a pressure for conformity. Groupthink is characterized by a reduced tendency to consider other alternatives because of a perception (which may not be valid) that a group consensus has been reached; group members begin to apply direct pressure to any member expressing doubt, no matter how justified, about the alternative currently under discussion. Those members who do have doubts then keep silent because they don't want to expose themselves to group censure. Groupthink creates an illusion of unanimity (Janis, 1982) that the individual members of the group accept because it is more comfortable to go along than it is to oppose the group. To lessen the impact of groupthink, the leader of the group should not initially offer an opinion. The tendency toward groupthink is accelerated when the manager heading the group starts the discussion by saying, "I want a full discussion of this issue, but I think we'll all agree that my proposal is the answer."

It is not uncommon for individuals after this type of meeting to discuss the group's decision and suddenly realize that it is a poor decision that is not really supported by the entire group. However, even at the level of senior managers, there is a powerful tendency for groupthink to turn otherwise competent individuals into individuals who go along with the group.

Groupshift

This is a special case of groupthink that has to do with risk. Discussion leads group members to gradually shift to a more extreme position in the direction toward which they were originally leaning. Thus, conservative individuals become more cautious and aggressive individuals are suddenly willing to take on more risk. The most

common form of groupshift involves increased risk taking. Why does this happen? The most plausible explanation is the diffusion of responsibility inherent in collective decision making encourages some people to take risks they otherwise would not consider because they cannot be held personally responsible for a poor decision (Clark, 1971). In other words, there is safety in numbers, especially when the subject is controversial or involves a major shift in policy.

Overcoming Groupthink and Groupshift

Groupthink and groupshift can occur because the decision-making groups are face-to-face interacting groups in which powerful pressure toward conformity can be exerted. How do we structure collective decision making to reduce the possibility of groupthink and groupshift? There are five options available to the corrections manager: brainstorming; the nominal group technique; the Delphi technique; electronic meetings; and the stepladder technique.

Brainstorming Brainstorming requires six to 15 participants to be seated at a round or U-shaped table instead of at the traditional rectangular conference table. The participants are encouraged to be informal and blurt out ideas as they are conceived in a "free wheel" format designed to generate a large number of ideas and alternatives in a short period of time. Conlin (1989: 32) notes there are four rules of brainstorming which must be strictly enforced: (1) no one is permitted to criticize an idea; (2) the wilder the idea, the better; (3) the group's focus is on the quantity of ideas, not their quality; and (4) each participant should "piggyback," i.e., combine suggested ideas or build on other ideas whenever possible. Conlin (1989: 32) notes, "As a meeting progresses, people blurt out more and more ideas as neurons make new connections in everyone's mind. The more connections, the more likely a group will find an innovative solution." One of the participants will have the responsibility of recording each idea on a flipchart that will be referred to during the more restrained discussion and structured analysis following the brainstorming session.

Brainstorming participants are not chosen at random. They must be knowledgeable about the problem under discussion and prepared to blurt out whatever idea comes to mind, no matter how bizarre or seemingly ridiculous. Time must be limited so that the participants feel a sense of urgency. It is also sound policy to include representatives from various departments. For example, returning to the cell-content policy issue, a brainstorming session on this issue would appropriately involve C.O.s., commissioned officers, employee union representatives, counselors, the superintendent's administrative assistant, and the facility Fire Safety Officer.

The Nominal Group Technique (NGT)

This technique restricts discussion during the decision-making process (Willis, 1979). Although the participants are physically present in the same room, they operate independently of each other to develop an objective ranking of alternatives. The correctional manager using the nominal group technique will first have the staff involved with a specific situation break down into groups of six to nine people. After the problem has been presented, each participant will write down as many solutions as possible, usually taking from five to 15 minutes. Then each participant, including the manager, will read one idea from his or her list. The manager will write each idea on a flipchart. There is no evaluation of the ideas allowed. This process continues until every idea has been recorded. At this point, questions to clarify specific ideas are permitted, but there is still no evaluation. Next, the manager passes out notecards and each participant ranks the five top ideas, with 1 being the best. The groups are given a break while the manager totals the rankings for each group and divides by the number of

people in the meeting. The five ideas with the highest scores are posted on the flipchart. Then the group is reconvened and group discussion will eventually produce a consensus about which idea is best. This process of private balloting greatly reduces group pressures to conform, but NGT is a very time-consuming process that can address only one narrowly defined problem at a time and should be reserved for the most critical problems and issues.

The Delphi Technique This approach to countering groupthink and groupshift was developed by the Rand Corporation in the 1960s. Instead of sponsoring a meeting, the correctional manager sends a questionnaire to every individual who should be involved in the decision-making process. For example, a Chief of Probation Services might develop a questionnaire that asks:

1. What are the five most common technical violations?
2. What are the most important factors involved in each technical violation?
3. What resources are available to reduce each type of technical violation?
4. How can we most effectively use the available resources?

This questionnaire is sent to every probation officer and supervisor in the jurisdiction. Once the Chief receives the responses they are recorded on a master form which is circulated among the respondents. After these initial responses have been reviewed, the probation officers and supervisors are asked to complete the questionnaire again. This process, which may take four or five cycles, is continued until a consensus is reached. Obviously, this can be a time-consuming process, but as Thomas (1980) notes: "What Delphi is, is a really quiet, thoughtful conversation, in which everyone gets a chance to listen." In addition, the process can involve a geographically disperse group of individuals without incurring the costs associated with bringing them together at one location. However, the full range of ideas that can be generated during face-to-face interactions may not be developed.

Electronic Meetings　Poole, Holmes, and DeSanctis (1991) note the emergence of an approach that blends the nominal group technique with computer technology. Electronic meetings involve groups of up to 50 people seated at a U-shaped table that has a computer terminal in front of each chair. As issues are presented to the participants they type their responses onto the computer screen, and individual comments, as well as aggregate votes, are displayed on a projection screens. The result is anonymity, honesty, and speed. There is no social conversation and brutal honesty is encouraged by the anonymity of the process. Drawbacks include the disadvantage presented to individuals who cannot type and the lack of recognition for individual ideas. Although the cost of developing this approach may intimidate some correctional managers, it is an idea that is likely to catch on as correctional managers become more comfortable with computer technology.

The Stepladder Technique　This technique was introduced by Rogelberg, Barnes-Farrell, and Lowe (1992). The stepladder technique reduces the tendency for group members to be unwilling to speak up by adding new members to a group one at a time and requiring each to present his or her ideas independently to the group, which has already discussed the issue at hand. The process begins with a pair of individuals who meet to discuss a specific problem. Then a third individual is added after independently considering the problem. There ensues a three-person discussion, which is joined by a fourth individual who has also independently considered the problem. This process continues until a consensus is reached. This approach allows individuals to reach independent conclusions prior to joining the group discussion. The group benefits from a continuous infusion of new ideas and group members feel more positive about their group experience than they do about the traditional group meeting (Rogelberg, Barnes-Farrell, and Lowe, 1992).

In addition to improving the decision-making process by minimizing groupthink and groupshift, the approaches presented can also serve the goal of employee empowerment because of the value placed on individual opinions and suggestions.

So far, we have discussed decision making in general terms, but understanding this complex process requires a more focused examination of the structure of decision-making. To accomplish this, we next look at three models of decision making.

MODELS OF DECISION MAKING

The study of organizational behavior (OB) has resulted in the identification of several models of the process of decision making: the optimizing model, the satisficing model, and the intuitive model.

Optimizing Model

This model postulates six steps (Harrison, 1981:53–57, 81–93) designed to maximize the effectiveness of decision making:

Step One—Ascertain the Need for a Decision　A problem must be identified and the need for a decision recognized. For example, the requirement that community corrections facilities be physically located in the community presents a wide range of problems and opportunities to community corrections managers. The situation we will use in examining the optimizing model involves the issue of site selection for a new community corrections facility. The decision to be made can be presented in the form of a question: Where in this city is the best site for a new 100-bed residential pre-parole facility for adult female offenders?

Step Two—Identify the Decision Criteria　Criteria represent all the facts and considerations that the decision maker perceives to be important in making the decision. Although there may be numerous criteria that can apply in any given situation, only those that are considered relevant by the decision maker will be considered. Sechrest (1992:88–103) has reported that correctional managers who do not fully understand the built environment of the community when they initiate a site selection for new prisons or community-based facilities can pay a price in poor decisions that have long-term negative consequences. In the case of our example, the Community Regional Director does not have the budget to build a new facility but does have a renovation budget. Therefore, the task is to find an existing structure that either meets the needs of the organization or can be renovated to meet those needs. To accomplish this task, the director forms a committee that develops a set of criteria intended to cover both possibilities. At this stage of the decision-making process, the committee recommends that the new facility should have the following:

1. A low proximity to high crime areas or areas with a history of urban unrest
2. A physical structure that meets all community fire safety and sanitation codes
3. A physical structure no higher than three stories that currently has adequate space for 25 group living areas, seven staff offices, a director's office, a kitchen, ten bathrooms, a laundry, and two visiting/recreational areas or
4. The capability to be renovated to meet the above requirements at a cost that will not exceed $500,000
5. Proximity to a variety of employment opportunities
6. Proximity to educational and vocational training
7. Proximity to police services
8. Proximity to other state correctional agencies for emergency support and assistance, if needed
9. Proximity to a full-service hospital and emergency response medical services, including ambulance

10. Close proximity to fire protection services
11. Accessibility to public transportation and highway systems
12. Adequate public utilities
13. An available workforce
14. A supportive base of political and citizen support for the new facility (or a lack of resistance to the proposal)

There are numerous other criteria that could be considered, but our regional director accepts the committee's recommendation that the 14 criteria listed above are the most important.

Step Three—Allocate Weights to the Criteria The criteria listed above are not equally important. Those criteria considered to be the most important will be assigned a greater weight and have a greater influence on the decision. For our purposes, we will use a scale of 1 to 10 with 10 having the most importance. After due thought and consultation with other managers, committee members, and technical and support staff, the regional director determines the following set of rankings. Criterion 14 must have a ranking of 10 because the lack of public and political support will probably kill the project and all other criteria will become a moot point. Criteria 2, 3, 4, and 12 must be given a weight of 10 because the budget is fixed and the priority has to be the safety of the physical structure. Criteria 1, 7, 8, 9, and 10 have a ranking of 6; they are important, but the structure of the city is such that most areas will meet these criteria. Criteria 5 and 6 have a ranking of 4; most of the offenders eligible for community placement will have met their educational and training needs while incarcerated. Criterion 11 is ranked as 6 because the offenders are young and healthy enough to walk to work or school if public transportation is not available. Finally, criterion 13 is ranked as 1 because the new facility will provide lateral transfer opportunities for institutional staff.

Step Four—Develop the Alternatives

This involves listing all the alternatives that could possibly succeed in resolving the problem. No value ranking of alternatives is attempted at this point. Using a map of the city, and in consultation with Central Office and community agency representatives, the regional director determines that there are six available buildings that meet the criteria. The sites are an abandoned hotel at 1606 Wilson Avenue; an apartment complex at 1919 Jackson Street that has less than 10 percent occupancy; two large Victorian homes at 1865 Norman Street that could be renovated and joined; a hotel at 2318 Florida Avenue that has less than 25 percent occupancy; an abandoned hotel at 3425 Decatur Avenue; and a vacated Salvation Army shelter at 2425 Howard Boulevard.

Step Five—Evaluate the Alternatives

The decision maker must now critically examine each alternative, determining the strengths and weaknesses of each. Each alternative's strengths and weaknesses are then compared to the selected criteria to determine the best match or fit. A high-to-low value ("best fit") ranking of alternatives is developed. The "best fit" ranking will use a scale that awards the number of points to each criterion that are equivalent to its importance ranking. For example, Criterion 14 will have a value of 10 because it is ranked as having an importance of 10, but Criterion 13 will only have a value of 1 because its importance ranking is 1. Therefore, the best possible fit will be awarded a total of 95 points. Matching the alternatives to the ranked criteria, the correctional manager finds the following distribution of points:

ALTERNATIVE SITE	TOTAL POINTS
1606 Wilson Avenue	58
1919 Jackson Street	65
1865 Norman Street	61
2318 Florida Avenue	80
3425 Decatur Avenue	80
2425 Howard Boulevard	90

Step Six—Select the Best Alternative

The alternative that best meets ("fits") the most important criteria is the alternative with the highest problem-solving probability. In this case, the abandoned Salvation Army shelter turns out to meet the most important requirements.

Of course, the reality is that site selection may be a very difficult, controversial process in which site criteria change, or are given different values, as the site selection process moves forward. The emphasis, however, is always on a rational approach to decision making.

Rational Assumptions of the Optimizing Model

The optimizing model, often referred to as a model of rational decision making, assumes that (1) the decision maker can be fully objective and logical, (2) there is a single, well-defined goal to be achieved, (3) the decision maker can identify all relevant criteria and alternatives, (4) criteria can be assigned numerical values and be ranked by order of preference, (5) the decision criteria and alternatives, and the weights assigned to them, are stable over time, and (6) the final choice will provide the maximum benefits (Robbins, 1993:150).

However, as Gottfredson (1975) has noted, although decision makers may work to achieve rationality, such an accomplishment is probably impossible. Why is rationality probably impossible? Lindblom notes that it is "impossible to take everything important into consideration unless 'important' is so narrowly defined that analysis is in fact quite limited" (Lindblom, 1959:79–88). Recognizing this limitation leads us to the consideration in the next section of an alternative model.

Satisficing Model

The satisficing model (sometimes called the incremental model) is a model based on the concept of "bounded rationality," which is a term used to indicate that a manager's ability to make completely rational decisions is limited by such factors as an incomplete understanding of organizational goals, time pressures, inadequate information and resources, and problem complexity (Simon, 1976). Because neither the problem nor the alternative solutions are completely identified, managers cannot think in terms of the best or optimal solution. Rather, they must think in terms of a course of action that will "satisfice," that is, be satisfactory or "good enough." The result is a tendency to not look for optimal solutions and to settle for the first satisfying solution that comes along (Perrow, 1981:2).

In practice, therefore, decision makers typically identify a short list of the most obvious criteria and most apparent alternatives. In many situations, these alternatives are quite similar to the course of action currently being taken. Every potential solution does not receive a complete evaluation. The desired solution becomes not the optimum, but one that is "good enough." The satisficing model maintains the routine of the status quo. In the case of our female prepa-role center, for example, the Community Regional Director might decide to approach the site selection question by checking out the neighborhood where a community corrections facility already exists to see if there are any suitable locations near it. The practical result of this approach could well be selection of the abandoned Salvation Army shelter without ever considering the other five site alternatives.

Intuitive Model

The optimal and the satisficing models involve a conscious process of gathering information and a structured process of evaluating that information. The third model does not. Correctional staff commonly refer to their "gut level feeling" when discussing their rationale for a specific decision. Another term for gut level feeling is "intuition," an unconscious process based on accumulated experience in dealing with similar situations. Intuition can complement rational thinking and is most frequently used when eight conditions exist: (1) there is a high level of uncertainty, (2) there is little precedent for a

solution, (3) variables are less scientifically predictable, (4) facts are limited, (5) the facts that are available do not clearly lead to a decision, (6) data is missing or of little use, (7) there are several possible solutions, each presenting a good argument for acceptance, and (8) time is limited and there is pressure to reach the right decision (Agor, 1986). In the case of the female prerelease center example, the regional director might simply act on a gut level feeling that a Salvation Army shelter known to be vacant would be the ideal site.

There is a major drawback to intuitive decision making. It is a highly subjective process often influenced by personal prejudices or bias toward the subjects of the decision. Yet, many experienced correctional professionals will swear that their personal intuition, especially when it comes to predicting a particular inmate's behavior, is far superior to any prediction instrument. And that brings us to another issue. We have said that a decision represents a response to either a problem or an opportunity. But there is another way of discussing decisions, which is to see them as representing the manager's best prediction of future behavior.

THE DECISION AS PREDICTION

We choose one decision over another because of the element of prediction. Prediction involves the anticipation of the consequences a specific decision is most likely to have. A criterion that must always be considered when choosing among alternative courses of action is the decision maker's prediction of the consequences most likely to be associated with each alternative. Choosing alternative A over alternative B or C or D represents the decision maker's prediction that alternative A's consequences are most likely to successfully advance the mission.

Prediction in Case-Management Decision Making

Prediction is a concept that is most easily applied to case-management decisions. In case-management decision making, the employee(s) is asked to predict the most likely behavior of a specific offender in a specific situation—What is the likelihood that this inmate will escape from inside a walled institution or participate in a riot or take a staff member hostage or succeed in a specific treatment program? Under the actuarial model, case-management prediction involves assignment of an individual offender to a risk group based on a predicted answer to a specific risk-related question or set of questions. In the case of an inmate eligible for parole, the question is: Will this inmate complete parole before violating the law and/or the parole rules? The parole board can make one of two decisions: approve (alternative A) or deny (alternative B) the inmate's request for parole. The decision to deny parole will represent the prediction that the inmate has too high a probability of recidivism.

Because case-management decision making is such an integral part of correctional life, we now turn our attention to two case-management prediction models.

Case-Management Prediction Models

In case-management decision making, there are two types of prediction model: the clinical model and the statistical model (Klofas, Stojkovic, and Kalinich, 1990:239).

Clinical Model
The clinical model relies on the expertise of professionals trained to interpret individual data and predict future behavior. Clinical models involve assessments of individuals that focus on personality variables. Personality, educational, and vocational aptitude tests as well as structured interviews are used to develop an offender profile that can be used in the attempt to predict the behavior of the individual.

For example, DOC classification centers routinely require that all newly committed inmates undergo a classification process that includes a psychological evaluation based, in part, on such standardized test instruments as

the Minnesota Multiphasic Personality Inventory-2 (MMPI-2), the Milton Clinical Multiaxial Inventory-2 (MCMI-2), and the Wechsler Adult Intelligence Scale-Revised (WAIS-R). Reliance on the information gathered with these instruments must take into consideration the fact that mental health professionals disagree on the accuracy and reliability of test instruments in diagnosing behavior, let alone predicting it with certainty.

An argument can be made that relying solely on test data provides too narrow a base for decision making. While test scores can be useful in developing a general description of an individual's personality, and may be predictive of certain tendencies, they do not identify the actual behavior of that individual in life situations. That is, while a MMPI profile may lead a clinician to a conclusion that the subject of the evaluation is a psychopath, that diagnosis does not provide factual information about the specific negative behaviors that particular psychopath will commit. The generic diagnosis of psychopath tells the corrections professional that the inmate receiving that label is likely to be antisocial, antiauthority, impulsive, and prone to criminal behavior. Unfortunately, none of these terms identifies the specific negative behavior most likely to be associated with the individual diagnosed as psychopathic. Is this psychopath a drug addict? A sex offender? Unusually violent? A car thief? A serial killer? Will he or she present a higher than normal risk of escape or suicide or assault or parole violation or commission of new crimes? The diagnosis of psychopath says the answer to these questions may be yes. However, corrections professionals are not comfortable making critical decisions solely on the basis of test data that says the answer to your questions may be yes. Rather, correctional decision makers tend to base their decision making on a more concrete basis: the assumption that the best predictor of future behavior is past behavior. Therefore, they will prefer a prediction model that incorporates an individual's past behavior into the model. This recognition leads to our second model.

Statistical Model

Statistical models use mathematical formulas that incorporate individual information to produce probability estimates of behavior. Information on the offender whose behavior is being predicted is compared to information on a large sample of offenders with similar characteristics. For example, Greenwood (1982:50) reported that the best predictors of recidivism include (1) prior conviction for the same offense, (2) incarceration for more than 50 percent of the preceding two years, (3) a first conviction prior to age 16, (4) prior incarceration in a state juvenile facility, (5) drug use in the preceding two years, (6) juvenile drug use, and (7) employment of less than 50 percent of the preceding two years.

An example of a statistical model is the Level of Service Inventory-Revised (LSI-R) Risk/Needs Assessment instrument implemented by the Washington DOC for the purpose of assessing individual offender risk to the community as well as individual needs that require treatment intervention. The instrument uses 54 questions (rated as "Yes/No" or a "0 to 3" rating) organized in ten categories of risk factors found to closely correlate with criminality (criminal history, financial, accommodations, companions, emotional/personal, education/employment, family/marital, leisure/recreation, alcohol/drug problems, and attitudes/orientation). Question responses are used to identify high-risk offenders and the treatment interventions that can be implemented to reduce the risk. More specifically, the information generated by the LSI-R

- provides a convenient record of factors to consider prior to classification,
- identifies the high-risk offender and assists in the appropriate allocation of resources to those offenders,
- identifies treatment or targets programming needs for reduction of risk,
- assists in the decision-making process prior to placement into less secure facilities,
- assesses the likelihood of recidivism or maladaptive behaviors within a correctional setting,

- assists in predicting violation/infraction behaviors,
- is a quick and easy method of evaluating offender change as well as the Department's effectiveness in addressing factors of criminality (Washington Department of Corrections, 1998:4).

According to DOC managers, the LSI-R has been carefully researched for approximately 20 years, is used in 24 U.S. states, Canada, New Zealand, and the United Kingdom, and has been "validated and found to be uniquely predictive of offender outcomes" (Washington Department of Corrections, 1998:4).

Predictive Validity of the Two Models

Predictive validity refers to the accuracy of prediction. Empirical studies indicate that statistical models outperform clinical models. Gottfredson and Gottfredson (1986:247) state that "in virtually every decision-making situation for which the issue has been studied, it has been found that statistically developed predictive devices outperform human judgments." However, the predictive validity of current statistical models needs to be improved because they (1) are inaccurate in predictive ability, (2) explain very little of the variance in parole outcome, (3) use subjective variables, (4) fail to protect the public and provide equality to offenders, and (5) focus on recent events, not criminogenic causes (Gottfredson, 1979).

Unfortunately, in many instances of case-management decision making, flipping a coin may yield results that are just as accurate as the best instrument developed to date.

Prediction in Organizational Decision Making

In organizational decision making, there is often a discrepancy between the current situation and some desired situation that requires considering alternative courses of action. In the case of organizational decision making, the role of prediction is not as readily obvious as it is in case-management decision making, but nevertheless it exists. Managers must choose between a variety of possible policies, procedures, and rules in trying to decide which is the most likely to produce effective organizational behavior. For example, a managerial decision that employees should be publicly rewarded for positive job performance is based on the prediction that employees who feel appreciated will be motivated to work to achieve the mission (see Chapter 11). A manager's choice of a specific policy, procedure, or rule is based on the prediction of that choice as the one most likely to advance the mission. Successful prediction is based on accurate information.

In both case management and organizational decision making, managers have a limited ability to predict human behavior. This observation leads us to the issue of prediction errors.

PREDICTION ERRORS IN DECISION MAKING

A particularly serious consequence of flawed prediction models is prediction error. To understand prediction errors, we must briefly review the concept of base rates.

Establishing the Base Rate

The base rate for any given behavior can be defined as the proportion of individuals in a population who exhibit the behavior (Klofas, Stojkovic, and Kalinich, 1990:241). For example, how many inmates commit a crime while on parole? If 20 out of every 100 parolees commit new crimes (for a base rate of .20), then a manager predicting that no offender will commit a crime while on parole would be accurate 80 percent of the time and inaccurate 20 percent of the time. The problem is predicting which 20 of the 100 parolees will commit a crime?

For predictions to be useful, the model selected to predict the behavior of a specific individual must improve on the base rate. In our example of crimes committed while on parole, the model selected to predict parole success must have a failure rate of less than 20 percent if we are to conclude that the model is useful. Unfortunately, the base rate of many offender behaviors is relatively unknown and frequently much of the behavior we wish to predict is relatively rare (Klofas, Stojkovic, and Kalanich, 1990:242). Therefore, our ability to make accurate predictions of individual inmate behavior in any given situation is limited.

False Positives and False Negatives

These prediction errors are the most troubling due to their potential for causing enormous problems.

False Positive

A false positive involves predicting that a specific behavior will occur, but it does not. The long-term effects of a false positive can be extremely serious. For example, case-management decision making which inaccurately predicts parole failure for large numbers of incarcerated inmates can significantly decrease the number of inmates granted parole. The result can be increased overcrowding and the waste of scarce correctional resources. There is also an ethical issue involved. False positives can lead to a longer incarceration than is justified, thus harming the offender, the offender's family, and the taxpayer who must pay the costs of an unnecessary confinement. False positive rates for many inmate behaviors are extremely difficult to determine.

An example of a false positive in organizational decision making is the prediction that employee job performance will be improved by implementing a motivational policy that every mistake by an employee will result in swift and immediate punishment (see Theory X and Theory Y in Chapter 11); in actuality, rigidly applied punishment generates learned helplessness and resistance behaviors that decrease effective job performance.

False Negative

A false negative is a prediction that a specific behavior such as violence, escape, or recidivism will not occur. When correctional officials predict that a specific inmate will not engage in negative behavior, but the inmate does engage in that behavior, there can be serious consequences for public policy as affected by the media and the public's concern. A classic example of a false negative in case-management decision making is Robert "Mudman" Simon (Chapter 6), whose murder of a New Jersey state trooper led to public policy changes that had a dramatic impact on Pennsylvania DOC overcrowding.

An example of a potential false negative in organizational decision making is the assignment of youthful offenders to boot camps in accordance with a policy that predicts that the probability of future criminal behavior will be decreased by placement in an environment that teaches self-discipline and self-control. If the development of these usually positive characteristics somehow leads to a more disciplined but more successful criminal, as some critics fear, then the result could well be an increase in future criminal behavior.

The above discussion of decision making should provide some idea of the complexity of that process. But there is yet another issue to discuss. How do the hundreds of decisions made every day in a DOC come together to advance the organizational mission? The answer is found in yet another process: planning.

THE PLANNING FUNCTION

What is the role of planning in the decision-making process? Donnelly, Gibson, and Ivancevich (1971:57) noted that "the planning function includes all the managerial activities which lead to the definition of goals and the determination of appropriate means to achieve those goals." Certo (1985:79) defined planning as "the process of determining how the organization can get

where it wants to go." Or, we can say that the primary purpose of the planning function is to coordinate and improve decision making at every level of the organization.

The planning function consists of four elements: (1) establishing goals and fixing their priority, (2) forecasting future events that can affect the accomplishment of goals, (3) making plans operational through budgeting, and (4) stating and implementing policies that direct organizational behavior toward mission success (Donnelly, Gibson, and Ivancevich, 1971:57). Successful planning involves coordinating the decision-making processes required by these elements to achieve (1) a reduction in both organizational and personal risk by increasing the safety and well-being of staff, inmates, and the community, (2) a decreased risk that budgets will be reduced, (3) an increased probability of achieving organizational goals, and (4) a reduced likelihood that the careers of managers will be cut short by unforeseen events that should have been anticipated. Managers typically engage in two types of planning: short-term and strategic.

Short-Term Planning

Short-term planning is focused on maintaining the routine day-to-day security, programming, offender management, and physical plant functions of the organization. In general, short-term planning is a process defined by the fiscal year. For example, a superintendent anticipating the completed construction of 200 new beds during the upcoming fiscal year will need to plan for the increased demand the additional inmates will place on basic medical, food service, laundry, treatment, employment, and recreational resources.

In order for managers to successfully project their need for the next fiscal year's expenditures, they must be aware of the DOC's strategic planning process. Short-term planning will fail if managers are unaware of strategic planning issues.

Strategic Planning

Strategic planning can be defined as "a disciplined effort to produce fundamental decisions and actions that shape and guide what an organization . . . is, what it does, and why it does it" (Bryson, 1988:5). In corrections, strategic planning involves a focus on the achievement of long-term goals essential to the routine operation of the correctional organization. The Profile of the Louisiana DPSC's Master Plan represents an example of this type of planning.

Strategic planning differs from short-term planning because it creates a vision of what the organization should be in the future and details how that vision can be achieved. It employs "a set of concepts, procedures, and tools" (Bryson, 1988:12) with the goal of helping the organization to

1. Develop effective strategies
2. Clarify future direction
3. Establish priorities
4. Consider the future consequences of decisions being made today
5. Develop a coherent and defensible basis for decision making
6. Exercise maximum discretion in the areas under organizational control
7. Make decisions across levels and functions
8. Solve major organizational problems
9. Improve organizational performance
10. Deal effectively with rapidly changing circumstances
11. Build teamwork and expertise (Bryson, Van de Ven, and Roering, 1987).

Strategic planning is translated into action through a process of establishing sets of operative goals, matching staff activities to goals, and establishing a budget.

A Note of Caution Although strategic planning can be beneficial, Barry (1986) warns that a strategic planning approach is not appropriate when the organization is in a state of chaos because of severe financial difficulties, or a lack of leadership, or lacks the skills, resources, or commitment of key

decision makers so essential to producing a sound plan. Such an organization will likely find strategic planning to be an exercise in futility because the willingness, or ability, to do the hard work critical to successful strategic planning is absent.

Having made that statement, it should be noted that there is one type of strategic planning that must always be attempted, regardless of the circumstances. That is strategic planning for correctional emergencies.

Strategic Planning for Correctional Emergencies

A correctional emergency is any event that can disrupt orderly facility operation; cause deaths, injuries, and property damage; and jeopardize public safety (Figure 10–1). Correctional emergencies are organized into four categories: (1) inmate-precipitated emergencies such as riots or escapes, (2) facility fires and technological failures, (3) natural emergencies such as floods and hurricanes, and (4) human emergencies such as nuclear accidents and hazardous waste spills (Freeman, 1996c:18).

Process of Emergency Planning

Strategic planning for correctional emergencies (emergency planning) relies on a process of ongoing analysis and evaluation designed to (1) establish vulnerability to 25 potential emergency situations, (2) rank the probability of occurrence of each type of emergency, (3) develop inventories of internal and external emergency management resources, (4) train staff to respond appropriately to every stage of the emergency life cycle, (5) test the emergency plan, and (6) provide for review and analysis after each test and/or actual emergency (Freeman, 1996c).

According to the Federal Emergency Management Agency (FEMA) (1990:2), effective emergency planning consists of four phases of sequential staff activity organized around the emergency life cycle:

1. *Mitigation:* Mitigation activities either prevent the occurrence of an emergency,

FIGURE 10–1   Correctional emergencies can range from easily manageable building fires to full scale riots that compromise the integrity of the entire institution. Courtesy of the Office of Archives, Federal Bureau of Prisons.

reduce vulnerability, or minimize the adverse impact of the emergency. Prevention of a flood emergency can be achieved by not building a prison on a flood plain. A vulnerability to hurricanes can be reduced by building new prisons as far away from the coast as possible. Minimizing riot impact can be achieved by installing interior fences that prevent rioting inmates from taking over the entire prison.

2. *Preparedness:* Preparedness activities involve the pre-emergency activities that are used to support or enhance response to the emergency: vulnerability assessment, resource inventory, planning, training, and emergency plan testing.

3. *Response:* Response activities are designed to reduce injuries, casualties, physical plant damage, and risk of harm to the community during the emergency.

4. *Recovery:* Recovery involves the activities directed toward returning the facility to normal operation. Recovery may last for years and pose as great a challenge as the emergency, especially if basic life support systems have been destroyed.

Focus of Emergency Planning

Correctional managers have traditionally been most concerned with the inmate-precipitated emergency and the history of emergency plan development reflects the role of inmate riot behavior in changing organizational behavior. Only four DOCs reported having a written emergency plan in place prior to the 1971 Attica riot. Twenty-five years later, an additional 25 DOCs had developed written emergency plans, many of them clearly motivated by the Attica riot. The South Dakota DOC wrote their emergency plan in 1993 after one of their prisons experienced a riot. Modification of Pennsylvania DOC emergency plans occurred after the 1989 Camp Hill riots. Extensive review of Ohio DRC emergency plans was undertaken after the 1993 Southern Ohio Correctional Facility in Lucasville riot (Freeman, 1997a).

Correctional managers, however, cannot afford to ignore the potential for other types of emergencies. For example, on August 11, 1997, more than 4,000 inmates at the Texas Department of Criminal Justice's Liberty complex had to be evacuated because of liquefied petroleum gas spewing through a two-inch hole in a Chevron pipeline and drifting in a cloud of flammable gas toward the prison complex (Horswell, 1997).

Private Sector and DOC Emergency Planning

Although most DOCs rely on in-house staff for emergency plan development, some have turned to the expertise of the private sector, as illustrated by the example of Kansas in Box 10–1. One potential drawback to the Kansas DOC approach is that too extensive a reliance on the private sector may decrease correctional staff commitment to the strategic-planning process that has been outlined in this section.

BOX 10–1 THE KANSAS DOC APPROACH TO EMERGENCY PLANNING

All prison systems face the possibility of experiencing emergency situations. These emergencies may range from isolated incidents such as inmate-on-inmate assaults to group actions such as work stoppages and large-scale violent events. Any emergency situation has the potential to place the lives of correctional staff, inmates, and possibly the public at risk. The primary mission of the Kansas Department of Corrections is public safety. Thus, the Secretary of Corrections is committed to developing an emergency preparedness strategy that will provide the highest degree of readiness possible.

In August 1995, the National Institute of Corrections awarded the Department a short-term technical assistance grant to assist with an evaluation of the Department's emergency preparedness system. From September 17, 1995, through September 19, 1995, two National Institute of Corrections consultants conducted an on-site review of emergency procedures at four of the Department's major correctional facilities. In addition, the consultants provided a three-day management training seminar September 20–22, 1995. During the management seminar, areas for improvement in the Department's current emergency preparedness system were identified, including the need to provide emergency plan training to all employees of the Department.

In November 1995, the Department contracted with LETRA Inc. for the design and implementation of a comprehensive emergency preparedness system. LETRA Inc. has been working with prisons and jails on emergency preparedness for over 20 years. LETRA's emergency preparedness system has been implemented in an estimated 20 of the 50 state correctional systems. In addition to assisting the Department in revising the current emergency plans, LETRA will train up to 14 staff as emergency preparedness instructors. The training program is five weeks in length and will begin in February 1996. Following instructor training, the certified instructors will provide training in emergency preparedness to the more than 3,000 employees of the Department. This training should be completed by September 30, 1996. Following training, LETRA will assist the Department in developing a number of emergency simulations. These simulations will be designed to field test the Department's ability to respond to both minor and major emergency situations. Emergency drills using the newly developed simulations are scheduled to begin in October 1996.

Source: Kansas Department of Corrections. *Corrections Briefing Report* (1996): 3.15.

FISCAL PLANNING

A fundamental element in both short-term and strategic planning is the budget process. In fact, the budget represents a planning process that functions as the primary mechanism for exercising managerial control over the organization's resources. Some basic principles of the budget process were provided in Chapter 5. To briefly summarize, a budget is a financial plan that expresses the correctional managers' best estimate of the scope and cost of future operations. The budget is also a mechanism for monitoring and controlling organizational behavior.

The Budget Process

Budgeting is a systematic process, generally conducted on a yearly basis (July 1 to June 30 for state and county correctional organizations and October 1 to September 30 for the Federal Bureau of Prisons). Correctional organizations typically use a "bottom-up" approach to creating the budget. This is also known as the "all levels" approach (Bennett and Hess, 1992:188) and is a process that allows every level of management to provide input into creating the budget. First-level managers know the needs of the employees they supervise and can include items that might be overlooked by middle and top managers who are more focused on the "big picture." Laundry supervisors, for example, are more likely to realize that the laundry equipment needs replacing than is the superintendent. Their contribution to the budget request will be a description of the needed replacement equipment, the number of machines needed, and the estimated cost. Therefore, the most effective budget preparation process is the one that moves up, not down, the chain of command. For this process to be most effective, managers should ask for input from their employees.

In the case of the DOC, once every level of management has had its input, the superintendents, community corrections directors, and Central Office directors provide a written budget request and justification for all personnel, programmatic, security, inmate services, and physical plant maintenance and construction costs to the chief fiscal officer in Central Office. That person then reviews and combines the field requests into a comprehensive budget request that is submitted to the governor's office after approval by the Commissioner.

Once the budget has been approved through the legislative process, specific allocations are made by the Commissioner and the Central Office fiscal chief, and the money is spent in accordance with the original justifications. Successful achievement of operative goals without exceeding the budget is a key element in any evaluation of a manager's effectiveness.

Structuring the Budget Process

There are three critical elements in a successful budget process: establishing priorities, reviewing previous expenditures, and making realistic assumptions.

Establishing the Priorities   The official goals constituting the mission generate a complex set of operative goals, each of which must be prioritized and a determination made of the resources necessary for its accomplishment. Therefore, each goal will have a cost factor associated with it. A budget, in its simplest form, can be thought of as a list of prioritized goals and associated costs. Each priority will have three associated costs: human resources, direct costs, and indirect costs (Streeter, 1983). Human resource costs include salaries; Social Secu-

rity matching contributions; retirement contributions; workers' compensation; maternity leave, health, life, and disability insurance; and vacation, sick, and personal days.

Direct costs cover line items that can be specifically associated with a service. For example, the direct costs associated with the supervision of parolees or probationers would include vehicles (including gasoline, oil, recommended routine maintenance); security equipment such as handcuffs, radios, firearms, body armor; computers; electronic monitoring devices; phones; office supplies; anticipated overtime; travel and training expenses; and building/office maintenance supplies.

Indirect costs cover the expenses associated with the technostructure and support staff. These include, for example, costs associated with communications, data processing and analysis, information management, recordkeeping, general supplies, and training services.

Review of Previous Expenditures   The actual cost of the achievement of past goals provides a realistic basis for projecting the cost of future goals. The cost for specific departments and specific functions will be known. The information contained in the illustrative Figures in the remainder of this section provide a variety of information that is useful in this review process.

Making Realistic Assumptions   Every year new challenges arise, new programs are developed, and old programs are modified or eliminated. Correctional management is not a static process. Therefore, budgeting is not a static process. Managers must look into the future to determine if there will be significant changes affecting the budget and to discern the nature of these changes. This is a benefit of strategic planning. It provides a formal structure for anticipating change. Many assumptions will be based on information provided by the Management Information Service Bureau (MISB), which we briefly considered earlier in this chapter. For example, Figure 10–2 shows the inmate population growth trend in the Arizona DOC for the period of 1972–2002. If this projection is correct, then DOC managers know that all inmate-related expenditures will have to increase at a specific rate that can be converted into dollars. This is a reasonable assumption that, if ignored, will produce an inadequate budget.

Defining the Total Budget

The total budget for a correctional organization can be broken down into three main components: the operating budget, the capital budget, and the revenue budget.

Operating Budget   The operating budget provides an estimate of the actual cost of operations for each department in the organization and for the entire organization. For example, Figure 10–3 provides an overview of the 1998 allocation for juvenile Intensive Supervision Probation (ISP) and aftercare services in the Community Corrections Division of the Kansas DOC. Examination of this data provides the anticipated cost of each of the 29 units that comprise the Community Services division as well as the total cost of that division.

Capital Budget   This budget category reflects the potential expenditures for major fixed and movable equipment. Fixed equipment includes buildings and related expenditures such as new roofs, asbestos removal, electronic perimeter surveillance systems, modular housing, and any other high-cost component of the physical plant. Moveable equipment includes such items as computers, copy machines, x-ray equipment, vehicles, and other major equipment items that are expected to last longer than one year. Generally, the definition of capital assets is regulated by a state revenue office or the Auditor General because the issue of what is a capital asset and what is not can be open to debate. The most common method of determining a capital asset involves the creation of a financial criterion. For example, a piece of equipment that costs $500 or more will be a capital asset and any equipment under $500 will be included in the operating budget. Table 10–2 provides an example of the proposed capital expansion budget for the North Carolina DOC. Clearly the North Carolina managers have evaluated their long-term capital expansion needs, developed a plan for the future, and tied the package together with appropriate requests in annual budget submissions.

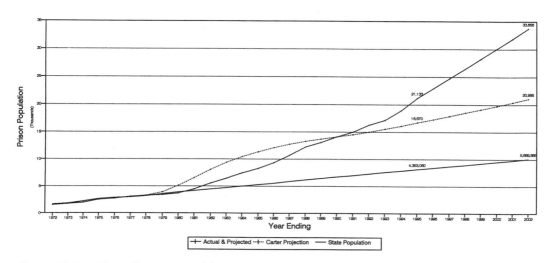

FIGURE 10–2   Arizona Department of Corrections: Prison Population Growth Trend, Fiscal Year 1972 to Fiscal Year 2002. Source: Arizona Department of Corrections. *1995 Annual Report* (1996): 10.

	AGENCY NAME	FY1997 JUV FUNDS	FY1997 FUNDED ADP	FY1997 9MO AVG ADP	FY1998 REC ADP	FY98 REC JUV FUNDS
1	AT	$28,336.00	8	10.9	13.92	$49,311.51
2	BLM	$95,634.00	27	28.1	29.84	$105,707.02
3	CEK	$88,550.00	25	35	35.81	$126,848.43
4	CB	$106,260.00	30	40.5	39.79	$140,942.70
5	CL	$70,840.00	20	21.8	21.89	$77,518.48
6	DG	$134,596.00	38	53.9	54.71	$193,796.21
7	JO	$230,230.00	65	88.7	89.53	$317,121.06
8	LV	$67,298.00	19	24.8	24.87	$88,089.18
9	MG	$53,130.00	15	26.8	28.84	$102,165.02
10	NWK	$88,550.00	25	26.2	30.84	$109,249.02
11	RN	$191,268.00	54	81.3	82.56	$292,419.23
12	RL	$116,886.00	33	42.5	41.78	$147,989.83
13	SFT	$88,550.00	25	18.3	19.90	$70,471.35
14	SG	$354,200.00	100	155.6	149.22	$528,535.11
15	SH	$134,596.00	38	49	48.75	$172,654.80
16	SCK	$46,046.00	13	16.1	15.92	$56,377.08
17	SEK	$70,840.00	20	28.3	27.85	$98,659.89
18	SU	$99,176.00	28	30.9	31.83	$112,754.16
19	WY	$247,940.00	70	93.9	89.53	$317,121.06
20	02D	$53,130.00	15	10.1	12.93	$45,806.38
21	04D	$70,840.00	20	20.7	20.90	$74,013.35
22	05D	$123,970.00	35	39.6	39.79	$140,942.70
23	08D	$159,390.00	45	52	51.73	$183,225.50
24	09D	$106,260.00	30	27.1	27.85	$98,659.89
25	1228D	$134,596.00	38	26.6	27.85	$98,659.89
26	13D	$113,344.00	32	31.6	32.83	$116,296.16
27	22D	$70,840.00	20	23	22.88	$81,042.05
28	24D	$28,336.00	8	3.5	6.97	$24,683.40
29	25D	$212,520.00	60	74.4	74.61	$264,267.55
TOTAL:		$3,386,152.00	956	1181.2	1195.74	$4,235,328.00
UNIT ALLOCATION:		$3,542			$3,542	

TOTAL STATEWIDE ALLOCATION:

JUVENILE ISP	$3,485,328.00
JUVENILE AFTERCARE	$750,000.00
	$4,235,328.00

Please note the following:
FY97 funding is for non-aftercare juvenile offender services only (i.e., FY97 aftercare funds are not included).
FY98 funding includes aftercare and non-aftercare juvenile offender services.
Although FY98 funding assumes funding for all of FY98, the contract between JJA and KDOC only addresses the first half of FY98.

FIGURE 10–3 Kansas Community Corrections Juvenile Offender Services Funding for Fiscal Year 1998. Source: Kansas Department of Corrections. *Budget; "Narrative Information"* (1997a).

TABLE 10-2 North Carolina DOC proposed capital expansion projects. Source: North Carolina Correction Enterprises. *Annual Report* (1995): 15–16.

Project Description	Inmate Positions	1996–97 Capital Costs	Comments
Fresh Produce Distribution DOC Caswell Co., Tyrrell Co., Caledonia	125–150	$7,452,580	Complete construction of Fresh Vegetable Warehouse at Caswell Co., and Caledonia will be finished with refrigeration and mechanical equipment necessary for fresh produce distribution. Construct new Fresh Produce warehouse at Tyrrell Co. Work Farm.
License Tag Plant Replacement Facility	60	$4,150,000	Construct new License Tag Plant within secure perimeter of new Warren Correctional Institution.
Cannery Replacement Facility	75–100	$3,400,000	New Cannery required to accommodate projected inmate population of 32,000. Current facility designed to accommodate 10,000 inmates, built in 1959.
Laundry Consolidation Facility (Consolidate existing Broughton Hospital Laundry and Craggy Laundry)	125–150	$5,600,000	Construct new 50,000 SF Laundry facility at Marion Correctional Institution to replace Broughton Hospital Laundry and Craggy Laundry. Project includes new laundry equipment.
Custom Cabinet Shop	35–50	$4,671,840	Construct new Custom Cabinet Plant at Lumberton Correctional Institution. Correction Enterprises currently employs no inmates at LCI.
Box Carton Plant	30	$3,351,120	Construct Box Carton Plant at Hyde Correctional Center. DOC Enterprises to coordinate with Hyde Co. Economic Development for possible private sector industry.
Modular Workstation Plant	50–75	$2,782,800	Construct Modular Workstation Plant at Pasquotank Correctional Institution. PCI currently has no Correction Enterprises operations.
Reserve to Construct a 15,000 SF facility for Private Sector Program	100–125	$ 2,563,920	Construct a 15,000 SF building to accommodate private industry within a medium security institution.

TABLE 10-2 (Continued)

Project Description	Inmate Positions	1996–97 Capital Costs	Comments
Reupholstery Plant	30–50	$ 1,904,040	Construct Reupholstery Plant at the planned 624 bed Southern Piedmont Correctional Institution.
Western Area Print Plant	100–125	$ 3,000,000	Construct Print Plant at the planned 624 bed Southern Piedmont Correctional Institution.
Expand Janitorial Products Plant	20–35	NONE	Expand current operation to second shift at existing plant to determine if plant space expansion is necessary.
Metal Products Plant		NONE	Deferred-Two existing Metal Products Plants meet present and foreseeable future needs.
Greenhouse and Plot Farming Area		N/A	SEE PRIORITY # 1
Sewing/Tailoring Plant		NONE	Deferred-Existing Sewing/Tailoring Plants in addition to new Columbus Sewing Plant (currently in pre-construction design development) can meet present and foreseeable future needs.
Mattress, Athletic Equipment, Reupholstery Plant		NONE	Deferred-Mattress production is to be consolidated into annex of existing operation at Moore Co. Athletic Equipment dropped at this time due to low market demand. Reupholstery addressed separately in this document.
Data Entry, CADD, Microfilm Operation		NONE	Deferred-At this time, market analysis does not support the construction of this facility.
Furniture Refurbishing Plant		N/A	Deferred-Most furniture is now particle board with veneer finish and cannot be refurbished.
TOTALS	810–1,010	$38,876,000	

Revenue Budget As fiscal conservatism requires correctional organizations to find sources of revenue other than the taxpayer, there is an increasing reliance on the use of a revenue budget that documents the receipt of funding from other sources, such as the offenders. Box 10–2 illustrates the budget summary of the Florida DOC and provides an example of the operating, capital, and revenue budgets for a very large system.

The function of the total budget is to translate organizational goals into numbers by quantifying the intentions of the top managers as they strive to accomplish the mission. For example, the Profile at the beginning of the chapter noted that the Louisiana DPSC Master Plan included an inten-

tion of adding 3,007 additional beds. This intention is quantified in a strategic planning budget (Figure 10–4) that provides a time frame for the creation of the additional beds between 1995 and 1998 and the projected cost of the new beds at each site. The development of this strategic planning financial document translates management's intentions into a plan of action.

The Budget as a Cost-Containment Mechanism

A budget is a useful cost-containment mechanism because it specifies the anticipated costs of specific operations. This specificity can pro-

---

BOX 10–2 FLORIDA DOC BUDGET SUMMARY

TOTAL APPROVED BUDGET: .... **$ 1,643,223,982**

OPERATING FUNDS

Expenditures by Budget Entity:

Department Administration	$	32,633,814
Custody and Care		1,156,316,857
Community Supervision		237,023,235
Education and Job Training		24,470,895
TOTAL OPERATING FUNDS	$	1,450,444,801

FIXED CAPITAL OUTLAY FUNDS

EXPENDITURES BY PROJECT CLASSIFICATION:

To Provide Additional Capacity Through Expansion and New Construction		56,678,633
To Maintain Existing Facilities and Meet Requirements of Regulatory Agencies		12,916,870
TOTAL FIXED CAPITAL OUTLAY FUNDS	$	69,595,503

LOCAL FUNDS

VOLUME OF COLLECTION ACTIVITIES:

Cost of Supervision Fees	$	22,489,760
Restitution and Court-Ordered Payments		41,771,895
Subsistence and Transportation Fees		7,747,200

INMATE BANKING ACTIVITIES:

Total Deposits	$	60,810,457
Total Disbursements		61,093,887
June 30, 1997 Total Assets		4,772,774

INMATE WELFARE FUND ACTIVITY:

Merchandise Sales	$	33,742,776
Gross Profit From Sales		9,429,177
Inmate Telephone Commissions		15,369,953
June 30, 1997 Retained Earnings		21,327,190

Source: Florida Department of Corrections. *1994–1995 Annual Report: The Guidebook to Corrections in Florida* (1995): 16.

PROJECTED NEW STATE BEDS ^
October 20, 1995

FY	New Beds	New/Location	Costs	Description
95/96	192	Avoyelles Correctional Center	$1,382,506.00	Increased density of dormitory population
95/96	192	Winn Correctional Center	$1,555,724.00	Increased density of dormitory population
95/96	192	Allen Correctional Center	$1,595,354.00	Increased density of dormitory population
95/96	224	Louisiana State Penitentiary	$ 997,066.00	Increased density of dormitory population and other minor adjustments
95/96	120	Dixon Correctional Institute	$ 233,160.00	Laundry conversion; beds will be used to absorb Unit 6 closure
95/96	200	La. Correctional Institute for Women	$2,760,000.00	New dormitory (construction)
95/96	80	W. Baton Rouge Work Release Facility		Cooperative Endeavor/CRC
Subtotals	1200	New Beds for FY 95/96	$8,523,810.00	
96/97	478	Caddo Detention Center	$7,349,497.00	Geriatric/Infirm and North La. ARDC
96/97*	132	Elayn Hunt Correctional Center	$1,572,620.00	Boot Camp Dormitory & Support (construction)
96/97	35	Rapides Work Release Facility		Amendment to Cooperative Endeavor
Subtotals	645	New beds for FY 96/97	$8,922,117.00	
97/98*	128	Elayn Hunt Correctional Center	$ 2,500,000.00	New Cellblock (construction)
97/98*	128	Dixon Correctional Center	$ 2,500,000.00	New Cellblock (construction)
97/98*	594	Elayn Hunt Correctional Center	$33,000,000.00	**Skilled Nursing/Mental Health Unit (construction)
97/98	104	Avoyelles Correctional Center	$ 2,700,000.00	New Cellblock (Construction)
97/98	104	Winn Correctional Center	$ 2,700,000.00	New Cellblock (Construction)
97/98	104	Allen Correctional Center	$ 2,700,000.00	New Cellblock (Construction)
Subtotals	1162	New beds for FY 97/98	$46,100,000.00	
	3007	**Grand Total New State Beds Projected thru FY 97/98**	**$63,545,927.00**	

Notes:

^ New state beds include state prisons, privately-operated prisons and community rehabilitation/work release centers under contract to the DPS&C.

* Projected fiscal year during which beds will become operational; contingent upon funding, construction, etc.

** If Federal funds are approved, the state will only be liable for approximately $8,250,000 of this cost.

Source: Budget Requests, Project Letters, etc./Office of the Secretary

FIGURE 10–4   Louisiana DPSC Projected New State Beds. Louisiana Department of Public Safety and Corrections. *Master Plan: October 1995* (1995):39.

vide a basis for evaluation of managerial performance because it provides a quantitative indicator of how well a manager is using the resources provided. In the case of Louisiana, the time frame and cost estimates in the Master Plan provide a method of evaluating progress toward accomplishment of the specific goal of creating additional beds.

Because the budget process is a process of assigning a financial cost to each category of organizational behavior, it can be a means of giving direction for productivity improvement by providing a basis for comparison and a mechanism for determining where expenditures are out of line. For example, Figure 10–5 presents the Fiscal

Summary of Average Inmate Costs (FY 1996-1997)					
Category	Average Population	Total Per Diem	Operations	Health Services	Education Service
Total All Department Facilities (Excluding Private)	61,664	$48.44	$38.67	$8.81	$0.96
Total Major Institutions (Excluding Private)	58,863	49.20	38.97	9.23	1.00
Adult Male	47,316	44.28	37.20	6.21	0.87
Youthful Offender	2,663	54.43	45.85	4.61	3.97
Reception Centers	5,747	72.74	44.99	27.49	0.26
Female Institutions	2,397	67.32	45.24	20.29	1.79
Specialty Institutions	740	103.73	60.31	41.35	2.07
Private Institutions (3)	2,167	46.33			
INDIVIDUAL MAJOR INSTITUTIONS					
Residential Facilities	Average Population	Total Per Diem	Operations	Health Services	Education Services
ADULT MALE					
Apalachee Correctional Institution (CI)	1,542	$47.77	$36.91	$8.90	$1.96
Avon Park CI	1,239	44.11	38.09	4.39	1.63
Baker CI	1,257	39.49	32.76	5.44	1.29
Calhoun CI	1,265	35.51	31.42	2.97	1.12
Century CI	1,501	36.09	31.89	3.70	0.50
Charlotte CI (1)	1,044	54.36	37.22	16.39	0.75
Columbia CI	1,251	41.24	33.18	7.28	0.78
Cross City CI	990	46.05	39.41	4.63	2.01
Dade CI (2)	981	69.38	55.82	12.32	1.24
DeSoto CI (2)	1,220	52.09	44.50	6.21	1.38
Everglades CI	1,242	37.92	32.39	5.34	0.19
Florida State Prison	1,393	52.74	44.60	7.95	0.19
Gainesville CI	617	41.77	37.79	3.64	0.34
Glades CI (1)	856	70.09	60.82	8.25	1.02
Gulf CI	1,451	40.87	35.53	5.08	0.26
Hamilton CI (2)	1,421	48.03	40.29	6.49	1.25
Hardee CI	1,346	39.92	35.57	3.69	0.66
Hendry CI	1,342	42.40	37.20	4.33	0.87
Hernando CI	426	42.67	37.77	4.38	0.52
Holmes CI	1,406	36.00	31.29	3.65	1.06
Jackson CI	1,306	36.81	32.48	3.72	0.61
Lake CI (2)	902	47.24	37.49	8.41	1.34
Lawtey CI	733	45.73	36.73	8.55	0.45
Liberty CI	1,450	34.72	29.82	4.26	0.64
Madison CI	1,321	36.38	30.72	4.95	0.71
Marion CI	1,273	44.03	37.19	5.25	1.59
Martin CI	1,339	52.93	44.72	7.44	0.77
Mayo CI (1)	916	45.72	40.22	5.02	0.48
New River CI	1,719	34.96	28.77	4.47	1.72
Okaloosa CI	970	40.26	35.07	4.75	0.44
Okeechobee CI (2)(3)	806	50.45	44.60	5.54	0.31
Polk CI	1,307	41.00	34.45	5.13	1.42
Putnam CI	416	52.09	45.74	6.01	0.34
Quincy CI	352	44.85	40.86	2.79	1.20
River Junction CI	478	46.23	39.32	6.30	0.61

INDIVIDUAL MAJOR INSTITUTIONS CONT'D. NEXT PAGE

FIGURE 10–5   Florida DOC Inmate Cost per Day by Facility. Source: Florida Department of Corrections. *1996–1997 Annual Report: The Guidebook to Corrections in Florida* (1997): 34–35.

INDIVIDUAL MAJOR INSTITUTIONS					
Residential Facilities	Average Population	Total Per Diem	Operations	Health Services	Education Services
ADULT MALE					
Santa Rosa CI (2)	334	$69.98	$63.37	$6.10	$0.51
Sumter CI	1,629	37.20	32.40	3.49	1.31
Taylor CI	1,003	39.13	33.13	5.79	0.21
Tomoka CI	1,325	44.75	36.10	8.37	0.28
Union CI	1,702	62.30	48.00	14.11	0.19
Walton CI	1,214	35.94	31.95	3.37	0.62
Washington CI	1,031	41.32	30.29	10.78	0.25
Total Adult Males	**47,316**	**44.28**	**37.20**	**6.21**	**0.87**
YOUTHFUL OFFENDER					
Brevard CI	1,179	45.01	38.97	3.32	2.72
Hillsborough CI	373	74.22	60.67	8.58	4.97
Indian River CI	279	69.36	59.64	2.76	6.96
Lancaster CI	832	53.88	44.32	5.28	4.28
Total Youthful Offenders	**2,663**	**54.43**	**45.85**	**4.61**	**3.97**
RECEPTION CENTERS (MALE)					
Central Florida Reception Center	1,880	68.64	45.46	22.90	0.28
North Florida Reception Center	2,069	78.23	41.80	36.17	0.26
South Florida Reception Center	1,798	70.72	48.19	22.30	0.23
Total Reception Centers	**5,747**	**72.74**	**44.99**	**27.49**	**0.26**
FEMALE INSTITUTIONS					
Broward CI (4)	526	102.74	63.81	36.90	2.03
Florida CI (1) & (4)	1,031	65.21	45.01	17.96	2.24
Jefferson CI	840	47.75	33.90	12.75	1.10
Total Female Institutions	**2,397**	**67.32**	**45.24**	**20.29**	**1.79**
SPECIALTY INSTITUTIONS					
Corrections Mental Health Institution	82	307.88	192.81	112.24	2.83
Zephyrhills CI	658	78.25	43.78	32.50	1.97
Total Specialty Institutions	**740**	**103.73**	**60.31**	**41.35**	**2.07**
TOTAL DEPARTMENT INSTITUTIONS (EXCLUDING PRIVATE)	**58,863**	**49.20**	**38.97**	**9.23**	**1.00**
PRIVATE INSTITUTIONS (1) & (6)					
Bay CI	708	45.04			
Gadsden CI	753	47.57			
Moore Haven CI	706	46.32			
Total Private Institutions	**2,167**	**46.33**			
COMMUNITY FACILITIES					
Community Correctional Centers	2,369	30.25	30.25	0.00	0.00
Contracted Facilities (5)	177	35.22	35.22	0.00	0.00
Probation & Restitution Centers	255	50.42	50.42	0.00	0.00
Total Community Facilities	**2,801**	**32.40**	**32.40**	**0.00**	**0.00**
TOTAL ALL DEPARTMENT FACILITIES (Excluding Private)	**61,664**	**$48.44**	**$38.67**	**$8.81**	**$0.96**

(1) These facilities reflect inflated per diems due in part to decreased population resulting from renovation or replacement of dorms.
(2) Due to opening and phase-in of these facilities during the fiscal year, average inmate population was relatively low, resulting in inflated per diem costs.
(3) These facilities exclude debt service costs which if included would increase the department's average adult male per diem by $0.25 and the private institution's per diem by an average of $5.77.
(4) Also serving as reception centers for female inmates.
(5) Amounts shown are net of daily inmate subsistence payments for inmates on work release, which contractors are allowed to retain as a credit to their billing.
(6) South Bay and Lake City CF are not included because they opened late in the Fiscal Year (Feb.) and inmate cost-per-day would be substantially inflated by the start-up. State-run institutions that opened late are also not listed.

FIGURE 10–5 (Continued)

Year 1996–1997 budget summary for each correctional unit in the Florida DOC and Figure 10–6 provides a breakdown of overall expenditures by service category. Combined, these types of data sets, compiled on a yearly basis, provide a useful means of making a gross comparison of expenditures over a specific period of time.

Control Through the Audit A much more detailed comparison of expenditures is achieved through the audit process. Budgets are subject to audit by accountants within the organization and those employed by an external auditing agency. The purpose of an auditing process is straightforward. It is a mechanism "to make those placed in

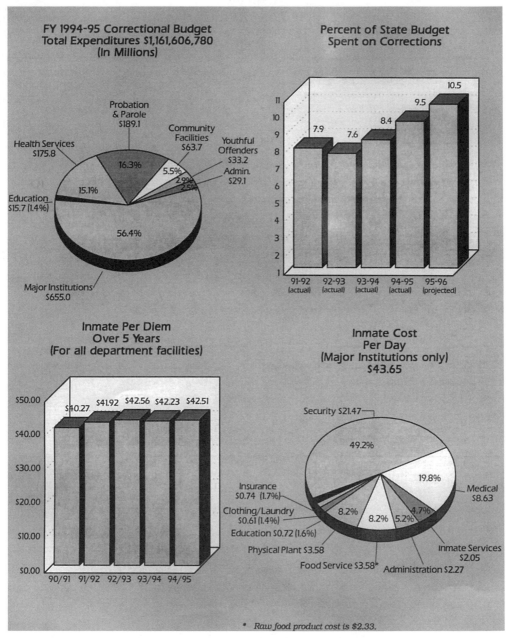

FIGURE 10–6   Florida DOC Overall Expenditures. Source: Florida Department of Corrections. *1994–1995 Annual Report: The Guidebook to Corrections in Florida* (1995): 19.

authority and given the responsibility over resources accountable to the people they serve. . . . Accounting provides the scorecard, and auditing is designed to ensure that the scorecard is correct" (Livingston, 1990:110).

Auditors can compare annual summaries (such as those presented in Figures 10–5 and 10–6) with both the projected cost of each facility and service category and the actual expenditures in previous years to determine if changes need to be made. Of course, such a process involves a much more detailed breakdown of expenditures and a consideration of such factors as inmate population growth and expansion of the number of personnel assigned to the organization. A comprehensive audit of even a small prison may take months, depending on whether irregularities are found. At the field level, budget analysts carefully scrutinize every expenditure to ensure that it is within budget parameters.

The audit process is not limited to financial issues. Correctional managers concerned about nonbudgetary issues such as creating correctional officer (C.O.) diversity, for example, can also use statistical reports for comparison purposes. For example, Figure 10–7 and Box 10–3 show the statistical breakdown of female and minority C.O.s in the Michigan DOC in 1995. Correctional managers in the year 2005 who need to see if diversity goals have been reached can compare a 2005 data set with the 1995 data set and draw appropriate conclusions about making any policy corrections.

THE BUDGET PROCESS AND ORGANIZATIONAL STRUCTURE

Because of the highly specialized nature of budget preparation and forecasting, every

	1993	1994	1995
White Males	57.7%	57.0%	56.8%
White Females	22.4%	22.5%	22.7%
Black Males	8.5%	8.4%	8.1%
Black Females	8.0%	8.2%	8.4%
Other Males	2.3%	2.8%	2.8%
Other Females	1.1%	1.1%	1.2%
TOTAL	100.0%	100.0%	100.0%
Individuals with a Disability	5.6%	5.7%	5.6%

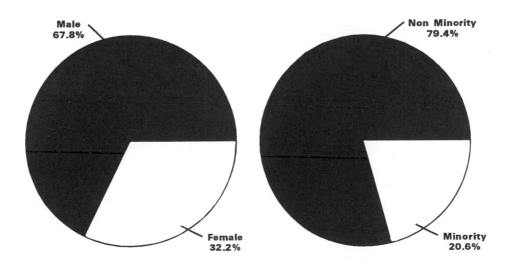

1995 Workforce: Gender **1995 Workforce: Race**

FIGURE 10–7 Michigan DOC Female and Minority C.O.s. Source: Michigan Department of Corrections. *1995 Statistical Report* (1996a).

BOX 10–3 NUMBER OF MICHIGAN DOC EMPLOYEES AS OF OCTOBER 21, 1995

Location	Total Employees	Total Minority Employees	Total Corrections Officers*	Total Female Corrections Officers	Total Minority Corrections Officers
Alger Maximum Correctional Facility	310	22	194	28	14
Baraga Maximum Correctional Facility	297	16	191	24	13
Earnest C. Brooks Correctional Facility[1]	553	170	294	88	113
Camp Program	984	89	523	76	58
Carson City Correctional Facility[2]	565	52	308	59	27
Central Office	455	103	0	0	0
CFA Central Region Office	136	18	0	0	0
Chippewa Correctional Facility[3]	634	62	333	41	45
G. Robert Cotton Correctional Facility	413	80	284	61	61
Florence Crane Women's Corr. Facility	202	12	109	36	6
Charles Egeler Correctional Facility	650	114	241	47	42
Field Operations & Administration	1,958	641	239	68	122
Richard A. Handlon MTU	322	48	162	24	22
Huron Valley Men's Correctional Facility	351	122	214	53	94
Gus Harrison Correctional Facility[4]	568	95	316	67	59
Ionia Maximum Correctional Facility	381	56	264	39	44
Ionia Temporary Correctional Facility	219	22	113	24	12
Kinross Correctional Facility[5]	550	68	334	41	48
Lakeland Correctional Facility	276	31	162	34	24
Macomb Correctional Facility	336	120	195	59	81
Marquette Branch Prison	426	19	235	18	13
Michigan Reformatory	438	49	231	34	39
Michigan State Industries	155	16	0	0	0
Mid-Michigan Temporary Corr. Facility	245	24	130	28	15
Mound Correctional Facility	354	185	231	76	119
Muskegon Correctional Facility	322	74	160	36	42
Newberry Correctional Facility**	210	24	144	22	21
Oaks Correctional Facility	321	16	205	33	14
Riverside Correctional Facility	487	54	273	41	39
Ryan Correctional Facility	356	241	237	93	182
Saginaw Correctional Facility	339	59	193	49	39
Robert Scott Correctional Facility	368	204	199	112	153
Standish Maximum Correctional Facility	308	17	191	36	11
SPSM - Central Complex	738	143	502	78	109
SPSM - South Complex	312	50	180	35	28
Thumb Correctional Facility	293	53	165	47	41
Western Wayne Correctional Facility	309	172	180	58	121
TOTAL	**16,141**	**3,341**	**7,932**	**1,665**	**1,871**

Source: Office of Personnel and Labor Relations (Administration and Programs).
* Includes Corrections Officers, Corrections Medical Aides, Resident Unit Officers and Work Camp Supervisors.
** Newberry Correctional Facility expected to begin operations in January 1996.
INCLUDES: [1]Muskegon Temporary Correctional Facility;   [2]Carson City Temporary Correctional Facility;
[3]Chippewa Temporary Correctional Facility;   [4]Adrian Temporary Correctional Facility;
[5]Hiawatha Temporary Correctional Facility.

Source: Michigan Department of Corrections. *1995 Statistical Report* (1996a): 180–182.

correctional organization has developed a fiscal department. For example, Figure 10–8 shows the Administrative Services Division of the Arizona Department of Corrections.

In Arizona, the Bureau of Management and Budget develops the DOC's operating budget requests, controls and monitors expenditures, conducts special management studies, and oversees position control (the number of employees needed to efficiently operate a specific department, facility, or program). The Bureau of Business and Finance is responsible for payroll, accounting, contracts administration, purchasing, equipment inventory, safety/loss control, and risk management functions. The Facilities Activation Bureau determines security and space needs for all new facilities, establishes criteria for all new construction, recommends preventative maintenance and repairs to DOC structures and systems, and compiles the historical cost and replacement values of the DOC's land and holdings. The Bureau of Management Information Services is responsible for data processing and computer systems development and maintenance. These departments provide the strategic apex with the current and historical information needed for effective planning through a process called "variance analysis."

Variance Report   Variance analysis involves a comparison of actual costs against what was budgeted and an analysis of any differences that have occurred. For example, if $500,000 was budgeted for drug treatment programming at a particular prison, but the actual amount expended was greater or smaller than this amount, correctional managers need to know the source of this variance if future fiscal planning is to be more accurate: "[T]he variance report provides data on budgeted and actual performance and shows the extent of each deviation where it has occurred. According to preestablished tolerance limits, the manager is expected to take appropriate corrective or postperformance action, or both" (Bittel, 1989:188).

Thomsett (1988:73) has suggested that the reporting of variances should not be viewed as a problem. Rather, it should be seen as an opportunity to provide guidance to management. The budget is a planning and monitoring tool and a variance is not a sign that mistakes have been made. Rather, they suggest that control needs to be exerted over income or expenses. A variance provides a clue to problems: weak or incomplete assumptions, excessive spending, or lack of control. The variance report provides a mechanism for recommending solutions.

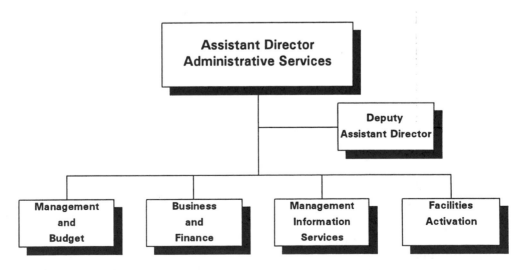

FIGURE 10–8   Arizona DOC Administrative Services Division. Source: Arizona Department of Corrections. *1995 Annual Report* (1996).

SUMMARY

Effective decision making is an essential function at every level of the correctional organization. Regardless of the model used, the goal of decision making is to advance the mission. The planning function coordinates decision making and provides staff with the information and direction they will need to accomplish the organizational mission. Unfortunately, planning is useless if organizational policy, procedures, and rules are not understood and accepted by the staff. Understanding and acceptance are the goals of communication and motivation, two processes that are examined in Chapter 11.

Discussion Questions

1. Why does the author say a decision is a response to both a problem and an opportunity?
2. What is the most effective approach to individual decision making in a correctional organization? Why?
3. How can a manager reduce the effect of groupthink and groupshift on the collective decision-making process?
4. How does planning coordinate decision making?
5. How can managers minimize the negative consequences of false positives and false negatives?
6. How would you incorporate emergency planning into the routine operations strategic planning activities of a prison?
7. How does the budgeting process assist managers?

Critical Analysis Exercise: An Engineering Marvel in the Texas Department of Criminal Justice

The Facilities Division of the Texas Department of Criminal Justice (TDCJ) is responsible for the concept, design, and contract administration of approved construction projects performed by both in-house construction and outside contractors. The division is involved in all stages of every construction project, beginning with the selection of an architect and the creation of the construction bid documents, the project bid and award of the contract, and management of the project until completion. A major accomplishment of Facilities staff in the early 1990s was the building of 75,000 prison beds in two years at a cost that was less than half that of the national average for prison construction. The division completed 94 different building projects ahead of schedule and under budget. Components of the construction program included 10 state prisons, 4 transfer units, 14 substance abuse treatment facilities, 18 state jails, 4 private prisons, 3 medical centers, and 1 intermediate sanction facility for parole violators. The Facilities Division also oversaw the addition of 13,876 beds at 29 existing units in an emergency building program that spanned only 16 months. So rapid was the construction that during 1995 nearly one prison unit a week was being completed and turned over to the TDCJ for occupancy.

In 1996, the Facilities Division was instructed to add 12,000 high-security beds over the next two years at a cost of $26,000 per cell, fully 20 percent less than 1994 prices. Planning for these additional beds included use of a simple building design, inmate laborers, building components provided by prison industries, closed-circuit TV monitoring, motion detection sensors, a wire perimeter, and self-contained cellblocks (Texas Department of Criminal Justice, 1996).

Critical Analysis Questions

1. Before planning for an expansion of this magnitude can begin, what decisions must be made?
2. From what sources should information for these decisions be obtained? How will it be organized?

3. Which categories of Central Office and field personnel would be involved in planning?

4. What are the most likely challenges to be encountered?

5. What alternative courses of action should be available to address these anticipated challenges?

11

Communication and Motivation: Shaping Employee Behavior

Learning Objectives

After completing this chapter, you should be able to:

- Define communication and outline the seven elements of a communication model.
- Contrast formal and informal networks of communication.
- List and define the eight barriers to effective communication.
- Explain the role of the correctional manager in promoting two-way communication.
- Apply needs theory to the development of a comprehensive set of employee empowerment strategies.

Key Terms and Concepts

Communication
Source
Message
Receiver
Communication
Model
Encoding
Channel
Feedback
Informal
Communication
Vertical
Communication
Barriers to
Communication
Motivation
ERG Theory
Theory X and
Theory Y
System Review
Quality Circles
Job Enrichment
Employee
Recognition
Ceremony
Decoding
Formal
Communication
Lateral
Communication
Communication
Networks
Rumors
Maslow's
Hierarchy
Motivation–
Hygiene
Employee
Empowerment
Total Quality
Management
Deliberative
Mentoring
Incident
Management
System

The process of communication is the dynamic transmission of meaning from one person to another. For it to be successful, the information must not only be imparted, but it must be understood. Accordingly, the speaker who is not heard or the writer who is not read, does not communicate. Only when one is understood has communication taken place.

Stephen P. Robbins

*There is no way an organization can hope to achieve and maintain com-
bined congruency in a dynamically complex milieu unless it is able to
motivate ordinary people to perform in extraordinary ways. . . . This will
not occur unless the organization manages its human assets and
resources with the same zeal, talent and persistence with which it
manages its other resources.*

Kenneth D. Mackenzie

Profile: The *Communicator*

The *Communicator* is the official newsletter of
the Ohio Department of Rehabilitation and
Correction (ODRC). The publication serves the
dual roles of increasing communication and
motivation. Typical of the publication is the
July 1996 issue that announced the winner of
the Ronald C. Marshall Award for the 1996
Correctional Officer (C.O.) of the Year at a
banquet attended by 350 people. Twenty-
seven other C.O.s were also recognized for
their outstanding performance. The July issue
contained a brief profile of each of the 28 C.O.s
and also reported on the Division of Parole
and Community Services Employee Recognition Awards Luncheon. In addition, the July
issue informed employees of the success of the
ODRC's use of the employee team approach to
problem solving, joint labor–management
training sessions designed to promote a
union–management partnership, the success
of the community corrections component of
ODRC, and the conviction of 47 inmates who
participated in the 1993 Easter riot at the
Southern Ohio Correctional Facility. An
article on the development of the Incident
Command System, a set of procedures
designed to reduce the loss of life and
property during emergency situations, and the
training of 9,000 employees in the approach,
was presented. The July issue concluded with
coverage of the annual Employee Recognition
and Memorial Service, which honored
employees killed in the line of duty (*Communicator,* 1996).

In 1997 The *Communicator* introduced the
Gold Star Award and highlighted the events of
the annual Gold Star ceremony in which
employees were recognized for saving lives,
apprehending criminals, planning multimillion dollar buildings, and working with

victims of crime. The Quality Services
Through Partnership (QSTP) program that
involves employees in a team approach to
problem solving was outlined. Seven teams—
Community Service Team, Morale Activity
Team, Pilot Dog Team, Mail Team, Visiting
Team, Recycling Team, and Security Team—
were cited for their contributions to the
ODRC. In addition, the ODRC's mentoring
program, new inmate mental health services,
the ODRC Internet web site, the work of a
Victim Impact Panel, and inmate involvement
in Black History Month were reviewed (*Communicator,* 1997).

The Profile presents an example of a management tool that recognizes that communication and motivation are two essential
elements of effective organizational behavior. Communication and motivation processes occur on both the formal and
informal levels of the organization. Formal
communication is a process in which managers send formal messages that define the
organization's mission, goals, policy, rules,
and procedures. Informal communication,
the "grapevine," is an employee-centered
process in which messages may support or
conflict with official messages. Motivation
is the process of persuading people that it is
in their best interests to accept and act in
accordance with formal messages. Individual motivation is influenced by the managers' use of specific employee empowerment
strategies. Individual motivation can also be
influenced by individual and peer group
factors. The effective correctional manager
uses communication and motivation processes to empower correctional employees.

COMMUNICATION: SENDING THE MESSAGE

The decision-making and planning elements of environmental design create an interlocking set of official messages meant to direct employee behavior in accordance with the organizational mission. But creation of these messages is not the end of environmental design. Before staff can act upon management's messages, they must receive them. The process through which individuals receive messages is communication.

Communication can be defined as "[t]he act of transmitting thoughts, feelings, opinions, and information to others" (Masters, 1994:214). Communication is an interactive process that can be formal or informal. The formal level is defined by the organization's chain of command. The informal level is most often defined in terms of the peer group structure: the personal relationships that exist among individuals. Communication can be intraorganizational (within the organization) or interorganizational (between organizations). No matter how well-defined the mission might be, it will not be achieved if managerial expectations are not transmitted to and understood by the individuals expected to achieve the mission.

A COMMUNICATION MODEL

Communication is an exchange relationship composed of seven components: (1) the communication source, (2) encoding, (3) the message, (4) the channel, (5) decoding, (6) the receiver, and (7) feedback (Berlo, 1960:30–32). The function of this relationship is to transfer meaning from one individual or group to another individual or group.

Source

The source begins the process of communication by encoding a thought. Any individual within or outside of the organization may be a source. The purpose of communication is to (1) be understood—to get something across to another individual so they know exactly what you mean, (2) to understand others—to know the intentions of others, (3) to gain acceptance for specific ideas, and (4) to produce action or change in an individual or group of individuals (Plunkett, 1983:78). Coursen (1980:11) has noted "there are no set formulas for communicating effectively, in fact good communication varies according to the needs of a situation, what works under one set of circumstances may be useless or even harmful under another." Thus, a source may engage in a variety of strategies intended to achieve the above goals.

Encoding

Communication is the exchange of symbols representing thoughts, feelings, opinions, and information (Farace, Monge, and Russell, 1977). A symbol is a representation of a thought, feeling, opinion, or piece of information that can be recognized by the receiver. The symbols transfer meaning from the source to the receiver and can be verbal (including written) or nonverbal. In verbal communication, symbols take the form of words, sentences, paragraphs, diagrams, charts, and pictures. In nonverbal communication, symbols are in the form of nonwritten, nonspoken physical attributes of the environment or person. For example, the prison perimeter tower with its armed, uniformed C.O. conveys a powerful message of coercive power. The facial expressions, hand gestures, body positioning, hair style, tone of voice, and personal use of clothing of all individuals may convey messages. Nonverbal communication is the foundation for human relationships: "Some anthropologists believe that more than two-thirds of any communication is transmitted on a nonverbal level (Okun, 1992:47–48).

Message

The message is the meaning that is transmitted through verbal and nonverbal communication. It is the actual physical product created by source encoding. It is presented through verbal or nonverbal communication. Effective messages are in clear standard

English that avoids jargon and language intended to impress rather than inform. Communication should be conversational, not formal or academic, and in tune with the principle of KISS—Keep It Short and Simple (Bennett and Hess, 1992:89). The more convoluted the message, the less likely that it will be understood. A simple rule of thumb is never use 20 words to express what can be said in ten. For example, a sentence such as "The express intent of this written policy is to officially establish the standards of behavior by which Probation Officers will conduct themselves during the authorized discharge of their officially designated duties so that issues of controversy, community sensitivity, legal liability, and professional misconduct will be held to a minimum" is cumbersome and boring. More effective is the sentence "The following policy establishes the Probation Officer Code of Ethics and Conduct."

Channel

This is the medium through which the message travels. The channel is selected by the source. Formal channels follow the chain of command and transmit messages related to the jobs of employees and the expectations of management. Policy directives, read-at-roll-call memos, meetings, news conferences, speeches, and newsletters represent formal communication methods. Formal communication is often in the form of one-on-one conversations and verbal channels are often preferred because they are fast, allow for immediate feedback, and are inexpensive.

Written Communications The drawback to verbal communications is that they are temporary; there is no permanent record of them unless they have been taped. This lack of permanence can interfere with accountability, especially if there is a dispute over the content of the communication. Therefore, in the interests of formalization, correctional managers rely extensively on written notes, memos, letters, reports, manuals, policies, procedures, rules, and official newsletters. However, these methods also have disadvantages: they are slower, often

more expensive, do not permit immediate feedback, and are impersonal. This last element deprives both sender and receiver of valuable nonverbal signals that might increase message understanding.

Informal Channels Informal channels, the "grapevine," are organized along social and informal group lines that exist inside and outside of the chain of command and are used to convey personal and social information.

Decoding

This involves the interpretation of the message, a process that is dependent on the ability to read and to listen effectively.

Listening Listening is the weakest link in the communication process (Montgomery, 1981:65) because most people have not been trained to listen. The receiver is often preoccupied with other matters or distracted by other individuals or background events and noise (this may be in the form of physical noise, such as occurs in a cellblock or on a busy street, or it may be in the form of too much information bombarding the receiver—an information overload). Because listening is such an important skill, formal training should provide employees and managers with the following guidelines for effective listening: (1) be interested in the message, (2) consciously resist all distractions, (3) look at the speaker, (4) do not let personal biases get in the way of the message, (5) try to understand both the words and the implied message, (6) work hard to understand difficult ideas or material, (7) don't hesitate to ask questions, and (8) be nonjudgmental (George, 1985:67). Effective listening is fundamental because faulty decoding can produce serious consequences, such as misinterpretation of expectations and orders or missing information crucial to making the right decision in a specific situation.

The issue of implied messages is critical. For example, an inmate who says, "Tomorrow would be a good day to call off sick, Officer Smith" may be attempting to communicate a message that a riot has been planned or another inmate is planning to physically assault the officer. A probationer who says "Sometimes I just get so sick of this rehab program I could scream" may be signaling a desire to terminate a mandatory program without permission.

Receiver

The receiver is the object to whom the message is directed, that is, the target audience. In the case of the *Communicator*, the target is three specific groups: the employees being honored, all ODRC employees, and the public. How each of these groups receives the message depends on their personal characteristics, such as age, gender, educational level, prior experience, and ability to listen effectively. The tone of the communication will also differ depending on the nature of the receiver. Messages to offenders and employees frequently take the form of providing information about specific behavior that is expected and behavior that is to be avoided—the normative rules and regulations for both groups. These messages are task-specific and often dry in tone. However, communications to the public are most effective if they are informative, friendly, use appropriate humor, and are designed to persuade and convince, not order or demand.

Feedback

Feedback represents a check on how successful the source has been in transmitting the message. Feedback establishes whether understanding has occurred. The response of the receiver, or lack of response, can inform the source if the message has been understood and accepted. This is why it is so important to ask questions. Questions indicate that the receiver is interested in the message and attempting to actively understand it.

Feedback Mechanisms The establishment of a formal inmate grievance system and the employee suggestion box system are attempts by managers to provide a formal feedback mechanism. Inmates who file Section 1983 litigation in federal court and employees who file union grievances are also using a formal feedback mechanism. Informal offender and employee feedback can be achieved through the casual conversations created by the Management by Walking Around (MBWA) approach. Inmate sitdown strikes or collective violence, such as riots, and employee use of the "blue flu"(employees calling in sick in mass) also represent informal feedback mechanisms.

Applying the Communication Model to Corrections

The communication model as it applies to corrections can be illustrated by examining a communication process designed to handle a situation all too familiar to correctional managers: selecting the site for a new correctional facility. Dorworth (1995) has described the communication process by which the Bureau of Prisons (BOP) secures community support for a new federal correctional facility. This process has eight specific steps, each of which is designed to encourage open communication.

Step 1 After initial selection of a potential community site, the site selection specialist obtains information from the community to determine (1) if the community has expressed an interest in having a correctional facility, (2) the general economic conditions in the community and whether the community is "pro-growth," and (3) if the community has ever attempted to secure a correctional facility.

Step 2 The site selection specialist contacts the director of the local economic development authority to seek sponsorship of the proposed facility.

Step 3 After an initial conversation with the director, the site selection specialist follows up with a letter expressing interest in the community and outlining all of the economic benefits associated with a correctional facility. Site-specific criteria are discussed and it is emphasized that the site should be free of wetlands and severe topography that might create an environmental constraint on construction and operation. At this point the site selection specialist begins to actively solicit feedback from elected officials, community leaders, and groups interested in community expansion projects.

Step 4   The site selection specialist visits the community and meets with community leaders and small groups that have expressed an interest in the proposed project. The goal is to create support for the concept of the project before there is any actual discussion about a specific site. The benefits (particularly jobs and economic stability) of having a BOP facility in the community are stressed and the site selection specialist encourages questions from citizens and the media. Questions are answered, citizens and media are invited to tour BOP facilities and talk to community leaders near those facilities, and the preliminary nature of the proposal is stressed. Media questions about local support are referred to community leaders.

Step 5   Once community support is achieved, the site selection search focuses on specific areas in the community that meet predetermined design criteria. Each site is evaluated in terms of potential socioeconomic and environmental effects.

Step 6   The site selection specialist holds a series of public meetings designed to inform the general public about the proposed project. The meeting is informal, includes a variety of BOP representatives, and provides a video presentation: "A Federal Correctional Institution in Your Community." The video addresses the most common community concerns and the meeting ends with a question-and-answer period.

Step 7   If sufficient community support exists, the BOP commissions an environmental consultant to develop a full-scale environmental impact statement on each potential site and conduct a public "scoping" hearing. The final impact statement will address all community concerns expressed by the community and involved regulatory agencies, such as the Environmental Protection Agency (EPA). Ultimately, one site will be selected and approved by the director of the BOP.

Step 8   Prior to activating the facility, the BOP hosts a job fair, a business seminar, and an open house for members of the community. Once the facility is operational, BOP members are appointed to a community relations board and community volunteers are recruited for involvement in facility educational and religious programs. This approach can be used whether the facility is a prison or a community corrections center.

Diagraming the Model

The BOP communication strategy for new facility siting can be presented as follows:

	Message		Message		Message
Source	→ Channel	→	Receiver	→	Feedback
	(Encoding)		(Decoding)		
(BOP)	Letters		Elected Officials		
	Conversations		Town Leaders		
	Meetings		Interest Groups		
	Video		Citizens		
	Q and A		Media		

The feedback from the receivers will tell the BOP how effectively they have presented the message that a correctional facility is an asset to a community, not a liability.

The communication model that has been presented describes the transmission of messages, but the process of communication is not fully explored until two communication fundamentals—direction and networks—are also examined.

COMMUNICATION FUNDAMENTALS: DIRECTION AND NETWORKS

The flow of communication is not haphazard or random. It is an integral part of the organizational structure and culture.

Direction of Communication

Communication flow has two dimensions: lateral and vertical. Both dimensions play an important role in structuring the formal and informal communication relationships that exist within the correctional organization.

Lateral Communication

This is communication that takes place among individuals within a specific work group and among individuals in work groups that are horizontally equivalent. It is communication between equals. C.O.s discussing a new overtime scheduling policy, superintendents engaging in policy discussions at the monthly Central Office superintendent's meeting, and probation officers discussing problems they are encountering with Intensive Supervision Probation (ISP) clients are all examples of communication among members of the same work group. An example of communication between members of work groups that are horizontally equivalent would be a discussion about special diets for diabetics between the Food Services Director and the Medical Department Director.

Vertical Communication

This is communication between individuals or groups that are located at different levels of the organizational structure. The vertical flow of information can be upward or downward.

Downward Vertical Communication

This type of communication flows from a higher level to a lower level. It is communication between nonequal individuals. When a superintendent tells the deputy superintendents to review visiting room policy and submit a recommendations report in two weeks, downward vertical communication is taking place. Other examples of downward communication include policy memos and statements of procedures and written rules, the issuing of a verbal reprimand by a supervisor, and a lieutenant personally commending the cellblock sergeant after conducting the weekly inspection.

Upward Vertical Communication   This type of communication flows from a lower level to a higher level. When superintendents initiate discussions of issues with the Commissioner, they are engaging in upward vertical communication. For inmates, any communication with staff is upward. For staff, upward communication may take the form of incident reports concerning inmate behavior, requests for leave, questions about policy, and union grievances. Upward communication alerts managers to specific offender and staff concerns.

Networks of Communication

The flow of communication is directed through networks. In this process, messages flow through formal and informal channels whose structure takes specific forms.

Formal Networks

Formal networks tend to be vertical, conform to the chain of command, and provide official work-related information. The organization chart is a written representation of the formal communication network.

Informal Networks

The informal network is the "grapevine" or "rumor mill." The grapevine is a powerful mechanism of lateral communication that has three important features: (1) it is not controlled by management, (2) many employees perceive it as more reliable and believable than information transmitted through the formal network, and (3) it serves personal, not organizational, interests (Newstrom, Monczka, and Reif, 1974:12–20). The informal network is a primary source of rumors (unofficial information that may or may not be accurate).

Nature of Rumors   Rumors serve four purposes (Hirschhorn, 1983:49–52): (1) they structure and reduce anxiety, (2) help make sense of limited or fragmented information, (3) signal the source's status or power, and (4) may serve as a vehicle to organize group members into coalitions. For example, C.O.s who read a newspaper article about the governor expressing a desire to explore prison privatization as an option may express high levels of anxiety. This anxiety may be reduced by a rumor that the governor is only talking about one prison, not the entire system, and that prison ("which is not our prison") has been targeted because its staff has allowed too many escapes. The C.O. who is the source of this rumor may be perceived as having inside information or being connected to powerful outsiders who know what the governor is thinking. Over time, this C.O. may be able to use that status as a means of organizing other C.O.s into a coalition dedicated to educating the public about the negatives associated with privatization.

Regardless of their purpose, rumors are a fact of life managers cannot avoid. Uncontrolled rumors that convey inaccurate information can upset organizational stability.

Managerial Response to Rumors Many managers shrug off rumors as just another thorn in their side and try to ignore them. Unfortunately, ignoring a rumor is frequently perceived as proof that the rumor is true. Managers must therefore develop a personal strategy of rumor control. This strategy can include (1) announcing timetables for making important decisions, (2) making written and verbal explanations of decisions and behaviors that are being questioned, (3) presenting the downside as well as the upside of current decisions and future plans (this provides a more objective perspective than the rumor), and (4) openly discussing worst-case scenarios to reduce anxiety and unspoken fantasies (Hirschhorn, 1983:54–56).

Although managers are frequently told about rumors, they must not become part of the rumor network because of the degree of credibility that will be given to any rumor they are responsible for disseminating. Rather, the manager should react to rumors by carefully listening and then providing as much factual information to counter the rumor as it is possible to provide.

Barriers to Effective Communication

While the above managerial approaches for responding to rumors can minimize their negative impact, there are other barriers to effective communication: (1) preconceived ideas, (2) denial of contrary information, (3) use of personalized meanings, (4) lack of motivation or interest, (5) noncredibility of the source, (6) lack of communication skills, (7) poor organizational climate, and (8) use of complex channels (DuBrin, 1978). These barriers can distort the message and produce unanticipated receiver responses.

Preconceived Ideas Preconceived ideas about the information being transmitted often leads to decoding that supports the preconceived idea, not the message. A rumor frequently is a preconceived idea verbally communicated from an informal source to a receiver. Preconceived ideas can easily result in selective perception, that is, we project onto the official message our personal characteristics, beliefs, attitudes, interests, expectations, and experiences. Selective perception may lead to stereotyping that creates misunderstandings, personal defensiveness, blaming each other for problems, and rule violations (Kagehiro and Werner, 1981). Where stereotyping exists, managerial messages are likely to be interpreted in terms of those stereotypes.

Denial of Contrary Information Messages that conflict with information already accepted as valid are often denied or rejected. This is a reason why rumors can be so damaging. If the rumor is received before the official memo, the memo may be discounted because the message contained in the rumor has already been accepted by the receiver. For example, probation managers attempting to implement electronic monitoring for house arrest probationers may find their probation officers (P.O.s) questioning the information they are given because of media speculation and in-house rumors that the new program will result in employee layoffs or involuntary transfers to other offices.

Use of Personalized Meanings The words chosen by the source may have a different meaning for the receiver, especially if they occupy different vertical levels. A superintendent who talks about the need to "meet recruiting goals for minority groups" may find line staff referring to "quotas" and "reverse discrimination in hiring." Inmates hearing a manager say, "We have a budget deficit this year so we can't install telephones on the yard," may interpret those words to mean that the staff are not interested in increasing the ability of inmates to call home. A manager who tells employees that "the budget is tight this year so we really have to trim the fat" may mean what? This type of statement is open to a broad range of interpretations, many of which can arouse unnecessary anxiety and feed the rumor mill.

Lack of Motivation or Interest Both the source and the receiver must be interested in the message. A lack of interest may occur because the receiver is simply not receptive—is upset, angry, tired, or preoccupied with more urgent matters. Or the written communication may be messy because of poor copy quality, illegible handwriting, faint print, and cross-throughs and write-overs. Or interest may be eroded by the behavior of the source or receiver, or both. Buchholz and Roth (1987:80–82) have suggested that there are six behavioral obstacles to effective communication: (1) flatly proclaiming that another individual is wrong, (2) practicing one-upmanship or flaunting authority to demonstrate personal superiority, (3) displaying an inability to recognize the possibility of making a mistake, (4) telling others how to do every facet of their job, (5) manipulating people to get them to act in a certain way, and (6) showing indifference to another individual's opinions and attitudes. Indifference can be displayed by such simple gestures as "frowning or raising eyebrows, shaking the head, yawning, sigh-ing, leaning back, avoiding eye contact, gazing around the room, taking irrelevant notes, or changing the subject" (Buchholz and Roth, 1987:82).

Noncredibility of the Source Credibility depends on status in the organization, the topic of discussion, and the reliability of past information. A superintendent will be expected to be a more credible source of information about the prison budget than a block officer because their different positions in the organizational structure determine the degree of access to budget information. An employee or manager with a reputation for "telling it like it is" will generally have higher credibility than an individual known for being evasive, spreading unfounded rumors, being malicious, or actually lying.

Lack of Communication Skills Individuals who lack active listening and feedback skills often have difficulty in receiving, collecting, recording, and disseminating information. Increased awareness of this obstacle is the reason why DOC training academies now include a variety of communication-relevant courses (such as "report writing" and "principles of effective communication") in their curriculum.

Poor Organizational Climate An insistence on formality and rigid adherence to the chain of command often discourages active communication between sources and receivers, creates polarization between organizational levels, and encourages the use of the informal network. For example, when the superintendent is not easily accessible, there is a tendency for staff to be eager to receive gossip about that superintendent.

Use of Complex Channels The more vertical levels any given communication must pass through, the more likely the message will pass slowly and be altered. Overreliance on the use of complex channels promotes the filtering of information, especially when the organizational climate is poor. In a machine bureaucracy, sources engaging in upward communication may tell the managers only what they believe the managers want to hear. For example, prison medical staff who believe a proposed policy of mandatory inmate HIV testing may be harmful, not beneficial, may be fearful of openly opposing the proposal because of the vertical distance between themselves and the Commissioner. They publicly endorse the idea while privately condemning it. The more vertical levels in an organization, the greater the likelihood of filtering.

Communication with the Community

The discussion about direction and networks can also apply to communication between the correctional organization and the various agencies in the community with which correctional personnel must communicate. The flow of communication is upwardly vertical when correctional managers are talking to elected officials and lateral when talking to groups like the media (lateral because there is no authority hierarchy present). The formal network consists of the Public Information Officer (PIO) and any correctional managers authorized to present the organization's viewpoint to the community. The informal network is composed of those employees who casually talk about their organization with neighbors, relatives, and friends. The informal network may also involve employees who "tip off" the media to embarrassing internal situations. The barriers to communication are also relevant in this discussion. For example, take the issue of noncredibility. The reluctance of some correctional managers to communicate with the media (expressed by one superintendent in the statement, "What the media is about is controversy, chaos, and confusion") because they do not trust the media to be factual encourages media distrust of corrections and the use of stereotyped images of correctional staff. Or the communication of rumors about prisons' decreasing property values and exposing

the public to an increased risk of assault may short-circuit the communication efforts of a site selection specialist.

THE CORRECTIONAL MANAGER AS A PROMOTER OF TWO-WAY COMMUNICATION

Whether it is intraorganizational or interorganizational, the most useful form of communication is two-way communication, which effective correctional organizations consciously attempt to promote. Effective managers learn how to provide, and encourage, an environment that promotes open communication at both the individual and the organizational level.

Individual Level

At the individual level, correctional managers must frequently engage in "leveling." That is, when they see an employee engaging in inappropriate or unproductive behavior, they must describe to that employee the specific behavior.

Effective Leveling Effective leveling can be accomplished by following six principles (Dreyfus, 1990; Jennings, 1993). First, describe the specific behavior of concern. The most accurate description is the one based on personal observation, but information received from another individual can also be used once the manager has asked sufficient questions to determine its validity. For example, a Probation Supervisor might be concerned about a probation officer who swears at clients and then slams down the phone when the client responds negatively to the verbal abuse, especially if this behavior has become a pattern. It is this specific behavior which will be the focus of the leveling. Second, explain the negative impact of the specific behavior on performance. For example, a probation officer who is verbally abusive is not going to gain client trust or invite the kind of conversations that can signal the need for an intervention. Thus, the probation officer will be doing harm to the client, and might even be endangering the public. Third, do not speculate about the employee's attitude. Speculating on attitude can lead to unproductive confrontation. Fourth, do not generalize or suggest causes of the poor performance or unacceptable behavior. Allow the employee to provide the explanations. Fifth, do not make judgmental statements. Employees who believe they are being judged often become so defensive that they do not receive the message. Sixth, speak in a calm, unemotional voice. Yelling, screaming, or even raising your voice will show a loss of control that can lead the employee to believe the criticism is a personal attack. The manager who loses emotional control is sending the wrong message. The leveling process must be driven by the goal to communicate in such a way that the employee understands, and accepts, the need to change a specific behavior.

The Language of Effective Leveling Buchholz and Roth (1987:82–85) suggested that there are certain phrases that managers can use to promote leveling. For example, "I see it like this" or "I hear you saying" is more effective than "You're wrong." The phrase "We're going to have to work this out because we need to come up with an answer" is more effective than "Let me tell you how to do your job." And "I understand how you feel" is certainly much more effective than "What you think doesn't matter." Positive words should be accompanied by positive behaviors: maintaining eye contact, keeping to the subject, smiling, nodding, and paying full attention to what the other person is saying. Leveling should include positive observations that will allow the employee to know that their strengths, not just their weaknesses, have been recognized.

In addition, leveling should always take place in privacy and the manager should do everything possible to ensure that the employee has had the opportunity to formulate a response.

Organizational Level

On the organizational level, effective communication is dependent on the willingness of managers to develop trust by showing that they care about employee perceptions and will consider those perceptions in decision making.

Effective Communication Behavior To create a sense of trust, managers must engage in six behaviors. First, they must openly communicate—information and feelings must be actively shared. The more employees recognize the commonalities they share with their managers (such as a concern for employee safety, fairness in decision making, and detection of offender misconduct), the more likely they are to see those managers as individuals instead of authority figures. MBWA is an excellent vehicle for sharing information and feelings. Second, managers should supply the background information about new policies or modifications of current policy so employees will understand the reasoning behind change. Third, managers must be honest with employees and talk to them as one adult to another. Employees strongly resent any approach perceived as patronizing. Fourth, managers should continuously solicit employee suggestions and ideas and follow through on any communication received from an employee. The manager who says, "I'll get back to you on that," but fails to do so will quickly sour manager–employee relations. Nobody likes to feel their question or opinion is not valued. Fifth, managers must avoid sarcastic remarks, even if they are intended as a joke. An employee should never be the target of a sarcastic remark because the power differential between manager and employee makes it very difficult for the employee to accept the manager's statement that the remark represents "kidding around because we have a great relationship." Finally, the effective manager removes roadblocks, irritants, and sources of frustration instead of creating them (Sandler, 1988; Jennings, 1993). One of the most effective methods of removing roadblocks is to develop clear and concise policies, procedures, and rules.

One final comment on manager–employee communication: Referring back to the admonition to never make jokes at an employee's expense, the damage that can be done by such behavior can be extensive. For example, on April 1, 1998, a Youth Center counselor on duty at a Pennsylvania county juvenile facility was interrogated by two city police officers who grilled him for 15 minutes about allegations of sexual harassment of a female employee (Decker, 1998). The interrogation was so authentic that the employee believed he was going to lose his job, be arrested, and lose custody of his two daughters. The ordeal finally ended when his supervisor entered the room and yelled, "April Fools'."

The result of this "harmless prank"? The employee collapsed and has since been diagnosed as suffering from post-traumatic stress disorder. He suffers flashbacks and has been unable to return to work since the incident. He is receiving workers' compensation and counseling. There is also a high likelihood of litigation against the facility and the county.

The successful transmission and understanding of a message is not enough, however, because effective behavior does not automatically follow accurate message decoding. In order for the message to be converted into the desired behavior, the receiver must accept the message. Acceptance of the message is the goal of motivation, which we consider next.

MOTIVATION: ACCEPTING THE MESSAGE

Motivation can be defined as an internal state that activates and gives direction to personal thoughts, feelings, and actions (Lahey, 1992:292). It is characterized by the desire to accomplish a goal with the expectation of receiving some personal benefit or reward. For example, an employee who desires promotion will work hard, assume progressive responsibility, and make known his or her willingness to do whatever is necessary to achieve the promotion. The employee who does not desire promotion may settle into a pattern of good performance, but no desire for more responsibility. For correctional managers, motivation involves developing a strategy designed to help employees accept official messages as a means of achieving their personal goals. Every manager must face a fundamental challenge: What can I do to meet the needs of my employees in such a way that they will be motivated to act in the best interests of the organization? The challenge for correctional managers is how to create and maintain motivation in a stressful work environment. We can understand the scope of that challenge by reviewing needs theory.

Overview of Needs Theory

As was noted in Chapter 1, the Human Relations movement (1920s–1940s) and the Contingency Approach (1950s–1960s) ushered in the development of psychological theories that influenced the environmental design philosophy of correctional managers. Of particular interest are the motivation theories of Abraham Maslow, Clayton Alderfer, Frederick Herzberg, and Douglas McGregor. We begin our discussion by briefly reviewing Maslow's concept of motivation as a function of a hierarchy of needs.

Maslow's Hierarchy of Needs

Abraham Maslow (1954) postulated a hierarchy of five needs within every individual. A need can be defined as the internal drive to accomplish a particular goal (Luthans, 1973:392). Maslow's five categories of need areas follows:

1. Physiological: Satisfaction of hunger, thirst, shelter, sex, and other bodily needs is necessary to ensure the physical survival of the individual. Physiological needs must be met before the other needs can be fulfilled.

2. Safety: People need to know that they are free from the threat of physical and emotional attack by aggressors, that they are in an environment in which they are safe and comfortable.

3. Social: These are belonging needs. People need to be able to show and receive affection, acceptance, and friendship. They need to belong to social groups.

4. Esteem: An individual's self-esteem is dependent upon internal factors such as self-respect, autonomy, and achievement and external factors such as status, recognition, and attention.

5. Self-Actualization: These needs center around the personal desire to achieve personal growth and self-fulfillment.

Maslow's needs hierarchy is typically conceptualized as a five-level pyramid with the first two steps composed of lower-order needs (physiological and safety) and the upper three levels composed of higher-order needs (social, esteem, and self-actualization, respectively). According to Malow, as each need is satisfied, it loses strength as a motivator, and the next level of need becomes dominant and assumes the role of motivator. The individual will strive to satisfy these needs by engaging in specific behavior, which may be quite different than the behavior required at a lower level. As higher-order needs become dominant, the individual moves up the hierarchy, one level at a time in a steplike progression that ultimately leads to the highest level: self-actualization. Thus, the ability to motivate any given individual depends on the ability to determine what level of the hierarchy that individual is currently on and focus on satisfying the needs specific to that level. Maslow proposed that lower-order needs are satisfied by the environment (through money, benefits, and job security) while higher-order needs are satisfied internally.

Managers influenced by Maslow's theory strive to meet their employees' lower-order needs so they will be motivated to seek satisfaction of their higher-order needs, a result that should work to the organization's benefit. While this hierarchy theory is intuitively attractive, research has found no support for the thesis that a satisfied lower-order need automatically activates movement to the next need level (Lawler and Suttle, 1972; Rauschenberger, Schmitt, and Hunter, 1980). When a theory is not validated by research, it becomes necessary to rework that theory.

ERG Theory

Clayton Alderfer (1969) recast Maslow's hierarchy into three groups of core needs:

1. Existence: This group of core needs is concerned with basic survival and includes Maslow's physiological and safety needs.

2. Relatedness: This group is concerned with the desire to maintain important interpersonal relations. It corresponds to the social need and the external esteem needs identified by Maslow.

3. Growth: These needs correspond to the self-esteem and self-actualization needs identified by Maslow.

What does this theory offer that Maslow's did not? First, the rigid, steplike progression proposed by Maslow does not reflect the way people actually behave. Alderfer proposed that more than one need may affect a person's behavior at any one time. In fact, all three need categories may be operating simultaneously. Alderfer also suggested that if the gratification of a higher-order need is not achieved, the desire to satisfy a lower-order need will increase. This second concept introduced a frustration-regression dimension into the discussion of motivation. That is, when a higher-order need is frustrated, the desire to satisfy a lower-order need may become increasingly more powerful. This refocus on a lower-order need constitutes regression. For example, the sergeant passed over for promotion to lieutenant (and denied the anticipated status, prestige, and external boost to self-esteem) might suddenly attend union-sponsored events never previously attended, and actively support the union in union–management conflicts.

Alderfer redefined motivation as a more complex process than that envisioned by Maslow. The implication for correctional managers is that effective motivation of employees requires the identification and satisfaction of multiple needs operating concurrently. The complexity of this task is increased by the fact that any discussion of motivation must take two types of job-related factors into consideration, which we examine next.

Motivation–Hygiene Theory

Frederick Herzberg approached the issue of motivation with the question: "What do people want from their jobs?" In other words, what is it about a job that makes an employee satisfied? What is it about a job that motivates an employee to not only keep the job but to be productive? He presented his answer by identifying two job-related factors: satisfiers and dissatisfiers (Herzberg, Mausner, and Snyderman, 1959).

1. Satisfiers (motivators): The factors associated with job satisfaction are those elements of the job that individuals find to be intrinsically rewarding. Individuals who feel good about their jobs cite such factors as achievement, recognition, the work itself, responsibility, advancement, and personal growth.

2. Dissatisfiers (hygiene factors): The factors associated with job dissatisfaction tend to be extrinsic—organizational policy, procedures, and rules; supervision; interpersonal relationships; salary and benefits; and working conditions.

Herzberg proposed that the opposite of dissatisfaction is not satisfaction, as is intuitively believed. Removing hygiene factors

from the work environment does not automatically make dissatisfied employees more satisfied. Rather, the opposite of dissatisfaction is no dissatisfaction and the opposite of satisfaction is no satisfaction. The practical implications of this somewhat esoteric statement are that the manager who works to increase salary, benefits, and general working conditions will find that subordinates are satisfied with their jobs, but they do not feel any urge to set higher personal performance standards. Herzberg argued that when hygiene factors are adequate, people will be content but not motivated to improve performance because the improvement of hygiene factors creates only a short-term increase in job satisfaction, not long-term motivation. This may explain why C.O. morale in many prisons remains low despite dramatic increases in salary and benefit packages. Herzberg argued that motivation could be created only through an organizational emphasis on motivators.

Assessing the Needs Preferences of Employees

In a 1966 survey conducted by the U.S. Chamber of Commerce, first-line managers in 24 organizations were asked to rank ten morale factors in the order in which they believed these factors would be important to their employees. Then the employees of these supervisors were asked to rank the same morale items in order of their importance. Their perception of what was important was markedly different (Table 11–1). The employees placed an emphasis on the satisfaction of higher-order, intrinsic needs while the managers were focused on lower-order, extrinsic factors. Although correctional employees were not the focus of this study, there is no reason to believe that the findings would be any different in corrections. The study raises the obvious question: How can managers view the same morale factors so much differently than their employees? The answer may lie in the managers' perception of their employees. A manager's approach to the task of employee motivation depends on the manager's fundamental assumptions about

TABLE 11–1   Manager and employee rankings of morale factors

Manager Rankings	Employee Rankings
Good wages	Full appreciation of work done
Job security	Being included in on things
Promotion/growth opportunity	Understanding of problems
Good working conditions	Job security
Interesting work	Good wages
Loyalty to employees	Interesting work
Tactful disciplining	Promotion/growth opportunity
Full appreciation of work done	Loyalty to employees
Understanding of problems	Good working conditions
Being included in on things	Tactful disciplining

the personal characteristics of the employees and the nature of the relationship that must exist between managers and workers.

Theory X and Theory Y

Douglas McGregor (1960) proposed that the methods chosen by a manager to motivate employees are a function of that manager's personal assumptions about the nature of human beings. There are two sets of assumptions (one negative, one positive) about human nature that McGregor termed Theory X and Theory Y.

Theory X   The Theory X manager views subordinates as individuals who (1) inherently dislike and will attempt to avoid work as much as possible, (2) avoid responsibility and require formal direction, and (3) lack ambition because of a preoccupation with personal security. Therefore, employee motivation requires coercion, control, and active threats of punishment if organizational goals are to be achieved. Employees are the instruments through which the work is done, but they are not considered to have the ability to play a role in decision making and problem solving. In fact, in many instances, they are viewed as part of the problem, not part of the solution. Thus, the organizational structure will be one in which the power and communication flow down the chain of command and the management style will be one of strictly enforcing the roles and personally overseeing every aspect of employee job performance. Trust will be limited and the manager–employee relationship is often one of mutual suspicion, which allows small problems to quickly grow into large problems. During Pre-DOC Corrections, autocratic wardens like Joseph Ragan typified the Theory X manager. These managers often achieved organizational goals but ultimately limited organizational effectiveness by not recognizing the potential of their employees and attempting to actualize it.

Theory Y   The Theory Y manager views subordinates as individuals who (1) regard work as a natural activity, (2) will exercise self-direction and self-control if they are committed to organizational goals, (3) can accept and seek responsibility, and (4) are able to make innovative decisions if allowed to do so. The Theory Y manager believes that employees are capable of self-actualization, are intrinsically motivated, and can contribute to the organizational good if organizational structure so permits. Increasingly, correctional managers have realized that a Theory Y management style is best suited to managing the complexity of the correctional organization created by bureaucratization.

The above theories provide a useful description of communication and motivation, but how are managers to apply these concepts to the management of their employees? The answer is that the organizational culture will have to be modified to encourage employee empowerment. (Note: We have not exhausted the various needs theories that have been used to explain human behavior; discussion of theories relating to achievement-power, goal setting, equity, and expectancy is deferred until Chapter 12).

EMPOWERMENT OF CORRECTIONAL EMPLOYEES

The brief review of communication and needs theory that has been provided above suggests that correctional managers should strive to develop an organizational culture based on four principles. First, the organization will benefit from a communication process that is open, honest, and involves a two-way exchange of information, beliefs, attitudes, and perceptions. Second, employees have intrinsic needs that can provide a powerful source of motivation that should be recognized and supported by managers. Third, employees possess skills and abilities that can benefit the organization if the organizational culture encourages their involvement in organizational problem-solving and decision-making processes. Fourth, the most productive approach to motivation is the Theory Y approach, which recognizes the potential of employees to grow as individuals and professionals. Acceptance of these principles has resulted in correctional managers' engaging in a variety of strategies designed to create a positive organizational culture that translates employee potential into effective organizational behavior. The strategies we will examine are the system review, Total Quality Management, deliberative mentoring, job enrichment, the Incident Management System approach to emergency response, and formal employee recognition ceremonies.

We begin with the approach that encourages upward communication by recognizing that every employee has the potential to spot organizational deficiencies and suggest remedies.

System Review

The system review is a managerial tool designed to solicit employee perceptions of the effectiveness of existing organizational functions and suggestions for their improvement. Box 11–1 provides an overview of the Kansas DOC use of system review. This approach encourages upward communica-

tion. Employees are given the formal authority to review organizational policy, procedures, and rules from their perspective—the perspective of the receiver of official messages—and then become a source of messages to management about the effectiveness of those policies, procedures, and rules. The knowledge that managers are eager to hear the opinions of employees provides a powerful motivation to improve individual and organizational performance.

BOX 11–1 THE KANSAS DOC SYSTEM REVIEW

In July 1995, Secretary Simmons initiated a correctional system review process with the objective of improving both the efficiency and effectiveness of departmental operations. The review process was structured in two phases, with the first phase designed to identify ideas and the second phase, to review and evaluate them. Community corrections agencies were also asked to conduct similar reviews, since their operations are funded with state grants.

In KDOC, 2,000 ideas were identified by over 380 employees who either turned in individual suggestions or who participated in one-time Idea Group brainstorming sessions. To accomplish the initial screening of these suggestions, eight review teams were established, each of which was chaired by a System Management Team member. Of the suggestions received, over 600 addressed general administration issues (including correctional facility administration). Approximately 450 addressed personnel and other human resources issues. Smaller numbers were assigned to the other review team subject categories, including: 311 to inmate management, 231 to information systems, records and fiscal, 151 to staff development and training, 125 to offender programs, and 108 to parole services and community corrections. Within categories, preliminary counts of frequently mentioned topics include:

- wages and benefits (52 suggestions received)
- special training needs (51)
- employee uniforms (50)
- paperwork and forms (45)
- mail (45)
- staffing issues (44)
- food service (39)
- inmate clothing (29)
- offender fees and charges (28)

Because of the volume of suggestions received, the review teams performed an initial screening to identify those measures on which a decision could be made quickly. In the initial screening, review teams recommended that approximately 5 percent of the total be implemented (either immediately or after preparation of a plan) and 22 percent be rejected. They recommended that most (approximately 60 percent) of the suggestions, however, be evaluated further before an implementation decision is made. In 10 percent of the cases, review teams found that the proposal had already been implemented or addressed in some manner.

The Department's Management Team has reviewed those proposals recommended for implementation by the review teams. To date, decisions have been made to pursue implementation of 38 separate initiatives resulting from this process. Some examples of these initiatives include: streamlining processes for promotion applications and position vacancy announcements, computer system modifications to improve

user efficiency, prohibiting inmate-to-inmate correspondence, energy conservation through temperature controls in inmate housing and recreation areas, modifying laundry schedules for inmate blankets, use of disposable jumpsuits for inmates released to court or detainer, use of maintenance agreements for inmate ice machines financed from Inmate Benefit Funds, eliminating new purchases of riding mowers, and modifying training exams to reduce the use of paper.

A more complete summary of the review process to date is contained in *System Review-Status Report,* which is available for review at each facility, regional parole office, and the Central Office. The review process is not yet complete, and work will continue in further evaluating the suggestions received.

Source: Kansas Department of Corrections. *Corrections Briefing Report* (1996): 3.13.

While many correctional organizations do not have a formal system review process, the seeds of such an approach can be seen in employee suggestion programs that encourage employees to submit written suggestions to correct procedural deficiencies. The identification of procedural deficiencies may then lead to the use of a Total Quality Management approach, which is considered next.

Total Quality Management

A popular motivational tool based on Theory Y logic is Total Quality Management (TQM), which in practice is often referred to as a "quality circle." A quality circle is a group of eight or ten nonmanagement individuals from the same work unit who meet regularly to identify and analyze problems, recommend solutions, and take corrective

FIGURE 11–1   Total Quality Management provides an excellent means of bringing all levels of staff together to engage in problem solving. Courtesy of the Office of Archives, Federal Bureau of Prisons.

actions (Hatry and Greiner, 1984:1). Although management typically retains authority over the implementation of recommended solutions, the quality circle often plays a defining role in the decision-making process. Advocates of quality circles argue that this approach promotes employee personal growth and helps make organizational behavior more effective (Figure 11–1).

This team-oriented approach to problem solving is increasingly being used in correctional organizations. An outstanding example of TQM is the ODRC's Quality Services Through Partnership Program (QSTP) presented in the Profile at the beginning of the chapter. The QSTP approach is founded on two principles. First, a structured process is used to focus efforts on improving system functions. This is more productive than employees merely seeing a problem and assigning blame for it. Second, improvement in an organization requires a full partnership between unions and management.

To elaborate on the Profile material, the ODRC Morale Activity Team hosted a successful Correctional Officer's week and developed future plans for a staff wellness program to teach stress management approaches. The Pilot Dog Team established policy and procedures for using dogs and implemented the inmate handler selection process. The Mail Team improved mail handling and security operations. The Visiting Teams developed survey instruments designed to provide information for upgrading inmate visiting procedures and areas. The Recycling Team developed a recycling program. The Security Team improved unit locking mechanisms and added security devices to state vehicles. At a more local level, a team at the Ross Correctional Institution, concerned that employees preferred food from the vending machines and were avoiding the employee dining room, developed a new and improved employee dining room that featured improvements in food selection, the appearance of inmate workers, the method of payment, and the overall look of the room (*Communicator,* 1997:2). Team accomplishments are periodically acknowledged in formal ceremonies dedicated to that specific team, and this recognition provides both information and motivation.

Structuring the Total Quality Management Process

Phillips and McConnell (1996:345–350) outline a six-stage process of TQM management that emphasizes its multidisciplinary approach to problem solving by core employees.

Stage 1—Select a Task or Identify a Problem

A problem or needed task can be identified by managers, employees, or both. Every area of correctional operation has the potential to contain problems. Whether it is low employee morale, budget overruns, conflicts over work schedules, inadequate physical facilities, inmate-related challenges, or labor relation issues, the TQM approach can be applied as a problem-solving mechanism. The area we will identify to illustrate this process is a prison Diagnostic and Classification Unit responsible for classifying 1,000 inmates every 30 days. The identified problem is that many inmates are not being classified in 30 days. The result is a backlog in transfers to other prisons and unit overcrowding.

Stage 2—Gather the Facts

After a problem has been identified, the team must establish the facts of the situation. Since many problems involve the failure to achieve a specific task in the manner stipulated by policy, the TQM team will first determine how the classification task is to be performed. Information will be gathered from a variety of sources: written policies and post orders, work schedules, observation of every step of the process, statistical reports, special incident reports documenting classification-related problems, and samples of record-keeping and work performance forms.

When the TQM team has established how the task is to be accomplished, they must review their information to determine how employees are actually performing the task. A fundamental rule to remember is that many problems are the result of a discrepancy between what is required and what is actually being done. The question then becomes why that discrepancy exists.

Stage 3—Reduce the Problem to Subproblems as Necessary

Many correctional challenges are too large to be addressed as a whole. It is sometimes necessary to divide a large issue into smaller, more manageable issues. For example, after the gathering of relevant information the following subproblems in our Diagnostic and Classification Unit problem may have been identified. First, there are inadequate numbers of secretarial staff to process the steady stream of data from counselors, psychologists, and block officers. Second, the secretarial equipment is antiquated: the secretaries use electric typewriters instead of computers. Third, the secretaries have low morale because of the workload and tight deadlines; they complain of burnout, take excessive amounts of sick and personal leave, and are generally unresponsive to the need to make deadlines. Fourth, there is no formal system for ensuring that inmates are classified in the order that they are received. It is not uncommon for inmates to be overlooked by the classification staff and initial testing and interviews delayed until the 30-day period is almost over. Then staff have to scramble to play catch-up and the result is confusion and disorder. Fifth, the Business Office manager enforces a rule that limits the quantity of psychological and educational testing material that can be ordered at any given time. The result is that test administrators frequently must delay the testing of new receptions because new supplies of tests have not been received. Finally, there is a high turnover in secretarial and classification staff because of the monotony and intensity of the deadline-driven work and new staff are not immediately employed in the unit because of the mandatory four weeks in the training academy. The result is a chronic shortage of staff.

Stage 4—Challenge Everything

The TQM team must take nothing for granted. Making assumptions can be a fatal flaw in any problem-solving process. Therefore, the team should examine and challenge every step of the process in order to determine how things are actually being done and why they are being done that way. It is always possible that efficiency can be increased by eliminating specific steps, combining them, or improving the manner in which they are performed. The sequence of activities should be reviewed to determine if changing the sequence, or assigning specific steps to other individuals, would improve the process.

Stage 5—Develop an Improved Method

Once a tentative solution has been proposed for each subproblem, the subsolutions can be combined to create a total problem solution. In the case of our Diagnostic and Classification Unit problem, for example, the proposal for an improved classification method could include the following elements. First, the unit's secretarial complement should be increased. Second, classification staff, including secretaries, should be rotated every six months to less-stressful work areas so that the high-stress work is more evenly distributed. Such a recommendation would, of course, have to be reviewed in terms of the collective bargaining agreement (CBA) governing the work performed by treatment staff and secretaries. Third, purchase computers and train all secretarial staff in their use. Fourth, develop and implement an accounting system to match inmate receptions with achievement of each step of the classification process. Fifth, change the rule enforced by the business manager unless that violates a state law. Sixth, schedule new employees for training on a staggered schedule instead of them all going at once.

Prior to implementation, the new method must be carefully evaluated to determine that the deficiencies in the current method have actually been corrected. The impact of this new system on employees must be examined because any change in a correctional organization is unsettling and may have unintended consequences. Questions must be asked: Will the proposed changes increase efficiency and morale or will efficiency be increased at the price of employee morale? How will the secretaries react to the challenge of learning to operate computers?

Will the proposed solutions be possible given the constraints of budget, CBAs, and the other issues correctional managers must take into consideration? Trial runs of the proposed solutions should be undertaken before new procedures are implemented.

Stage 6—Implement and Follow-Up

Once the proposed solution has been implemented, correctional managers must carefully assess the effect of the changes and be prepared to make mid-course corrections as they are identified. It is essential to listen to employee concerns and suggestions as the new procedures are activated. The employees will be the first ones to realize what is and what is not working. Ignoring their suggestions at this point will defeat the purpose of using a TQM approach. Major changes require careful follow-up and observation before all the bugs are worked out and goals achieved.

So far, we have assumed that every employee has the potential to participate in organizational problem-solving and decision-making processes. Now, we narrow our focus to the employee who is being groomed to assume a leadership position.

Deliberative Mentoring

Mentoring is a personal development and growth process that involves an experienced individual working with a less-experienced individual for the express purpose of developing the skills and abilities of the less-experienced person. Mentoring can be accomplished on an informal or a formal basis; however, the focus of our discussion is deliberative, or formalized mentoring. Deliberative mentoring is a formal communication and motivation process that involves a single mentor working purposefully with one of more learning partners. Formal mentoring can occur at every level of the organization, but it is most frequently used as a method of training potential leaders by giving them the opportunity to see the totality of the operation prior to promotion. A deliberative mentoring program has four elements: participant self-evaluation, getting together, planning projects, and evaluating projects (Andring, 1997).

Participant Self-Evaluation   Before beginning a mentoring relationship, mentors should engage in a process of self-examination to evaluate personal strengths and weaknesses and identify what they have to offer a less-experienced partner. This process will help avoid mistakes as well as identify for the mentor personal areas that could benefit from growth activities, such as those offered through National Institute of Corrections (NIC) seminars. Mentors should also identify why they are seeking a mentoring relationship and clarify goals that will help achieve positive results.

The individual being mentored should also engage in a self-examination process designed to identify personal strengths, weaknesses, and goals for the relationship. They must evaluate their ability to learn and benefit from the relationship. Personal motivation is a critical element. If it is high, the employee will do the hard work required in deliberative mentoring. If motivation is low, then the tendency to drop out because of time pressures, workload, or other external factors may triumph. An effective mentoring program involves hard work and a stretching of abilities, so the accurate assessment of the personal motivation of both participants is crucial.

Getting Together   After the self-examination process has been completed, the partners should mutually define the parameters of the mentoring experience by establishing (1) the length of the mentoring relationship, (2) the frequency and time of meetings, (3) the responsibilities of each partner, (4) the specific projects to be undertaken, (5) the goals to be achieved, and (6) the process for evaluating progress. A mentoring relationship can be a one-time experience or it can be a long-term relationship carried out over a period of years. For example, a superintendent grooming a deputy as a replacement when it's time to retire is likely to want a long-term relation-

ship that will involve shared experiences in every aspect of the organization.

Planning Projects   Mentoring will likely involve outside reading assignments and participation in professional training seminars, but the most valuable component will be involvement in projects that can be incorporated in the assigned workload. However, to be useful, these projects must take the individual being mentored outside of the normal work activity and provide sufficient challenge to foster the acquisition of new skills, knowledge, and ability. The individual should be challenged to see the organization from a new perspective, to engage in projects that are outside of the current area of expertise. For example, a captain in a mentoring relationship should be involved in a treatment-oriented project that requires a different perspective than that usually acquired while rising through the security ranks.

Projects should not be imposed. Rather, they should be based on a mutual agreement that the project will help create new skills and abilities. Prior to approval of a specific project, goals and evaluation criteria should be mutually decided.

Evaluating Projects   Using the preapproval evaluation criteria, both partners can identify how well specific goals have been achieved, what skills or abilities were enhanced or learned, what made the learning experience successful or hindered it, and what the next step in the mentoring process should be. The evaluation process should be continuous with a frank exchange of information occurring at each meeting. Strengths and weaknesses must be continually evaluated and mentoring assignments adjusted as needed. The best form of deliberative mentoring uses a flexible approach, not rigid adherence to an original plan of action.

Job Enrichment

Although deliberative mentoring will not be an option open to every employee, it is possible to engage in a process of job design that can strengthen those employees not being mentored. A job enrichment strategy involves a focus on improving the quality of work, especially routine work, by adding variety, creating a deeper personal interest and involvement in the job, increasing responsibility, and permitting greater decision-making autonomy. This often accompanies a job enlargement approach in which an employee is assigned additional duties. Two examples of job enrichment strategy are the unit management system and flextime.

Unit Management System

The BOP implemented a unit management system at the National Training School for Boys in 1966 as a pilot project and the concept gradually spread throughout the system. Unit management is a TQM approach in the sense that it uses teams of employees for problem solving and decision making, but it is also a job enrichment approach because it permanently assigns employees to a specific housing unit. The essential components of the unit management approach consist of "a small number of inmates (50 to 120) who are permanently assigned together and a multidisciplinary staff (unit manager, case manager(s), correctional counselor(s), full or part-time psychologist, and clerk typist) whose offices are located adjacent to the inmate housing unit, and who are permanently assigned to work with the inmates of that unit" (Lansing, Bogan, and Karacki, 1977).

Advantages of Unit Management   Unit management divides the inmate population into manageable groups, each with a sense of group identity, and increases the frequency of employee–staff contacts so that small problems can be addressed before they become large problems. It is an approach that increases communication between employees and inmates and between employees in different job categories. It allows for a more individualized classification and treatment process and creates an inmate observation process that

is more effective at identifying potentially serious problems in the early stages of development. The quality and speed of decision making is increased, which reduces inmate frustration and anxiety (U.S. Bureau of Prisons, 1975). As of 1995, unit management had spread to at least 14 DOCs (Houston, 1995:258). But unit management also has its critics.

Disadvantages of Unit Management

Houston (1995:260–261) noted three disadvantages of the unit management approach. First, this approach is expensive. Costs for a prison using unit management are higher than the costs of a facility using the traditional approach of departmental segregation. Unit management is labor intensive and does not take advantage of economy of scale benefits (i.e., correctional staff are responsible for a smaller number of inmates than they could efficiently manage).

Second, unit management requires a strategic planning approach. It cannot be implemented overnight. Funds must be requested and allocated, new positions added to the complement, opponents to the change persuaded that it is a positive change, staff training and education planned and accomplished, and, in many cases, renovation of the physical plant. This can be a time-consuming, stressful process that harried managers may not want to undertake.

Third, unit management threatens the distribution of power in the organizational structure. Managers may perceive increased employee responsibility and autonomy as a threat to their position power and a challenge to their traditional authority. There is a sense in which this perception is accurate because unit management does redistribute power to some degree. However, it also provides organizational benefits and managers must recognize that any loss of position power can be offset by the value of increasing organizational effectiveness.

Flextime Systems

Flextime is any work schedule that differs from the traditional way of structuring employee schedules. It is, in fact, a discretionary work week. In most flextime systems, there are two requirements: a core time when the employee must work and a total number of hours that must be worked each day (Carrell, Jennings, and Heavrin, 1997:220). For example, probation officers on a forty-hour-a-week schedule might be required to work at least eight hours a day with the core time being 10 A.M. to 12 Noon and 1:00 P.M. to 3 P.M. (one unpaid lunch hour). The scheduling of the remaining hours, within specified time spans (such as 6:00 to 10:00 A.M. and 3:00 to 7:00 P.M.) is at the discretion of the employee. The advantages of flextime include a gain in productive hours, increased job satisfaction, reduction in early-morning tension, more efficient planning of the daily activities, and decreased traffic congestion to and from work (Fleuter, 1975). The use of flextime can be extended to every job category, including C.O.s. The value of flextime is that it gives employees a sense of being able to control (within reasonable limits) their schedules, which can be adjusted to accommodate personal needs. This translates into savings in employee turnover, absenteeism, and tardiness (Carrell, Jennings, and Heavrin, 1997:219–220).

A variation on flextime is the staggered start approach that allows employees to determine when they will start their work day on the condition that they then must work the full number of hours for that day. This approach lacks the true freedom of choice that is the hallmark of a flextime system, but it does increase, to some extent, employee control over their personal lives. We now move to a more radical form of employee empowerment, one which defies traditional thinking in a critical area of organizational activity: the response to emergency situations.

Incident Management System

The activation of a correctional organization's incident management system (IMS) historically has been accomplished through the traditional command and control structure contained within the chain of command that is the backbone of the organizational structure.

Traditional Command and Control Structure This structure requires that the emergency plan can only be activated by the organization's top manager or appropriate designee. Typical wording in the emergency plan manual is "During an emergency situation, the Warden, or highest ranking official on duty, shall have absolute and total authority for decisions made affecting the institution, the emergency and security of the premises" (Avoyelles Correctional Center, 1995:9).

All emergency response direction comes from managers through the regular chain of command. The most senior staff providing direction to line staff is the traditional corrections approach to emergency response because it conforms so closely to the flow of power and communication that occurs during the normal daily routine. It is the approach with which both managers and employees are most comfortable, but it is an approach that can cause delays in the effective response to an emergency system. However, the Arizona DOC has adopted a model of emergency response direction that empowers every employee.

Arizona DOC Incident Management System This IMS was implemented with the goal of effectively managing resources in such a way that little problems don't have the time to become big problems. The element of the Arizona IMS that most distinguishes it from the traditional command and control structure is the policy that the first C.O., regardless of rank, to identify an emergency in progress becomes the Incident Commander charged with directing the response: "The first arriving officer on the scene not directly involved in the incident is to assume command" (Arizona Department of Correction, 1993:2). Those staff already involved in the emergency situation cannot assume command, but they are authorized to accept direction from the first noninvolved C.O. who arrives on the scene. They do not have to wait for managers to arrive.

The Incident Commander also has the authority to direct the activities of managers in accordance with the established emergency plan as they arrive on the scene. Managers arriving on the scene do not automatically assume command as would be the case in the traditional command and control structure. Although there *may* be a transfer of command authority as managers arrive, "Command is normally transferred *ONLY* to improve the quality of the command organization and the effectiveness of the incident being managed" (Arizona Department of Correction, 1993:3).

Thus, the arrival of a ranking officer on the incident scene does not mean that command authority is automatically transferred to that officer. Command authority is only transferred when a specific transfer of command process has been initiated and completed. Off-site managers such as the DOC Commissioner or Central Office directors who want to provide direction or advice may do so without assuming command. All specialized response teams arriving at the scene of the emergency report to the Incident Commander, even if managers senior to the Incident Commander are physically present in the area.

The Arizona IMS also provides for an effective communication process by requiring that every instance of radio communication be in the form of plain language, that is, there should be no call signs or confusing code labels such as "Red Rock Leader to Green Eagle Support." All radio transmissions are to use the job title of the individual involved in the communication. If the officer assigned to escort duty is being radioed, for example, the term to be used is "escorts."

The Arizona IMS represents a highly controversial approach to emergency response management because it provides employees with a potential level of authority historically reserved for senior managers. But this process empowers employees and can increase employee commitment to the organization. To be effective, however, both employees and managers must be trained prior to implementation of the system.

Employee Recognition Ceremony

Finally, we come to the strategy that officially recognizes the successful efforts of employees. The culmination of strategies designed to improve both communication and motivation is the employee recognition ceremony. This strategy has already been noted in the Profile at the beginning of the chapter, but the ODRC is only one of many correctional organizations that formally recognize employee achievements. An almost universal motivator in corrections is the Employee Awards Program, the only difference among correctional organizations is how the program is structured. Some organizations have an annual awards ceremony while others have them on a quarterly basis. For example, in 1995, the Arizona DOC honored 145 employees in its quarterly Employee Awards Program. Five employees were Employee of the Year, another was recognized for valor, and one employee received an award for a suggestion submitted to the Employee Suggestion Program. Other awards included 69 Meritorious Service Awards, 6 Lifesaving Awards, and 52 Length of State Service Awards honoring those employees with 20, 25, or 30 years of service (Arizona Department of Corrections, 1996:15).

In addition, the American Correctional Association (ACA) sponsors the annual E. R. Cass Award, which recognizes outstanding correctional employees, and the ACA's official publication, *Corrections Today*, annually publishes the profiles of employees nominated by colleagues as representative of the "Best in the Business."

SUMMARY

Communication and motivation are intertwined processes that shape the ability of the employees of any correctional organization to achieve the mission. Managers who want to improve organizational behavior must understand the theoretical foundations of these processes and strive to convert theory into practice by developing specific employee empowerment strategies. But receiving, understanding, and accepting the message are not the only determinants of organizational behavior. For organizational behavior to be effective, employees must be socialized to the expected norms and values of the organization. The next chapter examines employee socialization through professionalization and the conditions that will promote this process.

Discussion Questions

1. How can managers use their understanding of the seven elements of the communication model to increase employee motivation?
2. What actions can managers take to overcome the eight barriers to effective communication?
3. How can each correctional employee apply motivation theory to increase inmate motivation to enter treatment programs?
4. Which needs theories are most useful for correctional managers attempting to motivate subordinates? Why?
5. Which needs theories are most useful in overcoming barriers to effective communication? Why?
6. What are the pros and cons of each employee empowerment strategy presented in this chapter?
7. Which employee empowerment strategies will be most effective in a prison? In a community corrections facility? Why?

Critical Analysis Exercise: Gender Differences in Communication

Deborah Tannen (1991) has extensively explored the issue of how gender can create oral communication barriers. Tannen has found that the way men and women use speech reflects fundamental gender differences in how relationships are viewed. Men use their speech to emphasize status while women use speech to create an emotional connection. Women speak and hear a language of connection and intimacy while men speak and hear a language of status and independence. So, for many men, conversations serve the twin purposes of expressing independence and maintaining a status in a hierarchical social order. For many women, conversations are a vehicle for seeking emotional closeness; confirmation and support are sought and provided. When men hear a problem, they assert a desire for independence and control by providing solutions while women, hearing the same problem, view the resulting conversation as a means of promoting closeness and gaining support and connection. Men are often more direct than women in conversations and more likely to openly criticize. In fact, men often criticize women for the frequency of their use of apologies. When a woman says "I'm sorry," men tend to interpret that phrase as a sign of weakness, an indication that the woman is accepting blame when he knows she's not to blame. But the woman also knows she's not to blame. The phrase is being used to express regret, as in "I know we both feel bad about this situation." The next time you see a man and a woman in a store or on a street nearly run into each other, observe who is the first to say "Excuse me." It will probably be the woman, even if it was the man who was not watching where he was going.

Meier and Foley (1991:6) have reported that gender differences between men and women are also evident in their listening and speaking styles. When listening, men make irregular eye contact, infrequently nod or make humming sounds, may continue another activity while speaking, interrupt in order to speak, and ask questions designed to analyze the speaker's information. However, women when they are listening have uninterrupted eye contact, frequently nod and make humming sounds, usually stop other activities, wait for pauses in order to speak, and ask questions designed to elicit more information.

When speaking, men have few pauses in the flow of words, may abruptly change the topic, speak until interrupted, speak louder than the previous speaker, make frequent use of "I" and "me," rarely engage in personal self-disclosure, and their use of humor is often based on kidding or making fun of others. Women, when speaking, have frequent pauses, connect their information to a previous speaker's information, stop speaking when the information is delivered, use the same volume as the previous speaker, use "us" and "we," engage in self-disclosure, and frequently use humor that is not based on kidding or making fun of others.

Critical Analysis Questions

1. What stereotypes and misunderstandings can result from gender differences in communication?
2. How can these differences be effectively communicated to managers and employees?
3. In terms of the communication model presented in this chapter, who has the most effective listening and speaking style—men or women? Defend your answer.
4. How can a manager effectively motivate staff to understand and accept gender differences in speaking and listening?

12

The Professionalization of Correctional Employees: Selection, Training, and Evaluation

---

Learning Objectives

After completing this chapter, you should be able to:

- Define professionalization as a socialization process.
- Identify the role of selection, training, and evaluation in promoting professionalization.
- Describe an effective basic training program.
- Outline the variety of in-service training programs available to correctional line staff and managers.
- Define and critique individual evaluation methods.
- Summarize the strengths and weaknesses of ACA accreditation.
- Relate the principles of equity and expectancy theory to developing an environment conducive to professionalization.

Key Terms and Concepts

Professionalization
Job Description
Open-Ended Questions
Basic Training
Emergency Management Teams
Personal Trait Model
MBO Model
ACA Accreditation
Equity Norm
Expectancy Theory
Job Analysis
Selection Process
Structured Questions
Training
In-Service Training
Individual Evaluation
Goal-Setting Theory
Organizational Evaluation
Equity Theory
Equity Tension
Achievement-Power Theory

If you want one year of prosperity, grow grain. If you want ten years of prosperity, grow trees. If you want one hundred years of prosperity, grow people.

Chinese proverb

Profile: An Overview of American Correctional Association Accreditation

Correctional accreditation began in 1974 with the creation of the Commission on Accreditation for Corrections. Charged with the task of creating a body of professional standards against which correctional organizations could be evaluated, the Commission merged in 1986 with the American Correctional Association (ACA). ACA accreditation standards are extremely useful to correctional managers because of the variety of organizational needs they meet. First, the standards can be used as a reference source by staff responsible for training new employees and introducing them to the complexity of corrections. Second, they provide a professionally organized reference to guide the activities of busy managers who want to upgrade their policy and operations manuals. Third, the standards provide a comprehensive set of guidelines for the top managers bringing a new facility on line. Fourth, they provide the framework for a checklist to be used by inspectors from the Central Office's Evaluation Unit who need a recognized set of criteria for evaluating every facet of facility operation. ACA accreditation standards serve as a useful reference when developing organizational activities to professionalize correctional employees.

Corrections is an exceedingly complex business that requires employees capable of achieving a mission that often contains conflicting elements of the punitive control, rehabilitation, justice, and actuarial models. New correctional employees enter the organization with differences in personal history, attitudes, and perceptions of the job. Because of these differences, every employee must undergo a process of socialization known as "professionalization": an ongoing process that defines and reinforces professional conduct. Professional conduct, in turn, is behavior that advances the organizational mission. Professionalization has three elements— selection, training, and evaluation—that are found within the technical and support sub-

systems of the correctional organization. Selection involves the determination of which individuals in the applicant pool have the most potential to successfully handle the challenges of correctional work. Training converts that potential into professional behavior by providing the knowledge, skills, and techniques necessary to achieve the mission. Evaluation is a feedback mechanism that compares individual and organizational performance to predetermined criteria and identifies professional conduct that should be rewarded and behavioral deficiencies that must be corrected. Professionalization is most effectively achieved in an organizational culture in which employees have an expectation that their efforts will be appreciated and rewarded.

A MODEL OF CORRECTIONAL EMPLOYEE PROFESSIONALIZATION

A correctional organization is only as effective as its staff is professional. A staff will be professional only when correctional managers have developed a system of turning inexperienced civilians into corrections professionals. How do we define the corrections professional? For our purposes, we will define a corrections professional as a skilled human service worker who uses legitimate authority to help inmates adjust to the reality of prison life and to minimize custodial repression, and who applies skill and ingenuity to humanizing the prison environment. Professionalization is to be achieved through a systemic process of selecting, training, and evaluating a diverse workforce of high-quality and committed employees and maintaining a working climate where all staff at all levels are provided with training, supervision, encouragement, support, and opportunities to develop their full professional potential (Minnesota Department of Corrections, 1995:19). Correctional managers are especially concerned with developing professional correctional officers (C.O.s) because this is the largest employee group and the group that has the most daily contact with, and control over, inmates (Figure 12–1).

In order to become a corrections professional, socialization to the mission and the goals of the organization must be accomplished. This is usually done through a three-stage professionalization process that can be diagrammed as follows:

Selection + Training + Evaluation = Professionalization

Each of these stages requires specific managerial behavior.

CORRECTIONAL EMPLOYEE SELECTION PROCESS

A critical management function is the hiring of staff through a selection process that complies with all applicable federal and state laws (Skrapec, 1988:49–52). The typical selection process can be diagrammed as follows:

Job Analysis →Recruitment→ Application → Pre-employment Tests →Interview→ Background Check →Conditional Offer of Employment →Medical Examination →Employment

At any stage in this process the applicant can be rejected, but rejection has to be on the basis of a failure to comply with job-related criteria. The first step in an effective employee selection process is to conduct a job analysis of every category of position within the organizational structure.

Job Analysis

A job analysis is the process of developing a detailed description of the specific tasks involved in a job, determining the relationship of that specific job to other jobs in the organization, and ascertaining the knowledge, skills, and abilities to successfully perform the job (Ghorpade, 1988). The product of a job analysis is a job description: a written description of the ideal candidate

FIGURE 12–1 The role of the correctional officer as only a control agent, as depicted in this Pre-DOC Corrections picture, has been replaced by the expectation that correctional officers will be human service professionals. Courtesy of the Office of Archives, Federal Bureau of Prisons.

for the position. The job description is used to inform potential applicants of the requirements of a job as well as provide specific guidelines for training and monitoring the performance of the individual hired for the position.

An example of a typical corrections job description is provided in Box 12–1. Any person interested in becoming a parole officer for the Missouri Department of Corrections (DOC) Board of Probation and Parole will have a clear idea of what the job entails and their match to the position requirements. This job description contains qualifications for employment that are job-related. An employee selection process that uses non-job-related factors increases the probability of hiring false positives: applicants who are poor choices who eventually generate negative behavior, high turnover, negative publicity, and inmate litigation.

BOX 12–1 PROBATION AND PAROLE OFFICER I

DEFINITION

This is professional adult probation and parole work in a district office of the Board of Probation and Parole.

An employee in this class conducts investigations for the courts and the Board of Probation and Parole and supervises clients/offenders who are on probation or parole or incarcerated in the Department of Corrections. Work includes checking social history information on clients/offenders, preparing reports, and formulating placement plans. Emphasis is on working with the client/offender in the community, including adjustment to the community. Administrative and technical supervision is provided by a professional superior; however, the employee is expected to exercise considerable discretion and independent decision

making in the performance of work within established policies and procedures.

Any one position may not involve all of the specified duties or knowledge, skills and abilities, nor are the listed examples exhaustive.

EXAMPLES OF WORK

Conducts investigations on clients/offenders for the circuit courts and/or the Board of Probation and Parole; collects and verifies data through the interview process and review of historical records; evaluates information and incorporates into records and reports.

Assesses the needs and risk levels of clients/offenders for appropriate supervision strategies such as individual counseling or referral to internal programs or community resources.

Maintains ongoing records of supervision activity and submits reports thereof to the designated legal authority, as required.

Contacts clients/offenders in their home, place of employment, or place of confinement and counsels them regarding personal or adjustment problems.

Attends court to receive court assignments and/or make reports.

Secures and verifies information from incarcerated adult clients/offenders concerning their home life, family relationships, work history, and related pertinent personal and social factors.

Serves on a classification team; evaluates the client/offender's institutional adjustment, attitude toward society and release plans; makes recommendations relative to job assignments, transfers, disciplinary actions, etc.; prepares and maintains casework records and reports.

Assesses classification status and prepares reclassification analysis for program eligibility determination.

Counsels clients/offenders on work release; coordinates programs activities; assists in the solution of problems with employers, correctional center staff, and others; prepares and maintains casework records and reports.

Conducts background and resource investigations of clients/ offenders for determination of eligibility for recognizance bond.

Cooperates with law enforcement and public and private social agencies in matters relating to probationers and/or parolees.

Performs other related work as assigned.

EXAMPLES OF KNOWLEDGE, SKILLS, AND ABILITIES

Working knowledge of the general methods of social casework and job placement as applied to probation and parole work.

Working knowledge of the methods of obtaining social and personal information and developing case histories.

Working knowledge of human behavior, attitudes, and motivation and ability to apply this knowledge to casework and the rehabilitation of criminal offenders.

Working knowledge of the causes of crime and related issues of substance abuse and mental illness.

Ability to conduct interviews with hostile or reluctant individuals and to maintain contacts with employers, social agencies, the courts, and the general public.

Ability to implement plans of supervision with the client/offender.

Ability to exercise job authority in an appropriate and productive manner.

Ability to prepare accurate and complete case records and reports.

EXPERIENCE AND EDUCATION QUALIFICATIONS

The following entrance requirements are used to admit or reject applicants for merit system examinations, or may be used to evaluate applicants for employment in positions not requiring selection from merit system registers. When applicable, equivalent substitution will be allowed for deficiencies in experience or education.

One year of experience as a Correctional Services Trainee under the Missouri Merit System.

OR

One year of professional experience in adult probation and parole or corrections casework, and graduation from an accredited four-year college or university with specialization in criminal justice, social work, sociology, or psychology. (Graduate work in the specified education areas may be substituted on a year-for-year basis for the stated experience. Additional qualifying experience, substance abuse counseling or closely related work may be substituted on a year-for-year basis for deficiencies in the stated education. Two years of less related social casework, employment interviewing or counseling may be substituted for each year of deficiency in the stated education.)

Source: Missouri Department of Corrections. "Job Descriptions." *Department Manual—Job Descriptions* (1997).

Job analysis is not limited to line staff positions. It is also applied to correctional manager positions. The structure of the manager's job description will be the same as the job descriptions for line staff, but the content will markedly differ. For example, the definition of a Probation and Parole District Administrator II in the Missouri DOC is as follows:

An employee in this class is responsible for the administration of all probation and parole services in a moderate to large size district field office. Work includes planning, directing, and ensuring the professional performance of duties and compliance with established policies, procedures, and rules; overseeing resource development and utilization; developing and maintaining public relations; supervising, directly and through subordinate supervisors, a moderate to large sized professional and support staff; and directing the general office management functions. Work involves participation in the formulation of divisional policies and procedures. General supervision is received from a Probation and Parole Administrator or other designated superior; however, the employee is expected to exercise considerable discretion and independence in directing the assigned office within established policies. (Missouri Department of Corrections, 1997.)

This job description clearly articulates the management functions as outlined by Henri Fayol in Chapter 1. Regardless of the position under discussion, job descriptions provide a written overview of the organization's expectations and minimum requirements to fill the position. Note that both of the job descriptions presented above require the individuals in those positions to exercise "considerable discretion and independence" but limit that exercise with the phrase "within established policies."

Recruitment Process

The most common techniques used for correctional recruitment are walk-in applica-

tions, employee referrals, newspaper and magazine advertisements, brochures, and campus recruiting (Gilbert, 1988:39). As of 1987, only 16 DOCs used radio advertising and only nine DOCs used television advertising (Benton and Nesbitt, 1987). The broader the target audience of recruiting efforts, the larger the applicant pool. For this reason, an effective recruitment campaign will use as many media outlets as possible and provide potential applicants with a description of (1) the role of the agency in the criminal justice system, (2) the duties associated with the position being sought, (3) the skills required for effective performance, (4) the minimum credentials for employment, and (5) selection procedures. The more specific the information provided to applicants, the better their ability to determine if they should apply for the position.

Application Process

The application for employment form is a standardized document, usually based on Civil Service criteria, which provides an overview of the applicant: name, address, educational background, employment record, and personal experience. It may ask about criminal convictions, usually with a statement that a conviction does not automatically make the applicant ineligible. Other information, such as race, age, military status, or disabilities, may be asked for on a voluntary basis for Personnel Department Affirmative Action monitoring purposes. But, as Bittel (1989:135) has noted, the following information cannot be required by an application form: race, religion, age, national origin, gender, marital status, disabilities, arrest history, and physical capabilities. The correctional managers in charge of developing the application must be able to demonstrate that every application question is relevant to the job. These criteria also apply to the interview stage.

Pro-Employment Testing

Correctional organizations routinely require applicants to take three types of tests designed to predict job performance. The first type of test consists of a written exam designed to assess levels of general knowledge, job-specific knowledge, and the ability to use knowledge in problem-solving situations.

The second type of test consists of a psychological test battery designed to determine if applicants have the psychological makeup to handle the complexity and rigors of the job. For example, in the New York DOC, all C.O. applicants must undergo a pre-employment psychological screening battery: the Minnesota Multiphasic Personality Inventory (MMPI), the Inwald Personality Inventory (IPI), the Correction Officer Interest Blank, and a face-to-face clinical interview (New York Department of Corrections, 1995:4). The use of psychological testing to screen C.O. applicants is not without some controversy. Skrapec (1988:56–57) reported that there is no agreement on which psychological instruments are most appropriate because there is inadequate evidence that any of the above instruments reduces the frequency of prediction errors. However, Davis (1992) reported that 14 DOCs using psychological tests report an improved ability to select candidates, reduce turnover rates, and screen out false positives.

Finally, agility tests measuring physical capabilities can be done at any stage of the selection process. However, "measuring an applicant's physical or psychological response to the agility test would be considered medical and, therefore, cannot be done before a conditional offer of employment is made" (Rubin, 1995a:116).

Technology and the Testing Process   A Pennsylvania DOC study of their requirement that C.O. applicants be tested in a written exam and then undergo an oral exam found that the written test was sufficient to predict job performance. Acting on this finding, the Pennsylvania DOC and state Civil Service Commission have created a video-based exam that includes written portions and 12 video-based scenarios designed to assess applicant observation skills, problem-solving ability, and ability to follow verbal instructions. The applicants answer questions in a booklet based on the

information presented in the video. Future plans include placement of the exam questions on the computer screen. Moving to a single-part test by eliminating the oral exam is expected to save $500,000 per year (*Corrections Professional,* 1997a:2).

Interview

The New York DOC interview process is designed to evaluate C.O. applicants on the basis of the following: interview behavior, employment history, interpersonal relationships, arrest history, motor vehicle infractions, military history, MMPI results, IPI results, aggression/violence history, alcohol/drug abuse, and psychiatric history (New York Department of Correctional Services, 1995:5). The applicant is rated on a five-point scale in accordance with pre-established criteria. A rating of 4 or 5 results in psychological disqualification.

Structuring the Interview
Interviews should be structured, that is, they should use a predetermined set of questions that are relevant to the specific position under consideration: "the most valid interviews use a consistent structure and ask applicants questions that require answers giving detailed accounts of actual behaviors they have displayed on the job" (Robbins, 1993:563). Structured interviews are best for assessing the applicant's intelligence, level of motivation, and interpersonal skills (Robbins, 1993:562) and are accomplished by asking highly structured questions and open-ended questions. An example of a highly structured question is: "What was your job classification in the military?" Open-ended questions, on the other hand, may be like the following:

- Why do you want to become a probation officer?
- What was the most difficult part of your last job?
- Why was that the most difficult part?
- What did you do to handle that part of the job?

- What are your strengths and weaknesses as an employee?
- What was the most challenging situation you have ever encountered on any job?
- How did you handle that situation?

A particularly useful type of open-ended question is the scenario question. For example, "You are a correctional officer working a block with 250 inmates in it. You see two inmates fighting at the far end of the block. What do you do?"

Interviewers must remember that they are to ask every candidate the same set of questions. Although follow-up questions can be used to allow an applicant to elaborate on an answer, every applicant must have the opportunity to answer every question. The interview process may involve one interview by a committee or it may involve a two-stage process in which a screening committee refers the most eligible candidates to a final interview with one or two key decision makers. The one-interview approach is usually most appropriate for entry-level positions.

Pitfalls to Avoid in the Interview Process

Lineback (1987:135) has suggested the following interview pitfalls that interviewers should try to avoid:

1. Do not form an opinion early in the interview. Force yourself to remain neutral throughout the interview. Be on the alert for any biases that may surface at the beginning of the interview. If these are not recognized, the interview may become a way of confirming an initial negative opinion of an applicant.

2. Be aware that back-to-back interviews may create a situation in which an opinion of the current applicant may be unduly influenced by the opinion of the last applicant.

3. Avoid the "halo effect." This is a natural tendency to assume that an appli-

cant who is strong or weak in one area will be strong or weak in all other areas.

4. Do not view the interview as a method for disqualifying applicants. Rather, regard it as a method for assessing strengths and weaknesses and hire for strength, not to avoid weaknesses. Know the position and the qualifications of the ideal candidate for that position. Look for specific skills and levels of motivation when interviewing.

5. Do not forget that the interview is a two-way process. The effective interviewer will give information as well as receive it and attempt to sell the applicant on the organization as a good place to work.

The development of a standardized rating form is an effective way to help avoid these pitfalls. A standardized form will incorporate a rating scale (usually 1 to 10, with 10 the highest rating) and will list each question and the number of points its answer should be given.

Background Check

Background checks can be undertaken prior to or after the interview. Because of the time and money a comprehensive background check can entail, it is most cost-effective to reserve this element of the selection process for applicants recommended for employment on the basis of the interview(s). At a minimum the background check should gather the following information:

1. Employment History. This includes dates of employment, work performance, job titles, promotions, supervisory reports, and eligibility for rehire. Past employers may be reluctant to release more than the dates of prior employment because of a fear of being sued by former employees if they divulge too much information. For this reason, interview questions should address the applicant's perception of previous work experience.

2. Educational History. This is more easily confirmed.

3. Criminal History. Local police, state police, and FBI records are readily available to correctional managers and records should be carefully scrutinized for crimes that may preclude hiring. However, any rejection of an applicant based on criminal history must be in accordance with the guidelines and opinion of the organization's attorneys since this is a very complicated area.

4. Community References. A check of the references listed on the employee application should be undertaken if for no other reason than to confirm that the reference actually knows the applicant and is qualified to express an opinion about them.

5. Professional Licenses. If a professional license is needed for a position, the appropriate licensing agency should be contacted for confirmation that the applicant's license is in good standing with the official accrediting agency.

Again, all questions must be job-related. The background check cannot be used as a fishing expedition. At this point, the correctional manager should be in a position to make a conditional offer of employment to those applicants whose nonmedical information indicates that they are best suited for the position. However, the offer will not be final until the applicant has undergone a medical examination.

Medical Examination

Medical examinations are defined as "procedures or tests that seek information about the existence, nature, or severity of a person's mental or physical impairment, or that seek information regarding an individual's physical or psychological health" (Rubin, 1995a:116). In accordance with the Americans with Disabilities Act (ADA) requirements, the medical examination occurs after the conditional offer of employment. It cannot be used to screen out applicants prior to a conditional offer of employment, and medical results can be used to withdraw a conditional offer of employment only if managers are unable to make a reasonable accommodation for the applicant's disability because the necessary changes would constitute an undue hardship. The Equal Employment Opportunity Commission (EEOC) requires that managers not place those individuals with disabilities at the bottom of the hiring list; reranking based on postoffer exams must be communicated to the applicant.

Once the selection process is completed, the successful applicants are given an employment date. However, completion of the selection process is just the beginning of professionalization. Training must now develop applicant potential.

TRAINING: THE FOUNDATION OF PROFESSIONALIZATION

The first training academy for C.O.s was opened in New York City in 1930. Commissioned by Federal Bureau of Prisons Director Sanford Bates, the school provided a three-month training program with a curriculum that included the history of crime and punishment, crime statistics, types and functions of prisons, inmate characteristics, prison discipline, and classification and segregation (McShane, 1996:118).

Training has three socialization goals: (1) preparing staff to act decisively and correctly in a broad spectrum of situations, (2) creating greater productivity and effectiveness, and (3) fostering cooperation and unity of purpose (Josi, 1996:121). These goals are achieved through a systematic process of providing a basic training program, in-service training programs, and specialized skills training.

Basic Training

It would be difficult to find a correctional organization that does not require preservice training of new employees. The length of any given basic training program depends on the classification of the employee. As a general rule of thumb, the most sophisticated training programs require noncustody employees (clerical and treatment staff) to have at least 80 hours of preservice training and personnel such as trades and maintenance and food service supervisors to have 120 hours. Camp and Camp (1996b:113) reported that the typical C.O. must complete 228 hours of preservice training, undergo a probationary period that averages 8.9 months, and receive 40 hours of annual in-service training.

Training Curriculum

The emphasis in basic training is on a balanced approach to provide information and skills development in (1) organizational policy, (2) organizational structure and functions, (3) basic security techniques, (4) the interpersonal relations and communication skills required to manage an offender population, (5) legal and medical processes, and (6) techniques of emergency preparedness. Typical of DOC basic training programs is the six-week C.O. basic training program offered by the California DOC at the Richard A. McGee Correctional Training Center. The training methods used include lectures, videotapes, outside speakers, and hands-on application of specific skills, especially those required for basic security and emergency response. The training curriculum comprises ten subject areas (California Department of Corrections, 1997:10–21). Box 12–2 provides a listing of the subject areas, courses in each area, and (in parentheses) the number of hours per course. Course instructors are certified in their specialty areas and the curriculum is subject to periodic review and modification.

BOX 12–2 TRAINING CURRICULUM OF THE CALIFORNIA DOC

Category A—Communications: Community Relations (2); Introduction to Communications (5); Radio Communications (2); Report Writing 1, 2, and 3 (12); Orientation to Crime Victims Program (1).

Category B—Supervision: Discretionary Decision Making (3); Supervisory Skills I, II, III, and IV (10); Inmate/Staff Relations (4).

Category C—Ethics: Ethics and Professionalism (2); Staff Rights and Responsibilities (4); Sexual Harassment (2); Courtroom Testimony (4).

Category D—Effects/Use of Force: Effects of Force (4); Firearms Safety and Familiarization (12); Firearms Range Training and Qualification (40); Chemical Agents (8); Weaponless Training (8); Side Handle Baton 1, 2, and 3 (12).

Category E—Security/Custody: Crime Scene Preservation and Investigation (6); Key and Tool Control (3); Inmate Disciplinary Process (4); Officer/Hostage Survival (4); Count Procedures (2); Body and Cell Search, Practice and Grading (8); Transportation of Prisoners and Application of Restraint Gear (8); Orientation to Prison Gangs (4); Disturbance Control (2).

Category F—Medical/Health and Safety: First Aid (8); Fire Safety (2); Unusual Inmate Behavior (3); Acquired Immune Deficiency Syndrome (AIDS) (2); Drug ID (4).

Category G—Records Keeping: Inmate Property and Appeals Process (4); Inmate Work Incentive and Time Keeping (4).

Category H—Physical Training/ Stress Management: Orientation to Physical Training (1.5); Physical Training (25); Physical Training Testing (3); Stress Management (2).

Category I—Orientation to Corrections/Justice System: Meet with CCPOA (2); Study Habits (1); Inspection/Drill (1); Defensive Driving (3.5) ; Overview of the Criminal Justice System (2); Law and Search and Seizure (8) ; Constitutional Rights Law (4); Orientation to the California Department of Corrections (4); On-the-Job Training (16).

Category J—Administrative Process: Check-In Orientation (12); Personnel/Accounting and Data Processing (5); Exam (2); Squad Meetings (4); Delta College Registration (1); Weekly Exams (7); Company Inspections (4); Squad Evaluations (2); Graduation Practice (4); Graduation (6).

Evaluation of Student Performance

Typically, correctional instructors measure student performance by testing basic information retention through written tests and observation of skills application exercises. Courses like First Aid require the students to meet state certification standards. In California, there is an evaluation schedule consisting of weekly exams on Mondays, inspections on Tuesdays and Thursdays, and squad meetings on Wednesdays and Fridays (California Department of Corrections, 1997a:22).

Correctional instructors must be well versed in a variety of educational techniques because of the varying levels of new employees, especially C.O.s. Blair and Kratcoski (1992) found that 27 percent of C.O.s have at least a bachelor's degree, 67 percent have a high school diploma or its equivalent, and

only 6 percent have less than a high school education. These figures are impressive given the results of a national survey that found that the minimum educational standard for C.O. employment in 1992 was "less than a high school diploma for 13 states (25.5 percent), a GED or high school diploma in 22 states (43.1 percent), and a high school diploma or more for 16 states (31.4 percent)" (Sechrest and Josi, 1992:8).

Basic Training Affiliated with Community Colleges

Basic training also takes place in locations other than a DOC training academy. While state DOCs have the luxury of sufficient funding to develop a training academy, many local jails are not as fortunate. An example of an innovative strategy designed to meet county jail training needs is preservice training at community colleges. For example, the Cattaraugus County Campus of Jamestown Community College in Olean, New York, offers a regionalized 12-week preservice training program for C.O.s that provides full training and certification prior to employment. The curriculum offered is comparable to that offered by DOC training academies, includes a two-week jail internship, and is cost-effective because the students pay the tuition. Proponents of this approach report increased employee professionalism (Crawford, 1995:158).

FIGURE 12–2 Special protective equipment is a requirement for every Correctional Emergency Response Team. Courtesy of the Ohio Department of Rehabilitation and Correction.

Advancing Professionalization Through In-Service Training

Basic training provides a foundation for professional behavior, but it is not the end of the training process. Every employee must be involved in an ongoing in-service training process designed to develop and maintain specific sets of skills (Figures 12–2 and 12–3).

In-Service Training

Certain employee skills must be periodically updated. Skills such as cardiopulmonary resuscitation (CPR) and first aid techniques are annually updated through a required recertification process. Other in-service programs are provided as needed. For example, in the 1980s the threat of AIDS transmission inspired such enormous employee fear that

FIGURE 12–3   Members of Correctional Emergency Response Team practice a variety of techniques for effectively managing serious inmate-precipitated emergencies. Courtesy of the Ohio Department of Rehabilitation and Correction.

FIGURE 12–3 (Continued)

special AIDS education programs were developed in virtually every correctional organization. Many DOCs offer "train-the-trainer" programs that provide specialized curriculums to selected staff who use that training to teach specific skills to other employees in their facility. The in-service training component can be extensive. Box 12–3 presents a list of the 113 courses that can be offered by the North Carolina DOC Office of Staff Development and Training (North Carolina Department of Corrections, 1996).

In addition to basic, in-service, and train-the-trainer programs, the potential for

FIGURE 12–3   (Continued)

correctional emergencies to confront employees at any time requires a form of specialized in-service training referred to as emergency management training.

BOX 12–3 NORTH CAROLINA DOC IN-SERVICE TRAINING COMPONENT

Administrative Matters, Review and Testing
Administrative Remedy procedures
Advanced Arrest, Search & Seizures
Advanced Revolver Training
Advanced SAMNA
Advanced Unarmed Self-Defense
AIDS
AIDS Policy Training for Key DOP Staff
AIDS/HIV Policy Implementation Trainers
Air Pack Refresher

Asbestos Awareness Training
Audio/Video Documentation of Anticipated Use of Force
Basic Overview & Procedure Training for State Accounting System
Basic SAMNA Training
Basic SAMNA Word Processing
Bomb Threats and Discoveries
Behavioral Therapy Techniques
Breath-Alcohol Tester (BT-2)
Case Analysis Training (Interview Techniques)
Case Management
Lesson Plans for Chaplains
Chemical Training for South Central Area PFRT
Child Abuse & Child Neglect Awareness
Commercial Drivers License
Communicating Effectively
Computers–Introduction
Conflict and Crisis Management

Contraband and Techniques of
Search (816)
Correctional Managers & the Media
DAPP Office Management
Diabetes Mellitus
Diagnostic Center Directory
Disciplinary Grievance Procedures
Phase I & II
Distribution of Medications by
Correctional Officers
DOP Terminal Training
DCI
Drug Testing Policy
DC –121–R's in General
DOS and Text File Training
Drug Free Work Place
Extradition Officers Training Program
EAP Orientation for Employees
EHA Equipment Procedures
Workshop
Electronic House Arrest Program
Emergency Generator
Employee Time Report
Employee Conduct & Personnel
Evacuation Plan & Use of Emergency
Exits & Keys
Evaluating Instructor Effectiveness
Extinguishment of Fires in Central
Prison Maximum Security Cell-
blocks
Fingerprinting (204)
Fire Alarm Systems Maintenance
Fire Truck Training
Food Service Supervisors: Basic
Human Nutrition Diet Therapy
& Food Service Management
Grievance Investigators
Hazardous Materials Communication
Hazardous Communications Standards
Hostage/Riot
Human Interaction
How to Build a Hazardous Commu-
nications Program
How to Conduct a Monthly Safety
Inspection
How to Identify and Manage Haz-
ardous wastes
Identifying and Solving Crime-
Related problems

Identifying Passive Inmates
Infection Control in the Penal
Environment
Inmate Mental Health Needs and
DOC Mental Health Services
Inmate Health Screening
Inmate Administrative Remedy
Procedure
DOP Inmate Health Screening
Interpersonal Communication &
Staff Relations Skills
Interpersonal Communication for
Correctional Personnel
Introduction to SAMNA Spreadsheet
Introduction to Computer (Office
Management)
JC-80 Computer Training
LPN Certification for IV Therapy
Mailing Procedures for Department
of Corrections
Management by Objectives Training
for Center Superintendent
Nursing Aspects of Inmates Experi-
encing Disturbances of the
Integumentary System
Office Safety Computer Workstation
Officevision/400–Introduction
Occupational Exposure to Blood-
borne Pathogens in Dentistry
Oral and Written Communication
DOP Orientation to Medical Review
of NC, Inc.
Pepper, Oleoresin Capsicum (OC),
Spray
Personal Safety in the Office Envi-
ronment
DOP Presentence Diagnostic Program;
Purpose, Process, Procedure
Prevention of Transmission of
Human Immuno Deficiency
Virus & Hepatitis B Virus—A
Guide for Probation Parole
Office Staff
Prevention of Transmission of
Human Immuno Deficiency
Virus & Hepatitis B Virus—DOC
Staff
Preventative Intervention
Techniques

Preparing for Court and Testifying in Court

PPO Advanced Legal Powers & Duties of PPO (506) Part I

Protection Against Occupational Exposure to AIDS Virus for DOC

Procedure for PRN Controlled Substances South Piedmont Area Correctional Centers

Professional Write

Preparation of Mental Health Treatment

Performing Urinalysis with Microscopic Exam

Road Officers Training

Safety Inspection Training Video

Safety Representatives Conference and Workshop

Self-Care for Chaplains

Rules for the Correctional Staff Hostage

DOP—Sexual Offender Treatment

Scoring Rorschach by Exner's System

PPO 11 (Advanced Techniques of Search, Transporting Violators & Use of Mechanical Restraints (506) Part II

DOP-Testing Orientation

Use of Scott Air Pak II-A

Ventilation System—Operations & Maintenance

What to Expect When OSHA Inspects

Work Performance Review

Writing to Communicate

Written Communication

The Criminal Mind

In reviewing this list of courses, note the emphasis placed on legal, medical, technological, and communication issues. The increasingly sophisticated nature of the correctional work environment is clearly reflected in this curriculum.

Source: North Carolina Department of Corrections, 1996.

Emergency Management Training

Life in corrections is not always routine. Emergencies occur, often with a serious loss of life and property. The fundamental goal of emergency management training is to prepare every correctional employee to effectively respond to an emergency. The primary principle underlying this type of training is that emergencies are most often unexpected and the ability of every staff member to effectively respond to emergencies is best nurtured through a skills application approach. Training can involve any or all of the following: (1) orientation and education sessions that formally train staff in the knowledge necessary for emergency plan implementation, (2) walk-through drills that require staff to physically perform response activities, (3) functional drills that train employees to perform specific functions such as using fire extinguishers, (4) evacuation drills to train staff in the proper procedures to rapidly evacuate specific prison buildings, and (5) full-scale exercises designed to simulate an actual emergency and provide employees with an opportunity to sharpen their emergency management skills (Federal Emergency Management Agency, 1993:22–23).

The full-scale emergency exercise provides the best opportunity for employees to learn emergency management. In a prison, this type of exercise can range from a simulated fire in a housing unit to a simulated riot involving the entire facility. In community corrections, it can involve a residential facility caught in an urban riot, the search for a resident who has not returned from furlough, or the procedures to be followed when a probationer has removed an electronic-monitoring device. A full-scale exercise is conducted in accordance with six basic principles: (1) Central Office staff or community emergency management professionals, not facility staff, plan the emergency simulation, (2) the simulated emergency is scheduled for a time outside of the normal working hours, that is, it does not happen between 8 A.M. and 4:30 P.M. on a weekday, (3) there is no advance warning provided to the staff who are being evaluated, (4) evaluators make an extensive use of "wild cards" (i.e., present unexpected situations to team members who think they have everything under control) during response and recovery, (5) there is a full participation by community emergency resources, and (6) outside evaluators conduct the on-site evaluation of staff performance and make suggestions for further training (Freeman, 1996c:172).

Emergency Management Team Because effective emergency response is such an extremely complicated process, it is necessary for correctional managers to create emergency management teams. Depending on the nature of the emergency, an institutional or community correctional facility may, during the course of the emergency, require the use of one or all of the following:

Fire Safety Team—Responsible for fire prevention activities, fire safety training, and response to fires.

Correctional Emergency Response Team—Uses controlled force to manage inmate disturbances ranging from an inmate refusing to leave his cell to full-scale riots.

Hostage Negotiation Team—Responsible for negotiating with inmate hostage takers for the safe release of all hostages.

Intelligence Unit—Gathers information about inmate leaders, gangs, and any inmate-related activities or plans that may threaten institutional security.

Medical Response Team—Provides for the medical care of employees and inmates hurt during the course of any emergency.

Special Transportation Unit—Responsible for the safe evacuation of employees and offenders from a correctional facility severely damaged in an emergency.

Damage Assessment Team—Provides a postemergency estimate and prioritization of necessary facility repairs.

Damage Repair Team—Makes the prioritized repairs.

Escapee Recovery Team—Enters the community for the purpose of capturing escaped offenders.

Posttraumatic Assessment Team—Determines the amount of postemergency psychological trauma and makes referrals to appropriate counseling providers.

Criminal Prosecution Team—Gathers evidence of offender criminal activity and helps prepare cases and witnesses for the prosecution of offenders.

Litigation Response Team—Prepares the defense against postemergency litigation and assists employees who will testify.

Information Management Team—Responsible for coordinating the communication process during an emergency situation.

Command Post Recording Team—Documents all decisions made by top managers during an emergency response.

Media/Community Information Group—Provides the media and community with accurate information during and after an emergency. Has the primary responsibility for rumor control.

Architectural Assessment Team—Evaluates physical plant design in terms of emergency prevention and response needs.

Stepdown Committee—Coordinates the recovery activities of a correctional facility that has experienced an emergency (Freeman, 1996c:29–40).

The selection process for membership in any of the above teams is straightforward. Any employee who volunteers for assignment to a specific emergency management team is interviewed, may have to undergo psychological testing and physical agility testing, and has his or her work record thoroughly evaluated before being accepted on the team. Acceptance is based on the ability to meet specific team-related criteria. For example, volunteers for a hostage negotiation team are expected to have a knowledge of corrections, inmates, and human behavior; sufficient intelligence to translate conflict resolution theory into practice; a high tolerance for frustration and the ability to remain calm in threatening situations; the ability to handle high levels of stress; strong verbal skills; a position that does not have the authority to make command decisions; and the ability to work well with other correctional employees, especially C.O.s (Freeman, 1996c:31). Once selected, emergency management team members undergo the formal training previously described with an emphasis on simulated emergencies.

Training the Managers

Our focus thus far has been on the training of line staff, but correctional managers also require specialized training. In the early 1990s, state DOC leadership began to recognize the need to train managers to be leaders. Taking the lead in this effort have been the South Carolina and the California DOCs

(Gengler and Riley, 1995:104). In 1993, South Carolina began a program called Leadership SCDC that provides intensive training to 50 correctional managers and community leaders each year. The program consists of 6 two-day sessions (scheduled throughout the year) that cover leadership, environment and the economy, education, governance, total quality management, health and human services, and cultural diversity. In 1994, California opened the Leadership Institute, which offers a six-week curriculum that covers leadership inventories, communication and goal-directed leadership, the hands-on approach to news media interviews and court and legislative testimony, ethics and motivation, "moving from vision to reality," and short-term and strategic planning. This program is conducted over a six-month period and requires some course work to be completed upon return to the job site. Box 12–4 presents the curriculum of the Leadership Institute. A review of this curriculum provides an insight into the complexity of correctional leadership.

BOX 12–4 LEADERSHIP INSTITUTE CURRICULUM

Week 1. Introduction to Leadership (Kalinich)

> Overall Learning Objective: Understand basic concepts of leadership, visionary leadership, and participatory decision making. Understand fundamental aspects of problem analysis and problem-solving techniques in a participatory decision-making environment.

Day 1.   Taking a Leadership Perspective
           Learning Objectives:

1. Identify the elements of paradigm shifts.
2. Identify the paradigm shifts expected of participants.
3. Identify three perspectives for understanding organizations.
4. Identify the elements and process of critical thinking.
5. Apply problem analysis techniques and critical thinking to CDC problems.
6. Apply the basic rules of collaborative team work and group dynamics.
7. Identify the significance of paradigm shift, critical thinking and problem analysis, and team work to leadership.

Day 2.   Defining Yourself as a Leader
          Learning Objectives:

1. Identify the need for future planning and visionary leadership.
2. Identify the differences between leadership and management.
3. List individual leadership traits, skills, and behaviors.
4. Identify the beliefs and behaviors of visionary leaders.
5. Identify the focus and functions of visionary leadership.
6. List the essential methods of visionary leadership.
7. Apply the process of participatory decision making and identify its motivational impact.
8. Identify the benefits of participation and working as a team.

Day 3.   Developing Your Leadership Inventory
          Learning Objectives:

1. Utilize the leadership self-assessment tool, Organizational Inventory, to determine the human leadership resources within your organization.
2. Develop an inventory of the leadership skills within the organization and those skills needing development, or introduction through   group   discussion.
3. Analyze your leadership skills and how you use them through self-assessment.
4. Exchange information on your leadership skills and improve your ability to work as teams.
5. Gauge your ability and comfort level in employing leadership skills.
6. Identify your personal group leadership skills.
7. Apply visionary planning techniques through a team problem-analysis framework.

Day 4.   Organizational Analysis Process
          Learning Objectives:

1. Identify the elements of an organization's mission. Identify the constraints or forces that "mold" an organization's mission.
2. Identify the major forces that "mold" CDC's mission.
3. Apply WOTSUP analysis to identify the top strengths and weaknesses of CDC.
4. Determine the impact of CDC weaknesses on team CDC problem(s).
5. Determine the top five CDC weaknesses that can be improved.

Day 5.   Creating a Vision for CDC Organizing and Leading Teams
          Learning Objectives:

1. Identify actual current CDC mission.
2. Create CDC mission for 2001.
3. Identify key visionary leadership skills that will be required to realize 2001 CDC mission.
4. Apply 2001 mission and identified leadership skills to group problem(s), analysis.

5. Identify how teamwork is affected by integrity (commitment, trust, clarity of purpose and goals, and communications).
6. Identify the process of facilitating individual participation and creativity.
7. Identify the process of sustaining individual and group motivation.
8. Identify the importance of interpersonal communication skills in teamwork.

Week 2. Contingent, Transformational, and Visionary Leadership
Overall Learning Objective: To familiarize the participant with the component parts of contingency leadership, transformational leadership, and visionary leadership, to develop multiple approaches to problem solving, and to provide access to the use of computer technology to enhance organizational decision making.

Day 1.   The Context of Leadership in Corrections Learning Objectives:

1. Identify attributes and characteristics of effective leaders.
2. Define key elements of contingency leadership.
3. Employ contingency leadership through the identification of five steps to success.

Day 2.   Contingency Planning in Corrections
Learning Objectives:

1. Identify steps to developing a contingency plan.
2. Identify steps to environmental scanning and show relevance to corrections.

Day 3.   Transformational Leadership in Corrections
Learning Objectives:

1. Identify steps to transforming correctional organizations.
2. Identify various organizational paradigms.
3. Identify characteristics of effective teams within organizations.

Day 4.   Information Systems and Leadership Goals
Learning Objectives:

1. Identify future issues facing the CDC.
2. Identify elements of leadership training and implications for future use.

Day 5.   Visionary Leadership and Corrections
Learning Objectives:

1. Identify future issues facing the CDC.
2. Identify elements of leadership training and implications for future use.

Week 3. Leadership, Law, and Ethics (Stojkovic)
Overall Learning Objective: To identify models of ethical thinking and how they relate to the workings of the CDC. Additionally, to identify methods for motivating correctional employees within the CDC.

Day 1.   Ethical Reasoning and Corrections
Learning Objectives:

1. List the types of ethical reasoning.
2. Identify ethical theories and corrections.
3. Create an "Ethical Checklist" for the CDC.

Day 2.   Ethical Behavior and Corrections
Learning Objectives:

1. Explore and identify the ethical source of the top 5 goals of the CDC.
2. Identify the relationship between ethics, goals, and Mission Statement of the CDC.
3. Identify the relationship between ethics, goals, and departmental policies.

Day 3.   Defining Ethical Standards Within Corrections Learning Objective:

1. Create ethical standards for the CDC.

Day 4.   The Motivation Process and Corrections
Learning Objectives:

1. Identify motivation factors.
2. Identify motivational methods.
3. Develop a motivational plan for correctional employees.

Day 5.   Implementation of Motivational Plan and Practical Exercise
Learning Objective:

1. Implement a motivational plan for the CDC.

Week 4.   Transitional Planning and Organizational Transformations
Overall Learning Objective: Examine the relationships among leadership, organizational culture, and strategic vision. Explore methods for analyzing internal culture. Learn the general contributions of evaluation to systematic thinking and strategic planning. Apply concepts to CDC problems and issues.

Day 1.   Organizational Culture and Leadership
Learning Objectives:

1. Examine the notion of organizational culture.
2. Define organizational culture.
3. Develop a plan for analyzing internal culture.
4. Analyze elements of CDC culture.

Day 2.   Evaluation in Visionary Leadership Learning Objectives:

1. Review the benefits of program and project evaluation for developing strategic vision.

2. Identify the components of evaluation and the process of evaluation planning.
3. Develop an understanding of types of evaluation based on what is to be evaluated.

Day 3. Evaluation in CDC Problems Learning Objectives:

1. Examine methods of evaluation appropriate to various CDC issues.
2. Discuss development of evaluation plans.
3. Explore issues related to communication and use of evaluation information.

Day 4. Group Processes and Leadership Learning Objectives:

1. Examine research on group processes and strategic vision.
2. Discuss the Leadership Institute experience and extend to CDC issues and strategic vision.
3. Redefine and increase specification of group projects.

Day 5. Group Project Planning Learning Objectives:

1. Continue to develop and refine statement of group problems.
2. Identify information requirements relevant to group projects.
3. Organize and plan for collection of information by group.

Week 5. Visionary Leadership: Strategic Planning and Planning for Implementation (Lovell)
Overall Learning Objective: To focus on key processes of these key processes by example, using group sessions and the contexts of the CDC themes being addressed across the leadership groups.

Day 1. Policy Planning and Transformational Leadership Learning Objectives:

1. Identify key elements of policy planning and relate these to transformational leadership.
2. Develop comprehensive strategies by group to address CDC themes previously identified.

Day 2. Strategic Planning: Goal and Problem Identification, Forecasting Learning Objectives:

1. Discuss problem and goal identification issues and techniques. Apply these by group to CDC themes.
2. Discuss forecasting issues and techniques. Apply these by group to CDC themes.

Day 3. Strategic Planning: Generating and Testing Alternatives Learning Objectives:

1. Discuss overall considerations regarding generation and testing of alternatives for implementation. Apply these by group to CDC themes.
2. Review techniques for generating and testing alternatives. Apply these by group to CDC themes.

Day 4.   Implementation Planning: Key Elements and Techniques
         Learning Objectives:

1. Discuss key elements in implementation planning. Apply these by group to CDC themes.
2. Review techniques for controlling implementation and drafting implementation plans. Apply these by group to CDC themes.

Day 5.   Benefit-Cost Analysis: Summary
         Learning Objectives:

1. Discuss general considerations and issues in using benefit-cost techniques. Apply these by group to CDC themes.
2. Summarize and discuss the week's work and transition to week 6.

Week 6. CDC and the Media and Legislative Process
         Overall Learning Objective: To identify strategies for correctional leaders when interacting with the media. Introduce correctional leaders to the legislative processes and activities of the department.

Day 1.   Media
         Learning Objective:

1. Steps in how to deal with the media.

Day 2.   Crisis Communications and a Practical Media Exercise
         Learning Objective:

1. Methods to communicate in a crisis situation.

Day 3.   Practical Exercise, the CDC Public Information Policy
         Learning Objective:

1. Identify the CDC Public Information Policy.

Day 4.   Legislative Process and Corrections (A.M.) Learning Objectives:

1. Discuss relationship between CDC and the legislative process.
2. Discuss various and develop conceptual models of the various constituency groups that politically impact CDC.
3. Discuss the process, format, and culture of the legislature.
4. Discuss the relationship between the CDC and the executive branch of government. Identify Final Strategies for Presentations (P.M.) Participant Feedback to Institute Staff

Day 5.   Group Presentations and Luncheon

Source: California Department of Corrections. *Leadership Institute Curriculum* (1997c).

Many of the managers who have attended these programs say that their ability to perform has been enhanced by the structured opportunity to develop new skills in both management and leadership (Gengler and Riley, 1995:107). In California, managers not accepted into the Leadership Institute can still receive training through curriculums offered to first- and second-line supervisors, support staff, correctional sergeants, lieutenants, and captains.

Training is an increasingly sophisticated process that often requires a level of expertise not found within the correctional organization, especially if it is small. But, as we shall see next, correctional managers have an outside source of training expertise and assistance available to them.

National Institute of Corrections as a Training Resource

We already considered in Chapter 9 the role of the National Institute of Corrections (NIC) in providing management and leadership training. In addition, the NIC also provides training in several other areas of corrections.

Development of Training Curriculums

Instructors and training program coordinators in prisons, jails, and community corrections agencies can receive technical assistance in the identification of training needs, strategies for training development and delivery, evaluation of training programs, management of training systems, and the training-for-trainers approach (National Institute of Corrections, 1997:6). Combined, these five areas of assistance can provide any correctional organization with the structure it needs to provide effective basic, in-service, and specialized training.

NIC Jails Division This branch of the NIC offers technical assistance and training seminars in such areas as policy and procedure development, jail security, legal issues, facility review, standards and accreditation, suicide prevention, medical services, classification, data management, jail industries, and inmate job training and placement (National Institute of Corrections, 1997:4).

NIC Executive Leadership Program for Women In the early 1990s, the NIC Prisons Division decided to confront the challenge of the underrepresentation of women in top correctional management positions. A leadership curriculum was designed to enhance the promotion potential of those female correctional employees interested in career advancement (Moss and Rans, 1997:116–119). The curriculum was developed after administration of an Organizational Culture Questionnaire (OCI) to 48 directors of corrections. The OCI revealed that women must move more frequently than men (44 percent of women directors had worked at three to five correctional agencies during their careers while only 20 percent of men had moved that frequently) if they wish to advance their careers and must work longer hours (78 percent of women directors worked more than 56 hours per week compared to 44 percent of male directors). The OCI also revealed that women needed to develop competency in three specific leadership areas—strategic, communication, and consensual. Strategic competency involves the ability to analyze the impact of decisions by using a long-term and big-picture approach to problem solving. Communication competency involves the ability to clearly state goals and expectations while maintaining a precise and constant flow of information. Consensual competency involves the ability to collect input and opinion from a variety of individuals as part of the decision-making process.

A five-day Leadership program was developed around the need to develop these competencies and three goals were articulated: (1) to provide executive leadership development for women in corrections, (2) to establish strategies for women's long-term promotional success, and (3) to facilitate planning that supports personal learning and career opportunities. The first program in September 1994 involved primarily women who report directly to Commissioners of corrections. By the end of Fiscal Year 1997, 100 women had participated in the program. Program participants frequently return to the program as members of the training faculty and are responsible for the development of similar programs in their agencies.

Overall satisfaction with the program has been very high and it has evolved to now have three phases. Phase I is the original five-day leadership program. Phase II is a three-day follow-up training program that emphasizes strategic thinking—the ability to formulate and implement organizational change. Phase III has extended the leadership program to directors of corrections.

Training is the second stage in employee socialization. We now turn to the third stage: evaluation of individual and organizational effectiveness. Professionalization requires a periodic evaluation of both the individual and the organization to identify professional conduct that should be rewarded and behavioral deviations that should be corrected.

EVALUATING INDIVIDUAL PERFORMANCE

The evaluation of individuals is typically accomplished by measuring personal performance of assigned tasks against predetermined criteria. The most commonly used set of criteria is the job description. For example, a captain assigned to evaluate the effectiveness of a lieutenant would first look at the job description for that position. Box 12–5 displays the job description of a corrections lieutenant:

BOX 12–5 CORRECTIONAL LIEU-TENANT JOB DESCRIPTION

Provides supervision to Corrections Officers and Corrections Sergeants.
Assigns and reviews the work of Corrections Sergeants, and serves as second-level supervisor to Corrections Officers.

Ensures all training requirements are met.
Tours and monitors the facility to ensure that staff performs duties in accordance with oral and written instructions.
Resolves security problems related to the work by applying the rules and regulations which govern the specific problem.
Writes and submits security/other reports and operating procedures as instructed or established by written policy.
Ensures that reports are clear, complete, and concise.
Reviews all logbooks and policy books and updates or replaces as needed.
Schedules security staff to ensure appropriate coverage of posts as outlined in the approved post audit and duty roster.
Completes and submits daily time-keeping records on time worked and leave used.
Ensures that time-keeping procedures are adhered to.
Approves/denies leave requests of Sergeants.
Monitors leave balances to ensure that leave requests are appropriate and leave balances are not lost.
Ensures time records are maintained accurately and are submitted to the Employee Relations office in a timely and appropriate manner.
Conducts sanitation and security inspections pursuant to agency policies.
Takes necessary steps to resolve issues or reports identified problems to higher supervision, as appropriate.
Gathers written and oral information relating to problems with inmates or staff.
Determines actions needed and recommends or initiates actions as appropriate.

Provides counseling and guidance to staff and inmates.

Responds to inmate and staff grievances.

Evaluates work performance of staff and inmates.

Serves as a member of various committees for custody review, work assignments, and recommendations for work release/furloughs, etc.

Performs other duties as assigned.

Source: Virginia Department of Corrections. *Position Descriptions* (1996).

Principles of Effective Individual Evaluation

Employee evaluation is most effective when it involves a yearly written review of individual employee performance that is communicated in a face-to-face meeting with the manager. The evaluation should also be designed to create a feedback process, which provides a rationale for the reinforcement of professional conduct through rewards or the correction of deficiencies through counseling or formal disciplinary action.

Reinforcement of Professional Conduct

The reinforcement of professional conduct can be accomplished through the use of intrinsic or extrinsic rewards. Robbins (1993:585) noted that performance evaluation plays a relatively small role in reward decisions in organizations where unions exist. The ability of correctional managers to reward outstanding employee performance through the use of extrinsic rewards such as pay raises or promotion is severely restricted by collective bargaining agreements (CBAs). However, intrinsic rewards in the form of more responsibility, opportunities for professional growth, and participation in decision making can be provided through the development of the employee empowerment methods discussed in Chapter 11.

Correction of Deficiencies The correction of personal deficiencies usually involves a process of counseling, stated expectations for improvement, and an established time frame for that improvement to be produced. Disciplinary action is a possibility, depending on the nature of the deficiency, as long as it is administered in accordance with the CBA.

Models of Individual Evaluation

There are two models of individual evaluation particularly relevant to corrections. The first model is highly subjective and rates personal traits. The second model measures achievement of concrete, time-defined performance objectives.

Personal Trait Model

This model, frequently referred to as a "graphic rating scale," typically uses a rating system (unsatisfactory—average—good—superior—excellent) to score a checklist of personal traits such as loyalty, quantity and quality of work, decisiveness, depth of knowledge, ability to communicate, planning, honesty, effort, appearance, ability to accept criticism, attitude, initiative, and cooperation.

This model, although relatively easy to develop, administer, and apply to a variety of different job classifications, is highly subjective and criteria for evaluation are vague and rarely defined. A major drawback to the personal trait method is a strong tendency for managers to provide "Aunt Fanny" evaluations, where everyone is rated as *good*. There are a number of possible explanations for this tendency. First, terms such as *loyalty, cooperation, attitude,* and *decisiveness* are difficult to quantify, can have many different meanings, and may seem unrelated to the job. Second, many managers are reluctant to criticize because they don't want to offend the employees they supervise. Third, managers often feel unprepared for, and thus try to avoid, the confrontations that can arise when an employee feels an evaluation is unfair and accuses the manager of personal bias and lack of objectivity (National Academy of Corrections, 1984). Consequently, this model has little practical usefulness because research has failed to establish any significant relationship between the traits being measured and individual performance. Numerous studies have established that trait criteria are largely useless in evaluating employee performance (Butler and Yorks, 1984).

Management by Objectives Model

The management by objectives (MBO) model attempts to eliminate the above problems by evaluating individual performance in terms of well-defined, concrete, measurable objectives organized within a time frame. MBO is a product of goal-setting theory (Locke, 1968) and is based on the assumption that the intention to work to achieve a specific goal is a major source of motivation; goals provide structure for individuals by telling them what needs to be done and how much effort will be required to accomplish them. But in order to produce the required level of performance, goals must be specific and there must be feedback to let the individual know if progress is being made. MBO reflects the mission statement by developing a specific hierarchy of operative goals for units and individuals and requires individual managers and employees to mutually identify goals and structure goal achievement and evaluation in terms of four criteria (Carroll and Tosi, 1973): goal specificity, participative decision making, an explicit time period, and performance feedback.

Goal Specificity MBO evaluation criteria are negotiated and less subjective than the criteria in the personal trait model. Goals are presented in the form of specific objectives that are concrete and measurable: to reduce C.O. overtime by 12 percent; to increase inmate bed capacity by 8 percent; to submit all reports no later than 30 days after an assignment has been given; to increase the number of inmate basketball

courts by the end of the fiscal year; to classify every new inmate within 30 days of reception. For another example, the MBO objectives for a Food Services Manager might be to (1) increase the variety of the inmate evening meal by the addition of three entrees by March 15, 1999, (2) develop a comprehensive proposal (including all cost estimates) for a 200-seat expansion of the main inmate dining room and submit the proposal by June 30, 1999, (3) complete training of the inmate crew for the new auxiliary kitchen by April 15, 1999, (4) assist Maintenance in developing a vegetable garden expansion plan for submission by May 1, 1999, (5) complete installation of the new food services computer inventory system by June 30, 1999, and (6) ensure that the four new Food Services Instructors have completed their training by April 30, 1999.

If the goals are not specific, concrete, and measurable, MBO is doomed to failure before it is even implemented.

Participative Decision Making MBO requires managers and subordinates to jointly choose the goals and determine how and when goal accomplishment will be measured. The participation of subordinates in this process is expected to provide them with a sense of personal responsibility for achieving the goals because they play a role in determining the priority of certain activities.

Specific Time Period Each objective has a specific time period in which it is to be completed. Less difficult objectives may have a target date of three to six months. More difficult objectives will have target dates of nine to 12 months. The setting of an end date by which the goal is expected to be accomplished provides an incentive for the employee that encourages time management and efficient planning.

Feedback on Performance The employee receives continuous informal feedback on performance supplemented by periodic formal review and evaluations by management. Performance without feedback leaves an employee without the guidance so critical to maintaining high levels of performance or improving on low levels.

Is MBO Successful? Kast and Rosenzweig (1979:168) noted that MBO programs have been used successfully by a number of business organizations interested in integrating organizational and individual goals. The most successful programs appear to be those that are applied to all individuals within an organization, not just selected individuals with performance problems. However, Ford (1979) found that MBO is not a panacea. It will not effectively motivate employee performance if the following factors are present: (1) unrealistic expectations regarding results, (2) lack of top management commitment, and (3) an inability or unwillingness of management to allocate rewards based on performance. One of the most difficult obstacles to implementation of a successful MBO program in corrections is the reluctance of some managers to share decision making and goal setting with their subordinates. This can lead to the lack of commitment that short-circuits the program.

The evaluation of individual performance provides a picture of how well each individual is performing assigned tasks, but what about the organization as a whole? Is the organization achieving its mission? There is only one way to answer this question. Organizational performance must be evaluated.

EVALUATING ORGANIZATIONAL PERFORMANCE

Although most correctional organizations have internal audit units responsible for the periodic evaluation of the performance of the various departments on the organizational chart, these audits typically cannot perform an evaluation of the total organization at a specific point in time. During one year the focus may be accounting procedures, with a shift in focus to information management systems the following year.

This department- or function-specific approach allows problems to develop unnoticed in areas not being audited. For example, serious violations of the confidentiality provisions governing information management systems may go unnoticed because uncontrolled employee access to computer data banks has developed while the internal audit unit is focused on the organization's accounting procedures.

The most effective method of evaluating organizational effectiveness at a specific point in time is to use a multigoal, multimeasure approach (Blomberg, 1983) that rates the organization in terms of compliance with a set of objective, predetermined standards. The ACA accreditation process is an example of such a process.

American Correctional Association Accreditation Process

The heart of the ACA accreditation process is 463 performance standards designed to provide an objective measurement of effectiveness for every relevant area of correctional operation. These standards are contained in the 1,880-page *Standards for Adult Correctional Institutions* (3rd ed.), where they are organized into categories, sections, and subsections.

There are five functional categories into which the standards are grouped: Part One—Administration and Management; Part Two—Physical Plant; Part Three—Institutional Operations; Part Four—Institutional Services; and Part Five—Inmate Programs.

Each category is divided into sections. Administration and Management, for example, has seven sections: Section A—General Administration; Section B—Fiscal Management; Section C—Personnel; Section D—Training and Staff Development; Section E—Case Records; Section F—Information Systems and Research; and Section G—Citizen Involvement and Volunteers.

Finally, each section is then divided into subsections. Section C (Personnel), for example, is subdivided into: Personnel Policy Manual; Staffing Requirements; Equal Employment Opportunity; Selection and Promotion; Probationary Term; Provisional Appointments; Criminal Record Check; Physical Examination; Drug-free Workplace; Performance Reviews; Compensation and Benefits; Personnel Files; Code of Ethics; Confidentiality of Information; and Employee Assistance Program. Each subsection contains a sufficient number of standards to address the subject (American Correctional Association, 1990:xvi–xxii).

The ACA annually reviews its standards and makes revisions that reflect the increasing professionalization of the field. For example, in 1997, the ACA added a visitation policy requirement for correctional facilities and a standard that juvenile training schools develop and adopt a health assessment policy for each new reception (*Corrections Professional,* 1997a:7).

Defining the Standards

The 463 ACA standards are classified as being either mandatory or nonmandatory. The mandatory standards cover such areas as safety and emergency procedures. An example of a mandatory standard is the following:

3-4200: Written policy, procedure, and practice provide for a comprehensive and thorough monthly inspection of the institution by a qualified fire and safety officer for compliance with safety and fire prevention standards. There is a weekly fire and safety inspection of the institution by a qualified departmental staff member. This policy and procedure is reviewed annually and updated as needed.

Every mandatory standard must be met if accreditation status is to be granted. The nonmandatory standards cover routine operational issues such as: "3-4206: There is a written plan for preventive maintenance of the physical plant." Ninety percent of the nonmandatory standards must be met for accreditation status to be awarded.

Accreditation Audit

Most DOCS have developed Accreditation and Standards Units staffed by Accreditation Managers. Their preparation for an ACA accreditation audit frequently includes "mock" audits and visits by managers from other institutions to evaluate local policies and procedures and correct deficiencies before the official audit. The ACA accreditation audit itself involves a three-person team of independent auditors (i.e., they are not employees of the facility or DOC whose facility is being evaluated) who conduct a three-day visit on-site during which they rate organizational compliance with the 463 standards. In addition to reviewing all policy and procedures manuals, the auditors talk to offenders and staff to learn their perceptions of how well the organization functions. The role of the auditors is to determine if each standard is covered by written policy and whether that policy is known to and being properly used by staff.

At the end of the third day of their visit, the audit team meets with the facility staff in an exit interview, reviews the team findings, and either awards or withholds accreditation status. The exit interview is frequently a very emotional experience for staff. Facilities failing the initial audit can ask for a re-audit after correction of deficiencies. Facilities earning accreditation can ask for re-accreditation every three years. In 1991, more than 1,000 facilities and programs were involved in the ACA accreditation process. In the opinion of one observer, "[t]his shows that as corrections professionals we believe accreditation is truly the foundation of our profession" (Phyfer, 1992:8).

Scope of Accreditation

The Profile at the beginning of the chapter suggested that the accreditation process can be of value for both the new facility and the established facility. But it can have other value as well. For example, proponents of ACA accreditation argue that it can be a particularly powerful tool for managers who are concerned about inmate litigation or operating under court order. Black and Nestlerode (1989) described the success of the

Larimer Country Detention Facility in using accreditation to reduce inmate litigation. Roberts (1992:52) reported the "rehabilitation" of the Kansas State Penitentiary, after three years of accreditation efforts, from a prison with enormous deficiencies "to a state-of-the-art correctional facility." And after the Louisiana Department of Public Safety and Corrections earned accreditation, U.S. District Judge Frank Polozola issued a court order on September 25, 1996, that ended judicial supervision at 100 of the 105 Louisiana state and parish prisons, effective April 1, 1997 (Clayton, 1996:125).

One warning must be noted here, however: the ACA standards represent *minimum* standards for correctional organizations. If a facility fails to achieve accreditation, its managers may find that failure a prominent part of class action inmate litigation.

Is Accreditation Achieving Its Potential as a Management Tool?

The answer to this question is not yet clear. There are two areas of concern: the line staff perception of the accreditation process and the question of process effectiveness.

Line Staff Perception of Accreditation

Czajkowski et al. (1995), in evaluating 566 responses to a national survey of accredited facilities and programs in the United States and Canada, found that managers view the accreditation process more favorably than do line staff. While managers tended to see accreditation as a management tool that effectively increased the allocation of resources, improved relations with outside agencies, provided justification for budget requests, and allowed for more efficient evaluation of staff compliance with policy, line staff viewed the process as lacking tangible benefits, creating unnecessary work, and negatively affecting staff morale. The researchers concluded that managers seeking accreditation status need to recognize the additional workload that process places

on line staff and make a concerted effort to provide them with extra support (Czajkowski et al., 1995:49). For example, it is easy for a top manager to direct employees to label and inventory all the fluid containers in their work area, but it may take line staff days or weeks to accomplish this task. If the impact of this additional work on busy employees is not recognized, accreditation may become yet another source of job-related stress.

Is the Process Effective? In August, 1982, David Bazelon, Senior Judge of the First U.S. Circuit Court of Appeals in Washington, D.C., resigned from the Commission on Accreditation for Corrections, charging that the Commission (1) refuses to allow public involvement in the accreditation process, (2) uses "inherently unreliable" audit techniques, (3) will not accept constructive criticism, (4) has priorities that are "fundamentally flawed," (5) has conflicts of interests with the facilities it is evaluating, and (6) has allowed accreditation to become a "propaganda vehicle for corrections" (Bazelon, 1982:20).

Judge Bazelon was particularly concerned about the structure of the ACA accreditation process. Because participation in the process is completely voluntary in most states, very few correctional organizations are actually required by law or court order to undergo accreditation. If managers do apply on behalf of their facility for accreditation, they may reject ACA-appointed auditors they believe will be too strict, schedule the audit (instead of it being unannounced), elect to not correct deficiencies, and withdraw from the process at any time. Moreover, the auditors are themselves correctional employees, which raises questions about their objectivity. Judge Bazelon warned that "[t]he commission has broken faith with the public and has betrayed the promise of accreditation. In resigning, I urge my fellow commissioners to change their present course. If they do not, this country will have lost one of the last, best hopes for reforming . . . our prison system" (Bazelon, 1982:24).

Eight years after Judge Bazelon's resignation, Rauch (1990) noted that the debate over accreditation had produced two schools of thought. The first school charges that accreditation standards are so high they can only be met by "country club prisons." The second school charges that accreditation is such an easy process that any facility can achieve the status (Rauch, 1990:100). While unable to conclusively determine which of the two schools of thought on the issue was correct, Rauch (1990:100–101) did note that in 1988, 594 superintendents expressed an interest in accreditation, but only 28 percent actually sought and achieved the status. Rauch concluded that "[t]his clearly shows that many correctional facilities in the United States are being run below ACA standard requirements, widely recognized as the minimum level considered adequate by the correctional profession" (Rauch, 1990:134).

Suggestions for Improvement

To encourage a higher degree of participation in ACA accreditation, adoption of a multi-tiered system of accreditation modeled along the lines of the Joint Commission on Accreditation of Healthcare Organizations (JCAHO) has been proposed (Branham, 1993:16). JCAHO guidelines provide for (1) accreditation with commendation, (2) accreditation for "substantial compliance" with standards, and (3) conditional accreditation, which requires correction of specific deficiencies and a second audit before full accreditation can be awarded. This approach allows for recognition that a facility is trying to perform up to recognized standards and substantial or conditional accreditation provides the motivation to work harder that may not be provided by a simple pronouncement that the organization has failed the audit.

Selection, training, and evaluation are all essential components in the correctional employee socialization process. But there is one more consideration. Is the correctional environment conducive to professionalization?

Creating an Environment Conducive to Professionalization

The chapter epigraph suggests that the "growing" of people is the most productive activity in which an organization can engage. Professionalization is a method for growing people. However, in order for professionalization to flourish, correctional managers must be aware of two powerful influences on individual motivation: the individual employee's perception of how fairly they are being treated by the organization and their expectation of being rewarded for their efforts. We can examine these two influences by briefly reviewing equity and expectancy theory.

Equity Theory

Equity theory brings to managerial awareness a fundamental issue of fairness: the comparative worth of job inputs and job outcomes. Inputs are defined as what an individual puts into the job (effort, duties, and performance). Outcomes are defined as the benefits the individual receives as a result of their inputs (salary, benefits, promotional opportunity). These can be expressed in terms of the ratio inputs:outcomes. If the ratio is perceived to be equal, then a condition of equity exists and the employee perceives that he or she is being treated fairly. But if the ratio is unequal, equity tension exists.

A potential source of conflict in any organization is that employees routinely compare their inputs and outcomes with the inputs and outcomes of others in order to establish an "equity norm" (Adams, 1963). The comparison can be with co-workers, friends, neighbors, past jobs, or individuals in other organizations who are performing work perceived as comparable. If the ratio of inputs to outcomes among individuals, or groups, is perceived to be equal, then the employees making the comparison will feel that they are being treated fairly. If the ratios are not equal, then one employee (or group of employees) will feel that they are being treated less fairly than the employees with whom they are making the comparison. For example, C.O.s making $8,000 less than correctional counselors may strongly believe that they are being underpaid, while the counselors are being overpaid, because the officers perceive their job to be much more demanding and dangerous. Jail C.O.s making $10,000 a year less than prison C.O.s may feel undervalued because they believe the jobs are equivalent. The result in both cases is equity tension.

Equity Tension as a Source of Motivation

J. Stacy Adams (1965) has proposed that equity tension can be an important source of motivation. Similarly, Greenberg (1989) suggested that motivation that is inspired by equity tension can lead employees to make the following changes:

1. Change their inputs (not work as hard). On an individual level, this takes the form of taking more time to do less. An example is the probation officer who stops for a half-hour coffee break before visiting a client instead of going directly from the office to the probationer's home.

2. Change their outcomes, that is, become more productive. Counselors, for example, can increase the number of classification summaries they produce per week.

3. Distort perceptions of self. Employees can conclude that they actually work harder than everybody else, although management refuses to recognize that fact.

4. Distort perceptions of others. Employees can decide that the employee with the higher pay is the recipient of manager favoritism or that the employee with lower pay doesn't have as attractive a job as previously thought.

5. Choose a different referent. The employee can make a comparison with a friend or relative who is not doing as well and conclude that they are doing better than those individuals.

6. Leave the field. The employee can resign and obtain a job in a more attractive organization.

Reducing Equity Tension

If it is not managed properly, equity tension can result in poor employee morale, overuse of the grapevine, failure to achieve organizational goals, and the active sabotage of policy and vandalism of property. The effective correctional manager will recognize that equity tension may be a part of organizational life, understand that the employee has six options when it comes to responding to that tension, then strive to motivate employees to choose the option of changing their outcomes by increasing the perception of fairness in the organization. To assess the current perception of fairness, effective managers will periodically use anonymous surveys to determine if changes in operating procedure need to be made.

Carrell and Dittrich (1978) reported that the most frequently used strategy of decreasing equity tension within an organization involves a combination of (1) reclassifying jobs that appear to be inequitably paid, (2) basing promotions on objective measures of performance, (3) training supervisors to distribute the workload more fairly, (4) reviewing pay differences to make sure they are justified, (5) allowing employees more latitude in planning and controlling their work, and (6) ensuring that policies, procedures, and rules are uniformly applied and enforced. Thus, the effective correctional manager will attempt to use MBO and all the employee empowerment strategies considered earlier in Chapter 11.

Union CBAs represent an external attempt to create equity by restraining managerial discretion in the distribution of reward, but they have not totally eliminated the ability of managers to differentially reward. For example, managers retain a certain amount of discretion in promotion (for example, being able to choose one of the top three on a promotion list) and there are abundant opportunities for promotion in corrections during periods of rapid prison construction. However, it is not enough that the manager has the authority to confer a promotion. Employees have to believe that they can receive that promotion. This brings us to expectancy theory.

Expectancy Theory

An expectancy is belief in the likelihood that an event or outcome will occur when specific tasks are accomplished. Victor Vroom (1964) proposed that the strength of a tendency to engage in a specific behavior depends on (1) attractiveness of the outcome—the importance the individual places on the potential outcome or reward, (2) performance–reward linkage—the degree to which the individual believes that performing at a particular level will lead to attainment of the desired outcome, and (3) effort–performance linkage—the probability perceived by the individual that a given effort will lead to the expected performance.

This is a theory of self-interest that understands employees to be motivated by the offers of rewards that they value if they perceive that the tasks necessary to achieve those rewards are reasonable, that is, within their capabilities. The strength of an individual's motivation to engage in expected behavior depends on the strength of that individual's perception that required tasks can be accomplished and that accomplishment will be appropriately rewarded. Managers, according to expectancy theory, can motivate subordinates by directly linking performance to all forms of rewards. Thus, the employee who desires promotion, and anticipates vacancies in the management ranks in the near future, may be motivated to reach high levels of performance through a promotions process that clearly links promotion to hard work. The mechanics of awarding a promotion will be very similar to the applicant selection process described

earlier in this chapter in that the interview will consist of job-related questions and the criteria for selection will be well-defined. This focus on job-related criteria will reinforce the perception that hard work can, and will be, rewarded.

In addition to promoting professionalization, an organizational environment in which employees believe that they are being treated fairly—that hard work will lead to desired rewards—can significantly reduce the stress levels discussed in Chapter 3.

SUMMARY

The professionalization of correctional employees through implementation and maintenance of effective selection, training, and evaluation systems in an environment conducive to individual professionalization would appear to constitute the final element of an environmental design structured to achieve the mission. But there is another process that must be addressed. Correctional managers must effectively develop an ethical structure within which employees can exercise discretionary decision making. This process will be discussed in the next chapter.

Discussion Questions

1. How does professionalization create professional conduct?
2. What are the elements of effective employee socialization?
3. What types of correctional training are available?
4. How does a training curriculum like that of the California Department of Corrections professionalize employees?
5. Why is the MBO model of individual employee evaluation more useful to employees and managers than the personal trait model?
6. What are the most important achievements of ACA accreditation?

7. How would you improve the ACA accreditation process?
8. How can correctional managers effectively apply equity and expectancy theory to the motivation of employees?

Critical Analysis Exercise: Today's New Hire—Tomorrow's Manager?

Correctional managers involved in the selection process are defining the candidate pool from which future correctional managers and leaders will come. Therefore, when they assess applicant motivation to perform well they should remember that David McClelland (1961) has suggested that motivation is based on three needs: achievement, power, and affiliation.

The need for achievement represents a drive to excel; to achieve in relation to a set of standards; to strive to succeed with success being the result of personal efforts, not other factors. Individuals with a high need to achieve seek concrete, ongoing feedback about their ability to manage challenges. The need to achieve is intrinsic. It is not rooted in a desire for the trappings of success. High achievers avoid tasks perceived as too easy or too difficult. They prefer situations that are moderately challenging (a 50-50 chance of success) where they can assume personal responsibility for finding solutions and receive rapid feedback to tell them if they are making progress. They readily accept the responsibility for success or failure.

Power entails the need to have an impact, to influence and/or control the behavior of others. Individuals with high power needs like to be in charge, enjoy competitive and status-oriented situations, and are more concerned with status and prestige than they are in effective performance.

Affiliation is the desire to be liked and accepted by others. Those individuals with a high affiliation need value friendship, cooperative situations where teamwork is emphasized, and relationships based on mutual understanding.

The most effective managers have a high need for power and a low need for affiliation (McClelland and Burnham, 1976). Why do power needs translate into managerial effectiveness more successfully than achievement or affiliation needs? Because the individual with a high need to achieve may be so focused on personal performance that insufficient attention is paid to how subordinates are performing. Specific direction may not be provided and subordinate errors are likely to be overlooked. And individuals with a high affiliation need may not be able to make the tough management decisions. A strong desire to be liked hinders decision making that can result in hurt feelings, animosity, and resentment. Thus, a promotion decision that the manager with high power needs may make in a matter of minutes may be agonized over for weeks by the manager with a high affiliation need. In addition, the high affiliation individual may be so intent on achieving group consensus on a policy that no decisions are made. Thus, people with high power needs tend to be effective managers if those needs are channeled into the service of the mission.

Critical Analysis Questions

1. How would you structure interview questions to identify an applicant's achievement, affiliation, and power needs?
2. How can training channel power needs into a useful direction?
3. How will individual evaluation methods identify these needs?
4. How will organizational evaluation methods identify these needs?
5. Do you agree that individuals with high power needs make the most effective correctional managers? Why or why not?

13

Social Responsibility and Ethical Behavior

Establishing a set of meaningful ethical standards demonstrates that members of the profession recognize the importance of their role in society and are willing to take responsibility for the conscientious exercise of their authority.

James H. Falk Sr.

Profile: Social Responsibility— Contributing to the Greatest Good

James Houston (1995:306) argues that correctional organizations have a responsibility to the community that includes more than confining, supervising, and/or rehabilitating offenders. Because the behavior of any given correctional organization will have an influence on individuals, groups, and society in general, correctional managers have a moral and ethical obligation to make that influence positive. That is, correctional organizations must engage in behavior that is guided by a philosophy of social responsibility grounded in five principles.

1. There is an obligation to maximize the greatest good for the greatest number. All decision making must be guided by this principle.

2. The organization should always be open to input from the community and willing to disclose the full extent of its operations. An organization that is behaving responsibly has nothing to hide from the public.

3. The short-term and long-term costs and benefits of any new activity or project must be evaluated before that activity or project is initiated. The impact of projects (such as prison construction) on the community must be carefully considered. Although Houston does not use the phrase, the third principle can be summed up as "being a good neighbor."

4. There must be a careful evaluation of every hidden economic cost and benefit associated with the operation of the organization. The organization must be guided by the public's willingness to pay. It must not hide costs from the taxpayers.

5. There must be a full utilization of all organizational resources for the benefit of the community. The skills of offenders and staff alike must be used to assist the community in resolving problems and meeting challenges. Resources that can benefit the community should not be withheld from that community. Correctional managers who provide inmate labor to assist communities threatened by natural disasters such as forest fires, floods, hurricanes, and winter storms are putting this fifth principle into practice.

Management's adoption of and adherence to these five principles will send a powerful message that the organization understands its social obligation to the individuals and groups touched by its sphere of activity.

The Profile presents the fundamental principle that every correctional organization has a responsibility to be socially responsible. Correctional managers guided by a philosophy of social responsibility will direct and organize employee behavior in accordance with written and verbal behavioral standards built on a foundation of morality, ethics, and the law. These standards will be incorporated into the organizational culture through a process of environmental design that strives to instill a strong sense of ethics in managers and employees alike. The key to promoting a climate of social responsibility is the ability and willingness of correctional managers to serve as role models by behaving in accordance with moral, ethical, and legal principles. Social responsibility is achieved through ethical behavior.

MORALITY, ETHICS, AND THE LAW

The fundamental principle to be explored in this chapter is that ethical behavior achieves the goal of social responsibility. To define ethical behavior we must first examine the relationship among morality, ethics, and the law.

Morality

Morality serves as the foundation for structuring ethical behavior by providing rules concerning how we should treat others and how others should treat us in our daily interactions inside, and outside of, the job (Heifetz, 1992). Morality deals with issues involving "the distinction between right and wrong in relation to human action or character" (Ferdico, 1992:284). It is rooted in religious principles and community values and is organized around such concepts as sin, right versus wrong, and the judgment of behavior as good or bad.

The term *moral behavior* is applied to the broad context of an individual's entire life—"the sum of a person's actions in every sphere of life" (Pollock, 1994:5). Moral behavior is behavior that is in accordance with religious principles and community values: honoring your parents, respecting the rights of others, obeying the law, revering life, being honest, showing compassion, and helping people in need. It is accepted behavior because it involves activities that enhance self-respect and confidence, develop personal integrity and integrity in relationships, and actualize personal potential without harming others (James and Jongeward, 1976).

Immoral behavior is behavior that violates religious or community values: lying, cheating, inflicting wanton pain, taking advantage of other people, breaking the law, practicing deceit, and abusing, degrading, or humiliating another person. These are unacceptable behaviors because they involve activities that exploit individuals, threaten their safety and security, reduce self-respect and limit the use of free choice (James and Jongeward, 1976).

Ethics

Ethics is a field of study. It is the philosophical study of morality and is often referred to as the study of values (Starling, 1993), the study of right and wrong, duty, responsibility, and personal character (Close and Meier, 1995), or the study of good and bad conduct (Pollock, 1994:4). There are three ethical perspectives that are important in our discussion of corrections: ethics of purpose, ethics of principle, and ethics of consequence.

Ethics of Purpose　　Aristotle (384–322 B.C.), a philosopher in ancient Greece, proposed that people are inherently good and will seek to do good things. Therefore, the means used to achieve goals will be positive and human activity is intrinsically directed toward achieving "good ends." This view of individuals as inherently good suggests that individuals will strive to reach their highest potential (Scruton, 1982). Thus, ethical behavior is that behavior that functions in the service of achieving human potential.

Ethics of Principle　　Immanuel Kant (1724–1804), a German philosopher, proposed that reason is the foundation of human actions. He believed that every individual has inherent worth (goodness) and that clear reasoning would result in the creation of rules and principles to guide every individual's actions toward other people. The product of these rules would be a society governed by the principle that individuals should always treat others in the way that they themselves wish to be treated. Kant believed that reason dictates a universal law of morality applicable to every individual and every situation. Put another way, people have the intellectual and emotional capacity to create rules designed to guide individuals in the direction of treating others in a just manner. The result of individual adherence to these rules will be ethical behavior and a moral society.

Ethics of Consequence　　John Stuart Mill (1806–1873), an English philosopher and political economist, believed that the result of any given action determines the morality of that action. The purpose or principle behind the action was not the important factor. An action is "right" if it creates more happiness than unhappiness. In other words, the morality of any action is judged by the consequences of that action. Therefore, individuals and organizations should strive to do the greatest good and the least harm. This is the fundamental proposition of the social responsibility model presented in the Profile. The application of this theory involves a conscious calculation of the costs and benefits of alternative courses of action and a determination of the action that will create the greatest happiness. The individual, or organization, that is consistently striving to do the greatest good is engaging in ethical behavior.

Correctional managers who understand, and accept, the fundamental propositions contained in an ethics of purpose, ethics of principle, and ethics of consequence will strive during environmental design to develop policy, procedures, and methods that create socially responsible organizational behavior.

Defining Professional Ethics

Because individuals have different perceptions of morality and ethics, it is necessary for organizations and professions to provide a unifying and consistent ethical guidance for their members as they strive to achieve social responsibility. This guidance is provided through professional ethics, which is the application of ethical principles to the behavior of a profession or group (Pollock, 1994:5). Ethical behavior can be defined as the behavior required by "the accepted principles of right conduct or practice governing a particular group or profession" (Ferdico, 1992:164). Guy (1990) observed that ethical behavior is characterized by caring, honesty, accountability, promise-keeping, pursuit of excellence, loyalty, fairness, integrity, and respect for others. Professional ethics provide the intellectual framework that individuals can use to define specific job-related behaviors as right or wrong, at least as judged from the organizational perspective.

The content of any given set of professional ethics is derived from the internal and external environment. The organization provides organizational policy, procedures, and rules. The external environment provides sets of regulations, standards, and guidelines that are designed to exercise an external control of organizational behavior. Regulations typically come from specific quasi-judicial regulatory governmental agencies—such as the Occupational Safety and Health Agency (OSHA) or the Environmental Protection Agency (EPA)—and often specify sanctions for noncompliance. Standards may come from professional organizations such as the American Correctional Association (ACA) and are often used as a basis for accreditation. Guidelines may come from a professional group such as the American Psychological Association.

Professional ethics rest on a foundation of ethics of purpose, principle, and consequence. Correctional managers and employees whose behavior is guided by professional ethics will (1) promote the proposition that individuals can achieve their potential (ethics of purpose), (2) treat individuals in the manner we all wish to be treated (ethics of principle), and (3) attempt to make decisions that do the most good for the most people (ethics of consequence). The result will be an organizational culture that promotes social responsibility.

Law

Laws are the formal, written rules that govern societal behavior. Because laws require organizational behavior to be both constitutional and legal, they function as an external control mechanism that prohibits organizational and employee behavior that is unconstitutional and/or illegal. Unconstitutional behavior, such as a DOC policy that bars Muslim spiritual leaders from holding church services for Muslim inmates, is subject to judicial review, as discussed in Chapter 7. Illegal and unconstitutional behavior, such as the physical abuse of inmates, makes employees and managers subject to arrest, prosecution, and legal sanctions, including incarceration. Because the Rule of Law applies to corrections just as it does to every other element of the criminal justice system, we might conclude that an organization's ethical system cannot require an employee to engage in behavior which is prohibited by the law. But, is this conclusion accurate? No, it is not. It is not accurate because of the paradox of professional ethics.

PARADOX OF PROFESSIONAL ETHICS

Professional ethics present a paradox. Although the behavior of correctional employees is expected to be both moral and legal, activities defined as ethical by corrections frequently involve behavior that would be immoral and/or illegal if it occurred outside of the job. Yet correctional employees are not arrested for engaging in this behavior. The paradox is that such behaviors are not only permitted; they are required by the employee's job description. Failure to perform them can result in the employee's being subjected to administrative disciplinary action. Consider, for example, the following examples.

The strip search is a routine prison procedure, based on the use of coercive power, that forces the inmate to submit to an activity that can produce powerful feelings of personal humiliation and degradation. A correctional officer (C.O.) using coercive power to force any individual outside of the job to undergo a strip search would be engaging in immoral behavior (the violation of both religious and community values) as well as in illegal behavior (the violation of numerous laws). However, when on the job, if the officer conducts an inmate strip search for the sole purpose of achieving the operative goal of maintaining security by searching for contraband, and acts to minimize inmate humiliation (i.e., the search is conducted in as private a setting as security considerations permit), then the officer has behaved in an ethical manner—the behavior is in accordance with professional ethics.

Take another example—death by lethal injection. The death penalty is highly controversial; there are individuals who believe that it represents state-sanctioned murder. In a state whose laws provide for imposition of the death penalty, the sentence of the court must be imposed by a lethal injection team composed of C.O.s. The officers who take the inmate to the death chamber and strap him to the chair or gurney are assisting in the termination of a human life. This participation in the formal execution process is ethical behavior. Therefore, behavior which is otherwise defined as immoral and/or illegal, is considered to be a legitimate correctional activity by both elected officials and the judiciary because it advances the organizational mission created through public policy formulation or implements an order of the court. However, such activities as strip searches and carrying out the death penalty are exceptions to the law only if they occur on the job and are conducted in accordance with written organizational policy which deliniates a constitutionally acceptable method of engaging in those activities.

Defining Unethical Behavior Unethical behavior is behavior that violates organizational policy, procedures, and rules and/or external regulations, standards, and guidelines. Correctional managers are most concerned about unethical behavior that is intentional and causes harm to others. To briefly return to the two examples above, an officer conducting a strip search for purposes of achieving sexual gratification, revenge, or intimidation is behaving in an unethical manner. And members of the lethal injection team who beat a Death Row inmate to death because he has provoked them are engaging in unethical behavior. In both instances, the breach of professional ethics provides grounds for disciplinary action, criminal prosecution, and civil litigation.

Ethical behavior advances the goal of social responsibility. But how are correctional employees to know which behaviors are ethical and which are not? The answer to this question is found in the codes of ethics and of conduct, which we consider next.

CODE OF ETHICS

The decentralization of corrections has produced a powerful need to replace supervisory control with employee self-control in decision making. The foundation of this self-control is the organization's code of ethics. A code of ethics is organized around a set of very broad principles that comprise those ideals to which the members of the organization or profession should adhere (Falk, 1995:112). The ACA Code of Ethics (see Box 13–1) provides a set of guidelines that provide the foundation for every correctional organization's code of ethics.

BOX 13–1 ACA CODE OF ETHICS

Preamble

The American Correctional Association expects of its members unfailing honesty, respect for the dignity and individuality of human beings, and a commitment to professional and compassionate service. To this end, we subscribe to the following principles.

Members shall respect and protect the civil and legal rights of all individuals.

Members shall treat every professional situation with concern for the welfare of the individuals involved and with no intent of personal gain.

Members shall maintain relationships with colleagues to promote mutual respect within the profession and improve the quality of service.

Members shall make public criticism of their colleagues or their agencies only when warranted, verifiable, and constructive.

Members shall respect the importance of all disciplines within the criminal justice system and work to improve cooperation with each segment.

Members shall honor the public's right to information and share information with the public to the extent permitted by law subject to individuals' right to privacy.

Members shall respect and protect the right of the public to be safeguarded from criminal activity.

Members shall refrain from using their positions to secure personal privileges or advantages.

Members shall refrain from allowing personal interest to impair objectivity in the performance of duty while acting in an official capacity.

Members shall refrain from entering into any formal or informal activity or agreement which presents a conflict of interest or is inconsistent with the conscientious performance of duties.

Members shall refrain from accepting any gifts, service, or favor that is or appears to be improper or implies an obligation inconsistent with the free and objective exercise of professional duties.

Members shall clearly differentiate between personal views/statements and views/statements/positions made on behalf of the agency or Association.

Members shall report to appropriate authorities any corrupt or unethical behaviors in which there is sufficient evidence to justify review.

Members shall refrain from discriminating against any individual because of race, gender, creed, national origin, religious affiliation, age, disability, or any other type of prohibited discrimination.

Members shall preserve the integrity of private information; they shall refrain from seeking information on individuals beyond that which is necessary to implement responsibilities and perform their duties; members shall refrain from revealing nonpublic information unless expressly authorized to do so.

Members shall make all appointments, promotions, and dismissals in accordance with established Civil Service rules, applicable contract agreements, and individual merit, rather than furtherance of personal interests.

Members shall respect, promote, and contribute to a workplace that is safe, healthy, and free of harassment in any form.

Adopted August 1975 at the 105th Congress of Correction. Revised August 1990 at the 120th Congress of Correction. Revised August 1994 at the 124th Congress of Correction.

Source: Reprinted with permission of the American Correctional Association, Lanham, MD.

While the specific wording and format of a code of ethics varies from organization to organization, the principles expressed in that code should comply with both the letter and spirit of the law and have a strong moral foundation. For example, the Code of Ethics for the Wisconsin Department of Corrections (DOC) expresses four principles:

- High moral and ethical standards among state officials and employees are essential to the conduct of free government.
- The purpose of the Code of Ethics is to help public officials and state employees "avoid conflicts between their personal interests and their public responsibilities."
- The Code of Ethics will ensure high standards of public service, and
- Will strengthen the confidence of the public in their state government (Wisconsin Department of Corrections, 1991:1).

However, the Missouri DOC Code of Ethics holds correctional personnel to a somewhat different set of standards:

- Employees will be diligent in their responsibility to record all information which could contribute to sound decisions affecting offenders or public safety.
- When making public statements, employees will clearly distinguish between those that are personal views and those that are statements and positions on behalf of the Department.
- Employees will maintain the integrity of private information and will neither seek personal data beyond that needed to perform their responsibilities nor reveal any information to anyone not having authorization for use of such.
- Any employee who is responsible for Departmental personnel actions will make all appointments, promotions, or dismissals on the basis of merit only and not in furtherance of personal or partisan interests.
- Employees will report without reservation any corrupt or unethical behavior which could affect either the offenders or the integrity of the Department (Missouri Department of Corrections, 1995:4).

Regardless of the specific principles, the written code of ethics provides a framework of standards designed to structure professional behavior. But standards are not enough. Terms such as "corrupt or unethical behavior" must be concretely defined if ambiguity and misinterpretation are to be avoided. The code of ethics must be complemented by a written code of conduct that contains specific Dos and Don'ts of behavior.

CODE OF CONDUCT

Codes of conduct differ depending on the characteristics of the correctional organization, its history, and the predominant concerns of the top managers. For example, The Wisconsin DOC Code of Conduct places a great deal of emphasis on the issue of avoiding conflicts of interest. Wisconsin managers define a conflict of interest as:

Striving for or acquiring substantial personal gain as a consequence of performing the duties of a public office or working in a state position, or, as a consequence of abusing or misusing the power and prestige of an office.

Or

Applying or allowing to be applied undue influence in making official decisions or recommendations, or taking a course of action as part of the duties of a public office or state position (Wisconsin Department of Corrections, 1991:1).

The Wisconsin Code of Conduct then defines specific standards of conduct and provides examples of situations and behaviors that would constitute a conflict of interest. For example, a conflict of interest would exist when a member of the Wisconsin DOC:

1. Secures outside employment that conflicts with the official duties and responsibilities of the state position—for example, a probation officer accepting employment as a consultant for a private corrections organization that receives referrals from the probation officer's department.

2. Accepts fees or reimbursement when representing the correctional organization at public events.

3. Sells, leases, or makes a profit from a product produced while fulfilling the responsibilities of state employment—for example, a computer technician who develops a parole failure prediction model for the DOC, then sells the software to a private company.

4. Accepts an award from a noncorrectional organization—for example, a superintendent being named Man of the Year by a company that has bid on a highly lucrative construction project at the superintendent's prison.

5. Accepts anything of monetary value from a private contractor—for example, a Commissioner who accepts a free ride on a corporate aircraft to attend a professional conference.

In contrast, the Missouri DOC Code of Conduct has a broader focus, although it does prohibit managers and employees from engaging in conflict of interest situations. The Missouri Code embodies the philosophy that every correctional employee and manager is expected to maintain professionalism during the performance of their duties; refrain from discrimination, use of illegal drugs, and harassment; avoid nepotism and political activity or outside employment that constitutes a conflict of interest; feel free to join a labor organization; and make use of DOC-provided counseling and rehabilitation programs if an alcohol or illegal drug problem exists.

The sorts of employee behavior most frequently prohibited by codes of conduct include the following: violating any policy, rule, or procedure; engaging in the abuse of offenders, including the use of abusive, profane, or threatening language; lying about job-related matters, including falsification of reports; willful destruction of state or offender property; possession of unauthorized weapons, explosives, or other dangerous devices; fighting, assault, or horseplay; sharing confidential information with unauthorized individuals; neglect of duty, including sleeping on duty; being on duty in a condition unfit to perform the job; possessing or using drugs or alcohol in the workplace; accepting gifts or gratuities from offenders, their family and friends, or any other individual; and engaging in any activity that will harm the organization.

The importance of a written code of ethics and code of conduct cannot be overemphasized. Pollock (1994:95–96), in discussing the importance of ethics in law enforcement, formulated a statement of purpose that applies equally well to corrections:

Ideally, a set of ethics will help the officer make decisions in a lawful, humane, and fair manner. A code of ethics also helps to engender self-respect in individual officers; self-pride comes from knowing they have conducted themselves in a proper and appropriate manner. . . . Further, a code of ethics contributes to mutual respect among police officers and helps in the development of an esprit de corps or a group feeling toward common goals. Agreement over methods, means, and aims are important to these feelings. As with any profession, an agreed-upon code of ethics is a unifying element and one that can help define the occupation as a profession, since it indicates a willingness to uphold certain standards of behavior.

How does the code of ethics achieve such positive outcomes? How does it promote the goal of social responsibility? First, it structures discretionary decision making. Second, it inhibits corruption.

STRUCTURING DISCRETIONARY DECISION MAKING

As has been noted in previous chapters, the growth of correctional organizations in response to a wide range of internal and external environmental challenges reduces the span of control enjoyed by managers and increases the number of decisions to be structured through formalization. However, the extent of decentralization makes it impossible for formalization to cover every possible decision that must be made. The result is an increase in discretionary decision making at every level of the organization.

Discretion can be defined as "the right or power to act according to one's own judgment . . . or conscience in choosing between two or more alternative courses of action. The term 'discretion' implies the absence of a hard and fast rule" (Ferdico, 1992:143). Discretionary decision making can be influenced by a variety of factors that can be grouped into two categories: legal and extralegal.

Legal Factors The term *legal* can be defined as fulfilling the requirements of the law, not contrary to law, or compliance with formal or technical rules (Ferdico, 1992:260). Legal factors are case-related factors such as charge seriousness, evidence of inappropriate behavior, and criminal record. These are considered to be legal fac-

tors whether the situation is that of a hearing examiner conducting a misconduct hearing, a parole board considering a parole recommendation, or a Commissioner setting prerelease eligibility criteria.

Extralegal Factors Extralegal factors are any factors that are considered in addition to the legal factors. Analysis of any instance of discretionary decision making must involve an understanding of the type of extralegal factors that may influence a decision (Blumstein et al., 1983). There are four categories of extralegal factors: (1) situational factors, which include community attitudes, subcultural values, and behavioral norms that apply to a situation, and the nature and location of the situation in which the decision is being made; (2) decision maker characteristics, which include demographic factors such as age, race, gender, education, perception of the role of the decision maker, and the decision maker's attitudes toward the offender; (3) offender characteristics, which include demographic factors such as age, race, gender, class, and attitude toward the decision maker as reflected in demeanor and other behavior; and (4) organizational factors, which include organizational structure, mission statement, goals, budget, and offender/employee management policy, procedures, and rules.

When organizational policy does not specifically address a decision-making situation confronting a correctional employee, the employee will attempt to resolve the situation by making a decision based on the combination of legal and extralegal factors that appear to be most relevant. The factors considered relevant are often chosen on the basis of the employee's experience with similar situations, individuals, or organizations. If that experience has been negative, the result may be a use of discretion that violates the basic principles of social responsibility.

For this reason, extralegal factors in decision making are of concern to correctional managers, which is often reflected in training curriculums. For example, the Pennsylvania DOC basic training curriculum contains a course titled "Cultural Sensitivity" that examines a specific set of extralegal factors:

This module examines values and prejudices and how they develop at the same time. Emphasizes respect for different cultures and their values. Module discusses discrimination, prejudice, and the problems they cause for corrections staff. Explores racial stereotypes and stresses the need to treat people as individuals. Looks at various populations within our institutions and their influence on staff/ operations (Pennsylvania Department of Corrections, 1996:3).

Because legal and extralegal factors can come into conflict in any given decision-making situation, correctional employees must be alert to the possibility of ethical dilemmas.

Defining the Ethical Dilemma

An ethical dilemma that confronts the decision maker has three defining characteristics. First, the situation or issue requires that one or more choices be made. Each choice has the potential to result in a breach of acceptable behavior (Zinn, 1993) or is part of a situation in which an individual must choose between equally unsatisfactory alternatives (Davis and Aroskar, 1978). Alternatives are equally unsatisfactory when the choice involves competing values and loyalties (Loewenberg and Dolgoff, 1988), conflicting core ethical values (Walker, 1993), or conflicting moral claims (Davis and Aroskar, 1978). Each obligation, interest, or value can be satisfied by a different behavior. It is the need to make a choice among opposing behaviors, values, or interests that creates the conflict at the heart of the ethical dilemma. An important source of conflict in corrections is created by the opportunity to abuse discretion through a subordination of

legal factors to extralegal factors. The abuse of discretion can be defined as "an unreasonable, arbitrary, or unconscionable action taken without proper consideration of the law and facts" (Ferdico, 1992:143). An abuse of discretion can occur when professional ethics collide with personal needs and philosophy, decision maker and offender personal characteristics, subcultural pressures, and/or external pressures.

The second characteristic of an ethical dilemma is that the individual is aware of the conflict. This awareness often stems from the decision maker's knowledge that his or her personal actions or inaction will affect the lives of others (Heifetz, 1992). The greater the potential impact on the lives of others, the greater the stress the decision maker is likely to experience while trying to resolve the conflict. Thus, ethical dilemmas can be an important source of job-related stress.

The third characteristic is that the individual is uncertain about how to resolve the conflict (Millstein, Dare-Winters, and Sullivan, 1994). It is this uncertainty that creates the job-related stress. Decision makers who are taught to identify, confront, and resolve ethical dilemmas will be less vulnerable to this type of job-related stress.

Examples of Ethical Dilemmas   There is no category of correctional employee that is immune to ethical dilemmas. Correctional managers who must choose between funding much-needed inmate drug treatment programs or purchasing body armor for the C.O.s because the budget is inadequate to meet both needs are facing an ethical dilemma. The need to provide inmate programming collides with the need to maximize C.O. safety. There can be negative consequences resulting from both decisions. The failure to provide programming can lead to inmate idleness, promote dissatisfaction, and hinder rehabilitation. The failure to provide body armor can result in an officer's death and union, media, and political criticism.

C.O.s constantly make low-visibility discretionary decisions that reward positive behavior and penalize negative behavior. Privileges such as extra TV time, phone calls, job assignments, cell changes, place in the shower rotation, and the opportunity to "visit" on the block are often given in reward, or denied as punishment, solely at the discretion of the C.O. More formalized activities such as conjugal visits, prerelease status, transfers, furloughs, and parole recommendations may be greatly influenced by C.O. behavioral reports. Formal punishments, in the form of withdrawal of privileges, punitive transfer, cell restriction, disciplinary segregation, and loss of good time are initiated by the C.O.'s filing of a misconduct report. Inmate control is physical and involves the use of handcuffs, shackles, come-along holds, batons, and, in extreme circumstances, the use of firearms. Any one of these decisions can involve a conflict between legal and extralegal factors and the resolution of the ethical dilemma can significantly affect inmate morale and employee stress levels.

Prison treatment staff work in an environment dedicated to control of the offender. The goals of control and treatment are in constant conflict and Pollack (1994:188–190) has noted that as a result of this prevailing conflict, treatment staff experience mixed loyalties. They are employed by the state, but their professional training requires them to act in the best interests of their clients. For example, treatment staff are bound by professional codes of ethics that hold client confidentiality to be sacred. But the correctional organization's professional ethics emphasize the importance of security issues. The need to respect confidentiality can conflict with the need to maintain a high level of facility safety and security. For example, an inmate who mentions in a counseling session that he has been smoking marijuana or is considering an escape attempt will create an ethical dilemma for the counselor. The resolution of such a dilemma has consequences. Failure to report this type of information to the security staff can result in criminal activity that threatens security and causes media and political criticism. Reporting the information can destroy the counseling relationship and hinder rehabilitation.

Probation and parole personnel are not immune to issues of choice and conflict. Consider the issue of supervision fees. Fiscal and political reality require that correctional managers live within tight budgets. The Constitution requires that certain services be provided to offenders. How are both needs to be met? As noted in an earlier chapter, there is a growing trend toward charging inmates for medical services and assessing community-placed offenders a fee for correctional supervision. The dilemma here is that while making offenders pay for state-provided services generates income and creates positive public relations, it may also impose a financial hardship that negatively affects an inmate's family.

Role of Professional Ethics in Discretionary Decision Making

Discretionary decision making involves choices that have a potential for negative consequences, especially if the situation has created an ethical dilemma. Professional ethics provides an intellectual framework for evaluating alternative courses of action; in so doing, it increases the probability of making the choice most likely to advance the organizational mission by promoting a reliance on legal factors and a careful scrutiny of extralegal factors. Take, for example, the issue of the use of force.

Structuring Discretion in the Use of Force One of the most important employee behaviors to be structured by professional ethics is the use of force. The Federal Bureau of Prisons has created a model document concerning this issue entitled "Use of Force and the Application of Restraints on Inmates (Falk, 1995:112–113). This document stipulates that force is to be used only as a last resort after all other reasonable efforts to resolve the conflict situation have failed and that the amount of force must be the minimum necessary to gain control of the inmate and protect safety, property, and institutional order. The code of conduct stipulates the method and degree of force to be used in specific situations, precautions to ensure health and safety, documentation and reporting of use-of-force incidents (including the use of video equipment whenever possible), procedures for the care of inmates after the incident, and requirements for ongoing use-of-force training of employees. The document also includes a section on the use of chemical agents and nonlethal control devices that outlines the justification and procedures for using these devices (Falk, 1995:112). Correctional managers need to review their codes of conduct as the technology of nonlethal control devices evolves. The National Institute of Justice has been engaged in a process of developing less-than-lethal technologies (stun guns, stun belts, and laser defense systems) that can be applied at local, state, and federal levels. As these devices come onto the market and enter into correctional use, it is imperative that codes of conduct be amended to govern their use.

Codes of ethics and conduct do not guarantee that the "right" choice will always be made. Negative consequences do result from ethical decisions. Honest mistakes are made often because of a lack of relevant information. In such a situation, all the decision maker can do is examine the process that led to the choice, learn the lessons to be learned, and then apply that knowledge when other discretionary decision situations arise.

Unfortunately, discretionary decision making can also result in a choice of behavior that is unacceptable by any set of professional standards—behavior that clearly breaks the law and violates ethical principles. That behavior is corruption.

INHIBITION OF CORRUPTION

McCarthy (1996:231) defines corruption as "the intentional violation of organizational norms (i.e., rules and regulations) by public employees for personal material gain." The primary difference between an ethical dilemma and corruption is the conscious violation of professional ethics for the specific purpose of personal material gain; this is the root of any act of corruption. Engaging in corrupt behavior is grounds for disciplinary action (including dismissal), arrest, and incarceration.

Corruption in corrections includes (1) theft from inmates, visitors, staff, and the organization; (2) trafficking in contraband—drugs, alcohol, money, and weapons smuggled into the prison in exchange for money, drugs, or sexual services; (3) the embezzlement of funds from inmate or prison accounts and materials from warehouses; and (4) misuse of authority (McCarthy 1996:232). The misuse of authority most frequently involves one, or all, of the following activities: the acceptance of inmate payoffs for special consideration in receiving legitimate prison privileges, such as choice cells or job assignments; the acceptance of inmate payoffs for special consideration in obtaining or protecting illicit activities such as drug sales, gambling, and prostitution; and extortion, that is, threatening to physically or programmatically harm an inmate if no payoff is forthcoming (McCarthy, 1981). The most blatant, and potentially most dangerous, form of corruption involves staff trafficking in contraband.

Employees who engage in corrupt behavior may do so because of a desire for increased income, resentment of the organization, an inability to resist temptation, or as a result of being compromised by an inmate adept at manipulation. Whatever the reason, the consequences are always serious. The employee loses both career and reputation, may gain a criminal record, and, if the corruption has been serious enough, be incarcerated. And the negative publicity generated by media coverage of the event will smear the reputation of the organization and the profession.

The role of professional ethics in inhibiting corruption is to clearly establish for every employee the expectations of the organization and provide a warning that corrupt behavior is totally unacceptable. Codes of ethics affirm that only socially responsible behavior will be accepted and rewarded.

Respecting the Ethical Principles of Other Organizations

When correctional managers develop a code of ethics and a code of conduct, they must be sensitive to the fact that some of their employees are also governed by ethical principles promulgated by professional organizations in their field of expertise. For example, the American Correctional Health Services Association (ACHSA) has promulgated a set of ethical standards governing the conduct of medical personnel employed in corrections. Prison is an unusual environment for medical personnel and correction's focus on control, deterrence, and discipline runs counter to the medical profession's emphasis on curing, healing and relieving suffering. Thus, there is an "inherent tension between the values of the two 'cultures'" (Thorburn, 1995:82).

In order to reduce this tension, correctional managers should be sensitive to ACHSA principles that require medical personnel to (1) abstain from any participation in executions, (2) not participate in such activities as "escorting inmates, forced transfers, security supervision, strip searches or witnessing use of force," (3) perform security body-cavity searches only when they are in "a patient–provider relationship with an inmate," and (4) perform involuntary medical care procedures only when there is a serious threat to the life of the inmate (Thorburn, 1995:83). Medical staff are expected to respect the functions of other employees, but they should not be expected to engage in behavior that violates their field's professional ethics. This must be incorporated by the effective correctional manager when promulgating the organization's code of ethics.

Is a Written Policy All That Is Needed?

The answer to this question is no. Written policy concerning ethics and standards of conduct in and of itself will not achieve the objectives of structuring discretion and inhibiting corruption. Although there is a lack of research studying the effectiveness in corrections of codes of ethics and conduct, it is possible to look at code of ethics research in other areas and reach some tentative conclusions. Mathews (1988:63–82), using data from a variety of studies on 485 corporations conducted between 1973 and 1980, found that there is little relationship between formal codes of ethics and organizational violations. Codes of conduct did not result in fewer violations. In many cases, they represented window dressing instead of an effective form of self-regulation.

Clearly, then, written policy by itself will not create an ethical organizational culture. Policy must be reinforced by correctional managers who actively strive to create an organizational culture that is dominated by ethical principles. Such a culture will be defined by the six elements we consider in the next section.

PROMOTING AN ETHICAL ORGANIZATIONAL CULTURE

Chapter 3 emphasized that the organizational culture has a profound effect on employee socialization. In order for a correctional organization to achieve the goal of social responsibility, it is necessary for both managerial and employee behavior to be strongly influenced by an organizational culture that is grounded firmly in a well-articulated set of ethical principles. A correctional organization that is striving to achieve or has already achieved an ethical organizational culture will be characterized by the following:

1. Managers who are role models for ethical behavior
2. A focus on ethical issues during the discharge of basic personnel management functions
3. An ethics ombudsman and/or ethics committee

4. Ethics as a core component in the training curriculum
5. Active use of an internal affairs unit
6. Development of a model for ethical group decision making

We begin with the most critical element of promoting an ethical organization: the managers.

Managers as a Positive Role Model

Hambrick and Mason (1984) pointed out that the comments by and behavior of managers are extremely important to the employees they supervise. There must be a high correlation between words and behavior. That is, managers must actively demonstrate that they will not engage in unethical decision making or corrupt activity or turn a blind eye to instances of either behavior. Managers must set the example by behaving in an ethical manner. They must instill in employees a sense of ethics.

Robert Briody, psychologist at the Mabel Bassett Correctional Center in Oklahoma, has offered eight suggestions for instilling a strong sense of ethics in correctional employees (Briody, 1997:1, 8–9).

1. Managers should watch for signs of a breakdown in ethics among staff such as property damage, a pattern of tardiness and calling in sick, violation of policy, lack of participation in organizational activities, and "playing dumb" during investigations of alleged staff misconduct.

2. Managers should police themselves. They should set the example by personally adhering to high ethical standards.

3. Managers should share with staff how ethics are factored into their decision making. They should emphasize that decisions should reflect the greatest good for the greatest number and it is this principle that should guide employee decision making.

4. Policy should expressly state that employees have both the authority, and obligation, to let other employees know when they are bending the rules.

5. The code of ethics should generate a code of conduct that is specific. For example, a code of ethics statement that staff are not permitted to exploit offenders for personal gain should be reinforced by code of conduct prohibitions against employees' bringing inmates contraband, engaging in sexual relations with them, or having a relationship with their families. Policy should emphasize that every employee has a responsibility to report employee misconduct.

6. Sanctions should be applied to employees who attempt to cover up the misconduct of other employees.

7. When employees do come forward to report employee misconduct, the managers should protect them from retaliation. The possibility of having an anonymous tip line to preserve anonymity has been suggested by Joe Marchese, President of the International Association of Corrections Training Personnel in 1997.

8. Managers must ensure that training programs use moral dilemmas that are demonstrated through employee role-playing and problem-solving exercises. A source of curriculum material to accomplish this objective is the National Institute of Corrections leadership program considered earlier in Chapter 9. The leadership program focus on ethics provides correctional managers and trainers at the organizational level with a readily available resource for an ethics curriculum.

Personnel Management Processes

An essential element of the promotion by correctional managers of an ethical organizational culture is incorporating ethical considerations into fundamental personnel management processes. In other words, as correctional managers engage in basic personnel management processes, there is ample opportunity to present an ethical message. We will examine three areas.

Selection and Promotion

The background check of a prospective employee may be the first indication that an applicant has the potential to engage in unethical behavior. The presence of a criminal history or negative reports from former employers, school officials, or the military will provide a warning flag. Interview questions in both the selection and the promotion process should reflect ethical concerns. Applicants for employment, for example, can be asked: "What types of behavior would you consider to be wrong?" and "What would you do if you saw another employee (or a supervisor) doing something that you know to be wrong?" Candidates for promotion can be asked to "Provide a summary of our code of ethics and tell us how you have applied that code in your present position" and "Name three situations in which you confronted an employee about unethical behavior. What was the behavior and how did you handle the situation?" Candidates for promotion should have their correctional work history carefully reviewed for possible ethical concerns before a final decision is made. The promotion process should be just as rigorous as the initial selection process that brings employees into the organization.

Keeping the Process Free of External Environmental Influences Political involvement in the hiring, promotion, and dismissal process can undermine the effort to promote social responsibility. Individuals who owe their allegiance to a politician, not the correctional organization, may believe they are above the rules and regulations because they are protected by a powerful outsider who can circumvent internal attempts at control. Managers should be grateful for Civil Service rules and collective bargaining agreements (CBAs) because they significantly reduce the ability of politicians to manipulate the personnel processes designed to screen out, or remove after hire, those individuals oriented toward unethical decision making and/or corruption. Managers must fight any effort to weaken Civil Service and the collective bargaining process because these mechanisms prevent a return to the days when prisons were staffed by the unqualified friends and relatives of the professional politicians (O'Hare, 1923:161).

Revision of Current Policy

McCarthy (1996:239) has suggested that managers review, and revise where necessary, their current policy structure to ensure that it includes the following: (1) publication of guidelines for discretionary rewards and punishments so that low-level discretionary decision making is more visible, (2) periodic supervisory review of low-level decision making, (3) application of psychological and background screening to all prospective employees to improve the overall quality of new hires, (4) police checks of prospective employees, and (5) improvement of overall working conditions with an emphasis on professionalism.

In line with the last of McCarthy's suggestions, the mechanisms for employee empowerment considered in Chapters 11 and 12 can play a role in structuring discretionary decision making. For example, the unit management concept, although usually discussed in terms of enhancing communication and decision making, can also be viewed in terms of structuring the use of discretion. The closer-than-normal working relationship between managers and employees required by unit management provides an opportunity to detect the inappropriate use of discretion as well as present a proper model of behavior. Although not a panacea, an alert manager working closely with staff is in a better position to detect and correct inappropriate uses of discretion than the manager who is secluded in an office.

Deliberative mentoring provides the opportunity for experienced managers to observe a talented subordinate's use of discretion and to model effective approaches to discretionary decision making; Total Quality Management (TQM) allows both managers and employees to review processes in terms of ethical considerations. Even if these employee empowerment approaches are not used, managers should enact an open door policy that encourages employees to bring their ethical concerns and issues to them.

Positive Reinforcement of Ethical Behavior

Ethical conduct must be reinforced. Written commendations and selection as Employee of the Month certainly can be useful awards, as can fast-tracking for promotion whenever possible. If no other avenue is open, a verbal commendation or a note in the personnel record for an employee who has acted in an ethical manner can reinforce ethical behavior. Managers should never underestimate the power of positive communication.

The Ombudsman and Ethics Committee

Mathews (1988:137), in examining unethical behavior in corporations, has suggested two types of structural change that can be applied to correctional organizations. First, top correctional managers can create an Ombudsman Office that makes available an impartial individual skilled in conflict resolution who can play an active role in resolving ethical dilemmas. This measure has the potential to reap positive results as long as employees are convinced that the ombudsman is truly impartial and has the authority to intervene in conflict situations. Second, the correctional organization can establish an official Ethics Committee that includes every level of management, union representatives, and community representatives who are expert in ethical questions. There is no reason why a correctional organization cannot have both an Ombudsman Office and an Ethics Committee.

Structuring the Ethics Committee   The Ethics Committee should meet once a month, without exception, and have the authority to inquire into every aspect of organizational behavior, interview employees who have observed unethical or corrupt behavior, and enforce official prohibitions against retaliation against whistle blowers. To be effective, however, an Ethics Committee has to be more than a group of people who meet once a month to listen to employees. There must be a specific job description for the committee, just as there is a job description for every correctional employee. The mission of the committee must be defined in terms of the organization's ethical policies.

In addition to the duties stated above, Mathews (1988:138–141) suggested that the Ethics Committee (1) write the organizational code of ethics and periodically review and revise it as new ethical situations arise, (2) organize and conduct bimonthly workshops, using an outside expert as a facilitator, that systematically target employees at each organizational level, (3) use evaluation and follow-up techniques to measure presession and postsession attitudes and beliefs toward unethical and illegal behavior and determine workshop effectiveness with content revision undertaken as indicated, (4) include in employee newsletters a section titled "Ethics" in which specific dilemmas and resolutions are discussed, and (5) encourage discussions of ethics through such devices as bulletin board postings. The Ethics Committee's work must be reinforced through inclusion of an ethics component in the training curriculum.

Training Curriculum

Every correctional training curriculum should include an ethics component designed to provide a basic understanding of ethical principles and teach employees how to recognize an ethical dilemma, analyze it, and make the choice that produces a socially responsible decision. Every correctional training curriculum structures its presentation of ethical issues in a different manner. For example, the R. A. McGee Correctional Training Center of the California DOC provides an ethics course designed to "foster discussion about values, ethics/integrity and principle as they relate to correction's decision-making. . . . As the students express opinions and listen to those of their peers, their attention is focused on analyzing the parameters of their own value system" (California Department of Corrections, 1997a). In contrast, the Pennsylvania DOC basic training curriculum has a course titled "The Professional Image," which explains the DOC code of ethics with an emphasis "on professional demeanor both on and off duty" (Pennsylvania Department of Corrections, 1996:1).

As part of a pragmatic training approach, the guidelines developed for business executives by Laura Nash (1981:82) should be incorporated into any ethics curriculum. Nash proposed that individuals confronted with making a tough ethical decision should be trained to ask themselves the following questions:

1. Have you defined the problem accurately?
2. How would you define the problem if you stood on the other side of the fence?
3. How did the situation occur in the first place?
4. To whom and to what do you give your loyalty as a person and as a member of the corporation?
5. What is your intention in making this decision?
6. How does this intention compare with the probable result?
7. Whom could your decision or action injure?
8. Can you discuss the problem with the affected parties before you make your decision?
9. Are you confident that your position will be as valid over a long period of time as it seems now?
10. Could you disclose without qualm your decision or action to your boss, CEO, the board of directors, your family, society as a whole?
11. What is the symbolic potential of your action if understood? If misunderstood?
12. Under what conditions would you allow exceptions to your stand?

Classroom discussions that emphasize these principles can help every level of correctional employee examine the issue of social responsibility in a productive way. Of particular value in ethics training is the use of scenarios (case studies) that present concrete examples of a variety of ethical dilemmas.

Scenario Training

The ethical dilemmas presented earlier in this chapter can easily be converted into scenario (case study) exercises. For example, for new employees, the following scenario can provide the opportunity for discussion and role playing:

You are a C.O. who witnesses another C.O. using excessive force against an inmate who is a chronic problem on the block. This verbally abusive inmate has provoked an officer who is having marital problems. That officer has responded with a brutal beating that has hospitalized the inmate. Two other C.O.s have testified that the inmate was beaten by a group of inmates who the officers are not able to identify. You are asked by an internal affairs investigator if you have any information to provide. What do you say?

In this scenario, a crime has been committed by a fellow officer. Discussion can center around issues of legality, morality, ethics, the influence of the organizational culture on employee behavior, and personal feelings about a fellow officer who "snapped" because of marital problems.

Correctional managers, or potential managers, can discuss the following scenario:

You are the superintendent of a state prison (or county jail) and you have put out a proposal for construction of a second perimeter security fence. Seven companies have provided construction bids. You receive a call from the president of the company that has provided the lowest bid. You have seen this individual on a number of social occasions and consider him to be honest and genuinely supportive of corrections. The company president mentions that he was talking to some of your C.O.s at a Little League game and they informed him that the organization's budget did not have adequate funding to purchase body armor for the emergency response team. The president offers to provide the equipment in the form of a contribution, no strings attached. You believe there is no hidden agenda because his company has already been publicly awarded the contract. What do you do? Accept the equipment which your C.O.s need and run the risk of somebody alleging the equipment was a subtle bribe? Or refuse it and risk the lives of your officers?

In this scenario, the issue is how decisions may be perceived. Discussion can center around how employees, the media, and the public perceive management decisions; the need to avoid any decision that will even raise a suspicion of unethical or corrupt behavior; and the way in which unfounded allegations can harm credibility. The influence of extralegal factors on decision making in general can also be incorporated into the discussion.

Structuring the Discussion Collins and Page (1992) have suggested an ethical analysis model that can be very useful in ethics training, especially scenario training. After presentation of the material, the following process will govern the discussion and analysis:

1. Each individual will write his or her solution to the dilemma. This forces the individual to examine basic assumptions about the issue under review.

2. The participants meet in groups of three or four to share their individual answers and reach a consensus on a solution. This process tests the viability of the solution and presents alternative solutions for examination.

3. All of the small group solutions are shared with the larger group, which must then reach a consensus.

4. In order to reach a consensus, the group must measure each solution against the following questions: Will the solution help more people than it will hurt? How can those hurt recover? Is this a win-lose solution? What values does this solution reinforce? What values does this solution violate?

5. After reaching a consensus, the group discusses that consensus in terms of our three ethical perspectives: (1) Ethics of purpose: Does the solution help achieve the potential of individuals and the organization? (2) Ethics of principle: Does the solution treat those affected in the way the decision makers would like to be treated? (3) Ethics of consequence: Is the solution going to do the most good and the least harm for most people?

Unfortunately, there are always a small number of correctional employees who fail to receive or accept the message of social responsibility. Therefore, the ethical standards of the correctional organization must be officially enforced.

Internal Affairs Unit

Most DOCs have an internal affairs unit (often designated as the Office of the Inspector General, the Office of Professional Responsibility, the Special Services Unit, or the Inspections and Investigations Division), which is charged with the official responsibility of investigating all allegations of employee misconduct. The head of the unit typically reports directly to the Commissioner and, if allegations of employee misconduct are verified, submits a formal report to the Commissioner with a recommendation for action. Reports of investigative findings may result in prosecution as well as administrative disciplinary action taken in accordance with the controlling CBA(s).

A typical example of a correctional internal affairs unit is the Arizona DOC Inspections and Investigations Division, which has two bureaus dedicated to social responsibility. The Administrative Investigations Bureau conducts employee investigations and consists of internal affairs, background investigations, and polygraph examination units. The Criminal Investigations Bureau investigates and arrests individuals committing, or attempting to commit, crimes directly related to DOC operations (Arizona Department of Corrections, 1996:22).

The information presented thus far in this section of the chapter provides a foundation for incorporating a strong sense of ethics into the organizational culture. But there is one initiative left to consider. Correctional managers must aggressively ensure that all group decision making is structured in terms of ethical principles.

Developing a Model of Ethical Group Decision Making

Marvin T. Brown (1990) has provided a model of ethical group decision making that is essential to the design of an organizational culture that will emphasize social responsibility. This model of decision making has five elements, which we examine in turn.

Policy Proposal This is the proposed course of action in response to a question that states a problem or a challenge. For example, in response to the question "What can we do about the rising number of HIV-positive inmates being received?" a policy proposal might be: "We should require all new receptions to undergo mandatory HIV testing and physically segregate the HIV-positives from general population." This coupling of a problem with a suggested solution is the beginning of the group decision-making process. The remainder of the process must include ethical considerations.

Observations The group shares the information about the problem that is currently available—the amount of increase in HIV-positive inmates, the risk they represent to employees and other inmates, the cost of testing and segregation, the legal issues involved in both activities, the possible psychological consequences of testing and segregation. This is essentially a fact-finding stage and the facts must be reliable. Therefore, a considerable amount of research and expert testimony may be required before proceeding to the next step. And intellectual honesty requires that all the facts be presented to the group. Half-truths and speculations should be avoided. The facts presented must be true.

Value Judgment The group will evaluate the facts and the proposal based upon the group's value system. There are likely to be differences in individual values. A C.O. representative may place a very high value on protection of the employees through every possible means, including segregation, while a medical director may emphasize inmate confidentiality and treatment in the least-restrictive setting possible. However, value judgments should be humane, practical, and consistent with the organizational mission, code of ethics, and code of conduct.

Assumptions The values being expressed by individual group members are based on assumptions. The C.O. representative may assume, for example, that HIV infection can be the result of casual contact while the medical director is assuming that the psychological consequences of segregation actually constitute cruel and inhumane punishment. Assumptions must be stated and explored in terms of a basic criterion: are they responsible or irresponsible in view of the policy under consideration?

Opposing Views   The leader of the group must encourage the expression of opposing views. Not in a confrontational "I'm right, you don't know what you're talking about" manner, but in a way that allows the group to investigate and validate facts and assumptions. For example, the medical director might cite the massive body of research that invalidates the assumption that HIV infection is the result of casual contact. This is a process of identifying and narrowing areas of significant disagreement. If the observations are valid, the value judgments humane and practical, and the assumptions responsive to the problem, then the policy proposal will be ethical.

Guiding this decision-making process are the three theories of ethics presented earlier in the chapter. If correctional managers successfully promote consideration of these theories, groups charged with decision-making responsibility will, over time, automatically begin to structure decisions in terms of the criteria of developing potential, recognizing the inherent worth of people, and doing the most good for the most people.

SUMMARY

The need for correctional employees to engage in socially responsible decision making has been a part of corrections from the beginning of its existence, as has the need for correctional managers to create an ethical organizational culture. Managers can instill a sense of ethics by aggressively focusing on ethical issues during environmental design. Organizational decision making will be guided by an ethic of principle, purpose, and consequence only if correctional managers have recognized the need for socially responsible behavior. We turn in the next chapter to a consideration of the effective management of change.

Discussion Questions

1. What is the role of the code of ethics and the code of conduct in achieving social responsibility on an organizational and an individual level?
2. What ethical issues are prison treatment staff, C.O.s, maintenance and food service personnel, probation and parole staff, and managers in general most likely to encounter?
3. What would be an effective strategy for developing an ethical response to each issue identified in question 2?
4. What can be done to make ethics training effective?
5. What is the most effective means of achieving an ethical organizational culture in corrections?

Critical Analysis Exercise: Sexual Harassment in the Workplace

The Civil Rights Act of 1964 prohibits sex discrimination. A form of sex discrimination is sexual harassment, which can be defined as follows: unwelcome sexual advances, requests for sexual favors, and other verbal or physical conduct that enters into employment decisions and/or conduct that unreasonably interferes with an individual's work performance or creates an intimidating, hostile, or offensive working environment (Rubin, 1995b:1–2).

Sexual harassment can be either quid pro quo harassment or hostile work environment harassment. In quid pro quo harassment, an employee is forced to choose between submitting to sexual advances or losing a tangible job benefit, or even the job itself. An essential element of this form of harassment is the harasser's power to control the employee's employment and employment benefits. In order to establish quid pro quo harassment, the complainant must establish that the harassment was based on sex, consisted of unwelcome sexual advances, and a tangible economic benefit of the job was conditional on submission to the unwelcome sexual advances. The advances may be direct or implied (inviting the claimant out for drinks "to discuss promotional opportunities," for example).

Hostile work environment harassment is unwelcome conduct that is so severe or pervasive as to create an intimidating, hostile, or offensive atmosphere at work. There does not have to be a threat of the loss of a tangible work benefit for this type of harassment to exist and it can include third parties, that is, it may not be the direct result of the manager's actions. The totality of the circumstances are considered by the court in hostile work environment harassment because the issues of severity and pervasiveness are critical. The courts use a "reasonable person" standard (i.e., How would the average person respond to a similar situation?) in considering this type of harassment, and it is possible, although rare, for a single severe incident to be sufficient to establish sexual harassment.

Sexual harassment claims are usually brought under the Civil Rights Act of 1871 (42 U.S.C. Section 1983), the same section inmates have used so successfully in challenging conditions of confinement on constitutional grounds. Correctional managers can be held responsible for incidents of sexual harassment involving employees, inmates, and visitors. Therefore, it is in their best interest to be proactive in the area of sexual harassment by the development of appropriate policy, training, and active supervision, and by the willingness to administer appropriate disciplinary action.

Critical Analysis Questions

1. Does the organizational culture of corrections make sexual harassment inevitable? Defend your answer.
2. Is sexual harassment more likely in the prison than it is in community-based corrections? Defend your answer.
3. Cite examples of managerial behavior that could encourage subordinates to refrain from engaging in sexual harassment.
4. Are female managers more likely to act proactively against sexual harassment than male managers? If there is a difference in response, what would account for that difference?
5. What message(s) does staff sexual harassment send to the offenders under correctional jurisdiction?
6. How does sexual harassment undermine the ability of the organization to achieve the mission?
7. What specific actions can managers and co-workers take to prevent sexual harassment?

14

The Management of Organizational Change

Learning Objectives

After completing this chapter, you should be able to:

- Discuss the nature of correctional change.
- Define the role of the manager as change agent.
- Contrast the three adaptive change strategies.
- Summarize the challenges involved in technological and employee change.
- Identify the sources of personal and organizational resistance.
- Develop strategies to reduce the impact of resistance.
- Summarize the basic principles of ethical change management
- Apply models of organizational change to real-life situations.
- Explain the law of unintended consequences.

Key Terms and Concepts

Change
Unplanned Change
Change Agent
Innovation
Imitation
Technological Change
Security Technology
Organizational Development
Survey Feedback
Team Building
Resistance
Group Inertia
Status Quo
Freezing
Diagnosis
Feedback
Evaluation
Implicit and Deferred Resistance

Planned Change
Equilibrium
Adaptive Strategy
Cost-Minimization
Structural Change
Telemedicine
Holistic View
Sensitivity Training
Process Consultation
Intergroup Development
Structural Inertia
Lewin's Three-Step Model
Unfreezing
Action Research Model
Analysis
Action
Overt and Immediate Resistance

The essential task of modern management is to deal with change. Management is the agency through which most changes enter our society, and it is the agency that then must cope with the environment it has set in turbulent motion.

M. Ways

Previously, the conventional wisdom about organizations was "If it's not broken, don't fix it." Today, the new dictum seems to be "If it works, make it better." There is a shift from a posture of reaction to one that embraces change. The prevailing wisdom is changing because many of our organizations are now or will soon be in a state of crisis. . . . Many organizations are failing but others are doing well. All wonder if something terrible could happen to their organization. Thus, it seems prudent to anticipate and proactively manage change rather than to passively sit by until some crisis strikes.

Kenneth D. MacKenzie

Unfortunately, many correctional managers have learned that [their bosses have] as a motto, "Let sleeping dogs lie." More unfortunately, they have learned that "barking" or "attacking" dogs generally will not survive. This is not to argue that there cannot be change, we know that change is inevitable. The question is whether an executive chooses to be reactive or proactive . . . will simply ride the currents of change . . . or deliberately attempt to harness and control change. The former is crisis management, the latter is the kind of manager we should be training to assume mantles of leadership.

Kenneth J. Peak

Profile: Changing the Mission of Probation

John Rosecrance (1986) believes that probation departments are no longer viable organizations because they lack a clear-cut mission. He has noted that offenders, judges, academics, the public, the media, and elected officials have all lost faith with probation departments because of their high recidivism rates and argues that probation departments must be provided a new mission. Specifically, probation officers should no longer be charged with the responsibility of providing direct supervision of offenders. Nor should they be expected to provide counseling or therapy services for which they have neither the training nor the skills. If the Rosecrance proposal were legislatively enacted, the mission of the probation department would be to compile and present to the court offender evaluations. In effect, probation officers would become background investigators for the judicial system and be responsible for providing the traditional presentence investigation as well as in-depth investigations of violation reports, revocation hearings, and early termination requests. They would also conduct periodic follow-up progress report investigations at a judge's request. Counseling and all treatment services would be provided by agencies outside of the criminal justice system. Monitoring probationers would become a computerized function carried out by clerical employees of the court who would schedule revocation hearings as soon as probationer violations were detected. Rosecrance believes that the result of these changes would be to create an achievable task for probation departments that replaces the current probation function, which is so poorly defined that ineffective supervision is inevitable (Rosecrance, 1986:25–31).

The Profile provides an example of a sweeping change being proposed for a traditional correctional organization. A fundamental principle of effective environmental design is that organizational functions and structure must change in response to the challenges created by an increasingly turbulent internal and external environment. Of particular importance are public policy changes that affect the resources and mission of a correctional organization. Although organizations must change if they are to survive, change is threatening. Change involves loss—the loss of a comfortable routine, traditions, adequate resource level, friends, even the job itself. The process of replacing the old with the new can exact a high cost in terms of human stress. However, change also can represent a tremendous opportunity to improve the organization's capability to advance the mission. This chapter explores the nature of change and the role of the correctional manager as an effective change agent.

NATURE OF ORGANIZATIONAL CHANGE

Correctional managers must constantly respond to changing circumstances in the internal and external environment. The need to adapt functions and structure can be imposed from outside of the organization through any of the agencies of public policy formulation discussed in the preceding chapters. Change can be the result of managers' perceiving deficiencies in the current environmental design that require correction. And changes in the nature of the offender population (such as an increase in violent offenders) can signal the need for policy changes.

Defining Change Change is a deviation from the norm or from the traditional behavior of a group or organization. Although historically conservative, corrections, like every other organization in society, has to respond to deviations from the norm. Change is a process initiated by events or situations that upset the equilibrium of the organization. Managers respond to this dis-

turbed equilibrium by functioning as change agents who implement one, or all, of the three types of adaptive strategy considered below in an attempt to restore equilibrium. Adaptive strategies produce an effect, or effects, the magnitude of which can be used to measure response effectiveness.

Simply put, change involves doing things differently. It can be either planned or unplanned. Planned change is the result of conscious, deliberate, coordinated efforts by managers who have defined a problem and developed a solution. It is undertaken for the purpose of improving the organization's environmental design and advancing the mission. Unplanned change is the result of unanticipated events that are beyond managerial control. This type of change is frequently disruptive because managers and staff are not prepared to manage its consequences, which can be severe.

Both types of change have consequences. For example, the decision to increase the availability of community-based programming to inmates represents a planned change that entails a redistribution of the Department of Corrections (DOC) budget, an increase in the number of contracts with private vendors, and an increased emphasis on assessing individual inmate suitability for community placement in classification and programming processes. An increase in the number of HIV-infected inmates represents an unplanned change that results in staff and inmate fear based on ignorance, an increase in the need for specialized medical services (Figure 14–1), higher medical budgets, HIV-related litigation, more inmate deaths, and a rise in inmate and correctional officer (C.O.) stress levels.

Planned and unplanned change are not necessarily exclusive processes. Unplanned changes have consequences that can stimulate planning. For example, an increase in the number of HIV-infected inmates (as occurred nationally in the 1980s) is unplanned, but the consequences noted above must be addressed through a process of planned change. Staff and inmate education programs are restructured to include

FIGURE 14–1   HIV Center at the California Medical Facility at Vacaville. Courtesy California Department of Corrections.

material on AIDS, medical budgets are revised to cover the increased cost of AIDS medications, and policy revisions to direct staff behavior in managing HIV-infected inmates are developed and disseminated.

Change is unavoidable. Just as unavoidable is the fact that effective change requires management.

THE CORRECTIONAL MANAGER AS CHANGE AGENT

Managers are charged with the responsibility of implementing changes in organizational functions and structure. A manager is a change agent: an individual who acts as a catalyst and assumes the responsibility for managing the process of change. Change is managed through the use of three types of adaptive strategy: innovation, cost-minimization, and imitation.

Innovation Strategy

Innovation strategy makes changes for the sake of meaningful innovation, not for mere cosmetic change. Examples of innovation strategy are the historical emergence of probation and parole as an alternative to incarceration; the expansion of community-based corrections alternatives such as halfway houses, house arrest, work release, Intensive Supervision Probation (ISP), and residential treatment programs; and the implementation of restorative justice concepts that will be examined in Chapter 15.

Cost-Minimization Strategy

Cost-minimization strategies of the type discussed in Chapter 5 seek to reduce the cost of the overall operation of the organization. Given the demands of fiscal conservatism, any adaptive strategy chosen by correctional managers must be carefully evaluated to determine if it can also qualify as a cost-minimization strategy. Managers concerned about the effectiveness of their cost-control activi-

ties may attempt to evaluate effectiveness through a comparison of their basic statistical data with that of other DOCs. An example of this approach is provided in Box 14–1.

BOX 14–1 STATISTICAL PROFILE: RANKING OF STATES

State	Incarceration Rate Rank	Inmates Per 100,000 Population[1]	Adult Institution Population[1]	Violent Crime Rate Rank[2]	Adult Institutions Operating Costs (in millions)[3]	Operating Costs Per Citizen	Costs Per Citizen Rank	State Population[2] (in thousands)	State Population Rank
Alabama	7	439	19,098	12	$159.4	$38.07	41	4,187	22
Alaska	27	256	2,738	15	$116.2	$193.99	1	599	48
Arizona	6	448	18,809	18	$243.6	$61.89	20	3,936	23
Arkansas	18	355	8,916	23	$112.3	$46.33	37	2,424	33
California	14	382	124,813	2	$2,848.4	$91.26	5	31,211	1
Colorado	26	272	9,954	24	$209.6	$58.78	24	3,566	26
Connecticut	19	331	14,427	31	$354.7	$108.24	4	3,277	27
Delaware	12	391	4,324	19	$76.1	$108.71	3	700	46
Florida	10	404	56,052	1	$1,058.6	$77.39	9	13,679	4
Georgia	9	417	30,292	17	$464.6	$67.17	15	6,917	11
Hawaii	40	170	3,246	43	$61.0	$52.05	29	1,172	40
Idaho	29	253	2,861	41	$47.9*	$43.59	39	1,099	42
Illinois	23	302	35,614	7	$668.9	$57.19	25	11,697	6
Indiana	28	256	14,826	29	$318.0	$55.66	28	5,713	14
Iowa	38	180	5,090	38	$133.6	$47.48	33	2,814	30
Kansas	31	239	6,090	28	$166.9	$65.94	16	2,531	32
Kentucky	24	281	10,724	30	$179.1	$47.27	35	3,789	24
Louisiana	2	514	23,333	4	$191.8	$44.66	38	4,295	21
Maine	47	113	1,468	48	$58.7	$47.38	34	1,239	39
Maryland	11	392	20,887	6	$364.3	$73.37	10	4,965	19
Massachusetts	43	165	10,072	10	$213.0	$35.43	44	6,012	13
Michigan	8	423	40,220	11	$1,062.0	$112.05	2	9,478	8
Minnesota	**49**	**100**	**4,573**	**37**	**$113.1**	**$25.04**	**48**	**4,517**	**20**
Mississippi	13	385	10,631	32	$85.0	$32.16	46	2,643	31
Missouri	20	321	16,957	16	$220.0	$42.03	40	5,234	16
Montana	36	192	1,654	46	$31.9	$38.02	42	839	44
Nebraska	45	148	2,449	36	$55.7	$34.66	45	1,607	37
Nevada	5	456	6,745	9	$79.0	$56.88	26	1,389	38
New Hampshire	42	167	1,895	47	$42.1	$37.42	43	1,125	41
New Jersey	22	307	24,471	22	$539.9	$68.52	12	7,879	9
New Mexico	34	216	3,704	8	$109.7	$67.88	13	1,616	36
New York	17	361	65,962	3	$1,283.8	$70.55	11	18,197	2
North Carolina	21	314	22,650	20	$564.1	$81.22	8	6,945	10
North Dakota	50	75	522	50	$8.6	$13.54	49	635	47
Ohio	16	369	41,156	26	$618.9	$55.80	27	11,091	7
Oklahoma	4	501	16,306	21	$196.9	$60.94	22	3,231	28
Oregon	41	169	6,723	27	$187.1	$61.71	21	3,032	29
Pennsylvania	33	224	27,071	33	$730.0	$60.59	23	12,048	5
Rhode Island	37	185	3,049	34	$88.8	$88.80	6	1,000	43
South Carolina	3	504	19,646	5	$174.5	$47.90	32	3,643	25
South Dakota	32	227	1,636	45	$22.5	$31.47	47	715	45
Tennessee	25	278	14,397	13	$344.8	$67.62	14	5,099	17
Texas	1	545	100,136	14	$1,600.0	$88.74	7	18,031	3
Utah	44	154	2,948	39	$87.1	$46.83	36	1,860	34
Vermont	46	138	1,182	49	$37.5	$65.10	17	576	49
Virginia	15	374	24,822	35	$324.1	$49.93	30	6,491	12
Washington	35	198	10,650	25	$332.3	$63.24	19	5,255	15
West Virginia	48	106	1,941	44	$23.0	$12.64	50	1,820	35
Wisconsin	39	172	9,206	42	$327.0	$64.91	18	5,038	18
Wyoming	30	247	1,174	40	$23.0	$48.94	31	470	50

[1]U.S. Department of Justice, Bureau of Justice Statistics, Prisoners under jurisdiction of state correctional authorities — June 30, 1994

[2]FBI Crime in the United States - 1993
[3]The Corrections Yearbook 1994 - Adult Corrections, published by the Criminal Justice Institute, Inc. (*Corrected number provided by the Idaho Corrections Department.)

Source: Minnesota Department of Corrections. *1994–1995 Biennial Report* (1995): 26.

It must be noted, however, that such a comparison can provide at best only a very rough evaluation of effectiveness because the number of variables that can affect operating costs is almost endless. Therefore, this approach has limited utility, although it is frequently used by legislators concerned with the high cost of corrections. The Commissioner of the Arizona DOC, for example, might find legislative critics demanding to know why Arizona has correctional costs of $61.89 per citizen while Alabama, with approximately the same inmate population, has costs of only $38.07 per citizen. Such a comparison is obviously unfair, but it is one that managers frequently have to contend with when the critics of correctional budgets take aim.

Imitation Strategy

Imitation strategy involves learning how other organizations (including those outside of corrections) are meeting specific challenges and then adapting those solutions to correctional challenges. Telemedicine (Box 14–2) provides an excellent example of an imitation strategy that appears to have the potential for success.

BOX 14–2 TELEMEDICINE IN THE FEDERAL BUREAU OF PRISONS

Prison systems are responsible for holding prisoners in custody and providing for their care and treatment, including health care. The delivery of health care to prisoners is a demanding, expensive responsibility for prison systems and often presents a threat to the good order and security of a prison facility. Often DOCs have difficulty in delivering medical care necessary for the continued health maintenance of the inmate in a prison setting. Typically, the prison provides primary health care within the

---

walls and wire, and must deliver secondary and tertiary health care for acutely ill inmates in the community. Under the Constitution of the United States, DOCs cannot deliberately be indifferent to the medical needs of inmates. Consequently, the inmate in need of health care that cannot be delivered inside the correctional facility must be transported into the community.

However, removing the inmate to the community for health care takes the offender outside the envelope of security provided by the institution. The walls and wire no longer surround the inmate. Inmates will exploit this security weakness inherent in outside medical trips by faking illness. This presents a very difficult situation for prison officials who must determine if the medical situation is legitimate, an escape plot, or some other scheme. Also, providing guard services for transporting an inmate with a legitimate illness to the community is very costly. The use of Telemedicine in corrections provides an opportunity to overcome some of these difficulties.

Telemedicine in Corrections

Telemedicine is the use of electronic signals to transfer information from one site to another in order to provide medical services. It is the use of advanced telecommunications technology to provide and enhance the practice of medicine. A television broadcast between a physician and a patient in which both can see and talk to one another on a screen would be an example of Telemedicine. The first use of Telemedicine occurred in 1959 when the University of Nebraska College of Medicine used microwave to connect the Nebraska Psychiatry Institute to the state mental hospital

112 miles away. The scope of depth of telemedicine has increased in recent years to include a wide variety of complex equipment and numerous medical specialties.

The Georgia DOC established Telemedicine in their prison hospital and connected with their remote correctional facilities. According to the Georgia DOC, the use of Telemedicine reduced the number of transfers to the prison hospital and, overall, reduced health care costs. The Texas Department of Criminal Justice has also used Telemedicine successfully for several years.

The Federal Prison System established Telemedicine 1996 in cooperation with the Veteran's Administration (VA) and the Department of Defense (DOD). The VA in Lexington, Kentucky, served as the "host" site from which the VA physicians provided service to the inmates. The prison "hub" sites at which the inmates received physician services from the VA were located in Allenwood, Pennsylvania, Lewisburg, Pennsylvania, and Lexington, Kentucky.

The implementation of Telemedicine in corrections presents some obstacles, but they can be overcome. The equipment is complex and costly. To overcome the complexity of the equipment, training for all users is mandatory, and joint training with all users is especially necessary. Equipment and telecommunications costs are being addressed and are expected to drop rapidly in the coming years.

Anticipated Benefits

A major benefit of telemedicine is the improvement of security. Telecommunications greatly reduces the need for transporting inmates to physicians in the community since the physicians are available inside the institution through the use of telecommunications. The elimination of "town trips" enhances security since inmates do not have to be moved from the secure confines of the correctional facility. The transportation of inmates outside the secure perimeter for medical treatment presents the opportunity for an inmate to escape or for violence to occur against correctional staff or the general public.

Second, a reduction in the demand in health care is also anticipated. Inmates will create their own medical problems in order to get a town trip. Theoretically, if an inmate knows he or she will not get a town trip, they are less likely to feign illness. Third, not unlike the private sector, correctional systems are experiencing dramatically increasing health care costs. Telemedicine should serve to reduce those costs. One significant portion of the overall health care costs is the cost of security that is needed when an inmate is taken on a town trip for health care. This may involve paying correctional officers overtime or providing them compensatory time. In either case, it is a cost in staffing that can be avoided through the use of Telemedicine. Fourth, the use of Telemedicine will improve inmate access to health care. The availability of the Telemedicine consult within the walls and the wire will reduce the constraints caused by transporting an inmate outside of an institution. Health care staff will be able to schedule inmates for a visit to a specialist without the concerns of a security detail for outside escort. Fifth, through Telemedicine BOP providers can receive continued medical education. Videotapes from accredited institutions that provide continued medical education are now available for broadcast to several sites. Additionally, providers will be working with the specialist directly and will probably learn from this experience.

Early results indicate correctional facilities may have the potential for being the most effective sites for Telemedicine because of transport and security savings. Telemedicine has been demonstrated to be useful for situations in which physical barriers prevent or hinder the contact between patients and health care providers and the availability of special information is key to proper medical management. Both conditions are a key aspect of correctional health care.

Source: Dr. Ronald J. Waldron, Ph.D., Senior Deputy Assistant Director, Health Services Division, Federal Bureau of Prisons, and C. Allan Turner, D.P.A, Senior Fellow, Mount Vernon College.

The interest of an increasing number of state DOCs in building super-max institutions based on the federal models in Marion, Illinois, and Florence, Colorado, which had their origins in Alcatraz, are also examples of imitation strategy (Figures 14–2 and 14–3). Similarly, boot camps represent an attempt to duplicate the U.S. military's success in transforming raw recruits into organized and disciplined individuals. In general, correctional managers are eager to learn about any program or initiative that will improve organizational effectiveness, but they are understandably fearful of using unproven strategies. Being the architect of a failed strategy can cost a manager any hope of future advancement.

Having now considered the above three adaptive strategies as mechanisms for organizational change, we must ask the obvious question: What is it that managers change? The answer is they change organizational structure, technology, and people. As we have noted throughout this book, organizational complexity and formalization increase, and centralization decreases, as organizations grow in response to environmental challenges. Put another way, structural change involves a process of task redefinition that requires a subsequent rearrangement of tasks, authority/reporting relationships, and communication channels. Every major challenge associated with the bureaucratization of corrections (such as workforce diversification, professionalization, community corrections, and privatization) has resulted in major structural change

Therefore, our emphasis in what remains of this chapter will be on the issues associated with technological and employee change.

TECHNOLOGICAL CHANGE

The information society and computer dependency became a fact of life by 1989 (Archambeault, 1996:301) and have added a new vocabulary in the lexicon of correctional managers. Virtually every correctional organization now uses computers, with varying degrees of sophistication, for basic data management and many superintendents now routinely use computers to track critical data. Computer-assisted instruction (CAI) and computer-based training (CBT) are being used in inmate programs to teach a variety of courses. CBT, in the form of simulation training, is slowly becoming a reality in many correctional training academies and may eventually replace videotapes. Increasingly, computer-assisted monitoring of offenders (CAMO), commonly used in house arrest, "may become the single most significant sentencing and correctional alternative of the twenty-first century" (Archambeault, 1996:307) despite serious concerns about the ethics of extending state control too deeply into the offender's community life.

Archambeault (1996:310–311) has predicted that in the near future correctional agencies may be using artificial intelligence (AI) computer technology to manage ever-

FIGURE 14–2   The U.S. Penitentiary at Marion, Illinois, represents the modern super-max prison. Courtesy of the Office of Archives, Federal Bureau of Prisons.

FIGURE 14–3   Alcatraz is the prototype for the modern super-max prison. Courtesy of the Office of Archives, Federal Bureau of Prisons.

FIGURE 14–4   The modern prison control center is technologically dominated. Courtesy of the Ohio Department of Rehabilitation and Correction.

growing offender data systems. Some researchers have suggested that new technologies for corrections will include x-ray equipment capable of detecting explosives, drugs, and weapons; rapid eye scanners to detect drug use; air-sniffing equipment that can detect drugs and weapons when placed in prison ventilation systems; and the routine use of night vision goggles (Allen and Simonsen, 1998:457). Currently, DOCs are heavily investing in electronic perimeter and interior surveillance systems that are computer-controlled (Figure 14–4).

The Federal Bureau of Prisons Office of Security Technology in 1997 began a search for new useful technologies for use in the BOP's 91 facilities (*Corrections Professional,* 1997a:9). Six of the most promising technologies were the following:

1. Handheld, noninvasive drug-detecting screening systems that use an ion technology and can be programmed to detect 30 different narcotics on the hands and clothing of visitors.

2. An electronic facility access control system.
3. A heartbeat detector that can be used at sally ports to detect inmates trying to escape in a vehicle.
4. A satellite vehicle tracking system that allows the BOP to track the location of transport buses and have two-way communication with them nationwide.
5. A firearm simulation program (Beam Hit) that uses a laser system and computerized target to teach employees how to correctly aim and fire a weapon without using expensive ammunition.
6. Personal body alarms that provide the exact location of an individual within a facility.

As these technologies are field-tested and found to be viable, they will inevitably be adopted by state and local correctional facilities. But there is more to technology than the hardware. Managers must know how, and when, to integrate it into the existing organizational processes.

The Manager and Technology

The task for the manager considering the use of technology is fourfold: (1) to develop a working knowledge of technology as it comes onto the market, (2) to identify the technology most useful to the organization, (3) to secure adequate levels of funding, and (4) to provide appropriate levels of staff training. Technology often represents a profound change for correctional staff, a change that can be met with resistance from employees who fear they cannot master the skills required to use the new devices.

Bogard (1993) has suggested that the manager entering the world of technology adopt a proactive strategy based on ten fundamental rules. First, recognize that the more complex and sophisticated the technology, the higher the probability of mechanical problems and difficulty in training staff. Managers must avoid the temptation to purchase a more complex system than is needed. Second, use a consultant who can analyze the organization's technological needs and make appropriate recommendations. Third, avoid being a guinea pig. Do not be the first to use a new product. Wait until the bugs have been worked out (this is in line with correction's historic reliance on imitation strategy.) Fourth, establish and stick to a budget. This is a fundamental reality of fiscal conservatism. Fifth, be skeptical about manufacturer claims. Ask questions and be ready to challenge claims that sound too good to be true (because they will almost always turn out to be too good to be true). Sixth, demand past performance data that will help determine long-term effectiveness. Seventh, require manufacturer installation and provision of adequate warranties. Eighth, always include line staff in the selection and evaluation process. Ninth, demand long-term, unconditional warranties that protect the budget. Ten, require training as part of the package. Don't put staff in the position of using trial and error to operate and repair the equipment. We can add an eleventh point to those presented by Bogard. The correctional manager must develop appropriate technology-related policy, disseminate it to all levels of employee, and ensure that it is incorporated into the training curriculum, both basic and in-service.

Following the above strategy will increase the probability of making technology an ally instead of an enemy. However, no matter how functional the structural change or productive the technology, the greatest challenge involved in any change process is the task of changing employee attitudes and behavior.

CHANGING THE PEOPLE OF THE ORGANIZATION

As organizational functions, structure, and technology change, employees must adapt to those changes. They must learn new skills, change attitudes that are no longer appropriate, and function in an organizational environment that is becoming increasingly complex. Changing behavior is a process that involves communication, motivation, and decision making; it poses significant challenges to the manager because most individuals are reluctant to change. They are comfortable with their current routine, traditions, work practices, relationships, attitudes, and behavior. Because change threatens this comfort, resistance to change may be the most significant challenge the change agent will encounter.

RESISTANCE TO CHANGE

While change is often proposed for valid reasons, many correctional staff are resistant to it. However, resistance to change is not necessarily bad or irrational. It can provide stability and predictability of behavior and prevent the chaotic randomness that would occur if employees simply did things the way they felt like doing them on any particular day. Resistance can also stimulate a healthy debate about controversial subjects that will ultimately lead to a better decision. But resistance to change is negative when it hinders or prevents the effective use of an adaptive strategy that will advance the mission. Resistance can present itself in two forms. It can be overt and immediate or implicit and deferred.

Overt and Immediate Resistance   Overt and immediate resistance is the easiest to manage. A staff strike, work slowdown (or threat of such action), or manager–employee verbal confrontations created by a controversial change (or proposed change) constitute overt and immediate resistance. Kotter and Schlesinger (1979:106–114) reported that these behaviors can be directly addressed, and a solution reached, through the use of such resistance-deflating techniques as education and communication; employee participation in the decision-making process;

provision of staff support in the form of counseling and new skills training; negotiation to resolve differences of opinion; manipulation of staff by distorting the facts, withholding information, and creating false rumors; and coercion through demotions or dismissals.

A word of caution is needed. Manipulation and coercion, while they may appear to be productive in the short-term, often produce long-term negative effects in the form of employee anger and resentment. Education, communication, participation, support, and negotiation are the preferred tools of an effective manager.

Implicit and Deferred Resistance   This type of resistance simmers and festers. The signs may initially be subtle: loss of loyalty to the organization; lowered motivation to work; a profound reluctance to take the initiative in even routine situations; an increase in mistakes and costly errors in judgment; increased use of sick, vacation, and emergency leave; a general attitude of just working for the pay check. Eventually, the symptoms of stress that we considered in Chapter 3 become overtly manifest. The most effective method of managing implicit and deferred resistance is to prevent it through the approaches that are discussed below.

The sources of resistance can be either personal or organizational. The effective correctional manager is able to accurately analyze the sources of resistance and devise effective solutions.

Personal Sources of Resistance

Steers (1977:167) has identified ten personal sources of resistance to organizational change: (1) misunderstanding the purpose of the change, (2) failure to see the need for the change, (3) fear of the unknown, (4) fear of loss of power, status, and security, (5) lack of involvement in the change, (6) habit, (7) vested interests in the status quo, (8) group norms and role expectations, (9) threats to

existing social relationships, and (10) conflicting personal and organizational objectives. These sources can be seen in the following experience of the Michigan DOC when it implemented a hearing examiner system in the late 1970s.

Changing the Michigan DOC Inmate Disciplinary Policy   The Michigan DOC attempted in 1979 to implement the due process provisions of *Wolff v. McDonnell* (1974). Disciplinary decisions were taken out of the hands of the C.O.s and became the responsibility of a Central Office Hearings Division, which employed attorneys to visit the institutions and conduct disciplinary hearings in accordance with *Wolff*'s due process requirements.

Correctional officers who were accustomed to having their word accepted unconditionally in matters of inmate misconduct were suddenly confronted with a system that appeared to put inmates on an equal level. Officers, in general, interpreted such a change as another example of "liberalism's" interference in their world, saw no need for such a change, and feared its long-term effects. They felt devalued; they were frustrated at having to manage inmates they had written up but whom a hearing examiner had found not guilty; they resented the lack of input in the policy change; and they had to modify well-ingrained habits. Those officers who were comfortable with the traditional approach to inmate management realized that the relationship between officer and inmate had changed. C.O.s no longer had autocratic power. Their ability to use discretion had been sharply decreased and personal needs for power and control had been curtailed by the organizational need to come into compliance with a judicial decision.

Officer resentment of the change in inmate disciplinary policy and procedures was intense, fueled by a perception that DOC top management was oblivious to the reality of the officers who had to enforce the rules. The hearing officers sent into the institutions were viewed as biased toward inmates. Dismissals of poorly written misconduct reports were seen as evidence that the new disciplinary system was unworkable. The view of C.O.s at the State Penitentiary in Southern Michigan was summarized in the following Task Force on Violence memo from Deputy Warden Elton Scott to Warden Mintzes:

[D]ue process is a major cause of violence being perpetuated in this facility. Most people indicated that there were no sanctions and the residents know it. The supervisors indicated that the staff feels that there is nothing they can do to the residents and they feel frustrated. The task force felt Lansing should let the institutional people run the institution and not the Lansing people, whom [sic] for the most part, have not worked in an institution. Times have changed and the Policy Directives and Operational Procedures do not apply. The task force felt that the violence really started and could be correlated with the inception of the Hearings Division (Useem and Kimball, 1989:123).

The correctional officer resistance to the new hearing examiner system took the form of a breakdown in inmate discipline caused by fewer and fewer officers writing inmates up for rules violations that had traditionally resulted in automatic segregation time. Officers throughout the system came to distrust the Lansing-based DOC Commissioner and his management staff.

Reality Versus Officer Fears But what is the reality of the hearing examiner system? Sixteen years after its implementation, Michigan DOC statistics (Figure 14–5) reveal that officer fears of being unable to maintain control in the face of a system operating in favor of the inmates were groundless. In the vast majority of cases, Michigan DOC inmates are found guilty of the alleged misconduct. The Michigan experience is a powerful reminder that fear of the unknown can generate fears and stress levels that are not warranted by the actual consequences of the implemented change.

Threat Posed by Change Can Be Real
Employee fears about change are not, however, necessarily irrational or groundless. As Kanter (1984) pointed out, sometimes the threat posed by an intended change is real. The fact is that change can create winners and losers. That is, some individuals or units can increase their power or gain a larger share of organizational resources as the result of a change. Because correctional budgeting often involves a zero-sum process, this means that some other individual or unit loses power or resources. In extreme cases, individuals may lose their jobs.

For example, in 1994, managers at the Wayne County (Michigan) Juvenile Detention Center were confronted with a Department of Justice review that had found numerous violations in the areas of medical care, programming, grievance procedures, and offender abuse. As a result, the facility lost its state license. New managers brought in to "clean house" determined that their priority had to be changing the organizational culture of the facility. To accomplish this change, they did the following:

1. Outside trainers were brought in to teach leadership and management skills to managers and supervisors.
2. Hiring standards were revised to require two years of experience or a college degree in sociology, psychology, or a related field.
3. The interview process for line staff was changed to require a one-day interview process that includes a tour.
4. Employees who abused juveniles were prosecuted through the efforts of a newly created special investigation unit.
5. All policy was enforced.
6. Eighty hours of staff training, more than the state requirement, was made the standard.

Institution	Total Cases	Total Charges	Charges Not Guilty	Percent of Charges Not Guilty	Charges Dismissed	Percent of Charges Dismissed	Total Percent Not Guilty & Dismissed
Adrian Temporary	610	643	52	8.1%	9	1.4%	9.5%
Alger Maximum	1,444	1,632	62	3.8%	67	4.1%	7.9%
Baraga Maximum	3,068	3,745	74	2.0%	69	1.8%	3.8%
Earnest C. Brooks	2,623	2,886	59	2.0%	77	2.7%	4.7%
Camp Program	3,866	4,106	246	6.0%	125	3.0%	9.0%
Carson City	2,503	2,818	111	3.9%	90	3.2%	7.1%
Carson City Temporary	615	664	15	2.3%	16	2.4%	4.7%
Chippewa	3,510	3,979	219	5.5%	148	3.7%	9.2%
Chippewa Temporary	1,608	1,848	81	4.4%	55	3.0%	7.4%
G. Robert Cotton	2,402	2,634	109	4.1%	81	3.1%	7.2%
Florence Crane Women's	949	1,037	82	7.9%	42	4.1%	12.0%
Charles Egeler	1,675	1,883	158	8.4%	72	3.8%	12.2%
Richard A. Handlon MTU	8,445	9,709	553	5.7%	521	5.4%	11.1%
Gus Harrison	2,527	2,877	195	6.8%	72	2.5%	9.3%
Hiawatha Temporary	924	980	85	8.7%	22	2.2%	10.9%
Huron Valley Men's	2,406	2,716	144	5.3%	60	2.2%	7.5%
Ionia Maximum	4,033	4,700	74	1.6%	152	3.2%	4.8%
Ionia Temporary	1,273	1,358	53	3.9%	19	1.4%	5.3%
Kinross	1,510	1,667	138	8.3%	51	3.1%	11.3%
Lakeland	766	802	66	8.2%	9	1.1%	9.4%
Macomb	1,630	1,792	147	8.2%	77	4.3%	12.5%
Marquette Branch	2,687	3,193	107	3.4%	115	3.6%	7.0%
Michigan Reformatory	3,800	4,462	180	4.0%	191	4.3%	8.3%
Mid-MI Temporary	846	930	31	3.3%	25	2.7%	6.0%
Mound	1,549	1,794	198	11.0%	110	6.1%	17.2%
Muskegon	3,356	3,704	177	4.8%	136	3.7%	8.5%
Muskegon Temporary	809	873	33	3.8%	21	2.4%	6.2%
Oaks	2,238	2,497	70	2.8%	66	2.6%	5.4%
Res. & Elec. Programs	3,737	4,190	230	5.5%	119	2.8%	8.3%
Riverside	1,854	2,043	99	4.8%	62	3.0%	7.9%
Ryan	1,106	1,283	106	8.3%	33	2.6%	10.8%
Saginaw	1,637	1,764	137	7.8%	32	1.8%	9.6%
SAI	102	114	0	0.0%	1	0.9%	0.9%
Robert Scott	1,998	2,421	264	10.9%	180	7.4%	18.3%
SPSM - Central Complex	2,630	2,920	224	7.7%	124	4.2%	11.9%
SPSM - South Complex	1,138	1,256	106	8.4%	40	3.2%	11.6%
SPSM-R&GC	312	343	8	2.3%	10	2.9%	5.2%
Standish Maximum	1,967	2,156	98	4.5%	129	6.0%	10.5%
Thumb	953	1,077	71	6.6%	27	2.5%	9.1%
Western Wayne	1,676	1,842	118	6.4%	73	4.0%	10.4%
TOTAL	**82,782**	**93,338**	**4,980**	**5.3%**	**3,328**	**3.6%**	**8.9%**

FIGURE 14–5 Major Yearly Misconduct Statistics: Yearly Totals—1995. Source: Michigan Department of Corrections. *1995 Statistical Report.* (1996): 165.

7. All managers were trained to teach by example.
8. Communication with juvenile court judges was increased.

9. A media liaison position was created.
10. The community was invited into the facility and a program of having a parent group come in each week

and for holiday dinners was initiated.

11. Community tours and solicitation of community suggestions were begun.
12. Employees who could not adjust to the new procedures and rules were fired.

Clearly, in view of the above, some of the detention center staff could define themselves as "losers"; however, as a result of these planned changes, the facility regained its state license and "in many ways has become a model for other detention centers" (*Corrections Professional,* 1997c:4).

While the personal source of employee resistance is important, the manager functioning as a change agent must understand and accept that there also exist organizational sources of resistance that can be quite difficult to overcome.

Organizational Sources of Resistance

Organizations, by their nature, are conservative (Hall, 1987:29). They actively resist change. There are six major sources of organizational resistance: (1) structural inertia, (2) limited focus of change, (3) group inertia, (4) threat to expertise, (5) threat to established power relationships, and (6) threat to established resource allocations (Katz and Kahn, 1978:714–715.) We will briefly examine each of these sources.

Structural Inertia
Organizational survival depends on developing mechanisms that promote stability. Applicant screening criteria are designed to admit only a certain type of individual into the organization. These individuals are then trained to engage in specific behavior that will promote stability. Policy, procedures, and rules have a central goal of achieving stability. Successful performance evaluations, and subsequent promotion, depend on the ability to conform to the organization's expectations.

Changing the organizational structure requires changing the mechanisms designed to promote stability. For example, the Profile at the beginning of the chapter presents John Rosecrance's proposal that the mission of probation departments be dramatically changed. What are the practical implications of such a proposal? Consider the Kansas DOC Community Corrections table of organization presented in Figure 14–6. This organization chart is the product of a mission "to enhance public safety and enforce offender accountability through the cost-effective use of community based supervision and control intervention" (Kansas Department of Corrections, 1997b). If Kansas adopted John Rosecrance's proposal, what organizational changes would occur? We can only speculate, but following the principle that changes in function result in changes in structure, we might find the following:

1. Mission statement would be changed to read: "To improve the quality of judicial decision making by providing in-depth investigative reports of probationer's backgrounds."

2. Functions such as program consultants, management systems analyst, funding oversight, program director, and local advisory board would almost certainly be eliminated because they would no longer be needed.

3. Existing local community corrections staff would have to be reoriented to a dramatically different role. Increased levels of stress would have to be monitored and treated.

4. Applicant screening procedures would be modified to emphasize the ability to effectively investigate and report findings. Job qualifications would be more oriented toward paperwork and less toward people.

5. Promotion criteria would change to reflect the increased value being placed on the ability to write effectively.

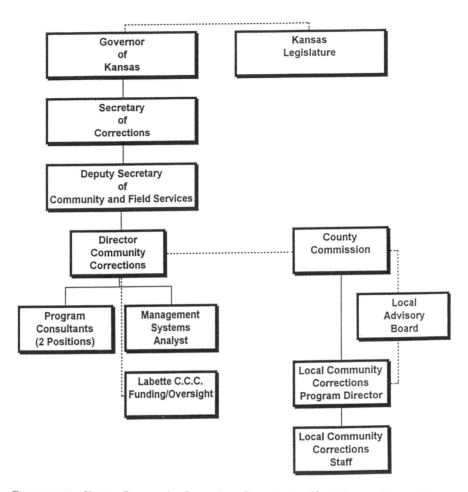

FIGURE 14–6   Kansas Community Corrections Organization Chart. Source: Kansas Department of Corrections, 1997b.

6. Policy, procedure, and rules manuals would undergo significant reorganization to reflect the new priorities.

7. Employees with a high need for human service–oriented work might leave, resulting in high levels of employee stress, dissatisfaction, and turnover.

8. The training curriculum would be dramatically changed with a far greater emphasis on the development of investigative and formal communication skills.

The list could go on, but the central point here is that the negative aspect of bureaucracies' being so successful in achieving stability is the enormous inertia associated with that stability. Inertia is a powerful force to overcome because people prefer to have stability. It makes their lives predictable and gives them a sense of control and power. The changes we have listed constitute a dramatic disruption of the stability mechanisms in place in the pre-Rosecrance probation department. Because disruption is the opposite of stability, employees frequently cling to the old way of doing things as long as they can. Therefore, our changes would most likely be slow in coming.

Slow Change Is Not Necessarily Bad   A slow process of change is not necessarily a negative. Rapid structural changes can be dangerous, at least in the short term, as the

Texas DOC learned during the early 1980s when Judge Wayne Justice's ruling in *Ruiz v. Estelle* forced it to dismantle the Building Tender system and find another method of controlling the inmate population. To accomplish that goal, Texas officials utilized an imitation strategy. They looked at other DOCs and adopted the policy of using C.O.s to directly supervise inmates. Thousands of new C.O.s were hired and Texas underwent the painful process of applying a new system of control to inmates conditioned to the Building Tender system. Initially, the results were negative:

In 1984 and 1985, a total of 52 inmates were murdered and over 700 were stabbed in Texas prisons. More serious violence occurred in those two years than had occurred in the previous decade. As the disorder mounted, inmate participation in treatment and education programs became erratic, inmate living quarters ceased to sparkle, and recreational privileges were curtailed. Hailed only a decade earlier as one of the nation's best penal systems, TDC became one of the very worst (DiIulio, 1987:206).

In Texas, an entire DOC had to undergo dramatic change in a short period of time. It can be argued that Texas could have achieved its current status with far less chaos if the necessary changes had been made more gradually, although the fact that the change was externally imposed by a court that the Texas DOC viewed as hostile would undoubtedly have increased the difficulty of implementing the changes no matter what time frame was in place. However, this level of massive change becomes increasingly rare as correctional professionalization increases. In general, changes with a limited focus occur far more frequently.

Limited Focus of Change
Look at any DOC organization chart and the number of interdependent departments is

obvious. Managers cannot change the policy in one department without that change having an effect on other departments. Changes that are limited in scope tend to be nullified by the larger organization. For example, a policy change in the Education Department to offer classroom instruction in the evening is likely to be nullified by a lack of corresponding change in recreational and visiting hours. Inmates given the opportunity for evening classes are likely to ignore that opportunity if it prevents recreation and visits. For this reason, managers focused on limited change must coordinate that change with other areas of operation.

Group Inertia
Group norms embedded in organizational subcultures can act as a constraint on behavioral changes. Union members may, as individuals, support a certain change but act to block it because of the official union position. For example, a probation or parole officer may be personally willing to accept compensatory time off for hours worked beyond the 40-hour week as an option to overtime pay because this allows flexibility in personal scheduling. But the union position may be that hours in addition to the standard 40 are always to constitute overtime for which money is received. The probation/parole officer who is a good union employee will refuse the option of compensatory time off. This may derail a manager's attempt to introduce a flextime system that will extend coverage to evenings and weekends.

Threat to Expertise
Change may threaten the expertise of specialized groups. For example, the use of business consultants may be resisted by correctional industry managers who fear that they will be shown to be deficient in current manufacturing and marketing methods. Proof of such deficiency is embarrassing and might endanger their employment. Correctional counselors might resist the contracting of counseling services to private drug and alcohol experts.

Threat to Established Power Relationships

Historically, the introduction of treatment personnel and female and minority correctional officers, as discussed in Chapter 3, threatened the power of the traditional white male correctional officer (Figure 14–7) because these individuals were perceived as having a dramatically different set of values and attitudes about offenders and the nature of corrections. White male officers feared that these new values and attitudes would reduce their authority and place them at greater risk. Employee empowerment is frequently perceived by correctional managers as threatening because it involves a sharing of decision-making authority and, in some instances, more control over the allocation of resources. Any redistribution of decision-making authority may be viewed as threatening the status and authority of managers. The introduction of unit management, in particular, is often resisted because it takes authority from managers and gives it to line staff. Very few people are willing to relinquish authority no matter how valid the argument for that relinquishment.

Threat to Established Resource Allocations

Change that will reduce the level of resources a powerful group will receive is resisted. However, the ability of a correctional organization to fight change is limited, especially when that change is being driven by public policy based on political expediency. Chapter 4 emphasized the role of public policy formulation in defining the correctional mission. When public policy changes, the impact on the correctional organization can be dramatic. Such was the case in Michigan in the early 1980s.

In the late 1970s, Michigan DOC managers attempted to replace antiquated facilities with modern facilities to relieve severe overcrowding—in five years there had been an inmate population increase of 7,000. This

FIGURE 14–7   This picture of the Leavenworth staff taken in the late 1950s shows the lack of diversity that no longer exists in corrections. Courtesy of the Office of Archives, Federal Bureau of Prisons.

attempt ran headlong into powerful political forces responding to a public demand for tougher crime control policies. The political refusal to listen to correctional managers resulted in the death of a massive prison construction plan and the passage of legislation that severely limited the use of good time credits and restricted parole eligibility. These actions, combined with an unenforced court ruling that had found prison conditions unconstitutional, created a high level of disorder within the correctional system.

The situation was complicated further when, in response to a fiscal crisis, the state legislature reduced DOC funding for the 1980 fiscal year by $7.7 million. This resulted in the elimination of 69 staff positions statewide and a sharp reduction in the amount of overtime available to the C.O.s. For fiscal year 1981, the budget was cut by an additional $2.9 million and 125 more positions were eliminated. To reduce overtime, shifts were often operated below the officially designated "critical level" of the minimum number of officers needed to safely operate the prison. C.O.s complained bitterly and frequently voiced their fears of the growing potential for increased violence and the possibility of riot. Given this convergence of events, many observers predicted a high probability of inmate unrest and were proven correct. Over a five-day period in 1981, five Michigan state prisons experienced inmate riots at a cost of approximately $9 million dollars. Fortunately, there were no deaths or serious injuries (Useem and Kimball, 1989:121).

So, it should now be clear that change is a reality and that there are numerous sources of resistance to it. This brings us to the issue of how to effectively manage change.

EFFECTIVE MANAGEMENT OF CHANGE

Moorhead and Griffin (1989:754–755) suggest that the effective change agent will do the following:

Take a Holistic View   Because an organization's subsystems are interdependent, a manager who has tunnel vision (i.e., looks only at the department, process, or procedure to be changed) will likely ignore the potential impact of a specific change on other departments and their employees. The result may be confusion, stress, and interdepartmental conflict, all of which could have been avoided by taking a holistic view of the situation under consideration. Change agents must anticipate the impact of change on overall organizational behavior.

Secure Top Management Support
Change without the support of top management is doomed to failure. Employee resistance to change is often communicated to top management, and managers who have initiated controversial change without giving them prior notification, and soliciting their support, may find their jobs jeopardized. Top managers are very sensitive to the issue of unauthorized policy changes being made by subordinate managers.

Reward Contributors   Those employees who help effect needed changes should be publicly rewarded. Any of the reward mechanisms discussed in earlier chapters can be used to recognize the contributions of employees who actively assist the change agent.

Encourage Participation   Problems related to employee resistance can be reduced through a process of employee participation that gives a sense of personal control and power.

Foster Open Communication   Open communication is critical to defusing the power of rumors. Misinformation, uncertainty, and ambiguities can be reduced by a process of two-way communication.

These last two actions require some elaboration. How does the change agent encourage employee participation and foster open communication? This is actually an issue of employee empowerment and organizational culture. An organizational culture in which employees are empowered is more likely to smoothly effect change than a culture in which employees are expected to obey their superiors without question. There is a strategy that can be useful in creating an empowered organizational culture. That strategy is known as "organizational development."

Organizational Development

Organizational development (OD) is a Theory Y–based employee strategy designed to increase the level of employee–manager trust, (2) increase the frequency of confronting problems rather than ignoring them, (3) create a work environment where authority is based on expertise as well as position power, (4) increase the level of personal satisfaction among employees, and (5) increase open communication within the organization (French, 1969:24). OD rests on a foundation comprising the following five activities:

Sensitivity Training   This is a method (often referred to as "T-groups" or "encounter groups") of changing behavior through unstructured group interaction. Employees are brought together into a process-oriented group for the purpose of increasing awareness of their personal behavior. A professional facilitator assists the members in working together to increase their ability to empathize, listen, tolerate individual differences, and improve conflict resolution skills. Sensitivity training is an approach applicable to every group in corrections. In California, for example, correctional officers are sent to conflict-resolution training to learn how to efficiently handle the tension involved in staff–inmate and inmate–inmate conflict. The goal of this training is to teach correctional officers appropriate methods for reducing the potential for violence in conflicts.

Survey Feedback   This method uses a survey questionnaire to ask for employee perceptions concerning personal job satisfaction, communication effectiveness, decision-mak-

ing practices, coordination between units, and satisfaction with the job, peers, and managers. The survey constitutes a feedback mechanism that allows managers to identify potential weaknesses in organizational structure and processes and take corrective action before a serious problem develops. This method can assure employees that their opinions do count by demonstrating that their opinions can influence organizational behavior.

Process Consultation   This involves an outside consultant's assisting managers in evaluating some aspect of organizational effectiveness. The purpose of the consultant is to provide insight into organizational processes and provide a joint diagnosis of problem areas. Correctional managers frequently call on the National Institute of Corrections (NIC), professional consultants (often retired managers), private contractors, and, more rarely, academics to provide this service. Employee empowerment can occur when consultant recommendations for improvement of the work environment reflect employee input and are implemented.

Team Building   One of the most useful methods of empowerment is team building, which brings a group of employees together for the purposes of situation analysis, priority definition, goal-setting, and role clarification in a common endeavor. Unit management and Total Quality Management (TQM) groups are examples of team building.

Intergroup Development   This method seeks to change the attitudes, perceptions, and stereotypes that groups have of each other. A popular technique involves each group's independently listing their perceptions of another group. The lists are then shared and distortions in perception are discussed. The fundamental assumption of this approach is that a breakdown in stereotyping will increase the ability of employees to engage in team building and constructive problem-solving activities. As this ability increases, employees feel more capable and in control.

Can Organizational Development Be Successfully Applied to Corrections?

Hollander and Offermann (1990) advise that there are significant obstacles to achieving empowerment: a subculture of low commitment to and acceptance of organizational goals, fear of managerial retribution, managerial reluctance to delegate authority if subordinates' mistakes can lead to disciplinary action against the manager, employees who possess a low need for autonomy and want the security of being told what to do, and managers with a high power need. Historically, corrections has possessed all of these obstacles in abundance; however, this does not mean that empowerment is an impossible goal. Employee empowerment should be an integral part of environmental design if change is to be smoothly managed. But employee empowerment is not the only issue. There must also be an effective change process.

PROCESS OF ORGANIZATIONAL CHANGE

Change must be orderly effected, through a strategic sequence of activities. There are two models that can be of use in discussing this aspect of the change process: Lewin's three-step model and the action research model.

Lewin's Three-Step Model

Kurt Lewin (1951) proposed that successful organizational change follows three steps: unfreezing the status quo, movement to a new state, and refreezing the change to make it permanent.

Unfreezing the Status Quo
The status quo is a state of equilibrium that is often difficult to overcome. In order to unfreeze the status quo, managers must promote a strategy of increasing driving forces while decreasing restraining forces. Driving forces are the activities that direct behavior away from the status quo. They involve a set of managerial incentives offered to the employees affected by the proposed change. Restraining forces are the activities that support the status quo. Their influence must be reduced, often through use of a counseling or disciplinary approach.

Skolnick and Bayley (1986:222–223) have identified a change strategy in the police literature that can be applied to unfreezing the status quo in corrections. This strategy involves the following combination of increased driving forces and decreased constraining forces: (1) influencing younger staff to accept the change, then promoting them, (2) urging the retirement of older staff and replacing them with new, more malleable staff, (3) identifying and enlisting the assistance of older staff who will "buy into" the change, (4) training middle managers to ensure a prochange attitude, (5) promoting prochange managers in the field to increase their influence, and (6) applying coercive power to punish those employees fighting the change.

Movement to a New State
This stage involves the dissemination of new policy and implementation of the procedures and rules necessary to enact the change. In many respects, this is the easiest stage, although the change process must be carefully monitored to ensure that every employee understands the nature of the change(s) being undertaken and the rationale(s) for change.

Refreezing the Change
Once the change is in place, managers must closely monitor employee activities and take corrective action whenever an employee appears to be drifting back to the old behavior. Continuous reinforcement with formal rules and regulations is necessary until the change is incorporated into the routine and becomes habit. The promotion of individuals who support the new policy will help ensure change permanence.

Lewin has proposed a model that focuses on managing the change. What is not addressed is the issue of determining the nature of the change. Change can assume a multitude of forms. How is the manager to determine the most beneficial change? That can be accomplished through use of the action research model.

Action Research Model

Shani and Pasmore (1985) describe a change process based on the systematic collection and analysis of data prior to selection of a specific policy change. The importance of this approach is that it provides a scientific methodology for managing planned change. The process involves diagnosis, analysis, feedback, action, and evaluation, and frequently uses a consultant.

Diagnosis

Information concerning problems, concerns, and needed changes is gathered from each level of staff. This process involves personnel interviews, the use of surveys, and scrutiny of agency records. The focus is on establishing the need for change and the area of the organization most in need of change.

Westbrook and Knowles (1997:115–118) have outlined a diagnostic process that requires the change agent to take the following actions:

Differentiate Between Language and Event This is similar to the expression "The map is not the territory." The language used to describe a specific situation is not the actual situation. The change agent must focus on what is really being said, not just the language being used. For example, a decision maker examining the management of elderly inmates may be told "our older guys are falling through the cracks when it comes to programming." This is the language used to describe the situation. The situation is that the organization has not yet developed a policy that requires the counselors to meet with their elderly offenders on

a regular basis to ensure that their special physical and psychological needs are being evaluated and met.

Determine the Precision of the Information The change agent must determine if the information presented is fact or opinion. Are elderly inmates being ignored by their counselors? Or are they being seen with the same frequency as the younger inmates?

Determine the Cause Rather Than the Blame The fundamental purpose of a diagnostic process is to investigate a situation to determine its cause(s). Making judgments about employee competence or worth is counterproductive. In the case of the elderly inmates, if they are "falling through the cracks," the question is: "Why are they being seen less often than the younger offenders?" The question is not: "Who's to blame for this lack of contact?" Seeking out individuals to punish does not address a problem that may in fact be organizational.

Determine if There Is More Than One Cause Seldom do problems have one cause. Any change based on such an assumption is likely to fail to correct the problem. Problems usually have a combination of sources. In the case of our elderly inmates, the causes may include a lack of relevant policy, caseloads that are too large, the tendency of older inmates to blend into the background, and a lack of specialized programming.

The result of this four-pronged diagnostic process will be the formulation of a working diagnosis, that is, a tentative plan of action. The accuracy of the diagnosis can be checked by asking the following questions:

1. Does the diagnosis take into consideration all available information?
2. Does the diagnosis specify the degree of certainty of the information and the relative importance of the information?
3. Does the diagnosis include an examination of relationships among points of view?

4. Does the diagnosis specify problems, causes, events, persons, interactions, facts, evidence, and so on?

5. Is the diagnosis organized in such a way that it facilitates identification of the central problem to be solved? (Westbrook and Knowles, 1997:118.)

Analysis

The information is analyzed to determine perceived needs for change, specific problems, and any patterns of problem, especially those that cut across department boundaries. Dramatic changes in baseline statistical data—for example, changes in the rate of inmate reception (Figure 14–8)—can

Year	Year-End Population	Numerical Change	Percent Change
1981	13,180	- - -	- - -
1982	13,272	92	0.7
1983	12,882	(390)	(2.9)
1984	13,162	280	2.2
1985	16,003	2,841	21.6
1986	18,836	2,833	17.7
1987	21,930	3,094	16.4
1988	25,377	3,447	15.7
1989	29,321	3,944	15.5
1990	31,240	1,919	6.5
1991	33,018	1,778	5.7
1992	35,131	2,113	6.4
1993	36,474	1,343	3.8
1994	38,145	1,671	4.6
1995	38,854	709	1.9

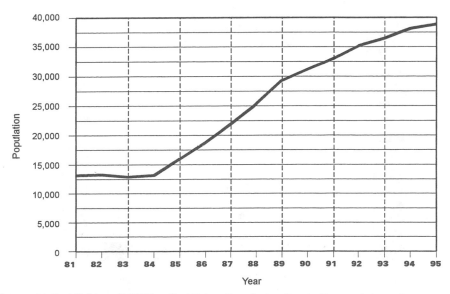

FIGURE 14–8   Michigan DOC Year-End Prison Population (Institutions and Camps). Source: Michigan Department of Corrections. *1995 Statistical Report* (1996a): 81.

serve as a warning of impending problems that will effect the entire department.

Clearly, based on the data in Figure 14–8, Michigan DOC managers engaged in strategic planning would have been alarmed by an increase of 25,000 inmates in a 14-year period and quickly realized that bed control would have to be both a short-term and a long-term priority. However, if in the future, a dramatic decrease in inmate populations occurs in Michigan (say, for example all mandatory sentencing was eliminated and a variety of drug laws are eliminated), DOC managers will have to readjust their vision of the future and decrease the emphasis on bed management.

A sharp increase in medical problems can also signal an issue that will need to be addressed during the strategic planning process. One such problem is AIDS (Figure 14–9). The increase in AIDS-related inmate deaths in Florida between 1990 and 1994 certainly waves a red flag to strategic planners in medical services that signals the need to make AIDS-related issues a planning priority. Conversely, if AIDS-related deaths level off or decrease in the future, priorities can once again be shifted.

Feedback

If change is to be effective, employees must believe that they have played a role in effecting that change. Feedback involves the sharing of information and analysis with the employees and the coordination of employee participation in developing a plan of action for initiating change. Feedback can be a significant help in reducing employee resistance because of the sense of responsibility that participation carries with it. For example, the counselors in our elderly inmate example could be invited to attend management meetings where the issue of elderly inmates is under discussion. This would allow them to review the data that has been gathered, provide direct input to decision makers, and react to proposed solutions before any policy is drafted.

Action

The specific activities necessary to implement the change are carried out. This phase of the change process constitutes a transition period during which staff stress levels may rise significantly, especially if the change affects a large number of departments and employees, or implementation is

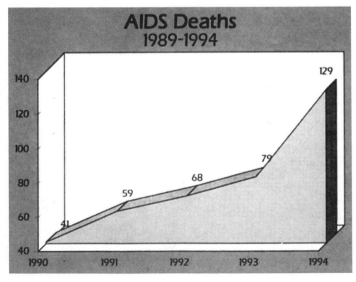

FIGURE 14–9   Florida DOC AIDS Deaths, 1989–1994. Source: Florida Department of Corrections. *1994–1995 Annual Report: The Guidebook to Corrections in Florida* (1995): 44.

taking longer than anticipated, as often occurs if the change involves new construction or extensive physical plant renovation. Correctional managers must carefully monitor employee and offender (if they are directly affected by the change) stress levels and be prepared to intervene if adjustment problems arise. Management by Walking Around (MBWA) can be effective during the transition period.

Evaluation

The change agent evaluates the effectiveness of the change that has been implemented, looks for problems, and initiates corrective actions. Evaluation of change effectiveness can be accomplished in part by "a look at the numbers"—compare the current numerical measurement of an event or situation with the previous numerical measurement. For example, on September 1, 1993, the Michigan DOC implemented a

zero-tolerance escape policy designed to "strengthen monitoring and accountability of prisoners in community programs" (Michigan Department of Corrections, 1996a:147). Zero-tolerance means that community-based program residents must adhere so strictly to their approved schedules that any deviation without mitigating circumstances is considered an escape requiring immediate apprehension and return to an institution. Based on the information presented in Figure 14–10, DOC evaluators concluded that "[w]alkaway escape returns increased sharply at first while prisoners got used to the policy, but the number of returns have since declined and stabilized" (Michigan Department of Corrections, 1996a:147).

Success in increasing inmate accountability is one measure of organizational effectiveness. Another measure is the reduction in escapes from prisons and camps (Figure 14–11) that

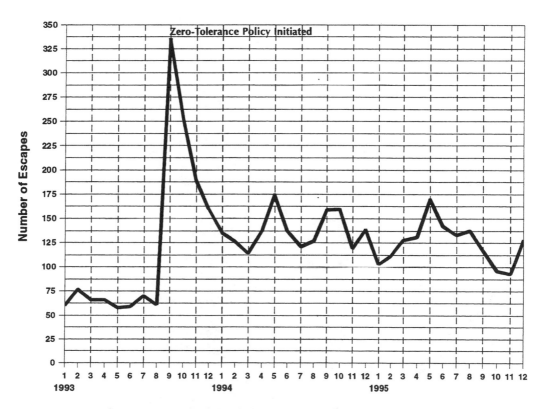

FIGURE 14–10 Michigan DOC Residential and Electronic Programs Walkaway Escapes, 1993–1995. Source: Michigan Department of Corrections. *1995 Statistical Report* (1996a): 147.

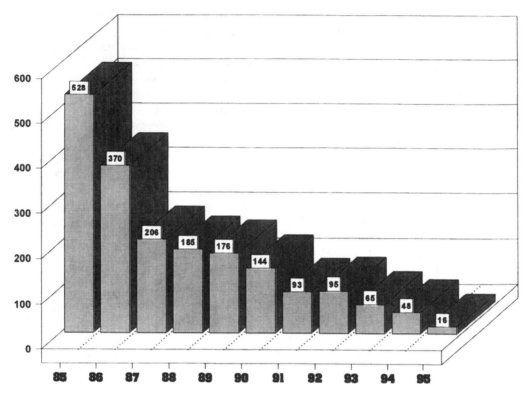

FIGURE 14–11   Michigan DOC Institution and Camp Escapes: Calendar Years 1985–1995. Source: Michigan Department of Corrections. *1995 Statistical Report* (1996a): 118.

results from improvements in staff training, technological advances, and improved security procedures. Managers reviewing the data in Figure 14–11 would conclude that their security improvement strategy had indeed been effective and could use this data to deflect any criticism of DOC security procedures. Future comparisons using the period of 1985 to 1995 as baseline data would quickly alert managers to any increase in escapes and the need to reevaluate security procedures.

The preceding models provide a structure for change management, but change agents must also understand that there is an ethical component involved.

RULES OF ETHICAL CHANGE MANAGEMENT

Employees and offenders can be harmed during any change process in the correctional organization. For this reason, correc-

tional managers need to develop and implement an ethical change management policy, i.e., a policy consistent with the basic ethical principles set forth in Chapter 13. An ethical change management policy requires correctional managers to structure the change process in such a way as to: (1) avoid people management failure; (2) objectively measure change effectiveness; and (3) be humane when change involves loss.

Avoiding People Management Failure

Employees have a fundamental right to know what is going on in the organization, especially if they are going to be affected by management actions. Managers unwilling to engage in two-way communication with their employees are inviting failure. Wismer (1979:31) identified seven managerial behaviors that can increase employee resistance to change. They are the failure to (1) be specific about the change, (2) show why the change is necessary, (3) allow people affected by the change to have a say in planning it, (4) consider the work group's habit patterns, (5) keep employees informed about the change, (6) prevent the creation of excessive work pressure during the change, and (7) deal with employee anxiety concerning job security or duties. Wismer (1979:31) also advocated that managers considering change should take group norms and habits into consideration, make only those changes that need to be made, and use proper problem-solving techniques (of the type presented in the above models).

Westbrook and Knowles (1997:115) suggested that the change agent can employ five strategies to minimize the negative impact of change. First, they can accept resistance as a natural reaction by understanding that change is a source of anxiety for many people. Second, they can encourage employees to express their concerns and any suggestions they have about a specific course of action. Third, they can inform all the employees of an impending change as soon as it has been determined that it should be made. Fourth, they can provide accurate knowledge of the proposed change, and its rationale. Fifth, the change agent can create employee interest and participation in the planned changes. One method of accomplishing this is to emphasize how the change will help employees better perform their duties.

Objectively Measure Change Effectiveness

The determination of change effectiveness cannot be arbitrary. The subjective evaluation of change effectiveness may harm the organization by permitting problems to remain undetected. The effectiveness of implemented change must be measured in some objective fashion so correctional managers can determine if goals prompting the change have been achieved. Objective measurement permits a more efficient identification of potential prob-

lem areas and possible solutions. One type of objective measurement is the use of performance-based standards, which focus on predetermined outcomes and goal attainments (Godfrey, 1997:94).

For example, the Office of Juvenile Justice and Delinquency Prevention (OJJDP) has funded the Performance-Based Standards Project to define juvenile correctional facility goals, objective criteria to measure performance, and a data collection protocol to measure facility performance (Godfrey, 1997). The project has determined that every juvenile correctional facility should strive to achieve three fundamental goals: (1) minimize fear among facility staff and residents, (2) minimize intentional injuries and accidents to staff and residents, and (3) minimize environmental risks within the facility. Sixty-three standards in the areas of safety, order, security, programming, health/mental health, and justice provide the objective criteria to measure success in achieving these three goals. The protocol instrument used to evaluate facility performance on each standard obtains data from general facility documents, juvenile and staff files, incident reports, and interviews with both juveniles and staff.

One standard involved in the goal to minimize intentional and accidental injuries to staff and residents, for example, is a requirement that facility staff protect residents from assault by other residents. To assess facility success in achieving this standard, performance is assessed based on the rate of injury to residents inflicted by other residents, looking for a decline over successive assessment periods. Additionally, the standards look for a classification system that considers juveniles' size, age, vulnerability to victimization, and nature of offense that is regularly used when making housing assignments. The data to be collected comes from incident reports (Godfrey, 1997:95).

Adoption of a performance-based measurement system can allow correctional managers to develop an objective database that can be routinely updated and evaluated over any number of years.

Be Humane When Change Involves Loss

For the manager, the realization that there are "losers" during any given change process imposes an obligation to administer that loss as humanely as possible. Specifically, any employees being negatively affected by change should be told as quickly as possible what is about to occur so they can make whatever plans they deem necessary. Letting people "twist in the wind" while rumors swirl around them will only create more rumors, bad feelings, and an expression of anger and resentment when the unwanted message is finally delivered. Employees should be given the opportunity to express their feelings about their loss and managers should devise ways to assist them in adjusting to their new status.

This brings us to one final consideration. No plan ever works exactly the way you think it will. This is known as the "law of unintended consequences."

THE LAW OF UNINTENDED CONSEQUENCES

Regardless of the change model used, managers must always be prepared to confront the law of unintended consequences: every change will have consequences that cannot be foreseen, no matter how diligent the planning activity or wise the planners. Introduction of the rehabilitation model, with all of its good intentions, created C.O. ambiguity, role conflict, and a host of alienation-related problems. The advent of community-based corrections had a widening effect that increased the number of offenders under correctional jurisdiction. The introduction of inmate programming and increased recreational opportunities gave rise to a popular public perception that inmates have it too easy and therefore prisons are failing to deter crime. A future unintended consequence of privatization may be governmental dependency on the private sector. Correctional managers must accept

that this law is immutable while striving to cover all the bases during change planning.

SUMMARY

Because change is inevitable, correctional managers must be effective change agents. They must understand basic principles of change management and develop the skills necessary to apply those principles to both planned and unplanned change situations. The most effective change process emphasizes an ongoing strategy of employee empowerment. The implementation of adaptive strategies must always be followed by evaluation and a willingness to make course corrections as they are required. We now turn to a topic that has a tremendous potential for organizational change: the future.

Discussion Questions

1. How does the staff subculture contribute to employee resistance to change?
2. What characteristics of the machine bureaucracy constitute an obstacle to change?
3. What actions can a manager take to effectively manage the change process from beginning to end?
4. What benefits does an organization derive from planned change?
5. What are the rules of ethical change management?
6. How would you factor the law of unintended consequences into a strategy of change management?

Critical Analysis Exercise: Architecture as a Reflection of Organizational Change

The architecture of a prison is the physical structure component of environmental design. Physical structure can complement or undermine the influence of policy, training, and evaluation. Historically, corrections has been dominated by the architecture of the fortress prison (sometimes referred to as the "Humphrey Bogart" prison) (Figure 14–12) . The fortress prison with its 30-foot walls and guard towers on the corners and over the gates was the typical prison at the end of the nineteenth century. Inmates were housed in massive cell-blocks with back-to-back rows of cells stacked three, four, or five levels high. This economical use of space resulted in thousands of inmates being jammed together into a very small physical area. Meals and recreation were concentrated at specific locations designed to service large groups of inmates in a short period of time. There was little programming space available. A classic example of the fortress prison is the Southern Michigan State Prison in Jackson, Michigan, which has housed as many as 6,000 inmates.

Recently, correctional managers have become interested in the construction of "new generation" prisons. These prisons have an architecture dramatically different from that of the fortress prison. Typical of this new generation prison is the Oak Park Heights correctional facility in Minnesota. Built into a hillside and earth sheltered, there are no gun towers and inmate housing is structured in a circular design containing eight 48-man units that are completely self-contained and separated from each other with all units connected by two corridors, one for inmate movement and one for staff movement. Each unit has its own dining, recreational, and laundry facilities. Several units contain Correctional Industries and others are dedicated to education, drug dependency, and sex-offender treatment programs. A separate mental health unit and a disciplinary segregation unit serve all units. The two tiers of cells in each unit face

FIGURE 14–12 What correctional philosophy and functions are suggested by this picture of the New York State Reformatory at Elmira? Courtesy of the Chemung Co. Historical Society.

a control room from which a C.O. can observe traffic flow and all inmate–staff and inmate–inmate interactions.

Critical Analysis Questions

1. How does architecture reflect the organizational mission?
2. Is the policy structure of a fortress prison equally applicable to a new generation prison? Why or why not?
3. What elements of the DOC mission statements presented in this book would you emphasize in the policy structure of a fortress prison? In a new generation prison? If both types of prison exist in the same DOC, would there be any difference in emphasis? Should there be? If there is a difference, what is the basis for that difference?
4. Does the fortress prison encourage an emphasis on custody and control to a greater extent than the new generation prison? Explain your answer.
5. Should the training of new correctional officers being assigned to a fortress prison differ from the training of officers being assigned to a new generation prison? Why or why not? If your answer is yes, how would the training differ?
6. Which type of prison is most likely to achieve American Correctional Association accreditation? What factors are most important in your answer?
7. Are policy, training, and evaluation more important than architecture in influencing the development of the professional officer? Defend your answer.

15
Future-Oriented Leadership

Learning Objectives

After completing this chapter, you should be able to:

- Outline a view of the major challenges that will confront correctional managers in the twenty-first century.
- Define restorative justice and contrast it with the public policy of the conservative revolution.
- Summarize the advantages of a corrections of place.
- Contrast the tough time prison with the traditional prison.
- Discuss the challenge that changing workforce demographics present to correctional managers.
- Outline the four major challenges for correctional managers.
- Define the ten competencies of the future-oriented leader.

Key Terms and Concepts

Sandin v. Connor
Community Corrections
Retributive Justice
Corrections of Place
Reparative Probation
Workforce
Future-Oriented Leadership
Prison Litigation Reform Act
Distributive Justice
Restorative Justice
Hot Spots
Tough Time Prison
Demographic Changes
Ten Competencies

Corrections is in the hands of men and women who think of themselves as professionals. For years far into the future, they will be preoccupied with applying their skill and their technology to the maintenance of control over vast numbers of prisoners.

John P. Conrad

Profile: Looking Toward the Future

[The following comments were prepared especially for this book by Reginald A. Wilkinson (Figure 15–1), Director of the Ohio Department of Rehabilitation and Correction and former President of the American Correctional Association.]

Corrections managers today are fortunate to be riding the cusp of change. While we may sometimes long for the "good old days" when predictability was our byword, it is an exciting time to be in this field. The decisions we make, the paths we follow, the options we choose—these will combine to map the future of corrections.

Outside forces also shape our future. News of crime, especially as portrayed on television, has brought a sense of immediacy and danger into America's living rooms. Our citizens list the fear of crime as an overriding concern in their lives. Public officials have responded with "get tough on crime" legislation. In many

FIGURE 15–1   Director Reginald A. Wilkinson, Ohio Department of Rehabilitation and Correction. Courtesy of Ohio Department of Rehabilitation and Correction.

jurisdictions, indefinite sentences and the hope of parole for many have been curtailed or eliminated. As a result, our prison populations will continue to grow, inexorably consuming more and more resources. It is conceivable that a taxpayer backlash will ensue, with a demand for more prudent use of expensive prison beds. Fortunately, a push for community-based sanctions and a greater range of creative punishments for nonviolent offenders is already in effect in various locales.

The influence of the courts on how prisons are managed is also in flux. The pendulum of public opinion and court decisions is swinging away from inmate rights and toward society's and victims' rights. For instance, a 1995 decision by the U.S. Supreme Court, *Sandin v. Connor,* has significantly limited the ability of inmates to claim due process rights in the prison environment. The recently enacted Prison Litigation Reform Act expresses the concerns of Congress and imposes substantial limitations on a prisoner's right to bring litigation and on the federal courts' ability to monitor prison management. Many states are also writing legislation to curb frivolous inmate lawsuits.

There is a need to put the "community" back into community corrections. Increasing attention is being given to the notion of restorative justice, which gives victims and communities a more profound role in the justice process. Restorative, or "community," justice is long overdue.

If, indeed, community sanctions are imposed on nonviolent offenders, prisons will increasingly become the repository for the more violent, predatory, and remorseless criminals. A greater concentration of violent offenders may create more tension among inmates and between inmates and staff. Added incidents of violence can be anticipated, resulting in more injuries or worse, and a requirement for more disciplinary cells.

Currently, prison populations are a mix of short-term offenders and "Lifers," definite and indefinite sentenced inmates, the young and the old. This diversity is reflected in a wide variety of program offerings. If populations become more long-term, programming must evolve accordingly. Corrections professionals will need to perfect the tenets of managing the long-term offender.

Prisoners facing decades of incarceration will also need tools with which to battle becoming institutionalized—not only as a humane gesture, but also to prepare for their survival after their eventual release.

Many of us have determined that removing predatory and other dangerous offenders from the population improves safety and security systemwide. By developing "super-max" prisons, we can isolate offenders in one facility. While this concept has come under some criticism, the benefits appear to outweigh the negatives: staff and inmates are safer; problem offenders participate in targeted, in-cell programming; super-max staff receive specialized training in working with dangerous prisoners; policies and procedures are specific to problem offenders without restricting the privileges of the general population; segregation cells in other facilities can be used more effectively when not clogged by repeat offenders; and finally, the super-max facility becomes a disincentive for seriously negative behavior.

Many prison populations are also becoming older. Geriatric care and programming are definite necessities for the immediate future. The older offender requires specialized programming and an environment that is more slowly paced. Similarly, more people will be dying in prison, not only due to longer sentences but also because of scourges such as AIDS and drug-resistant tuberculosis. It may be wise to develop "theme" units for those special needs.

Ameliorating the need for accommodating specialized populations is the concept of prototype prisons. We are no longer bound by the traditional—and costly—high stone walls and guard towers. Agencies are now encouraged to save time and money by designing and building "prototype" prisons. These simplified architectural plans can be utilized over and over again—modified slightly to fit security needs and the terrain. At the same time, high-tech security systems replace and augment human perimeter forces, improving accuracy and allowing us to use valuable manpower resources elsewhere in the facility.

As a society, we face the dilemma of young offenders who commit unimaginable crimes. Gang bangers, those who don't end up bleeding in the street, are also increasingly becoming our wards. What is to be done with these young castoffs of society? Many want to see these youth "rehabilitated." Others want them banished from society. Our adult prisons will be facing mounting numbers of ever-younger inmates serving, in some cases, very long sentences. An entirely new programming genre will have to be developed, possibly including gang member "recovery" programs to help young offenders achieve a productive life outside the counterfeit gang "family."

Training, also, will become more diverse. Reflecting the prison population, our employees will have to become better versed in supervising and caring for the very young, the very old, the mentally ill, and the infirm. The roles of custody and treatment, once sharply delineated, must continue to meld.

According to personnel pundits, the work "face" will also change as work "force" diversity continues to evolve. The corrections profession, once the sole purview of white males, has made significant progress in the past decades. The richness, creativity, innovation, and multiple viewpoints generated by a diverse workforce must continue to be encouraged and cultivated.

The next ten years will reveal whether the privatization of prisons will maintain its present momentum. If so, the evolution from public to private management may prove to be painful to correctional traditionalists. Debate on the pros and cons, rights and wrongs, of "punishment for profit" will rage back and forth. In the end, the profit margin and public opinion may be the determining factors on how much of the corrections profession will be outsourced to for-profit providers.

As communications, information, and networking become more and more accessible to the general public, we can expect a greater degree of interest in our profession. Just as victims' rights groups have used communications and the media to educate all of us about their needs and rights, other special interest groups will want to have a say in how we conduct our affairs.

The phrase "knowledge is power" has been a traditional mainstay of our profession. Proponents of this Jurassic school of thought will be left behind with the dinosaurs as the rest of us discover the multitude of benefits that information technology has to offer. The sharing of data, research, and intelligence is facilitated. "Surfing the net" brings us a world of creative ways to address our individual needs. Networking and benchmarking enriches all our agencies as we share what works and what doesn't. The inculcation of teamwork and interagency cooperation serves to make problem solving and decision making more relevant and more acceptable to our employees.

Other technological advancements such as less-than-lethal weaponry and improved surveillance and detection devices make the future, both near and far, exciting and unpredictable.

There's an old Arab saying that goes, "May you live in interesting times." We should count ourselves lucky that we do, indeed, live in interesting times.

Director Wilkinson has presented a concise summary of the challenges that correctional managers in the twenty-first century will have to confront. The ability to effectively manage these challenges will be influenced by the impact of changes in public policy on mission formulation and resource allocation. The continued use of an unprecedented rate of incarceration is simply untenable. As the number of incarcerated offenders, and the costs associated with that incarceration, continue to increase, the demand for a rational response to crime should also increase. The first element of a rational response could be an increase in the use of community corrections for the majority of offenders who are nonviolent. The second element could be creation of the tough time prison for those offenders judged to be too dangerous to remain in the community. The environmental design of correctional organizations in the twenty-first century will be influenced by public policy changes, changing workforce demographics, and the ability of current managers to become future-oriented leaders.

CURRENT STATUS OF CORRECTIONS

What is the current status of American corrections? Its policies and procedures continue to be driven by the massive prison overcrowding created by the conservative revolution. As of February 3, 1997, the number of incarcerated Americans was 1,630,940. To put this figure in perspective, on the same day, the population of Houston, Texas, was 1,700,000; the population of Nebraska was 1,650,000; the number of U.S. university graduate students was 1,700,000; and the number of active U.S. military personnel was 1,500,000 (*Time*, 1997:14). Between 1990 and 1996, America's adult prison population increased, on average, 7 percent per year with the rate of growth dropping slightly to 5.2 percent in 1997. The largest increase in the number of state inmates was for violent offenders, an increase of 179,500 (Bureau of Justice Statistics, 1998). The projected cost of the new construction required to house this level of increase is $26 billion in new prison construction and $12 billion in new jail con-

struction (Peak, 1997:381). It is estimated that the "three strikes" statute in California alone will cost an additional $5.7 billion and add an additional 276,000 inmates to the state prison system over the next 30 years if it is not changed or eliminated (Skolnick, 1995:4). The National Council on Crime and Delinquency estimates that if other states continue to amend their sentencing laws, $351 billion will be needed for corrections in the next ten years (*Corrections Digest,* 1994:1).

Can America continue to fund this level of increase? It is difficult to see how the answer could be anything other than no. The taxpayer well is going dry, despite military cutbacks and welfare system dismantling. There is a growing concern that expenditures to corrections are diverting funding from education and social service programs. Take California, for example. Ten years ago, the budget for higher education was two and a half times the budget for corrections. In 1994, California's $3.8 billion corrections budget was equal to the entire higher education budget. By the year 2000, corrections is predicted to require 18 percent of the entire state budget while higher education will be allocated less than 1 percent (Zimbardo, 1994:7–8; Skolnick, 1995:4). Cutbacks in higher education are a liability as America moves into a future that requires a highly educated workforce.

The End of the Prison Building Boom?
However, the predictions of a continuing prison building boom may be wrong. Lemov (1997) reported that there are strong indicators that states are beginning to reject the concept of building out of prison overcrowding. First, the leaders in building out—California, Texas, North Carolina, Florida, and Virginia—are near the end of their five- and ten-year building programs and are projecting that they will have sufficient beds to handle future increases. Second, political leaders are showing an increased reluctance to continue to divert money from social programs (like higher education) into corrections. The long-term

cost of operating new prisons is beginning to be realized. Third, the incarceration rate is slowly dropping, down from 8 percent in 1996 to 5 percent in 1997. In many states, such as Florida, the projected population increases are far higher than what has materialized. North Carolina, for example, will finish construction of three new prisons, but they will not be opened unless the inmate population begins to increase. Texas has 6,000 of its 30,000 new prison beds sitting empty. Finally, estimates of the consequences of three-strikes legislation may have been faulty because states have frequently overestimated the number of felons who would be affected.

The issue of incarceration as a primary method of responding to crime goes beyond cost, however. The success of this approach is also an issue. A growing number of individuals believe that the mission of prisons to protect society has failed because "they cannot remove the criminal element totally from our midst, they cannot protect society on any long-term basis, and they cannot (and do not) rehabilitate in any systematic way" (Farrington, 1992:23). Economics and the perception that prisons have failed to address the crime problem suggest that a shift in public policy will be required in the near future.

NEW DIRECTIONS IN PUBLIC POLICY

Morgan-Sharp and Sigler (1996) suggest that a public policy shift from a preference for punishment to one of treatment as a disposition for criminal offenders may now be on the horizon. Support for this position is seen in a growing body of research suggesting that the public's attitude is not as punitive as is often depicted in the press or perceived by elected officials (Cullen and Gendreau, 1988).

To cite a few examples, Doble and Klein (1989) found that Alabama citizens, if educated about prison costs and the nature of offenders, were willing to tolerate a much

lower level of incarceration and support work and community service programs. In Ohio there was strong public support for early parole based on good behavior and participation in education and work programs (Skovron, Scott, and Cullen, 1989). Bennett (1991) reported on a study by the American Justice Institute that found public support for community-based programs such as intensive supervision, boot camp, drug treatment programs, and restitution centers. The Figgie Report (1985) found mixed support for parole: only 8 percent of the public believed that parole should be abolished; 24 percent felt it should be retained in the form that it existed at the time of the study; and 61 percent said the parole system does need reorganization. Doble (1987) has reported findings of support for crime prevention through social programs. Mande and English (1989) reported no evidence of a "lock 'em up and throw away the key mentality" in Colorado. Rather, they found public acceptance of community treatment of offenders. A 1991 Wirthlin Group national poll found 80 percent of Americans favoring a community sentence for nonviolent offenders (Irwin and Austin, 1997:58–59). Finally, Applegate, Cullen, and Fisher (1997) found strong support in Ohio for correctional treatment programs and the idea that the primary aim of incarceration should be rehabilitation.

Shifting Public Policy from Punishment to Treatment   Branham (1992) has proposed a public policy shift that includes the following elements. First, sentencing structures will be transformed through the repeal of all mandatory sentencing statutes. Second, every legislature will be required to prepare detailed correctional impact statements before enacting any legislation that has the potential to increase the number of people under correctional supervision. Third, judges will sentence in accordance with sentencing guidelines that reserve prison space for violent offenders and include a range of community-based options, including the extensive use of means-based fines as sanctions. Thus, those offenders with financial resources can be hit in the wallet. Fourth, judges will be able to employ a sentencing structure that allows a graduated response to violations of community-based sanctions. That is, automatic revocation of probation and parole leading to incarceration will be replaced by a system of increased supervision, special conditions, and fines.

In addition, Branham has proposeed the development of policy provisions for a wide range of alternative sanctions for nonviolent offenders and probation/parole violators; provision of adequate funding levels for treatment programs designed to reduce recidivism; and a mandatory requirement that from 3 percent to 5 percent of the correctional budget be earmarked for research targeting a broad range of correctional effectiveness issues.

Morgan-Sharp and Sigler (1996:248) caution that a continuing public concern with the perceived increase in the amount and seriousness of violent crime may moderate legislative action. They are probably right. The fear of crime is so deeply ingrained in the public psyche by the mass media that it is unlikely that there will be a dramatic repeal of mandatory sentencing or emptying of the prisons in the immediate future. In fact, the push for increased sentence length continues in many areas of the country. To cite one example, in November 1994, Oregon voters approved Measure 11, an initiative that increased minimum sentences and is expected to create a need for 10,000 more beds in the Oregon DOC by 2004 (Bryant and Taylor, 1996:96). As long as drug use is viewed as a cause of crime, large numbers of drug offenders will probably continue to be incarcerated.

However, there is always the law of unintended consequences to consider. For example, as Lemov (1997:33) has noted, the Oregon law is currently being used by prosecutors as a lever to increase plea-bargaining, and the projection of the need for 10,000 new beds has been reduced by 14 percent.

Instead of a wholesale repeal of "get tough on crime" laws, there will most likely be a retuning of existing statutes to permit certain types of offender to go into community corrections instead of incarceration. Morgan-Sharp and Sigler (1996) believe that any public opinion shift in the direction of treatment-oriented reform and moderation of the punishment paradigm will take the form of an expansion of community corrections. If a public policy shift toward community corrections does occur, how will managers use this resource?

ENVIRONMENTAL DESIGN OF COMMUNITY CORRECTIONS

Scott (1996:172) suggested that probation-based intervention programs in the future will be expected to address issues such as "literacy, drug treatment, job counseling, mental illness, and parenting skills in the struggle to help probationers succeed." In order to address these treatment needs, as well as carry out the role of supervision and surveillance, probation departments will need to develop increasingly sophisticated risk-assessment instruments and rely more extensively on computer technology. Scott (1996:174) further suggested that the probation department of the future will have bullet-proof, lightweight clothing; biomedical monitoring; and reliable electronic surveillance technology. Probation departments will work much more closely with government education and job training agencies and specialized treatment programs for such difficult clients as sex offenders may become the norm. Strict control of the offender's community environment will be the hallmark of the future probation office. It is almost certain that parole departments will move in the same direction.

However, Scott has also sounded a note of warning. Because historically the swings of the pendulum in public policy concerning crime and punishment have rarely involved any degree of meaningful planning, correctional managers must try to prepare for a sudden dumping of large numbers of offenders into probation and parole systems that have not received additional resources.

The focus of a public policy shift toward community corrections may well have two additional dimensions: the implementation of restorative justice and creation of the tough time prison.

RESTORATIVE JUSTICE: WAVE OF THE FUTURE?

A concept that is currently being reintroduced into public discussion is the policy of restorative justice: a paradigm shift from a punishment philosophy that ignores both victim and community. Eglash (1977) identified three models of criminal justice: (1) retributive justice based on punishment, (2) distributive justice based on rehabilitation, and (3) restorative justice. Eglash noted that the first two models have three deficiencies: a focus on the actions of offenders, a denial of victim participation in the process of justice, and passive offender participation. Restorative justice corrects these deficiencies.

Restorative Justice Perspective

Restorative justice shifts the focus of attention to the harmful effects of offender behavior and actively involves both victims and offenders in the justice process.

Rejecting the "Get Tough on Crime" Approach Restorative justice is the antithesis of the "get-tough-on-crime" approach. It rejects the fundamentally punitive mechanisms of chain gangs, hard labor, harsh boot camp regimens for juvenile offenders, and proposals to end such "amenities" as television, smoking, and weight lifting, all of which are designed to frighten offenders into going straight, despite the evidence that such programs do nothing more than provide a false sense of justice being accomplished. Restorative justice is based on a belief that the extensive use of punishment as deterrence has failed

because this approach does not meaningfully include victims and offenders in making decisions about criminal sentences. Its focus is on self-management and control, problem solving, and attitude changes (Immarigeon, 1995). Restorative justice can be formally defined as a process that focuses on the injury resulting from the crime and works to repair that injury by shifting the role of the offender from passive recipient of punishment to active participant in reparation. It is a community-based model for criminal justice intervention that engages the offender, the community, and the victim, although victim involvement is voluntary. In the restorative justice model, accountability on the part of the offender means taking responsibility for the harmful behavior and acting to repair the harm. Accountability on the part of the community means providing support for the victim and opportunity for the offender to repair the harm through community service (Minnesota Department of Corrections, 1995:12).

Changing the Mission of Corrections

The mission of corrections under a restorative justice public policy structure could be modified to emphasize a significant expansion of community corrections by replacing a punitive orientation with a "place" orientation. The term *corrections of place* embodies the concept that the focus of corrections is no longer on offender punishment but is rather directed toward community safety and the quality of community life:

The corrections system can broaden its focus beyond the supervision of offenders to include such activities as working with victims, organizing community groups, and developing crime prevention strategies for specific crime problems. The central question becomes "What short- and long-term approaches promote a safer community?" Any answer has to recognize that offenders are members of the community and important consumers of safer streets (Clear, 1996:53).

Restorative justice can borrow from the law enforcement concept of policing hot spots to develop an approach that allocates high levels of correctional resources to those areas of the community with large proportions of identified offenders—a geography-based allocation of correctional resources. A corrections of place (Clear, 1996) shifts correctional personnel from the world of the prison to the larger world of the community through an emphasis on crime prevention and community involvement.

Correctional employees can engage in crime prevention by emphasizing relapse prevention through an intensive system of communication with the offender and the people in the offender's life. Correctional employees, in effect, can become guardians of the community who are constantly on the lookout for signals of reoffending and work with offenders, victims, the police, community leaders, and other government agencies to make community safety a priority. For example, Vermont is pioneering the concept of reparative probation, a program designed to bring offenders face to face with five community members at a community meeting designed to negotiate a detailed plan for the offender to repay both the victim and the community. The plan can include community service work, restitution, victim–offender mediation, decision-making programs, skills development, and any approach that will bring offender and community together.

However, community involvement is not a one-way street. It is not enough for corrections to reach out to the community. The community must also accept its responsibility to support offenders and receive them back into the community—to give them a second chance by providing employment opportunities, mentoring, and guidance. In a corrections of place, managers will co-locate services with other community services in order to bring corrections out of a prison context into a community context.

Will the Public Accept Restorative Justice? Steele and Quinn (1995) noted that a number of public opinion surveys have elicited high levels of support for restorative justice and that "a growing body or research in North America and Europe is finding that the process of mediating conflict between crime victims and offenders provides many benefits to the parties involved, the community, and the justice system" (Steele and Quinn, 1995:530).

The National Institute of Corrections and Restorative Justice

The National Institute of Corrections (NIC) has been interested in restorative justice since 1993. In 1997, the NIC Information Center conducted a national needs assessment that targeted 300 community and corrections agencies with a victim orientation or interest. Five areas of needed assistance were identified:

- Establishing and maintaining community involvement and partnerships (82 percent)
- Identifying funding and resources (68 percent)
- Defining and implementing community and restorative justice processes (65 percent)
- Involving offenders in the sanctioning process (62 percent)
- Developing strategies for working with victims (60 percent) (Dooley, 1997:111).

The NIC has disseminated information on the concepts of restorative justice through (1) the use of national satellite two-hour video conferences downlinked to more than 350 sites in the United States and Canada, (2) seminars, (3) development of a curriculum package that includes lesson plans, participant materials, and other training-related resources, and (4) five regional symposia developed in conjunction with the National Institute of Justice (Dooley, 1997:112–114).

But what about that proportion of offenders who are too dangerous for restorative justice? They will always be present in our society and corrections must be prepared to manage them. It is possible that the nation will address this issue by continuing to build super-max prisons, but these may well be self-defeating if such prisons do not change offender attitudes. Quinlan (1993) has proposed a less punitive approach: the tough time prison.

THE TOUGH TIME PRISON

For the truly dangerous offenders, J. Michael Quinlan, former Director of the Federal Bureau of Prisons, recommends incarceration in a tough time prison. A tough time prison, as proposed by Quinlan, would be a cost-effective alternative to traditional incarceration and would be characterized by (1) a spartan environment of limited family visits and phone calls, no television, and virtually no personal property; (2) a carefully structured program of work, drug treatment, and educational programming; (3) a rigorously enforced due process decision-making structure; and (4) highly trained, professional staff. The recruitment of educated employees and a high level of sophisticated training would be essential elements of developing tough time prison managers and staff to ensure that a proper balance between treatment and rigorous discipline would be consistently maintained. The tough time prison would not be isolated from the community; partnerships with community organizations would be valued (Quinlan, 1993:61).

Effective use of the tough time prison would require a classification process designed to screen out particularly dangerous inmates, such as violent offenders and organized crime leaders. In the tough time prison, an inmate would receive two days' credit for every day served. Release from prison would be followed by a community corrections component that would provide strict supervision, regular drug testing, and reincarceration for criminal behavior or rule violations (Quinlan, 1993:61).

Cearly, the history of corrections suggests that corrections-related public policy changes in one form or another will occur in the future. But there is another external challenge on the horizon: the demographics of the workforce is changing.

CHANGING WORKFORCE DEMOGRAPHICS

The American workforce of the twenty-first century will likely bear little resemblance to the white, male-dominated workforce that has historically characterized corrections. Four converging demographic trends in American society will have an impact on corrections that will require its managers to develop new organizational models to "permit flexibility, employee participation, and proactive human resource strategies" (Gido, 1996:273).

Johnston (1987), in a comprehensive workforce analysis, identified the four demographic trends. First, the U.S. population and the current workforce is aging while the number of "replacement youth" in the labor pool is declining by 2.7 million. Second, new-job creation will be concentrated in occupations emphasizing literacy, problem solving, communication, and analysis skills. The growing legal and technological complexity of the correctional work environment is rapidly moving corrections toward the day when a high school diploma will not equip employees for the responsibilities they must assume. Employees who are reading at eighth-grade levels cannot be the corrections worker of the future. Third, women will make up about 60 percent of the new entrants into the workforce between 1990 and 2000. This means that women will most likely cease being a numerical minority in corrections. Fourth, blacks, Hispanics, and other minorities will make up about 57 percent of labor force expansion in the 1990s. Many of these individuals could be immigrants with poor educational backgrounds and a lack of the most sought after technological skills.

Four Challenges for Correctional Management

These demographic shifts will combine to create four challenges correctional managers cannot ignore (Gido, 1996:275–276). The first challenge involves the availability of individuals qualified to work in corrections. Gido suggested that correctional mangers will face a rapidly approaching future in which competition for higher-paying skilled jobs, and a shrinking labor pool, in the private sector will drive up salaries to a level corrections will not be able to match. As a result, corrections may be confronted with a recruitment pool consisting to a large extent of semiskilled and unskilled workers: the same type of pool Pre-DOC Corrections drew from when physical strength, the ability to use force, a submissive deference to authority, and a high tolerance for routine were the only job requirements.

In order for the unskilled or semiskilled worker to perform in the increasingly complex correctional environment, corrections will have to dramatically increase its training budgets. The length of basic training will have to be extended with an increased emphasis on developing remedial reading and writing skills. In-service training time and frequency of programs will also need to be increased. The question is whether correctional budgets will be adequate to meet this challenge. As fiscal conservatism demands greater efficiency, training budgets may well be cut. An imperative for environmental design will be the creation of a policy structure that will enhance the ability to retain (and retrain) experienced employees.

The second challenge, created by the shrinking pool of "replacement youth," will be the increased retirement of experienced staff and managers who will have to be replaced by individuals who, in many cases, may not have the qualifications for the position. The dilemma of an inadequate depth of the managerial pool is already occurring in DOCs where rapid prison construction has had the unintended consequence of diluting the overall number of suitable management candidates. As experienced managers retire or are promoted to fill the vacancies created by new prison construction, their vacancies are being filled by line staff who may not be adequately prepared for the position. This situation is likely to become progressively more serious as the overall number of "replacement youth" in the societal labor pool decreases. The negative consequence of having too many inexperienced managers can be dramatic, expensive mistakes.

The third challenge derives from the increased number of women and minorities in the labor pool. Will correctional managers be able to develop the race- and gender-sensitive recruitment and retention policies necessary to draw women and minorities into a field traditionally dominated by white males, some of whom do not want to see that dominance eroded further than has already occurred since the 1960s? Can managers develop the proactive strategy that will end sexual and racial discrimination in corrections?

The fourth challenge involves employee empowerment. The introduction of unit management in prisons and a diversified role of probation and parole officers has, to some extent, flattened the organization chart in corrections. Will this trend toward employee participation continue?

The questions created by the changing nature of the workforce present powerful challenges, but each challenge can be successfully met. The key to meeting them will be found in the exercise of future-oriented leadership.

EXERCISE OF FUTURE-ORIENTED LEADERSHIP

How should we define the future-oriented leader? Gray, Stohr-Gillmore, and Lovrich (1990), in a study of Washington State Police, defined future-oriented managers as individuals who possess the following three qualities: (1) an acceptance of the need to implement a participatory management philosophy at every level of the organization; (2) a willingness to sponsor continuous, long-term training in participatory management and team building that applies training to problems existing at every organizational level; and (3) a willingness and ability to establish "verteams" (vertical teams) to enhance information exchange and make policy recommendations at every level. These measures have the effect of decreasing centralization and empowering employees.

The future-oriented leader will engage in a proactive strategy of environmental design that defines challenges and resources, and attempts to involve every level of employee in organizational problem solving. The leaders of the future must possess a respect for strategic planning and the knowledge that employees can be motivated to accomplish tasks that sometimes seem impossible. The correctional leaders of the future are those managers who accept the need to be proactive in achieving the following four goals.

First Goal The first goal is to transform the correctional employee from a passive worker in a paramilitary machine bureaucracy to a professional with a participatory role in a professional bureaucracy. Mease (1993:2) has suggested that such a transformation will involve structural innovations such as revising the basic rank system, replacing military titles with selected personnel grades, and decreasing the number of authority levels. Fundamental to participatory management is an environmental design that places a high priority on training employees from the first day of employment to handle higher levels of responsibility and periodically offers opportunities for increased participation in decision making. To successfully achieve this goal, correctional leaders must confront organizational inertia head-on by rejecting the "We've always done it this way" philosophy.

Second Goal The second goal is to reject the traditional managerial approach of circling the correctional wagons behind the wall or fence and concentrating on keeping inmates inside and the community outside. Leaders should not be afraid to educate the public to question self-defeating public policies that bloat prison populations and drain the tax coffers. The historical fear of political retaliation that has made corrections the victim of policy based on political expediency must be replaced by a collective decision to exert leadership in the formulation of public policy affecting corrections. A good place to start would be the strong public advocacy of the restorative justice model and elimination of mandatory sentencing structures.

Third Goal The third goal is to begin to seriously utilize research findings when meeting with political leaders and during the formulation of correctional policy decisions. Lovell (1994), in a study of a DOC, determined that with rare exception most correctional managers are reluctant to involve their organization in research studies because of concerns that research findings will be used against the agency by a disgruntled employee or lend ammunition to the critics of corrections. However, there is a compelling reason for managers to put aside their fears and willingly enter into a research relationship with academia and other private and public research organizations. How else are managers, elected officials, and the public to know what truly works and what is just hype? Instead of fearing the results of research, managers should encourage research, particularly in the areas of employee empowerment, leadership development, offender programming, and privatization.

Fourth Goal To accomplish the first three goals, current correctional managers must commit to an ongoing personal development program that emphasizes the mastery of the ten correctional leadership competencies noted by Moss and Rans (1997:118) in their discussion of the NIC Correctional Leadership Competency model:

1. Innovation. Feeling comfortable in a rapidly changing environment, taking risks, and actively considering new and untested approaches to old and new problems.

2. Strategy. Analyzing the future impact of decisions by using a strategic planning approach that attempts to anticipate and address future organizational needs.

3. Excitement. Operating with a high level of energy that will keep employees stimulated, enthusiastic, involved, and committed.

4. Communication. Stating well-defined goals and expectations while maintaining a precise and constant flow of information in a two-way communication process.

5. Delegation. Enlisting the talents of others to help meet goals by providing the opportunity to engage in important projects that require the exercise of autonomous judgment and decision making.

6. Feedback. Letting others know in an honest and straightforward manner how well they have performed and communicating the specific improvements in performance that are expected.

7. Management Focus. Gaining satisfaction from leading, directing, organizing, and controlling the efforts of employees in the attempt to meet official and operative goals.

8. Production. Advocating a strong bottom-line orientation, stating high expectations for oneself and employees, and motivating every member of the organization to grow and achieve.

9. Consensus. Soliciting opinions and suggestions from peers and employees to inform the decision-making process.

10. Empathy. Showing a genuine concern for the needs of other people by developing supportive relationships with them.

In addition, we can add the competencies of demonstrating a high level of ethical behavior in one's personal and professional life and showing a willingness to work with individuals and groups outside of the correctional organization.

SUMMARY

The future of corrections is a future of challenges. The failure of punishment-oriented approaches has demonstrated the urgent need for a shift to community-based corrections and a philosophy of restorative justice that actively brings together corrections and the community. Correctional managers must address the challenge of punitive public policies, overcrowded prisons, and a dramatic shift in workforce demographics that may drain corrections of its most experienced managers just when it needs them the most. Most important, the managers of corrections must be individuals capable of, and willing to provide, future-oriented leadership. Change often comes slowly to corrections, but change is possible and challenges can be met. Today's corrections professionals are proving that truth every day.

Discussion Questions

1. In reviewing the Profile, are there any significant issues you would have added? If so, what are they?
2. How would you determine which offenders should be placed in the community under a policy of restorative justice?
3. What might be a hidden danger(s) in a policy of restorative justice? How would you plan to reduce this danger(s)?
4. Will the tough time prison lower recidivism more effectively than the traditional prison? Defend your answer.
5. What are the risks and benefits associated with correctional managers' becoming leaders?

Critical Analysis Exercise: Bringing the Best and the Brightest into Corrections

One indisputable fact of life is that the key to any organization's success is its people. If employees are intelligent, motivated, proactive, and responsive to challenge, then the probability of successful achievement of the mission is increased. The challenge confronting the correctional manager is twofold. First, how do you attract the best and the brightest to enter such a demanding work environment? The vast majority of high school and college graduates, even if they are interested in criminal justice, rarely think of entering corrections. Second, once the best and the brightest are brought into corrections, how can they be retained? What can be done to keep the best and the brightest in a field that urgently needs them?

Critical Analysis Questions

1. What incentives could be provided to attract highly qualified individuals to work in a prison?
2. What incentives could be provided to attract highly qualified individuals to work in community corrections?
3. What structural/design changes would be most effective in attracting highly qualified individuals into corrections?
4. What public policy changes will enhance the ability of corrections to attract highly qualified individuals?
5. What would you personally require from corrections to motivate you to enter the profession?

References

Adams, J. Stacy. "Toward an Understanding of Inequity." *Journal of Abnormal Psychology* 67 (1963): 422–436.

———. "Inequity in Social Exchanges." In *Advances in Experimental Social Psychology,* edited by L. Berkowitz, 267–300. New York: Academic Press, 1965.

Adler, Freda, Gerhard O. W. Mueller, and William S. Laufer. *Criminal Justice.* New York: McGraw-Hill, 1994.

Advisory Commission on Intergovernmental Relations. *Jails: Intergovernmental Dimensions of a Local Problem, A Commission Report.* Washington, DC: U.S. Government Printing Office, 1984.

Adwell, S., and L. E. Miller. "Occupational Burnout." *Corrections Today* 47(7) (1985): 70, 72.

Agor, W. H. "The Logic of Intuition: How Top Executives Make Important Decisions." *Organizational Dynamics* (Winter 1986).

Alabama Department of Corrections. *Request for Proposal for Contracted Medical Services* (1991).

Alderfer, Clayton P. "An Empirical Test of a New Theory of Human Needs." *Organizational Behavior and Human Performance* (May 1969): 142–175.

Alexander, Kim. *Deep Pockets: 1991–1992 Top Ten Contributors to California Legislative Campaigns.* Sacramento, CA: Common Cause, 1993.

Alexander, Myrl E. Foreword to *Prisons and the American Conscience: A History of U.S. Federal Corrections,* by Paul W. Keve. Carbondale: Southern Illinois University Press, 1991.

Allen, Harry E., and Clifford E. Simonsen. *Corrections in America: An Introduction.* 8th ed. Upper Saddle River, NJ: Prentice Hall, 1998.

Alpert, G. P., and C. R. Huff. "Prisoners, the Law and Public Policy: Planning for Legal Aid." *New England Journal of Prison Law* 7 (1991): 307–340.

American Correctional Association. *Final Report of the Task Force on Victims of Crime.* Laurel, MD: ACA, 1988.

———. *Standards for Adult Correctional Institutions.* 3rd ed. Lanham, MD: ACA, 1990.

———. *Gangs in Correctional Facilities: A National Assessment (Preliminary Result)* (1993) (unpublished).

———. *Directory of Juvenile and Adult Correctional Departments, Institutions, Agencies and Paroling Authorities.* Lanham, MD: ACA, 1997.

American Jail Association. "Policy Statement on Correctional Privatization." *Journal of Contemporary Criminal Justice* 7(1) (1991): 69.

American Probation and Parole Association. "Special Issue: Incorporating Victim Services." *Perspectives* 18(3) (1994).

Andring Sr., Ronald. "Deliberative Mentoring: Creating Tomorrow's Leaders by Design." *Corrections Today* 59(6) (1997): 109–111.

Appel, Alan. "Requirements and Rewards of the Americans with Disabilities Act." *Corrections Today* 57(2) (1995): 84–86.

Applegate, Brandon K., Francis T. Cullen, and Bonnie S. Fisher. "Public Support for Correctional Treatment." *Prison Journal* 77(3) (1997): 237–258.

Archambeault, William G. "Impact of Computer Based Technologies on Criminal Justice: Transition to the Twenty-First Century." In *Visions For Change: Crime and Justice in the Twenty-First Century,* edited by Roslyn Muraskin and Albert R. Roberts, 229–316. Upper Saddle River, NJ: Prentice Hall, 1996.

Arizona Department of Corrections. *Incident Management System Manual* (1993).

———. *1995 Annual Report* (1996).

Arkansas Department of Corrections. *Annual Report: 1994–1995* (1996).

Ashforth, B. E., and R. T. Lee. "Defensive Behavior in Organizations: A Preliminary Model." *Human Relations* (July 1990): 621–648.

Auerbach, Barbara J., George E. Sexton, Franklin C. Farrow, and Robert H. Lawson. *Work in American Prisons: The Private Sector Gets Involved.* Washington, DC: U.S. Department of Justice, 1988.

Ault, Allen L., and Robert M. Brown, Jr. "Correctional Excellence: Leadership Development." *Corrections Today* 59(2) (1997): 134–137.

Austin, James. "Using Early Release to Relieve Prison Overcrowding: A Dilemma in Public Policy." *Crime and Delinquency* 32(4) (1986): 404–502.

———. "Correctional Options: An Overview." *Corrections Today* 57(1) (1995).

Austin, James, and Melissa Bolyard. *The Effectiveness of Shorter Prison Terms.* San Francisco: National Council on Crime and Delinquency, 1993.

Austin, James, and Patricia Hardyman. *The Use of Early Parole with Electronic Monitoring to Control Prison Crowding.* San Francisco: National Council on Crime and Delinquency, 1992.

Avoyelles (Louisiana) Correctional Center. *Policy and Procedure, No. 02–05–013* (1995).

Baack, Jane, Norma Carr-Ruffino, and Monique Pelletier. "Making It to the Top: Specific Leadership Skills." *Women in Management Review* 8(2) (1993): 17–23.

Bacharach, S. B., and E. E. Lawler. *Power and Politics in Organizations.* San Francisco: Jossey-Bass, 1980.

Bachman, J. G., D. G. Bowers, and P. M. Marcus. "Bases of Supervisory Power: A Comparative Study in Five Organizational Settings." In *Control in Organizations,* edited by A. S. Tannenbaum, 236. New York: McGraw-Hill, 1968.

Baird, Christopher S., and Dennis Wagner. "Measuring Diversion: The Florida Community Control Program." *Crime and Delinquency* 36 (1990): 112–125.

Baker, H. G. "The Unwritten Contract: Job Perceptions." *Personnel Journal* (July 1985): 37–41.

Banisky, Sandy. "The Grumpier the Inmates, the More Happy the Sheriff." *Patriot-News* (Harrisburg, PA), 19 February 1996, A1, A8.

Barnard, Chester I. *The Functions of the Executive.* Cambridge, MA: Harvard University Press, 1938.

Barnet, Jay, and Ricky W. Griffin. *The Management of Organizations: Strategy, Structure, Behavior.* Boston: Houghton Mifflin, 1992.

Baron, Robert A. *Behavior in Organizations: Understanding and Managing the Human Side of Work.* Boston: Allyn and Bacon, 1983.

Barrineau III, H. E. *Civil Liability in Criminal Justice.* 2nd ed. Cincinnati: Anderson, 1994.

Barry, B. W. *Strategic Planning Workbook for Nonprofit Organizations.* St. Paul, MN: Amherst H. Wilder Foundation, 1986.

Bartollas, Clemens, and John P. Conrad. *Introduction to Corrections.* 2nd ed. New York: Harper Collins, 1992.

Bartollas, Clemens, and Stuart Miller. *Correctional Administration: Theory and Practice.* New York: McGraw-Hill, 1978.

Bass, B. M., and B. J. Avolio. "Developing Transformational Leadership: 1992 and Beyond." *Journal of European Industrial Training* (January 1990): 23.

Bazelon, David L. "The Accreditation Debate: Two Views." *Corrections Magazine* 8(6) (1982): 20–26.

Beck, Allen J., and Peter M. Brien. "Trends in the U.S. Correctional Populations: Recent Findings from the Bureau of Justice Statistics." In *The Dilemmas of Corrections*, edited by Kenneth C. Haas and Geoffrey P. Alpert, 43–63. 3rd ed. Prospect Heights, IL: Waveland Press, 1995.

Becker, Robert. "The Privatization of Prisons." In *Prisons: Today and Tomorrow*, edited by Joycelyn M. Pollock, 382–412. Gaithersburg, MD: Aspen, 1997.

Beilen, Thomas, and Peter Krasnow. "Jail Prototype Leads to Faster Construction, Lower Costs." *Corrections Today* 58 (2) (1996): 128–131.

Belknap, J. "Women in Conflict: An Analysis of Women Correctional Officers." *Women and Criminal Justice* 2(2) (1991): 89–115.

Bell, Adam. "Plan Brewing to Put Ban on Coffee, Tea at State's Prisons." *Evening News* (Harrisburg, PA), 9 July 1996, A1, A8.

Bennett, Lawrence A. "The Public Wants Accountability." *Corrections Today* 53(5) (1991): 92–95.

Bennett, Wayne W., and Karen M. Hess. *Management and Supervision in Law Enforcement.* St. Paul, MN: West, 1992.

Bennis, Warren. *On Becoming a Leader.* Reading, MA: Addison-Wesley, 1989.

———. "Canceling the Doppelganger Effect." *Training and Development Journal* (December 1990): 36–37.

Bennis, Warren, and Burt Nanus. *Leaders: The Strategies for Taking Charge*. New York: Harper and Row, 1985.

Benton, F., and C. Nesbitt. *Questions and Answers About Correctional Personnel Management: Prison Personnel Management and Staff Development. Volume II, Summary of the National Survey.* College Park, MD: ACA, 1987.

Benton, F. W., Ellen Rosen, and Judy Peters. *National Survey of Correctional Institution Employee Attrition*. New York: Center for Public Productivity, 1982.

Berlo, D. K. *The Process of Communication*. New York: Holt, Rinehart, and Winston, 1960.

Bernsen, Herbert L., and Glenn E. Gauger. "ADA's Impact–Requirements for Cell and Housing Design." *Corrections Today* 57(2) (1995): 96–102.

Bershad, Lawrence. "Law and Corrections: A Management Perspective." *New England Journal of Prison Law* 4 (1977): 49–82.

Biskupic, Joan. "Court Gives States Leeway in Confining Sex Offenders." *Washington Post*, 24 June 1997, A01.

Bittel, Lester R. *The McGraw-Hill 36 Hour Management Course*. New York: McGraw-Hill, 1989.

Black, James W., and William Nestlerode. "Accreditation: Setting a Standard for Excellence." *Corrections Today* 51(1) (1989): 108–109.

Blair, Robert, and Peter Kratcoski. "Professionalism Among Correctional Officers: A Longitudinal Analysis of Individual and Structural Determinants." In *Corrections: Dilemmas and Directions*, edited by Peter J. Benekos and Alida V. Merlo. Cincinnati: Anderson, 1992.

Blau, J. R., S. C. Light, and M. Chamlin. "Individual and Contextual Effects on Stress and Job Satisfaction." *WOC* 13(1) (1986): 131–156.

Blau, P. M. "A Formal Theory of Differentiation in Organizations." *American Sociological Review* (April 1970): 201–218.

Blish, Randy. Editorial cartoons in *Tribune Review* (Greensburg, PA), February 1997.

Blomberg, T. "Diversion's Disparate Results and Unresolved Questions: An Integrative Evaluation Perspective." *Journal of Research in Crime and Delinquency* (1983): 20, 24–38.

Blumstein, Alfred, Jacqueline Cohen, Susan E. Martin, and Michael H. Tonry. *Research on Sentencing: The Search for Reform*. Washington, DC: National Academy Press, 1983.

Bogard, David M. "Making the Right Technology Choices." *Corrections Today* 55(2) (1993): 74, 76, 78.

Botkin, James W., Elmandjra Mahdi, and Malitza Mircea. *No Limits to Learning*. New York: Pergamon, 1979.

Bowker, Lee H. *Prisoner Subcultures*. Lexington, MA: Lexington, 1977.

Branham, Lynn S. "Accreditation: Making a Good Process Better." *Federal Probation* 57(2) (1993): 11–16.

Branham, Lynn S. *The Use of Incarceration in the United States: A Look at the Present and the Future*. Chicago: ABA, 1992.

Braun, Peter J., Alma G. McKinney, and the Florida Team. "Facing Tomorrow Today—Diversity and Staff Development in Corrections." *Corrections Today* 57(3) (1995): 92–95.

Brennan, Edward T. "On the Inside Looking Out." *Albion News* (Albion, PA), 12 February 1997, 19.

Briody, Robert. "Eliminate 'Code of Silence' Breeding Ground with Top to Bottom Approach: Leaders Must Specifically Address Ethics with Staff." *Corrections Professional* 3(3) (1997): 1, 8–9.

Brock, Horace R., Charles E. Palmer, and John Ellis Price. *Accounting Principles and Applications*. 6th ed. New York: McGraw-Hill, 1990.

Brodsky, C. M. "Work Stress in Correctional Institutions." *Journal of Prison Jail Health* 2(2) (1982): 74–102.

Brown, Marvin T. *Working Ethics Strategies for Decision-Making and Organizational Responsibility*. San Francisco: Jossey-Bass, 1990.

Brown, Paul W. "The Martial Arts: A CO's Best Defense." *Corrections Today* 58(4) (1996): 74–79.

Brown, Stanley D. "What to Look for When Contracting for Beds." *Corrections Today* 58(1) (1996): 44–47.

Bryant, Neil, and Bill Taylor. "Oregon Increases Local Control of Community Corrections." *Corrections Today* 58(7) (1996): 96–97.

Bryce, Robert. "A Lock on Prisons: Big Business Behind Bars." *Current* (November 1993): 6.

Bryson, John M. *Strategic Planning for Public and Nonprofit Organizations*. San Francisco: Jossey-Bass, 1988.

Bryson, John M., A. H. Van de Ven, and W. D. Roering. "Strategic Planning and the Revitalization of the Public Service." In *Toward a New Public Service,* edited by R. Denhardt and E. Jennings. Columbia, MO: Extension Publications, 1987.

Buchholz, Steve, and Thomas Roth. *Creating the High-Performance Team.* New York: John Wiley, 1987.

Buentello, Salvador. "Combating Gangs in Texas." *Corrections Today* 54(5) (1992): 58–60.

Bulmer, P. R. "Alcohol and Drug Testing in the Workplace." In *The Americans with Disabilities Act: Access and Accommodations,* edited by N. Hablutzel and B. T. McMahon, 155–167. Orlando: Paul M. Deutsch Press, 1992.

Bureau of Justice Statistics Bulletin. *Prison and Jail Inmates, 1995.* Washington, DC: U.S. Department of Justice, August 1996.

———. *Felony Sentences in the United States, 1994.* Washington, DC: U.S. Department of Justice, July 1997a.

———. *Prison and Jail Inmates at Midyear 1996.* Washington, DC: U.S. Department of Justice, January 1997b.

———. "Prisoners in 1997." Washington, DC: U.S. Department of Justice, August 1998.

Burns, James MacGregor. *Leadership.* New York: Harper Torchbooks, 1978.

Butler, R., and L. Yorks. "A New Appraisal System as Organizational Change: GE's Task Force Approach." *Personnel* (January-February 1984): 31–42.

California Department of Corrections. *Inside Corrections: Public Safety, Public Service* (1996a).

———. *Prisons Without Walls* (1996b).

———. "Basic Correctional Officer Academy Curriculum." *Training Academy Manual of Instructions and Regulations* (1997a).

———. *Basic Training Curriculum* (1997b).

———. *Leadership Institute Curriculum* (1997c).

Camp, Camille Graham, and George M. Camp. "Correctional Privatization in Perspective." *Prison Journal* 65(2) (1985): 14–31.

———. *Management of Crowded Prisons.* Washington, DC: NIC, 1989.

———. *The Corrections Yearbook: Adult Corrections 1995.* South Salem, NY: Criminal Justice Institute, 1996a.

———. *The Corrections Yearbook 1996.* South Salem, NY: Criminal Justice Institute, 1996b.

———. *The Corrections Yearbook 1997.* South Salem, NY: Criminal Justice Institute, 1997.

Camp, George, and Camille Camp. *Private Sector Involvement in Prison Services and Operations.* South Salem, NY: Criminal Justice Institute, 1984.

Cardarelli, A., and M. M. Finkelstein. "Correctional Administrators Assess the Adequacy and Impact of Prison Legal Services Programs in the United States." *Journal of Criminal Law and Criminology* 65 (1974): 91–102.

Carrell, Michael R., Daniel F. Jennings, and Christina Heavrin. *Fundamentals of Organizational Behavior.* Upper Saddle River, NJ: Prentice Hall, 1997.

Carrell, Michael R., and John E. Dittrich. "Equity Theory: The Recent Literature, Methodological Considerations, and New Directions." *Academy of Management Review* 3(2) (1978): 202–210.

Carroll, Leo. *Hacks, Blacks, and Cons: Race Relations in a Maximum Security Prison.* Lexington, MA: D. C. Heath, 1974.

———. "Race and Three Forms of Prisoner Power: Confrontation, Censoriousness and the Corruption of Authority." Paper presented at the ASC (American Society of Criminology) meeting, Tucson, AZ (1976).

———. "Race, Ethnicity and the Social Order of the Prison." In *The Pains of Imprisonment,* edited by R. Johnson and H. Toch, 181–201. Beverly Hills: Sage, 1982.

———. "Judicial Intervention." In *Encyclopedia of American Prisons,* edited by Marilyn D. McShane and Frank P. Williams III, 268–275. New York: Garland, 1996.

Carroll, S. J., and H. L. Tosi. *Management by Objectives: Applications and Research.* New York: Macmillan, 1973.

Caudron, Shari. "Subculture Strife Hinders Productivity." *Personnel Journal* (December 1992): 60–64.

Certo, Samuel C. *Principles of Modern Management: Functions and Systems.* 3rd ed. Dubuque, IA: William C. Brown, 1985.

Chamber of Commerce of the United States. *Washington Review* (1966).

Chandler Jr., A. D. *Strategy and Structure: Chapters in the History of the Industrial Enterprise.* Cambridge, MA: MIT Press, 1962.

Chase, G., and E. G. Reveal. *How to Manage the Public Sector.* New York: McGraw-Hill, 1983.

Cheek, F. E. *Stress Management for Correctional Officers and Their Families.* College Park, MD: ACA, 1984.

Cheek, F. E., and M. D. Miller. "The Experience of Stress for Correction Officers: A Double-Bind Theory of Correctional Stress." *Journal of Criminal Justice* 11(2) (1983): 105–120.

Child, J., and R. Mansfield. "Technology, Size, and Organization Structure." *Sociology* (September 1972): 369–393.

Chilton, Bradley. *Prisons Under the Gavel: The Federal Takeover of Georgia Prisons.* Columbus, OH: Ohio State University Press, 1991.

Cialdini, R. B. "Indirect Tactics of Image Management: Beyond Basking." In *Impression Management in the Organization,* edited by R.A. Giacalone and P. Rosenfeld, 45–71. Hillsdale, NJ: Lawrence Erlbaum Associates, 1989.

Clark, Charles S. "Prison Overcrowding." *The Congressional Quarterly Researcher* 4(5) (1994): 97–120.

Clark, Cherie L., David W. Aziz, and Doris L. MacKenzie. *Shock Incarceration in New York: Focus on Treatment.* Washington, DC: NIC, 1994.

Clark III, R. D. "Group-Induced Shift Toward Risk: A Critical Appraisal." *Psychological Bulletin* (October 1971): 251–270.

Clayton, Susan L. "In Louisiana: State Regains Control of Prison System." *Corrections Today* 58(7) (1996): 125.

———. "Making a Difference for Victims and Inmates." *Corrections Today* 59(6) (1997): 71.

Clayton Jr., Obie, and Tim Carr. "The Effects of Prison Crowding upon Infraction Rates." *Criminal Justice Review* 9 (1984): 69–77.

Clear, Todd R. "Toward a Corrections of 'Place': The Challenge of 'Community' in Corrections." *National Institute of Justice Journal* 231 (1996): 52–56.

Clear, Todd R., and George F. Cole. *American Corrections.* 3rd ed. Belmont, CA: Wadsworth, 1994.

Clear, T. R., J. D. Hewitt, and R. M. Regoli. "Discretion and the Indeterminate Sentence: Its Distribution, Control, and Effect on Time Served." *Crime and Delinquency* 24 (1978): 428–445.

Close, Daryl, and Nicholas Meier. *Morality in Criminal Justice.* New York: Wadsworth, 1995.

Cohen, Fred. "The Discovery of Prison Reform." *Buffalo Law Review* 21 (1972): 855–887.

Cohen, Stanley. *Visions of Social Control: Crime, Punishment and Classification.* Oxford: Polity Press, 1985.

Cohen, Warren. "Need Work? Go to Jail." *U.S. News and World Report* 120(25) (1996): 66–67.

Cohn, A. W. "The Future of Correctional Management." *Federal Probation* 45 (1991): 12–16.

Coleman, Troy, and Rebecca Furr. "The Americans with Disabilities Act: Crisis or Challenge for Workforce 2000?" *Public Management* (April 1992): 4–8.

Collins, Denis, and Laura V. Page. "Teaching Business Ethics: A Practical Guide and Case Studies." *Small Business Forum* (Spring 1992): 63–80.

Collins, William. "Employee Legal Issues." In *Encyclopedia of American Prisons*, edited by Marilyn D. McShane and Frank P. Williams III, 300–306. New York: Garland, 1996.

Collins, William C. *Correctional Law for the Correctional Officer.* Laurel, MD: ACA, 1993.

Collins, William. "Employee Legal Issues." In *Encyclopedia of American Prisons*, edited by Marilyn D. McShane and Frank P. Williams III, 300–306. New York: Garland, 1996.

———. "The Eighth Amendment in Prison: Does the Supreme Court Know Where It Is Going?" In *The Dilemmas of Corrections: Contemporary Readings*, edited by Kenneth C. Haas and Geoffrey P. Alpert, 269–287. 3rd ed. Prospect Heights, IL: Waveland Press, 1995.

Communicator. "The Gold Star—A Higher Standard." *Communicator* (Spring 1996).

———. "The Best in the Business." *Communicator* (July 1997).

Conlin, Joseph. "Brainstorming: It's Not as Easy as You Think." *Successful Meetings* (September 1989): 30–34.

Connecticut Department of Corrections. *Annual Report: 1994–1995* (1996).

Conrad, John P. "The Pessimistic Reflections of a Chronic Optimist." *Federal Probation* 55(2) (1991): 4–9.

Contract Between the State of Ohio and the Ohio Civil Service Employees Association AFSCME Local 11, AFL–CIO (1994–1997).

Cooper, P. J. *Hard Judicial Choices: Federal District Court Judges and State and Local Officials.* New York: Oxford University Press, 1988.

Corrections Alert. "Supreme Court to Decide if ADA Applies to Prisons." *Corrections Alert* 4(21) (1998): 1–2.

Corrections Digest. "Senate Crime Bill Will More Than Double American Prison Population by Year 2005." *Corrections Digest* (March 1994): 1–4.

Corrections Journal. "Virginia Department to Allow Face-to-Face Press Interviews." *Corrections Journal* (August 1997): 1–2.

Corrections Professional. "ACA Establishes New Accreditation Standards, Makes Revisions." *Corrections Professional* (November 21, 1997a): 7.

———. "BOP Tests Five Technologies." *Corrections Professional* 3(7) (1997b): 9.

———. "Changing a Troubled Facility's Culture: A Michigan Success." *Corrections Professional* 3(7) (1997c): 4.

———. "Officials Not Negligent Despite Rape of Prison Librarian." *Correctionals Professional* 3(5) (1997d): 14.

———. "Pennsylvania COTs Take Video Exam." *Corrections Professional* (November 21, 1997e): 2.

———. "Inmate with Tourette's May Have ADA Case, Court Rules." *Corrrections Professional* 3(11) (1998): 12.

Cory, B. "Progress and Politics in Resolving Inmate Grievances." *Corrections Magazine* 8(5) (1982): 20–24.

Cotton, Barbara L. "The Challenge to Balance Efficiency, Mandates and Costs." *Corrections Today* 57(6) (1995): 78–81.

Coursen, D. "Communications in the Open Organization." Contract No. 400–77–0099. Washington, DC: National Institute of Education, 1980.

Cox, V. C., Paul B. Paulus, and G. McCain. "Prison Crowding Research: The Relevance for Prison Housing Standards and a General Approach Regarding Crowding Phenomena." *American Psychologist* 39(10) (1984): 1148–1160.

Crawford, Thomasine F. "Community College Delivers Preservice Training That Works." *Corrections Today* 57(5) (1995): 156–158.

Cressey, Donald. "Contradictory Directives in Complex Organizations: The Case of the Prison." In *Prison Within Society*, edited by Lawrence Hazelrigg, 494. Garden City, NY: Doubleday, 1969.

Cressey, Donald R. "Prison Organizations." In *Handbook of Organizations*, edited by Chames G. March, 1025. Chicago: Rand McNally, 1965.

Cronin, Thomas, Tania Cronin, and Michael Milakovich. *U.S. v. Crime in the Streets.* Bloomington, IN: Indiana University Press, 1981.

Crouch, Ben. "Pandora's Box: Women Guards in Men's Prisons." *Journal of Criminal Justice* 13 (1985): 535–548.

Crouch, Ben, and James Marquart. "On Becoming a Prison Guard." In *The Keepers,* edited by Ben Crouch and James Marquart. Springfield, IL: Charles C. Thomas, 1980.

Crouch, Ben M., Geoffrey P. Alpert, James W. Marquart, and Kenneth C. Haas. "The American Prison Crisis: Clashing Philosophies of Punishment and Crowded Cell Blocks." In *The Dilemmas of Corrections: Contemporary Readings*, edited by Kenneth C. Haas and Geoffrey P. Alpert, 64–80. Prospect Heights, IL: Waveland Press, 1995.

Culbertson, Robert G., and Ralph A. Weisheit, eds. *"Order Under Law:" Readings in Criminal Justice.* 5th ed. Prospect Heights, IL: Waveland Press, 1997.

Cullen, F., B. Link, N. Wolfe, and J. Frank. "The Social Dimension of Correctional Officer Stress." *Justice Quarterly* 2 (1985): 505–533.

Cullen, Francis T., Edward J. Latessa, Velmer S. Burton Jr., and Lucien X. Lombardo. "The Correctional Orientation of Prison Wardens: Is the Rehabilitative Ideal Supported?" *Criminology* 31(1) (1993): 69–92.

Cullen, Frank, and Paul Gendreau. "The Effectiveness of Correctional Rehabilitation: Reconsidering the 'Nothing Works' Debate." In *The American Prison: Issues in Research and Policy*, edited by Lynn Goodstein and Doris Layton MacKenzie, 23–44. New York: Plenum Press, 1988.

Curran, John J. "Priority for Parole—Agencies Must Reach Out to the Media and the Community." *Corrections Today* 51(1) (1989): 30–34.

Currie, Elliott. "Crime, Justice, and the Social Environment." In *Public Policy, Crime, and Criminal Justice,* edited by Barry W. Hancock and Paul M. Sharp, 51–67. Upper Saddle River, NJ: Prentice Hall, 1997.

Czajkowski, Susan M., Peter L. Nacci, Nancy Kramer, Shelley J. Price, and Dale K. Sechrest. "Responses to the Accreditation Program: What Correctional Staff Think About Accreditation." *Federal Probation* 49(1) (1995): 42–49.

Dahl, R. "The Concept of Power." *Behavioral Science* 2(3) (1957): 201–215.

Dallao, Mary. "Prison Construction Trends." *Corrections Today* 59(2) (1997): 70–72.

Dallas Morning News. "Guard Set Off Jail Riot, Report Says '96 Arizona Incident Caused an Estimated $130,000 in Damage." Feb. 9, 1998.

Dalton, Erin. "Leaders Convene to Assess Correctional Technology Needs." *Corrections Today* 59(4) (1997): 82–85.

Davidson, Theodore R. *Chicano Prisoners: The Key to San Quentin.* New York: Rinehart and Winston, 1974.

Davis, Anne J., and Mila A. Aroskar. *Ethical Dilemmas and Nursing Practice.* New York: Appleton, 1978.

Davis, S. P. "Survey: Programs and Services for Female Offenders." *Corrections Compendium* 9 (1992): 7–20.

Deal, T. E., and A. A. Kennedy. "Culture: A New Look Through Old Lenses." *Journal of Applied Behavioral Science* (November 1983).

Decker, Theodore. "'Joke' Not Funny, Worker Asserts." *The Patriot News,* May 16, 1997, A–1, A–10.

deGroot, Gabrielle. "Hot New Technologies." *Corrections Today* 59(4) (1997a): 60–62.

———. "Reducing Inmate Lawsuits." *Corrections Today* 59(6) (1997b): 77.

Del Carmen, Rolando. "Legal Issues and Liabilities in Community Corrections." In *Probation, Parole and Community Corrections: A Reader,* edited by L. Travis, 47–72. Prospect Heights, IL: Waveland Press, 1985.

Delong, R. *Liability of Corrections Administrators for Failure to Train or Failure to Supervise Training.* Paper presented to the Seminar for Managers of Staff Training sponsored by the National Institute of Corrections, University of Texas at Arlington, September 22, 1980.

Denhardt, Robert B. *Theories of Public Organization.* Monterey, CA: Brooks/Cole, 1984.

Deschenes, Elizabeth Piper, Susan Turner, and Joan Petersilia. "Diverting Offenders from Prison: An Evaluation of Minnesota's Intensive Community Supervision Program." In *Correctional Contexts: Contemporary and Classical Readings,* edited by James W. Marquart and Jonathan R. Sorensen, 374–384. Los Angeles: Roxbury, 1997.

DiIulio, John J. *Governing Prisons: A Comparative Study of Correctional Management.* New York: Free Press, 1987.

———. *No Escape: The Future of American Corrections.* New York: Basic Books, 1991.

Doble, John. *Crime and Punishment: The Public's View.* New York: Public Agenda Foundation, 1987.

Doble, John, and Josh Klein. *Prison Overcrowding and Alternative Sentences: The Views of the People of Alabama.* New York: Public Agenda Foundation, 1989.

Donnelly Jr., James H., James L. Gibson, and John M. Ivancevich. *Fundamentals of Management.* Dallas: Business Publications, 1971.

Donohue, Stephen A., and Anthony J. Greloch. "Keeping It Simple: Design Techniques Can Enhance Security." *Corrections Today* 59(4) (1997): 90–92.

Donziger, Steven R. "The Prison–Industrial Complex." In *"Order Under Law": Readings in Criminal Justice,* edited by Robert G. Culbertson and Ralph A. Weisheit, 319–337. 5th ed. Prospect Heights, IL: Waveland Press, 1997.

Dooley, Mike. "The NIC on Restorative Justice: A Brief History of the NIC's Involvement in Community Justice." *Corrections Today* 59(7) (1997): 110–114.

Dorworth, David J. "BOP Provides Blueprint for Siting New Facilities." *Corrections Today* 58(2) (1995): 114–117.

Downs, John, and Jorda Elliot Goodman. "Zero-Based Budget." In *Dictionary of Finance and Investment Terms,* 481. New York: Barron's Educational Series, 1985.

Dreyfus, J. "Get Ready for the New Workforce." *Fortune,* 23 April 1990, 165–181.

Drory, A. "Politics in Organization and Its Perception Within the Organization." *Organization Studies* 9(2) (1988): 165–179.

Drucker, Peter. *The Effective Executive.* New York: Harper and Row, 1967.

Dubrin, A. J. *Human Relations: A Job Oriented Approach.* Reston, VA: Reston, 1978.

Duchon, D., S. G. Green, and T. D. Taber. "Vertical Dyad Linkage: A Longitudinal Assessment of Antecedents, Measures, and Consequences." *Journal of Applied Psychology* (February 1986): 56–60.

Duffee, David. "The Correctional Officer Subculture and Organizational Change." *Journal of Research in Crime and Delinquency* 12 (1975): 155–172.

———. *Correctional Management.* Englewood Cliffs, NJ: Prentice Hall, 1980a.

———. *Correctional Management: Change and Control in Correctional Organizations.* Prospect Heights, IL: Waveland Press, 1980b.

———. *Corrections Practice and Policy.* New York: Random House, 1989.

Durham, Alexis M. *Crisis and Reform: Current Issues in American Punishment.* Boston: Little, Brown, 1994.

Dwyer, Diane C., and Roger B. McNally. "Public Policy and Prison Industries for the 1990s." In *Critical Issues in Crime and Justice,* edited by Albert R. Rhodes, 277–295. Thousand Oaks, CA: Sage, 1994.

Dye, Thomas. *Understanding Public Policy.* 4th ed. Englewood Cliffs, NJ: Prentice Hall, 1981.

Earnest, Ed. "Youth Day Treatment Program Works for Alabama." *Corrections Today* 58(5) (1996): 70–73, 140–141.

Edna McConnell Clark Foundation. *Seeking Justice: Crime and Punishment in America.* New York: Edna McConnell Clark Foundation, 1995.

Edwards, Calvin R., and Jeff Wrigley. "Staff Mentoring: A Valuable Human Resource Tool Used by the Bureau of Prisons." *Corrections Today* 57(3) (1995): 100–102.

Eglash, Albert. "Beyond Restitution: Creative Restitution." In *Restitution in Criminal Justice,* edited by Joe Hudson and Burt Galloway, 91–99. Lexington, MA: Lexington, 1977.

Enos, Richard, and Stephen Southern. *Correctional Case Management.* Cincinnati: Anderson, 1966.

Etzioni, Amatai. *A Comparative Analysis of Complex Organizations.* New York: Free Press, 1961.

Evening News. "Drop in Parolees Crowd Prisons: Simon Murder Case Makes Board Wary of Release." *Evening News* (Harrisburg, PA), 24 August 1995, B1, B10.

———. "State Plans Jail-Tower Guard Cuts: Reduction in Overtime at 5 Prisons Is The Aim." *Evening News* (Harrisburg, PA), 19 January 1996, B1, B4.

Fabello, Tony. *Sentencing Dynamics Study.* Austin, TX: Criminal Justice Policy Council, 1993.

Fairchild, E. S. "Politicalization of the Criminal Offender: Prisoner Perceptions of Crime and Politics." *Criminology* 15(2) (1977): 287–295.

Falk Sr., James H. "Developing a Code of Ethics So COs Know How to Respond." *Corrections Today* 57(4) 1995: 110–113.

Fandt, P. M., and G. R. Ferris. "The Management of Information and Impressions: When Employees Behave Opportunistically." *Organizational Behavior and Human Decision Processes* (February 1990): 140–58.

Farace, R., P. Monge, and H. Russell. *Communicating and Organizing.* New York: Random House, 1977.

Farkas, Charles M., and Philippe DeBacker. "There Are Only Five Ways to Lead." *Fortune* 133(1) (1996): 109–112.

Farrell, D., and J. C. Petersen. "Patterns of Political Behavior in Organizations." *Academy of Management Review* (July 1982): 405–407.

Farrington, Keith. "The Modern Prison as Total Institution? Public Perception versus Objective Reality." *Crime and Delinquency* 38(1) (1992): 6–26.

Fayol, Henri. *Industrial and General Administration.* Paris: Dunod, 1916.

Federal Emergency Management Agency. *Guide for the Development of State and Local Emergency Operation Plans* (1990).

———. *Emergency Management Guide for Business and Industry* (1993).

Feeley, Malcolm M., and Jonathan Simon (1992). "The New Penology: Notes on the Emerging Strategy of Corrections and Its Implications." *Criminology* 30(4) (1992): 449–474.

Ferdico, John N. *Ferdico's Criminal Law and Justice Dictionary.* St. Paul, MN: West, 1992.

Ferris, G. R., G. S. Russ, and P. M. Fandt. "Politics in Organizations." In *Impression Management in the Organization,* edited by R.A. Giacalone and P. Rosenfeld, 155–156. Hillsdale, NJ: Lawrence Erlbaum Associates, 1989.

Fiedler, Fred A. *A Theory of Leadership Effectiveness.* New York: McGraw-Hill, 1967.

Fiedler, Fred A., M. M. Chemers, and L. Mahar. *Improving Leadership Effectiveness: The Leader Match Concept.* New York: John Wiley, 1977.

Fields, Gary. "Privatized Prisons Pose Problems." *USA Today* 11 November 1996, 3A.

Figgie Report. *Part V Parole: A Search for Justice and Safety.* New York: Research and Forecasts, Inc., 1985.

Finn, Peter, and Dale Parent. "Making the Offender Foot the Bill: A Texas Program." *National Institute of Justice: Program Focus.* Washington, DC: U.S. Department of Justice, 1992.

Flannagan, T. J. "Discretion in the Prison Justice System: A Study of Sentencing in Institutional Disciplinary Proceedings." *Journal of Research in Crime and Delinquency* 19(2) (1982): 216–237.

Fleuter, Douglas. "Flextime—A Social Phenomenon." *Personnel Journal* (June 1975): 318–319.

Florida Department of Corrections. *1994–1995 Annual Report: The Guidebook to Corrections in Florida* (1995).

———. *1996–1997 Annual Report: The Guidebook to Corrections in Florida* (1997): 34–35.

Follet, Mary Parker. *The Creative Experience.* New York: Longmans, Green, 1924.

Foote, Caleb. *The Prison Population Explosion: California's Rogue Elephant.* San Francisco: Center on Juvenile and Criminal Justice, 1993.

Ford, C. H. "MBO: An Idea Whose Time Has Gone?" *Business Horizons* (December 1979): 49.

Ford, Marilyn. "Community Relations." In *Encyclopedia of American Prisons,* edited by Marilyn D. McShane and Frank P. Williams III, 102–105. New York: Garland, 1996.

Fox, J. *Organizational and Racial Conflict in Maximum Security Prisons.* Boston: D. C. Heath, 1982.

Franke, R. H., and J. Kaul. "The Hawthorne Experiments: First Statistical Interpretations." *American Sociological Review* (October 1978): 623–643.

Freeman, Robert M. "Correctional Staff as the Villain and the Inmate as Hero: The Problem Is Bigger Than Hollywood!" *American Jails* 10(3) (1996a): 9–16.

———. "Pre-emergency Planning for Post-emergency Litigation." *Corrections Today* 58(4) (1996b): 98–105, 128.

———. *Strategic Planning for Correctional Emergencies.* Lanham, MD: ACA, 1996c.

———. *Evaluation of Staff Preparedness for Correctional Emergencies: A National Survey of State Departments of Corrections.* Paper presented at the March meeting of the Academy of Criminal Justice Sciences, Louisville, KY, 1997a.

———. In *Prisons: Today and Tomorrow,* edited by Joycelyn M. Pollock, 270–305. Gaithersburg, MD: Aspen, 1997b.

French, J. R. P., and B. Raven. "The Bases of Social Power." In *Group Dynamics,* edited by D. Cartwright and A. Zander, 259–269. 3rd ed. New York: Harper and Row, 1968.

French, W. L. "Organizational Development: Objectives, Assumptions, and Strategies." *California Management Review* 12(2) (1969): 23–35.

Fry, Lincoln J., and Daniel Glaser. "Gender Differences in Work Adjustment of Prison Employees." *Journal of Offender Counseling, Services and Rehabilitation* 12 (1987): 39–52.

Fulton, Betsy, Amy Stichman, Lawrence Travis, and Edward Latessa. "Moderating Probation and Parole Officer Attitudes to Achieve Desired Outcomes." *The Prison Journal* 77(3) (1997): 295–312.

Furniss, Jill R. "The Population Boom." *Corrections Today* 58(1) (1996):38–43.

Gaes, Gerald G. "The Effects of Overcrowding in Prison." In *Crime and Justice,* edited by Michael Tonry and Norval Morris, 95–146. Vol. 6. Chicago: University of Chicago Press, 1985.

Gailiun, Michelle. "Telemedicine Takes Off." *Corrections Today* 59(4) (1997): 68–70.

Gandy, Jeffrey, and Victor V. Murray. "The Experience of Workplace Politics." *Academy of Management Journal* 23(2) (1980): 237–251.

Gardiner, John A., and Theodore R. Lyman. *Decisions for Sale, Corruption and Reform in Land Use and Building Regulations.* New York: Praeger, 1978.

Garmire, Bernard L. *Local Government Police Management.* 2nd ed. Washington, DC: International City Management Association, 1982.

Gatland, Stanley D., and Bill Bowers. "Too Many Cooks in the Kitchen?" *Corrections Today* 59(2) (1997): 78–82.

Geary, David C. "Are You a Leader or a Manager?" *Public Relations Journal* (August 1990): 16.

Geiger, Doren, and Mark Shea. "The GENIE System." *Corrections Today* 59(4) (1997): 72–75.

Gengler, William, and Connie Riley. "Two States' Training Programs Lead the Way into the 21st Century." *Corrections Today* 57(3) (1995): 104, 105, 107.

Gentry, J. T. "The Panopticon Revisited: The Problem of Monitoring Private Prisons." *Yale Law Journal* 96 (1986): 353.

George Jr., Claude S. *Supervision in Action: The Art of Managing Others.* 4th ed. Reston, VA: Reston Publishing, 1985.

Georgia Department of Corrections. *Annual Report Fiscal Year 1996: Tough Issues, Hard Facts* (1997).

Gerstein, L. H., C. G. Topp, G. Correll. "Role of the Environment and Person When Predicting Burn-out Among Correctional Personnel." *Criminal Justice Behavior* 14(3) (1987): 352–369.

Gest, Ted. "New War Over Crack." *U.S. News and World Report*, 16 November 1995, 82.

Ghorpade, J. V. *Job Analysis: A Handbook for the Human Resource Director.* Englewood Cliffs, NJ: Prentice Hall, 1988.

Gido, Rosemary L. "Organizational Change and Workforce Planning: Dilemmas for Criminal Justice Organizations for the Year 2000." In *Visions for Change: Crime and Justice in the Twenty-First Century,* edited by Roslyn Muraskin and Albert R. Roberts, 272–282. Upper Saddle River, NJ: Prentice Hall, 1996.

Gilbert, Michael J. "Recruiting." In *Prison Personnel Management and Staff Development*, edited by F. Warren Benton and Charlotte A. Nesbitt, 37–47. College Park, MD: ACA, 1988.

Gleason, Jerry L. "York County OKs Prison Expansion." *Patriot-News* (Harrisburg, PA), 19 September 1996, B6.

Godfrey, Kim. "Performance-Based Standards." *Corrections Today* 59(3) (1997): 94–97.

Goins, Ted. *Institutional Research.* Richmond, VA: Branch Cabell, 1994.

Goldberg, K., and Y. Breece. "An Overview: The History of Prison Industries." *Correctional Industries Association Newsletter* 5(3) (1990).

Gottfredson, D. M. *Decision Making in the Criminal Justice System: Review and Essays.* Rockville, MD: National Institute of Mental Health, 1975.

Gottfredson, M. R. "Parole Guidelines and the Reduction of Sentencing Disparity: A Preliminary Study." *Journal of Research in Crime and Delinquency* 16 (1979): 218–231.

Gottfredson, Stephen D. "Fighting Crime at the Expense of Colleges." *Chronicle of Higher Education* (January 20, 1995).

Gottfredson, Stephen D., and Don M. Gottfredson. "Accuracy of Prediction Models." In *Criminal Careers and "Career Criminals,"* edited by Alfred Blumstein, Jacqueline Cohen, Jeffrey A. Roth, and Christy A. Visher, 212–290. Vol. II. Washington, DC: National Academy Press, 1986.

Graber, Doris. "Evaluating Crime-Fighting Policies: Media Images and Public Perspective." In *Evaluating Alternative Law Enforcement Policies,* edited by Ralph Baker and Fred A. Meyer Jr., 179–199. Lexington, MA: D. C. Heath, 1979.

Graen, G., M. Novak, and P. Sommerkamp. "The Effects of Leader–Member Exchange and Job Design on Productivity and Satisfaction: Testing A Dual Attachment Model." *Organizational Behavior and Human Performance* (August 1982): 109–131.

Gray, K., M. K. Stohr-Gillmore, and N. P. Lovrich. "Adapting Participatory Management for a Para-military Organization: The Implementation of TEAMS in the Washington State Patrol." MS (1990).

Greenberg, J. "Cognitive Reevaluation of Outcomes in Response to Underpayment Inequity." *Academy of Management Journal* (March 1989): 174–184.

Greenwood, Peter. *Selective Incapacitation.* Santa Monica, CA: Rand, 1982.

Grieser, R. C. "Organizational Models of Prison Industries." Paper presented at the American Correctional Association's Conference of Prison Industries, Chicago, 1987.

Guy, Mary E. *Ethical Decision Making in Everyday Work Situations.* Westport, CT: Quorum Books, 1990.

Haas, Kenneth C. "Judicial Politics and Correctional Reform: An Analysis of the Decline of the 'Hands–off' Doctrine." *Detroit College of Law Review* 4 (1977): 796–831.

Haas, Kenneth C., and A. Champagne. "The Impact of *Johnson v. Avery* on Prison Administration." *Tennessee Law Review* 43 (1976): 275–306.

Hall, Richard H. "Intraorganizational Structure Variation: Application of the Bureaucratic Model." *Administrative Science Quarterly* 7 (1962): 295–308.

———. *Organizations: Structures, Processes, and Outcomes.* 4th ed. Englewood Cliffs, NJ: Prentice Hall, 1987.

Hambrick, Donald C., and Phyllis A. Mason. "Upper Echelons: The Organization as a Reflection of Its Top Management." *Academy of Management Review* 9 (1984): 193–206.

Hambrick, M. C. "The Correctional Worker Concept: Being Connected in the 90s." *Federal Prison Journal* (Winter 1992): 11–14.

Hancock, Barry W., and Paul M. Sharp. *Public Policy: Crime and Criminal Justice.* Upper Saddle River, NJ: Prentice Hall, 1997.

Hardy, C. "The Contribution of Political Science to Organizational Behavior." In *Handbook of Organizational Behavior,* edited by J. W. Lorsch, 103. Englewood Cliffs, NJ: Prentice Hall, 1987.

Harris, M. Kay, and D. P. Spiller Jr. *After Decision: Implementation of Judicial Decrees in Correctional Settings.* Washington, DC: U.S. Department of Justice, 1977.

Harrison, E. F. *The Managerial Decision-Making Process.* 2nd ed. Boston: Houghton Mifflin, 1981.

Hatry, H. P., and J. M. Greiner. *How Police Departments Better Apply Management-by-Objectives and Quality Circle Programs.* Washington, DC: U.S. Department of Justice, 1984.

Hawkins, Gordon. "Prison Labor and Prison Industries." In *Crime and Justice: An Annual Review of Research,* edited by Michael Tonry and Norval Morris. Vol. 5. Chicago: University of Chicago Press, 1983.

Hawkins, Richard, and Geoffrey P. Alpert. *American Prison Systems: Punishment and Justice.* Englewood Cliffs, NJ: Prentice Hall, 1989.

Heifetz, Milton D. *Easier Said Than Done.* New York: Prometheus Books, 1992.

Hellriegel, D., and J. W. Slocum. *Organizational Behavior.* St. Paul, MN: West, 1979.

Hemmons, Craig. "The Origin of Correctional Health Care Standards." *Corrections Now* 2(1) (1997): 1–2.

Henry, Nicholas L. *Public Administration and Public Affairs.* 3rd ed. Englewood Cliffs, NJ: Prentice Hall, 1986.

Hepburn, John R. "The Exercise of Power in Coercive Organizations: A Study of Prison Guards." *Criminology* 23(1) (1985): 145–164.

———. "Prison Guards as Agents of Social Control." In *The American Prison: Issues in Research and Policy,* edited by Lynne Goldstein and Doris MacKenzie, 191–206. New York: Plenum Press, 1989.

Herbert, Wray. "Troubled at Work: The Courts Are Skeptical About Mental Disability Claims." *U.S. News and World Report,* 9 February 1998, 62–64.

Hershey, Paul, and Ken Blanchard. "So You Want to Know Your Leadership Style?" *Training and Development Journal* (February 1974): 1–15.

———. *Management of Organizational Behavior: Utilizing Human Resources.* 4th ed. Englewood Cliffs, NJ: Prentice Hall, 1982.

Herzberg, Frederick, B. Mausner, and B. B. Snyderman. *The Motivation to Work.* New York: John Wiley, 1959.

Hickey, Thomas J. "National Prison Project." In *Encyclopedia of American Prisons,* edited by Marilyn D. McShane and Frank P. Williams III, 329–330. New York: Garland, 1996.

Hill, G. W. "Group versus Individual Performance: Are N +1 Heads Better Than One?" *Psychological Bulletin* (May 1982): 517–539.

Hirschhorn, L. "Managing Rumors." in L. Hirschhorn (ed.), *Cutting Back.* San Francisco: Jossey-Bass (1983): 49–52.

Hoffmann, Brian, Gary Straughn, Jack Richardson, and Allen Randall. "California Electrified Fences: A New Concept in Prison Security." *Corrections Today* 58(4) (1996): 66–68.

Hollander, E. P., and L. R. Offermann. "Power and Leadership in Organizations." *American Psychologist* (February 1990): 179–189.

Holton, N. G., and M. E. Jones. *The System of Criminal Justice.* 2nd ed. Boston: Little, Brown, 1982.

Honnold, J. A., and J. B. Stinchcomb. "Officer Stress." *Corrections Today* (December 1985): 46–51.

Hood, J. B., and B. A. Hardy Jr. *Workers' Compensation and Employee Protection Laws in a Nutshell.* St. Paul, MN: West, 1983.

Hornblum, A. "Are We ready for the Privatization of American Prisons?" *The Privatization Review* (Autumn 1985).

Horswell, Cindy. "Gas Cloud Forces Evacuation at 3 Prison Units." *Houston Chronicle,* 11 August 1997.

House, Robert J. "A Path-Goal Theory of Leader Effectiveness." *Administrative Science Quarterly* (September 1971): 321–338.

Houston, James. *Correctional Management: Functions, Skills, and Systems.* Chicago: Nelson-Hall, 1995.

Howard, A. E. D. "The States and the Supreme Court." *Catholic University Law Review* 31 (1982): 375.

Hudson, Arthur. "Changing Our Approach to Managing Stress." *Corrections Today* 56(2) (1994): 20–21.

Huggins, M. Wayne. "Changing Public Perception is Everyone's Responsibility." *Corrections Today* 54(2) (1992): 58–60.

Hunzeker, Donna. "Bring Corrections Policy into the 1990s." *State Legislative Report* 17(5). Denver: National Conference of State Legislatures, 1992.

Illinois Department of Corrections. *Insight into Corrections Fiscal Year 1995—Annual Report* (1995).

———. *Fiscal Year 1996 Annual Report* (1997).

Immarigeon, Russ. "Prison Bailout." *Dollars and Sense* (July/August 1987).

———. "Correctional Options: What Works?" *Corrections Today* 57(7) (1995).

Ingley, Stephen. "Privatization: Yet Another Nonsolution." *Corrections Today* 58(7) (1996): 26–27.

Irwin, John. "The Changing Social Structure of the Men's Correctional Prison." In *Corrections and Punishment*, edited by D. Greenberg, 21–40. Beverly Hills: Sage, 1977.

———. *Prisons in Turmoil.* Boston: Little, Brown, 1980.

Irwin, John, and James Austin. *It's About Time: America's Imprisonment Binge.* 2nd ed. New York: Wadsworth, 1997.

Ivancevich, J. "An Analysis of Control, Bases of Control, and Satisfaction in an Organizational Setting." *Academy of Management Journal* (December 1970): 427–436.

Jacobs, James B. *Stateville: The Penitentiary in Mass Society.* Chicago: University of Chicago Press, 1977.

———. *Guard Unions and the Future of Prisons.* Cornell University (Ithaca, NY): Institute of Public Employment, 1978.

———. "Sentencing By Prison Personnel: Good Time." *UCLA Law Review* 30(2) (1982): 217–270.

———. "The Prisoners' Rights Movement and Its Impacts." In *Correctional Contexts: Contemporary and Classical Readings,* edited by James W. Marquart and Jonathan R. Sorensen, 231–247. Los Angeles: Roxbury, 1997.

Jacobs, James B., and Lawrence Kraft. "Integrating the Keepers: A Comparison of Black and White Prison Guards in Illinois." *Social Problems* 25 (1978): 304–318.

Jacobs, James B., and Harold G. Retsky. "Prison Guard." *Urban Life* 4 (1975): 5–29.

James, Muriel, and Dorothy Jongeward. *Born To Win: Transactional Analysis with Gestalt Experiments.* Reading, MA: Addison-Wesley, 1976.

Janis, I. L. *Groupthink.* Boston: Houghton Mifflin, 1982.

Jenne, D. L., and Robert Kersting. "Aggression and Women Correctional Officers in Male Prisons." *Prison Journal* 76(4) (1996): 442.

Jennings, Daniel F. *Effective Supervision: Frontline Management for the 90s.* St. Paul, MN: West, 1993.

Johnson, Frank M. "The Constitution and the Federal District Judge." In *The Dilemmas of Corrections: Contemporary Readings,* edited by Kenneth C. Haas and Geoffrey P. Alpert, 210–222. 3rd ed. Prospect Heights, IL: Waveland Press, 1995. Originally printed in *Texas Law Review* 54 (1976): 903.

Johnson, Robert. *Hard Time: Understanding and Reforming the Prison.* Monterey, CA: Brooks/Cole, 1987.

———. *Hard Time: Understanding and Reforming the Prison.* 2nd ed. Belmont, CA: Wadsworth, 1996.

———. In *Prisons: Today and Tomorrow,* edited by Joycelyn M. Pollock, 26–51. Gaithersburg, MD: Aspen, 1997.

Johnston, W. *Workforce 2000.* Prepared for the U.S. Department of Labor. Indianapolis, IN: Hudson Institute, 1987.

Josi, Don A. "Selection and Training." In *Encyclopedia of American Prisons*, edited by Marilyn D. McShane and Frank P. Williams III, 118–122. New York: Garland, 1996.

Junsaker, Philip L., and Johanna S. Junsaker. "Decision Styles—In Theory, In Practice." *Organizational Dynamics* 10 (1981): 23–26.

Jurik, Nancy C. "Individual and Organizational Determinants of Correctional Officer Attitudes Toward Inmates." *Criminology* 23(3) (1985): 523–539.

———. "Striking a Balance: Female Correctional Officers, Gender Role Stereotypes, and Male Prisons." *Sociological Inquiry* 58 (1988): 291–305.

Jurik, Nancy C., and Gregory J. Halemba. "Gender, Working Conditions and the Job Satisfaction of Women in a Non-Traditional Occupation: Female Correctional Officers in Men's Prisons." *The Sociological Quarterly* 25 (1984): 551–566.

Kagehiro, D., and C. Werner. "Different Perceptions of Jail Inmates and Correctional Officers: The 'Blame the Other—Expect to Be Blamed' Effect." *Journal of Applied Social Psychology* 11(6) (1981): 507–528.

Kamerman, Jack. "Correctional Officer Stress and Suicide." *American Jails* 10(3) (1996): 23–28.

Kansas Department of Corrections. *Corrections Briefing Report* (1996).

———. "Narrative Information." Division of the Budget (1997a).

———. Personal letter from Robert Sanders, Director of Community Corrections Services (1997b).

Kanter, Rosabeth Moss. *Men and Women of the Corporation.* New York: Basic Books, 1977.

———. *Managing Change—The Human Dimension.* Boston: Goodmeasure, 1984.

Kast, Fremont, and James E. Rosenzweig. *Organization and Management: A System and Contingency Approach.* 3rd ed. New York: McGraw-Hill, 1979.

Katz, Robert L. "Skills of an Effective Administrator." *Harvard Business Review* (September–October 1974): 90–102.

Katz, D., and R. L. Kahn. *The Social Psychology of Organizations.* 2nd ed. New York: John Wiley, 1978.

Kauffman, Kelsey. "Prison Officers' Attitudes and Perceptions of Attitudes: A Case of Pluralistic Ignorance." *Journal of Research in Crime and Delinquency* (July 1981): 272–292.

———. *Prison Officers and Their World.* Cambridge, MA: Harvard University Press, 1988.

Kazimer, Leonard J. *Principles of Management: A Programmed-Instructional Approach.* 3rd ed. New York: McGraw-Hill, 1974.

Kent, Russell L., and Sherry Moss. "Effects of Sex and Gender Role on Leader Emergence." *Academy of Management Journal* 37(5) (1994): 1335–1346.

Kentucky Department of Corrections. *Commonwealth of Kentucky Justice Cabinet Department of Corrections: In Review 1994–1995* (1996).

Kerle, Ken. "The Jail Image and the Caring Factor." *American Jails* 10 (3) (1996): 5.

Kinkade, Patrick T., and Matthew C. Leone. "The Privatization of Prisons: The Warden's View." *Federal Probation* 56(4) (1992): 58–65.

Kipnis, D., S. M. Schmidt, C. Swaffin-Smith, and I. Wilkinson. "Patterns of Managerial Influence: Shotgun Managers, Tacticians, and Bystanders." *Organizational Dynamics* (Winter 1984): 58–67.

Kissel, P., and J. Seidel. *The Management and Impact of Female Corrections Officers at Jail Facilities Housing Male Inmates.* Boulder, CO: NIC, 1980.

Klofas, John, Stan Stojkovic, and David Kalinich. *Criminal Justice Organizations: Administration and Management.* Belmont, CA: Wadsworth Publishing, 1990.

Klofas, John M., and H. Toch. "The Guard Subculture Myth." *Journal of Research in Crime and Delinquency* 19 (1982): 238–254.

Koehler, Richard J. "Like it or Not: We Are News." *Corrections Today* 51(1) (1989): 16–17.

Koontz, Harold, Cyril O'Donnell, and Heinz Weihrich. *Essentials of Management.* 4th ed. New York: McGraw-Hill, 1986.

Korn, Richard R. "Litigation Can Be Therapeutic." In *The Dilemmas of Corrections: Contemporary Readings,* edited by Kenneth C. Haas and Geoffrey P. Alpert, 335–343. 3rd ed. Prospect Heights, IL: Waveland, 1995.

Korn, Richard, and Lloyd W. McCorkle. "Resocialization Within Walls." *Annals* 293 (1954).

Kotter, John. *A Force for Change: How Leadership Differs from Management.* New York: Free Press, 1990.

Kotter, John P. *Power in Management.* New York: AMACON, 1979.

Kotter, J. P., and A. Schlesinger. "Choosing Strategies for Change." *Harvard Business Review* (March-April 1979): 106–114.

Kouzes, James M., and Barry Z. Posner. "Eye of the Follower." *Administrative Radiology* (April 1986): 55–56, 58, 63–64.

———. *The Leadership Challenge.* San Francisco: Jossey-Bass, 1987.

———. *The Leadership Challenge: How to Get Extraordinary Things Done in Organizations.* San Francisco: Jossey-Bass, 1988.

———. "The Credibility Factor: What Followers Expect from Their Leaders." *Business Credit* (July/August 1990): 24–28.

Labecki, Lee Ann S. "Director's Note." *Data Bits* 1(1) (1996): 1–12.

Lahey, Benjamin B. *Psychology: An Introduction.* 4th ed. Dubuque, IA: Wm. C. Brown, 1992.

Lansing, Douglas, Joseph B. Bogan, and Loren Karacki. "Unit Management: Implementing a Different Correctional Approach." *Federal Probation* 41 (March 1977): 43–49.

Lasky, G. L., B. Gordon, and D. J. Strebalus. "Occupational Stressors Among Federal Correctional Officers Working in Different Security Levels." *Criminal Justice Behavior* 13(3) (1986): 317–327.

Lawes, Lewis L. *Twenty Thousand Years in Sing Sing.* New York: Ray Long & Richard R. Smith, 1932.

Lawler III, E. E., and J. L. Suttle. "A Causal Correlation Test of the Need Hierarchy Concept." *Organizational Behavior and Human Performance* (April 1972): 265–287.

Lazarus, R. S., and S. Folkman. *Stress, Appraisal, and Coping.* New York: Springer, 1984.

Legnini, Mark W. "Developing Leaders vs. Training Administrators in the Health Services." *American Journal of Public Health* 84(10) (1994): 1569–1573.

Lemov, Penelope. "The End of the Prison Boom." *Governing* (August 1997): 32–33.

Lewin, Kurt. *Field Theory in Social Science.* New York: Harper and Row, 1951.

Lillis, J. "Prison Escapes and Violence Remain Down." *Corrections Compendium* 29(6) (1994): 6–21.

Lindblom, Charles E. "The Science of Muddling Through." *Public Administration* 19 (1959): 79–88.

Lindquist, C. A., and J. T. Whitehead. "Burnout, Job Stress, and Job Satisfaction Among Southern Correctional Officers: Perception and Causal Factors." *Journal of Criminal Science* 10(4) (1986): 5–26.

Lineback, L. Kent. *Being the Boss: The Craft of Managing People.* New York: Institute of Electrical and Electronics Engineers, 1987.

Linton, John. "Inmate Education Makes Sense." *Corrections Today* 60(3) (1998):18.

Livingston, John Leslie. "Accounting and Management Decision Making." In *The Portable MBA.* New York: John Wiley, 1990.

Locke, Edwin A. "Toward a Theory of Task Motivation and Incentives." *Organizational Behavior and Human Performance* (May 1968): 157–189.

Loewenberg, Frank, and Ralph Dolgoff. *Ethical Decisions for Social Work Practice.* Itasca, IL: F. E. Peacock, 1988.

Logan, Charles H. "Well Kept: Comparing Quality of Confinement in Private and Public Prisons." *The Journal of Criminal Law and Criminology* 83(3) (1992): 577–613.

Logan, Charles H., and Sharla P. Rausch. "Punish and Profit: The Emergence of Private Enterprise Prisons." *Justice Quarterly* 2(3) (1985): 303–318.

Lombardo, Lucien. *Guards Imprisoned: Correctional Officers at Work.* New York: Elsevier, 1981.

Louisiana Department of Public Safety and Corrections. *Master Plan: October 1995* (1995).

Lovell, Rick. "Research Utilization in Complex Organizations: A Case Study in Corrections." In *The Administration and Management of Criminal Justice Organizations: A Book of Readings,* edited by Stan Stojkovic, John Klofas, and David Kalinich, 518–538. 2nd ed. Prospect Heights, IL: Waveland Press, 1994.

Lunden, Walter. "The Tenure and Turnover of State Prison Wardens." *American Journal of Correction* (November-December 1957): 14.

———. *Organizational Behavior.* New York: McGraw-Hill, 1973.

Luthans, Fred. "Successful vs. Effective Managers." *Academy of Management Executive* (May 1988).

Lyles, Richard I. *Practical Management Problem Solving and Decision Making.* New York: Van Nostrand Reinhold, 1982.

Maanen, J. Van, and E. H. Schein. "Career Development." In *Improving Life at Work,* edited by J. R. Hackman and J. L. Suttle, 58–62. Santa Monica, CA: Goodyear, 1977.

MacKenzie, Doris Layton, and Claire Souryal. "Multisite Evaluation of Shock Incarceration." In *Correctional Contexts: Contemporary and Classical Readings,* edited by James W. Marquart and Jonathan R. Sorensen, 385–400. Los Angeles: Roxbury, 1997.

MacKenzie, Kenneth D. *The Organizational Hologram: The Effective Management of Organizational Change.* Norwell, MA: Kluwer Academic, 1991.

Mactavish, Marie. "A Correctional Leadership Practices Model." *Corrections Today* 59(1) (1997): 60–61, 70.

Mahan, Susan. "State Prisons Broke Growth Records in '95." *Patriot-News* (Harrisburg, PA), 30 January 1996, B8.

Maier, N. R. F. "Assets and Liabilities in Group Problem Solving: The Need for an Integrative Function." *Psychological Review* (April 1967): 239–249.

Mande, Mary J., and Kim English. *The Effect of Public Opinion on Correctional Policy: A Comparison of Opinions and Practice.* Colorado Department of Public Safety, Division of Criminal Justice, 1989.

Mann, Michael, ed. *The International Encyclopedia of Sociology.* New York: Continuum, 1984.

Marquart, James W., and Jonathan R. Sorensen. *Correctional Contexts: Contemporary and Classical Readings.* Los Angeles: Roxbury, 1997.

Marsh, Harry L. "News Media." In *Encyclopedia of American Prisons,* edited by Marilyn D. McShane and Frank P. Williams III, 332–333. New York: Garland, 1996.

Martin, John Barlow. *Break Down the Walls*. New York: Ballantine Books, 1954.

Martin, S.J., and S. Ekland-Olson. *Texas Prisons: The Walls Came Tumbling Down*. Austin, TX: Texas Monthly Press, 1987.

Maslow, Abraham. *Motivation and Personality*. New York: Harper and Row, 1954.

Masters, Ruth E. *Counseling Criminal Justice Offenders*. Thousand Oaks, CA: Sage, 1994.

Mathews, M. Cash. *Strategic Interventions in Organizations: Resolving Ethical Dilemmas*. Newbury Park, CA: Sage, 1988.

Mayo, Elton, and F. J. Roethlisberger. *Management and the Worker*. Cambridge, MA: Harvard University Press, 1939.

McCarthy, Bernard J. "Exploratory Study in Corruption in Corrections." Ph.D. diss., Florida State University, 1981.

————. "Keeping An Eye on the Keeper: Prison Corruption and Its Control." In *Justice, Crime, and Ethics,* edited by Michael C. Braswell, Belinda R. McCarthy, and Bernard J. McCarthy, 229–241. 2nd ed. Cincinnati: Anderson, 1996.

McCarthy, Belinda Rogers, and Bernard J. McCarthy Jr. *Community-Based Corrections*. 2nd ed. Belmont, CA: Brooks/Cole, 1991.

McClelland, David C. *The Achieving Society*. New York: Van Nostrand Reinhold, 1961.

McClelland, David C., and D. H. Burnham. "Power Is the Great Motivator." *Harvard Business Review* (March-April 1976): 100–110.

McCormack, Wayne. "The Expansion of Federal Question Jurisdiction and the Prisoner Complaint Caseload." *Wisconsin Law Review* (1975): 523, 536.

McDonald, Douglas C. "The Cost of Corrections: In Search of the Bottom Line." In *Research in Corrections 2,* edited by Joan Petersilia, 1–25. Washington, DC: NIC, 1989.

McGregor, Douglas. *The Human Side of Enterprise*. New York: McGraw-Hill, 1960.

————. In *The Professional Manager*, edited by Caroline McGregor and W. G. Bennis. New York: McGraw-Hill, 1967.

McShane, Marilyn D. "Correctional Officers." In *Encyclopedia of American Prisons,* edited by Marilyn D. McShane and Frank P. Williams III, 117–118. New York: Garland, 1996.

McShane, Marilyn D., and Frank P. Williams III. *The Management of Correctional Institutions*. New York: Garland, 1993.

McShane, M., F. Williams, K. McClain, and D. Shichor. "Examining Employee Turnover in Corrections." *Corrections Today* 53(5) (1991): 220–225.

Mease, E. "Community Policing and the Police Officer." *NIJ Perspectives on Policing*. Washington, DC: U.S. Department of Justice, 1993.

Meddis, Sam Vincent, and Deborah Sharp. "Prison Business Is a Blockbuster." *USA Today*, 13 December 1994, 10A.

Meier, Peg, and Ellen Foley. "War of the Words." *Minneapolis Star Tribune, First Sunday,* 6 January 1991, 5–8.

Michaelsen, L. K., W. E. Watson, and R. H. Black. "A Realistic Test of Individual versus Group Consensus Decision Making." *Journal of Applied Psychology* (October 1989): 834–839.

Michigan Department of Corrections. *1995 Statistical Report* (1996a).

————. *Meeting The Challenge of Public Safety* (1996b).

Miles, R. E., and C. C. Snow. *Organizational Strategy, Structure, and Process*. New York: McGraw-Hill, 1978.

Mileti, D. S., D. F. Gillespie, and J. E. Haas. "Size and Structure in Complex Organizations." *Social Forces* (September 1977): 208–217.

Miller, D. "The Structural and Environmental Correlates of Business Strategy." *Strategic Management Journal* (January-February 1987): 55–76.

Miller, Marsha L., and Bruce Hobler. "Delaware's Life Skills Program Reduces Inmate Recidivism." *Corrections Today* 58(5) (1996): 114–117, 143.

Millstein, Kathleen, Kate Dare-Winters, and Sally Sullivan. "The Power of Silence: Ethical Dilemmas of Informed Consent in Practice Evaluation." *Clinical Social Work Journal* 22(3) (1994): 317–329.

Miner, F. C. "Group Versus Individual Decision Making: An Investigation of Performance Measures, Decision Strategies, and Process Losses/Gains." *Organizational Behavior and Human Performance* (February 1984): 112–124.

Minnesota Department of Corrections. *1994–1995 Biennial Report* (1995).

Mintzberg, Henry. *The Nature of Managerial Work*. New York: Harper and Row, 1973.

————. *Power in and Around Organizations*. Englewood Cliffs, NJ: Prentice Hall, 1983a.

————. *Structure in Fives: Designing Effective Organizations*. Englewood Cliffs, NJ: Prentice Hall, 1983b.

———. "The Structuring of Organizations." In *The Strategy Process*, edited by Henry Mintzberg and James Brian Quinn, 330–331. 2nd ed. Englewood Cliffs, NJ: Prentice Hall, 1991.

Mishra, Jitendra. "The ADA Helps—But Not Much." *Public Personnel Management* 24(4) (1995): 429–441.

Missouri Department of Corrections. "Employee Standards." *Department Manual*, Policy No. D2-11 (1995).

———. "Job Descriptions." *Department Manual* (1997).

Mitchell, Christopher, Andrea Emodi, and William Loehfelm. "Developing an Inmate Program That Works." *Corrections Today* 58(5) (1996): 88–90.

Mitford, Jessica. *Kind and Usual Punishment*. New York: Knopf, 1973.

Montgomery, Robert L. "Are You a Good Listener?" *Nation's Business* (October 1981): 65–68.

Moore, J. "Prison Litigation and the States: A Case Law Review." *State Legislative Report* 8 (1981): 1.

Moorhead, Gregory, and Ricky W. Griffin. *Organizational Behavior*. 2nd ed. Boston: Houghton Mifflin, 1989.

Morgan-Sharp, Etta, and Robert T. Sigler. "Sentencing into the Twenty-First Century: Sentence Enhancement and Life Without Parole." In *Visions for Change: Crime and Justice in the Twenty-First Century*, edited by Roslyn Muraskin and Albert R. Roberts, 237–252. Upper Saddle River, NJ: Prentice Hall, 1996.

Morris, Norval, and Michael Tonry. *Between Prison and Probation: Intermediate Punishments in a Rational Sentencing System*. New York: Oxford University Press, 1990.

Morton, Joann B., and Judy C. Anderson. "Implementing the Americans with Disabilities Act for Inmates." *Corrections Today* 58(6) (1996): 86–90, 140.

Moss, Andie, and Laurel Rans. "Executive Leadership for Women." *Corrections Today* 59(7) (1997): 116–119.

Mullen, J., K. Chabotar, and D. Cartow. *The Privatization of Corrections*. Washington, DC: NIJ, 1985.

Mullen, Rod, John Ratelle, Elaine Abraham, and Jody Boyle. "California Program Reduces Recidivism and Saves Tax Dollars." *Corrections Today* 58(5) (1996): 118–123.

Munsterberg, H. *Psychology and Industrial Efficiency*. Boston: Houghton Mifflin, 1913.

Mushlin, M. *Rights of Prisoners*. 2nd ed. Colorado Springs, CO: Shepard's, 1993.

Nash, Laura. "Ethics Without the Sermon." *Harvard Business Review* 59 (1981): 79–91.

National Academy of Corrections. *Correctional Supervision–Instructors Manual* (1984).

National Institute of Corrections. *NIC Service Plan for Fiscal Year 1998: Training, Technical Assistance, Information Services*. Washington, DC: U.S. Department of Justice, 1997.

National Institute of Justice. *Shock Incarceration in New York*. Washington, DC: U.S. Department of Justice, 1994: 9.

———. *National Assessment Program: 1994 Survey Results* (1995a).

———. Update. *NIJ Survey of Wardens and State Commissioners of Corrections* (May 1995b): 1–2.

National Victim Center. *National Victim Services Survey of Adult and Juvenile Corrections and Parole Agencies, Final Report*. Arlington, VA: National Victim Center, 1991.

Neubauer, David W. *America's Courts and the Criminal Justice System*. 5th ed. New York: Wadsworth, 1996.

New York Department of Correctional Services. *Psychological Screening Program for Correction Officer Applicant* (1995).

New York Department of Corrections. *Incident of Tuberculosis Infection Among New York State Prison Employees* (1996).

Newstrom, J. W., R. E. Monczka, and W. E. Reif. "Perceptions of the Grapevine: Its Value and Influence." *Journal of Business Communication* (Spring 1974): 12–20.

North Carolina Correction Enterprises. *Annual Report* (1995).

North Carolina Department of Corrections. "Basic Correctional Officer." *Topical Area Headings and Minimum Instructional Hours (1996)*.

O'Hare, Kate R. *In Prison*. New York: Alfred Knopf, 1923.

Ohio Contract Between the State of Ohio and District 1199 of the Health Care and Social Services Union, Service Employees International Union, AFL–CIO (1994–1997).

Ohio Department of Rehabilitation and Correction. *Annual Report: Fiscal Year 1994* (1996).

Okun, Barbara F. *Effective Helping: Interviewing and Counseling Techniques.* 4th ed. Pacific Grove, CA: Brooks/Cole, 1992.

Oregon Department of Corrections. *Prohibited Inmate Conduct and Processing Disciplinary Actions* (1996).

Ott, J. Stephen. *The Organizational Culture Perspective.* Pacific Grove, CA: Brooks/Cole, 1989.

Owen, B. *The Reproduction of Social Control: A Study of Prison Workers at San Quentin.* New York: Praeger, 1988.

Paulette, Thomas. "Making Crime Pay: Triangle of Interests Creates Infrastructure to Fight Lawlessness." *Wall Street Journal,* 1 March 1994, A1.

Peak, Kenneth J. "Peeking Over the Rim: What Lies Ahead." In *Crime and Justice in America: Present Realities and Future Prospects,* edited by Paul F. Cromwell and Roger G. Durham, 374–390. Upper Saddle River, NJ: Prentice Hall, 1997.

Pearson, Frank S., and Alice G. Harper. "Contingent Intermediate Sentences: New Jersey's Intensive Supervision Program." *Crime and Delinquency* 36 (1990): 75–86.

Pennsylvania Department of Corrections. Basic Training Course Syllabus (1996).

Perrow, Charles. "The Analysis of Goals in Complex Organizations." *American Sociological Review* 26 (1961): 854–866.

———. "Disintegrating Social Sciences." *New York University Educational Quarterly* (Winter 1981): 2–9.

Petersen, Cheryl Bowser. "Doing Time with the Boys: An Analysis of Women Correctional Officers in All-Male Facilities." In *The Criminal Justice System and Women,* edited by Barbara R. Price and Natalie J. Sokoloff, 437–460. New York: Clark Boardman, 1982.

Petersilia, Joan. "House Arrest." *Crime File Study Guide.* Washington, DC: NIJ, 1988.

Petersilia, Joan, and Susan Turner. "Intensive Probation and Parole." In *Crime and Justice: A Review of Research,* edited by M. Tonry. Chicago: University of Chicago Press, 1993.

Pfeffer, J. *Power in Organizations.* Marshfield, MA: Pitman, 1981.

Philadelphia Inquirer. "New U.S. Law Targets Suits by Inmates." *Phildadelphia Inquirer,* 23 May 1996, A30.

Philliber, Susan. "Thy Brother's Keeper: A Review of the Literature on Correctional Officers." *Justice Quarterly* 4 (1987): 9–37.

Phillips, Richard L., and Charles R. McConnell. *The Effective Corrections Manager: Maximizing Staff Performance in Demanding Times.* Gaithersburg, MD: Aspen, 1996.

Phyfer, George M. "Accreditation: Corrections' Foundation." *Corrections Today* 54(3) (1992): 8.

Pisciotta, Alexander W. *Benevolent Repression: Social Control and the American Reformatory–Prison Movement.* New York: New York University Press, 1994.

Plunkett, W. Richard. *The Direction of People at Work.* 3rd ed. Dubuque, IA: Wm. C. Brown, 1983.

Pollock, Joycelyn M. *Sex and Supervision: Guarding Male and Female Inmates.* New York: Greenwood Press, 1986.

———. *Ethics in Crime and Justice: Dilemmas and Decisions.* 2nd ed. Belmont, CA: Wadsworth, 1994.

———. "Women in Corrections: Custody and the 'Caring Ethic.'" In *Women, Law, and Social Control,* edited by Alida V. Merlo and Joycelyn M. Pollock, 97–116. Boston: Allyn and Bacon, 1995.

———. "The Social World of the Prisoner." In *Prisons: Today and Tomorrow,* edited by Joycelyn M. Pollock, 218–269. Gaithersburg, MD: Aspen, 1997.

Poole, Eric D., and Robert M. Regoli. "Alienation in Prison: An Examination of the Work Relations of Prison Guards." *Criminology* 19(2) (1981): 251–270.

Poole, M. S., M. Holmes, and G. DeSanctis. "Conflict Management in a Computer-Supported Meeting Environment." *Management Science* (August 1991): 926–953.

President's Commission on Law Enforcement and the Administration of Justice. *The Challenge of Crime in a Free Society.* Washington, DC: Government Printing Office, 1967.

President's Task Force on Victims of Crime. *Final Report.* Washington, DC: Government Printing Office, 1982.

Progrebin, M., and E. D. Poole. "The Sexualized Work Environment: A Look at Women Jail Officers." *The Prison Journal* 77 (1997): 41–57.

Quinlan, J. Michael. "News of the Future: Carving Out New Territory for American Corrections." *Federal Probation* 57(4) (1993): 59–63.

Quinn, James B. *Strategies for Change: Logical Incrementalism*. Homewood, IL: Irwin, 1980.

Rahim, M. A. "Relationships of Leader Power to Compliance and Satisfaction with Supervision: Evidence from a National Sample of Managers." *Journal of Management* (December 1989): 545–556.

Raia, Anthony P. *Managing by Objectives*. Glenview, IL: Scott, Foresman, 1974.

Ramirez, Anthony. "Privatizing America's Prisons, Slowly." *New York Times,* 14 August 1994, sec. 3, p.1.

Rauch, W. Hardy. "Too Tough, Too Easy, or Just Right?" *Corrections Today* 52(3) (1990): 100, 134.

Rausch, Erwin. *Balancing Needs of People and Organizations: The Linking Elements Concept*. Washington, DC: Bureau of National Affairs, 1978.

Rauschenberger, J., N. Schmitt, and J. E. Hunter. "A Test of the Need Hierarchy Concept by a Markov Model of Change in Need Strength." *Administrative Science Quarterly* (December 1980): 654–670.

Reichman, Nancy. "Managing Crime Risks: Toward an Insurance-Based Model of Social Control." *Research in Law, Deviance and Social Control* 8 (1986): 151–172.

Reilly, Mark, and Jim Grothoff. "Packaging the Process." *Corrections Today* 59(2) (1997): 74–76.

Ressner, Jeffrey. "Dr. Tim's Last Trip." *Time* 147(18) (1996): 72–73.

Rhine, Edward E. "Parole Boards." In *Encyclopedia of American Prisons*, edited by Marilyn D. McShane and Frank P. Williams III, 342–348. New York: Garland, 1996.

Riley, William. "A Dual Approach: Washington Penitentiary Stresses Prevention and Reaction." *Corrections Today* 54(5) (1992): 68–71.

Riveland, Chase. "Being a Director of Corrections in the 1990s." *Federal Probation* 55(2) (1991): 10–11.

Robbins, Ira P. "Privatization of Corrections: Defining the Issues." In *The Dilemmas of Corrections: Contemporary Readings,* edited by Kenneth C. Haas and Geoffrey P. Alpert, 585–600. 3rd ed. Prospect Heights, IL: Waveland Press, 1995.

Robbins, Stephen P. *Managing Organizational Conflict: A Nontraditional Approach*. Englewood Cliffs, NJ: Prentice Hall, 1974.

———. *Organizational Behavior: Concepts, Controversies, and Applications*. 6th ed. Englewood Cliffs, NJ: Prentice Hall, 1993.

Roberts, John W. "James V. Bennett (1894–1978)." In *Encyclopedia of American Prisons,* edited by Marilyn D. McShane and Frank P. Williams III, 55–58. New York, Garland, 1996.

Roberts, Raymond N. "How Accreditation Helped Revitalize a Penitentiary Under Court Order." *Corrections Today* 54(3) (1992): 52, 54, 56.

Robinson, Dana Gains. "The 1990s: From Managing to Leading." *Supervisory Management* (June 1989): 5–10.

Regelberg, S. G., J. L. Barnes-Farrell, and C. A. Lowe. "The Stepladder Technique: An Alternative Group Structure Facilitating Effective Group Decision Making." *Journal of Applied Psychology* 72 (1992): 651–657.

Rosecrance, John. "Probation Supervision: Mission Impossible." *Federal Probation* 50(1) (1986): 25–31.

———. "Getting Rid of the Prima Donnas: The Bureaucratization of a Probation Department." *Criminal Justice and Behavior* 14(2) (1987): 138–155.

Rosefield Jr., H. A. "Self-Identified Stressors Among Correctional Officers." Ph.D. diss., North Carolina State University, 1981.

Ross, R. R., and T. G. Barker. *Incentives and Disincentives: A Review of Prison Remission Systems*. Ottawa, Canada: Ministry of the Solicitor General of Canada, 1986.

Rotemberg, Julio J., and Garth Salener. "Leadership Style and Incentives." *Management Science* 39(11) (1993): 1299–1318.

Rothschild, J. "Towards a Feminine Model of Organization." Working paper, Department of Sociology, Virginia Polytechnic Institute and State University (1991).

Rubin, Paula N. "The Americans with Disabilities Act's Impact on Corrections." *Corrections Today* 57(2) (1995a): 114–120.

———. *Civil Rights and Criminal Justice: Primer on Sexual Harassment*. Washington, DC: National Institute of Justice, 1995b.

Rudovsky, D., A. L. Bronstein, and E. I. Koren. *The Rights of Prisoners*. New York: Bantam, 1983.

Rushing, W. A. "Organizational Size, Rules, and Surveillance." In *Organizations: Structure and Behavior,* edited by J. A. Litterer, 396–405. 3rd ed. New York: John Wiley, 1980.

Ryan, Mick, and Tony Ward. *Privatization and the Penal System: The American Experience and the Debate in Britain.* New York: St. Martin's Press, 1989.

Salahi, David L. "California University Costs." *Los Angeles Times,* 29 March 1994.

Salavik, Gerald R., and Jeffrey Pfeffer. "Who Gets Power and How They Hold onto It: A Strategic Contingency Model of Power." *Organizational Dynamics* 5 (Winter 1977): 3–21.

Sandler, Len. "Rules for Management Communication." *Personnel Journal* (September 1988): 40–44.

Schein, Edgar H. *Organizational Culture and Leadership.* San Francisco: Jossey-Bass, 1985.

Schroeger, D. "The Course of Corrections in Missouri, 1833–1983." *Manual of the State of Missouri.* Jefferson City, MO: Office of the Secretary of State, 1983/1984.

Schwartz, A. E., and J. Levin. "Better Group Decision Making." *Supervisory Management* (June 1990): 4.

Schwartz, Jeffrey A. "Promoting a Good Public Image: Effective Leadership, Sound Practices Make the Difference." *Corrections Today* 51(1) (1989): 38–42.

Scott, Lori. "Probation: Heading in New Directions." In *Visions for Change: Crime and Justice in the Twenty-First Century,* edited by Roslyn Muraskin and Albert R. Roberts, 172–183. Upper Saddle River, NJ: Prentice Hall, 1996.

Scruton, Roger. *A Dictionary of Political Thought.* New York: Hill and Wang, 1982.

Sechrest, Dale K. "Locating Prisons: Open Versus Closed Approaches to Siting." *Crime and Delinquency* 38(1) (1992): 88–104.

Sechrest, D. K., and D. A. Josi. *National Correctional Officers Education Survey.* Riverside, CA: Robert Presley Institute of Corrections Research and Training, 1992.

Securities and Exchange Commission. *Annual Report of Form 10–K Under the Securities Exchange Act of 1934 for the Fiscal Year Ended December 31, 1993: Corrections Corporation of America* (1994).

Seligman, Daniel. "Making Crime Pay." *Fortune* (June 1992): 111–112.

Seltzer, J., and B. M. Bass. "Transformational Leadership: Beyond Initiation and Consideration." *Journal of Management* (December 1990): 693–703.

Shani, A. B., and W. A. Pasmore. "Organization Inquiry: Towards a New Model of the Action Research Process." In *Contemporary Organization Development: Current Thinking and Applications,* edited by D.D. Warwick, 438–448. Glenview, IL: Scott, Foresman, 1985.

Shannon, Douglas. "Correctional Executives: Who's Leading the Way?" *Corrections Today* 49(1) (1990): 48, 94.

Shaw, Linda R., Paula W. MacGillis, and Keith M. Dvorchik. "Alcoholism and the Americans with Disabilities Act: Obligations and Accommodations." *Rehabilitation Counseling Bulletin* 38 (1994): 108–123.

Shawver, Louis, and R. Dickover. "Research Perspectives: Exploding a Myth." *Corrections Today* 48(5) (1986): 30–34.

Shepperd, Robert A., Jeffrey R. Geiger, and George Welborn. "Closed Maximum Security: The Illinois Supermax." *Corrections Today* 58(4) (1996): 84–87, 106.

Sickle, Darlene Van. "Avoiding Lawsuits: A Summary of ADA Provisions and Remedies." *Corrections Today* 57(2) (1995): 104–108.

Silverman, Ira J., and Manuel Vega. *Corrections: A Comprehensive View.* St. Paul, MN: West, 1996.

Simon, Herbert A. *Administrative Behavior.* 3rd ed. New York: Free Press, 1976.

Simon, Paul. "Prison Wardens Dispute Politicians on Anti-Crime Solutions; Simon Sets Wedn. News Conference to Release Survey Results." Press release, December 19, 1994a.

———. Press Conference Concerning the U.S. Senate Judiciary Committee Prison Survey. December 21, 1994b.

Simon, Rita J., and Judith D. Simon. "Female C.O.s: Legitimate Authority." *Corrections Today* 50(5) (1988): 132–134.

Skinner, B. F. *Science and Human Behavior.* New York: Free Press, 1953.

Skinner, Wickham, and W. Earl Sasser. "Managers with Impact: Versatile and Inconsistent." *Harvard Business Review* 55 (1981): 140–148.

Skolnick, Jerome H. "What Not to Do About Crime— The American Society of Criminology 1994 Presidential Address." *Criminology* 33(1) (1995): 1–13.

Skolnick, J. H., and D. H. Bayley. *The New Blue Line: Police Innovation in Six Cities.* New York: Free Press, 1986.

Skovron, Sandra Evans, Joseph E. Scott, and Francis T. Cullen. "Prison Crowding: Public Attitudes Toward Strategies of Population Control." *Journal of Research in Crime and Delinquency* 25 (1989): 150–169.

Skrapec, Candice. "Assessment and Selection." In *Prison Personnel Management and Staff Development*, edited by Warren Benton and Charlotte A. Nesbitt, 49–63. Lanham, MD: ACA, 1988.

Slate, Risdon N. "Stress." In *Encyclopedia of American Prisons*, edited by Marilyn D. McShane and Frank P. Williams III, 129–131. New York: Garland, 1996.

Smith, Alexander B., and Harriet Pollack. "The Bill of Rights in the Twenty-First Century." In *Visions for Change: Crime and Justice in the Twenty-First Century*, edited by Roslyn Muraskin and Albert R. Roberts, 157–169. Upper Saddle River, NJ: Prentice Hall, 1996.

Sommers, Pat. "Inmates Will Pay for Victims' Rights." *Mercury Online* (Pottsville, PA), 1 July 1997.

Sonnenstuhl, W. J. "Contrasting Employee Assistance, Health Promotion, and Quality of Work Life Programs and Their Effects on Alcohol Abuse and Dependence." *Journal of Applied Behavioral Science* 24 (1988): 347–364.

Starling, Grover. *Managing the Public Sector.* 4th ed. Belmont, CA: Wadsworth, 1993.

Steele, Myron, and Thomas J. Quinn. "Restorative Justice: Including Victims in Community Corrections." In *The Dilemmas of Corrections: Contemporary Readings*, edited by Kenneth C. Haas and Geoffrey P. Alpert, 524–532. 3rd ed. Prospect Heights, IL: Waveland Press, 1995.

Steers, R. M. *Organizational Effectiveness: A Behavioral View.* Santa Monica, CA: Goodyear, 1977.

Stogdill, Ralph M. "Personal Factors Associated with Leadership: A Survey of the Literature." *Journal of Psychology* 25 (1948): 35–64.

Stojkovic, Stan. "Social Bases of Power and Control Mechanisms Among Prisoners in a Prison Organization." *Justice Quarterly* 1(4) (1984): 511–528.

———. *An Examination of Compliance Structures in a Prison Organization: A Study of the Types of Correctional Officer Power.* Unpublished manuscript, University of Wisconsin, Milwaukee, 1987.

Streeter, John V. "A Cost-Analysis Technique for Police Services." *The Police Chief* (November 1983): 42–44.

Sykes, Gresham M., and Sheldon Messinger. "The Inmate Social System." *Theoretical Studies in the Social Organization of the Prison.* New York: Social Science Research Council, 1960.

Tannen, Deborah. *You Just Don't Understand: Women and Men in Conversation.* New York: Ballantine Books, 1991.

Tannenbaum, Robert, and Warren H. Schmidt. "How to Choose a Leadership Pattern." *Harvard Business Review* (March/April 1958): 95–101.

Taxman, Faye S. "Intermediate Sanctions: Dealing with Technical Violators." *Corrections Today* 57(1) (1995): 46, 50–51, 54–57.

Taylor, Frederick W. *Principles of Scientific Management.* New York: Harper, 1911.

———. *Scientific Management.* New York: Harper, 1947.

———. "Time Study, Piece Work, and the First Class Man." In *Classics in Management*, edited by Harwood F. Merrill. New York: American Management Association, 1960.

Texas Department of Criminal Justice. *Annual Report for 1995* (1996).

Thomas, Charles W. "Growth in Privatization Continues to Accelerate." *Corrections Compendium* (April 1994): 5–6.

———. *Private Adult Correctional Facility Census.* 8th ed. Gainesville, FL: Private Corrections Project, University of Florida, 1995.

———. "Beyond a Reasonable Doubt." *Corrections Today* 58(7) (1996): 26–27.

Thomas, Lewis. *The Media and the Snail.* New York: Bantam Books, 1980.

Thompson, Arthur P., and Wesley Ridlon. "How ADA Requirements Affect Small Jail Design." *Corrections Today* 57(2) (1995): 122–126.

Thompson, Cheryl W. "D.C. to Close Two of Three Halfway Houses, Send Most Employees to Lorton." *Washington Post,* 24 July 1997, D03.

Thomsett, Michael C. *The Little Black Book of Budgets and Forecasts.* New York: AMACOM, 1988.

Thorburn, Kim Marie. "ACHSA Adopts Code of Ethics to Guide Health Professionals." *Corrections Today* 57(6) (1995): 82–83.

"Number of the Week." *Time,* 3 February 1997.

Toch, Hans. "Is a 'Correctional Officer,' By Any Other Name, A 'Screw?'" *Criminal Justice Review* 3(2) (1978): 19–35.

Toller, William, and Basil Tsagaris. "Managing Institutional Gangs: A Practical Approach Combining Security and Human Services." *Corrections Today* 58(6) (1996): 110–111, 115.

Tosi, H. L., J. R. Rizzo, and S. J. Carroll. *Managing Organizational Behavior.* Marshfield, MA: Pitman, 1986.

Tracey, Diane. *10 Steps to Empowerment*. New York: William Morrow, 1990.

Travis, Lawrence F., Edward J. Latessa Jr., and Gennaro F. Vito. "Private Enterprise and Institutional Corrections: A Call for Caution." *Federal Probation* (December 1985): 11–16.

Trends in Offender Characteristics. GAO/PEMD–90–4FS. Washington, DC: U.S. Government Accounting Office, 1989.

Trout, Craig H. "BOP Overview: Taking a New Look at an Old Problem." *Corrections Today* 54(5) (1992): 62–66.

Turner, W. B. "When Prisoners Sue: A Study of Prisoner Section 1983 Suits in the Federal Courts." *Harvard Law Review* 92 (1979): 610–663.

Uniform Crime Report. *Crime in the United States, 1986*. Washington, DC: U.S. Department of Justice, 1986: 41.

Uniform Crime Report. *Crime in the United States, 1991*. Washington, DC: U.S. Department of Justice, 1991: 5.

U.S. Bureau of Prisons. *Preliminary Evaluation of the Functional Unit Approach to Correctional Management* (1975).

Useem, Bert, and Peter Kimball. *States of Siege: U.S. Prison Riots 1971–1986*. New York: Oxford University Press, 1989.

U.S. General Accounting Office. *Improved Prison Work Programs Will Benefit Correctional Institutions and Inmates* (1982).

———. *Federal Prisons: Trends in Offender Characteristics* (1989a).

———. *Prison Crowding—Issues Facing the Nation's Prison System* (1989b).

U.S. President's Commission on Law Enforcement and Administration of Justice. *The Challenge of Crime in a Free Society*. Washington, DC: Government Printing Office, 1967.

Vander Zanden, James W. *Social Psychology*. 3rd ed. New York: Random House, 1984.

Vaughn, Michael S. "Listening to the Experts: A National Study of Correctional Administrators' Responses to Prison Overcrowding." *Criminal Justice Review* 18 (1993): 12–25.

Virginia Department of Corrections. *Position Descriptions* (1996).

Vogel, Brenda. "Advances in Technology and Strategic Thinking." *Corrections Today* 58(4) (1996): 120–122.

Vredenburgh, D .J., and J. G. Maurer. "A Process Framework of Organizational Politics." *Human Relations* (January 1984): 47–66.

Vroom, Victor H. *Work and Motivation*. New York: John Wiley, 1964.

Walker, Donald B. "Privatization in Corrections." In *Correctional Counseling and Treatment*, edited by Peter C. Kratcoski, 570–585. Prospect Heights, IL: Waveland Press, 1994.

Walker, Katey. "Values, Ethics, and Ethical Decision-Making." *Adult Learning* 5(2) (1993): 13–14.

Walker, Samuel. *Sense and Nonsense About Crime: A Policy Guide*. 2nd ed. Pacific Grove, CA: Brooks/Cole, 1989.

Wallace, Donald H. "Prisoners' Rights: Historical Views." In *Correctional Contexts: Contemporary and Classical Readings*, edited by James W. Marquart and Jonathan R. Sorensen, 248–257. Los Angeles, CA: Roxbury, 1997.

Washington Department of Corrections. "Case Management System" (1998).

Ways, M. "Tomorrow's Management: A More Adventurous Life in a Free-Form Corporation." *Fortune,* 1 July 1966.

Weber, Max. *The Theory of Social and Economic Organizations*. Edited by T. Parsons. Translated by A. M. Henderson and T. Parsons. New York: Free Press, 1947.

Weinberg, R .B., J. H. Evans, C. A. Otten, and H. A. Marlowe. "Managerial Stress in Corrections Personnel." *Corrective and Social Psychiatry and Journal of Behavior Technology Methods and Therapy* 31(2) (1985): 9–45.

Weisburd, David, and Ellen F. Chayet. "Good Time: An Agenda for Research." *Criminal Justice and Behavior* 16(2) (1989): 183–195.

———. "Good Time Credit." In *Encyclopedia of American Prisons*, edited by Marilyn D. McShane and Frank P. Williams III, 220–223. New York: Garland, 1996.

Weisz, William J. "Employee Involvement: How It Works at Motorola." *Personnel* 62 (1985): 29.

Welch, Michael. *Corrections: A Critical Approach*. New York: McGraw-Hill, 1986.

Welsh, Wayne N. "Jail Overcrowding and Court-Ordered Reform: Critical Issues for the Future." In *Visions for Change: Crime and Justice in the Twenty-First Century,* edited by Roslyn Muraskin and Albert R. Roberts, 199–214. Upper Saddle River, NJ: Prentice Hall, 1996.

Westbrook III, C. F., and F. E. Knowles, Jr. "Managing Change." *Corrections Today* 59(4) (1997): 114–118.

Whitehead, J. T. "Intensive Supervision: Officer Perspectives." In *Intermediate Punishments: Intensive Supervision, Home Confinement, and Electronic Surveillance,* edited by B. R. McCarthy, 67–84. Monsey, NY: Criminal Justice Press, 1987.

Whitehead, J. T., and C. A. Lindquist. "Correctional Officer Job Burnout: A Path Model." *Journal of Research in Crime and Delinquency* 23 (1986): 23–42.

Wilkinson, Reginald A., and Peggy Ritchie-Matsumoto. "Collaborations and Applications." *Corrections Today* 59(4) (1997): 64–67.

Willis, R. E. "A Simulation of Multiple Selection Using Nominal Group Procedures." *Management Science* 25 (1979): 171–181.

Wilson, James Q. *Thinking About Crime.* New York: Random House, 1975.

Wisconsin Department of Corrections. "Chapter 2—Code of Ethics." *Employee Handbook* (1991): 1–7.

Wismer, J. "Organizational Change: How to Understand It and Deal with It." *Training* 16(5) (1979): 28–32.

Wren, D. A. *The Evolution of Management Thought.* 3rd ed. New York: John Wiley, 1987.

Wright, Kevin. "Successful Prison Leadership." *Federal Probation* 55(3) (1991): 5–7.

———. *Effective Prison Leadership.* Binghamton, NY: William Neil, 1994.

Wright, Kevin, and William G. Saylor. "A Comparison of Perceptions of the Work Environment Between Minority and Non-Minority Employees of the Federal Prison System." *Journal of Criminal Justice* 20(1) (1992): 63–71.

Yackle, Larry W. *Reform and Regret: The Story of Federal Judicial Involvement in the Alabama Prison System.* New York: Oxford University Press, 1989.

Young, Jock. "Recent Developments in Criminology." In *Developments in Sociology,* edited by M. Haralambos. London: Causeway Press, 1988.

Zaner, Laura O. "The Screen Test: Has Hollywood Hurt Corrections' Image?" *Corrections Today* 51(1) (1989): 64–66, 94–98.

Zimbardo, Philip G. *Transforming California's Prisons into Expensive Old Age Homes for Felons: Enormous Hidden Costs and Consequences for California's Taxpayers.* San Francisco, CA: Center on Juvenile and Criminal Justice, 1994: 1–16.

Zimmer, Lynn E. *Women Guarding Men.* Chicago: University of Chicago Press, 1986.

Zinn, Lorraine M. "Do the Right Thing: Ethical Decision-Making in Professional and Business Practice." *Adult Learning* 5(2) (1993): 7–8.

Zoglin, Richard. "Tim at the Top." *Time* 144(24) (1994): 76–81.

Zupan, Lynn. "Gender-Related Differences in Correctional Officers' Perceptions and Attitudes." *Journal of Criminal Justice* 14 (1986): 349–361.

Zupan, Lynn. "The Progress of Women Correctional Officers in All-Male Prisons." In *The Changing Roles of Women in the Criminal Justice System,* edited by Imogene Moyer, 323–343. 2nd ed. Prospect Heights, IL: Waveland Press, 1992.

Cases Cited

Bell v. Wolfish, 441 U.S. 520 (1979)

Bounds v. Smith, 430 U.S. 817 (1977)

Brown v. Board of Education of Topeka, 347 U.S. 483 (1954)

Coleman v. Peyton, 302 F.2d 905 (4th Cir. 1966)

Cooper v. Pate, 378 U.S. 546 (1964)

Daniels v. Williams, 474 U.S. 327 (1986)

Gagnon v. Scarpelli, 411 U.S. 778 (1973)

Griffin v. Wisconsin, 483 U.S. 868 (1987)

Holt v. Sarver, 309 F. Supp. 362 (E.D. Ark. 1970), aff'd, 442 F.2d 304 (8th Cir. 1971)

Johnson v. Avery, 393 U.S. 483 (1969)

Monroe v. Pape, 365 U.S. 167 (1961)

Morrissey v. Brewer, 408 U.S. 471 (1972)

Palmigiano v. Garrahy, 443 F. Supp. 956 (Rhode Island, 1977)

Pugh v. Locke, 406 F. Supp. 318 (M.D. Ala. 1976)

Rhodes v. Chapman, 452 U.S. 337 (1981)

Ruffin v. Commonwealth, 62 Va. (21 Gratt.) 790 (1871)

Ruiz v. Estelle, 503 F. Supp. 1265 (S.D. Tex. 1980)

Ruiz v. Estelle, 688 F.2d 266 (5th Cir. 1982)

Sandin v. Connor, 115 s.ct 2293 (1995)

Smith v. Wade, 461 U.S. 30 (1983)

Sostre v. McGinnis, 442 F.2d 178 (2d Cir. 1971)

State v. Morris, 48 CrL 1498 (Ha. Sup. Ct. 1991)

Walker v. Rowe, 791 F.2d 507 (7th Cir. 1986)

Westbrook v. State, 133 Ga. 578 (1909)

Wilson v. Seiter, 111 S. Ct. 2321 (1991)

Wolff v. McDonnell, 418 U.S. 539 (1974)

Index